Personality Assessment

Third Edition

Personality Assessment
Third Edition

Richard I. Lanyon
Leonard D. Goodstein

JOHN WILEY & SONS, INC.

New York • Chichester • Brisbane • Toronto • Singapore • Weinheim

To Barbara and Jeanette

This text is printed on acid-free paper.

This publication is designed to provide accurate and authoritative
information in regard to the subject matter covered. It is sold
with the understanding that the publisher is not engaged in
rendering professional services. If legal, accounting, medical,
psychological, or any other expert assistance is required, the
services of a competent professional person should be sought.

Library of Congress Cataloging-in-Publication Data:

Lanyon, Richard I., 1937–
      Personality assessment / by Richard I. Lanyon, Leonard D.
Goodstein. — 3rd ed.
            p.   cm.
      Includes indexes.
      ISBN 0-471-55562-2 (cloth : alk. paper)
      1. Personality assessment.   I. Goodstein, Leonard David.
II. Title.
BF698.4.L34   1997
155.2'8—dc20   96-18061

Printed in the United States of America

10   9   8   7   6   5   4   3   2   1

Preface to the
Third Edition

More than twenty years have elapsed since the original publication of *Personality Assessment*. Our basic aim remains the same: to present a relatively brief but comprehensive account of the area of psychological inquiry and practice usually identified as *personality assessment*. Our basic approach has also remained the same: we describe the major methods and techniques used, including some discussion of their underlying rationale and manner of development, and we give a survey of the most central contemporary issues and problems involved in this ever expanding area.

The rapid development of the field in the 1970s led to a number of additions and changes in the second edition, published in 1982. Chapters on computer-based assessment and on areas of special application, such as the assessment of children, forensic psychology, neuropsychology, and the effects of particular demographic factors, were added. The text was also expanded to reflect developments in behavioral assessment, the use of biographical data, the technology of assessment, and the increasingly legalistic atmosphere surrounding psychological practice in general.

The changes in the field of personality assessment over the past fifteen years have been more fundamental and far-reaching than those of the previous decade. These changes, whose roots can be traced back for a considerably longer period of time, can be regarded as defining a new level of technical sophistication, one that shows real promise for ultimately shedding the prescientific origins of personality assessment and for redefining it as an area of applied science. The changes include: the increasing differentiation of assessment for practical, diagnostic purposes from assessment for purposes of theoretical study; a greater acceptance of traits and an increased sophistication in understanding them as a fundamental aspect of personality; advances in the conceptual and psychometric technology of test construction; and a rapidly increasing availability of high-speed computing power and the multivariate statistical procedures associated with it. We have embedded our discussion of each of these trends within the existing structure of the second edition. The developments in the application of personality assessment technology to the workplace, however, are sufficiently important to warrant a new, separate chapter.

These changes inevitably make the third edition longer and more technologically oriented than the earlier editions. We have nevertheless tried to maintain the text at the level of the advanced undergraduate and beginning graduate reader. As such, we hope that it will continue to be useful in a wide variety of academic and professional training settings, including psychology, counseling, social work, management assessment and development, and medicine. To restate our original goals, the book is not intended as a manual for developing proficiency in the practice of personality assessment or in the use of any specific assessment device. Such skills are the product of carefully directed study and extensive supervised practice. Rather, it is intended as a general introduction to the area of personality assessment; it lays the groundwork for the concurrent or later development of practical proficiency.

In preparing the third edition, we have benefited from continuing feedback contributed by students and colleagues, and we have tried to improve the manuscript accordingly. We are grateful to several members of the secretarial staff at Arizona State University for their able assistance—in particular LaVaun Habegger, Evelyn Pajewski, and Sharon Lindsay. As always, we appreciate the willingness of our families to accommodate our needs and priorities as we have worked on this project.

RICHARD I. LANYON
LEONARD D. GOODSTEIN

Contents

CHAPTER ONE

History of Personality Assessment

The ways in which people behave have always been of interest. They are of immediate interest to family, friends, and neighbors, for whom the behavior is likely to have direct consequences. Also, most of us like to feel that we have at least some general understanding of human behavior. Thus, the development of a capacity to understand and predict individual human behavior is of both immediate personal interest and general social interest.

The field of personality assessment—*systematic* efforts to understand and predict the behavior of individuals—has a long history. A prehistoric cave dweller might have attempted to gauge the intentions of an approaching stranger by observing the stance of the visitor, or the cast of the visitor's eyes. This appraisal might be regarded as an early effort at personality assessment. The later use of soothsayers and oracles to determine the veracity of peace offers from an enemy could be similarly viewed. Many other informal procedures preceded the development of modern scientific and professional psychology. Because of their historical value and because they illuminate some of the methodological issues involved in all personality assessment, we discuss several of those procedures here, concentrating on astrology, palmistry, and phrenology, which are still practiced to some degree despite their ascientific development and rather dubious contemporary status. These methods are considerably older than any current professional assessment technique.

ASTROLOGY, PALMISTRY, AND PHRENOLOGY

Astrology, the attempt to forecast events on earth through observation of the fixed stars and other heavenly bodies, is thought to have originated about 25 centuries ago in Mesopotamia. Their belief that the stars were powerful gods led the ancients to conclude that human affairs could be foretold by study of the heavens. Personality and the course of events in each individual's life were determined by consulting a horoscope (the configuration of the stars at the moment of birth). Personality assessment for an individual was accomplished by noting the moment of birth and then getting the appropriate predictive information from one of a number of elaborate manuals or almanacs, not unlike the daily horoscopes still found in many newspapers. The extensive knowledge of the physical world, developed during the scientific revolution, has done much to reduce serious interest in astrology, but it still remains popular with many people.

The notion that human lives are predetermined by the configuration of the stars at the moment of birth seems extremely naive, and there is absolutely no serious evidence for the existence of a relationship between time of birth and personality. Why then does the popularity of the notion persist, much to the discomfort of most professional psychologists? One reason for this persistence is the Barnum effect (described below). Another is the general fascination that cosmic or supernatural notions hold for the public. Books such as *Cosmic Influences on Human Behaviors* (Gauquelin, 1973) and *Supernature* (Watson, 1973) cater to this fascination by dressing up the pseudoscientific notions of astrology in the trappings of formal research and scholarship. It might perhaps be most appropriate to view current astrology and similar areas of interest as belonging to the entertainment industry, with its emphasis on packaging whatever will "sell," irrespective of most other considerations.

Analogous to astrology is the technique of *biorhythms,* a method for personal prediction developed initially by Sigmund Freud's colleague Wilhelm Fliess and promoted by George Thommen (1973). According to the theory of biorhythms, day-to-day effectiveness is governed by a position on three "cycles"—physical, emotional, and mental—that are fixed according to the moment of birth and are not otherwise modifiable. Because each of the cycles has a different period, they can periodically combine to produce "triple-low" days, on which things are likely to go badly, and "triple-high" days, when the opposite will be true. The more cycles stacked against us on any particular day, the more things are likely to go wrong, and vice versa. With the advent of preprogrammed microcomputers, people can predict their potential effectiveness for any given day almost instantaneously.

There is no apparent reason why this scheme would give any useful information, and a number of empirical studies (e.g., Schaffer, Schmidt, Zlotowitz, & Fisher, 1978) have shown conclusively that it does not. There *are* changes in one's energy level and motivation over time. What is inconceivable on the basis of contemporary understanding of developmental biology is that the pattern of these changes should be fixed absolutely by the moment of one's birth. Nevertheless, the notion of biorhythms has attracted a cult of "true believers" and has been commercially promoted as a viable approach to the prediction of human behavior.

Palmistry refers to the determination of an individual's characteristics by interpreting the various irregularities and folds of the skin of the hand. Palmistry is known to have existed as a standardized system in China as early as 3000 B.C., although its early beginnings and theoretical roots are lost in antiquity. In palmistry, importance is given to the lines of the hand, as well as to the swellings, or monticuli, between these lines. Each of these "signs" is interpreted in a specific manner. A large Mound of Saturn, the portion of the palm directly below the third joint of the middle finger, indicates wisdom, good fortune, and prudence. By "reading" these signs, palmistry provides for a comprehensive assessment of individuals. Note that the two charts shown in Figure 1.1, taken from the palmistry literature and representing a right hand and a left hand, present the basic features rather differently. The complete absence of any reasonable explanation for the

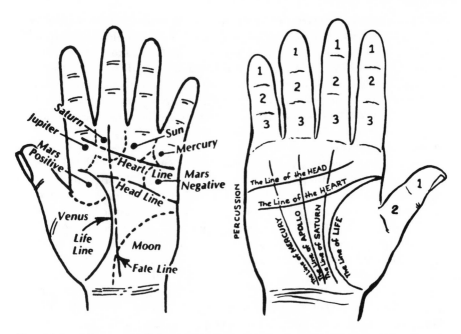

Figure 1.1   These two palmistry charts present the basic features of the left and right hands rather differently. (Source: Left, from Wade, 1992, p. 12. Copyright © 1992 Globe Communications Corp. Right, from **The Key to Palmistry** *by Leona Lehman, 1963, p. 14. New York: Bell Publishing.)*

interpretive inferences, coupled with the clear knowledge that the monticuli and other characteristics of the hand can be changed by physical exercise, leads to a dismissal of palmistry as superstition and quackery.

Nevertheless, people claiming to be practitioners of this ancient art can still be readily found today, and booklets purporting to teach palmistry are available in many supermarkets and drug stores (e.g., Wade, 1991). Much of the claimed success of palmists would seem to depend on their ability to respond to cues such as voice, general demeanor, and dress, which are more relevant for assessing personality than are the "signs" of palmistry. Still another possibility is that the palmist offers such generalized trivial statements (e.g., "Although you have considerable affection for your parents, there have been times of great discord") that they could apply to virtually anyone.

Meehl (1956) suggested the phrase *Barnum effect* to "stigmatize those pseudosuccessful clinical procedures in which patient descriptions from tests are made to fit the patient largely or wholly by virtue of their triviality; and in which any nontrivial, but perhaps erroneous, inferences are hidden in a context of assertions or denials which carry high confidence simply because of the population base rates" (p. 266). Tallent (1958) labeled this method of personality assessment as involving the *Aunt Fanny* error because it contains mostly information that would be true of anybody's "Aunt Fanny." The degree to which any personality assessment procedure involves the Barnum or Aunt Fanny effect because it produces trivial, highly generalized personality descriptions always needs to be carefully evaluated.

Phrenology, the art of personality assessment through the measurement of the external shape of the human skull, was given its major impetus by Franz Joseph Gall, a German physician and anatomist, late in the 18th century. This comparatively recent attempt to develop a complete system of personality measurement deserves a more careful scrutiny, for several reasons: (a) there were reasonable theoretical assumptions underlying the system, (b) the system is completely empirical and thus open to scientific inquiry, and (c) the history of phrenology is recent enough to have provided fairly complete documentation.

Gall's basic assumption was that the human brain is the locus of control over human behavior, a view now accepted uniformly by psychologists. At the turn of the 19th century, however, the operation of the cerebral cortex was poorly understood, and the prevailing scientific view favored a strict localization of cortical action, with each function or faculty centered in a definite and specific region of the brain surface. The sizes of these regions created corresponding and observable alterations in the shape of the skull, which could be used by the phrenologist to assess the many characteristics of the individual, including personality. For example, a protrusion of the skull in the area of "honesty" would indicate an honest individual. Like astrology and palmistry, phrenology enabled its practitioners to give a complete personality assessment, based in this case on the protrusions and contours of the skull (see Figure 1.2). The basic assumptions concerning the specificity of cerebral functioning and the formation of the skull have now been clearly disproven, thus discrediting the theory on which phrenology rests.

Gall was essentially empirical in his approach to the development of phrenology. He attempted to relate behavior to brain functioning and skull shape through personal observation. To gather information about the brain, he examined the skulls of living persons and then attempted to study their brains through autopsy after death. He also examined the skulls of persons in mental hospitals, prisons, colleges, and other places where individuals of exceptional deficiencies or endowments could be found, hoping to be able to relate skull shape with the characteristics that had brought these persons together. Although this early attempt at the development of an empirical science of personality assessment is both noteworthy and laudable, it points up the danger of unverified personal observations as the sole source of data in a scientific endeavor. The need for cross-validation of personal observations—that is, the objective demonstration of the same relationships in an independent setting by other observers—is as crucial today as it was in Gall's time.

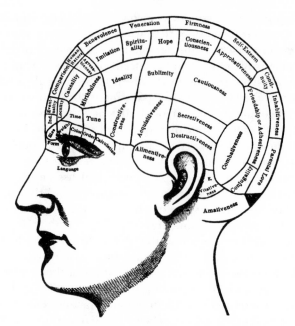

Numbering and Definition of the Organs

Amativeness, Love between the sexes.
Conjugality, Matrimony—love of one.
Parental Love, Regard for offspring, pets.
Friendship, Adhesiveness—sociability.
Inhabitiveness, Love of home.
Continuity, One thing at a time.
Vitativeness, Love of life.
Combativeness, Resistance—defense.
Destructiveness, Executiveness—force.
Alimentiveness, Appetite—hunger.
Acquisitiveness, Accumulation.

Secretiveness, Policy—management.
Cautiousness, Prudence—provision.
Approbativeness, Ambition—display.
Self-Esteem, Self-respect—dignity.
Firmness, Decision—perseverance.
Conscientiousness, Justice, equity.
Hope, Expectation—enterprise.
Spirituality, Intuition—faith—credulity.
Veneration, Devotion—respect.
Benevolence, Kindness—goodness.

Figure 1.2   A skull chart reflecting the beliefs of phrenologists. (**Source: Phrenology: A Practical Guide to Your Head** *by O. S. Fowler and L. N. Fowler, 1969, p. xviii. New York: Chelsea House.*)

Paradoxically, it was not the lack of scientific validity of Gall's position that drew the most serious objections. Rather, the most strenuous indictments were based on philosophical grounds (Davies, 1955). The critics of phrenology insisted that Gall's position was not unproved but unprovable; and even if provable, it was immoral. The confirmation of phrenology, according to these critics, would involve an acceptance of atheism and fatalism and a denial of moral responsibility. The same issues are raised in objection to contemporary deterministic views of human behavior. In the face of this violent and emotional criticism, the phrenologists themselves became defensive and dogmatic. What had originally been regarded as tentative and experimental became dogma and gospel. Phrenology thus deteriorated from an experimental science, albeit one based on inadequate assumptions, into a religion-like cult that was closed to any self-examination or modification based on new data. The change doubtlessly served to hasten its fall from the respectability it once enjoyed.

The use of stable physical signs to assess personality characteristics is common to both palmistry and phrenology. The search for clear-cut relationships between the physical attributes of an individual and his or her psychological characteristics has been continual, not unlike the unending concern about the relationship between mind and body. This concern had an early expression in the *humoural theory,* an ancient physiology that remained current through the Middle Ages. The theory proposed four "ingredients": blood, phlegm, yellow bile (choler), and black bile (melancholy). The particular proportion of these four ingredients in different people determined their "complexions" (or personality characteristics), their physical and mental qualities, and their unique dispositions. It was thus claimed that, by reading the physical signs of the relative amounts of these humours in a given individual, his or her distinctive personality could be determined.

Although a more complete understanding of the physiology of the human body has long put the humoural theory into disuse, the assumption that human personality is a reflection of the physical body can be found in the modern work of Sheldon and his colleagues (Sheldon, Stevens, & Tucker, 1940). Sheldon's theory of *somatotypes* divides people into three major types: the ectomorph, who is thin and fragile; the mesomorph, who is powerful and muscular; and the endomorph, who is round, soft, and fat. According to the theory, each of these ideal types has a specific personality that is an innate consequence of that particular body build. Because most individuals are combinations of these three body types, the personality characteristics are determined by the relative proportions of the body-type factors in their individual somatotype. Sheldon's theory has been the subject of considerable controversy, and the evidence for its validity is at best equivocal (Herman, 1992). Nevertheless, it is consistent with the age-old preoccupation with discovering a simple link between mind and body.

There *are* significant relationships between certain physical signs (e.g., trembling, sweating) and personality characteristics (e.g., anxiety), and these relationships, though far from perfect, can be utilized in assessment. The unsuccessful attempts, throughout history, to rely on physical signs appear to have at least one of the following two characteristics: first, reliance on a theory which postulates that personality characteristics are *caused* by particular physical attributes; and second, lack of any logical connection between the physical sign and the personality attribute.

Astrology, palmistry, and phrenology—together with such methods as crystal ball gazing, tea leaf reading, and physiognomy (personality assessment from facial features)—have not survived scientific investigations of their usefulness, and the practice of such dubious procedures is considered charlatanism today. Yet, as we have seen, certain aspects of these approaches continue to be identifiable in current psychological thinking—an indication

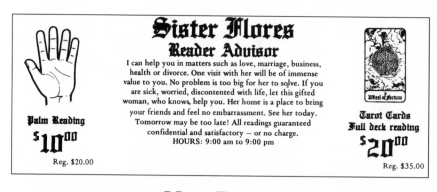

Figure 1.3   Coupons advertising palmistry and similar services are regularly distributed in some major metropolitan areas.

that they do have some current influence. Practitioners of these procedures can readily be found in many communities. The coupons shown in Figure 1.3 were distributed in the Phoenix area together with addresses and telephone numbers.

It should not be assumed that the practitioners can never do better than chance in personality assessment. Some of these persons are sensitive to the same subtle cues that trained mental health professionals use in their intuitive personality assessments. The charge of charlatanism arises from the attempts of phrenologists and palmists to insist that their understanding of the person being studied results from the application of some technique or procedure that has now been demonstrated to be ineffective or useless for that purpose, rather than from their superior intuitive assessment skills.

INFLUENCE OF PSYCHOLOGICAL MEASUREMENT

Scientific personality assessment has its roots in the study of individual differences through psychological measurement. Most students of individual differences date the opening of this area of inquiry at 1796, when a Greenwich astronomer's assistant, Kinnebrook, was dismissed because he had constantly observed the times of stellar transits almost one second later than his superior. It was later realized that this difference in reaction time was a stable one, and that people differed from each other in this and other measurable characteristics in a similarly stable fashion.

The study of individual differences was given considerable impetus by Darwin's work on evolution. To study the effects of human genetics, it would be necessary to identify clearly the individual differences in those behaviors that had adaptability and survival value for humanity. Sir Francis Galton, a famous British scholar of the 19th century, became interested in the inheritance of these differences and devoted the later portion of his life to their study. Although there had been previous attempts to categorize and measure what Galton called "intellectual faculties," Galton himself was the initiator of the measurement of the nonintellectual faculties, known more commonly at that time as "character and temperament."

Galton discussed the measurement of several such faculties in the *Fortnightly Review* of 1884. His statement "that the character which shapes our conduct is a definite and durable 'something,' and therefore . . . it is reasonable to attempt to measure it," bears a strong resemblance to most contemporary views of personality. Further, Galton proposed that the measurement of character should involve the same approach as "that which lies at the root of examinations into the intellectual capacity," and he briefly discussed methods for the measurement of "emotion" and "temper," using what we might term the *behavior sample approach*. For example, he suggested measuring emotion by means of instruments to record physiological changes in the individual during real-life stress situations. To investigate the practicality of this procedure, Galton himself actually wore a pneumocardiograph over his heart while delivering an important public lecture. He also suggested measuring pulse rate and changes in limb volume with the withdrawal of blood— measures that are still used in psychophysiological research laboratories for studying emotional reactions. With regard to temper, Galton pointed out that small boys were expert in measuring the temper of a dog (i.e., how much teasing a dog would tolerate before responding negatively), and he was convinced that similar techniques could be developed for the assessment of good and bad temper in humans.

The study of individual differences in the United States was pioneered by James McKeen Cattell, who took his doctorate in Leipzig with the pioneer of experimental psychology, Wilhelm Wundt. Cattell also worked briefly with Galton in England, then returned to the United States in 1888 and established the Psychological Laboratory at the University of Pennsylvania. Although his interests were mainly in the areas of psychophysics, perception, and reaction time, Cattell had a strong influence on the development of other psychological measurement devices, including personality tests, through his support for the practical utilization of psychological knowledge (Boring, 1929, pp. 532–540).

At about the same time, in France, Alfred Binet, who had become enthusiastic about Galton's work on individual differences, began a series of studies of eminent persons in the arts and sciences. Binet used a standard series of experimental tasks, including observations on body types, head measurements, and handwriting. Some of these interests appeared to reflect the influence of phrenology (which was then current) and other pre-scientific notions, and Binet, who was a careful and objective investigator, later discarded them as not leading to useful understanding of the persons being studied. Binet also began a series of investigations into mental functioning (which included personality), using a wide variety of tasks involving word knowledge, reasoning, and numerical ability. These investigations led to the development of the now famous Binet tests of intelligence. Some of his tasks, which involved telling stories about pictures and identifying inkblots, were antecedents of what are now known as the "projective" tests of personality.

Thus, prior to 1915, research on the measurement of personality was preceded by work on the measurement of skills or abilities, and it grew out of the early academic interest in the measurement of human individual differences. The faculties of character or temperament were considered to be "real," as were reaction times and perceptual abilities, in much the same sense as physical characteristics such as height and weight. Galton had introduced the use of direct behavior samples in real-life situations, and his work had stimulated considerable interest in both the United States and France. Two of Galton's followers, Karl Pearson and Charles Spearman, were playing a major part in the development of statistical procedures that provided powerful tools for later work in assessment.

At about this time, an English scientist named Webb (1915) published what seems to have been the first major attempt to summarize the important aspects of character through the intensive study of a large number of subjects. He obtained ratings of a large group of school- and college-age males on 40 or more qualities that had "a general and fundamental bearing on the total personality." The ratings were obtained from persons who knew the subjects well, and the resulting data were treated by an early form of statistical procedures which are now known as *factor analysis*. They were interpreted to indicate that the most basic aspect of personality was "consistency of action resulting from deliberate volition, or will." Webb's study is noteworthy both for its use of judges' ratings (i.e., estimates by experts) and for its sophisticated statistical techniques. Webb also summarized two previous studies that had approached the scientific study of personality through the use of what he called the "biographic method," an analysis of written personal life histories. These can be regarded as forerunners of the present-day "biographical data blank" approach to personality assessment.

INFLUENCE OF ABNORMAL PSYCHOLOGY

At about the same time that academic psychologists were developing their interest in the measurement of normal human capacities and individual differences, other investigators were becoming involved in the formal assessment of *abnormal* human behavior. This interest stemmed from the practical need to classify and categorize the various kinds of psychopathology as well as the more theoretical need to gain a better understanding of the phenomena under scrutiny. Closely related to these efforts were the parallel attempts of Binet to develop clinical tests that would identify children who lacked the mental capacity to benefit from schooling and provide theoretical information about their intellectual limitations.

It is generally considered that the earliest attempts at personality assessment with psychopathological cases involved word association procedures. Emil Kraepelin, the renowned German psychiatrist who was primarily responsible for our current psychiatric classification procedures, made some use of a "free association test" as early as 1892, and Sommer, one of his colleagues, suggested its use for differentiating various kinds of mental disorder in 1894 (Anastasi, 1988, p. 17). In the word association technique, the subject is presented with a stimulus word, frequently from a standardized list of such words, and is asked to respond as quickly as possible with the first word that comes to mind. The list is usually presented more than once, because different responses to the same word are believed to indicate a problem area. A record is made of the responses and of the reaction time to each presentation. The technique had been used by Galton and Cattell for assessing individual differences.

The use of word association as a method for the identification of unconscious personality conflicts was advanced by Carl Jung. Jung (1910) developed a standardized list of words that were regarded as especially useful in detecting areas of conflict or disturbance. Excessively long reaction times, failures to respond, misunderstandings of the stimulus words, and other emotional reactions such as stammering and blushing were key indications.

Another, more formal approach to the use of word association was developed by Kent and Rosanoff (1910). They deliberately omitted from their standardized list words that were especially likely to call up personal experiences, and they developed norms of common responses by administering the list to 1,000 normal persons. By comparing the responses of normal persons with those of psychotics, they were able to demonstrate that the psychotics gave strikingly fewer common responses than normals and that these differences were large enough to be of diagnostic significance in individual cases. Thus, the word association test can be regarded as the first practical psychometric device for identifying emotionally disturbed persons, although it is little used for this purpose today.

A similar concern with problems of adjustment led Heymans and Wiersma (1906) to develop a list of symptoms indicative of psychopathology.

This list, revised by Hoch and Amsden (1913) and later by Wells (1914), was influential in generating the early self-report personality inventory. The first such inventory was Woodworth's (1919) Personal Data Sheet, which was developed during World War I to diagnose the ability of soldiers to adjust satisfactorily to the stresses and strains of military life. With not enough psychologists or psychiatrists available to interview each draftee personally about his emotional status, some more economical method was sought. A Committee on Emotional Fitness was appointed by the National Research Council to work on this problem under the chairmanship of Robert S. Woodworth. Their solution was a paper-and-pencil inventory (entitled the Personal Data Sheet to allay suspicion about its real purpose), which was a standardized psychiatric interview in printed form (see Symonds, 1931). The questions were based on common neurotic symptoms and on reports of symptoms that were actually observed in men who had not been able to adjust to war and its stresses.

The questions dealt with physical symptoms ("Do you ever feel an awful pressure in or about your head?"); fears and worries ("Are you troubled with the idea that people are watching you on the street?"); adjustment to the environment ("Do you make friends easily?"); unhappiness and unsociability ("Are you troubled by shyness?"); dreams, fantasies, and sleep disturbance ("Are you frightened in the middle of the night?"); plus some miscellaneous items. The score on this questionnaire was the number of items answered in the direction considered to be typical of maladjustment or psychoneurosis. Over 200 questions capable of being answered yes or no were initially assembled. On the basis of preliminary testing with both college men and draftees, the list was reduced to 116. However, the armistice came before the final form could be used in practice. Later called the Woodworth Psychoneurotic Inventory, this self-report inventory was the forerunner of the many paper-and-pencil personality tests in use today.

Following Woodworth's original work, there were several rather immediate attempts to adapt his questionnaire to other groups (such as schoolchildren, juvenile delinquents, and college students), essentially by modifying the wording of the questions. A variation of the questionnaire procedure was developed by Pressey and Pressey (1919), whose X-O Test presented the subject with lists of words rather than questions. Subjects were asked to read the list and designate the words that they regarded as wrong (such as spitting, smoking, recklessness), or that made them nervous or anxious (such as loneliness, sin, pain), and those that involved their likes or interests (such as camping, reading, kissing).

Thus, by 1920, there was a firm beginning of a structured and empirical approach to personality measurement—one based on the academic study of individual differences and the clinical assessment of psychopathology. In the subsequent decades, there has been an explosion of interest in personality assessment. The lines of development are much less clear, however, and there is much cross-fertilization of ideas and research. Let us try to untangle the basic threads of the later influences on this burgeoning field.

INFLUENCE OF PSYCHOANALYSIS

As noted previously, the clinical assessment of individuals suffering from some form of psychopathology influenced the development of personality assessment. Within this context, psychoanalytic theory, with its view that personality is best understood as a series of levels and that the causes of psychological disturbances are hidden deep below the level of conscious awareness, became predominant. In the psychoanalytic view, the most important and useful means of understanding an individual is an analysis of the hidden elements of his or her functioning, not the overt behavior that is readily available for superficial scrutiny. To psychoanalysts, the data yielded by the self-report inventories then available were of limited utility. Of related importance was the rising influence of Gestalt psychology, with its implication that the personality of the whole individual was more than the simple sum of discrete behaviors or traits.

These trends came together in a well-known development in the history of personality assessment for clinical purposes. Hermann Rorschach, a Swiss psychiatrist, had been using the perception of inkblots as an approach to theoretical problems in psychology when he made the empirical discovery that the results could be used for making differential psychiatric diagnoses. His major work was published in German in 1921 but did not appear officially in English until 1942 (Rorschach, 1942/1951). Although earlier investigators had used inkblots as free association material, they had limited themselves to an analysis of the thematic content. Rorschach's contribution was to attempt a systematic analysis of the subject's concern with the *formal* aspects of the blots (such as color, shading, apparent movement) and whether the subject used the whole or parts of the blot in responding. He believed that these different perceptual approaches were related to different psychological processes, or "structures," of the personality, and he advocated further research into this perceptual task, using an empirical, statistical orientation. Rorschach's work was seminal both in stimulating research with his inkblots and in the development of other minimally structured stimulus situations, to which responses can be elicited and analyzed for the purpose of personality assessment. Rorschach's plans for greater validational research on his technique were interrupted by his untimely death at the age of 37.

Rorschach's inkblot technique soon found favor among clinicians, especially those of a psychoanalytic orientation, as a means for assessing the state of the unconscious mind. Its use in this manner is somewhat ironic; Rorschach used his inkblots primarily as a means of addressing theoretical problems in experimental psychology, and only secondarily as an empirical means of assigning patients to psychodiagnostic categories (Rorschach, 1921/1942). In fact, he specifically stated that "the test cannot be considered as a means for delving into the unconscious" (p. 123). Nevertheless, the technique eventually became the most widely used procedure for exploring both the content and structure of the deeper aspects of personality within psychoanalytic theory. More recently, Exner and his colleagues have done very extensive work in an attempt to put the Rorschach on a sounder footing psychometrically and to develop it further as a comprehensive instrument for assessing personality and psychopathology (Exner, 1986, 1991; Exner & Weiner, 1982).

The popularity of the Rorschach technique and the development of other, similar procedures for examining the hidden or covert aspects of personality led Frank (1939) to term these approaches to personality assessment *projective* techniques. Projective methods were conceptualized as those that present subjects with a situation for which there are few clearly defined cultural patterns of response, so that they must "project" on that ambiguous field a "way of seeing life, . . . meanings, significances, patterns, and especially . . . feelings" (Frank, 1939, p. 403). According to Frank, a projective test involves the presentation of a stimulus situation that elicits the idiosyncratic meaning and organization of the individual's private world, bringing them to the testing situation in response to the test demands. Frank regarded these methods as indirect; they tap the pattern of internal organization and structure of personality without disintegrating or modifying the pattern as it exists, much in the manner of an X ray.

What are the other projective methods? The word association method, which is seldom used nowadays in clinical practice, has already been discussed. A group of procedures that Lindzey (1961) called *constructive techniques* was developed by Henry A. Murray and his colleagues at Harvard University in the 1930s (Morgan & Murray, 1935; Murray, 1938, 1943). Murray, who had a strong interest in literary creation, developed the Thematic Apperception Test (TAT), in which subjects create stories about ambiguous pictures. According to Murray, the content of the stories reflects the subjects' past experiences and present needs. A similar constructive approach was involved in Van Lennep's (1951) Four Picture Test, developed initially in the 1930s, and in such later instruments as the Blacky Pictures (Blum, 1950) and the Children's Apperception Test (Bellak, 1954). Another widely used group of projective procedures involves an analysis of the subject's own creative drawings and paintings. Although figure drawings of a man had been used for some time as a convenient method of estimating intelligence (Goodenough, 1926), it remained for Buck (1948a, 1948b) and Machover (1949) to popularize them as a projective method for personality assessment.

INFLUENCE OF PSYCHOMETRICS

At the same time that some psychologists were busy developing and using projective approaches to the assessment of personality, others were busy with the further development and refinement of personality inventories. This work, although directly related to Woodworth's original Personal Data Sheet (Symonds, 1931), was conducted by psychologists who in many cases possessed sophisticated skills in test construction and statistics, together with a clear understanding of the complex problems of test reliability and validity. It emphasized the measurement of a person's discrete traits or aspects rather than a global assessment of the whole personality.

The advantages of inventories were: they could be readily administered to many individuals in a group; scoring was rapid and objective; and statistical procedures could be used in establishing norms, internal consistency, the relationship between test scores and other behavioral measures, and other characteristics of the instruments. There were difficulties also. The test items involved in these instruments often reflected the more superficial and obvious aspects of overt behavior, and their susceptibility to deliberate faking posed many problems in interpreting the scores obtained. Goldberg (1971a) published an exhaustive historical survey of personality scales and inventories, and the interested reader is referred to his work for more extensive information in this area.

The item content of most early inventories was chosen for its face validity; that is, items were included if the test developer thought they would elicit different responses from well-adjusted as compared to poorly adjusted subjects. The Bell Adjustment Inventory (Bell, 1939) is an example of this approach to item selection and test construction.

A different and more sophisticated technique for item selection is the *empirical* approach: the actual responses of different subject groups are examined to determine which responses are characteristic of each group. Only those items that can be actually shown to differentiate the groups are included in the final form of the test. The empirical approach, used by Rorschach in the original development of his psychodiagnostic procedure, was also employed by Edward K. Strong (1927) in the development of the Strong Vocational Interest Blank, the forerunner of the current Strong Interest Inventory. Although a full discussion of interest measurement is beyond our scope here, Strong's work is noteworthy because it presents an important early model of the empirical approach to test construction. The empirical technique was also involved to some extent in the construction of the Bernreuter Personality Inventory (Bernreuter, 1939) and in the Humm-Wadsworth Temperament Scale (Humm & Wadsworth, 1935). The latter was a direct predecessor of the more carefully developed Minnesota Multiphasic Personality Inventory (MMPI) (Hathaway & McKinley, 1940, 1951), and its successors, the MMPI-2 and the MMPI-A (Butcher et al., 1992; Hathaway & McKinley, 1989).

We have already alluded to the troublesome problem caused when some subjects avoided giving socially undesirable answers to inventory items; for example, they failed to admit to being nervous, rather than making the more personally appropriate responses. The MMPI attempted to deal with this problem by including several *validity scales,* such as the Lie scale, which give some measure of a tendency to respond in the socially acceptable manner. Concern with this problem also led to the development, in the 1940s, of the forced-choice technique, which was subsequently used by Edwards (1953) in his Personal Preference Schedule. Because the forced-choice procedure requires subjects to endorse one of two items matched for social desirability (or undesirability), it was presumed that responses would not be limited to social desirability.

Goldberg (1971b), commenting on the proliferation of personality inventories, made a distinction between two kinds of inventories, based on the reasons for their development. The first group of inventories was developed in response to pressures from society to deal with specific applied problems. This category included the inventories dealing with the problem of personal adjustment (previously discussed), those measuring satisfaction and success in vocational choice, and those tapping aspects of academic achievement beyond what is predictable from measures of scholastic aptitude or intelligence. The second group of inventories was based more on conceptions of the structure of individual differences than on any societal or real-life considerations, and was viewed as stemming from theoretical concepts about the nature of personality. This group included the inventory measures of introversion-extroversion and masculinity-femininity, and those based on three influential theories of individual differences: (a) Spranger's (1928) classification of "personal values"; (b) Murray's (1938) scheme for ordering manifest needs; and (c) the Myers-Briggs approach to assessing Carl Jung's types (Briggs & Myers, 1943). Although Goldberg's classification scheme was developed only for inventory measures of personality, it has clear relevance for other personality assessment methods.

PSYCHOANALYSIS VERSUS PSYCHOMETRICS

Most of the specific instruments and the methodological issues introduced in the preceding sections will be discussed in greater detail later. What, however, can be said about the present relationship between these two major historical influences—psychoanalysis and psychometrics—and the two major approaches to assessment they spawned—the projective technique and the self-report inventory? Over the years, there has been a persistent tendency on the part of most followers of these two traditions to have a strong negative emotional bias toward work in the other tradition. This tendency was undoubtedly heightened in 1939 by Frank's use of the label "projective techniques" with the explicit statement that these instruments provided indirect measures of personality structure, and by the implication that the era's more traditional inventories were not coming to grips with the real stuff of personality.

The most important consequence of this development of two antagonistic points of view has been the loss of much clinical and scientific interchange between the two opposing camps and the loss of cross-fertilization that might have advanced the entire process of personality assessment. There have been a number of methodologically sound attempts to integrate the two traditions, such as the Holtzman Inkblot Technique (Holtzman, Thorpe, Swartz, & Herron, 1961), the Defense Mechanisms Inventory (Ihilevich & Gleser, 1986), the Incomplete Sentences Task (Lanyon & Lanyon, 1980), and the Roberts Apperception Test (McArthur & Roberts, 1982). However, these efforts have generated relatively little enthusiasm on either side.

INFLUENCE OF VOCATIONAL AND INDUSTRIAL PSYCHOLOGY

While clinical psychologists were directing their efforts toward the detection and evaluation of maladjustment through either inventories or projective techniques, interest was also developing in the assessment of other aspects of human personality, especially nonskill characteristics that might contribute to vocational success. Although maladjustment per se was often seen as an important factor in determining vocational failure, interest was focused more specifically on factors within the range of normal functioning that determined people's choices of vocation and their long-range vocational success and satisfaction.

The Strong Vocational Interest Blank (now the Strong Interest Inventory), noted earlier, was originally developed in 1927 by empirically comparing the expressed interests of successful persons in a variety of occupations. By asking persons who were established in different occupations to express their preferences among activities such as "visit an art gallery" and "collect coins," Strong was able to identify a number of interests that were differentially correlated with success in specific occupations. He reasoned that, if successful persons in a vocation could be differentiated on the basis of their expressed interests, then new persons with similar interests would more likely be successful in that vocation than would newcomers with dissimilar interests. More than 60 years of research with Strong's instrument and its successors has shown substantial support for this basic hypothesis. The Strong Vocational Interest Blank and a number of similar interest inventories began to be routinely used by vocational counselors for career guidance and by industrial psychologists for selection purposes.

Vocational and industrial psychologists began to assess other variables as well. For example, large differences in effective job performance were found among persons of approximately equal ability level. Those who did well seemed to have more drive or a stronger motive to achieve than those who did poorly. It was hoped that the assessment of this characteristic would result in improved counseling and selection procedures. McClelland, Atkinson, Clark, and Lowell (1953) responded to this particular challenge by developing a highly reliable scoring scheme for achievement motivation, based on the Thematic Apperception Test. The development of the Edwards Personal Preference Schedule (Edwards, 1953, 1959), using a modified self-report inventory approach, was another response to the need for instruments to assess motivational aspects among normal persons.

Psychologists started to realize that as people progressed up the vocational ladder from assembly line worker through supervisory roles and into management, interpersonal relationships became more and more important as a determinant of success. Consequently, it began to become necessary for psychologists to evaluate interpersonal factors as part of their routine work of management selection and management development. The earlier paper-and-pencil inventories, with their focus on psychopathology, were clearly unsuited for such purposes, and a new generation of inventories was developed, tapping aspects of everyday psychological functioning such as sociability, dominance, flexibility, and various dimensions of interpersonal style. Instruments whose origins were motivated in part by the needs of vocational and industrial psychology include the California Psychological Inventory (Gough, 1957, 1987), the Fundamental Interpersonal Relations Orientation (FIRO) Scales developed by Schutz (1967), Jackson's (1967, 1974) Personality Research Form, the Jackson Personality Inventory (Jackson, 1976), the Executive Profile Survey (Lang & Krug, 1983), and the Hogan Personality Inventory (Hogan, 1992).

Another product of the real world of work was the observation that items of personal history, as recorded on a written application blank, appeared to have value in predicting success in specific work settings. This observation resulted in the development of the weighted biographical data sheet (England, 1961), which provides an alternative to the established psychological "testing" approach to assessment.

To digress for a moment, the use of biographical data for clinical purposes has been well established. For example, the Phillips (1953) scale for predicting outcome in schizophrenia was a method of estimating the premorbid adjustment of psychiatric patients by assigning differential weighting to various items in the patient's case history, mainly those behaviors involving heterosexual interests and relationships. Biographical data have also been used for many years in the development of base expectancy tables to predict whether a prisoner is likely to violate parole if it is granted (e.g., Burgess, 1928). In view of the central role accorded case history information in professional mental health work, it is somewhat surprising that no widely used clinical instrument of this type exists. Preliminary work by Briggs (1959) and others indicated that such instruments could be developed and showed their potential for clinical use.

Another approach to personality assessment is the behavior sample technique pioneered by Galton (1884), described previously. Here, the behaviors of interest are evoked in the laboratory or in a controlled field setting. The primary assumption underlying this approach is direct and simple: the frequency or ease with which the behaviors are aroused in test situations is related to the frequency with which they occur in ordinary real-life settings.

Perhaps the best known of the early attempts to use the behavior sample approach is that of Hartshorne and May (1928) in their studies of honesty and deceit. A more complex use is found in the *assessment center* procedure, which is designed to gain a better understanding of particular groups of individuals or to select candidates for difficult or high-level positions. The use of this procedure for assessing a particular group of individuals, such as architects or mathematicians, was pioneered by psychologists at the University of California's Institute of Personality Assessment and Research (IPAR). Their research reports (e.g., MacKinnon, 1975) tended to offer strong support for this type of complex, behavior-sample approach.

One of the first uses of the assessment center method for personnel selection was in the U.S. Office of Strategic Services' clinical assessment project during the Second World War (OSS Assessment Staff, 1948), where persons were selected for counterintelligence and spying operations. The candidates were brought together in small groups for several days of evaluation by a group of assessors at a remote residential site or assessment center. Many different kinds of data were made available to the panel of assessors, including psychological tests and interview transcripts. What was unique, however, was observation of the participants in a variety of situational tests that were developed as representative samples of the work to be done. For instance, one of the situational tests developed for the OSS assessment program was a stress interview in which interrogators attempted to break down the "cover story" the candidate had developed. Despite considerable difficulty, data were obtained to indicate the positive contribution of the assessment center concept for selecting spies. Among the several problems inherent in this approach are how the many behavioral indexes (such as test scores and ratings) should be weighted, how to combine them into a single predictor, and how to develop criterion measures. Taft (1959) provided an interesting and illuminating summary of many of the issues involved in the multiple-method approach to assessment and selection.

Motivated in part by the OSS experience, a multiple-method assessment program was conducted to study the selection process for the profession of clinical psychology (Kelly & Fiske, 1951; Kelly & Goldberg, 1959). However, results were disappointing. Using ratings of later professional success as the criteria, neither the individual measures nor the combined ratings yielded useful predictions. In trying to explain the relative failure, the authors noted that the subjects involved were already highly selected and rather homogeneous in a number of important respects, all of which would attenuate the obtained correlations. A similar study with more promising results was reported by Holt and Luborsky (1958), using psychiatric residents as the subjects.

The assessment center methodology has been widely adopted as the procedure of choice in the selection and development of middle-level managers. Based on the early work of the American Telephone and Telegraph Company (Bray & Grant, 1966), these centers have been shown to provide reliable and valid predictions against ratings of job success (Bray, 1982; Thornton & Byham, 1982). Predictions have been based on situations with a high degree of real-life behavioral relevance. One advantage of the behavior sample approach in this situation is its relatively high degree of acceptance by participants; another is that its predictive validity and its obvious face validity make it less susceptible to legal objections based on equal employment opportunity legislation. Research indicating the superiority of multimethod assessment is discussed in Chapter Eight and assessment center technology is further described in Chapter Nine.

INFLUENCE OF MODERN BEHAVIORISM

The mainstream of American academic psychology has always been rather behavioral in orientation, and the 1960s and 1970s saw a strong movement to extend this orientation into clinical psychology. This movement, largely associated with the rise of behavior modification and behavior therapy, also has its implications for personality assessment. Assessments prepared by persons working from traditional positions, based either on self-report inventories or projective techniques, have typically emphasized the underlying personality structure or the inner predispositions of the person. There has been little interest in considering the contextual or situational determinants of the person's behavior. Rather, the assumption in traditional assessment has been that an understanding of personality, referring to inner dispositions, is all that is necessary for making predictions about future behaviors.

Behaviorally oriented psychologists have called for greater specificity of predictions and, most particularly, for a thorough study of the environmental circumstances that are necessary for a particular behavior to be evoked (Mischel, 1968, 1977). Many behavioral psychologists also believe that an individual's self-statements and self-predictions are often as accurate in predicting the person's behavior as the more indirect and expensive evaluations by trained personality assessors. The underlying rationale is phenomeno-logical. The crucial determinant of the person's behavior in a situation is believed to be the person's awareness of the behavioral contingencies in the situation, and only the person has access to that awareness.

Another important characteristic of the behavioral approach is its em-phasis on the person's behavior, or what a person *does* in various situations, rather than on inner dispositions, or what a person *is*. Thus, instead of rely-ing on generally available and commercially published personality tests, be-havioral psychologists prefer to develop "tailor-made" assessment devices in which the particular stimulus situation of interest to the psychologist is rep-resented in as accurate and detailed a manner as possible. As an early ex-ample, in measuring fear, a population of potentially fear-arousing stimuli was identified and a representative sample of items was drawn from it and presented to the person in a variety of ways. In assessing fear of snakes, the items included written descriptions; slides, pictures, or movies; vivid fan-tasies of snakes; and actual snakes (Lang & Lazovik, 1963). Similar proce-dures were developed for assessment in interpersonal areas such as marital discord and parent–child problems (O'Leary & Wilson, 1987). The similar-ity of this approach to the behavioral sample approach of the assessment center should be readily apparent. Use is also made of the *continuity as-sumption,* in which internal or covert behaviors such as thoughts and feel-ings are viewed as responses similar to overt or external behaviors, and are subject to the same principles as external behaviors (Thoresen & Mahoney, 1974). The growing field of behavioral assessment is considered in detail in Chapter Five.

RESURGENCE OF TRAIT PSYCHOLOGY

For the past hundred years and more, many students of human behavior have been sympathetic to the viewpoint that the basis for human personal-ity is best understood in terms of a finite number of basic *traits* or personal characteristics. In this approach, a bar-chart can be constructed for each of us, depicting the amount of each trait that we possess. The terms *faculty psy-chology, character,* and *temperament* all belong to this general approach to per-sonality. Two basic questions arise from the trait approach:

1. How many basic traits are there, and what are they?
2. How can they be assessed?

A variety of different possible answers to the first question were offered in the 1940s and 1950s by Thurstone (1949, 1951), Guilford (1940, 1947), Guil-ford and Martin (1943a, 1943b), Eysenck (1952, 1953b), and Cattell (1946, 1950). In the subsequent two decades, the increasing popularity of applied behavioral psychology, with its emphasis on situations and environments as the causes of human behavior, pushed trait psychology into a back seat (e.g., Mischel, 1968). However, a major resurgence of interest in trait psychology has taken place since that time, supported by greater research sophistication in defining and measuring traits. The result has been the emergence of the *five-factor model of personality* and its related variants (Digman, 1990; Goldberg, 1993; Wiggins & Pincus, 1992). Current researchers are reaching beyond this simple structural pattern to explore the relationship of basic traits to personality disorders (Costa & Widiger, 1992), the use of circular or circumplex trait models (Pincus & Wiggins, 1990), questions of trait "width" and hierarchical structure (Hampson, John, & Goldberg, 1986), and trait stability over the life span (Costa & McCrae, 1986).

The most popular answer to the question of how to measure traits has been the same for many years: through the use of factor analysis and its variants. Indeed, the resurgence of interest in trait models of personality has gone hand in hand with the rapid development of new multivariate statistical procedures, such as confirmatory factor analysis, that were made feasible by the availability of high-speed computer technology. Thus, specific trait models of personality, and procedures for assessing them through factor-analytic personality questionnaires, have developed simultaneously, and a number of tests based on the five-factor model are now available (e.g., Costa & McCrae, 1992b; Hogan, 1986, 1992). This work is described in more detail in Chapters Three and Nine.

INFLUENCE OF BEHAVIOR GENETICS

We have just seen how theories or models of personality with a trait orientation have become a powerful force in their field, with strong implications for assessment. Underlying trait theories has often been the assumption that traits are biologically determined. Galton (1884), for example, believed that character was hereditary, and Gall's phrenology tied faculties directly to the brain. More recently, Cattell (1950) and Eysenck (1960) expressed a similar view, which was also implied in the temperament research of Buss and Plomin (1975).

The view that personality is biologically or genetically determined, at least in part, is unpopular in American society, as is the view that there is a substantial genetic component to intelligence. It is an American tradition to believe that everyone is born with comparable potential, and that we can be all we want to be if we devote enough time and effort to it. This viewpoint is reflected in behavioral psychology with its emphasis on situations rather than dispositions as the causes of behavior.

Starting in the mid-1970s, research evidence from studies of twins began to indicate that as much as half or even more of the variation in major personality characteristics is due to genetic factors (Loehlin & Nichols, 1976; Tellegen et al., 1988). Although there is some controversy concerning the age at which such effects become evident and measurable (Plomin, Coon, Carey, DeFries, & Fulker, 1991), the fact of genetic influences on personality now appears to be well established (Heath, 1991).

The implications of these findings for personality assessment are:

1. They reinforce belief in the existence of a simple, basic framework or structure for personality.
2. They encourage the possibility of exploring physiological or biological measures, or at least of relating basic personality concepts to corresponding biological concepts.
3. They narrow the distinction between traits and "temperaments," a term traditionally used for patterns of behavior that are assumed to be innate.
4. They lend credence to the stability of personality characteristics across the life span (Costa, McCrae, & Arenberg, 1980), and they support the current enthusiasm for assessment devices based on trait models of personality.

INFLUENCE OF SOCIAL PSYCHOLOGY

We began the chapter with a discussion of humans' abiding interest in understanding the behavior of others, and the manner in which "naive" persons have gone about achieving this understanding. We conclude with the same topic but from a different perspective. Social psychologists have long been interested in understanding how nonpsychologists go about understanding others—assessing other people's intentions, motives, interpersonal likes and dislikes, and other important characteristics. Social psychologists term this area *person perception,* and we can assume that at least some of the operations engaged in by clinical psychologists during interviewing and therapy fall within this topic. Clinicians were naive perceivers of others long before they became psychologists, and these early patterns of perception probably continue to function largely unchanged.

Not unexpectedly, our physical appearance is a primary determinant of how we are perceived by others. A large number of research studies support the conclusion that the impression we make is influenced by physical attractiveness and neatness of dress and grooming, plus a number of other immediately obvious characteristics, such as the wearing of glasses. To cite a specific example, Dion, Berscheid, and Walster (1972) found that physically attractive people are seen by others as more sensitive, more interesting, more sociable, more exciting, and kinder than less attractive people.

The impressions we form of others come not only from various static or structural elements of appearance but also from a variety of kinetic or fluid elements, such as gestures and body movements. Body contact, proximity, orientation of body, posture, looking or gazing, and the nonverbal elements of speech have all been studied (Argyle, 1972). In general, these cues are utilized to make judgments about such characteristics as attractiveness or likability, about emotional states such as depression or anxiety, and about status and role. Judgments appear to rely heavily on "display rules," or conventions that have established the appropriate behaviors for a variety of situations (Goffman, 1959).

One important finding from the research on person perception is that, as we collect data about other people, we tend to rely on *central traits* in forming our impressions. That is, certain bits of data about a person are given greater weight than other bits, and we ordinarily use these more central bits to organize our impressions. The seminal experiments of Asch (1946) demonstrated that the *warm–cold dimension* was a central trait. For instance, when the adjective *warm* was used to describe another person who was to be judged, over 90% of the experimental subjects described the target person as *generous,* and more than 75% used *humorous* as a descriptor. Other constructs, such as *polite* or *blunt,* when applied to the subjects, did not generate such a strong halo effect about the target person, leading Asch to conclude that only certain descriptors or traits were central ones. Asch's work, supported and elaborated by a number of subsequent investigations, is useful in helping us to understand how we often form a rather clear impression of another person, even with a minimum of information.

A basic question is, of course, the accuracy of such impressions. There is no clear answer to this question. However, there is evidence˜ (Norman & Goldberg, 1966; Passini & Norman, 1966) that central traits or dimensions of personality are, at least in part, a function of the way in which observers tend to use the trait names rather than of the observed person's actual characteristics. In other words, our judgments about others can be in part a function of the way we structure our interpersonal world and might not be primarily a function of the way others behave.

There appear to be three kinds of central traits around which observers organize their judgments of others: *evaluation,* where judgments are organized around a good–bad dimension; *potency,* where strong–weak or hard–soft is used as the dimension; and *activity,* where the dimension is active–passive or energetic–lazy (Rosenberg & Sedlak, 1972). These dimensions are particularly apparent in direct ratings of traits and in trait-sorting tasks, where judges are asked to describe a target person by selecting from a list of traits those that best describe them. There is obvious congruence between this group of three dimensions and those previously identified by Osgood in his work with the Semantic Differential (Osgood, Suci, & Tannenbaum, 1957).

One important reason why people observe another person is to know the person's intentions or motives (Heider, 1958). Such knowledge makes that other person's behavior understandable and predictable. Two basic models of this process have been proposed—the intuitive and the inferential. The phenomenological and Gestalt psychologists have argued that the person-perception process is intuitive, immediate, organized, and direct, and is based more on some innate, human mechanism than on learning (e.g., Allport, 1937, 1961). The inferential view, on the other hand (e.g., Sarbin, Taft, & Bailey, 1960), suggests that judgments about others are built up from cues provided by the person and are based on learned, general principles of human behavior. The inferences operate much like syllogisms in which the underlying characteristics of the person are judged in terms of *general constructs* or postulates.

Consider the syllogism:

People who wear glasses are intelligent.

This person wears glasses.

Therefore this person is intelligent.

The major premise ("People who wear glasses are intelligent"), the one on which the entire inferential process depends, is a general construct developed from (a) past experience, (b) an organized set of beliefs that constitutes, in effect, a personality theory, (c) an analogy, or (d) the uncritical acceptance of a proposed construct from others. These constructs, which are part of what the observer brings to the person perception, produce the beauty in the beholder's eye. The usefulness of such constructs depends on their "truthfulness," or predictive validity.

One general set of constructs is called *stereotypes* (Lippmann, 1922), widespread beliefs about the characteristics of persons who belong to certain definable groups (racial, ethnic, national, social, sex, or age) or who possess certain salient physical qualities (height, weight, hair coloring, facial characteristics, handicaps, or deformities). Many stereotypes contain some truths, but these truths are typically distorted and exaggerated by the language used to express them. More important, there is considerable danger that people tend to use stereotypes in an overspecific manner and that every member of a certain group is assumed to have exactly the same characteristic. Nevertheless, stereotypes do constitute one important source of our initial constructs about other people.

The minor premise ("This person wears glasses") involves placement of the person in the class defined in the major premise. This process involves an examination of the many cues provided by the person. When the cues clearly establish class membership, we draw a conclusion based on that membership. Hathaway (1956a) demonstrated that only a handful of cues (including gender, age, and intelligence) provide an adequate basis for assignment to group membership, and that much of our inaccuracy in making predictions about others stems from using cues that are insufficiently valid. To summarize, whether or not the inferential model of Sarbin et al. (1960) accurately reflects all instances of person perception, it would seem to be useful in understanding a great many of them.

Social psychologists recently have centered much of their research attention on the process of *attribution:* how people go about assessing and evaluating the intentions and motives of others. When we observe a behavior of others, we believe that the person did it either by *volition* or because of *situational circumstances*. For example, a person who is successful is seen either to have tried hard or to have been given an easy task. Analogously, failure is explained either by insufficient effort or by inability to cope with a task that was too difficult.

It is important to recognize that people tend to be held responsible for their behavior when they are free to choose, but are not seen as responsible for responding to external compulsion. Many of our judgments about the moral quality of others depend on how we attribute motivation or responsibility. Did some POWs become traitors voluntarily, or did they simply yield to the inevitable and overwhelming pressure of their captors? Was Patty Hearst a voluntary colleague of her bank-robbing captors or did she simply break down under extreme duress?

The body of research now available suggests that the answer to such questions is different for the actor and the observer. As summarized by Jones and Nisbett (1971), there is a "persistent tendency for actors to attribute their actions to situational requirements, whereas observers tend to attribute the same actions to stable personal dispositions" (p. 2). In other words, we tend to perceive that our own actions are controlled by the environment and not by some internal need or predisposition, but we believe that others act in the same way because of their personal dispositions and not because of the influence of *their* environment. Thus, we may regard our affectional overtures to another person as due to a covert invitation (or possibly inebriation), but we are much more likely to regard such behavior in others as evidence of their licentiousness. "I am just a victim of circumstances, but he's a dirty old man."

Perhaps the simplest way of explaining this pervasive finding is that we have a great deal more information available about our own inner needs, our own past history, and how we experience our own environment than we do about other people. Also, we have a large library of data about our own past reactions in similar and dissimilar situations, whereas we must interpret the behavior of others from a normative or modal frame of reference. These tendencies tend to combine to produce a view of other people as a package of personality traits, even as we see ourselves as a package of underlying values and strategies that are brought into behavior by particular circumstances. Some psychologists, like Mischel (1968), believe that this approach to ourselves is also a potentially more accurate way of perceiving other persons, compared to our typical way of seeing them as driven by underlying traits. In any event, the data seem rather clear. We tend to attribute our own behavior to external causes and the behavior of others to internal causes.

Attribution theory has considerable relevance to the practical problems of personality assessment (Brehm, 1976). Psychologists make many attributions concerning their clients; indeed, much clinical work is motivated by the need to reach some conclusion about the underlying intentions or motives of those with whom we are working. As Shaver (1975) noted, "insight" by a client in therapy can be seen as basically a correct attribution of causation (or, at least, one that matches that of the psychologist), and much of our therapeutic work with clients has the goal of changing their attributional systems. Valins and Nisbett (1971) expanded on this idea. In their analysis, clients frequently make attributions of abnormality or inadequacy about themselves that have very negative consequences. These attributions are developed without any checking with peers, because the behavior for which causation is sought is bad or shameful, or because it is assumed that others would not have had similar experiences. The erroneous causal attribution ("I am emotionally disturbed" or "I am sick") exacerbates the problem by creating even further distance between the person and his or her peers.

In summary, attribution theory, which began as a theory of "naive psychology," has important implications for the process of personality assessment in a broad sense. In particular, we need to beware of the general tendency to attribute the behavior of others to underlying, internal traits, without considering how such attributions may be a function of a pervasive tendency to externalize causation that has little to do with the target person but much to do with people in general.

SUMMARY

A number of assessment methods, such as phrenology, astrology, and palmistry, are fascinating to many laypersons but are not regarded as having the documented utility required for their serious consideration by trained professional workers in personality assessment. Turning to the professionally recognized assessment instruments, two historical trends can be seen in their development. The first is traceable to early academic interest in measuring individual differences, and it has its most important consequences in contemporary paper-and-pencil inventories, the self-report personality tests. The second originated in the need for understanding clinically abnormal behavior, and it is seen as leading to the interest in and development of projective techniques.

There has been long-standing conflict between the proponents of projective techniques and psychologists interested in psychometrically oriented assessment procedures. Some differences may exist between the two approaches, especially in their historical development, but the overemphasis placed on the differences has probably been detrimental to the development of the science of personality assessment.

Several other areas have had a significant impact on personality assessment. Within the fields of vocational and industrial psychology, procedures such as the Strong Vocational Interest Blank (now the Strong Interest Inventory) were developed for career guidance and vocational selection. Also, a variety of inventories have been developed for assessing motivation and personality variables within the normal range, and biographical data and behavior samples have been used for assessment purposes. Such procedures came together in the assessment center technique, which was used for the selection of intelligence agents during World War II and has been widely adopted as the procedure of choice in selecting middle-level management personnel in business and industry.

Another influence in the development of personality assessment has been modern behaviorism with its emphasis on a thorough study of the environmental circumstances that are necessary for a particular behavior to be evoked, as opposed to the more traditional approach of viewing the causes of behavior as residing within the person. A renewed interest in trait psychology, and the study of genetic factors underlying personality development, have also helped to shape contemporary personality assessment. A further influence has been the field of social psychology, and particularly the area of person perception, referring to the study of the manner in which laypersons go about achieving an understanding of others. One manner of organizing judgments about others involves three dimensions: (a) evaluation, (b) potency, and (c) activity. A recent framework for studying how people assess the intentions and motives of others is attribution theory. Research findings in this area suggest that we tend to view our own behavior as controlled by the environment but that of others as due to personal dispositions.

CHAPTER TWO

Concepts and Definitions

In understanding any human enterprise, it is important not only to understand *what* is being undertaken, but also to understand *why* a particular course of action is being pursued. Why do psychologists undertake the task of personality assessment? What are the benefits that this enterprise can offer? In general, psychologists assess personality for two reasons: first and primary, to assist our understanding of the behavior of a particular person, that is, the *clinical assessment* of a single individual; and second, in the context of psychological research and theory building, to advance our *general knowledge* of human behavior.

The major use of personality assessment instruments in professional psychology has been in the first context, the assessment of the individual. The aim is to come to some decision about the future course of action of a specified person or to make a prediction about his or her unique future behavior. This professional use has been the main reason for the development and continued existence of most of the better known assessment devices.

With regard to the second use of assessment, researchers in psychology employ personality assessment techniques for a number of reasons. Some wish to study a particular personality concept—such as authoritarianism, ego strength, or loss of control—either for its own sake or within the framework of some theoretical approach to personality. Another research reason for utilizing assessment techniques could be in the context of achieving a better understanding of a certain pattern of behavior, such as managerial behavior or a particular clinical syndrome. A third reason might be to reduce the range of individual differences within subject groups on a research task by sorting the subjects according to a distinctive personality characteristic. For example, a researcher evaluating the effects of a psychotherapy procedure such as relaxation training might decide to examine high-anxiety and low-anxiety subjects separately because it is suspected that these subjects will differ in their ability to relax. Or, it might be decided to separate field-dependent and field-independent persons in an investigation of ability to solve a managerial in-box problem. In research uses of assessment, the interest is typically in group differences rather than in a particular individual or in understanding the implications of the findings for the individual. Researchers are primarily interested in how the overall results shed light on some general fact or behavioral law that is reflected in the behavior of people in their experiments.

It would appear that the two major themes or influences that have defined and shaped our current knowledge in personality assessment are: (a) our involvement in solving applied, practical problems and (b) our interest in a better theoretical understanding of human functioning. We have previously noted that Goldberg (1971a) drew a similar conclusion after discussing the rise of interest in personality inventories. His conclusion might well be extended to include the entire field of personality assessment, as it seems clear that the interplay between these two themes—the applied or individual, and the general or theoretical—has strongly influenced our present stage of development in personality assessment. Let us further examine these themes in order to enhance our understanding of basic concepts and issues. We focus our discussion on the clinical or practical role of assessment and introduce theoretical aspects as appropriate.

PERSONALITY ASSESSMENT: THE EMPIRICAL APPROACH

We begin with an analysis of personality assessment procedures that utilize empirical knowledge. Taking a simple example, assume we have evidence that a particular response or set of responses (for instance, a score on a self-report personality inventory or a set of responses to the ambiguous stimuli of a projective test) is highly correlated with some nontest behavior (the criterion). It might be that high scores on the ABC test are known to be highly correlated with success in door-to-door selling, or that a large number of animal responses on the XYZ test are highly correlated with unsuccessful rehabilitation following release from a mental hospital.

In the *empirical approach* to personality assessment, the psychologist would need only to administer either of these tests, compare the obtained results with the empirical research findings, and make a prediction as to the probability of success or failure of the individual in either door-to-door selling or posthospital rehabilitation. The psychologist usually neither knows nor is concerned about the psychological or theoretical connection between the individual's test responses and the behavior to be predicted. In the empirical approach, it is not necessary to understand *why* there is a connection between high scores on the ABC test and selling behavior; it is sufficient to know that such a relationship reliably exists. Naturally, it is important to know the limiting conditions of this empirically derived relationship; that is, to know the particular groups of individuals and kinds of selling for which this relationship holds, and the circumstances under which it might break down. If we presume, however, that such information is available and that the individual is drawn from the segment of the population covered by a known empirical relationship, we can use this knowledge for prediction or decision making about that individual. The empirical approach might be schematically represented as follows:

Information from assessment procedures	→	Previous empirical findings	→	Decision about the individual

Depending on such factors as the size of the relationship between the predictor and the criterion, the representativeness of the original empirical data, and the similarity of the current criterion to the original one, the professional psychologist will be more or less correct in the prediction or decision. Because there is a relatively small number of steps and inferences between the data and the decision, and it is not difficult to make periodic checks of the accuracy of the previously reported relationship, the probability of serious error is not great. However, it has been argued by Peak (1953), Loevinger (1957), and others that a purely empirical approach, with a total reliance on observed relationships, is limited and superficial. The psychologist will not be able to develop any understanding, except on a primitive correlational level, of *why* the decision was a useful one.

The empirical approach to assessment involves a basic assumption of *interpersonal behavior consistency;* that is, there are enduring patterns of behavioral responses that transcend situations and can be tapped and used for understanding particular individuals and people in general. The search for an understanding of these enduring characteristics of persons serves to identify the entire field of personality as an area of inquiry. Although a concern with the *nature* of these enduring characteristics is clearly the province of the more theoretically based approaches to personality assessment, the empirical approach must also assume their existence. It is particularly important to understand this assumption, because some psychologists who are identified with the behavioral approach to assessment have questioned the existence of significant enduring characteristics. This theoretical trend, which minimizes the importance of general and enduring characteristics as determinants of behavior, was seen in its most radical form in the 1960s (e.g., Kanfer & Saslow, 1965; Mischel, 1968; Peterson, 1968). The major question asked today is not so much whether enduring interpersonal characteristics can be identified as whether they have importance for the field of personality theory, and in particular for assessment. In the *behavioral assessment* movement, primary emphasis is placed on the current situational determinants of behavior and on the relevant rewards and punishments that are contingent on these behaviors. Thus, the understanding and prediction of individual behavior is based not so much on an assessment of "underlying personality" as on an analysis of the actual behavior and the context in which the behavior occurs. We return to these issues later in the chapter.

PERSONALITY DESCRIPTION AND PERSONALITY ASSESSMENT

In the empirical approach to personality assessment, the professional psychologist moves directly from the obtained data to the prediction or decision, without considering any intervening processes. The empirical approach is data-based, and its use is limited to those situations in which the test data, usually psychometric in nature, have been shown to be of predictive value.

In actual practice, this limitation turns out to be a serious one. The data may predict door-to-door salesmanship, but there is also interest in sales potential in a whole variety of situations. Similarly, although empirical data may refer to success in posthospital rehabilitation, related situations such as postprison rehabilitation are also of interest.

It could be argued that all that is required under these circumstances is to extend the empirical approach to these new situations—that is, collect additional new empirical data in each specific situation of interest. Unfortunately, because of the high cost of collecting and processing data—in terms of time, money, and other resources—this is usually not what happens in practice. Rather, the existing data are interpreted in more general terms, using the nonspecific language of personality description, and then they are used for prediction or decision making. Thus, persons scoring high on the ABC test become characterized in general terms, such as high in "salesmanship," and persons giving many animal responses to the XYZ test, are described as low in "rehabilitation potential." In other words, rather than simply basing the decision on the empirical findings, as was true in the empirical approach, the personality description approach treats the assessment information as data about some inferred but stable psychological state. This inferred state (a) allows more general conclusions to be drawn about the test respondent, and (b) presumably permits predictive statements to be made on a broader range than would be acceptable by simply extending the empirical findings into the additional situation. The personality description approach to assessment might be schematically represented as follows:

Information from assessment procedures	$\rightarrow$	Personality description (inferred psychological state)	$\rightarrow$	Decision about the individual

It is possible to regard this approach to clinical or individual assessment as being theoretical, but we prefer not to do so. Our reasons are: (a) beyond common sense, very little "theory" is involved, and (b) the choice of the concepts involved in this kind of procedure is primarily determined by pragmatic rather than theoretical considerations. Thus, our decision to use the ABC test of "salesmanship" or the XYZ test of "rehabilitation potential" would be made because we are interested in the behaviors that presumably can be predicted by these instruments, and minimal "theory" is involved either in developing the tests for this use or employing them in this practical manner.

It seems advisable to state more precisely what we mean by a *theory*. Marx and Hillix (1973) identified three general meanings in contemporary psychological writings. The most general use is in reference to any conceptual process in science, in contrast with the empirical, or observational, aspects. A second use is in reference to any generalized explanatory principle, one that ordinarily involves a statement of functional relationships among variables. The third use, which Marx and Hillix (and the present writers) have endorsed as the preferred one, refers to a group of logically organized or deductively related laws, usually based on empirical observations. This usage is more closely aligned with those of the more developed sciences, and it has a closer relationship to the concept of a *system,* which, within psychology, refers to a cluster of theoretical propositions and methodological biases. Taking the third usage as the criterion, it is readily apparent that there are few viable personality theories. In the remainder of our text, the term *theory* is restricted to this third usage, and much of what is often termed "theory" is regarded by us as rational, a priori, or commonsensical.

The reader should note that there is nothing intrinsically incorrect, either theoretically or methodologically, with the procedure of assessment through description. Indeed, if there were data available to suggest that the ABC test did identify those who would become successful salespeople in a variety of settings, or that the XYZ test could predict who would respond unfavorably to rehabilitation efforts under a number of different circumstances, no serious objections to this kind of procedure would be raised. Unfortunately, the literature in personality assessment is replete with examples demonstrating that this is *not* the case. Rather, it would appear that indexes developed for predicting a characteristic such as salesmanship in a particular setting are often relatively specific to that particular setting, and that they become much less effective when the situation to be predicted differs in any substantial way. Therefore, it is always necessary to check, empirically, the generality of the prediction. The ABC test must be checked to see whether it works with new samples of people, who may be older or younger or better educated than the original sample, or to see whether it will predict life insurance sales as well as door-to-door sales of encyclopedias. If the generality of the conclusions is not empirically verified, there is a risk of making incorrect predictions and bad decisions, and, sometimes, of performing worse than if pure chance had been used to make the choices. In summary, the major problem involved in using such descriptive constructs as "salesmanship" or "rehabilitation potential" is that their looseness represents, to many potential users, a clear invitation for abuse.

Because nontest criteria for generalized tendencies such as salesmanship or rehabilitation potential are often extremely difficult to obtain, it is sometimes argued that psychologists should use peer ratings or expert ratings of these tendencies as the criteria for comparison of the test responses. The major problem with this approach is the unknown validity of the ratings. On what basis can it be assumed that peer or "expert" ratings of some generalized behavioral tendency are themselves correlated with the behaviors in question? The question is itself an empirical one, and, without evidence, it cannot be assumed that ratings can be substituted for more empirically based criterion data. Indeed, the very existence of these inferred generalized psychological states is questioned by the more behaviorally oriented psychologists. They tend to argue that success in a variety of selling situations is determined far more by the characteristics of the particular situation than by any internal psychological state of the salesperson, and that overlooking these situational variables reduces the accuracy of any predictions. We will return to this debate later in this chapter.

The procedure of using the empirical relationships between test scores and nontest behaviors to support the utility of an abstract, generalized construct introduces the important concept of *construct validity* (Cronbach & Meehl, 1955), which is further discussed in Chapter Six. What should be understood at this point is the existence of a frequent problem in the applied use of personality assessment procedures—the assumption that a test score or index is indicative of some generalized internal characteristic of the respondent in cases where there are precious few data available to support such an assumption.

THE LANGUAGE OF PERSONALITY DESCRIPTION

Before becoming involved with matters of theory in personality assessment, we will discuss the language that we tend to use to describe personality characteristics. Phrases like "sleeps more than usual," "works energetically on a problem," and "has never been observed to cry" represent rather clear and specific descriptions of directly observable behavior. In describing personality, however, either in our ordinary conversation or as professional psychologists, we usually wish to go further than this. We are usually interested in descriptive concepts that tap the more basic characteristics of the individual. Thus, we tend to use general descriptive concepts such as "lethargic," "energetic," and "stoic" rather than the more behaviorally specific phrases given above. Our language usage involves many of these general descriptive words that are employed in both lay and professional conversations to describe ourselves and others.

Cultural anthropologists have suggested that a study of the words used in a culture's ordinary conversation will provide clues as to what the culture regards as basic and important. The observation that the Eskimo language has many separate words denoting different kinds of snow (variations that, in English, would require multiword phrases) and that the Polynesian dialects contain single words indicative of complex kinship relations (e.g., my father's brother's wife) is seen as evidence that snow and kinship are important concepts in these cultures. Personality characteristics that are regarded as the more basic ones in our culture tend to be denoted by single words.

This view—that individual differences that are most important in daily human transactions have been encoded into natural, everyday language as single-word descriptors—was initially proposed by Allport (1937) and has been strongly supported by Norman (1963c) and Goldberg (1978a, 1982). A related assumption is that the English language contains many synonyms to provide the culture with nuances of meaning for these important human characteristics. To illustrate, consider the large number of separate words used to describe a person with a high energy level—for example, vigorous, energetic, active, lively, spry, brisk, pushy, and busy. However, there is no single-word descriptor of persons with skill in wiggling their ears.

We have just seen that the importance of an individual difference is linked to its representation in natural language. Both Gough (1965) and Cattell (1950, 1957), in their development of personality measures, deliberately used the occurrence of single-word descriptors in natural language to identify characteristics that are worth measuring. Gough selected "variables used for the description and analysis of personality in everyday life and in social interaction. It is theorized that such folk concepts, viewed as emergents from interpersonal behavior, have a kind of immediate meaningfulness and *universal relevance*" (1965, p. 295).

While Gough relied on informal procedures for developing his list of important characteristics, Cattell used the 17,954 trait names that Allport and Odbert (1936) had developed from *Webster's Second Unabridged Dictionary.* Allport and Odbert had synthesized this list into a briefer list of 4,504 names, which they regarded as "real traits." Cattell further reduced the list to 171 items by eliminating synonyms. A cluster analysis of peer ratings using the 171 descriptors yielded 36 clusters, which Cattell regarded as "surface traits." Several different factor analytic studies based on peer ratings of these surface traits led Cattell to conclude that there were 15 to 20 distinct factors, or "source traits," underlying the surface traits. These so-called primary personality factors are measured by his Sixteen Personality Factors Test (Cattell, Eber, & Tatsuoka, 1970). Thus, by a distillation process involving a combination of common sense and statistics, Cattell was able to reduce almost 18,000 characteristics to a list of 16.

Norman (1967) used the 17,954 characteristics listed by Allport and Odbert, plus 170 additional terms selected from *Webster's* third edition, to develop a list of 7,300 descriptors. He eliminated terms that were obscure, ambiguous, purely physically descriptive, or purely evaluative (such as awful, bad, or fine). The remaining 7,300 trait words were then sorted into three categories by Norman and his colleagues, using the criterion of consensus. The three categories were: (a) stable traits (e.g., daring, imaginative, lazy, persistent), which accounted for approximately 40 percent of the total list; (b) temporary states (e.g., hesitant, sad, peeved, ranting), which also accounted for about 40 percent; and (c) social roles, relationships, and effects (e.g., employed, manageable, noted, respected), which accounted for the remaining 20 percent. In this manner, the list was differentiated into *traits*, or enduring response predispositions that have implications for intrapersonal and interpersonal adjustment, and *states*, which are more transitory and ephemeral. For example, anxiety as a trait would suggest a continuing, generalized condition of the individual; anxiety as a state would suggest a more transitory or temporary condition. One of the common confusions in personality description is that the presence of traits is often assumed from behaviors that are indicative only of states. When we are developing a personality description, as opposed to predicting a specific behavior in a specific situation, we are presumably trying to identify the individual's underlying, enduring response predispositions.

DISPOSITIONAL VERSUS SITUATIONAL DETERMINANTS OF BEHAVIOR

As indicated earlier in this chapter, a number of psychologists—in particular, Mischel (1968, 1973, 1977)—have minimized the significance of underlying, enduring response predispositions. Let us now examine in greater detail the objections to the significance of dispositional determinants. For convenience, the term *traits* is used for these underlying dispositional determinants, a usage typical of the field. (As explained later, this term is problematic and somewhat difficult to define.) Hogan, DeSoto, and Solano (1977), in summarizing the objections that have been raised to both the theoretical and practical utility of traits, discerned six major criticisms. First, "critics seem to assume that personality researchers define traits as enduring psychic or neurological structures located somewhere in the mind or nervous system" (p. 256). Or, as Mischel (1976) suggested, "traits are likely to have both a genetic and a biochemical source" (p. 166). Such a position tends to reify traits as much more than convenient abstractions or intervening variables, perhaps even suggesting that the neural or biochemical substrata can be specifically identified.

A second criticism involves an assumption that the bulk of personality assessment procedures measure traits, and it charges that validation of these procedures is impossible because there are no independent measures of traits. A third criticism involves an assumption that psychologists who use personality tests are necessarily wedded to trait theory. Because tests measure traits, psychologists who use tests must believe that "traits form the molecular structure of personality" (Hogan et al., 1977, p. 257).

A fourth criticism is that traits lack explanatory power. To explain an individual's hostility by recourse to an underlying trait of aggression is seen as essentially circular. A fifth objection is that there is little evidence for the consistency of traits within individuals across situations. Within subjects, it is argued, trans-situational differences in behavior are larger than any trait theory suggests they should be. The early Hartshorne and May (1928) studies on deceit are often cited as typical evidence for the lack of intraindividual consistency. Hartshorne and May concluded from their data that children's behavior was less a function of any internalized predisposition to be honest and more a function of the particular temptation. Proponents of the situational view of behavior (e.g., Mischel, 1968, 1973, 1977; Peterson, 1968) believed that the succeeding 50 years of research did nothing to change this conclusion. As Peterson stated: "This research suggested very strongly that traditional conceptions of personality as internal behavior dispositions were inadequate and insufficient" (p. 23). It should be understood that this is not an argument against the feasibility of understanding and predicting behavior, but against the view that prediction is better approached from internal rather than external determinants.

A sixth and last objection is that traits are concepts constructed by the external perceiver rather than some inner state of the actor. Here, the argument is that personality traits are best viewed not as properties of the individual but as value judgments placed on the behaving individual by observers. We encountered this position in Chapter One, in our discussion of attribution theory (Jones & Nisbett, 1971). It assumes that people's generalized tendencies to attribute the behavior of others to internal dispositions and their own behavior to external factors have produced a universally consistent way of understanding behavior, but one that distorts the true nature of human personality.

These objections were held to signal the demise, or at least the decline, of personality assessment as a useful enterprise (Bersoff, 1973; Cleveland, 1976; Mischel, 1977). However, each of the objections can be countered on both theoretical and empirical grounds. First, are traits really seen as biophysical systems? Allport (1937), Cattell (1950, 1957), and a few other writers seem to have favored that position, but the bulk of trait-oriented psychologists are nonspecific about the underlying nature of traits. Most psychologists who favor a trait approach do appear to agree that trait terms refer to stylistic consistencies in interpersonal behavior, but there is no agreement about the origins of the consistencies. Hogan et al. (1977) pointed out that it is reasonable to criticize these psychologists for not attempting to define traits, but it is not proper to assume that they necessarily adopt Allport's definition.

Second, are most personality tests really assumed to measure traits? As noted earlier, most test authors tend to be negligent in providing an explicit rationale for selecting their scales, or information as to how one should regard the behaviors that are presumably tapped. Some authors, such as Gough (1957, 1987), have explicitly specified that traits are *not* being measured. Rather, Gough intended that the scales of the CPI be used "to predict what an individual will do in a specified context, and/or to identify individuals who will be described in a certain way" (p. 56). Most test authors, however, are much less clear than Gough in regard to their intentions.

This argument applies also to the third criticism, that persons who use tests are necessarily committed to some kind of trait theory. As pointed out by Hogan, DeSoto, and Solano (1977), "one can use personality tests and adopt any of a number of views on the structure of personality, just as one can use a particle accelerator and adopt any of a number of views on the structure of matter" (p. 257). All that is necessary is clear evidence of the reliability and validity of the particular instrument for the intended purpose. Underlying this usage, of course, is also the assumption that individuals' behavior is significantly consistent from situation to situation.

The fourth criticism involves the explanatory power of traits. To some extent, taking a position on this issue depends on the *level* of explanation that is desired. One can "explain" the illumination of a room in terms of: flicking a light switch, or making a more thorough examination of the electrical generating system that provided the current to illuminate the light bulb, or raising questions about the nature of light. Each of these levels of explanation is useful at certain times and inadequate at other times. In the same way, traits as explanations can be seen both as adequate and as inadequate. The fact that there are certain regularities in human behavior and that one can use these regularities for purposes of individual prediction can be seen as an example of a low-level general law and thus as a valid explanation on that level. Such explanations give rise to further questions, and it is up to the individual scientist or practitioner to decide what particular level of explanation will be adequate for his or her particular purpose.

The fifth and most critical objection to trait theory is that there really is no evidence to support it. Citing as their primary evidence the generally low correlations of behavioral ratings across situations (typically, no higher than .30, accounting for less than 10 percent of the total variance), the critics of trait theory argued that there is no trans-situational consistency in human behavior except for that which occurs as a function of the similarity of environmental cues.

This situational argument, however, is open to rebuttal. First, trait theorists have never denied the importance of situational determinants of behavior. It is clear that situations differ widely in the constraints they place on human behavior. Some situations, such as participating in a church service or attending a lecture, provide substantial constraints. The expected behaviors are well known, and only grossly deviant persons significantly violate the behavioral norms involved. Other situations provide considerably more behavioral options, such as attending a large party or going to a public beach. Trans-situational consistency can only be expected to occur in situations where the relevant behaviors can be freely demonstrated.

A second point in rebuttal is that individual differences occur even in the face of strong situational cues. For example, some churchgoers carefully follow the church service, some fall asleep, and some daydream. Hogan et al. (1977) reminded us that in the now notorious Milgram (1974) obedience studies, in which the situational variables were extremely power-ful, over 30 percent of the subjects were nevertheless disobedient, refusing to administer the electric shocks. Such individual differences among peo-ple are clearly contrary to the situational position, just as findings of low trans-situational consistency are contrary to the position of trait theory proponents.

Traits differ in importance—importance to the culture, importance to the behaving individual, and importance to observing others. For instance, the stealing of pennies in the early work of Hartshorne and May (1928) in-volved a rather trivial behavior from most points of view, and thus is per-haps not a very compelling base from which to make generalizations. On the other hand, the McClelland et al. "need for achievement" (1953) is a much more central and important characteristic, and some consistency is necessary in order to regard it as a viable concept. Thus, a reasonable posi-tion would seem to be that only certain personal characteristics should be expected to have a high degree of generality across situations, and that con-clusions regarding trans-situational consistency in general should be based on findings in regard to important traits rather than trivial ones.

More recent investigators have concluded that there is greater consistency of individual behavior across situations than argued by Mischel and other trait critics (e.g., Oskamp, Mindick, Berger, & Motta, 1978; Sechrest, 1976). Hogan, DeSoto, and Solano (1977) drew attention to Block's (1971) work using Q-sort methodology to demonstrate the high stability of a number of personality characteristics over long periods of time, and to Strong's (1955) report of exceptionally high stability in vocational interests as measured by his Vocational Interest Blank over a 22-year period. The findings of Costa and McCrae (1986) in demonstrating trait stability over the life span are also significant here. Thus, a careful consideration of the relevant literature would appear to merit the conclusion that the state of affairs regarding trans-situational consistency and stability of traits is not as dismal as was once suggested. A more moderate view (e.g., Mischel, 1977; 1979) shows an emphasis on the importance of person–environment interactions, to be dis-cussed next.

An interesting and potentially important insight into the trans-situational consistency of behavior is found in the work of Bem and Allen (1974). These investigators obtained self-ratings on a number of traits such as friendliness and conscientiousness, plus ratings by parents and peers on the same traits. Subjects were also asked to rate their perceived *consistency* (vs. variability) on each characteristic. Bem and Allen hypothesized that trans-situational con-sistency would be found only in behaviors where the individuals perceived themselves as consistent. The results strongly supported their hypothesis. Correlations between self-ratings and others' ratings were much stronger for the low-variability subjects than for the high-variability subjects. For in-stance, the mean correlation for "friendliness" was .57 for the low-variability subjects but only .27 for the high-variability group. Bem and Allen concluded that it is possible to "predict some of the people some of the time " (p. 517), and that people are able to identify their own consistencies in a fairly direct fashion. One could further ask whether consistency itself might be a source trait worthy of further investigative efforts.

The sixth and final criticism is that people tend to overestimate the degree to which behavior of others is caused by underlying traits and underestimate the degree to which it is caused by external factors. Although research findings (e.g., Goldberg, 1978a; Nisbett, Caputo, Legant, & Marecek, 1973) apparently tend to support the actor-observer differences as postulated by attribution theory (Jones & Nisbett, 1971), a more careful analysis of the data raises serious questions about the strength and generality of these conclusions. As Goldberg (1978a) clearly pointed out, despite the strong tendency for subjects to use the situational response in describing themselves and the trait response for describing others, the fact that the situational response is also the "middle, neutral, average, uncertain, and ambiguous response" (p. 1028) makes these findings more difficult to interpret than it would initially seem, because the situational response can be viewed as "an amalgam of inconsistency, neutrality, and uncertainty" (p. 1027). The last word on this topic has by no means been written, but there may not be as much support for the attribution theory interpretation of trait concepts as the trait critics had once believed.

In sum, a careful review of the theoretical and empirical underpinnings of the six major criticisms that have been raised against the dispositional view of human behavior indicates that these arguments are themselves flawed and are less conclusive than their proponents have suggested. Personality assessment remains a healthy and thriving enterprise, and there is a steadily growing database to support the empirical utility of many of the standard assessment instruments. (The database is described and analyzed in the remainder of this volume.) Among the existing personality assessment instruments, many lack the psychometric properties required for legitimate use, and there are a number of important but unresolved theoretical and methodological questions in this field. These problems and issues are also covered, in what is intended to be a balanced fashion.

SITUATIONAL AND DISPOSITIONAL DETERMINANTS OF BEHAVIOR

There is little question that the situational critics of internal dispositions overstated their position, but it is equally true that psychologists, especially those interested in personality assessment, have paid too little attention to the situational determinants of behavior. As Bowers (1973) concluded: "Although it is undoubtedly true that behavior is more situation specific than trait theory acknowledged . . . situations are more person specific than is commonly recognized" (p. 307). Bowers, among others, believed that an interactionist view of human behavior, one in which neither the main effects of traits nor those of situations are seen as adequate to account for behavior, would be the only viable approach.

Bowers (1973) reviewed 11 published investigations in which it was possible to evaluate the relative magnitudes of the person and situation variables involved in the dependent behavior that was studied. Using analysis of variance techniques, he was able to partition the variance attributable to situations, to persons, and to the person-by-situation interaction. His conclusion was that, although the percentage of variance due to situations was less than the variance attributable to persons, the interaction of persons and settings accounted for a higher percentage than the effect of either person or situation alone. Similarly, an independent review of the research literature by Endler and Magnusson (1976) supported a view of behavior as a function of a continuous interaction process between the individual and the situations that he or she encounters.

In summary, with the waning of enthusiasm for the situational view of human behavior, there was a rise in the *interactional view,* in which it was argued that the causes of behavior lie in the interaction between person and environment. Endler and Magnusson (1976) went even further in postulating a *reciprocal causation* position. In their view, not only do events affect the behavior of people, but the person is also an active agent in influencing environmental events.

The interactional view of human behavior is not a new one in psychology. The early works of Woodworth (1920) and Murray (1938) were clearly in this tradition, as noted by Ekehammar (1974) and others. However, there is a lack of methodology and tools for assessing and classifying situations and environments. It is not enough to argue for an interactional point of view; a methodology for implementing this point of view is also needed, as well as theory to guide the efforts. Without theory and methodology, research into the prediction of human behavior will continue to focus heavily on traits or dispositions, where a plentiful supply of both theory and methodology can be found.

STRUCTURE OF PERSONALITY

As indicated in the preceding section, the development of a viable interactional approach to the study of personality requires the existence of an adequate taxonomy of environments and situations—ideally, with an appropriate theoretical basis. The same is true for the area of personality characteristics. The challenge is how to arrange the many traits and characteristics in some systematic, understandable, and logical fashion, such as the chemists have done for the elements in the periodic table. As noted previously, early work was done along these lines (Cattell, 1950, 1957; Norman, 1967), and in the past 15 years or so, a resurgence of interest in this area has occurred. As indicated in Chapter One, the scheme that is currently most popular is the five-factor model (e.g., Digman, 1990), which is discussed in later chapters. Several other models also deserve serious consideration. Wiggins (1980, 1982) proposed a *circumplex* model, in which traits that are polar opposites appear on diametrically opposite points in a circular scheme, and similar traits appear next to each other. Wiggins's model is shown in Figure 2.1. More recently, Wiggins and his colleagues (see Wiggins & Pincus, 1992) supplemented this model by incorporating aspects of the five-factor model.

A different approach to personality structure has been taken by Goldberg and his colleagues, who have proposed dimensions such as trait breadth and trait symmetry as ways of extending existing structural models (Hampson, John, & Goldberg, 1986). They have also proposed a *hierarchical* scheme, within which different traits may be at different "levels" according to these and other characteristics. Although only the five-factor model for organizing personality traits and characteristics has led to the significant

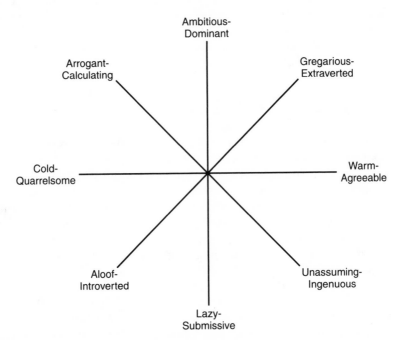

Figure 2.1   Wiggins's circumplex model of personality. (**Source:** *From Wiggins, 1980, p. 268. Copyright © 1980 Sage Publications. Reprinted by permission of Sage Publications.*)

development of test instruments, the other models are important contributions toward our increased understanding of the structure of personality.

If one considers science to be essentially a matter of the discovery of truth, then the problem is to determine how these personality characteristics are arranged in nature—that is, to discover nature's "building blocks." If, on the other hand, one's view of science is that scientists impose explanatory constructs on their observations of the natural world in order to assist them in understanding certain phenomena and that there is no "real order" to the universe, then the task is to develop useful explanatory constructs. In this latter view, the primary problem in the study of personality is to develop useful ways of organizing or conceptualizing personality structure and functioning. As stated earlier in this chapter, Cattell's work (1957, 1965) was a carefully reasoned presentation of the former ("discovery of the truth") viewpoint as applied to the organization of personality traits, George Kelly (1955) was a vigorous proponent of the latter ("creative") point of view, and the five-factor model and the approaches of Wiggins and Goldberg also tend to represent the creative viewpoint. It should be emphasized that the discovery point of view presumes only a single correct view of personality structure. The creative view accepts the proposition that there may be several different, and even equally useful, ways of viewing the structure of personality. Because most psychologists would appear to be implicitly, if not explicitly, committed to the creative view, the reader may begin to understand why there are so many different concepts and ideas about personality, personality structure, and personality assessment.

DEFINITIONS OF PERSONALITY

The problem of defining personality is a difficult one, and a very wide variety of definitions have been suggested over the years. Allport (1937) was able to delineate no fewer than 50 meanings for this term. Allport's analysis exhaustively traced the history of the concept of personality, beginning with the early antecedent *persona,* which referred to the theatrical mask first used in Greek drama, and documented its diverse meanings in such fields as theology, philosophy, sociology, linguistics, and psychology.

Even when the matter of defining personality is approached from a purely psychological viewpoint, the diversity is great. In their text on personality theory, Hall and Lindzey (1978) stated that "no substantive definition of personality can be applied with any generality" (p. 9). The historical and theoretical reasons for this diversity of thought and lack of agreement among psychologists are complex and lengthy, and the reader is referred to the text by Maddi (1989) for a careful discussion of the issues.

Hall and Lindzey (1978) argued that personality is best defined by "the particular empirical concepts which are part of the theory of personality employed by the observer" (p. 9). The typical *measures* of personality in use today, however, tend to be atheoretical. As early as 1941, Angyal was concerned that most personality tests involved the measurement of elements of personality that are random or arbitrary, such as leadership, dominance, or anxiety. Although these kinds of measures may be of practical utility, they do little to advance either the science of personality study in general or the technology of personality assessment in particular. Even today, only a handful of personality questionnaires exist for which there is a careful discussion of the rationale underlying the selection of their scales. The most potent factor in scale development would seem to be simple historical precedent. The few exceptions include the previously mentioned scales developed by Gough (1957, 1987) and Cattell (1950, 1957), in which attempts were made to use the natural language of personality description as a base, the Myers-Briggs Type Indicator (Briggs & Myers, 1943), which is based on the typology of Carl G. Jung, and recent tests based on the five-factor model of personality.

In light of the lack of unification in both personality theory and personality measurement, it is difficult to develop a definition of personality that adequately comprehends all the diverse and contradictory elements involved in this complex and difficult field of endeavor. The best approximation that we can offer, one that reflects the concern of most psychologists for utility ahead of theory, is that personality is an abstraction for *those enduring characteristics of the person that are significant for his or her interpersonal behavior.* In using this definition, we are also mindful of Allport's (1937) insistence that personality is what the person *really is;* that is, it involves what is most typical and deeply characteristic of the individual. In using the concept of personality, we need to concentrate on those individual differences that are of greatest significance in the daily transactions of human beings with each other. Only by identifying and focusing our attention on such factors will we be able to discover those trait-by-situation interactions that can enable us to make more valid differential predictions than those obtainable from the individual effects of traits or situations.

All definitions of personality suggest many questions, and ours is no exception. What are the antecedents of these enduring characteristics? To what extent are they inherited, learned in early childhood, or developed in later life? Under what conditions and to what degree can they be expected to change? These and related questions bring us deeper into the subject of personality theory; indeed, around such questions are the major differences in personality theory found. These problems are actively dealt with by most of the major contemporary personality theorists (see Pervin, 1989, for lucid and readable accounts), each of whom takes a somewhat different stand. From the viewpoint of personality assessment, however, they need not be of direct concern here. The subject can be pursued with only minimal involvement in personality theory per se.

PERSONALITY THEORY AND PERSONALITY ASSESSMENT

Although it would be useful to have a universal, internally consistent conceptual language for personality description, none exists. As indicated in the earlier discussion of the structure of personality, there is much disagreement about how best to approach this task. Each of the major personality theorists has attempted to develop his or her own conceptual system, which has little or no integration with any other system. Most approaches to assessing personality have been theoretically neutral, but the personality descriptions produced by each have tended to involve the language of one or another personality theory. For example, psychoanalytic, or Freudian, theory considers that differences in personality stem from individual differences in the amount of available psychic energy (libido) or in the methods of handling this energy. Concepts such as ego, superego, and Oedipal conflict refer to mechanisms and processes in the flow of energy. Thus, an explanation of an individual's behavior as being due to a strong ego, or to unresolved Oedipal striving, would be using the language of Freudian personality theory. In another language system, that of "trait and type" personality theory, personality is described as a simple additive combination of many separate characteristics. A user of this language might say that the individual was very hostile, or had strong dominance characteristics, or was extroverted. As yet another alternative, if the language system of behavioral learning theory were applied to personality, the individual might be described as having failed to learn an appropriate discrimination or as behaving according to a certain reinforcement history.

To repeat, personality descriptions resulting from assessment procedures are often couched in the language of a particular personality theory. Readers must not be misled, however, into believing that the assessment procedures are therefore based on careful theoretical considerations. A few of the major methods of personality assessment do have some theoretical identification, but most are theoretically neutral, and the language of the assessment procedure is chosen according to the theoretical sympathies of the test constructor rather than because the assessment procedure is derived directly from the theory or satisfies its assumptions. Too often, the names of the concepts used in a procedure are substituted for those of another theoretical language system, without any significant difference either in the procedures involved or in the level of understanding achieved.

Which theory offers the best language to clarify the description of personality? There are no simple rules for assessing the relative merits of the existing sets of personality concepts, and certainly none on which the major theorists would agree. Hall and Lindzey (1978, Chapter One) suggested that the critical test of the utility of a theory is the amount of significant research it generates. Using this criterion of utility, the generally atheoretical nature of personality assessment procedures is a reflection of the continuing gap between the fields of personality assessment and personality theory.

THEORETICAL APPROACHES TO PERSONALITY ASSESSMENT

Let us try to see what is involved in the theoretical approach to clinical assessment. For the purposes of this discussion, we shall ignore the issue of which assessment procedures the psychologist chooses and how the information produced by these procedures is collected, analyzed, and integrated. We shall simply note that the information is processed and a description of the individual's personality is offered by the psychologist, phrased in the language of a particular theory of personality. For example, let us suppose that an individual being considered for psychotherapy is referred to a psychologist of Freudian persuasion for a personality evaluation. After completing the steps involved in a clinical personality assessment, the psychologist forwards a report, which includes the finding that the patient has an unresolved Oedipal conflict. The psychologist further recommends that the patient be seen in therapy by a dominant male therapist as the optimal arrangement for the resolution of the conflict. It should be clearly apparent that the conclusion that the patient requires a dominant male therapist does *not* stem directly from the assessment data but rather from some theoretical considerations on the part of the psychologist. This process might be schematically expressed as follows:

Information from assessment procedures	$\rightarrow$	Personality description	$\rightarrow$	Personality theory	$\rightarrow$	Decision about the patient

For this decision to be useful for the patient, three conditions must hold true: (a) the psychologist's interpretation of the assessment data must be correct within the framework of the particular personality theory that is being used; (b) the psychologist's understanding of the theory must be adequate enough to facilitate a decision that is consistent with the demands of the theory; and (c) the theory itself must be a useful one. If the patient subsequently *deteriorates* in therapy with a dominant male therapist, the psychologist will be somewhat at a loss to know why, because of the lengthy chain of inferences leading to the original decision. Any one of, or any combination of, the three conditions might not have held true. Or, the failure may have been a function of therapist incompetence, unfavorable changes in the real-life circumstances of the patient, or a multitude of other considerations.

On the other hand, suppose the patient improves in therapy. What could be concluded from this event? Success with one individual does not validate this rather long chain of inference; for one thing, the same extraneous factors listed above (favorable real-life circumstances of the patient or extreme competence of the therapist) may have been operating. Success by several dominant male therapists with several similar patients would take us further toward the desired validation but not the whole distance, because the chain of inferences might well contain redundancies or compensating errors. The validity of this approach to individual assessment cannot be adequately determined by observing the outcomes of decisions based on it, but must be investigated through careful step-by-step study of the inferential chain. In other words, validating the assessment technique is closely tied to validating the personality theory utilized in the chain.

COMPARISON OF THEORETICAL AND EMPIRICAL APPROACHES

To contrast the steps involved in this theoretical or inferential approach with those that would be involved in an empirical approach to the same problem, let us assume that the psychologist knows, from previously reported empirical research, that patients with certain kinds of responses on a particular assessment instrument improve more quickly with male than with female therapists. Faced with the decision of specifying the gender of a therapist for a prospective patient, the psychologist would administer this assessment instrument, compare the patient's responses with the empirical research findings, and make a decision as to a male or female therapist solely on that basis. Given the current state of personality theory, the clinician has a greater probability of correctness in decision making if the empirical rather than the theoretical approach is used. There are fewer steps and inferences between the data and the decision, which reduces the probability of error, and it is comparatively easy to recheck the correctness of the previously reported relationships.

It is possible to argue that the empirical approach is not personality assessment at all, at least not in any strict sense. The inferential step of attributing some underlying enduring characteristic to the respondent—that is, of making inferences about his or her personality—has, in a sense, been bypassed. However, empirical processes have traditionally been so closely tied with personality assessment, particularly in the context of establishing the validity of personality tests (see Chapter Seven), that they must be regarded an integral part of the field.

One might reasonably ask which of the two approaches—theoretical or empirical—generally should be the better one to use. There is no simple answer. On one hand, the existing theories of personality are not sufficiently explicit to offer any superiority to prediction through the theoretical approach. On the other hand, this approach offers more for the ultimate advancement of the field, so that its development will be slowed if empirical procedures are always favored for applied work.

It is possible, in principle, to develop an assessment instrument directly from a theory of personality. The individual's responses would then be immediately meaningful within the context of the theory, and no additional inferential activity by the clinician would be necessary. Thus, the step labeled "personality description" in the schematic on page 47 would be eliminated. Instruments that are clearly and explicitly based on theory include the Blacky Pictures Test (Blum, 1949, 1950) and the Defense Mechanisms Inventory (Gleser & Ihilevich, 1969; Ihilevich & Gleser, 1986). Although such approaches are scientifically rather sophisticated and offer much hope for the development of basic knowledge about personality, it must be stated again that personality theorizing is not sufficiently advanced for them to be generally useful at the present time.

METHODS OF PERSONALITY ASSESSMENT

Personality assessment refers to the process of gathering and organizing information about another person in the expectation that this information will lead to a better understanding of the person. Understanding the personality of another individual typically involves making some rather specific predictions about the future behavior of that person. Among the possible predictions could be probability of vocational success in a variety of areas, response to different kinds of psychological treatments, or probability of demonstrating certain socially undesirable behaviors. The task of the professional psychologist often involves participating in a variety of decisions concerning other people, based on assessments of their personalities.

All of us, however, are continually involved in gathering a variety of unsystematic information about the behavior of people around us, and we are continually, if not with complete awareness, making inferences about their personality characteristics from our observations. Statements such as "I know her pretty well" or "I've known him for a long time but I don't understand him at all" reflect our everyday ways of describing our knowledge of another's personality. Study of these informal processes of data collection and of the ways we organize and analyze the information is a fascinating endeavor. How well can one get to know another's personality in this manner? Are some people more effective in this respect than others? On what basis? What psychological processes are involved? These questions have been addressed within the framework of attribution theory, as discussed in Chapter One, and are most recently grouped under the heading of social perception (e.g., Zebrowitz, 1990).

The informal, or intuitive, processes by which one gets to know and understand people with whom one is closely involved are similar to those employed by the psychotherapist in understanding a patient. The informal approach is characterized by the large amount of time it requires and by its lack of specificity about the manner of both data collection and data analysis. Observers are expected to proceed with the task of understanding the other person at their own pace and in their own, nonspecified fashion.

Although the informal, intuitive approach is fascinating, it is not considered beyond this chapter. We are primarily concerned with the formal, systematic ways of going about the assessment task—the methods used by the professional psychologist in the formal role of expert assessor of personality. We shall emphasize the situations in which the psychologist or other professional person uses standardized assessment instruments in a systematic manner in the assessment situation. The interview, an unstandardized personality assessment technique but a major assessment method in use today, is also considered briefly.

How might standardized assessment tools be classified? Three groups of instruments can be identified. The first consists of instruments generally regarded as *personality tests*. Discussion of personality tests, both inventories and projective techniques, and of the many problems surrounding their use and interpretation, fills the major portion of this book. A second group of procedures uses either models of real-life situations or real life itself, in which the behavior of interest can be observed directly. For example, an instrument for assessing the subject's stress tolerance would consist of a structured and standardized situation in which the individual would be required to perform under some artificially produced stress. The situation normally would be arranged so that the behavior could be directly observed without the person's being aware of what was happening. This method of assessment, through the use of *behavioral observation,* is discussed in Chapter Five. A third group of instruments makes use of specific factual information about the individual's present status and past history, the kind of information that might be obtained from a biographical data blank or a carefully structured interview. This *biographical data method,* which is widely used in personnel selection in industry, is discussed in Chapter Six.

Some psychologists have felt that certain personality tests, notably the projective techniques, are more appropriately regarded as standardized situations for eliciting a behavior sample. They consider that the projective testing situation represents a standardized model of an interpersonal interaction with ambiguous demands, and that the entire situation—the projective test materials (such as inkblots or pictures), plus the examiner, plus the instructions, plus the immediate environment—constitutes the assessment instrument. This is a fruitful approach to the analysis and understanding of projective tests and their contribution to personality assessment; we, however, have taken the more straightforward and traditional approach of grouping projective techniques together with the other personality tests.

CHOICE OF ASSESSMENT PROCEDURES

How does the psychologist decide which instruments to use in a particular assessment situation? The psychologist traditionally uses an interview, tests, biographical and other case data such as supervisory ratings or school records, and additional assessment tools, in order to provide information about the individual under study. Although the steps involved in normal clinical assessment may be more organized than those in the informal intuitive method of assessment, there is still much variability among psychologists in their manner of both data collection and data analysis. No standard procedures for gathering data are followed universally by psychologists. The assessment instruments chosen by a particular psychologist will be a function of training and experience, idiosyncratic preferences, and familiarity with the current literature.

One recurring problem in choosing assessment methods involves deciding between formal personality tests and informal intuitive methods. Although it is usually not the case, let us assume, for purposes of this discussion, that the end results of the two methods would be comparably useful; that is, both methods would yield equally correct predictions.

In choosing between the methods, the *time factor* is one important consideration. It may well be that a decision must be reached about a patient by noon tomorrow because he or she is going on court trial or is being considered for discharge. To initiate a lengthy informal intuitive procedure at this stage would not be expedient. However, if the patient had previously been seen in psychotherapy for several months, the therapist could give an intuitive assessment very quickly.

Economic factors must also be considered in making a decision about which method to use. To assign an individual to an informal assessor for an extended period of time is obviously an expensive business and would rarely be done for the sake of assessment alone. However, if the person were a hospital patient in a well-staffed ward, a routine duty of the ward staff might well be to gather the informal data needed for such an assessment. Another situation where intuitive assessment would be prohibitively expensive is in the routine screening of large numbers of persons, such as for draft into the armed forces. Standardized assessment techniques, which can be administered to large numbers of persons simultaneously in a short time, have an obvious economic advantage.

Thus, the choice between these or any other assessment procedures will be influenced by considerations of practical efficiency. In this regard, a crucial factor will often be the availability of a person or persons who have been able to make the kind of observations necessary for an informal intuitive assessment over an extended period of time. If competent assessors of this type are available, they should generally be utilized. To state the conclusion another way, the decision as to which assessment method to use should ultimately be determined by the *relative gain* or payoff of the alternative courses of action.

There may be occasions when it is not justifiable to apply any assessment procedure at all. Taking all factors into consideration, if the losses (in time, expense, increased hostility of the patient, loss of staff morale) more than offset the gains (additional pertinent information about the individual, increased probability of making the optimal prediction or decision), then it would be better not to use any assessment procedure. Unfortunately, there has been little systematic research on the relative payoffs of assessment techniques. Further, many psychiatric hospitals, clinics, industries, and schools have been using the same assessment procedures routinely over many years, with little information about, or even interest in, the efficiency of these procedures. If an empirical evaluation of their efficiency were made, based on the time actually spent by clinical psychologists in traditional routine clinical assessment, much of this activity would likely be abandoned.

PERSONALITY TESTS AND ABILITY TESTS

As indicated previously, the major focus of this book is on personality assessment through the medium of standardized assessment instruments, typically referred to as *personality tests*. The more general term, *psychological tests*, includes, in addition to personality assessment instruments, an extensive array of devices for measuring *abilities*.

How might we differentiate between ability tests and personality tests? Some of the attributes of an individual that are typically regarded as personality traits could also, at times, be considered as abilities, especially when interpersonal interactions are involved. For example, are leadership and persuasiveness more appropriately considered as personality factors or ability factors? Any distinction between these two kinds of domains is arbitrary to some degree. Traditionally, the term *ability tests* has been used to identify instruments that assess skills or achievement in cognitive, intellectual, and motor areas. As an alternative, Cronbach (1984) suggested *maximum performance tests*, a term that conveys the following concepts: (a) individuals are expected to perform as skillfully as they can; and (b) there are specific right and wrong answers to the test items. Cronbach further suggested that personality tests might be better regarded as tests of *typical performance*, or instruments that are expected to identify the individual's typical modes of responding, where no particular response can be singled out as "right." The arbitrariness of the distinction is not eliminated by Cronbach's suggestions, but the types of individual differences involved in these two categories are made more specific.

One reason for discussing ability tests in the present context is that the methods and techniques employed in ability testing have provided important models for the development of personality tests. However, the degree of success enjoyed by ability tests has not yet been realized in the field of personality assessment. Although the predictions about real-life situations made from carefully constructed ability tests can be considered fairly satisfactory, the same cannot be said for personality tests. Some of the reasons for this difference lie in the lack of widely accepted personality concepts; others involve fundamental questions as to what is meant by "measurement." Nevertheless, personality tests modeled on the traditional ability-testing procedures have probably now reached their maximum degree of refinement. Thus, further improvements in personality assessment will probably have to come from new approaches to the problem rather than from further refinements of the traditional methods.

SUMMARY

Psychologists undertake personality assessment for two reasons, corresponding to two general themes underlying the development of the field: (a) the clinical assessment of individuals and (b) the advancement of knowledge of human behavior through research and theory. In clinical assessment, the simplest approach is prediction based on known empirical relationships between the assessment results and the behavior to be predicted. A disadvantage of this procedure is that it adds little to a broader understanding of the processes involved. One assumption basic to all traditional personality assessment procedures is that one's interpersonal behavior has some consistency over time and across different situations. This assumption is questioned in theoretical approaches to personality through behavioral learning theory, in which much greater emphasis is placed on environmental conditions in determining behavior at any time.

A common approach to personality prediction is to (a) construct a personality description by generalizing from known empirical relationships, and (b) make predictions on the basis of the description. This approach is sometimes regarded as "theoretical," but the term *theory* in the present text is reserved for more rigorous procedures involving sets of related laws. A serious problem with prediction from a general personality description is that the known empirical relationships are frequently generalized beyond their applicability.

There has been considerable debate as to whether personality is determined by traits or dispositions, as opposed to situational factors. Critics of the trait position point to the difficulty of obtaining independent evidence of traits' existence, their limited utility for predictive purposes, their limited explanatory power, and other problems. A reasoned position would seem to suggest that behavior is determined in part by both situations and dispositions, and that the causes of behavior probably lie in the interaction between person and environment. Further, it is suggested that each actively influences the other in a reciprocal manner.

Researchers have attempted to ascertain the structure of personality in our culture by identifying and analyzing the many thousands of trait words in the English language. There are two points of view about personality structure: (a) a "true" structure exists and will be eventually discovered, and (b) any number of structures may be imposed on natural human behavior in an attempt to understand it better. Proposals for the structure of personality have included the five-factor model, the circumplex model, and the complex hierarchical models. There is no agreed-on definition for the term personality; in this text, we adopt an atheoretical, practical definition of personality as *those enduring characteristics of the person that are significant for his or her interpersonal behavior.* Personality descriptions resulting from assessment procedures are usually couched in the specific language of one or another theory of personality, but this does not mean that the assessment is based on the theory. In fact, the science of personality is not yet sufficiently developed to permit a truly theoretical approach to personality assessment.

A variety of methods address personality assessment: informal and intuitive methods, interviewing, formal standardized procedures, biographical data, and behavior samples. Most of this book is devoted to a consideration of standardized assessment procedures. The choice of which assessment procedure to employ in any given situation depends on economic factors, the available time, and other aspects of practical efficiency.

In the development of personality assessment procedures, the well-established methods for assessing skills and abilities have generally been used as models. However, it appears that personality assessment procedures based on these models have now reached their maximum degree of refinement, and further developments will have to come from new approaches.

CHAPTER THREE

Objective Approaches to Personality Assessment

The previous chapters touched on a number of basic issues involved in developing and using personality assessment instruments. They include the problems of how the test situation can be standardized, what stimuli can be used to evoke meaningful and useful responses from test takers, and what type of responses should be observed in order to understand and predict those human behaviors usually subsumed under the rubric *personality.* This chapter and Chapter Four are specifically concerned with these issues. Following a discussion of the characteristics of assessment techniques, the most widely used assessment devices are examined. This procedure serves to present and illustrate the problems mentioned above and to give the reader some familiarity with current assessment devices and practices. Tests that have grown from the psychometric tradition, usually termed *inventories,* are also discussed in this chapter.

Projective procedures are discussed in Chapter Four. The terms *assessment technique, device, procedure,* and *test* have subtle differences of meaning, but are used here more or less interchangeably. *Technique* is somewhat preferred over *test* in referring to the traditional usage of projectives, where the criteria for structure and standardization, implied by the term *test,* may not be fully met.

CHARACTERISTICS OF STANDARDIZED ASSESSMENT PROCEDURES

An examination of the standardized assessment procedures in common use shows that they tend to meet the following conditions: (a) the stimuli to be used in the assessment process are identical for all respondents and are always presented in the same fashion; (b) there are available *norms,* or frequency distributions of responses, either formal or informal (intuitive), so that responses can be assigned to a specific place within an anticipated range; and (c) there are useful personality and behavioral correlates of the to-be-observed responses. We say that assessment procedures *tend* to meet these criteria because the strictness with which the criteria are employed, particularly the latter two, varies. Nevertheless, each of these elements is present to some extent in all techniques that are considered formal assessment procedures.

The previously mentioned conditions suggest three dimensions that could be useful in characterizing personality assessment procedures. The first dimension, which concerns the variety of relevant responses made by the test taker and observed by the examiner, might be termed the *degree of response structure.* This term does *not* refer to differences in the degree of structure imposed on the testing situation by the examiner. A high degree of structure or standardization of procedure is an important condition for any formal assessment device. Thus, the procedures for administering the Rorschach are, or should be, just as inflexible as those for the Minnesota Multiphasic Personality Inventory (MMPI).

Most paper-and-pencil personality inventories, such as the MMPI, can also be regarded as rather highly structured with respect to respondent behaviors, because the only responses to be made and observed are indications of "true" or "false" for a series of personal statements. Other responses by the test taker are discouraged by the preliminary instructions and tend to be ignored if they are made despite the instructions. The MMPI is taken either by sorting cards into "true" and "false" piles or by marking a true/false answer sheet. Variations in such behaviors as vigor or response time are not recorded, and neither the MMPI scoring procedure nor its interpretive system permits the use of such data. Rorschach's inkblot test, on the other hand, would be regarded as relatively unstructured in the present sense, because the examiner generally observes and records a wide range of respondent behaviors and considers all of them to be relevant response material. Included are the portion of the blot to which the person has responded; the stimulus characteristics of that portion of the blot—for example, the form, color, or shading that determined each given response; the actual content of each response; the respondent's body position and movement; changes in pitch, volume, loudness, and rate of speech; any spontaneous comments about the situation; and other features of the respondent's style of expression.

A second dimension on which assessment procedures differ is the degree to which published formal norms are available. Structured inventories, such as the MMPI, which allow a small range of relevant responses, more readily lend themselves to the development of formal norms. These norms are usually developed by the test authors and are presented in tabular form, frequently with conversion tables for easy translation into some standard score form. For example, the MMPI scales employ "T-scores," with a mean of 50 and a standard deviation of 10. Later research often provides specific norms for working with homogeneous groups of various sorts (e.g., Lanyon, 1968). Projective techniques, on the other hand, have a larger range of responses and generally do not have formal norms available. Instead, the clinician who uses these procedures must build informal norms based on personal experience, so that the development of skills in the use of projective techniques becomes complex and time-consuming. There have been some attempts to develop formal norms for these assessment procedures, especially for the Rorschach (e.g., Beck, Beck, Levitt, & Molish, 1961; Exner, 1986), but the results have by no means been generally accepted or integrated into clinical practice.

A third dimension that might be relevant for characterizing personality assessment devices is the usefulness of the instrument. By usefulness, we mean the extent to which the test taker's responses will permit understanding and prediction of some of his or her nontest behaviors. A very useful instrument would enable relatively precise predictions to be made about socially important behaviors, such as success in a particular occupation or prognosis in psychotherapy. Less useful instruments are either less precise in their predictions or deal with less significant social behavior, such as performance on an experimental laboratory task. The term *validity* is similar to usefulness, but it is more precise and refers to the existence of a demonstrated relationship between certain test responses and a particular nontest characteristic of the person. Thus, the number of validities (valid relationships) that a test possesses, and the importance or significance of these relationships, determine the test's usefulness. This topic is discussed more fully in Chapter Seven.

The position of an assessment instrument on each of these three dimensions (degree of response structure, availability of norms, and usefulness) is influenced to some extent by a more basic aspect of the instrument: the method of construction of the instrument, and, more particularly, the method employed in selecting and developing the stimuli. In general, there have been three major approaches to or strategies in the construction of formal assessment devices: (a) rational-theoretical, (b) empirical, and (c) factor-analytic. As discussed later, the current state of the art is to use all three strategies at different stages of test development. (Older tests are often based primarily on just one strategy.) For ease in understanding, each strategy is introduced separately here.

1. A test may be based on purely rational, face-value, or commonsense considerations. For example, the item "I frequently find myself worrying about something" might appear in a test of manifest anxiety because it would be reasonable to assume that, on an a priori basis, manifestly anxious subjects would be more likely than nonanxious subjects to respond affirmatively to this item. Rationally derived tests are developed by selecting or constructing stimulus materials that *seem* to tap the behavior in which the test author is interested. A test might also be devised to be congruent with a particular theoretical view of personality, and it would assess concepts within that theory. The Blacky Pictures Test (Blum, 1950), which involves drawings portraying the adventures of the pup Blacky and its family, is an example of a theoretically derived personality test—in this case, based on traditional psychoanalytic theory. The test taker's responses to the drawings are scored and interpreted as indexes of the amount of conflict in the various psychoanalytic stages of psychosexual development. Because, strictly speaking, no theories of personality meet the preferred definition of a theory (see Chapter Two) and most rationally based tests do involve some theoretical considerations, the discussion to follow considers rational and theoretically based tests together. Thus, a continuum of *rational-theoretical* derivation is conceptualized, with a priori inventories nearer to the rational end and tests such as the Blacky Pictures nearer to the theoretical end.

2. The basis for a test can be *empirical;* that is, there is an empirical basis for believing that the test should work in the manner described by the test author. Each test item might be selected according to its power to discriminate between two groups that are of interest—for example, people with sales potential, and people in general—or a global score of some kind might be devised to discriminate between two groups.

3. A test might be developed by searching statistically for clusters of items or stimuli with similar content; that is, clusters in which the test stimuli appear to be reflecting a single basic trait or characteristic. This strategy for test development is termed *factor-analytic,* reflecting the use of the statistical procedure of factor analysis. The variables thus identified are defined statistically, and the content of each cluster is examined to see what name is most appropriate for each variable.

The three approaches to test development have never been mutually exclusive. For example, even the development of the older empirically derived instruments has usually involved an initial rational or theoretical selection of items to be put to an empirical test. Similarly, the factor-analytic approach has usually followed some rational or theoretical assembling of the items. Each approach tends to complement the others and contributes uniquely to the potential of the test for validity in a variety of settings. Psychologists interested in personality and assessment have often tended to employ the word *theory* in a loose or colloquial sense. Thus, they might consider certain tests to have a stronger theoretical base than is credited to them here.

The remaining sections of this chapter discuss the application of these three strategies to the development of personality inventories. Chapter Four discusses their application in the development and use of projective techniques. Debate and research findings regarding their advantages, disadvantages, and relative merits are deferred until the end of Chapter Four.

RATIONAL-THEORETICAL INVENTORIES

Perhaps the most obvious approach to test development is the rational one, where the test items are expected to act as stimuli for directly eliciting the information that is of interest. Woodworth's Personal Data Sheet, described in some detail in Chapter One, is an early example of rational derivation. It asks the same questions that a psychiatrist or a clinical psychologist would ask when directly examining a patient to determine level of adjustment. As already noted, responses to such test items as "Do you sleep well?" or "Do you get rattled easily?" are assumed to be valid indexes of the level of adjustment of the respondent, in the same way that the responses to an oral examination are assumed to be valid. (More is said about these assumptions at the end of Chapter Four.) Next, we describe several of the better-known objective instruments in the rational-theoretical category: the Edwards Personal Preference Schedule, developed some forty years ago along almost purely rational lines; the Myers-Briggs Type Indicator, a theoretically based test designed to assess Jung's psychological types, and Jackson's Personality Research Form and the Jackson Personality Inventory—rational tests whose development includes some more recent advances in test construction technology.

Edwards Personal Preference Schedule (EPPS)

Edwards's (1954, 1959) avowed purpose in developing the EPPS was "to provide quick and convenient measures of a number of relatively independent normal personality variables" (1959, p. 5). The 15 variables, selected from the list of "manifest needs" proposed in the theoretical writings of Henry Murray (1938), include achievement, affiliation, deference, nurturance, and order. To assess each need, the EPPS uses nine brief statements that bear a rational, commonsense relationship to that need. Thus, the need for achievement is tapped by such statements as "I like to do my very best in whatever I undertake" and "I would like to accomplish something of great significance." Although the EPPS has sometimes been considered to be derived from Murray's theoretical views of personality, its reliance on commonsense considerations, particularly in item development, is much more basic.

The sophistication of the EPPS is found in its *forced-choice* format. Pairs of self-reference statements are presented simultaneously to the respondent, who, in each case, is to choose the more self-descriptive statement. There are 210 such choices, and the respondent can endorse the set of statements related to each need from zero to 28 times. Every need is paired three or four times. The strength of a particular need is determined by the number of times, out of the 28 options, that the respondent chooses or endorses the statements representing that need. Fifteen additional pairs are included, to evaluate the consistency or reliability of an individual's responses.

Why was the forced-choice technique employed? Edwards (1953, 1957) was concerned by his finding that the frequency of endorsement of any self-descriptive statement was highly related to the judged *social desirability* of that statement. The general issue of the complex effects of social desirability on personality test responses is dealt with in some detail in Chapter Seven; the discussion here simply indicates its role in the construction of the EPPS. Edwards decided, on the basis of his findings, that people ordinarily respond to a test item according to the social desirability of that item rather than according to its specific personality content. Thus, the failure to control for social desirability led to a failure to fairly evaluate the respondents' personality characteristics. Edwards attempted to circumvent this difficulty by arranging the EPPS statements in pairs within which the alternatives were approximately matched for social desirability, and by requiring respondents to endorse one statement from each pair. He reasoned that because the choice could not now be made on the basis of social desirability, persons must choose according to their own personality characteristics.

The development of the EPPS represented an innovative attempt to deal with the problem of social desirability, although subsequent research (e.g., Heilbrun & Goodstein, 1961a, 1961b; Rorer, 1965) has shown that the problem was not resolved. The forced-choice format reduced but failed to remove the influence of social desirability; more important, however, was the finding that the predictive usefulness or validity of such questionnaires is determined in part by the extent to which the factor of social desirability is still present. As already mentioned, this problem is explored in detail in Chapter Seven (see especially "Response Sets").

A forced-choice format also raises other problems. The respondent to the EPPS is asked, in effect, to distribute 210 endorsements over 420 items. Put another way, the respondent must indicate 210 points' worth of personality needs, regardless of whether this degree of "need" exists. As a result, an EPPS profile reflects a rank order of needs as they apply to the respondent. Such procedures, which allow comparisons of an individual's intraindividual characteristics but are limited in the degree to which they permit interindividual comparisons, are termed *ipsative,* and they raise special problems in the interpretation of test scores. Still another problem posed by the forced-choice format is that the scale scores thus obtained are not statistically independent of each other; an elevated score on one dimension will force a lower score on another dimension. Because most statistical operations assume the independence of scores, many studies involving the interrelationship of EPPS scores are difficult to interpret. Thus, it is generally concluded that Edwards's attempts to deal with the problem of social desirability were not completely successful. Instead, they created several new and difficult problems.

The rational derivation of the EPPS might still lead us to expect it to be a reasonably useful or valid instrument. Edwards (1959, p. 19) has shown that the scores are reasonably stable or reliable. But the reviews of the EPPS (Cooper, 1990; McKee, 1972) have been consistent in concluding that the evidence for its utility is, in general, poor, as well over 1,000 reported studies have attested. Nevertheless, it is still commonly used in some counseling settings (Drummond, 1984; Zytowski & Warman, 1982).

Myers-Briggs Type Indicator (MBTI)

Classifying or sorting individuals into various types is as old as humankind itself. It long preceded the development of any science of psychology. Katherine Briggs, who had no formal training in psychology, had begun developing a typology of her own early in the 20th century. When she read the English-language version of Carl Jung's *Psychological Types* in 1923, Briggs recognized his ideas as quite similar to hers, but more highly developed. She abandoned her efforts at creating her own typology and instead began to work on more fully understanding Jung's system. Together with her daughter, Isabel Briggs Myers, she developed a psychological inventory to measure these types.

In 1956, the Educational Testing Service (ETS) agreed to publish their instrument, primarily for research purposes. Over a period of almost 20 years, the instrument became a widely used research tool, both within ETS and by external, independent researchers. Finally, in 1975, ETS turned the publication of the instrument over to Consulting Psychologists Press, which made it available for both research and clinical use (Briggs, 1980; Briggs & Myers, 1985; Myers & McCaulley, 1985). In 1987, *Fortune* magazine (Moore, 1987) estimated that some 1.5 million persons had taken the instrument the previous year, making it the most widely used instrument for nonclinical purposes, especially for management development (Kroeger & Thuesen, 1988) and team building (Hirsh & Kummerow, 1990) in the business world.

The use of the MBTI by professional psychologists for traditional diagnostic purposes has been less enthusiastic. The reasons for this disfavor include a lack of interest in Jung and his theories, the fact that neither Myers nor Briggs was professionally trained, the limited availability of the instrument until fairly recently, and the cultlike intensity of some of its advocates. However, its acceptance by psychologists does seem to be increasing, especially in counseling and managerial assessment.

The current standard version of the MBTI, Form G, consists of 126 forced-choice items. Each item asks the respondent to choose which of two alternatives is more descriptive or appealing. The MBTI initially yields scores on four bipolar dimensions that stem from the writings of Carl Jung: (a) Extraversion-Introversion, indicating one's orientation toward life; (b) Sensing-Intuition, reflecting how one perceives; (c) Thinking-Feeling, relating to the basis of one's judgments; and (d) Judgment-Perception, concerning one's decision-making orientation to the external world.

Extraversion-Introversion, the best-known of these Jungian polarities, is viewed as a set of complementary attitudes or orientations toward life. Extraversion (E) involves a positive orientation toward the external world of people and relationships, a seeking for stimulation and information there, and an ease of interpersonal communication and sociability. Introversion (I), on the other hand, involves a positive attitude toward the inner world of concepts and idea, a turning toward that inner world for stimulation and information, and a thoughtful, contemplative detachment coupled with the enjoyment of solitude and privacy.

Sensing-Intuition involves two different approaches to perception. Sensing (S) refers to perceptions obtained via the five senses by direct experience, and Intuition (N) refers to perception via the unconscious, through hunch, sudden insight, discovery, or intuition.

Thinking-Feeling (TF) taps two different ways of coming to judgment. Thinking (T) is based on rationality and impersonal logic, and Feeling (F) is based on subjective values, either personal or group. The TF dimension is essentially one of tough- versus tender-mindedness, a distinction well known to psychologists.

The Judgment-Perception dimension ranges from Judgment (J), a concern with making decisions, developing closure, planning, and organizing, to Perceiving (P), a concern for information gathering, spontaneity, curiosity, and adaptability. The Judgment-Perception dimension is more implicit than explicit in Jung's work and represents one of the contributions of Myers and Briggs to his ideas.

Scoring the MBTI, by hand or computer, involves determining a weighted raw score for each pole of the four dimensions. A letter showing the direction of the preference is assigned for each dimension (E or I, S or N, T or F, and J or P) along with a number showing the reported strength of that preference. Although the scores are seen as continuous, each set of scores is reduced to a four-letter combination specifying which polarity is dominant in each pair (e.g., ENFP, ISTJ). Thus, a continuum of behaviors is reduced to a typology. For each of the 16 possible types, a detailed psychological description is provided that differentiates it from all others.

Based on the specific typology obtained, there is a complex way of determining dominant and auxiliary preferences, and these are also regarded as having interpretive behavioral implications. The difference between dominant and auxiliary functions is not well articulated in Jung's original writings and is another—fairly controversial—addition by Myers and Briggs. Our literature review revealed no empirical research supporting the use of this distinction, so extreme caution in its use for other than research purposes is suggested.

The interpretive literature pays some attention to the relative strength of the score in understanding the resultant behavior, but it strongly implies that knowing and understanding one's type is far more important (e.g., Kroeger & Thuesen, 1988). Although the psychometrics of the MBTI suggest that each of the measures is indeed a continuum, the interpretive literature suggests that the four polarities should be regarded as dichotomies rather than continua. The supporting statistical evidence for this position is weak (DeVito, 1985), and the matter of types versus continuous scores must be regarded as unresolved.

The relatively few published studies on the reliability of the MBTI tend to show acceptable internal consistency and, with the exception of the Thinking-Feeling continuum, satisfactory test–retest reliability over periods of up to several months. Myers and McCaulley (1985), for example, reported alpha coefficients of .76 to .84 for the four continuous scales with a sample of more than 9,000 cases. For much smaller samples, they report test–retest correlations ranging from .60 (for TF) to .89. Other investigators (see Carlson, 1985) have reported similar data.

Despite decades of research on the MTBI, remarkably little substantive validity data are available. The bulk of the published literature is concerned with internal consistency, correlations with other self-report inventories or self-descriptions, and differences in MBTI scores among various occupational groups (Carlson, 1985; DeVito, 1985), little of which directly addresses validity. In addition, a large body of unpublished theses and dissertations is methodologically flawed in one or more serious ways.

One substantial body of validity data was provided by the results of a 30-year research program at the Institute of Personality Assessment and Research (IPAR) at the University of California at Berkeley (Thorne & Gough, 1991). A sample of 614 well-educated persons was studied in depth with a battery of psychological tests that included the MBTI and several measures of intellectual and cognitive functioning. Ratings by trained observers were obtained in a variety of situations, including leaderless discussion groups, role plays, and informal social interactions. The observers were not aware of the psychological test scores.

Continuous scores on the four polarities were found to correlate substantially with a variety of other self-report measures. There were also significant correlations between observer ratings and MBTI scores. For example, compared to extraverts, introverts were seen as less happy, having problems in their home lives, and generally dissatisfied. On the other hand, introverts tended to do better on standard measures of intelligence, particularly on the verbal portions, and to obtain higher grades in college. Correlations were also reported for the other three MBTI scales. In addition, observer ratings on a specially constructed scale for each of the four MBTI dimensions correlated significantly with actual MBTI scores.

Several cautions apply to these results. Thorne and Gough (1991) pointed out that the high correlations between the Sensing-Intuitive dimension and the Judgment-Perception dimension suggest the need for considerable caution in interpreting these two dimensions separately. Also, the atypical nature of the IPAR sample raises a serious question about the generality of the findings.

Despite the lack of strong validity data, the MBTI is considered to offer promise as a theoretically derived instrument that taps important dimensions of human behavior. One critical issue is: Exactly what would constitute adequate evidence of the validity of the MBTI, in view of the philosophical nature of Jung's constructs and the resultant shortage of behavioral referents? A more useful approach might be to inquire about the practical value of MBTI scores in understanding others. The work of Thorne and Gough

(1991) is clearly a step in the right direction, but much more needs to be done before a positive conclusion can be reached. Meanwhile, a guarded view of the MBTI in individual assessment is recommended.

Personality Research Form and Jackson Personality Inventory

During the 1960s, a considerable amount of research was conducted on the methodology of constructing inventories. Jackson's (1967, 1984) Personality Research Form (PRF) was one of the first to capitalize on this increased sophistication, making it an early member of a new generation of personality assessment devices. The PRF was designed to assess 20 traits adapted (as was the EPPS) from the writings of Murray (1938). When first published, the PRF was offered in two parallel 440-item forms (AA and BB) and two parallel 300-item forms (A and B). In 1974, an improved and simplified 352-item version (Form E) was published. Based on his belief (Jackson, 1971) that the most satisfactory approach to the development of personality test items is a rational one, Jackson initially developed more than 100 items for each trait and refined the pool using a variety of careful psychometric procedures.

In particular, Jackson utilized *internal consistency* procedures—a study of the correlations between individual items and their intended scales—to ensure that the content of each scale was relatively homogeneous and that correlations between scales were fairly low. The resulting scales also have high content validity and relatively low correlations with social desirability. The average of the external validity coefficients reported is close to .5 (Jackson, 1984), which is notably higher than validity levels traditionally attained (Mischel, 1968). According to Hogan (1978), "it has been developed with extraordinary attention to psychometric detail and is in some ways a paragon of technical sophistication" (p. 1007). On the debit side, the samples used for test development, norms, and validity involved mainly college undergraduates. For use with that population, the PRF must be considered one of the most promising instruments in personality assessment.

In 1976, Jackson published another test, the Jackson Personality Inventory (JPI). Constructed (once again, using a rational approach) to assess traits that are somewhat more social or interpersonal in nature than those assessed by the PRF, the JPI was developed using essentially the same methods but an even higher degree of psychometric sophistication. The initial pool included more than 1,800 items, and the sequential item-selection steps included the use of a Differential Reliability Index (DRI), which helped suppress social desirability bias. Specifically, the DRI expressed each item's contribution to the meaning of its intended scale, beyond the correlation that was due to the effects of social desirability alone. Other details of construction are difficult to follow, but are summarized clearly by Goldberg (1978b). Correlations of the JPI scales with ratings of the traits by the respondents' peers show a high degree of empirical validity for some of the scales, and it would appear that the JPI has the potential for becoming a very useful test. As with the PRF, the subjects involved in construction, norms, and validation of the JPI were mainly college students.

Millon Clinical Multiaxial Inventory

First published in 1977, the Millon Clinical Multiaxial Inventory is now in its third revision (MCMI-III; Millon, Millon, & Davis, 1994). This 175-item true–false inventory was intended for use with psychiatric patients; in particular, it was designed to facilitate diagnoses using the American Psychiatric Association's (1980, 1987, 1994) *Diagnostic and Statistical Manual of Mental Disorders,* especially with regard to the expanded classification of personality disorders. It was constructed primarily on a rational basis, but has some empirical aspects. Its 22 scales include 8 personality style scales, 3 scales assessing severe personality patterns or pathological personality disorders, 9 scales for clinical symptom syndromes (such as anxiety, psychotic thinking, and alcohol abuse), and 2 validity scales. Because most items are scored on several different scales, many of the scales are substantially intercorrelated. Reviews of the MCMI (e.g., Choca, Shanley, & Van Denberg, 1992; Dana & Cantrell, 1988) have shown that the interpretive material, which is available most readily through computer-based interpretations, is mainly subjective in nature.

EMPIRICALLY BASED INVENTORIES

In a strictly empirical approach to developing a personality inventory scale, the items that generate responses with predictive value would be determined purely by trial and error. Rational or theoretical hunches about possible relationships would play no part. Such a strict approach is rarely followed, and most of the test instruments that are called empirical include rational or theoretical considerations in their derivation—especially the former. Inventories tend to be termed *empirical* if that was the primary strategy employed in their development.

The pure empirical approach is illustrated in constructing an inventory scale to assess the personality characteristic of *dominance.* The initial step is to identify a clear-cut and readily obtainable behavioral index of the attribute; that is, to formulate an *operational definition* of dominance. For our present purpose, we define dominance as "the characteristic involved in seeking elective public office." We then obtain a group of dominant persons (that is, people who have sought or are seeking elective office) and a group of nondominant persons (those who have not sought elective office). It is assumed that both groups are equally willing to cooperate in our undertaking and that they are matched on relevant characteristics such as age, education, and socioeconomic status.

Both groups are asked to respond to a large number of questionnaire items—let us say, 200. Items might inquire about subjects' likes and dislikes, interpersonal relationships, political orientation, or anything at all. In truly empirically based instruments, the items would be randomly selected from a universe of all such questionnaire items, if such a pool were available. In our hypothetical example, let us suppose that one of the items is "I like people with blue eyes," to be answered "true" or "false" by the respondent.

Let us further suppose that we learn, by comparing the responses of our office-seeking/dominant/criterion group with those of the non-office-seeking/nondominant/control group, that 90 percent of the criterion group have responded "true" to this item and only 15 percent of the control subjects have answered "true." We have discovered a diagnostic "sign" for identifying dominant people. Each of our 200 statements would be similarly examined, typically using rigorous statistical criteria, to determine whether it too is a sign of dominance. By identifying all the items that reliably differentiate our criterion and control groups, we would have constructed an empirical dominance scale, and a dominance score would be generated for each person by totaling the number of discriminating items that were answered in the criterion direction.

Depending on the level of significance established for the selection of items, at least some proportion of the items would have been identified as valid on the basis of chance alone. For example, if a 5 percent probability level is used to identify discriminating items, then 5 percent of the items in the total item pool will be "selected" by chance alone. Inclusion of such chance items is typically referred to by statisticians as committing a *type one error.* To guard against errors of this nature, it is imperative that the items selected be *cross-validated*—that is, administered to additional criterion groups that are demographically and otherwise similar to, but independent of, the original groups. In terms of our example, either the complete item pool, or a portion of it, should be administered to another group of persons identified as dominant and to another control group. Because the items selected by chance alone would not be the same in both administrations (except for a negligibly small percentage), those that are selected in both procedures can be assumed to be "true" discriminating items. A less elegant, but more typical, procedure for cross-validation is simply to test on a new group the discriminating power of a scale composed of items selected from the initial administration.

The method of empirical derivation, illustrated here with questionnaire items, can in principle be applied to any set of test responses, such as preference for geometric designs, responses to inkblots, or endorsement of self-descriptive adjectives. It is only necessary to establish that a reliable difference exists between the criterion and control groups in the proportions of responses to the stimuli. We next describe several common inventories whose primary basis of development was empirical: the Minnesota Multiphasic Personality Inventory (MMPI) and its successor, the MMPI-2; the California Psychological Inventory (CPI); and a recent addition to psychologists' armamentarium, the Personality Assessment Inventory (PAI). Discussed in Chapter Ten are two other tests that are primarily empirical: The Personality Inventory for Children (PIC) and the new adolescent form of the MMPI (MMPI-A).

Minnesota Multiphasic Personality Inventory (MMPI) and MMPI-2

The MMPI can be described as the most widely used personality or psychodiagnostic questionnaire and the most widely researched of all psychological tests. Data presented in *The Eleventh Mental Measurements Yearbook* (Kramer & Conoley, 1992) and other editions of this handbook suggest that the number of published references is probably in excess of 8,000, twice as many as for any other test. Literature on the MMPI tests continues to appear at a rapid rate.

Construction of the MMPI was begun in the late 1930s by Hathaway and McKinley (1940, 1951), who were motivated by their recognition of a need in both clinical psychiatric research and practice for an objective multidimensional instrument to assist in the identification of psychopathology. They were interested in developing an instrument that would provide for a comprehensive sampling of behavior that was of significance to psychiatrists, yet would offer a simple presentation so that it could be used with individuals of limited intelligence and education.

They compiled more than 1,000 items from psychiatric examination forms, psychiatry textbooks, previously published attitude and personality scales, and their own clinical experience, and prepared them in a self-report (true or false) format. The number of items was reduced to 550 through the course of revisions. The items are presented to the respondent either in a printed booklet or singly in a deck of small item cards. The test is scored for 10 or more basic psychiatric and personality scales, as well as three "validity" scales.

Generally speaking, each scale was empirically developed by contrasting the responses of nonpsychiatric control subjects with those of patients in a particular psychiatric diagnostic category, using the traditional system of diagnosis that stemmed from the work of Kraepelin in the late 19th century. More than 800 carefully studied psychiatric patients constituted the pool of clinical subjects, and approximately 1,500 control subjects were drawn from hospital visitors, normal clients at the University of Minnesota Testing Bureau, local WPA workers, and general medical patients. The individual diagnostic criterion groups generally numbered 50 or fewer, although some additional groups were utilized in efforts to improve the discriminating power of the scale. For example, more than a dozen scales were developed in an unsuccessful effort to obtain satisfactory discrimination among the subcategories of schizophrenia (Hathaway, 1956b, p. 108). The schizophrenia scale finally chosen for inclusion in the inventory was the fourth such scale attempted and proved to be the most satisfactory of both previous and subsequent efforts.

The usual method of item selection was to consider a basic pool of items that showed a statistically significant percentage of frequency difference between the responses of the criterion group and the control subjects. Items were excluded if the frequency of response for both groups was very high or very low, if they failed to differentiate among additional relevant groups, or if the group difference appeared to have an irrelevant basis, such as marital status. Further items were often eliminated from a scale if they showed an overlap in validity with some other diagnostic category. No item, however, was eliminated from a scale because its manifest content appeared unrelated to the category in question. The articles documenting the original construction and validation of the MMPI were reprinted by Welsh and Dahlstrom (1956).

In the construction of the basic MMPI scales, every effort was made to utilize responses only of psychiatric patients whose symptoms were clearcut and who were relatively free from psychiatric signs other than those qualifying them for their particular diagnostic category. The categories and the resultant scales are:

Scale 1. Hypochondriasis (*Hs*). These patients showed an exaggerated concern about their physical health, often with complaints about physical problems that in fact had a psychological basis.

Scale 2. Depression (*D*). Characterized by intense unhappiness, poor morale, and lack of hope about the future, these patients were relatively pure cases of depression.

Scale 3. Hysteria (*Hy*). These patients, who had been diagnosed "psychoneurosis hysteria," had psychologically based physical symptoms coupled with *la belle indifference* or bland unconcern about their condition.

Scale 4. Psychopathic Deviate (*Pd*). All the criterion subjects used in developing this scale had shown notable difficulties in social adjustment, with histories of delinquency and other antisocial behavior.

Scale 5. Masculinity-Femininity (*Mf*). This scale was derived from the responses of a rather small group of homosexual males, all of whom were relatively free of other psychopathology.

Scale 6. Paranoia (*Pa*). Although rarely diagnosed as having paranoia, these patients showed paranoid symptoms such as ideas of reference, suspiciousness, interpersonal sensitivity, feelings of persecution, and delusions of grandeur.

Scale 7. Psychasthenia (*Pt*). The subjects in this criterion group, mainly patients, showed unreasonable fears, high general anxiety, feelings of guilt, and excessive doubts.

Scale 8. Schizophrenia (*Sc*). These patients were all diagnosed as schizophrenic without regard to the various subtypes of the disorder.

Scale 9. Hypomania (*Ma*). These patients showed the milder degrees of manic excitement typically occurring in manic-depressive psychosis, characterized by excessive activity, easy distractibility, elevated mood, and a rapid but disjointed flow of speech.

One additional scale, social introversion-extroversion (*Si*), was later added to the nine basic clinical scales.

The three "validity" scales developed to enhance the clinical usefulness of the MMPI were constructed as follows. (a) The *L,* or lie scale, designed to provide a basis for evaluating the subject's general frankness, contains 15 rationally selected items reflecting socially desirable but rather improbable behaviors. (b) The *F,* or infrequency scale, intended as an aid to recognizing random or other invalid respondents, contains items that are answered in the same direction by at least 90% of the normal subjects, and is thus a measure of how similar the subject's responses are to those of people in general. (c) The *K,* or defensiveness, scale was developed as a correction or "suppressor" scale to improve the discriminating power of several of the clinical scales by correcting for varying degrees of subtle test-taking defensiveness. It was constructed by comparing the responses of normals with those of patients whose clinical scale scores were in the normal range and who could thus be assumed to have responded to the items defensively.

It soon became apparent that the MMPI could not be used successfully in the manner originally intended, because high scorers on a scale often did not fit into that particular diagnostic category. Further, it was recognized that large numbers of apparently normal people achieved high scores on the clinical scales. However, it was found that useful clinical and personality discriminations could be made by examining combinations or *patterns* of scores, and it is in this manner that the MMPI has come to be used. The large volume of research literature involving the MMPI was summarized through 1975 by Dahlstrom, Welsh, and Dahlstrom (1972, 1975). A number of empirically based interpretation manuals were developed in the 1970s, for adults (Gilberstadt & Duker, 1965; Lanyon, 1968; Marks & Seeman, 1963) and adolescents (Marks, Seeman, & Haller, 1974). Lachar's (1974) manual summarizes previous empirical and clinical literature on the MMPI and is set out in convenient form as an interpretive guide. More recently, textbooks have been published by Friedman, Webb, and Lewak (1989), Graham (1990), and Greene (1980); the latter includes material on the MMPI-2. A considerable amount of formal training and supervision with the test is needed to use these materials properly.

Although the MMPI has not been completely successful in its original purpose (the classification of psychiatric patients), there is much empirical support for its usefulness in identifying other aspects of personality functioning in the psychopathological domain. Empirical databases, or "cookbooks," for interpreting the MMPI, as previously listed, found increasingly wide use in the 1970s, and these have substantially increased the validity of the MMPI's use. (This topic is discussed in detail in Chapter Eight.) The development of computer interpretation services has had a further major impact on the use of this test. Automated interpretation is the subject of Chapter Eleven; for now, the reader should be aware that there are significant validity problems with many automated interpretation systems (Lanyon, 1987; Matarazzo, 1986).

Ever since the publication of the MMPI, interested psychologists have heeded the suggestion of Hathaway and McKinley to develop further scales from the item pool, for particular purposes. Dahlstrom, Welsh, and Dahlstrom (1975) listed a total of 455 scales, subscales, and indexes that had been proposed up to that time. Unfortunately, most of this later work lacked the care that was put into the development of the original scales, so that the utility of much of the additional work is quite questionable. However, special mention should be made of the Wiggins Content Scales (Wiggins, 1966), a set of 13 scales developed to represent the "content" clusters in the MMPI item pool. These scales have high internal consistency, are moderately independent, and have some demonstrated validity for college undergraduates (Wiggins, Goldberg, & Appelbaum, 1971), for psychiatric inpatients (Jarnecke & Chambers, 1977), and for male clients at a military medical facility (Lachar & Alexander, 1978).

One of the major practical problems in using the MMPI has been the length of time required to complete it. Because of the considerable redundancy in the item pool, a number of efforts have aimed to develop shorter forms of the instrument that would retain the original meaning of the scales. In the first of these attempts, Kincannon (1968) selected a representative sample of 71 items, most of which appeared on more than one scale; from these items, he projected the full scores on each of the scales. Items on Kincannon's Mini-Mult were reworded for use in an interview situation. Other short forms include Dean's (1972) 86-item Midi-Mult, the MMPI-168 of Overall and Gomez-Mont (1974), Faschingbauer's (1974) abbreviated MMPI (the FAM), and others. In general, there is relatively limited practical correspondence between profiles based on the full MMPI and those derived from short forms (McLaughlin, Helms, & Howe, 1983; Rand, 1979), and the validity evidence is rather weak (Butcher, Kendall, & Hoffman, 1980). The present authors endorse Greene's (1980) conclusion that the short forms are best regarded as new tests whose correlates need to be determined independently of the MMPI.

The MMPI is open to a number of criticisms. Perhaps the most frequently voiced concern is that some of the scales are highly correlated, indicating a considerable degree of redundancy. Block (1965) showed that many of the "pathological" items are highly similar in nature, creating a redundancy in items as well as scales. Other common criticisms have been that the test is too long, that it contains items about sex and religion that are offensive to many people, and that many normal persons achieve high scores on the clinical scales. Finally, it should be clearly noted that the MMPI was not designed for the assessment of normal personality, so that neither the items nor the scales are optimal for this purpose.

The MMPI-2. Suggestions for revising or improving the MMPI have appeared in the literature for years (e.g., Meehl, 1979; Norman, 1972). Such work was initiated in 1982 with the appointment of a committee by the University of Minnesota Press (Graham, 1990, p. 9). To maintain continuity between the MMPI and the MMPI-2, it was decided that the new test should be primarily a restandardization rather than a wholesale revision. The item pool would be improved by updating outmoded wording and removing objectionable items, and a new, more representative normative sample would be collected. In addition, 154 new items were written to represent potential new scales reflecting the broad content areas of the item pool, plus specific areas of clinical interest such as drug abuse, marital adjustment, and Type A behavior pattern.

The final form of the MMPI-2, published in 1989, contains 567 items and yields three separate sets of scales, each with its own profile form: (a) the original validity and clinical scales, (b) a set of 13 supplementary clinical scales, and (c) a set of 15 scales based directly on the content of the MMPI-2 items, analogous to the Wiggins (1966) scales described above. Several new "validity" scales were also developed, to increase the accuracy of assessing respondents' test-taking set. They include two rather complex measures of response consistency, VRIN (Variable Response Inconsistency) and TRIN (True Response Inconsistency), which help to determine whether the test subject may have responded in a confused or indiscriminate manner.

Compared to the MMPI, the MMPI-2 was standardized on a normative group that was much more representative of the United States. Approximately 2,900 subjects were tested in seven states, to produce a sample that was representative racially and in age distribution. The education and income characteristics of the sample were somewhat higher than average, however, and the south and southwest geographic regions were still not represented in the sample. As another way of increasing the meaningfulness of the clinical scales, the restandardization committee noted that the clinical scales of the MMPI are all positively skewed; but because they are skewed to different degrees, a given T-score on one scale does not represent the same percentile rank as the same T-score on another scale. To make the T-scores comparable in meaning, the average skewness was computed, and each scale was skewed just that amount. Using this procedure, a T-score of 65 represents the 92nd percentile on every scale; this is the level that is considered to have potential clinical significance. The use of *uniform T-scores* in this manner means that the pattern of an MMPI-2 profile differs a bit from its corresponding MMPI profile, but ongoing research suggests that, in most cases, the difference is not a serious one. Butcher, Dahlstrom, Graham, Tellegen, and Kaemmer (1989) emphasize that the changes in the MMPI-2 over the MMPI have significantly increased the reliability of test profiles, and that the huge accumulation of validity data on the MMPI can also be applied to the MMPI-2.

Not all writers agree with this optimistic view. For example, in a critical review, Helmes and Reddon (1993) concluded that the comparability of the two tests has not been established. Other continuing criticisms of the instrument in its new form include the reading level of the items, which is still too high for poorly educated clients (Duckworth, 1991); the continued overlap among the scales; and nonrepresentative norms. Nevertheless, the MMPI-2 represents a significant advance over the original instrument, and as validity data are gathered that are specific to the new test, its use will be on more solid ground.

The contemporary clinical use of the MMPI-2 is illustrated as follows. Figure 3.1 shows the MMPI-2 profile of an adult male client seeking help in a community mental health center. The numbers on the sides of the chart represent a standard score system with a mean of 50 and a standard deviation of 10. The K-correction has been added to the raw scores on the *Hs, Pd, Pt, Sc,* and *Ma* scales.

To give a satisfactory interpretation of these responses, we should have some idea of the *base rates,* or relative frequencies in the population of interest, of the various personal characteristics suggested by the test responses. (This concept is discussed in detail in Chapters Seven and Eight.) The most noteworthy psychological features of persons giving MMPI-2 profiles of the general pattern shown in Figure 3.1 (termed a "27" pattern, referring to the two highest scales in the range beyond a T-score of 65) are anxiety and depression. Thus, in a community mental health center, where the base rate of these characteristics is fairly high, we could suggest with considerable confidence that anxiety and depression are psychological problems of major concern to this client. If a psychiatric label is given, it would probably involve some category of anxiety or depressive disorder. Detailed information about such profiles, based on both empirical and clinical findings, has been developed through actuarial studies such as that of Gilberstadt and Duker (1965) and is reported with reference to the MMPI-2 by Butcher (1990) and by Graham (1990). For example, according to the Gilberstadt and Duker source, which is based on the characteristics of male patients seen in the psychiatry service of a Veterans Administration (VA) hospital, the most common (and discriminating) complaints of such clients include insomnia, obsessions, anxiety, depression, nervousness, tension, worry, tiredness, and

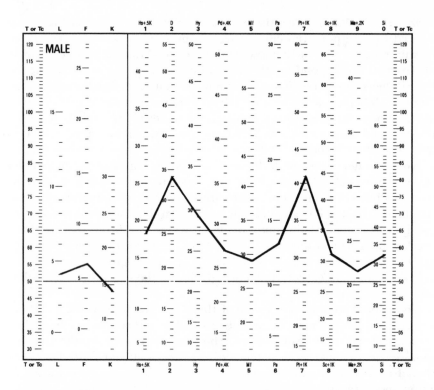

Figure 3.1   MMPI-2 profile suggesting anxiety and depression. (**Source:** *Minnesota Multiphasic Personality Inventory-2 (MMPI-2) Profile for Basic Scales. Copyright © 1989 the Regents of the University of Minnesota. All rights reserved. "MMPI-2" and "Minnesota Multiphasic Personality Inventory-2" are trademarks owned by the University of Minnesota.*)

gastrointestinal problems. Typically, they have high standards of performance, are capable of developing good emotional ties, and tend to become overwhelmed and dependent under accumulated stress. However, reality orientation remains good, and, in a hospital setting, improvement is usually fairly rapid.

California Psychological Inventory (CPI)

The California Psychological Inventory (CPI; Gough, 1957, 1987) was specifically designed for the multidimensional or multiphasic description of normal personality—the task to which the MMPI had, less appropriately, been put. Gough, who had a strong interest in devising measures with broad psychological and sociological relevance, used the empirical approach with a variety of criterion groups. The current version of the CPI, revised in 1987, contains 462 self-reference items, of which about 200 appear in the MMPI, to be answered "true" or "false" in the same manner as the MMPI.

The CPI yields scores on 17 personality scales, 3 "structural" scales, and 3 validity or response bias scales, most of which were constructed empirically. The empirical personality scales are: dominance, capacity for status, sociability, empathy, independence, responsibility, socialization, tolerance, achievement via conformity, achievement via independence, intellectual efficiency, psychological mindedness, and femininity. For some of these scales, the criterion groups were identified by a directly obtainable behavioral index. Thus, the socialization scale was derived by comparing the responses of juvenile offenders and high school disciplinary cases with those of normal high school students (Gough & Peterson, 1952); similarly, the achievement via independence scale employed criterion groups defined according to course grades (Gough, 1953). For other scales, where behaviorally based groups were more difficult to obtain, criterion groups were defined by judges' ratings. For example, the dominance scale was developed by asking fraternity and sorority members to nominate the five most dominant and five least dominant members of their group (Gough, McClosky, & Meehl, 1951).

Four of the scales were constructed through internal consistency analyses, utilizing a combination of the rational selection of items and statistical refinement of the initial item pool. These four scales are: (a) social presence, (b) self-acceptance, (c) self-control, and (d) flexibility. The utility of the scales was demonstrated by comparing the scores of a number of additional behavioral and personality groups. The three structural scales, added in the 1987 revision, reflect the general traits of internality vs. externality, norm-favoring vs. norm-doubting, and self-realization. These traits appear to have a loose correspondence to three of the "big five" traits, although the connection is not emphasized by Gough. The three scales, developed through a complex series of item analyses, are statistically independent of each other.

The three validity scales are similar in nature to the validity scales of the MMPI. The well-being scale, designed to identify persons who exaggerate their misfortunes, was empirically constructed by comparing the responses of normal subjects who simulated severe conflict with those of actual psychiatric patients. The good impression scale, also empirically developed, was designed to identify exaggeration of one's personality characteristics in the positive direction. The communality scale, similar to the MMPI *F* scale, indicates the degree to which one's responses are like those of most normal subjects.

To facilitate the clinical interpretation of individual CPI profiles, the scales were originally organized into four groups or clusters:

1. Measures of poise, ascendancy, and self-assurance.
2. Measures of socialization, maturity, and responsibility.
3. Measures of achievement potential and intellectual efficiency.
4. Measures of intellectual and interest modes.

This grouping of scales was generally supported by independent factor-analytic studies of the CPI (Crites, Bechtoldt, Goodstein, & Heilbrun, 1961; Mitchell & Pierce-Jones, 1960). The profile grid for the revised CPI continues to portray this scheme, which now involves three groups: (a) interactional or socially observable qualities; (b) internal values and control mechanisms; and (for the last two clusters) (c) stylistic variables related to different functional modes (Gough, 1987, p. 5). The three structural scales do not appear on the profile grid. Procedures for interpretation are based either on a scheme involving the three structural scales or on the individual personality scales. An adequate amount of validity data is presented.

The contemporary clinical use of the CPI is illustrated by Figure 3.2, which presents the CPI profile of a 41-year-old male research scientist who was tested as part of an industrial management development program. As with the MMPI, the numbers on the sides of the chart represent a standard score system with a mean of 50 and a standard deviation of 10. The 20 CPI scales are presented along the horizontal axis in the same order in which they were listed in the test.

Applying the interpretive rules suggested earlier, this man would be viewed as a self-assured, poised, rather forceful person with little self-doubt or uncertainty about himself. At the same time, his sense of responsibility, his willingness to accept rules and proper authority, and his self-control seem less well developed. His achievements, both those gained through conformance and those gained through independence, are probably modest. Quite aware of and sensitive to others, he is quite open to change and may even be impulsive at times. However, he appears rather satisfied with himself and can be rather closed-minded and intolerant of others, especially when he feels that his principles are being violated. One might conclude that this man is an ambitious and socially skillful individual who lacks the impulse control and conscientiousness necessary to realize his ambition. His sensitivity to others, coupled with his unwillingness or inability to respond completely to this awareness, might lead others to view him as manipulative and controlling.

This characterization was very much in keeping with the man's supervisory evaluations, which noted that he "has never realized his potential as a scientist." These evaluations further noted his very high needs for autonomy, making it very difficult for him to hear or accept supervisory feedback. His impulsiveness and his impaired interpersonal relationships led to a variety of morale problems in his laboratory, and he was generally regarded as having limited potential for higher managerial positions or promotions.

Personality Assessment Inventory (PAI)

Although the PAI was developed on a rational rather than an empirical basis, it is introduced in this section of the text because of its similarity to the

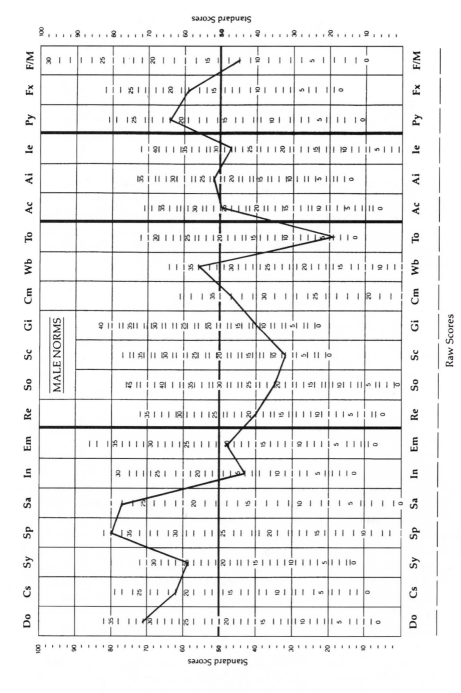

Figure 3.2 CPI profile suggesting mild personality problems. Reprinted with permission of Consulting Psychologists Press, Palo Alto, California.

MMPI-2 in purpose and structure. A new instrument (Morey, 1991) designed for the clinical assessment of psychopathology, its 22 scales include many of the same clinical syndromes as the MMPI, such as depression and schizophrenia. In contrast to the MMPI-2, which aimed for the best that could be done in updating the MMPI without upsetting the applicability of its extensive validity base, the development of this instrument carefully followed most of Jackson's (1967) procedures. Included were additional steps and procedures such as the use of four-point rating scales rather than the traditional true–false response form, and nationally representative norms. In the manner of the NEO-PI-R and the Hogan Personality Inventory (see below), most scales are composed of several homogeneous subscales, and the PAI embodies many other features that enhance its utility. The PAI *Manual* (Morey, 1991) is sophisticated and extensive, and presents a wealth of details characterizing the development of the PAI throughout its various stages.

Validity data in the *Manual* consist of correlations with scores on other tests, but no data involving other modalities such as overt behaviors, observer ratings, or independent diagnoses. Another limitation is the considerable redundancy among the scales and subscales, as shown in the matrix of intercorrelations and the factor loadings. However, these are relatively minor criticisms when compared with the high degree of care and sophistication that was employed in developing this state-of-the-art assessment device. Because of its newness, there is essentially no literature except for the *Manual;* however, the PAI has the potential to become a major tool in clinical assessment in the future.

FACTOR-ANALYTIC INVENTORIES

The third approach to the construction of personality tests is based on the statistical identification of clusters of related test items. An example can perhaps best introduce it. Suppose we have collected the responses of a large number of subjects to a number of test stimuli. The nature of the test stimuli is not important for the moment, except that they are usually selected to provide balanced coverage of the particular behavior domain in which the test constructor is interested. Thus, most of the tests that have been developed on the basis of this strategy involve self-reference questionnaire items, though in principle they could equally well involve inkblots or geometrical forms. Let us suppose that we have as stimuli 50 self-reference questionnaire items, all of which have been answered "true" or "false" by 500 subjects.

Because we are unsure, at this stage of our test development, of the characteristics our items are tapping, we might be seen as having responses to 50 different "scales," each of which had a possible "score" of 0 or 1. It would obviously be desirable to have a method for examining such a large mass of responses on other than an individual basis. We note that the responses to some items tend to be correlated, so that persons who answer "true" to item 13 are very likely to answer "true" to items 15, 25, and 36, and "false" to items 8 and 39. Other item clusters can be expected. In other words, a subject's "score" on any item in a cluster can, to some extent, be predicted by the "score" on other items; the items in each cluster are intercorrelated because they have a common basis for variability. The statistical procedure for identifying such clusters of items, or *factors*, is known as factor analysis. As might be expected, the first step in a factor analysis is to correlate every item with every other item. The resulting matrix of intercorrelations is then treated by a series of complex statistical procedures in order to identify the factors, or grouping of items. Incidentally, the same steps could be followed using scales rather than items, to determine the factorial structure of a multiphasic instrument such as the MMPI or CPI.

When a factor, or cluster of items, is identified in this manner, it is assumed generally that these items are tapping the same psychological variable, because they tend to elicit consistent responses. In our example involving 50 items, let us suppose that we have been able to identify four clusters, each with 10 items, and that the remaining 10 items did not correlate significantly with each other nor with any of the four identifiable clusters. Factor analysis has reduced our original 50 variables to 4, and we can describe individuals as they represent themselves by scores on 4 scales that could be derived to represent these factorial variables. If these 4 factors are reproducible by the same steps in other, similar groups of normal persons, then we might assume that we have isolated 4 central traits of normal personality structure.

What do factor-analytically-derived scales really measure, and how do we know what the factors mean? They have a specific statistical meaning, because they are defined in part by statistical procedures. We can also look for rational meaning, both in the original selection of the items and in what items contribute to the particular factor. For example, the composition of Welsh's MMPI factor *A* (Welsh & Dahlstrom, 1956) was such that he described it as a measure of anxiety or emotional upset. The procedure for naming factors is always rational or clinical, and empirical validity evidence must be accumulated before it can be concluded that the behavior domain involved in the factor is the same as that typically described by that name. Thus, the decision about the usefulness of terming Welsh's MMPI factor *A* an "anxiety factor" must depend partly on whether persons with high scores on that scale are judged to be clinically anxious. Although the meaning of a factor is built into it in a statistical sense, the full nature of its meaning is not made clear by the statistical procedures.

An additional question is whether factors are *real* traits, the psychological essence of personality. This question is highly complex and has given rise to a variety of views among researchers in this area. On the one hand, Cattell (1965) viewed the particular factors that he proposed as natural unitary structures in the domain of normal personality, natural elements that are logically equivalent to the atomic elements in the physical world. Eysenck (1953b) took a similar, although less extreme view. On the other hand, Jackson and Messick (1958) suggested that the major factors that are identified through the factor analysis of self-report inventories are mainly "response distortions" that should be regarded as distinct from the content of the scales. At the very least, however, factor analysis is a useful technique for studying the internal composition both of individual scales and of the several scales in a battery or in a multiphasic instrument.

In Chapter One, we introduced the resurgence of trait approaches to describing personality, a movement that has been accompanied by increasing agreement on the use of a five-factor framework, the *Big Five*. This framework has had a major positive impact on the use of personality tests in personnel assessment and selection. (Its emergence and development will be discussed in detail in Chapter Nine.) Here, we describe and evaluate the best known of the factor-based tests, both old and new. It has been shown that all reflect the five-factor model to some degree, and some are directly based on that model. Consistent with the technological advances in inventory construction during the late 1960s and the 1970s, the tests developed in the past 15 years are considerably more sophisticated than the earlier ones.

Guilford Tests

Guilford (1959), an early practitioner of test construction through factor analysis, sought the most parsimonious set of traits for describing normal personality functioning. After several factor analyses of many sets of self-report questionnaire items, he developed three separate inventories: (a) Inventory of Factors STDGR (Guilford, 1940), (b) Inventory of Factors GAMIN (Guilford & Martin, 1943b), and (c) Personnel Inventory (Guilford & Martin, 1943a). The Guilford-Zimmerman Temperament Survey (Guilford & Zimmerman, 1949) was developed later to cover, in a single inventory, 10 of the 13 traits of the original three inventories. These were: general activity, restraint versus rhathymia, ascendance, sociability, emotional stability, objectivity, friendliness, thoughtfulness, personal relations, and masculinity. Two empirically derived falsification scales, similar to the validity scales of the MMPI and CPI, were added later, together with a "carelessness-deviancy" scale similar to the MMPI *F* scale (Jacobs & Schlaff, 1955). Although there is evidence that some of these factorially derived scales do measure the traits for which they were named (Guilford, 1959, pp. 185–187), their relationships to other indexes of the same traits have generally been shown to be fairly minimal.

Thurstone Temperament Schedule

Thurstone (1949, 1951) performed his own factor analysis on Guilford's original data and concluded that 7 rather than 13 factors were sufficient to describe the main dimensions of personality. He developed the Thurstone Temperament Schedule to measure these factors, which he named active, vigorous, impulsive, dominant, stable, sociable, and reflective. As might be assumed, the same evaluative comments directed toward the Guilford instruments can be applied to Thurstone's test.

Sixteen Personality Factors Questionnaire (16 PF)

Based on extensive factor analyses of self-report inventories, biographical data, and behavior observation, Cattell (1965) defined 16 factors that he regarded as the "source traits" of normal personality structure, suitable for measurement on an inventory. Because some of these factors did not readily correspond to any readily named personality trait, he originally developed his own nomenclature, such as *parmia* (implying parasympathetic nervous system domination) versus *threctia* (implying susceptibility to threat) (Cattell, 1965, p. 95).

The 16 PF questionnaire was developed to assess these factors. There are two sets of parallel forms (A and B, with 187 items each; and shorter forms, C and D), plus Form E for persons with low reading skills. To ensure adequate reliability, it is recommended that more than one form be used. Variants of the 16 PF include the Clinical Analysis Questionnaire (Krug, 1980), the LEADR (Allen, 1985), the Adult Personality Inventory (Krug, 1982), and several versions for children and adolescents (see Chapter Nine). Cattell, Eber, and Tatsuoka (1970) and Karson and O'Dell (1976) published major reference works on the 16 PF, and the popularity of the instrument is shown by its relatively high volume of literature (Buros, 1978; Mitchell, 1985) and its frequency of use in practical settings (Piotrowski & Keller, 1989).

Despite the massive amount of psychometric effort that was devoted to the development of the 16 PF, the test has a number of serious deficiencies (Bloxom, 1978; Zuckerman, 1985). The writings on the construction of the test tend to be confusing and sometimes contradictory. The handbook (Cattell, Eber, & Tatsuoka, 1970) contains an enormous amount of validity data, but much of it is presented in a form that is very difficult to evaluate. Further, some of the claims about the uses of the test are simply not supported by the validity data (Walsh, 1978). Thus, the 16 PF should be used only with considerable caution.

NEO Personality Inventory

Out of the various efforts to represent the Big Five factor structure in the form of a personality inventory, the best known and most widely researched is the NEO Personality Inventory, now in its revised form, the NEO-PI-R (Costa & McCrae, 1992b). Development began in the 1970s with the recognition of the neuroticism (N), extraversion (E), and openness (O) dimensions.

NEO-PI-R Facet	Adjective Check List Items
Neuroticism facets	
N1: Anxiety	anxious, fearful, worrying, tense, nervous, –confident, –optimistic
N2: Angry Hostility	anxious, irritable, impatient, excitable, moody, –gentle, tense
N3: Depression	worrying, –contented, –confident, –self-confident, pessimistic, moody, anxious
N4: Self-Consciousness	shy, –self-confident, timid, –confident, defensive, inhibited, anxious
N5: Impulsiveness	moody, irritable, sarcastic, self-centered, loud, hasty, excitable
N6: Vulnerability	–clear-thinking, –self-confident, –confident, anxious, –efficient, –alert, careless
Extraversion facets	
E1: Warmth	friendly, warm, sociable, cheerful, –aloof, affectionate, outgoing
E2: Gregariousness	sociable, outgoing, pleasure-seeking, –aloof, talkative, spontaneous, –withdrawn
E3: Assertiveness	aggressive, –shy, assertive, self-confident, forceful, enthusiastic, confident
E4: Activity	energetic, hurried, quick, determined, enthusiastic, aggressive, active
E5: Excitement-Seeking	pleasure-seeking, daring, adventurous, charming, handsome, spunky, clever
E6: Positive Emotions	enthusiastic, humorous, praising, spontaneous, pleasure-seeking, optimistic, jolly
Openness facets	
O1: Fantasy	dreamy, imaginative, humorous, mischievous, idealistic, artistic, complicated
O2: Aesthetics	imaginative, artistic, original, enthusiastic, inventive, idealistic, versatile
O3: Feelings	excitable, spontaneous, insightful, imaginative, affectionate, talkative, outgoing
O4: Actions	interests wide, imaginative, adventurous, optimistic, –mild, talkative, versatile
O5: Ideas	idealistic, interests wide, inventive, curious, original, imaginative, insightful
O6: Values	–conservative, unconventional, –cautious, flirtatious
Agreeableness facets	
A1: Trust	forgiving, trusting, –suspicious, –wary, –pessimistic, peaceable, –hard-hearted
A2: Straightforwardness	–complicated, –demanding, –clever, –flirtatious, –charming, –shrewd, –autocratic

Figure 3.3   Scales, facets, and adjective checklist correlates of the NEO-PI-R. (**Source:** *Reproduced by special permission of the Publishers, Psychological Assessment Resources, Inc., from the* **NEO-PI-R Professional Manual** *by Paul T. Costa, Jr., Ph.D., and Robert McCrae, Ph.D., 1992, p. 49. Copyright 1978, 1985, 1989, 1992 by PAR, Inc. All rights reserved.*)

NEO-PI-R Facet	Adjective Check List Items
A3: Altruism	warm, soft-hearted, gentle, generous, kind, tolerant, –selfish
A4: Compliance	–stubborn, –demanding, –headstrong, –impatient, –intolerant, –outspoken, –hard-hearted
A5: Modesty	–show-off, –clever, –assertive, –argumentative, –self-confident, –aggressive, –idealistic
A6: Tender-Mindedness	friendly, warm, sympathetic, soft-hearted, gentle, –unstable, kind
Conscientiousness facets	
C1: Competence	efficient, self-confident, thorough, resourceful, confident, –confused, intelligent
C2: Order	organized, thorough, efficient, precise, methodical, –absent-minded, –careless
C3: Dutifulness	–defensive, –distractible, –careless, –lazy, thorough, –absent-minded, –fault-finding
C4: Achievement Striving	thorough, ambitious, industrious, enterprising, determined, confident, persistent
C5: Self-Discipline	organized, –lazy, efficient, –absent-minded, energetic, thorough, industrious
C6: Deliberation	–hasty, –impulsive, –careless, –impatient, –immature, thorough, –moody

Figure 3.3   (Continued)

Agreeableness (A) and conscientiousness (C) were added later. The subject pool for the development of the first three scales consisted of 2,000 male veterans; additional groups, studied later, balanced the biases of the earlier subjects. A large number of items were initially developed based on the trait assumed to underlie each construct, and a variety of item refinement procedures were employed, as well as factor analyses.

An important innovation in the NEO was the incorporation of *facets,* or homogeneous clusters of items within each factor-based scale. Costa and McCrae (1992b) recognized early that general traits may incorporate narrower, or more specific traits, and their work ultimately led to the development of six facets for each of the five factors. Figure 3.3 presents names for these facets, together with the adjectives that were found to be most frequently associated with them. The current norms are based on 500 men and 500 women selected from among previously studied normative groups to be representative of age, race, and education, although the mean educational level is still higher than average, especially for men. A wide range of validity data is offered in the *Manual,* including correlations with observer ratings and with corresponding concepts on other tests.

Several forms of the NEO are now available. In all of them, items are rated on a five-point scale from "strongly disagree" to "strongly agree." Each scale has 6 facets represented by 8 items, making a total of 48 items per scale and 240 items overall. The use of five-point rating scales rather than true–false items increases reliability while minimizing the length of the instrument. The basic form of the NEO is a self-report form (Form S); there are also observer report forms (Form A) with items written in the third person for either males or females. An abbreviated self-report form, the NEO Five-Factor Inventory (NEO-FFI), has 60 items, 12 from each scale. Norms are provided in the *Manual* for adults in general and also for college-age persons.

The reviews of the NEO to date have been positive. Widiger (1992) considered it the best representation of the Big Five dimensions and was especially impressed with the research on validity and reliability reported in the *Manual*. Hess (1992) also praised many aspects of the test's construction and validation. While the research evidence on the usefulness of the NEO as a comprehensive measure of personality is still accumulating, its usefulness as an employment screening device has been well established. We examine this evidence and provide a more comprehensive review of the importance of the Big Five factors in Chapter Nine.

Hogan Personality Inventory (HPI)

Another factor-analytic inventory that is consistent with the five-factor structure is the Hogan Personality Inventory (HPI; Hogan, 1986; Hogan & Hogan, 1992). Designed primarily for use in individual assessment situations, including personnel selection and career counseling, the HPI was developed in the context of Hogan's (1983) socioanalytic theory of personality, which relates basic human motivation to social behavior and personal development. Based in part on the theory and in part on continuing psychometric research with many personnel-related subject groups, Hogan found two of the Big Five variables to be better represented as two factors each, making a total of seven factors. Specifically, the extraversion factor is broken down into *ambition* and *sociability,* and the openness or intellectance factor is restated as *intellectance* and *school success.*

Construction of the HPI began in the late 1970s, and involved most of the item and scales development procedures originally proposed by Jackson (1967). Hogan pioneered the use of facets within factors, and called them *homogeneous item composites,* or HICs. The seven scales differ in the number of HICs they contain, ranging from four to eight. In regard to social desirability, Hogan believed that it was not a source of interference with test validity, but that self-enhancement ability should be viewed as a social skill. Because some HICs contain as few as three items, they may be of limited use when viewed alone, but they can be combined empirically to form six *occupational scales,* such as Service Orientation, Sales Potential, and Managerial Potential.

The HPI contains 206 items written at a fourth-grade level. Scoring and interpretation are done by computer, and although many thousands of subjects were involved in test construction and the development of norms, the specifics of this work are not presented in the HPI *Manual*. Nevertheless, the wealth of validity data that are reported suggests that it is a useful instrument, particularly for job-related assessments.

SUMMARY

This chapter introduces basic issues in the development of standardized personality assessment procedures. Such procedures tend to meet several conditions: (a) the stimuli and their manner of presentation are invariant, (b) norms exist for the responses of interest, and (c) the personality or behavior correlates of these responses are known. These conditions suggest several criteria for the classification of assessment devices: degree of response structure, completeness of norms, and degree of usefulness or validity. We have chosen a more basic classification: the manner in which the assessment stimuli were originally selected.

Three categories are employed: (a) rational-theoretical, where the stimuli have commonsense appeal and are based to a lesser or greater extent in a particular theory of personality; (b) empirical, where the stimuli are chosen solely on the basis of their demonstrated utility; and (c) factor-analytic, where the dimensions to be assessed are defined statistically. It is usual for all three procedures to be used today in the course of developing a particular test. The chapter discusses the application of these strategies to the development of personality inventories.

Some common inventories whose development is predominantly rational-theoretical have been described. The Edwards Personal Preference Schedule (EPPS) is a paper-and-pencil inventory yielding scores on 15 "need" scales. To counter the tendency to answer all questionnaire items in a socially desirable direction, Edwards employed the forced-choice technique of presenting the statements in pairs matched for social desirability. However, later research indicated that the validity of the test was not enhanced by this procedure. The Myers-Briggs Type Indicator is a paper-and-pencil inventory based on the typological theories of Carl Jung. It yields scores on four independent dimensions, leading to a classification in terms of one of 16 types. Despite almost 40 years of research, the evidence on the validity of the MBTI is sparse and it still must be regarded as a "promising" instrument. Two tests that represent a considerable advance in the sophistication of test-construction technology are the Personality Research Form (PRF) and the Jackson Personality Inventory (JPI).

In the purely empirical approach to test development, recognition of rational or theoretical connections is irrelevant because the stimuli are selected solely on the basis of their ability to lead to the desired description or prediction. The empirical approach is not often used alone. The Minnesota

Multiphasic Personality Inventory (MMPI), perhaps the best known of all personality inventories, was originally developed as an aid in classifying psychiatric patients into diagnostic groups. It was derived from an original item pool of more than 1,000 rationally selected statements by contrasting the responses of patients in each category with those of normal subjects. It is scored on 13 scales, most of which represent psychiatric categories, and there is a large amount of evidence for its research and clinical usefulness. The current version, the MMPI-2, has two additional sets of scales and is based on more representative norms. It was successful in dealing with some of the main disadvantages of the MMPI but not all of them. Because clinical interpretation involves patterns of scores rather than individual scales, a degree of skill is necessary in its use. The availability of empirical data bases, or "cookbooks," substantially increases the validity of MMPI interpretation.

The California Psychological Inventory (CPI) is somewhat similar to the MMPI but was designed to assess significant aspects of normal personality functioning. In its current version, there are 20 basic scales, most of which were derived empirically. They are grouped into four clusters: (a) poise, ascendancy, and self-assurance; (b) socialization, maturity, and responsibility; (c) achievement potential and intellectual efficiency; and (d) intellectual and interest modes. There are also three "structural" or traitlike scales. A considerable amount of normative and validity information is available for the CPI, and despite some redundancy among the scales, it appears to be a useful device. The Personality Assessment Inventory (PAI) is a new, rationally developed inventory to assess psychopathology. A potential competitor against the MMPI, it was developed using state-of-the-art item-and-scale construction procedures and appears to have excellent potential.

In the factor-analytic approach, complex statistical procedures are used to group items whose responses tend to be related to each other. The personality meaning of these item clusters, or factors, must be determined by other means. Guilford's several factor-analytically-derived inventories, of which the Guilford-Zimmerman Temperament Survey is most representative, assesses 10 such variables. In the Thurstone Temperament Schedule, developed from similar data, seven factors are thought sufficient to cover the range of normal personality functioning. Cattell's Sixteen Personality Factor Questionnaire assesses 16 such factors, or "source traits," which Cattel considered to be natural unitary structures, logically equivalent to atomic elements in the physical world.

Recent agreement over the existence of a five-factor structure (the Big Five) to represent normal personality functioning has led to the development of several promising tests. The best known is the NEO Personality Inventory–Revised, which represents the factors as neuroticism, extraversion, openness, agreeableness, and conscientiousness. Each factor has six facets or homogeneous clusters of items with separate scoring procedures and norms. In addition to the self-report form of the NEO, there are observer report forms and a short form with 60 items. In the Hogan Personality Inventory (HPI), which is oriented toward career counseling and personnel selection, two of the Big Five factors are split, making seven in all. In addition to these scales, the 41 homogeneous item composites (facets) have been empirically developed into occupational scales. A considerable amount of normative and validity data is available for a wide variety of personnel-related uses.

CHAPTER FOUR

Projective Assessment Instruments

In Chapter One, we traced the origin and development of personality assessment devices. One root of objective tests involved the need to find a solution to a practical problem: predicting which World War I military recruits might have adjustment difficulties. This need, together with the influence of psychological measurement, began a long tradition of structured personality inventories. Projective techniques also arose from a practical need to understand the inner workings of the mind, for it was believed that a knowledge of those workings could not be readily obtained by any other method. But the psychometric tradition has had relatively little impact on projective approaches to assessment. Reasons for this lack include the identification of projective methods with the clinical analysis of individuals, and the complex problems involved in trying to deal objectively with the infinite range of response possibilities that can be generated by projective tests. It is ironic that the originators of the two most widely known projective tests, the Rorschach and the Thematic Apperception Test, approached their work in a structured, quantitative vein. More will be said about this topic later in this chapter. First, let us review the best-known projective assessment procedures.

SENTENCE COMPLETION

Sentence completion is a technique or a method rather than a single specific instrument, although commercially marketed instruments representative of the method are available (Forer, 1950; Rotter, Lah, & Rafferty, 1992). The respondent is presented with a series of items consisting of the first few words of a sentence and is asked to provide an ending for each of these beginnings or stems. The stems are developed to elicit responses that illuminate various aspects of the individual's feelings and behaviors. Thus, the person's attitudes and feelings toward his or her mother are assumed to be tapped by the stem "My mother and I . . . ," and techniques for handling strong emotions are presumably seen in responses to the item "When I am angry or upset, I . . . ." Sentence stems in the third person are also employed, such as "His greatest wish was . . . ," and the projective hypothesis is used as a basis for reasoning that the responses to these third-person stems are informative about the subject's own desires.

Of the several commercially available instruments, the Rotter Incomplete Sentences Blank (ISB; Rotter, Lah, & Rafferty, 1992; Rotter & Rafferty, 1950) has perhaps enjoyed the widest use. In addition to qualitative, clinical inferences that might be drawn from the content of the individual's responses, the ISB contains a rationally derived quantitative scoring scheme that yields a single index of adjustment–maladjustment. There are 40 sentence stems, all of which are rather brief and nonspecific, such as "I feel . . ." and "Marriage . . . ." Each response is scored, with the aid of the examples provided in the ISB manual, on a seven-point rating scale for degree of maladjustment. The reasonably high levels of reliability and validity reported in the ISB manual for this maladjustment index were substantiated in subsequent studies (P. A. Goldberg, 1965), and Lah (1989) has provided further norms and other psychometric data.

In general, the available evidence about the usefulness of the sentence-completion method can be summarized as follows (P. A. Goldberg, 1965; Rabin & Zltogorski, 1985):

1. There is little research evidence to indicate that any of the formal aspects of responses to sentence-completion items, such as reaction time, response length, or grammatical or spelling errors, are systematically related to any personality-relevant behaviors. There is also little evidence to support the use of impressionistic or clinical analyses of the content of the responses, although adequate studies of such an approach are difficult to conduct.

2. The more structured approaches to content analysis, such as Rotter's scoring procedure, have been demonstrated to be useful. This finding is intuitively reasonable because an instrument developed to assess a single, clearly definable variable or dimension such as adjustment—maladjustment can be expected to be valid or useful for that particular purpose. Further, the focus on a single dimension tends to result in relative homogeneity of items, enhancing the consistency or reliability of the instrument, which, in turn, enhances usefulness. However, it should be pointed out that the clinician interested in describing and understanding a broad range of personality and behavior will probably be dissatisfied with an instrument yielding only a single score.

3. Employing first-person stems seems to provide somewhat more useful responses than employing third-person stems, although the evidence is equivocal.

4. The specificity of the content of a response can be controlled by the specificity of the sentence stem; that is, the stems can be worded so that the responses are more or less delimited. For example, the stem "Marriage . . ." elicits a wider range of responses than the stem "My marriage has been. . . ." It is unclear which of these two types of stems elicits the more significant responses.

To illustrate the use of the sentence-completion method, the first five sentence stems of the ISB are given here, together with the completions provided by an 18-year-old male college freshman who was seeking help for personal problems.

1. I like . . . music, leisure time, and sports.
2. The happiest time . . . is when I'm performing.
3. I want to know . . . what I don't know.

4. Back home . . . it's very nice.
5. I regret . . . many things, but only slightly.

The nature of the objective scoring system for degree of maladjustment is as follows. The original scoring manual (Rotter & Rafferty, 1950, p. 55) would give a score of *6*, representing the extreme of maladjustment, if the first stem, "I like. . . ," is completed with ". . . to know if I am going crazy." The response ". . . most everything" to this stem would receive a score of *0*, representing the extreme of adjustment. The response ". . . to observe people" would receive a score of *3*, the neutral category with respect to adjustment–maladjustment. The response given by the college freshman would be scored *2*, or slightly on the "adjusted" side of the neutral point. With the aid of similar scoring examples, the response given by the client to the second sentence stem would be scored *3*. The complete set of 40 responses given by this client yielded a total score of 134, placing him at about the 70th percentile with respect to maladjustment, according to the norms provided in the ISB manual.

Qualitative or subjective inferences are typically drawn from sentence-completion responses, although caution should be observed. The client's response to the second stem might be taken to suggest exhibitionistic needs. Dependency needs might be inferred from the fourth response. The fifth response, which contains a mild contradiction, might be interpreted as reflecting a personality conflict, perhaps involving guilt. Further evidence to support or contradict these tentative hypotheses would be sought from the remainder of the test.

Another structured sentence-completion test, the Incomplete Sentences Task (IST), was developed psychometrically to yield scores on three variables: (a) hostility, (b) anxiety, and (c) dependency (Lanyon, 1972; Lanyon & Lanyon, 1980). This test is noteworthy because it represents the application of all three test construction procedures to the development of what has traditionally been regarded as a projective test. Thus, preliminary sentence stems were written on the basis of a rationally developed universe of content for each characteristic, and were refined through factor-analytic procedures. Final selection of the stems was made empirically, by contrasting the responses of junior high school students whom teachers rated high and low on the criterion measures. Empirical cross-validation data supported the validity of each scale.

RORSCHACH PSYCHODIAGNOSTIC TECHNIQUE

Hermann Rorschach was a Swiss psychiatrist practicing in the early 1900s. He had an intellectual interest in fantasy, which he studied through perception of small, colored geometric forms (Zubin, Eron, & Schumer, 1965).

Finding that these geometric forms were too limited as stimulus material, he started to experiment with inkblots. When he began to use his patients as subjects for these perceptual experiments, he made the accidental discovery that there were stable relationships between certain inkblot perceptions and psychiatric diagnostic types. Encouraged by these findings, he began a more systematic investigation of the responses of a number of diverse patient groups and started to speculate about the reasons for these relationships.

Because Rorschach was primarily interested in perception, he paid particular attention to the formal aspects of the individual's responses rather than to the content. He noted the number of responses, the reaction time, whether the response was determined solely by the form of the response or whether color or perceived movement was also involved, and so forth (Rorschach, 1942/1951, p. 19). As part of his speculation, he developed fairly complex hypotheses about the relation of color and movement responses to the dimension of extroversion–introversion, based in part on Jung's theoretical interest in this dimension. Ironically, Rorschach believed that his technique had little to offer in understanding the unconscious. Despite his misgivings, the test was enthusiastically embraced by psychoanalytically oriented psychologists. By the 1940s and 1950s, it had become the cornerstone of their assessment procedures.

"The Rorschach" cannot be easily classified in terms of its construction and development. Some of the original interpretive hypotheses have an empirical base, some were based on rational or commonsense considerations, and some stemmed from Jungian personality theory. A variety of attempts to conceptualize the Rorschach within various other theoretical frameworks have been made; these efforts have been evaluated by Zubin, Eron, and Schumer (1965). However, the use of the Rorschach during its heyday, as reflected in the writings of Beck et al. (1961), Klopfer, Ainsworth, Klopfer, and Holt (1954), Rorschach (1942/1951), and many, many others, was based primarily on rational considerations—and, even then, there was a wide variety of approaches. Exner (1974) identified "at least five reasonably distinct Rorschachs. But when the potential combinations of these systems are considered, the possibilities become astronomical" (p. 14). Thus, the traditional use of the Rorschach has essentially been a subjective, individual enterprise.

In administering the Rorschach, the examiner shows the respondent a series of ten symmetrical inkblots, five achromatic and five chromatic, and asks for a description of what he or she can see in these blots: "What do they remind you of?" or, following Rorschach's original instruction, "What might this be?" The order of presentation is invariant, and the examiner records the individual's responses verbatim, including spontaneous comments, and any nonverbal behavior such as card turning. The respondent is permitted to give as many or as few responses as he or she wishes. Following this initial free-association period, there is an inquiry or posttest interview in which the examiner, bearing in mind an interest in the specific formal

Rorschach scoring categories, reads the responses back and asks the individual to specify the particular characteristics of the blot that determined each response.

As an illustration Figure 4.1 reproduces Card I from the ten Rorschach cards. Klopfer and Davidson (1962, p. 9) described some of the stimulus characteristics of this card as follows:

> *Card I is a fairly large over-all black-gray blot with four rather conspicuous white spaces. If one looks closely, small black spots may be observed outside the large blot material. The large black-gray area is easily subdivided into three parts: the center area and the two side areas. The first reaction of many people to this card is to use the whole blot and to see in it some winged creature. More imaginative or less constricted subjects use the whole blot in many different ways, sometimes projecting human movement onto it. Observing any of the smaller portions or using the white spaces by themselves is less frequent. However, it is not unusual for the white spaces to be used as part of a concept which involves the entire blot ("a pumpkin face," for example). In addition to the winged creature, the blot lends itself to the perception of human beings, especially a female figure in the center area. Persons who are concerned about their bodies may perceive a pelvis or some other anatomical concept in the entire blot.*

The traditional manner in which the Rorschach is used clinically can best be illustrated by discussing actual responses to a card. A 23-year-old female psychotherapy outpatient gave the following responses to Card IV in the ten-card sequence. The question marks in the inquiry phase indicate places where the examiner asked clarifying questions about the *location* of the percept ("What parts of the blot are you referring to?") and its *determinants* (for example, "What about the blot suggested a monster?").

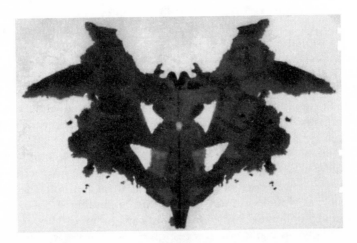

Figure 4.1   A reproduction of Card I from the ten Rorschach inkblots. (**Source:** *Hermann Rorschach, Rorschach®-Test. Copyright © Verlag Hans Huber AG, Bern, Switzerland, 1921, 1948, 1994.*)

Free Association Phase	Inquiry Phase
IV 1. Sort of looks like a monster with big feet.	A cute little thing. Really a dashing little monster. Such a friendly little guy. Got a big tail, though. (?) The whole blot. (?) Really looks like a monster, but a friendly one.
2. When I turn it round, it just looks like—when you mount an insect it has wings and legs— looks like a mounted insect. Sort of cute insect. Maybe a little moth.	You lay him out flat. Only partially mounted. Person hasn't finished yet. You can tell by the lighter color that its wings are turned over. (?) The lighter gray. (?) Again, the whole blot.

Klopfer and Davidson's (1962, p. 10) description of Card IV includes the following:

The blot material of Card IV appears massive, compact, yet indistinct in shape. This card is black-gray all over and highly shaded. Because of its massive structure and dense shading, it appears ominous to some people. Thus monsters, giants, gorillas, or peculiar-looking people are seen sitting or approaching, or the blot looks like a dense forest with mountains and lakes. The frequency of the giant, ape, or monster type of response has prompted some clinicians to refer to this card as the "father card." They believe that attitudes toward paternal authority are revealed because of the combination of masculine aggression and dependent needs related to shading. Subjects who are prone to select details for their responses may perceive the large side areas as "boots," or the top side areas as "snakes" or a "female figure diving." Two other areas that are easily delineated are the lower center portion and the small top center area, frequently associated with sexual responses.

The first response would be scored W F+ (H), indicating that the location of the percept was the whole blot (W), that the determinant was form, or shape (F), that the form perceived was appropriate or realistic (indicated by the + sign), and that the content of the percept was humanlike, but not distinctly human (H). The second response would be scored W FC′+ A, indicating a whole response (W), a realistic form integrated with the perception of achromatic color (FC′+), and animal content (A).

In traditional Rorschach interpretation, at least three kinds of material are considered to be significant: (a) the formal scoring categories (namely, the distribution of percepts over the various location and determinant categories), (b) the nature of the perceived content, and (c) the general language with which percepts are described. Only the most tentative hypotheses would be made from each individual percept, and heavy reliance is placed on the response pattern as a whole.

Predominance of W, or "whole," locations, when combined with a high level of form appropriateness, is traditionally interpreted as reflecting "the ability to organize material, to relate details, to be concerned with the abstract and the theoretical" (Klopfer & Davidson, 1962, p. 131). A high degree of form appropriateness is also considered to indicate a concern with reality. The presence of achromatic color responses in any quantity is interpreted as indicating either hesitation in responsiveness to external stimuli or a dysphoric mood. With regard to content and language, the client's recognition of a "monster" and the manner in which she divests it of its threatening nature ("cute," "little," "friendly") might be seen as illustrating one method of adjustment to perceived threat, by denying and even "reversing" the threatening elements. The fact that a satisfactory compromise is reached at the end of the inquiry ("a monster, but a friendly one") might be taken as a tentative indication that this particular defense mechanism—denial—operates satisfactorily for the client. This hypothesis might be tempered slightly after examining the next response, in which the percept has been reduced not only to an insect but a dead one, and the client again calls it "cute," perhaps suggesting that she still finds it necessary to reassure herself that no threat exists. Pinning it out on a board might be seen as yet a further attempt to distance herself from the threat. The use of "him" rather than "it" in the inquiry might be taken as a tentative cue that the threat has its basis in human interactions, particularly involving males. Statements such as these would be regarded as only tentative hypotheses, to be confirmed or negated by the client's responses to the other nine cards.

One of the traditional reasons offered for a relative lack of sound, validating evidence for the Rorschach test was that there were too many variations in administration and scoring. In the early 1970s, Exner (1974) reasoned that a single, standardized scoring system was required. Taking what he considered to be the most satisfactory elements from the various existing systems, he developed what he termed the Comprehensive System, using Rorschach's original work as a guide wherever possible. Together with his students and colleagues, he elaborated this system with many, many additional scoring variables and ratios, so that by 1990 the Comprehensive System had expanded Rorschach's handful of scoring variables to more than 100. Exner's current writings on the Comprehensive System are monumental indeed, with three volumes of text and a workbook, totaling nearly 2,000 pages (Exner, 1990, 1991, 1993; Exner & Weiner, 1982). Norms are available on all the variables for children, normal adults, and psychiatric patients (Exner, 1991).

Learning to score and interpret the Rorschach test by Exner's system is a formidable task. Despite the massive amounts of clerical and research information reported in the books, interpretation remains a complex process requiring a great deal of clinical training. Interestingly, the question of establishing the *validity* of the interpretive process, the extent to which it results in accurate interpretations, is not addressed in Exner's work. Thus, there is no scientific reason to conclude that the Comprehensive System is any more valid than the earlier, simpler scoring and interpretation procedures it was designed to replace.

The validity of the Rorschach is the subject of continuing controversy. Despite a total literature of more than 5,000 references and a recent increase in empirical studies (e.g., Exner & Andronikof-Sanglade, 1992), the overall empirical basis for interpreting this test remains thin. Reviewers who are identified with the field of projective techniques and with psychoanalytic theory tend to acknowledge the lack of evidence for predictive validity, but they believe that the strength of the test lies in its ability to assess personality processes (Weiner, 1986), to serve as a general source of information about a patient (Dana, 1978), to reveal aspects of motivation and personality not assessed by other instruments (Klopfer & Taulbee, 1976), or to serve as a standardized interview. Evidence for the utility of these applications, however, is mostly subjective in nature.

Careful analyses of different procedures for establishing the validity of the Rorschach have been made by Weiner (1977, 1986) and by Zubin, Eron, and Schumer (1965). The most frequently used approach has involved attempts to show the empirical validity of various signs, scores, indexes, or clusters of scores in predicting behavior or discriminating different groups. Either formal scores or aspects of response content can be involved. This approach highlights the low reliabilities of most of the signs or scores, a difficulty that greatly restricts the validities that can be achieved. Traditional Rorschach enthusiasts criticize this approach because it does not accurately reflect the manner in which experienced clinicians are thought to interpret the test—by relying on patterns or configurations of scores rather than on simple signs or scores.

A second approach to validity involves the matching of a series of Rorschach protocols with the case history belonging to each respondent. Success in matching is said to demonstrate validity in a holistic sense for the test. However, a major criticism, sufficient to preclude further use of matching as a validation strategy, is that many protocols and case histories can easily be matched on the basis of trivial or irrelevant variables, such as references to a particular geographic location, a specific occupation, or other personal data. A third approach, preferred by Weiner (1986) and termed the *conceptual approach,* is to assess construct validity (see Chapter Seven). Here, the challenge is to "formulate theoretical relationships that adequately link the personality characteristics being assessed with the condition being assessed or the behavior being predicted" (Weiner, 1977, p. 597). This is a "theoretical" approach, as described in Chapter Two, in which aspects of personality functioning serve as bridges between the test response and the behavior or prediction of interest (Exner & Weiner, 1982).

A fourth approach, which the present authors regard as the simplest and most direct, is the global strategy, in which the clinician makes predictions and interpretations about each patient from the Rorschach results as a whole, according to some structured format such as a Q-sort, checklist, or questionnaire. The same structured format is used by an independent criterion judge to describe each patient from nontest sources of information such as therapy notes or assessment center data, and the two sets of patient descriptions are compared for accuracy. Further details on the use of this approach are given in Chapter Seven, in an extended discussion of the reliability of projective techniques. As indicated earlier, none of these approaches has been very successful in demonstrating validity for the Rorschach.

HOLTZMAN INKBLOT TECHNIQUE (HIT)

As previously noted, some of the most serious difficulties with the traditional use of the Rorschach involved problems of formal measurement, such as lack of norms and unreliability. In 1954, a project was begun to develop "a completely new approach to inkblot testing, one which is designed from its inception to meet adequate standards of measurement while preserving the uniquely valuable projective quality of the Rorschach" (Holtzman et al., 1961, p. 10). The materials were specifically designed to tap the same variables as the Rorschach, yet the method was designed to correct a number of serious psychometric problems inherent in any quantitative use of the Rorschach, problems that stem from the great variation in number of responses from subject to subject.

Out of a very large number of inkblots produced by a variety of methods, Holtzman and his coworkers developed two parallel forms of 45 cards each. In preliminary investigations, the stimulus cards were administered to samples of normal persons (college students) and mental hospital patients. The two major criteria for selecting the final stimulus blots were that they should provide maximum discriminatory power between the two groups, and that the blots should enable maximum reliability of the scoring categories being studied. These categories included many traditional Rorschach variables such as (a) location, (b) form appropriateness, (c) color, (d) shading, and (e) movement—categories for which personality interpretation is based on rational grounds. Thus, the HIT, like the Rorschach, is best viewed as a rationally derived instrument, despite some empirical basis in the selection of the actual HIT stimuli.

The HIT cards are shown one at a time, and the individual is asked to give a single response to each card. The responses are then scored for 22 different variables, selected for their relative independence, reliability of scoring, and judged relevance for understanding personality. In addition to the five scoring variables already listed, they include: form definiteness, space, anxiety, pathognomic verbalization, and five different content categories. The advantages claimed for the HIT include:

1. Simplified psychometric treatment (all subjects give the same number of responses).
2. Independence of responses (each response is given to a different stimulus).
3. Utilization of existing Rorschach research to improve on the response elicitation properties of the cards.
4. Computation of reliabilities through the correlations between parallel forms.

A great deal of reliability information was developed by Holtzman et al. (1961), and it indicated that the stability or reliability of most scores was, for the most part, satisfactory. An exception was found in the relatively low test–retest reliabilities, some of which were lower than .5, even with intervals as short as one week between test and retest. Extensive normative data are available on children, normal adults, and psychiatric patients (Holtzman et al., 1961). There are substantial correlations between HIT scores and scores obtained from the Rorschach, suggesting that the same variables are indeed being tapped by these two instruments. On the other hand, very few significant relationships were reported between HIT scores and either scores from paper-and-pencil inventories or ratings of overt behavior. These findings were explained by Holtzman et al. as attributable to the fact that the significant variables in personality and psychopathology are neither directly observable nor measurable by inventories.

More recent reviews of the utility of the HIT have been mixed. In a handbook on the test, Hill (1972) took the view that interpretation is best regarded as a creative process, relying heavily on traditional beliefs regarding the meaning of projective responses. Reviews of the validity literature by Gamble (1972), Cundick (1985), and Dush (1985) adopted more scientific standards and concluded that the instrument has some degree of potential for personality assessment. Some reviewers have approached their evaluation of the HIT mainly in the context of comparing it with the Rorschach. It would seem more logical to regard it as a completely different test, to be evaluated on its own merits.

THEMATIC APPERCEPTION TEST

The Thematic Apperception Test, more commonly known as the TAT (Murray, 1943), is another traditional projective device that is rational-theoretical in nature. The stimulus materials consist of 31 cards—30 depicting various scenes and people, and one blank card. The standard presentation uses 20 cards chosen according to the respondent's sex and age, although fewer than 20 cards are generally used in the typical clinical presentation. The TAT is introduced as a "test of imagination," and the respondent is asked to tell as dramatic a story as possible when each card is shown. He or she is instructed that each story should include what has led up to the event depicted in the card, what is happening at that moment, what the people in the story are feeling and thinking, and the final outcome of the story. The examiner records the narrations of the stories verbatim. Murray (1943) also recommended that the examiner should attempt, in a posttest interview, to determine the source of the story—whether personal experience, friends, or books or movies.

Murray was not the first person to use the picture-story method, but he did the most to popularize it as both a clinical and a research tool. Apart from one or two isolated studies in the early 1900s, the earliest clinical application of the procedure was Schwartz's (1932) use of a Social Situation Picture Test as a diagnostic aid to psychiatric interviews with juvenile delinquents. The TAT was developed as a method for eliciting unconscious fantasy material from patients within a psychoanalytic context (Morgan & Murray, 1935). Indeed, the final selection of the TAT cards was based on how much relevant information the TAT responses contributed to understanding the personality characteristics of individuals who had already been studied in detail, using other methods.

Two rational assumptions guided Murray's initial work with the TAT: (a) that the attributes of the hero/heroine, or main character, in the story represent tendencies in the respondent's own personality; and (b) that characteristics of the main character's environment represent significant aspects of the respondent's own environment. Thus, the traditional use of the picture-story technique involves an interpretive analysis by the examiner, first, of the intrapsychic state of the individual, as reflected in descriptions of the story characters, and second, of the environmental pressures experienced, as reflected in descriptions of the characters' environments. For example, in the first TAT card, which shows a boy peering at a violin, the story might reflect the boy's resentment (an inner state) toward his parents, who insist on his practicing (an environmental pressure) when he wishes to do something else. Murray's (1938) own theoretical system would discuss these inner states as *needs* and the environmental or external pressures as *press*. However, the use of the TAT does not require the adoption of Murray's system, so this instrument cannot be regarded as having a strong theoretical base.

As with the Rorschach, there have been a number of attempts both to develop quantitative scoring schemes and to construct formal norms for the data derived from an analysis of TAT responses. Perhaps the most widely known scoring system is that of McClelland (McClelland et al., 1953). McClelland was concerned primarily with the *need achievement* dimension, and with assessing motivation in various research endeavors rather than clinical diagnosis. Another system is Eron's (Zubin, Eron, & Schumer, 1965), which has been shown to be useful in research but appears to have found little clinical application. Murstein (1963) has provided an excellent summary of a variety of scoring and interpretive schemes for picture stories. However, the typical clinical use of the TAT and the other picture-story methods remains rather informal and idiosyncratic.

Figure 4.2 shows one of the stimulus cards of the Thematic Apperception Test. According to Henry (1956), the stimulus properties of this TAT card are as follows:

Murray's description. *The portrait of a young woman. A weird old woman with a shawl over her head is grimacing in the background.*

Manifest stimulus demand. *An adequate accounting will include only the two figures plus some explanation of their being together in this position. Generally, the interpretation of subjects is about as Murray gives it. However, recently we have seen in female subjects over seventy interpretations in which the "weird old woman" becomes a gently smiling and helpful person. Close examination of the face of the older figure suggests that "weird" and "grimacing" are not necessary connotations.*

Form demand. *The two figures are the only major details. though the facial features of the older woman can be differentially perceived.*

Latent stimulus demand. *In subjects in the middle-age range, this appears to be a stimulus relating older to younger. Thus, for the mature woman, threats of old age appear prominent. In the younger adult, apprehension over control by an older woman appears more prominent. A basic stimulus selected by many subjects, especially women, is one which portrays the old woman as some symbolic representation of a part of the younger; her evil self, her self when aged, etc.*

Frequent plots. *Most generally, the younger woman bears a family relationship to the older woman who is influencing or advising in some way. In about one-third of the stories, the older woman is seen as adversely influencing. In about one-third of the stories, a second plot will appear in which the older woman is a symbolic representation of the younger woman.*

Significant variations. *Of importance here is the issue of whether the subject sees the two figures in the same reality plane (mother-daughter) or whether one is a symbolic representation (my bad self, me when old, etc.). In addition, if treated in this fashion, the particular ideas toward the good and evil or other parts of the self should be specially viewed. In the light of the possibility of some, especially older, subjects seeing the background woman as kindly, responses to her should probably be watched more carefully and attention paid to the extent to which projection rather than reality observation is involved in attributing adverse influences. (pp. 254–256)*

The following story was given by the same 23-year-old female who contributed the Rorschach material discussed earlier in this chapter.

Figure 4.2   A reproduction of one of the TAT stimulus cards. (Source: *Reprinted by permission of the publisher from* Thematic Apperception Test *by Henry A. Murray, 1943. Cambridge, MA: Harvard University Press. Copyright © 1943 by the President and Fellows of Harvard College; copyright © 1971 by Henry A. Murray.)*

Well, there's a young woman in the foreground and an older woman in the background, and the older woman looks as though she has planned something that will be harmful to the younger woman, who looks very naive. And in fact the older woman has planned to keep the younger woman captive, and to make her serve her, for the rest of the older woman's life. But although the girl is naive, she's also rebellious; and by asserting herself with other people and getting a group of friends she's able to move out of the—not exactly spell, but she's able to break the bond that the older woman has around her. Right now she's just beginning to realize that she is being put in a position like this, but she's still very much under the control of the older woman, because these two have lived together for a long time. In fact, the younger woman was raised by the older woman. She's still very much under her control as I said, and she has strong feelings of guilt and fear of facing the world on her own. But fortunately she is able to make friends. At this point, though, she hasn't broken the bonds and she feels very confused, like she's being drawn between two poles. Ultimately, she's able to go out and make friends, and getting to know people and the different ways they have from the ways the old woman had taught her, she's able successfully to face the older woman, and defy her control, and go out and live a life of her own.

This story follows the stimulus demands of the card to a considerable extent; that is, the client reacted to the card much like most people her age, although some aspects of her story are more dramatic than those usually given. But we would not be justified in coming to an immediate conclusion that she has any special problem in her relationships with older women. Also, a typical TAT interpretation would draw material from ten or more cards and would regard whatever hypotheses are gleaned from an individual story as quite tentative, to be strengthened or disconfirmed by the remainder of the stories. From the present story, the following details might be considered of interest.

The older woman's control over the younger is perceived as long-standing and as having caused some rather central personality problems. However, the younger woman is seen as taking the initiative in developing other relationships in order to provide emotional support for breaking away from the older woman, which she plans to do. Her ambivalence over these plans is seen in the use of the words "rebellious," "guilt," and "confused." The younger woman is perceived as displaying perhaps a somewhat lesser degree of anger and resentment toward the older than one would expect after having been trained as a lifelong captive and servant; and the severity of the confinement, together with the younger woman's expression of guilt rather than anger, suggests a situation where anger is repressed. There is also the younger woman's determination and ultimate success, though this comes about through defiance of the older woman rather than a resolution of conflict, again suggesting more anger than is overtly acknowledged.

Although themes of apprehension over control by an older woman are relatively common in stories given by younger persons to this picture, the strength of the conflict as represented by the guilt, the severity of the control exercised, and the absence of appropriate expressions of anger by the younger woman suggest the tentative hypothesis that such a conflict does exist for this client. The client's inability to resolve the fantasy conflict successfully lends further support to this hypothesis. A TAT analyst might also suggest that the client's ability to put forward a rational plan for the younger woman while still acknowledging her confusion and naïveté suggests good potential for improvement in psychotherapy. Naturally, the experienced clinician would search for additional support for these tentative hypotheses elsewhere in the client's TAT responses.

How useful or valid is the TAT as a personality assessment procedure? There is a large volume of literature on the TAT, but its status as a proven, clinically useful instrument is still in doubt. Many of the problems associated with the clinical use of the TAT—lack of standardized procedures and formal normative data, low reliabilities, overenthusiastic and undercritical acceptance of intuitive hunches about the supposed meaning of certain responses—are also present in the Rorschach and other unstructured techniques (Cohen, Swerdlik, & Smith, 1992).

One particularly troublesome problem with the TAT is the difficulty of determining whether an indicated need or personality characteristic will be present in the subject's overt behavior in real-life situations as opposed to existing only at the fantasy or unconscious level. This is especially important because the TAT is commonly regarded as helpful in understanding the content or "dynamics" of behavior; yet, for example, a person with strong needs for attention and recognition that are expressed overtly is very different behaviorally from a "Walter Mitty" character with equally strong needs that do not find behavioral expression because of some suppressive or inhibitory mechanism. Murstein (1963) summarized the research pertaining to one specific aspect of this problem: the relationship between the judged aggressiveness of the heroes or heroines in TAT stories and the overt aggressive behavior of the subject. He concluded that the relationship was generally positive but was complicated by the operation of a number of other variables, such as guilt over aggression, the objective amount of hostility depicted in the TAT pictures, and the specificity of the aggressive acts. According to Groth-Marnat (1990), the research on the relationships of TAT stories to real-life behavior continues to be equivocal.

An additional consideration is worth noting: the "hero assumption" described earlier. Lindzey and Kalnins (1958) were able to demonstrate the validity of this assumption in two rather important ways. First, they were able to show that the figures identified by respondents in a clinical interview as most like themselves were, indeed, the same as those judged to be the heroes or heroines in the TAT protocol. Second, the aggression ascribed by the respondents to the TAT heroes or heroines increased following experimentally induced frustration, but the aggression ascribed to other figures did not. These findings tend to support the assumption that the picture-story hero or heroine often does possess characteristics of the storyteller.

The popularity of the TAT gave rise to a number of other story construction tests. The Children's Apperception Test (Bellak, 1954) and the Michigan Pictures Test (Hartwell, Hutt, Andrew, & Walton, 1951) are rather similar in procedure to the TAT. In the Four Picture Test (Van Lennep, 1951), the subject is presented simultaneously with four colored pictures and is instructed to incorporate them in a story. In Shneidman's (1951) Make-a-Picture-Story Test, respondents are given various background scenes and cardboard cutouts of a large variety of people from which to construct their own pictures, to be used as a basis for stories. In general, these techniques are based on the same assumptions and utilize the same interpretive framework as the TAT, although much less evaluative research is available on them.

Special mention should be made of the Roberts Apperception Test for Children (RATC; McArthur & Roberts, 1982; Sines, 1985), which attempts to combine projective methodology with psychometric methods to improve reliability and validity. There is a structured scoring system for 13 content scales and 3 validity scales, norms for 4 different children's age groups, and global validity data. Despite the obvious potential superiority of the RATC to story construction tests that rely on subjective interpretation, Sines (1985) has pointed out that a number of quantitative systems were developed for the TAT (see Murstein, 1963) but have been little used. Thus, the RATC faces an uncertain future.

PICTURE-DRAWING TECHNIQUES

It is widely believed that creative works (especially in the fine arts, and drawing and painting in particular) reflect the personality of the artist. A demonstration of the validity of this assumption for trained artists, however, would not necessarily establish its validity for people with little or no formal artistic training. This latter assumption underlies the use of picture-drawing techniques in the assessment of personality characteristics.

The use of drawings in psychological evaluation was first popularized by Goodenough (1926), who developed a standardized procedure for evaluating the intelligence of children from their drawings of a man. As a result of a growing interest in interpreting the qualitative aspects of such drawings, two techniques have become widely used: (a) Buck's (1948a, 1948b, 1949)

House-Tree-Person, or H-T-P, technique, in which the respondent is required to draw first a house, then a tree, and finally a person, each on a separate sheet of paper, and (b) Machover's (1949) Draw-a-Person (DAP) test, where the respondent first draws a person of either sex and then is asked to draw a person of the opposite sex. In the interests of brevity, discussion here is confined to the Machover DAP. Most of the evaluative remarks are equally cogent for the H-T-P and other drawing procedures.

In administering the DAP, the respondent is given a pencil, an 8½ by 11-inch sheet of blank paper, and an instruction to "draw a person." The examiner inconspicuously observes the individual, noting such behavior as the total time involved, the sequence in which the drawing is completed, any spontaneous comments, and so on. When this drawing is completed, the individual is given a fresh sheet of paper and told, "Now draw a man [woman]." Machover recommends reassuring the respondent, if necessary, that the test has nothing to do with drawing skills, and persuading him or her to draw any parts that appear to have been omitted. It is also recommended that the individual be asked a series of questions to encourage free associations to the drawings, such as "How old is the person drawn?" and "Is he [she] married?"

The major portion of Machover's (1949) book is devoted to rules of interpretation involving the qualitative aspects of the drawings. These rules were apparently derived from the author's clinical experience as well as a variety of rational considerations, most of which reflect a psychoanalytic orientation. The rules provide for a description of the personality characteristics of the respondent with a strong emphasis on psychopathology. They include the following sets of categories: head, parts of the face, facial expression, neck, contact features (arms and hands, legs and feet, fingers, toes), other body features, clothing, structural and formal aspects, conflict indicators (erasures and shading), and differential treatment of the male and female figures. One of the rules that can be regarded as representative of rational considerations involves the interpretation of the manner in which the shoulders are drawn: "The width and massiveness of the shoulders are considered the most common graphic expression of physical power and perfection of physique" (p. 71). The rationale underlying some interpretations is more difficult to comprehend; for example, "The Adam's apple . . . has been seen mostly in the drawing of young males in an expression of strong virility or masculine drive. Special interest in the Adam's apple has been restricted to the sexually weak individual who shows little differentiation between male and female characteristics and is uncertain about his own role" (p. 58).

Figure 4.3 shows two drawings that were reported and interpreted by Hammer (1968), another leading authority in this area. Hammer's interpretation is given here.

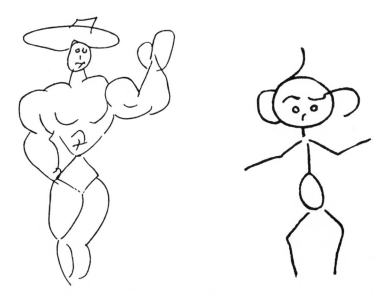

Figure 4.3   Drawings by an 18-year-old male showing surface and subsurface personality levels. (**Source: From Hammer, 1968, pp. 162–163. Used by permission of the publisher.**)

The nuanced language of drawing projection is particularly suited for stating the complexities and human contradictions as they balance and interrelate within a single personality. At such times, the apparent contradictions can be seen to possess an inner harmony, as in the musical statement and counterstatement of a fugue. [Figure 4.3], drawn by an eighteen-year-old male caught stealing a TV set, constitutes such a pictorial statement. Beneath the obvious attempts at an impressive figure of masculine prowess there are more subtle trends of the opposite: of inadequacy and inconsequentiality. The muscles of the drawn figure have been inflated beyond the hard and sinewy, into a puffy softness as if it is a figure made of balloons; the legs taper down to insubstantiality and, finally, absent feet, and an incongruous hat is placed on the boxer making comical his lifting of one gloved hand in victory. . . . On the one hand, emblematic of his defenses, his drawn achromatic person is the "twenty-year-old" boxer with muscles flexed and a weight-lifter's build. Beneath this inflated image, however, on the crayon drawing of a person—which, due to the impact of color, tends to tap the relatively deeper levels of personality (Hammer, 1958)—he offers now only a "six-year-old boy" who then looks even more like an infant than a child: with one curlicue hair sticking up and the suggestion of diapers on (. . . shown here in black and white). The ears are rather ludicrous in their standing away from the head and, all in all, the total projection in this drawing is that of an infantile, laughable entity, rather than the impressive he-man he overstated on the achromatic version of a person. Beneath his attempts to demonstrate rugged masculinity (which may have culminated into the offense with which he is charged), the patient experiences himself as actually a little child, dependent and needing care, protection, and affection. (p. 163)

Swensen (1957, 1968) and Roback (1968), in their reviews of the validity research literature on the DAP, concluded that there was little support for Machover's interpretations or hypotheses. Indeed, more of the data directly contradicted her assertions than supported them. Swensen further noted that the available evidence indicated the test–retest reliabilities of the various content and structural aspects of the drawings were quite low, although the overall quality of the drawings (rated according to their realism or correspondence to life) was fairly constant. The research also suggested that the judged overall quality of the drawing is related to the gross level of adjustment of the subject, and this finding has received more recent support from the work of Tharinger and Stark (1990). Swensen (1968) suggested that future research that controlled for overall quality of the drawings might possibly lead to more satisfactory findings with respect to specific personality variables. Johnson and Greenberg (1978), however, did control for quality of drawings and found essentially no significant personality correlates.

Some interesting findings were reported by Oas (1984), who developed a scoring system for *impulsivity* based mainly on subjects' behavior as reflected in their drawings. The measure was able to differentiate between independently defined impulsive and nonimpulsive adolescents, both normals and psychiatric patients. This illustration that a behaviorally oriented personal characteristic can be assessed from human figure drawings suggests that other behaviorally defined characteristics could also be validly assessed. Overall, however, the validity picture is rather negative. Nevertheless, the clinical use of picture-drawing techniques continues to be very high (Piotrowski & Keller, 1989; Sweeney, Clarkin, & Fitzgibbon, 1987). The work of Chapman and Chapman (1967) on the phenomenon of illusory correlations, discussed in Chapter Twelve, offers some possible explanations for their unabated popularity despite minimal evidence of validity.

BLACKY PICTURES TEST

In Chapter Two, we suggested that most attempts to develop personality assessment procedures have been theoretically neutral, although the personality descriptions that stem from them are often couched in the language of some particular personality theory. For an assessment procedure to be regarded as theoretically derived, the actual stimuli employed to elicit the relevant responses would have to be selected on the basis of a viable personality theory, and the entire assessment procedure would be closely interwoven with that theory. As stated previously, because there are no rigorous theories of personality, we have utilized a general classification of *rational-*

theoretical tests; and within this framework, the best-established test toward the theoretical end of the continuum is the Blacky Pictures Test developed by Blum (1949, 1950). Although it is rarely used nowadays (Lubin, Larsen, & Matarazzo, 1984), this test is worth studying in some detail as a clear-cut example of how personality theory serves as the foundation of an assessment device.

The Blacky test is based on the traditional psychoanalytic theory of psychosexual development, which holds that children typically pass through three distinct and critically important stages in their personality development. In the first, or oral stage, the child's primary preoccupation is with oral satisfactions—eating, sucking, chewing, and other stimulation involving the mouth. The anal stage is the period in which the child is made aware of the need for controlling eliminative functions and learns to achieve the required control. In the phallic stage, there is an awareness of the sexual organs as a source of satisfaction and a preoccupation with this satisfaction. Psychoanalytic theory involves a vast number of additional complexities, but what is important here is the notion that excessive deprivation, or excessive gratification, at any one of these stages may lead to the child's becoming "fixated" at that stage. That is, later personality characteristics, especially ways of handling conflict, may reflect the child's experiences at the fixated stage of development. Thus, a person who, as a child, received excessive gratification at the oral stage might develop an "oral dependent" personality: confronted with psychological conflicts, this person would expect to have needs met by others, with little effort on his or her part, in an adult restructuring of the helpless role of the suckling infant. A child who was deprived of gratification at the anal stage may develop "anal retentive" personality characteristics, such as strong feelings of possessiveness about material things, stubbornness, and hoarding behavior. These examples show how psychoanalytic theory regards the roots for adult behavior to be established in the early psychosexual development of the child.

It follows from the Freudian theory of psychosexual development that discovery of an individual's reactions and attitudes connected with the oral, anal, and phallic aspects of psychosexual development will provide significant information about the person's personality and about the sources of any overt or latent personality conflicts that may exist. The Blacky pictures are specifically designed to yield such information. The test materials consist of 12 cartoons portraying the life of Blacky, a puppy of indeterminate sex, and its family, consisting of Papa, Mama, and another sibling. Each scene was developed to tap what should be a potential conflict area for Blacky according to the psychoanalytic theory of psychosexual development. For example, the second picture, designed to assess "oral sadism," shows the puppy snarling while vigorously shaking Mama's collar in its teeth. The other pictures are similarly designed to measure such psychosexual concepts as anal sadism, penis envy, sibling rivalry, and guilt feelings. The respondent is presented with each picture, asked to make up a story telling what is happening and why, and then asked a series of multiple-choice questions about the pictures. Respondents are also asked which cards they like and dislike. It is assumed that these evaluations, together with the respondents' reports of Blacky's mood as unhappy, angry, frightened, and so forth, are indicative of the respondents' own responses to these potential conflict areas. Because the connections between the stimulus materials and the inferences to be drawn from responses to them are quite subtle, and because there is little general understanding of psychoanalytic concepts, the Blacky test does not require self-awareness on the part of the respondent and is typically regarded as a projective technique.

The scoring and interpretation of responses to the Blacky pictures are relatively complex procedures. Blum (1950, 1951) initially provided scoring directions for assessing the strength of 13 different psychosexual areas, and later proposed a 30-variable scoring system based on factor-analytic research on the previous scoring schemata (Blum, 1962). According to Sappenfield's (1965) review, the scoring of the Blacky test is sufficiently reliable for research purposes but is not adequate for individual clinical assessment.

How useful or valid is the Blacky test? It has been successfully used to demonstrate the validity of certain aspects of psychoanalytic theory, one of the primary purposes for which it was developed. One study showed a connection between the development of peptic ulcers and oral erotic conflicts (Blum & Kaufman, 1952); another confirmed the predictions made from psychoanalytic theory about paranoia, using the Blacky test responses of paranoids and other psychotic patients (Aronson, 1953).

There is little published evidence to support use of this test as a clinical assessment device. Nevertheless, its sophistication as a theoretically based instrument can serve as a model for this type of test construction.

BENDER VISUAL MOTOR GESTALT TEST

The Bender Visual Motor Gestalt Test (Bender, 1938, 1946), initially developed within the Gestalt school of psychology, also has an easily identified theoretical base. Originally an orientation for the study of perceptual phenomena, the Gestalt approach soon spread into virtually all aspects of psychological theorizing. Briefly, it was based in the notion that events could be understood only by studying them in their entirety, as opposed to studying their individual elements, because the *configuration* of the elements, a critical component of the "whole," would otherwise be lost.

Bender (1938) studied the visual-motor perceptual skill of young children from a Gestalt viewpoint, noting the gradual development of their ability to perceive "wholes" and relationships when shown drawings of incomplete figures and other simple patterns. Reasoning that the individual's entire psychological development was reflected in this particular aspect of functioning, Bender proposed that overall level of mental skill could be assessed from visual-motor perceptual performance, and she based her development of test materials on that assumption.

The test stimuli for the Bender-Gestalt consist of nine 4 by 6 inch cards, each of which contains one of the original patterns used in early Gestalt perceptual research studies. The respondent is shown the cards one by one and is asked to copy the patterns on a single sheet of blank 8½ by 11-inch white paper. Bender (1946) originally interpreted the drawings according to the principle that "any deviation in the total organism will be reflected in the final sensory motor patterns in response to the given stimulus pattern" (p. 4). For guidance in interpretation, Bender presented illustrations of (a) the responses of normal children at various age levels and (b) the response patterns of various psychologically disturbed groups that she considered to be identifiable with the instrument. Her assumption was that psychopathology is caused by early childhood trauma, which subsequently interferes with the maturation of the ability to perceive Gestalts, or "wholes."

Although it can be argued that any *quantitative* scoring of Bender-Gestalt responses would be inconsistent with the theoretical insistence of the Gestalt viewpoint (the "whole" is more than the sum of its parts), Bender (1938) did offer a tentative scoring scheme for measuring the maturational level of children, using their responses to the test stimuli. A number of other scoring systems have been developed for both adults (Hutt, 1977; Pascal & Suttell, 1951) and children (Koppitz, 1963, 1975).

The theoretical basis of the test indicates that its validity should be assessed, at least initially, from its degree of success in discriminating among subjects who differ in their development of the visual-motor Gestalt function, or the capacity to organize perceptual "wholes." A number of studies have shown that a fairly adequate mental age score can be derived from the test responses of children between the ages of 4 and 12 (Billingslea, 1963), a conclusion not inconsistent with Bender's initial assumption. It is also sometimes possible to make a gross differentiation of normal persons from various groups, especially those with cerebral brain damage, although these findings are less clear-cut (Billingslea, 1963; Golden, 1979) and there are other, more reliable ways to screen for brain damage (see Berg, Franzen, & Wedding, 1987).

The most common use of the Bender-Gestalt test has been in the domain of personality assessment. It is widely believed that a variety of qualitative aspects of a subject's Bender-Gestalt responses—such as the relative size of the drawing, the strength of the impression, and the relative placement of the figures on the page—are useful indexes to the personality of the individual (Groth-Marnat, 1990). However, empirical efforts to demonstrate these relationships have been unsuccessful (Kitay, 1972; Sattler, 1985). The negative findings should not be surprising in view of the fact that Bender's original theory and her selection of the test stimuli have only the most tenuous connection with personality functioning, at least on the level of the assessment of observable behavioral characteristics. Hutt (1977) reported significant differences between normals and a number of groups with various kinds of psychopathology. Factors such as intelligence were not controlled, however, and could well have been responsible for these differences.

In summary, the theoretical basis of the Bender Visual Motor Gestalt Test as a measure of personality functioning is not a sound one; neither the theory nor the test stimuli seem to be firmly grounded in personality functioning. It is thus not surprising to find that the test lacks validity for personality assessment.

THE THREE STRATEGIES IN PERSONALITY
TEST DEVELOPMENT

This chapter and the preceding one have described some of the best-known personality assessment instruments, typically called personality tests. They are all based on one or more of the three basic strategies for personality test development: (a) rational-theoretical, (b) empirical, and (c) factor-analytic. As discussed earlier, the current state of the art in developing personality measures is to utilize the complementary strengths of all three strategies, while minimizing the effects of their limitations. Thus, a balanced approach might involve the initial selection of test stimuli based on theoretical or rational considerations, with factor analysis used to attain internal consistency, and final refinement based on clear-cut empirical findings. Although this type of test derivation is both time-consuming and costly, it clearly is necessary in order to achieve satisfactory levels of validity. Let us examine the contributions and limitations of each strategy in more detail.

Rational-Theoretical Procedures

Rationally derived questionnaires seem to depend for their usefulness on at least three specific assumptions:

1. Respondents are competent to judge themselves with regard to the questions asked.
2. Respondents must be relied on to share the truth about which they are assumed to be aware.
3. Test stimuli are clear and unambiguous.

Most psychodynamic views of personality would tend to deny the validity of the first two assumptions. Such views hold that most people tend to hide unpleasant truths from self-awareness, as a way of avoiding the anxiety that the admission of these truths would arouse. Thus, individuals would be least likely to provide useful responses in the very aspects of personality where assessment is most important. In addition, most persons are well aware of the possibility of dissimulation—deliberately not revealing unpleasant truths about themselves because of the social consequences of admitting them. Both of these considerations are among the most frequently mentioned objections to rationally derived instruments.

Concerning the third assumption, the psychological meaning of the stimulus can be thought of as varying among persons in two ways: (a) as a consequence of the defensiveness just discussed, and (b) because of individual differences in meaning stemming from differences in individual experiences or personal learning history. Thus, the questionnaire stimulus "I often have headaches" may elicit an affirmative response from one subject for whom "often" is once a month, and a negative response from another subject for whom "often" is once a week. Selecting unambiguous stimuli is by no means a simple task.

These idiosyncratic differences in the psychological meaning of the stimulus materials originally gave rise to the concept of using test stimuli "projectively." The major assumption underlying projection in this sense is that individual differences in responses to ambiguous stimuli are functionally related to some underlying, habitual characteristics of individuals—their personality. An allied assumption is that the relationships between the stimuli and responses are known or knowable to the test developer on some rational basis. However, because of the subtle nature of these relationships, they are not readily known to the subject, thus reducing the effects of defensiveness or deliberate simulation on responses. As it turns out, this very subtle or tenuous nature of the relationship between test response and assumed personality characteristic provides the most serious objection to the traditional projective instruments.

Although the rational selection of the content of test stimuli often may not be a *sufficient* basis for usefulness or validity, it seems to be a *necessary* basis. That is to say, without some rational connection between the test response and the characteristic to be assessed or the criterion to be predicted, the likelihood of establishing a satisfactory level of validity is much reduced. Thus, an important consideration in selecting test stimuli is that the meaning of responses to the test stimuli should be inherent in the stimuli themselves or in the fashion in which they were selected.

A clear illustration of this point is found in the research reported by Norman (1963a, 1963b), using questionnaire items. Faced with assessing the personality suitability of candidates for desirable jobs (where the defensiveness of the respondents could be assumed to be high), Norman attempted to develop "subtle" items whose meaning would not be clear to the respondents. For several groups of college students, friends' ratings were obtained on five personality dimensions. These ratings were then used as personality criteria to be predicted from the students' responses to three sets of test stimuli. The first test employed personality-descriptive adjectives (obviously related to the criterion), the second required preference ratings for various occupational titles (intermediate in their relationship to the criterion), and the third required preference ratings for geometrical designs (very subtle in their relationship to the criterion). Using the criterion-groups approach, Norman constructed a series of personality scales from the results of each test. Only the scales based on the first test (the self-descriptive adjectives), which were the most obvious in their meaning, were at all consistently related to the criterion.

The importance of rationality in test stimuli was also illustrated by Duff (1965) using the MMPI. Following the lead of Seeman (1952, 1953), who had demonstrated that the MMPI contained both obvious and subtle items, and that subtle items were difficult for the test taker to simulate or "fake," Duff listed the MMPI items that originally had discriminated normal persons from persons with three particular psychiatric conditions: (a) conversion hysteria, (b) psychopathic personality, and (c) schizophrenia. Expert judges were then asked to indicate which items, on the basis of their content, appeared to be appropriate for one or another of these discriminations; that is, the judges were asked to pick out the items that one would rationally expect to be relevant for these discriminations. After identifying the rational or obvious (content-relevant) and the nonobvious or subtle (content-irrelevant) items in this manner, Duff compared the validity of the two kinds of items by examining the responses of patients in the appropriate diagnostic groups. His findings clearly indicated that the content-relevant items—that is, those with rational or face meaning—discriminated to a greater degree than the so-called subtle items.

Similar conclusions were drawn by Goldberg and Slovic (1967), who tested Berg's (1959) "Deviation Hypothesis." Berg had argued that the rational content of the test stimuli is unimportant, and he advocated the use of a greater variety of test stimuli, such as abstract geometric designs, requiring only that they should elicit enough variability of response to permit the discovery of empirical relationships. Like Duff, Goldberg and Slovic investigated the relationship between content validity and empirical validity for a variety of kinds of possible personality inventory items, including nonverbal items. They found that "items of low face validity generally had low validity coefficients, while items of high face validity had validities that were distributed over the entire range of the distribution (e.g., some presumably relevant items actually were valid discriminators, while others were not)" (p. 467). These findings directly contradict Berg's point of view and give further support to the notion that content validity is a necessary but insufficient basis for empirical validity.

In a major theoretical paper, Jackson (1971) mustered many arguments to support his contention that rational derivation was an absolute necessity. He regarded the most useful personality assessment measures as those that are constructed rationally and "derived from an explicitly formulated, theoretically based definition of a trait" (p. 232). Jackson emphasized the necessity of developing an item pool whose content adequately and representatively reflects the universe of content implied by the definition. He also advocated the use of items that could be regarded as both subtle and content-relevant. For example, the item "I think newborn babies look very much like little monkeys" initially appears to have no particular content relevance, but a moment's thought indicates that it could well represent the negative pole of the nurturance dimension. The value of Jackson's paper is in providing a sophisticated rationale and model for the rational-theoretical development of personality test items in a way that maximizes their potential validity.

Much of the evidence regarding the primacy of the rational approach has involved measures of normal personality functioning. It is possible that persons with severe psychological problems are less able to describe themselves accurately, and that the utility of rational procedures in assessing psychopathology is therefore much more limited, although Duff's (1965) research suggests that this might not be the case. Additional research evidence is needed on this question.

A word should be said about the theoretical end of the rational-theoretical continuum. Despite Jackson's exhortation, the present status of personality assessment instruments with a substantial theoretical base is equivocal. Relatively few such instruments are available, their contribution to the knowledge of personality function in either an applied or a theoretical sense has been minimal, and they tend to offer little to the practicing psychologist who is concerned with describing and understanding an individual person. Thus, their promise as the most sophisticated approach to the problem of understanding personality has not as yet been realized.

There are at least two reasons for this state of affairs. First, few approaches to personality fully qualify to be called theories. Further, contemporary psychological theorists have shown relatively little interest in developing new molar personality theories. Instead, far more attention is being given to constructing microtheories that attempt to deal with more limited behavior sequences than those typically subsumed under the rubric of personality. The personality theory that has been most viable in instigating the development of personality tests has been Freudian psychoanalytic theory, which can claim the Blacky Pictures Test, the IES (Id-Ego-Superego) Test (Dombrose & Slobin, 1958), and others.

The second reason for the atheoretical basis of current assessment devices is the preoccupation of psychologists who are interested in test development with psychometric technical refinements rather than with clinical usefulness. The increasing demand for a high level of technical specialization among psychometricians may have tended to isolate them from both the theorizing and the research in other areas, which might have important implications for test development. There is clearly a need for both technical sophistication and theoretical understanding in the area of personality test development.

One of the most frequent criticisms of personality inventories has been directed at the apparent ease with which responses can be distorted or faked by persons with the motivation to do so. Because it is now well established that content validity is a necessary component of a successful inventory scale, this concern is all the more salient. The main response to these concerns has been the use of so-called "validity" scales, such as *L, F,* and *K* on the MMPI, to detect and/or correct for such biases. With the recent increasing conceptual and psychometric sophistication in developing personality tests have come new and useful strategies for detecting deception. This work is discussed in more detail in Chapter Seven.

Empirical Procedures

The unique contribution of selecting test items or stimuli empirically is, of course, that it provides a built-in assurance that each item will be statistically related to the concept or characteristic in question. If this step is conducted before the final items or stimuli are selected, there is a greater likelihood that the test will "work" in practice—that it can be successfully cross-validated. Cross-validation involves a demonstration that the test continues to discriminate, using independent samples of the criterion and normal subjects.

The absolute necessity for cross-validation should be clearly understood. As a concrete example, let us imagine a pool of 1,000 self-reference questionnaire items that can be answered positively or negatively. If we take two arbitrary groups—for example, people with blue eyes and people with brown eyes—the two groups will differ in their responses to some of the items by sheer chance. Specifically, if we note the differences that would be expected to occur by chance less often than 5% of the time, we would identify about 5%, or 50 of the 1,000 items, that could be advanced as an empirically derived test for eye-color differentiation. Yet these items would have been selected on the basis of a statistical artifact and would probably have no stable relationship to eye color. Thus, if we repeated the item analysis on two different groups of blue- and brown-eyed subjects, the second resultant scale would contain 50 *different* items—another chance selection from the 1,000 items. Needless to say, neither of these two scales would be of any value in discriminating between further criterion groups. Because the extent to which empirically derived scales capitalize on chance variability is not always clear, independent demonstration of their discriminative ability is essential.

When a measure is developed only by empirical means, care is necessary in interpreting the personality attribute that an empirical scale is presumed to be measuring, because other differences between the criterion and control groups may distort the meaning of the scale. Thus, later research might demonstrate that the hypothetical dominance scale described in Chapter Three measures strength of political feelings rather than what is generally agreed to be meant by dominance, and it would therefore have little utility in identifying persons who are interpersonally dominant. This potential difficulty is avoided, of course, by using a rational-theoretical basis for developing the initial item pool, provided that the items that survive the empirical screening process continue to be a representative sample of the original item pool.

There is one other potential problem with the empirical method. The criterion groups are ordinarily selected to be pure, and often extreme, instances of the behavior domain to be tapped. We would use "obvious" schizophrenics in developing a schizophrenia scale, and highly dominant versus quite passive individuals in developing a dominance scale, even though we are typically interested in employing such scales to identify persons more in the middle of the continuum, rather then extreme individuals. Whether the items selected in such a fashion are either logically or empirically relevant for identifying less extreme instances of the phenomena is a moot point.

Factor-Analytic Procedures

As indicated in Chapter Three, factor analysis identifies clusters of items or other variables that are statistically correlated with each other. It is usually concluded that such items share common meaning and are therefore assessing aspects of some central or basic concept; many times, this is clearly the case. For instance, if 50 items were written to sample comprehensively the universe of content of the personality trait "friendliness," and if most of the items loaded on (were significantly related to) a single factor, then those items could be viewed as forming a scale of friendliness. But if there is no prior rational-theoretical meaning for the item pool, or if the factor analysis yields several different factors (correlated item clusters) rather than just one, then naming the factor or factors must be done very tentatively, with reliance on further research to determine more precise meanings.

A closely related issue has been raised in regard to the Big Five factors of personality. Does the fact of their consistent occurrence in factor analyses prove that there is a single "real" structure of personality, or are all such structures necessarily man-made? Mischel (1968), arguing for a variant of the second position, held that the five factors simply reflected in part "behavioral consistencies that are *constructed* by observers rather than actual consistency in the subject's behavior" (p. 43). However, Norman and Goldberg (1966) and Goldberg (1990b) were able to demonstrate that the factors are based on more than just semantic consistency, and (at least in part) reflect the nature of personality structure among the subjects.

The major contribution of factor analysis is thus in understanding the relationships among items and scales of personality tests. Usefulness, in any predictive sense, is not an intrinsic property of factorially derived scales (unless, like Cattell, we consider them to be assessing some "real" properties of the organism), but must be demonstrated empirically. The reported empirical validities of factor scales have in general tended to be rather low. The major exceptions are the two-factor structure, which has been consistently replicated, and the five-factor structure, for which there is also strong evidence.

Comparison of Strategies

The research on the importance of content validity, described above, is consistent with the comments we have made regarding the empirical and factor-analytic strategies for test construction—namely, that content relevance is a basic necessity no matter which test development strategy is used. There has also been research to compare the predictive effectiveness of each individual strategy in head-to-head contests. In an early study, Hase and Goldberg (1967) took the CPI items and constructed 4 sets of 11 scales each, developing each set by one of the major strategies of test construction, and viewing the rational and theoretical methods as separate approaches. The predictive validities of these 4 sets of scales were then compared against 13 criterion measures obtained from 200 college women, such as college achievement relative to ability, an experimental test of conformity, sorority membership, dating behavior, and peer ratings on a variety of personality traits, such as dominance, sociability, and responsibility. The main finding was that the 4 sets of scales were equivalent in validity when measured against the 13 diverse criteria. In addition, the obtained validity correlations were all significantly higher than those obtained from 2 additional sets of scales that had been devised for control purposes.

In a further study, Ashton and Goldberg (1973) tested Jackson's (1971) assertion that the validity of typical empirically developed scales could be surpassed by rational scales composed of items developed intuitively by trained item writers, and even by inexperienced item writers. In a complex and extensive study, existing CPI and PRF scales were compared with scales rationally developed by graduate students in psychology and by individuals with no formal psychology training. All scales were administered to 169 college females, and validity criteria consisted of the average rankings on the different dimensions by groups of peers. The most reliable of the rational scales constructed by untrained persons were essentially as valid as the empirical scales on the CPI, and "the most reliable scales constructed by psychology students and the PRF scales were of approximately equal validity, considerably higher than that of any of the CPI scales" (Ashton & Goldberg, 1973, p. 1).

The highest average validity correlations in the Ashton and Goldberg study were only around .35, but the study clearly demonstrated the advantages of the rational or intuitive approach to item development. Burisch (1984) reviewed 16 studies that compared scale construction strategies, which he termed *external* (empirical), *inductive* (factor-analytic), and *deductive* (rational). Although no approach showed consistent superiority over the others, Burisch concluded that the advantages of the rational approach (rational scales are easier to build, and they communicate information more directly to the assessor) made it the procedure of choice. All of these findings are consistent with the current state-of-the-art method, as described above: the initial development of an item or stimulus pool on a rational or theoretical basis, followed by the use of empirical *and* factor-analytic methods to select the best items.

Projective Techniques

The above discussion of the strengths and limitations of different test construction strategies has focused exclusively on inventories because the relevant literature has exclusively involved inventories. But the issues apply equally to the development of projective stimuli. What can we learn from the discussion that might advance our understanding of projective procedures? For one thing, Chapter Three showed that the best validities with projectives are obtained by using structured scoring systems based on relevant content. This observation is entirely consistent with the research-based conclusion that content relevance is an essential component of validity for inventories. In this regard, however, inventories can be scored rapidly (often, by computer), whereas the task of "scoring," or coding, the content of projective responses is time-consuming and introduces an additional source of unreliability into the measure. This is the price that must be paid for respondents' opportunity to give open-ended responses, rather than being constrained by a true–false or multiple-choice format.

Interpretation of the best-known of all projectives, the Rorschach, tends *not* to rely on content but on a series of variables that are very similar to response styles (see Chapter Seven). It is tempting to conclude that the validity of these variables (location, human movement, color, and so on) depends on the likelihood that they are *confounded with content*. Clear support for this position is found in a study by Gorham (1967), which is described in more detail in Chapter Ten. Using the Holtzman Inkblot Technique, Gorham was able to reproduce scores for the main scoring categories by using only the individual content of each of the first six words of the individual responses. Such results suggest that research with the Rorschach (and other projectives) should concentrate on content-based

variables. However, examination of the contemporary Rorschach literature shows that this has not been the case.

SUMMARY

This chapter describes the best-known projective techniques and discusses
the strengths and limitations of the three basic strategies for test construction. In the sentence-completion method, subjects write endings to a variety of sentence beginnings designed to elicit personality-relevant material.
This method has been most widely used in a "clinical" or impressionistic
manner, although several scorable forms are available, and research findings suggest that standardized content-based scales have the best validity.

In the Rorschach test, the subject is shown a series of ten inkblots, and
responses are categorized according to a number of formal characteristics.
The original discovery of stable differences in responses among groups of
psychiatric patients was made accidentally, and Rorschach's tentative speculations about the reasons for these differences are still regarded by many
clinicians as authoritative, despite much research evidence to the contrary.
The Holtzman Inkblot Technique (HIT) was designed to measure the basic
variables assessed by the Rorschach, while avoiding a number of serious psychometric problems inherent in the Rorschach. Although the HIT does
measure these variables satisfactorily, there is little evidence that it is useful in personality assessment.

Picture-story techniques, of which the Thematic Apperception Test (TAT)
is the most popular, require the subject to make up stories about pictures depicting personality-relevant scenes. It is generally assumed that the behaviors
and feelings of the main characters (heroes and heroines) of the stories reflect those of the subject. A number of standardized schemes exist for
scoring the content and other aspects of the stories, but the clinical use of
picture-story techniques is generally impressionistic. In picture-drawing
methods, the subject is given blank paper on which to draw something, often
a human figure. Apart from a gross relationship between the degree of realism of the drawing (if a human figure) and the subject's general level of adjustment, such drawings have not yet been demonstrated to have much value.

Perhaps the most theoretically oriented of the established assessment devices is the Blacky Pictures Test, based in the traditional psychoanalytic
theory of psychosexual development. A standardized scoring system is available, and there is evidence to indicate that the system provides valid information for research purposes. The Bender Visual Motor Gestalt Test,
designed within the theoretical framework of Gestalt psychology, assumes
that all phases of human development, including personality, are reflected
in perceptual functioning. It appears to yield a fairly satisfactory "mental

age" score for children, but seems to have no demonstrated validity for assessing personality.

Each of the three basic strategies for personality test development has its particular strengths and weaknesses, and the current state of the art in constructing tests is to utilize the complementary strengths of all three. Research has clearly shown that although a rational or content-related basis is necessary for items to have validity, it is not a sufficient basis. There are relatively few test instruments at the theoretical end of the rational-theoretical continuum, and promise of this approach has yet to be fulfilled. Recent advances in sophistication have tended to be psychometric rather than theoretical in nature.

Empirical procedures for selecting items contribute a built-in assurance that the items will be statistically related to the criterion of interest. However, cross-validation is essential in using the empirical approach. The major contribution of the factor-analytic approach is in understanding the relationships among items and scales and in leading to scales that are both internally consistent and conceptually distinct from other scales on the same test.

Research comparing the predictive effectiveness of each of the three basic strategies individually has tended to show no consistent superiority for any of them, and has supported the approach of capitalizing on the contributions of each. Although the psychometric issues discussed in this chapter apply equally to the development of projective tests and to inventories, they have been virtually ignored in the projective area. The desire to preserve the opportunity for open-ended responding on projective tests has precluded the use of much of the currently available psychometric technology.

CHAPTER FIVE

Behavioral Assessment

Chapter One discussed the influence of modern behaviorism on personality assessment. This influence has given rise to the development of an approach to assessment that differs considerably from the more traditional approaches considered thus far. This behavioral approach to assessment is the subject matter of the present chapter.

Let us restate and clarify a possible source of confusion that has been touched on earlier. If the topic of this book is *personality* assessment, what is the relevance of the direct assessment of *behavior*? As stated in Chapter One, the purpose of the book is broadly conceived as the understanding and prediction of the behavior of individuals. It was once believed that such understanding could come only from thorough study of "inner predispositions," or what people *are*, or what they *have*—in other words, their dynamics, needs, expectations, and underlying motivational forces. This view has been termed the "centralist" orientation to the study of humans (Murray, 1938); we have referred to it in Chapter Two as the *dispositional* view of the determinants of behavior. In the more recent, behavioral view, however, it is believed that the best understanding comes from a greater emphasis on studying the behavior itself and the context in which it occurs. In particular, the behavioral assessor tries to identify the *controlling variables* for the specified behavior. Some of these variables may be external to the person and some may be internal. Assessment of the external factors has been the major contribution of the behavioral assessment movement; however, new and different ways of assessing the relevant internal variables are now included in this framework. Some of the early and more radical behavioral psychologists believed that the assessment process could do without information about internal, or organismic, variables. As discussed in Chapter Two, this situational view of the determinants of behavior has now given way to the *interactionist* view, which takes the position that the causes of behavior lie in the interaction between person and environment.

DEVELOPMENT OF BEHAVIORAL ASSESSMENT

Behavioral assessment procedures have been widely used for many years in industrial and organizational psychology, and in a variety of research applications (e.g., Hartshorne & May, 1928; OSS Assessment Staff, 1948). They did not become popular in clinically oriented applications until the late 1960s and early 1970s. There are a number of possible reasons for this lag; the most obvious is that the overwhelming influence of the psychodynamic orientation, with its centralist philosophy, was not diminished until the rise of behavior therapy in the 1960s. Thus, many of the issues involved in the systematic observation of behavior were understood and documented well before the clinical use of behavioral assessment. What was introduced in the clinical context was behavioral learning theory, with its premise that behavior is controlled and that these controlling variables—antecedents (cues or stimuli) and consequences (reinforcers and punishers)—can be identified through systematic observation and then altered to result in more adaptive behaviors. Thus, the scope of behavioral assessment was significantly broadened by its acceptance into the realm of human adjustment problems.

There were other reasons why behavioral assessment procedures were slow to become a part of the clinical enterprise. Several generations of clinical psychologists had been taught to believe that the information that was critical to an in-depth understanding was "beneath the surface"—that is, neither accessible to consciousness nor displayed directly in overt behavior. A simple description of overt behavior might, in this view, be quite misleading in any attempt to understand what an individual is really like. Another reason was that direct observation is much more difficult to carry out successfully than is initially apparent. Much of the present chapter is devoted to an analysis of these problems.

Enthusiasm for behavioral procedures in clinical work rose. Parallel hope for an expanded science of behavioral assessment led in the late 1970s to the appearance of two journals devoted especially to this area: *Behavioral Assessment* and *Journal of Behavioral Assessment*. Over the following decade came the gradual realization that assessment should be multimodal (see Chapter Eight) for the greatest accuracy. Now, behavioral assessment typically does not stand alone but is one of several components in an overall assessment approach. This change is nicely reflected in the disappearance of the two journals mentioned above and the recent appearance of two others with a more general mission: *Psychological Assessment* and *Assessment*. Although behavioral assessment is now well integrated into the larger assessment enterprise, it is discussed separately in this chapter for ease of understanding.

Clinical Behavioral Assessment

The clinical use of behavioral assessment made its formal appearance in the late 1960s, and a number of definitions and descriptions were offered (Kanfer & Phillips, 1970; Kanfer & Saslow, 1965; Mischel, 1968; Peterson, 1968). Peterson's description is worth repeating.

> *What, in specific detail, is the nature of the problem behavior? What is the person doing, overtly or covertly, which he or someone else defined as problematic and hence changeworthy behavior? What are the antecedents, both internal and external, of the problem behavior and what conditions are in effect at the time the behavior occurs? What are the consequences of the problem behavior? In particular, what reinforcing events, immediate as well as distant, appear to perpetuate the behavior under study? What changes might be made in the antecedents, concomitants, or consequences of behavior to effect behavior change?* (Donald R. Peterson, The Clinical Study of Social Behavior, 1968. Reprinted by permission of Prentice-Hall, Inc., Englewood Cliffs, NJ.)

Several other issues relate specifically to the clinical use of behavioral assessment. The first and perhaps most important one has already been identified: clinical behavioral assessment implies an interactionist view of the causes of behavior—a product of both organismic variables (such as current physiological state and past learning history) and current environmental variables (Nelson & Hayes, 1979). Thus, both kinds of variables need to be assessed, and their relationship to the problem behavior of interest must then be determined.

A second point involves the broadened definition of "behavior" that has accompanied the development of behavior therapy as a practical enterprise. Mainstream behavioral psychologists once confined the term to *overt motor events* that can be publicly perceived and recorded. Nowadays, any type of activity is commonly called "behavior." Specifically, two other classes involving covert behavior are now included within the realm of behavior that is amenable to assessment and scientific study: *thoughts,* or cognitive behavior, and *feelings,* related to emotional-psychological behavior. Some human problems involve more than one of these response systems. For example, anxiety involves all three in varying degrees for various people, and there tends to be only a low or moderate degree of relationship among the three response systems (Lang, 1968; Turpin, 1991). Thus, reference to the behavioral assessment of anxiety is ambiguous; rather, one must talk about the assessment of a particular response system—or, better, all three response systems. The use of multimethod assessment procedures or multiple data sources in the assessment of a particular construct results in a higher degree of overall validity (see Chapter Eight).

A third topic in the clinical use of behavioral assessment is an extension of the expanded definition of behavior given earlier. In clinical applications, not only is the behavior of interest observed but so are antecedents and consequences—the variables thought to be controlling the behavior of interest. These controlling variables can also be covert (thoughts or feelings). For example, a feeling (such as anger) can trigger an overt motor behavior (such as a physical assault), which can be followed by a punishing thought ("That was bad; I shouldn't have done it"). It is tempting to take the simple view that the principles of learning theory that apply to overt behaviors also apply to covert behaviors, a hypothesis termed the "continuity assumption" (Thoreson & Mahoney, 1974). Bandura (1986), Meichenbaum (1986), and others have documented ways in which covert events, particularly thoughts, can function to control overt behavior. The continuity assumption serves as a foundational aspect of the thriving field of cognitive (or cognitive-behavior) therapy, a fairly recent development that has potential for bridging the psychodynamic and behavioral therapies (e.g., Hawton, Salkovskis, Kirk, & Clark, 1989).

A fourth topic involves the scope of the practical observations that are needed in a behavioral assessment for clinical purposes. The patient usually does not know what environmental events are controlling (triggering and/or reinforcing) the problem behavior. To determine what should be observed besides the problem behavior itself, a considerable amount of trial and error is usually involved. One common procedure is to have the client keep structured notes as to *when* and *where* each instance of the problem behavior occurs, and *what else* is happening at the time. Several sets of observations are usually needed, with feedback, before the client becomes proficient at the kind of behavioral detective work that needs to be done. Because of the complexity of most clinical problems, a somewhat oversimplified version of behavioral assessment as it applies to clinical practice is given here. The development of practical skills in this area requires a considerable amount of experience and supervision.

Framework for Behavioral Assessment

The various definitions of behavioral assessment, both clinical and nonclinical, are in agreement on the two basic steps of the process:

1. Selecting and defining the behavior of interest in concrete, observable terms.
2. Using standardized or systematic procedures for observing the behaviors and recording the observations in an appropriate manner.

These two basic steps are reviewed here. In an assessment for planning clinical behavior change, three further steps are involved:

3. Observing the events that are controlling the behavior of interest.
4. Making a behavioral formulation, that is, attempting to formulate in social learning theory terms exactly how this control is being maintained.
5. Surveying the available resources for behavior change, and selecting or designing an optimal treatment strategy.

The reader is referred to the work of Lanyon and Lanyon (1976, 1978) for a discussion of the three latter steps. For a detailed overview of assessment within the traditional operant framework of behavior modification, Kazdin (1994) should be consulted.

SELECTING AND DEFINING THE BEHAVIOR

Behavioral Assessment

Definition is closely associated with observation. In the modified logical positivist philosophy that underlies modern behavioral psychology, *definition* is itself operationally defined as public and reliable observation. Even though the definition of a behavior of interest would seem to be obvious, numerous writers have stressed the need for care and precision in this regard. For example, consider a behavior as simple as fingernail biting. A young adult female client requesting treatment for this problem was given a simple *event counter* and instructed to record every instance of fingernail biting each day for one week. On the next visit, she reported that she had had difficulty in deciding exactly what should qualify as biting. At various times, she would inspect a finger, wondering whether to bite; or, she would put a finger to her mouth but not to her teeth; or, she would close her teeth over a nail but not bite off any part of the nail. After discussion, it was decided that fingernail biting should be defined to include all times when a finger touched the mouth for any reason, except while eating or washing.

In addition to its use with concrete or easily observable events such as fingernail biting, behavioral assessment can be employed with behaviors that are abstract or vague. For example, as part of a project to improve the quality of care in a hospital emergency room, Komaki, Collins, and Thoene (1980) reported the use of an instrument designed to define and measure "tender loving care." This instrument (Figure 5.1) was utilized by personnel who were not directly involved in the provision of service, to record a sample of patient–staff interactions. Note how the *definition* of the variable of interest is essentially the same as the procedure for its *observation*.

In contrast to nail biting, defined by specifying a simple physical position, and tender loving care, defined as the sum of a number of elements, more complicated situations require a more complex approach. In their work with aggressive children and their families, Patterson, Reid, Jones, and Conger (1975) developed definitions of 14 basic "noxious behaviors" together with norms for (or base rates of the occurrence of) these behaviors.

Check the appropriate boxes for each patient-staff interaction:	Yes	No	N/A or N/O
1. Within 15 seconds	☐	☐	☐
2. Greeting	☐	☐	☐
3. Eye contact during greeting	☐	☐	☐
4. Introduction of ER record	☐	☐	☐
5. Eye contact during introduction	☐	☐	☐
6. Individualized comment	☐	☐	☐
7. Eye contact during comment	☐	☐	☐
8. Within arm's reach	☐	☐	☐
9. Time → Dr.	☐	☐	☐
10. Next step	☐	☐	☐

Figure 5.1   Data sheet used to record care in a hospital emergency room. (Source: *From Komaki, Collins, & Thoene, 1980, p. 107. Copyright © 1980 by the Association for Advancement of Behavior Therapy. Reprinted by permission of the publisher and the authors.*)

Included were behaviors such as "yell," "whine," "tease," and "destructiveness." Also developed for the same project were definitions of 19 different behaviors that occurred in the classroom setting. Some were appropriate, such as "complies," "appropriate interaction with peer," and "attending"; and some were inappropriate, such as "destructiveness," "noisy," and "inappropriate locale." Definitions of several of these behaviors are shown in Figure 5.2, and a segment of the recording sheet is reproduced in Figure 5.3. A considerable amount of training is required before the observers can use this scheme successfully. The coding system developed by Patterson and his colleagues has been modified by many other researchers to serve as the basis for coding different interactions. For example, in a study of interactions between chronic pain patients and their spouses, Romano et al. (1991) were able to develop a reliable and valid observational measure of pain-related interactions. Their seven categories of pain behavior are shown in Figure 5.4, together with examples and reliability coefficients. Other child and family behavior coding systems are discussed by Gross and Wixted (1988).

Sampling and Recording Procedures

Regardless of the particular method of observation employed, it is necessary to specify in advance the exact procedures that will be used to sample the behavior and to record it. Careful sampling is necessary to ensure that the measurements will be representative of the behavior as a whole. This is particularly important in naturalistic observation because the behavior of interest may vary widely under different conditions. One technique that has been developed to heighten representativeness is *time sampling,* which involves the systematic observation of subjects' behavior according to a prearranged schedule of observations. The interval between observations is established to maximize the representativeness of the ongoing behavior that can be observed and recorded. The observations in a time sample are usually frequent and brief. In studying preschool children at play many years ago, Barker, Kounin, and Wright (1943) observed and recorded the behavior of each child for one minute during each five-minute segment of a one-hour session. Barker and Wright (1955) suggested ways of collecting time samples in order to maximize the usefulness of the obtained data. They also developed a "day record," or complete behavioral log, of an individual child by having trained observers accompany the child throughout the entire day (Barker & Wright, 1951). Such a log would be of considerable interest for some purposes, but the question of the representativeness of the particular day under study would limit its overall utility in many ways.

The observer needs to strike a balance between completeness of observation, on the one hand, and efficiency, on the other. Sufficient time must be allotted to pilot observations to (a) become fully aware of the range of

Appropriate Behaviors	Inappropriate Behaviors
Co—Complies. This category can be checked each time the person does what another person has requested. For example, the teacher asks class to take out notebooks and pupil does; she asks for paper to be turned in and pupil obeys; pupil asks for pencil and teacher or peer supplies one; teacher tells class to be quiet and pupil is quiet.	*DS—Destructiveness.* Use of this category is applicable when a person destroys or attempts to destroy some object; for example, breaking a pencil in half, tearing a page from a book, carving name on desk, etc. This category is not to be used when the person is writing an answer or working out a problem on a desk with a pen or pencil.
IP+—Appropriate interaction with peer. Coded when the pupil is interacting with peer and is not violating classroom rules. Interaction includes verbal and nonverbal communication; for example, talking, handing materials, working on project with peer. The response for the peer is IP+ if the peer is *interacting* with the subject. The main element to remember in applying this code is that *an interaction is occurring* or one of the persons is attempting to interact. If two students are working on a social studies project, the code is IP+; if they are talking to each other or organizing a notebook *together,* the code is IP+; but if the subject is simply writing a report and the peer is writing, then the appropriate code is AT.	*NY—Noisy.* This category is to be used when the person talks loudly, yells, bangs books, scrapes chairs, or makes any sounds that are likely to be actually or potentially disruptive to others.
AT—Attending. This category is used whenever a person indicates by behavior that he/she is doing what is appropriate in a school situation: for example, looking at the teacher when he/she is presenting material to the class; looking at visual aids as the teacher tells about them; has eyes focused on his/her book while doing the reading assignment; writes answers to arithmetic problems; the teacher or peer looks at the child reciting. "Attending" is to be coded as a *response* when there is an indication that the subject is aware that a teacher or peer is attending to his/her actions.	*IL—Inappropriate locale.* This category is not to be used if rules allow for pupils to leave seats without permission and what the pupil is doing is not an infraction of other rules; for example, a pupil going to sharpen pencil would not be classified IL, unless he/she stopped and looked at neighbors on the way or unless this activity takes permission from teacher, etc.

Figure 5.2 Examples of definitions of appropriate and inappropriate classroom behavior as coded by Patterson, Reid, Jones, and Conger (1975).

Coding Sheet

Observer _____ Sheet No. _____ *1* _____ Subject *Jimmy*

Date _____ *2-26-76* _____ Academic Activity *arithmetic*

Structured _✓_ Unstructured _____ Group _✓_ Individual _ Transitional _____

```
_S_  AP  CO  TT+  IP+  VO  AT  PN   DS  Dİ    1  NY  NC  PL  TT-  IP-  IL  SS (LO) NA  IT  _S_
_P_  AP  CO  TT+  IP+  VO (AT) PN   DS  DI    2  NY  NC  PL  TT-  IP-  IL  SS  LO  NA  IT  _P_
_S_  AP  CO  TT+  IP+  VO (AT) PN   DS  DI    3  NY  NC  PL  TT-  IP-  IL  SS  LO  NA  IT  _S_
_P_  AP  CO  TT+  IP+  VO  AT  PN   DS  DI    4  NY  NC  PL  TT-  IP- (SS) LO  NA  IT  _P_
_S_  AP  CO  TT+  IP+  VO  AT  PN   DS  DI    5  NY  NC  PL  TT- (IP) IL  SS  LO  NA  IT   °
_P_  AP  CO (TT+) IP+ VO  AT  PN   DS  DI    6  NY  NC  PL  TT-  IP-  IL  SS  LO  Nᴵ·
_S_  AP  CO  TT+  IP+  VO  AT  PN (DS) Dİ    7  NY  NC  PL  TT-  IP-  IL  Sꞔ
_P_  AP  CO  TT+  IP+  VO  AT  PN   DS  DI    8  NY  NC (Pᴸ) TT-  IP
_S_  AP  CO  TT+  IP+ (VO) AT  PN   DS  DI    9  NY  NC  Pᴵ                      ꞌA  IT  _P_
_P_  AP (CO) TT+  IP+  VO  AT  PN   DS  DI   10  Nᵛ                      SS  LO (NA) IT  _S_
_S_  AP  CO  TT+  IP+  VO  AT  PN   DS  Dᴵ               IP-  IP-  IL  SS  LO  NA  IT  _P_
_P_  AP  CO  TT+  IP+  VO  AT  Pᴺᴵ            ᴾL  TT-  IP-  IL  SS  LO (NA) IT  _S_
_S_  AP  CO  TT+  IP+  Vᴼ              NY  NC  PL  TT-  IP-  IL  SS  LO  NA  IT  _P_
_P_  AP  CO  TTᴵ·          ᴵⱼI  29 (NY) NC  PL  TT-  IP-  IL  SS  LO  NA  IT  _S_
_S_  ᴬ ᴾ              ᴾN  DS  DI   30  NY  NC  PL  TT-  IP-  IL (SS) LO  NA  IT  _P_
                  vO  AT  PN   DS  DI   31  NY  NC  PL  TT-  IP-  IL  SS (LO) NA  IT  _S_
            ᴵ ᴵ+ IP+  VO (AT) PN   DS  DI   32  NY  NC  PL  TT-  IP-  IL  SS  LO  NA  IT  _P_
         ᵤᵣ  CO  TT+  IP+  VO  AT  PN   DS  DI   33  NY  NC  PL  TT- (IP) IL  SS  LO  NA  IT  _S_
_P_  AP  CO  TT+  IP+  VO  AT  PN (DS) DI   34  NY  NC  PL  TT-  IP-  IL  SS  LO  NA  IT  _P_
_S_  AP  CO  TT+  IP+  VO (AT) PN   DS  DI   35  NY  NC  PL  TT-  IP-  IL  SS  LO  NA  IT  _S_
```

Figure 5.3 Illustrative segment of recording sheet used to code the observations of appropriate and inappropriate classroom behaviors. From Patterson, Reid, Jones, and Conger (1975).

variability of the behavior under different conditions and (b) design a time-sampling procedure that adequately incorporates this variability. In Patterson et al.'s observation system for classroom behaviors (see Figure 5.2), "the target subject is observed at 15-second intervals for 12 minutes, and then randomly selected peers are observed in the same manner for six minutes" (Patterson, Reid, et al., 1975, p. 74). These authors also recommended sampling classroom behavior in both group and individual academic work. Haynes (1978, p. 78) listed five characteristics to be considered in deciding how to sample: (a) the rate of the behavior, (b) its variability, (c) its situational specificity, (d) possible changes over time, and (e) complexity of the recording system. Low-rate behaviors pose a special problem in time sampling. Continuous observation methods may be needed, perhaps using a participant observer rather than an outside observer.

Several other sampling questions must also be considered. Where there is a wide variety of potentially relevant behaviors, a choice must be made as to which events to sample. The question of *subject sampling* also arises when it is not realistic to observe all available persons; for example, in setting out to assess the overall level of discipline that is maintained in a city school system. Representative sampling of situations should also be achieved,

Behavior	Kappa	Content/Affect Descriptors	Examples
Nonverbal Pain	.59	Facial expressions of pain; stiff, slow or restricted movement; paraverbal pain expressions; use of supports; holding or massaging part of the body.	Grimacing, wincing; limping, halting, during walking; not bending back while moving to sitting position; grunting, groaning; use of cane or crutch.
Verbal Pain	.66	Statements indicating pain, functional limitations or concern with the same.	"I'd better not lift that because of my back." "Oh, that hurts."
Solicitous	.58	Statements inquiring about or exhibiting concern for the other's physical condition or comfort; offers of assistance; behavior discouraging the other from activity; physical assistance or taking over a task.	"Are you sure you should do that with your bad back?" "Here, let me help you with that." "I'll do that—you rest now."
Facilitative	.61	Compliments, agreement, praise, encouragement, humor; behaviors (other than pain or solicitous) accompanied by happy or caring affect.	"You look great." "I know you can do it."
Aggressive	.57	Expressions of disapproval, disagreement, or displeasure directed toward the other; threats, arguments; refusals of requests, behaviors (other than pain) accompanied by aversive affect (irritated, angry, or sarcastic facial expression or voice tone).	"You don't know what you're talking about!" "Do it yourself."
Distressed	.53	Complaints indicating displeasure with objects, situations, or persons other than spouse; self-derogatory statements; behaviors (other than pain or solicitous) accompanied by dysphoric (sad, crying), anxious, or whining effect.	"I'm really upset about my job." "I look terrible today." "I can't do anything right."

Figure 5.4   Seven categories of pain behavior and their reliabilities. (**Source:** *From Romano et al., 1991, p. 556. Copyright © 1991 by the Association for Advancement of Behavior Therapy. Reprinted by permission of the publisher and the authors.*)

Time	Circumstances	Additional Information Elicited by Therapist
8 A.M.	Woke up feeling depressed; sat on side of bed	
10:15 A.M.	Felt less depressed; got dressed and made coffee	Telephone rang; patient hates its sound and answered it to stop the ringing
10:30 A.M.	Depressed again; sat in kitchen	
11:45 A.M.	Less depressed; got ready for work and left apartment	Patient became anxious about being late, which would result in a reprimand and possibly being fired
5:30	Became depressed when arrived home; depressed all evening; watched TV	

Figure 5.5 One day's self-observation sheet for a depressed patient, recording all changes in depressive feelings, together with time and place. On the right are the therapist's notes after questioning the patient concerning correlated events. (Source: From R. I. Lanyon & B. P. Lanyon, 1976, p. 305. Reprinted by permission of John Wiley & Sons.)

because the frequency of the target behavior may vary according to the many different stimulus components of the context in which the behavior occurs. Mash and Terdal (1981) have provided a more complete discussion of each of these topics.

Methods of recording observational data have been mentioned earlier; an example appears in Figure 5.3. With both simple and complex behaviors, a choice must usually be made between recording *frequency* and recording *duration*. The nailbiting client described earlier was asked to record frequency by activating the event counter for every instance of the behavior. At regular intervals, perhaps immediately before each meal (the meal serves as a reminding cue), the tally would be transferred to a data sheet. For behaviors such as asthma attacks, studying, or insomnia, the duration of the behavior might be more important than the frequency, and a recording procedure such as a log sheet is often appropriate. Figure 5.5 shows an abbreviated portion of such a sheet for a patient suffering from depression.

METHODS OF OBSERVATION

Procedures for behavioral observation can be grouped into four categories: (a) uncontrolled, or naturalistic observation; (b) controlled, or structured observation; (c) self-observation; and (d) written self-reports. These procedures focus mainly on the target behaviors themselves, and there is relatively little literature on the assessment of controlling variables as required in clinical applications, except on an informal basis, as exemplified in Figure 5.5.

Naturalistic Observation

Naturalistic observation refers to the observing and recording of the behavior of interest by an independent observer exactly as it occurs in real life. For clinical applications, this approach has a substantial advantage over laboratory observation, because the real-life antecedent stimuli and the consequences of the behavior can also be observed directly.

A major disadvantage of naturalistic observation is its cost. However, it is often argued that, particularly in a clinical situation, any other type of observation is of limited value. Only with naturalistic observation can the relevant controlling variables be detected. Unfortunately, scientific methodologists in psychology have traditionally regarded data gathered by naturalistic observation as an unsatisfactory basis for the development of knowledge (e.g., Levine & Parkinson, 1994; Sackett & Larson, 1990), even though it has been frequently pointed out (e.g., Sarason, 1974; Westover & Lanyon, 1990) that the controlling variables for behaviors in the laboratory are usually different from those in the natural environment. This difference is particularly important in the assessment of real-life problem behaviors for which the controlling variables are obscure. For psychologists interested in real-life problems, naturalistic rather than laboratory observation is essential, at least until sufficient knowledge is gained so that an appropriate situation for controlled observation can be designed.

A second difficulty in naturalistic observation involves possible changes in the behavior being observed, originating from the observational process itself. In other words, the knowledge that one is being observed or judged often has direct consequences on the behavior under scrutiny. Increased motivation and higher performance, or anxiety and lowered performance, or studied indifference with no apparent performance change are all possible results. Consider, for example, a student teacher being evaluated by a supervisor who is sitting in the classroom, or an assembly line worker who knows that a time-study engineer is posted somewhere on the line. Any subject's awareness of being observed might produce atypical behavior at a time when the occurrence of typical behavior is an absolute necessity. Campbell (1957) called these influences "reactive effects of measurement." Another term is "guinea pig effects." Their effects on accuracy of measurement were reviewed in detail by Wildman and Erickson (1977). An illustration of guinea pig effects was reported by Moos (1968), who studied the behavioral effects of having psychiatric inpatients wear wireless transmitter microphones. In general, the effects were very small, but some of the more disturbed individuals tended to show substantial reactions to being observed.

A third difficulty of direct observation involves the observer's invasion of the subject's privacy. This problem is especially important in personality assessment, because many of the behaviors that should be observed, such as affection, aggression, and sexual identification, are typically regarded as personal and private. Problems of invasion of privacy are considered in more detail in Chapter Twelve.

One technique for reducing guinea pig effects involves *participant observation:* the observers themselves actively engage in a spontaneous fashion with the individual or group under study. Participant observation has been widely used by anthropologists studying other cultures. Psychologists have found it useful for a variety of purposes. In a famous study, psychologists joined a "Doomsday" sect that met together to await the end of the world (Festinger, Riecken, & Schachter, 1956). The psychologists, whose professional role was not revealed to the sect, observed and recorded the group's behavior before and during the time it became clear that the prophecy would not be fulfilled. Two of the difficulties mentioned earlier are present in this example: (a) the observer's questionable objectivity in observing and recording data under such circumstances, and (b) the ethical question of invasion of the sect's privacy.

Another strategy to reduce guinea pig effects has been to provide for invisible or hidden observation, so that the subject is not aware of the observer's presence. Hidden microphones, "candid cameras," one-way vision mirrors, and electromechanical devices to record subjects' movements in a chair or other piece of furniture represent some of the possible devices that can be used for unobtrusive observation.

Other sources of natural behavior samples may be found in historical records available on individuals: official school records, high school and college yearbooks, medical and dental records, and records of military service. This approach is widely used in clinical evaluations, where a personality picture and/or hypotheses about current problems may be assembled on the basis of available records. However, quantitative uses are much less frequent. In an early example, Barthell and Holmes (1968) were able to demonstrate that the high school yearbook entries of persons who were later diagnosed as either schizophrenic or neurotic differed in expected ways from a control group. Such measures, in which natural behavior documented in records is quantified in a meaningful manner, would appear to have promise for the future.

Despite its inherent problems, naturalistic observation represents an important aspect of behavioral assessment, and there is currently, among psychologists, considerable interest in finding ways to deal with the various difficulties that accompany this approach. Two further methodological difficulties—(a) bias due to the observer's own expectancies and (b) problems of reliability—apply equally to controlled observations and are discussed under that heading. One additional limitation will not be solved by better methods. Naturalistic observation tends primarily to permit the recording of public and frequent behavior, whereas many of the behaviors required for personality evaluation tend to be private and relatively infrequent. Responsiveness to stress, the handling of anger or sexuality, and reactions to tragedy fit this description and may not be observable naturalistically, even with improved methodologies.

Controlled Observation

The difficulties involved in data collection in naturalistic settings have led to the development of procedures for sampling behavior under more closely controlled conditions. These conditions offer opportunity for more careful and thorough observation, as well as the potential for sufficient environmental control to elicit behaviors of special interest. Of considerable importance are laboratory situations in which subjects are presented with a number of tasks or experiences under conditions more or less similar to real life, and are expected to function with the degree of effectiveness they would have in real life. These laboratory or controlled naturalistic observations have been used for many years in the context of personnel selection, industrial psychology, and personality research, where they have been referred to as *situational tests* or *work samples*.

Among the earliest situational tests were those employed by Hartshorne and May (1928, 1929) and Hartshorne, May, and Shuttleworth (1930) in their series of famous studies on the investigation of character, incorporating such traits as honesty, truthfulness, self-control, and persistence. Hartshorne and May assumed that character consisted of a series of responses or habits, and they attempted to measure these responses by sampling them directly. For example, in assessing honesty with money, children were given boxes of coins that had been secretly identified so that the experimenters could later determine which child had a particular box. Because the children were unaware of this arrangement, their honesty in handling money could be determined without their knowledge, under relatively naturalistic but controlled conditions.

Recognizing that honesty with money might be unrelated to other kinds of honesty, Hartshorne and May collected behavior samples that allowed the possibility of other types of dishonesty. Thus, children were given an impossible task to perform and were then asked to report their own scores. The extended work of these authors involved a wide repertoire of tasks concerned with general behaviors such as honesty and persistence. Although these and similar tasks have been used in a variety of research studies (e.g.,

Brock & Guidice, 1963), the procedures have neither been standardized nor widely used as routine assessment devices for practical purposes.

Situational tests have also been utilized to assess suitability for military and intelligence operations, with a special emphasis on determining characteristic modes of responding to stress. The principal feature of this type of assessment has been the intensive study, by a highly trained staff of observers, of a small group of candidates in a live-in program lasting several days and typically held at a remote and secluded site. These programs have made use of the traditional testing devices discussed in Chapters Three and Four, but particular emphasis has been placed on observing the candidates' reactions to the novel situation, to the continued pressure of scrutiny and evaluation, and to a series of specially designed stress situations.

In one such situation, designed to assist in the selection of military personnel for the Office of Strategic Services during World War II, candidates were required to construct a five-foot Tinkertoy® cube with the aid of two supposed helpers, who were really members of the evaluation team and who had been instructed to criticize, ridicule, and otherwise impede the candidate in completing the task (OSS Assessment Staff, 1948). The helpers carefully observed the candidate's reaction to the continual stress and frustration they were causing. In another instance, a group of candidates were given the task of crossing a stream and were provided with some materials to build a primitive bridge. They were then observed in their efforts to organize themselves into an effective work group to solve the task. Because the successful candidates operated throughout the world and performed a great variety of tasks, criterion measures were hard to obtain, making it difficult to assess the effectiveness of these particular selection procedures. Nevertheless, the correlations between overall suitability ratings and success in the field, as evaluated by such criteria as judgments by field commanders, ranged from .08 to .53, varying with the particular group studied and the criteria used (OSS Assessment Staff, 1948, p. 428). The assessment program had a fairly rigorous set of selection standards, which served to decrease any correlation between the observers' predictions and judged criterion performance.

The live-in assessment procedure has also been used in the past for selecting members of the British Civil Service (Vernon, 1950). The situational tasks employed were based on a thorough job analysis of the work for which the candidates were applying, and included committee tasks and the handling of routine paperwork. There was much opportunity for informal observation of the candidates throughout a three-day period, but no deliberately stressful situations were built into the assessment procedure. With a rather homogeneous group of university graduates, the median correlation between ratings of trained observers and independent on-the-job evaluations collected two years later was .41. The median correlation between the more traditional written ability tests and the evaluations was only .12, indicating that the trained observers were able to identify significant elements of potential success that were not otherwise detected.

The assessors in this example had a clear understanding of the psychological requirements of the criterion task and were able to arrange for assessment situations to elicit relevant behaviors. Similar positive results were reported with trainees at U.S. Army Officer Candidate Schools, using leadership performance exercises as the situational task (Holmen, Katter, Jones, & Richardson, 1956), and with police cadets, using a "clues" test, a situational exercise in police detection (Mills, McDevitt, & Tonkin, 1966). On the other hand, assessment procedures based on more traditional psychological tests, including a wide variety of personality tests, have not been particularly successful in predicting success in psychiatry (Holt & Luborsky, 1958) or in clinical psychology (Kelly & Fiske, 1951; Kelly & Goldberg, 1959).

A technique often used in live-in or "house party" assessments is the *leaderless group discussion* (LGD). In this procedure, which originated in the German and British military assessment programs (Ansbacher, 1951), a small group of candidates, typically fewer than 12, are asked either to "discuss something" or to discuss a specific problem, perhaps a topic of current political or social interest. For a business-oriented group, the topic might be a management problem, such as how to deal with an unsatisfactory employee. Because the procedure is otherwise unstructured and the group members are usually strangers to each other, the situation is rather ambiguous. There is opportunity to observe and rate behaviors like leading and following, social poise and self-presence, and "goal facilitation," which refers to the degree the individual helped the group accomplish its goal through making suggestions or enabling others to contribute.

Initial participation in an LGD is usually equated with attempted leadership (Bass, 1960, p. 115). Most of the talk is directed at influencing other members, either with procedural suggestions or with opinions on the topic under discussion. Attempted leadership, as defined in this manner, could be measured by determining the amount of time spent talking one-on-one, the total number of responses made, the degree of participation, or the total time spent talking within the group. Other ways of assessing the members of an LGD have included ratings of behaviors (e.g., "motivating others to participate") and checklists of behaviors (e.g., "led the discussion") to be completed by either the participants themselves or external, nonparticipating observers.

Perhaps the most extensive and formal way of categorizing the various kinds of behavior observable in this and other social interactions is by means of the Bales Interaction Check List (Bales, 1950). In this technique, observers categorize every response made in the group into one of 12 predetermined categories, such as *shows solidarity* (gives help or reward), *shows tension release* (jokes, laughs), and *asks for orientation* (asks for information, confirmation). At the present time, however, the Bales Interaction Check List is more of a research instrument than a functional assessment device.

In general, there is excellent historical evidence for the reliability of observing LGD behavior. For most of the available methods of quantifying the behavior, the average correlation between any two observers is typically between .8 and .9 (Bass, 1954). There is also sound historical evidence for the predictive value of LGD behavioral indexes. For example, Bass and Coates (1952) reported correlations of .40 to .45 between LGD scores and ratings of military officers by their superiors. Similar findings were reported for British foreign service officers (Vernon, 1950), British Civil Service employees (Vernon, 1950), and fraternity and sorority leaders and sales trainees (Bass, 1954). Thornton (1992), in summarizing the research on LGD, concluded that this method is "particularly effective in assessing group leadership skills, such as the ability to contribute good ideas and guide the discussion process" (p. 74).

The LGD procedure is a very good example of the utility of the situational test or work sample approach to personality assessment, particularly in the evaluation of characteristics such as leadership. Leadership involves the behavior of individuals in group settings, particularly their ability to structure, organize, and generally influence the group; such behavior is elicited and observable in the LGD and it provides information about the individual's behavior in other situations that require similar responses for effective performance. The LGD method continues to play an important role in today's assessment centers, which are typically used to identify leadership and management potential in both prospective and current members of the work force. In Chapter Nine we discuss the contemporary use of assessment centers in regard to leadership, and we also describe more traditional psychometric effects to measure such behavior.

One portion of a study by Gordon (1967) examined the relative utility of several assessment procedures, including individual situational work samples, in predicting failure of Peace Corps trainees to be selected for an overseas assignment. The subjects were 178 trainees in three different training programs. All were subjected to an intensive one-week live-in assessment program. The program included a variety of paper-and-pencil personality inventories of the type discussed in Chapter Four, a foreign-language learning task, and four specially devised situational work samples. In the latter, the subject was required to (a) develop a plan to build an infirmary on a South Seas island, (b) describe to a foreign national the American governmental system of checks and balances, (c) discuss American culture with an anti-American, and (d) enlist the aid of an Indian government official in a project to raise poultry. Prior to overseas departure, 74 trainees were rejected as unsuitable, although the personnel making this decision did not have access to the earlier assessment data.

In general, each of the various assessment approaches enabled predictions of failure to be made that exceeded chance expectation, but there were no worthwhile differences in efficiency of prediction among the various approaches. Gordon argued that the simplest and most economical method of predicting success in the overseas assignments should be used operationally for screening—in this case, the paper-and-pencil inventories. These issues of cost and efficiency need further careful research involving a variety of criterion situations. The additional question of the relative utility of the different procedures for predicting success in overseas assignments is as yet unanswered. Despite the increasing importance of overseas assignments in today's global economy, our review of the research literature turned up no recent studies of this important practical problem.

Clinical Use of Controlled Observation

The use of controlled observation procedures for the assessment of clinically related problems is a relatively recent development. Such procedures can be discussed under four headings: (a) structured interactions, (b) role-playing tests, (c) experimental analogs, and (d) physiological measures. Except for physiological measures, these procedures are analogous to the situational tests and work sample methods discussed earlier in the context of personnel selection.

Structured Interactions.   The assessment of interpersonal interactions through structured tasks employs the same definition and recording procedures as were described for naturalistic observation. Thus, Patterson, Hops, and Weiss (1975) extended earlier work with families of deviant children (Patterson, Reid, Jones, & Conger, 1975) to develop a system for the assessment of husband–wife interaction. The laboratory situation consisted of ten-minute sessions in which the couples attempted to resolve several areas of conflict. Similar structured observational assessment procedures have also been developed for assessing components of mother–child interaction (e.g., Forehand & Scarboro, 1975), characteristics of depressed women and their families (Hops et al., 1987), and interactions of parents with problem-behavior children (Lewin, Hops, Aubuschon, & Budlinger, 1988).

Role-Playing Tests.   In these tests, the subject knows that the situation is simulated but is asked to react as though in real life. In one of the first examples, McFall and Marston (1970) developed a tape-recorded behavioral role-playing test to assess assertive behavior. Subjects were required to respond to 16 hypothetical situations requiring assertiveness, and the degree of assertiveness that they displayed was determined by independent judges. The items were developed by an extensive test construction process; the researchers began with a list of over 2,000 situations calling for assertive behavior and reduced them through screening, factor analysis, and additional procedures. Other situations in which behavioral role-playing tests have been employed include the assessment of social skills in delinquent boys and college populations, and adaptive skills in alcoholics.

Complex characteristics that are not readily observable can also be assessed by procedures based on role-playing. McCallum and Piper (1990) developed a procedure for assessing *psychological mindedness,* in which the subject watches a videotape of a simulated parent–therapist interaction. Then the subject, role-playing the therapist, is asked for his or her general impressions of "What seems to be troubling this woman?" At other points, the videotape is stopped and the subject is asked questions such as "What does he mean by that?" The subject's responses are tape-recorded and scored by judges using a structured manual for a variety of criteria, including a nine-level schema defining increasing degrees of psychological mindedness. These levels, which are scorable with moderate interjudge reliability, are shown in Figure 5.6.

Bellack (1979) reported that the use of audiotaped or videotaped situations often resulted in data of low validity as compared to the use of real-life models for the role playing. Based on a series of studies investigating the validity of role-playing tests for social skills with psychiatric patients, he offered the following recommendations: each item should allow for multiple responses by both the subject and the model; ways of making the assessment procedure less stressful should be explored; more detailed descriptions should be provided, and subjects should preview them before responding; and careful attention should be paid to the degree to which

Level I	The subject identifies a specific internal experience of the patient.
Level II	The subject recognizes the driving force of an internal experience of the patient.
Level III	The subject identifies a result of a drive such that a causal link is made between an internal event and its resultant expression.
Level IV	The subject recognizes that the motivating force in the patient is largely out of her awareness or is unconscious.
Level V	The subject identifies conflictual components of the patient's experience.
Level VI	Subject identifies a causal link where the conflict is presented as generating an expression.
Level VII	Subject identifies a causal link where tension (fear, anxiety) is presented as motivating an expression.
Level VIII	Subject recognizes that the patient is engaging in a defensive maneuver.
Level IX	Subject recognizes that despite the defensive maneuver, the patient remains disturbed in some way by the conflict.

Figure 5.6   Nine levels of psychological mindedness assessed through role-playing. (Source: *From McCallum & Piper, 1990, p. 418. Copyright © 1990 by the American Psychological Association. Reprinted with permission of the publisher and authors.*)

certain situations have specific demand characteristics which might lead to the same response for all subjects.

Experimental Analogs.   This term refers to laboratory situations that are arranged to be as parallel as possible to real-life problem situations. These tests usually involve the assessment of specific instances of *nonverbal behavior*. An example is the *behavioral avoidance test* for assessing specific fears such as phobias of snakes or spiders. To make a quantitative assessment of snake phobics, Lang and Lazovik (1963) asked their subjects to move systematically closer and closer to a harmless snake, under structured laboratory conditions. Each successive step earned them a lower behavioral avoidance score. Thus, subjects who refused to go into the room at all earned a score of 19, those who were willing to get within 2 feet of the snake received a 4, and those who picked it up earned a 1. In addition to the behavioral avoidance score, Lang and Lazovik had subjects rate their subjectively experienced anxiety on a 10-point scale.

The experimental analog has also been used in situations involving interpersonal behavior. Drawing on a method pioneered by Paul (1966), Beidel, Turner, Jacob, and Cooley (1989) developed a behavioral assessment procedure for the phobia of being asked to give impromptu speeches. Subjects were asked to choose three of five possible topics and were given three minutes to prepare. The main behavioral measure of interest was overall speech duration. Observable signs of fear, such as trembling, hesitating, and sweating, as well as pulse rate and palmar sweat indexes, can also be obtained in this type of situation. Thus, experimental analog tests are suitable for gathering data in several different response modalities.

Another kind of experimental analog situation has involved a laboratory model not of the behavior itself but of the *process* thought to be involved. This method was pioneered in 1953 by Lindsley (1960), who arranged a simple operant reinforcement task for psychiatric inpatients, in which reinforcers such as candy or cigarettes could be earned by systematically pulling a plunger. This situation was seen as a "model" for assessing the nature of the factors that influenced the patients' behavior, and it revealed certain response characteristics that had direct clinical relevance (Kazdin, 1979). In a different application of this procedure, Marlatt (1978) summarized the use of operant methods to assess the intensity of alcoholics' need to drink and the factors that can cause variation in the intensity of that need. Overall, however, the study of operant processes has not been widely adopted as an assessment device.

Physiological Measures.   This fourth laboratory procedure involves the assessment of physiological states. It would indeed be convenient if psychologists were able to assess personality characteristics by measuring bodily responses, as characters in science fiction often do. In real life, only a few systems that may be relevant to personality and interpersonal behavior can be assessed. But psychophysiological assessment has made significant advances in the past 20 years or so, due to the development of computerized electronic equipment to monitor bodily responses, plus an understanding of the relationships among physiological, cognitive, and emotional response systems (Haynes, 1991).

A commonly assessed psychophysiological response is the overall level of bodily arousal. Research and theory suggest that the common element in such pleasant states as deep relaxation and meditation is a bodily state of low psychophysiological arousal (Blanchard & Epstein, 1978). The elusive notion of increasing one's level of mental health by reducing one's overall level of "stress and tension," which are themselves ambiguous and poorly defined terms, is probably related to the interest in learning to reach a state of physiological hypoarousal. Relevant bodily measures include degree of electrical activity in the muscles (electromyographic, or EMG levels), heart rate, blood pressure, electrodermal activity (correlated with sweat gland activity), and certain EEG (brain wave) patterns. Because each individual's pattern of these responses in relation to stressful stimuli is unique, research progress on using them in structured assessment procedures is slow. However, there does appear to be some overall relationship between reduced psychophysiological activity and reduced physical and mental "tension." Other documented findings include the relationship of mental stresses to cardiovascular measures (Steptoe & Johnston, 1991) and to other physiological components of anxiety (Turpin, 1991). The topic of psychophysiology is a highly complex one, and psychologists interested in psychophysiological assessment procedures require a comprehensive training in the basic knowledge of that area.

Two other uses of psychophysiological processes in assessment deserve specific mention. The first involves the assessment of sexual functioning, in either a research context or clinical assessment situations. Reviews have been provided by Becker and Kaplan (1990) and by Travin, Cullen, and Melella (1988). For males, the *penile plethysmograph* is used to measure increases in the size of the penis while viewing pictures or other stimuli causing varying degrees of sexual arousal. This procedure involves either a strain gauge, registering changes in electrical resistance as the circumference of the penis changes, or a pneumatic plethysmograph, consisting of an airtight hollow cylinder wherein changes in air pressure reflect changes in penis size. The laboratory assessment of sexual arousal in women is less well documented. Geer (1980) described preliminary work involving the assessment of vaginal changes by means of photoplethysmography, in which a small instrument containing a photoelectric cell and a light source is inserted into the vagina to register changes in vaginal blood volume.

The penile plethysmograph has met with both popularity and controversy over the past decade because of widespread interest in obtaining objective evidence of the presence or absence of tendencies toward sexual deviance. Based on the empirical literature on the instrument's accuracy, some of which is cited in the reviews mentioned above, it now appears clear that the results are too variable and inaccurate to be of use in legal settings. However, it can serve a useful function in treatment programs with clients who fully admit their problems and are motivated for change.

The second additional use of physiological assessment procedures is in lie detection. Test procedures record multiple measures of overall physiological arousal (such as heart rate, blood pressure, skin resistance, and EMG levels) while the individual is answering questions related to the topic of interest. The procedures are based on the premise that the pattern of such responses while lying is different from the pattern while telling the truth. Despite the popularity of lie detection procedures, research reviews tend to conclude that most of the claims for accuracy are exaggerated. Saxe, Dougherty, and Cross (1985) concluded that "neither available data nor theoretical analysis indicates that polygraph tests function as claimed by their proponents. Substantial numbers of both truthful and deceptive individuals may be misidentified through the use of polygraph tests, and the test can be 'beaten.' For most common uses of polygraph testing there is not even rudimentary evidence to support such use . . ." (p. 355). Currently, polygraph test results are excluded or severely restricted as evidence in the state and federal court systems (Bartol & Bartol, 1994). In addition, federal legislation in 1988 (see Chapter Nine) has virtually eliminated the use of the polygraph in its preemployment testing role.

Self-Observation

The view that self-reports can contain useful information about actual behavior has had a stormy history in psychology. Individuals' reports about their own behavior have traditionally been regarded with suspicion, both by psychodynamically oriented psychologists and by classical behaviorists. It has been fashionable to believe that self-observation does not usually correlate adequately with observation made by independent observers, and that it is therefore not a valid assessment procedure. More recently, however, there has been increasing support for the view that accurate and reliable self-observation is a learnable skill that can be efficiently taught by behavioral methods such as modeling and shaping (e.g., Bellack & Hersen, 1988). One very important factor gives overriding support to the practical use of self-observation: its *economy*. The self-observer is always ready and available, and is free of charge. Self-observation is particularly important in making an assessment of *covert* events, because it provides the only means of identifying and quantifying these events.

Methods of Self-Observation. The importance of self-observation as an integral part of behavioral evaluation and change is incompletely understood, and its technology is still in the early stages of development (Kazdin, 1994). Most methods of self-observation involve systematic note taking on index cards or in a notebook. Special tally sheets have been prepared for specific behaviors, such as studying and substance abuse (Yates, 1985). Wrist counters and similar devices, such as golf score or supermarket counters, can also be used, although they enable only the recording of frequencies and not the antecedent stimulus conditions (e.g., time and place) under which the behavior occurs, nor its consequences.

A person who is recording instances of nailbiting, which may occur many times each day, would approach self-observation differently from a person recording instances of anxious feelings, which may occur only once or twice per day but may last several hours each time. Yates (1985) presents an excellent discussion of a wide variety of practical self-observation techniques, plus sound practical advice on how to self-monitor. In one common procedure, the behavior therapist has patients construct their own recording sheets. (Figure 5.5 illustrates a depressed patient's recording sheet.) Taken over a one-week or two-week interval and expanded through inquiry by the therapist, such observations provide an overall frequency count of depressive episodes and their length, plus a listing of the stimuli associated with their onset and termination.

Teaching Self-Observation. Procedures for the teaching of self-observation skills are not systematized at the present time. As pointed out by Thoreson and Mahoney (1974), individuals are not "naturally" accurate self-observers, so that specific training is, in most instances, essential. These authors have listed a number of factors that have been shown to enhance the learning of self-observation: modeling, immediate accuracy feedback, systematic reinforcement, and the gradual transfer of the responsibility for recording from an external source to oneself.

Problems in Self-Observation. Many of the methodological difficulties encountered in self-observation are similar to those encountered when naturalistic observations are made by an independent observer. However, one specific type of problem, the reactive effects of measurement, takes on additional complexities. The reactive effect of self-observation has itself been successfully used as a behavior change procedure, although unsuccessful outcomes have also been reported (Nelson, 1977). A simple operant explanation of this effect might be given in terms of either self-punishment or self-reward. Thus, recording one's problem behaviors might call forth a self-statement such as "This is bad; I should do it less often" or "I'm doing a good job of cutting back." Kazdin (1974, 1994) has analyzed in detail the behavior-change properties of self-observation and has shown that its behavior-change effects are highly varied and often temporary, and that a variety of theoretical explanations are possible in addition to a simple operant view.

Problems and Challenges in Behavioral Observation

The area of the systematic observation of direct behavior has developed quite rapidly, and these developments are generally regarded as positive. However, critics consistently point to one serious area of difficulty, which encompasses several different facets: Behavioral assessment procedures have in general failed to incorporate the usual psychometric standards of validity and reliability that are expected of any structured psychological assessment method (e.g., Goldfried, 1979). This same warning has been offered in regard to the proliferation of projective techniques (e.g., Hartmann, Roper, & Bradford, 1979).

Reliability. A major area of concern is reliability of observation. The topic of reliability (defined as the *repeatability of measurement*) is discussed in detail in Chapter Seven); specific questions, as they apply to behavioral assessment, are examined here. We have already discussed the need to gather adequate samples (over time, situations, and subjects) of the behaviors to be assessed, and the reactive effects of the observation process on the behavior itself. Another problem related to reliability involves the observational skill of objective observers versus bias due to the observers' own expectancies. This effect is closely related to the better-known effect of expectancies on the outcome of psychological research (e.g., Rosenthal, 1966). Lipinski and Nelson (1974) listed three factors that appear to improve the accuracy of observers' reports: (a) knowledge of expected results, (b) evaluative feedback from another person, and (c) knowledge that reliability measurements are being made.

Observer reliability may be developed through specific training, and the more structured the system and the training, the better the reliability. For example, Hawkins, Berler, and DeLawyer (1984) demonstrated a high degree of reliability in coding verbal interactions from audiotapes based on an extensive manual and training exercises. The process of measuring reliability is itself reactive, so that different results may be obtained, depending on the contingencies available to the observer. Romanczyk, Kent, Diament, and O'Leary (1973) showed that not only was reliability higher when the observers knew that they were to be monitored, but it increased even more when they knew against whose work it would be checked.

Validity. As discussed in more detail in Chapter Seven, an assessment procedure is valid to the extent that it measures what it is supposed to measure. Because behavioral assessment involves the *direct sampling* of the behaviors of interest, the most important aspect of validity is content validity—the degree to which the assessment procedure does indeed take a representative sample of the "universe of content" of the behavior to be assessed. A more detailed discussion of this topic has been given by Foster, Bell-Dolan, and Burge (1988).

The use of contrived or laboratory assessment situations poses special threats to content validity. In clinical assessment, where the variables controlling the behavior (antecedents and consequences) must also be assessed, the use of contrived situations is even riskier. Thus, it is legitimate to ask whether such an approach can be valid at all. An appropriate response is that the potential for validity exists to the extent that the controlling variables that maintain the problem behavior in real life are also present in the laboratory situation. In other words, a basic condition must be that the laboratory situation resembles the real-life situation in all essential ways.

Two other psychometric concerns should be noted. First, there have been relatively few attempts to standardize behavioral observation procedures, and even fewer efforts to develop norms for the various procedures. Second, and of importance ranging beyond behavioral approaches to assessment, there is a strong need for multiple sources of assessment information regarding a particular behavior or concept. This principle is related to the recognition that many human events involve three simultaneous response systems (overt motor activity; thoughts or cognitive behaviors; and feelings) related to emotional-physiological behavior (see page 143); and that a satisfactory assessment procedure should sample all three. It should also be understood that each particular method or mode of assessment suffers from biases or limitations inherent in that mode, so that "multimethod" or "multimodal" procedures are needed to provide unbiased assessment. We discuss this topic further in Chapter Eight in regard to personality assessment on a broader scale.

Unsystematic Observations

Discussion, until now, has concentrated on situations where a trained observer studies a subject in some specific type of behavioral situation. The subject has also been "behaving" in a wide variety of real-life situations where untrained observers have been present. The child's behavior in the classroom, the employee's on-the-job performance, and the patient's behavior on the ward are all observed and should provide useful data for the purposes of personality assessment. The major problem in making use of informal and unsystematic observations is the manner in which these observations are to be collected from the observers, and particularly the form in which the observations are to be reported.

One approach is to ask the observer of an individual or a group to keep an *anecdotal record*. Observers—often, teachers or supervisors—are asked to make note of whatever behavior in their daily or routine contact they regard as "significant." They are encouraged to record exact details as soon as possible after the observation, and to be objective and descriptive in their reports. Any inferences observers make should be clearly identified as such. An anecdotal record developed over a period of time provides a rich though nonquantified account of behavior that is unrivaled for developing an individualized behavioral description. The consistency and individuality of certain behavioral observations—for example, seeking affection, refusing help, working diligently at a task, or volunteering for responsibilities—permit the reader of the anecdotal record to construct a personality "picture." The artistic, clinical nature of this process is clearly apparent.

To develop in anecdotal records a greater focus on behaviors that are of particular interest to the investigator, it is possible to utilize the *critical incident technique* originally developed many years ago by Flanagan (1954). This technique asks the observer to consider instances of behavior that are illustrative of a particular personality characteristic. Thus, a supervisor might be asked to observe and record examples of good or poor work performance, or a psychiatric ward nurse might be asked to record all instances of aggression. The observer is again required to record objectively the actual behavioral incidents, and it is the difficult task of the reader to draw inferences from this record. It can be appreciated that the values and attitudes of the observer are clearly a factor in making the observations. For example, a supervisor who regards quantity of output as the most important indicator of good work performance will probably record different critical incidents than would a supervisor who is primarily concerned about quality of product.

Anecdotal data are perhaps more widely used in another context. Potential employers often attempt to ascertain the suitability of a job candidate through *references*—that is, by requesting letters of recommendation or making a telephone inquiry about the applicant. Reference checks are usually of limited use; they typically consist of positive but vague generalities. An early comprehensive study of reference checks made by the U.S. Civil Service Commission (Goheen & Mosel, 1959) indicated that such inquiries did not even identify disqualifying factors, such as alcoholism, which were readily uncovered by field investigations. Letters that are negative take on particular weight because of their rarity in actual practice. One exception to these findings was in work with the Peace Corps, where, in our personal experience, reference checks produced considerable frankness on the part of respondents, yielding useful comparative information about applicants. In particular, a significant relationship was demonstrated between quantified ratings of reference checks and overseas success (Stein, 1966).

SUMMARY

Behavioral approaches to assessment are consistent with the view that important determinants of human behavior are to be found in environmental variables as well as personal variables, and, more specifically, in the interaction between person and environment. Behavioral assessment procedures have been widely used for many years in industrial and organizational psychology, but their widespread use in clinical contexts is relatively new. In clinical assessment, covert behaviors (thoughts and feelings) tend to be included within the general definition of behavior, and attention is also given to gathering information about the variables (antecedents and consequences) thought to be controlling the behavior. Two basic steps in all behavioral assessment are (a) selecting and defining the behavior of interest and (b) conducting systematic observation and recording. For clinical uses, further steps include observation of controlling variables, behavioral formulation, and design of an appropriate treatment strategy.

Observation can involve complex behaviors as long as they are defined in operational terms. Sampling and recording procedures must be specified in advance; a common procedure is time sampling, using a predetermined schedule. Behaviors may be observed according to either frequency or duration. Naturalistic observation refers to observing and recording the behavior of interest exactly as it occurs in real life. Difficulties include its cost, the reactive effects of measurement, and possible invasion of privacy. Reactive effects can be reduced through participant observation.

Controlled observations, also referred to as situational tests, involve structured or laboratory settings. Employers have used them for personnel assessment purposes for many years. One notable technique involving structured interaction is the leaderless group discussion, in which a small group of people are called on to discuss a specific topic. An opportunity is thus provided for the observation of interpersonal characteristics such as leadership and social poise. Clinical uses of structured interaction have included the assessment of couples, families, and parent–child interactions. In role-playing tests, the situation is more obviously simulated, but the subject is asked to respond as though in real life. Uses of role-playing tests have included the assessment of social skills, assertiveness, and job-related behaviors. Experimental analogs involve laboratory situations that are arranged to duplicate the salient components of the real-life problem situations under highly structured conditions. Specific fears, such as phobias of snakes, spiders, and public speaking, have been assessed in this manner. Physiological assessment has also been employed for clinical purposes in the measurement of blood pressure, heart rate, and sexual and other responses correlated with psychophysiological arousal. Lie detection tests also involve psychophysiological assessment.

Self-observation, despite traditional criticisms of this procedure, is becoming more widely used and can be viewed as a learnable skill. Structured procedures include the use of notebooks and tally cards. Many methodological difficulties remain to be solved, particularly the reactive effects of measurement. General criticisms of all behavioral observation procedures include the inadequate attention that has been paid to basic psychometric considerations such as reliability and validity.

Unsystematic observations are also employed in assessment. An observer might keep an anecdotal record, in which everything is noted that appears significant in daily contact with the individual. In the critical-incident technique, behavior that the observer considers particularly illustrative of the individual's behavior is noted. Letters of reference also constitute unsystematic observations about interpersonal behavior. Problems of the representativeness of the behavior reported are an obvious drawback in this approach.

CHAPTER SIX

Biographical Data and Interviews

The use of biographical information regarding recent and current behavioral events forms the very core of the traditional assessment process in a wide variety of applications. In selecting from among job applicants, for example, the hiring officer typically gathers background information and then interviews to get a "feel" for the person. The traditional procedure for diagnosing medical diseases has been to ask questions about previous health status and then to assess current complaints. In the mental health area, diagnosis has traditionally been based on a current status interview and an extended case history.

Research findings in the technology of assessment over the past four decades, discussed in Chapter Eight, have conclusively demonstrated the great importance of *structure* and *objectivity* in gathering personal data. The use of structured instruments for gathering biographical data and for coding interviews has been an integral part of assessment in personnel selection for many years; however, their introduction into the mental health assessment field is more recent. Another relatively new development is the blurring of a conceptual distinction between biographical or historical data, on the one hand, and current status or recent data, on the other. The traditional distinction between written self-report methods versus interview methods of data collection is also being eroded to some extent. For convenience in presentation, the use of biographical information (which usually involves written self-report methods) is reviewed, and then interview procedures are discussed. Because these categories are not mutually exclusive, there is some degree of overlap in the two sections.

BIOGRAPHICAL INFORMATION

The predictive power of biographical data has been well established. Studies in both personnel and clinical fields show that it is comparable or even superior to the use of formal tests (e.g., Childs & Kleinoski, 1986; Stokes, Mumford, & Owens, 1989). A traditional approach in personnel selection is the weighted biographical data sheet (England, 1961), where it is assumed that personal history items, obtainable from a formal written application blank, have predictive value for success or failure in a particular occupational setting. The items can be *demographic* (such as age, sex, marital status, and number of dependents), *experiential* (such as number of schools attended, age when first married, number of jobs held, and arrest record), or *behavioral* (such as recreational pursuits, hobbies, current reading matter, and consumption of alcohol). Items that correlate with some criterion of success or failure are identified statistically and are given differential numerical weights according to how predictive they are. In operational use, applications are "scored" according to these weights, and applicants are accepted or rejected depending on whether their totals surpass a cutting point previously established by empirical means. This procedure closely resembles the development of empirically derived personality inventories, such as the MMPI.

The weighted biographical data technique was successfully applied to the selection of life insurance salesperson as early as 1919. Using nine personal history items, with weights ranging from -2 to $+3$ and a cutting score of $+4$ on the complete blank, Goldsmith (1922) reported that 84% of the successful salespeople would have been selected and 54% of the unsuccessful ones would have been rejected. During World War II, scores on the Air Force Biographical Data Blank were found to correlate .30 with pilot success (Guilford, 1947). More recently, indexes on biographical data have been shown to correlate with Holland's six-factor typology of occupations (Eberhardt & Muchinsky, 1984), and also to predict job performance for a wide range of occupational areas (Owens, 1983). For example, James, Ellison, Fox, and Taylor (1974) demonstrated the use of biographical data to predict artistic performance, and Helmreich, Bakeman, and Radloff (1973) used such data to predict performance in Navy distress training. Using biographical data, Hough (1984) developed an *accomplishment record* that predicted success as an attorney in a federal agency. Hough's research supports the notion that the "habit of achievement" can be tapped by a standard, thorough analysis of a person's biographical data. This is a useful strategy in selecting professional people, who often resist psychological testing and insist that "My record speaks for itself." The research of Hough and others suggests that reliance on their record is valid.

Owens and Henry (1966) surveyed the literature on the successful use of biographical data to predict creativity in a variety of work settings. The criteria for successful performance in such studies included job tenure or longevity, productivity, amount of absenteeism, and size of salary. Because these criteria are not always highly correlated, it is important for investigators to decide which criterion is of primary importance in a particular setting.

There is controversy about the need for continual cross-validation or rechecking of the accuracy of biographical predictors. One study (Hughes, Dunn, & Baxter, 1956) reported that the usefulness of a weighted application blank "disappeared" within two years after it was put into operational use. It was surmised that the field management staff, who knew the item weights, were leading or guiding the applicants so that their blank would "pass" the cutting score. On the other hand, Brown (1978) demonstrated that a scoring key developed in 1933 was still valid 45 years later.

Another major application of the biographical or personal history data method is in psychopathology. Such information has traditionally formed an important basis for prediction and decisions about clients in mental health settings. Let us review some of these applications, both early and recent.

It has long been noted that patients in mental hospitals, especially those diagnosed as schizophrenic, differ in prognosis: some show rather prompt and good recovery, and others achieve little or no change. Beginning with the work of Wittman (1941) at Elgin State Hospital, a number of investigators have attempted to identify particular aspects of case history or biographical data that are associated with good and poor prognosis in schizophrenia. In general, schizophrenics with good prognosis (who subsequently recover) are found to have been better adjusted prior to the onset of the illness. They had less family psychopathology, more satisfactory heterosexual experiences, better vocational adjustment, and more general stability than those with poor prognosis (who recover very slowly or not at all). The terms *reactive* and *process* schizophrenia were used more or less synonymously with good and poor prognosis, respectively.

Zigler and Phillips (1960) extended this work by developing a formal biographical data measure of premorbid adjustment level. Their procedure was based on six personal history variables: (a) age, (b) measured intelligence, (c) education, (d) occupational level, (e) employment history, and (f) marital status. These variables were used to produce a composite measure of *social competence,* which was found to be related to the type of symptoms shown by the patients. Those with higher social competence scores tended to show symptoms that could be regarded as "turning against the self," and those with lower scores tended to show symptoms indicative of "avoidance of others" or "self-indulgence and turning against others."

From these and further findings, Zigler and Phillips (1962) concluded that the reactive-process distinction in schizophrenia might be better regarded as a social competence or social maturity dimension that could be assessed through personal history data, and that this dimension was potentially applicable to all of psychopathology rather than to schizophrenia alone. The importance of premorbid functioning in assessing mental disorder was formally recognized by its inclusion as a separate source of diagnostic information in the third and fourth editions of the *Diagnostic and Statistical Manual of Mental Disorders* (American Psychiatric Association, 1980, 1994). Specifically, Axis IV involves a formal rating scale for assessing a patient's level of premorbid functioning over the prior year.

Computers have made complex multivariate statistical procedures available and feasible. By combining them with the computer's ability to conveniently handle large data sets, an increasing number of researchers in mental health have focused on biographical data in their search for the origins of behavior disorders. This work has led to some important discoveries that have implications for prevention. For example, from a series of studies on biographical and other factors related to sexual assault, it has been concluded that some key variables distinguishing rapists and nonrapists are *attitudinal* in nature (Malamuth, Sockloskie, Koss, & Tanaka, 1991; Stermac, Segal, & Gillis, 1990). These attitudes, in turn, are related to distinct types of childhood situations and experiences, such as delinquency, hostile home environment, and the nature of sexual and sex-role behaviors modeled in the home. Other important research involving the use of biographical information as assessment data includes the study of the developmental pathways leading to externalizing problems in children, such as conduct disorders (McMahon, 1994), and to internalizing problems (Ollendick & King, 1994).

The relationship between stressful life events and mental health disorders is being increasingly studied as a research area in its own right. Some initial work in this area was done by Langner and Michael (1963), who sought to identify early stressful events in a person's life that were related to later difficulties. Influenced by the writings of Adolf Meyer, interest shifted to a focus on more recent events—within the previous 3, 6, or 12 months—as predictors of current mental health and general stress level. For example, Holmes and Rahe (1967) asked subjects to rate a number of life events according to the amount and duration of change in their accustomed pattern of life that would result from each event. These authors' Social Readjustment Rating Scale is a list of mean readjustment values for 43 different life events. The item "death of a spouse" was set at a value of 100, "pregnancy" was valued at 40, "change in residence" at 20, and "jail term" at 63. Subsequent researchers have extended the work of Holmes and Rahe into the development of other procedures for assessing stresses associated with life events. For example, Coddington (1972) studied life events as an etiological factor in diseases of children, and Kobasa (1979) attempted to explain why life stresses led to disorders in some people but not others. Kobasa found distinct personality differences between the two groups, which she characterized as differences in *hardiness*.

Instruments based on biographical data have been developed for the assessment of a variety of other specific characteristics. For example, Lanyon (1967a) developed a 20-item self-report questionnaire to measure social competence in male college students. Sample items from this questionnaire are shown in Figure 6.1. Validity was established by showing the relationship of scores to other measures of social effectiveness, including ratings by peers.

Another quantified instrument is the Survey of Heterosexual Interactions (SHI), reported by Twentyman and McFall (1975). The SHI, a written self-report measure of heterosexual avoidance in shy males, was derived after pilot study interviews with college females. It includes a biographical section, containing items about subjects' past dating behavior, and a section with questions assessing their ability to initiate and carry out interactions with women in specific social situations. A list of other instruments for specific functions has been developed by Haynes and Wilson (1979). One additional area is the assessment of children through biographical data reported by teachers and parents. This work is discussed further in Chapter Ten.

Multiscale Instruments

In response to the promise of biographical data as a source of assessment information, attention was turned to the development of structured

2. How many *different* girls did you date *up to the end* of your senior year in high school? <u>2 and more</u>

4. How frequently do you date at present? <u>more often than once a month</u>

5. How old were you when you began to date regularly? <u>up to and including 17</u>

6. How many serious physical illnesses have you had during your lifetime (those that have incapacitated you for 2 weeks or more)? <u>0 or 1</u>

8. Have you ever made a trip as much as 200 miles away from home (without your parents or other guardian) where you stayed overnight, *other than* visiting relatives? <u>yes</u> (yes or no)

9. Have you ever made such a trip as much as 1,000 miles away from home without a parent or other guardian? <u>yes</u> (yes or no)

10. How do you approach your school assignments?

    <u>X</u> Get them done ahead of schedule

    <u>X</u> Do them in the last few days, but always get them in on time

    _____ Rush them at the last minute, and sometimes get them in late

            Have habitual problems with getting them done on time, in spite of

    _____ adequate ability

11. How many times, in your lifetime, have you been spoken to by a policeman for any possible *traffic* offense, except parking? <u>0–3</u>

13. Who usually buys (i.e., selects) your clothes?

    <u>X</u> I do

    _____ my mother does (or similar person)

    _____ sometimes I do; sometimes my mother does

14. With how many social, recreational, or organizational activities were you affiliated during your last year in high school? <u>2 and more</u>

15. Of the activities in No. 14 above, in how many of these (if any) did you hold an office? <u>1 and more</u>

17. Do you drink at all now? <u>yes</u> (yes or no)

18. Do you participate frequently and regularly (once a week or oftener) in some nonorganized athletic activity (e.g., play handball with Joe on Thursdays)? <u>yes</u> (yes or no)

19. How often do you go to church? <u>any response other than "never"</u>

Note—Criterion answers are checked or inserted. No more than 1 point is scored for any one question.

Figure 6.1   *Sample items from the Biographical Survey III for assessing social competence in college males.* (**Source: From Lanyon, 1967a, p. 497. Copyright 1967 by the American Psychological Association. Reprinted with permission of the publisher and author.**)

multiscale instruments for making comprehensive assessments. The Minnesota-Briggs History Record (MBHR; Briggs, 1959; Briggs, Rouzer, Hamburg, & Holman, 1972) was originally developed for use with a nonclient informant but was later revised to be a self-report instrument. Items on the MBHR concern the client's life history, including such diverse areas as education, food preferences, and marital status. The client's responses are weighted and scored on seven or eight content scales: family disunity, health awareness, introversion, and so on.

A comprehensive instrument using biographical data for mental health assessment is the Missouri Automated Psychiatric History (MAPS; Eaton, Sletten, Kitchen, & Smith, 1971). The MAPS consists of approximately 200 items to be completed by a relative. They cover nine general categories, including depression and suicide, work and interpersonal relationships, childhood and adolescence, and genetic factors. Procedural checks showed satisfactory answering for almost all respondents (Eaton, Altman, Scheff, & Sletten, 1970), and test–retest reliability was comparable to that found in other studies using relatives as informants. The MAPS was subsequently refined through factor-analytic procedures and shortened to a 98-item instrument titled the Community Adjustment Profile System (CAPS; Evenson, Sletten, Hedlund, & Faintich, 1974). Separate norms for men and women were developed for scales assessing ten separate areas of adjustment, and construct validity was demonstrated (Hedlund, Sletten, Evenson, Altman, & Cho, 1977).

The early promise of developing quantified biographical data instruments that are analogous to the more traditional personality questionnaires was not fulfilled. Rather, research attention in this area moved toward the development of more detailed and accurate criteria for the traditional psychiatric categories, as reflected in the publication of the DSM-III in 1980, DSM-III-R in 1987, and DSM-IV in 1994. These developments are discussed later in this chapter.

Subjective Approaches

In addition to the structured use of objective personal history forms and biographical data forms, life-history data are also widely used for the assessment of adjustment-related characteristics in an informal or subjective manner. When provided with this diverse array of data, the skilled clinician can develop many hypotheses about the personality characteristics of the respondent, in much the same fashion that many clinicians approach a projective test protocol. Besides the content of the form, potential personality information can be provided by assessing aspects such as how neatly the form has been completed, how completely information has been provided, and differences in how various questions are answered. Today's job applicant who lists under the category of Health History the fact that he or she had "measles—July 1987" presumably has rather different bodily concerns than applicants who fail to record this rather trivial event.

The content of many specific items on these forms can provide relevant material about the personality of the respondent. A youthful applicant who reports owning an expensive sports car, although showing a modest income, has different needs and values from a person who reports owning several large life insurance policies. At least one commercially available form, the Worthington Personal History Blank (Spencer & Worthington, 1952), was specifically designed to maximize the availability of such data by deliberately minimizing the amount of structure provided for completing the form. For example, there is no information about whether pencil or pen should be used, or how the applicant's name is to be written (last name or given name first). Other similar sources of written clinical data include letters, diaries, and other personal documents (Allport, 1961). The problem common to all of them lies in developing adequate methods for evaluating the usefulness and accuracy of the inferences drawn by the clinician.

As previously mentioned, structured but nonquantified biographical data forms have been used for many years to aid in the diagnosis of mental health patients. Sometimes they are viewed as short-cut alternatives to the traditional case history interview, and sometimes they are used as independent sources of data in their own right. Indeed, many if not all mental health facilities have their own structured questionnaires designed to fit the circumstances of their particular operation. In view of the widespread nature of this data source, it is surprising that there is little standardization. Among the few questionnaires commercially available are the Giannetti On-Line Psychological History (GOLPH; Giannetti, 1986) and the Personal History Checklist (Schinka, 1989), both of which can produce a computerized report that presents the information in narrative form. Analogous questionnaires are available on children and adolescents. These and other computer-based procedures are discussed in more detail in Chapter Eleven.

Problems and Cautions

Overall, the use of biographical or life history data for personality assessment has substantial research support. However, the problems inherent in this method should not be overlooked. For example, items could be subject to falsification because the "correct," or socially desirable, answer can readily be ascertained. The giveaway wording undoubtedly poses a problem in many situations, but distortion may not be as widespread as might be thought. For example, Walsh (1967, 1968) showed that data collected by the self-report method were acceptably accurate even when respondents were given financial incentives to distort their responses. In their more recent review of the literature, Sackett and Larson (1990) came to much the same conclusion. Other potential problems involve the coaching of applicants in personnel selection situations, and uncertainties as to how much continued cross-validation of scoring procedures is needed. Finally, the clinical or subjective use of the data depends heavily on the skill and acumen of the individual clinician, and this process requires careful and realistic self-monitoring.

INTERVIEWING

An interview can be regarded as a special kind of conversation between two people: the interviewer (a trained professional, who is attempting to understand and assess the other person) and the subject, or interviewee. An interview is distinguished from ordinary conversation by its purposive and probing nature. Much has been written on this complex and involved subject (e.g., Bingham & Moore, 1959; Fear, 1978; Haynes & Wilson, 1979; Richardson, Dohrenwend, & Klein, 1965; Sackett & Larson, 1990; Swan, 1989), and only a broad outline of the interview, as used for personality assessment purposes, will be given here. The role of the interview in personality change or psychotherapy will not be discussed.

Content and Style

There are many ways of categorizing the interview process—intent, type of interviewer, type of interviewee, degree of structure, and so on. Regardless of how they are categorized, all interviews develop two kinds of information: information yielded by the *content* of the subject's responses, and information revealed by the subject's *style,* or manner of relating to the interviewer.

Let us first examine how different purposes impact the content of the interview. In intake interviews in a social service agency or mental hospital, interviewers concentrate on clarifying patients' presenting complaints, their previous efforts to alleviate these problems, and their expectations from the present situation. The basic questions in an intake interview involve why each patient is at the agency and whether the agency can provide appropriate services. In an employment interview, the focus is on occupational and educational history, job and personal skills, motivation for the present job and for future advancement, and general suitability for work with the prospective employer. The basic question is: Does the applicant have the competencies to fill the job successfully? In a personal or case history interview, the interviewer's concern is to obtain a complete set of data about the individual for a specific purpose, such as research or psychotherapy treatment planning. The emphasis is on gathering as much data about the person as possible.

The style of an interviewee's responses similarly receives differential attention, depending on the purpose of the interview. Considerable overlap occurs among the types of interviews. The clinical intake interviewer is alert to signs of depression, dissociation, flight of ideas, and other symptoms of pathology. In an employment interview, attention is paid to the interviewee's presentation of self—his or her manner of dress, articulation, and clarity of expression—plus other evidence as to how well the candidate will fit into the culture of the organization. The case study interviewer observes the interviewee for congruence between the content of the interview and the interviewee's expressed affect, the completeness of reports in various areas of the person's life, and so on.

The important point is that, as with a biographical data sheet, the information supplied in an interview is both rich and useful for assessment and prediction. Indeed, it can be weighted and scored as in the weighted application blank procedure discussed previously. If this is the case, why should an interview be employed rather than the less time-consuming and more readily available application blank or written biographical data questionnaire?

Why Interview?

There are at least four reasons why a face-to-face interview might be preferred. First, the interview is less structured and more flexible than the application blank. Interviewers can vary their approach and their questions to maximize the possibility of openness and truthfulness. (This procedure would not be possible in a highly structured and standardized interview where a predetermined schedule must be followed, such as interviews carried out by public opinion polls.) Second, and related to the advantage of flexibility, the interviewer has an opportunity to establish *rapport,* or interpersonal warmth, before proceeding. Rapport is considered highly important in enhancing the quality of the information elicited in interviews. Third, in assessment for mental health purposes, the client may be sufficiently disturbed or confused as to require careful individual attention in order to successfully communicate the needed information. Fourth, interviewing provides an opportunity to observe the subject directly in an interpersonal situation. The interviewer can study the subject's reactions—both the obvious ones, like blushing, stammering, and long hesitations, and the subtler ones, like oblique, noninformative answers—all of which suggest that a fuller exploration of the topic under consideration would be more appropriate.

The interviewee's total behavior in response to the interview situation is a sample of his or her interpersonal skills and manner of approaching and dealing with others. Less structured interviews, which offer subjects few or no clear directions and permit great latitude in the areas to be covered, clearly provide interpersonal behavior samples. Interviewers can deliberately play a special role in order to evoke responses to particular kinds of "others." For example, they can be deliberately casual and noncommittal, warm and sympathetic, or cold and rejecting. During World War II, the

OSS Assessment Staff developed stress interviews in which subjects were ha-rassed, criticized, pressured, and otherwise made uncomfortable in order to evaluate their resistance to stress (OSS Assessment Staff, 1948).

The Interviewer

It is most important for all professional interviewers to know something about their social stimulus value and to be aware of the modal type of in-terpersonal situation they establish for their interviewees. There is consid-erable research evidence (Gottschalk & Gleser, 1969; Kaplan & Saccuzzo, 1993; Zedek, Tziner, & Middlestadt, 1983) that the large differences that exist among interviewers may be an important variable in clinical practice and research. For the interview to yield an interpersonal behavior sample that is useful for assessment purposes, considerable training and experi-ence on the part of the interviewer are required.

There is much evidence about the subtle cues that interviewers provide, many of which are not deliberate, and about how these cues tend to guide and bias the outcome of the interview (Sackett & Larson, 1990). Interview-ers may tend to avoid probing in areas in which they themselves are anxious (Bandura, Lipsher, & Miller, 1960). Interviewer biases contribute to the general concern that is often expressed about the utility of the interview as an assessment device.

Validity of the Interview

How valid are the predictions made from interview data? The quite large body of research on this topic, especially in the area of employment inter-viewing, is reviewed in Chapter Nine in the context of discussing personal-ity assessment in the workplace. The findings are briefly summarized here. Two large reviews of the research literature showed surprisingly good abil-ity of employment interviewers to predict on-the-job performance ratings (Huffcutt & Arthur, 1994; McDaniel, Whetzel, Schmidt, & Maurer, 1994). Predictions based on well-structured employment interviews were consis-tently more valid than those based on unstructured interviews. Although a comparable body of research on interviewing in mental health settings is not available, it is assumed that the same conclusions would apply.

Interview Rating Instruments

If the most valid use of the interview is obtained in structured contexts, then one output of the interview should be a formal, structured rating. After a careful review of the research literature, Sawyer (1966) concluded that the interviewer's most useful function was to provide ratings or judg-ments in as objective a manner as possible, using structured instruments developed for that purpose. In response to this mandate, there was a rapid development of structured interview procedures, in both clinical and employment interviewing. Many of the early clinical instruments were designed for computer scoring and interpretation, using some of the computer technology discussed in Chapter Eleven. Interview rating instruments can be of two types: (a) those that are designed to summarize the interview after it has been conducted, and (b) complete interview guides that are to be utilized as a format in conducting the interview.

Interview Summary Instruments. One of the best-known interview instruments is the Brief Psychiatric Rating Scale (BPRS; Overall & Gorham, 1962; Overall & Klett, 1972). Designed to provide a brief and reliable evaluation of symptomatology in hospitalized psychiatric patients, the BPRS consists of 16 ordered-category ratings scales, each representing a carefully selected dimension. The original idea was that each of the scales should represent a "primary dimension" of individual difference in psychiatric symptoms. All dimensions involve seven-point scales ranging from "not present" through "moderate" to "extremely severe." Examples are: somatic concern, anxiety, emotional withdrawal, conceptual disorganization, and guilt feelings. Overall and Klett (1972) later provided more extensive data on the BPRS, which continues to be used, primarily as a research instrument (e.g., Weideranders & Choate, 1994).

The availability and promise of computer technology in the early 1970s gave rise to the development of interview summary instruments that could potentially be incorporated into a comprehensive mental health assessment system. One such instrument is the Missouri Automated Mental Status Examination Checklist (MS; Hedland, Sletten, Evenson, Altman, & Cho, 1977; Sletten, Ernhart, & Ulett, 1970). This instrument consists of a series of rating scales that cover the following areas of function: general appearance, motor behavior, speech and thought, mood and affect, other emotional reactions, thought content, sensorium, intellect, and insight and judgment. The interviewer conducts a normal psychiatric interview in which patients are encouraged to tell their own stories in an atmosphere of interest and concern. Ratings on 3-point scales are made at the completion of the interview.

A somewhat similar instrument is the Mental Status Examination Record (MSER; Spitzer & Endicott, 1971), a four-page computer form designed to provide an objective record of the traditional mental status categories via 121 checklist items and 156 rating scales. Computer processing of the MSER yields a score on each of 20 derived scales: anger-negativism, hallucinations, somatic concern, judgment, and so on. These scales, derived from factor analysis of the MSER protocols of 2,000 subjects (MSIS, 1973), are said to provide rapid identification of patients' most severely affected domains of behavior.

Interview Guides. In contrast to the above instruments, which were designed to be completed after the interview, other instruments are intended as structured guides to be utilized by trained interviewers. The Psychiatric Anamnestic Record (PAR; Spitzer & Endicott, 1971; MSIS, 1973) is a highly structured interview schedule that can be administered by personnel with relatively little clinical experience, provided they are specifically trained with the schedule. The format is a four-page booklet containing multiple-choice questions and rating scales designed to cover the information that is usually included in a clinical case history. A major section deals with psychopathological signs and symptoms, judged over two time periods: (a) from age 12 up to the past month, and (b) within the past month. Another is the Current and Past Psychopathology Scales (CAPPS; Endicott & Spitzer, 1972), which contains a section for assessing a patient's current status and a "past" section relating to psychopathology, personality characteristics, and academic, occupational, and interpersonal adjustment. Because the CAPPS incorporates a highly structured interview schedule, it can be administered by any specifically trained person. The information for completing the CAPPS can be limited to a single source, such as the patient, or it can be based on case records or other informants. Output consists of standard scores on 26 factor-based symptom summary scales: 8 are derived from the "current" section, and 18 from the "past" section. The dimensions reflected in the factors include: current—disorganization, reality testing-social disturbance, and depression-anxiety; and past—manic, depression-anxiety, and organicity.

The computer-oriented instruments described above were, for the most part, constructed with adherence to basic psychometric principles and substantiated with reliability and validity studies. They represented a movement to advance the technology of clinical assessment in general. But an event occurred in 1980 that took the field in a somewhat different direction: the publication of a massive revision of the "official" psychiatric diagnostic manual, the American Psychiatric Association's *Diagnostic and Statistical Manual of Mental Disorders, Third edition,* or DSM-III (1980). In this volume and in the subsequent revisions (DSM-III-R, 1987, and DSM-IV, 1994), strenuous efforts were made to objectify the definitions of all recognized mental disorders and to provide reliable rules for determining their presence or absence. This mammoth task is underpinned by empirical findings and by programs of ongoing research in many different geographical locations.

As an example, the DSM-IV diagnostic definition for obsessive-compulsive disorder is reproduced in Figure 6.2. Note that the criteria are specific, referring to past and/or present behaviors/thoughts/feelings. Each set of diagnostic criteria is accompanied by a detailed introduction to the disorder, plus attempts to define behaviorally the terms utilized in the criteria. Although the criteria are based on the best available research and scholarship,

■ **DIAGNOSTIC CRITERIA FOR 300.3 OBSESSIVE-COMPULSIVE DISORDER**

A. Either obsessions or compulsions:

Obsessions as defined by (1), (2), (3), and (4):

(1) recurrent and persistent thoughts, impulses, or images that are experienced, at some time during the disturbance, as intrusive and inappropriate and that cause marked anxiety or distress

(2) the thoughts, impulses, or images are not simply excessive worries about real-life problems

(3) the person attempts to ignore or suppress such thoughts, impulses, or images, or to neutralize them with some other thought or action

(4) the person recognizes that the obsessional thoughts, impulses, or images are a product of his or her own mind (not imposed from without as in thought insertion)

Compulsions as defined by (1) and (2):

(1) repetitive behaviors (e.g., hand washing, ordering, checking) or mental acts (e.g., praying, counting, repeating words silently) that the person feels driven to perform in response to an obsession, or according to rules that must be applied rigidly

(2) the behaviors or mental acts are aimed at preventing or reducing distress or preventing some dreaded event or situation; however, these behaviors or mental acts either are not connected in a realistic way with what they are designed to neutralize or prevent or are clearly excessive

B. At some point during the course of the disorder, the person has recognized that the obsessions or compulsions are excessive or unreasonable. **Note:** This does not apply to children.

C. The obsessions or compulsions cause marked distress, are time consuming (take more than 1 hour a day), or significantly interfere with the person's normal routine, occupational (or academic) functioning, or usual social activities or relationships.

D. If another Axis I disorder is present, the content of the obsessions or compulsions is not restricted to it (e.g., preoccupation with food in the presence of an Eating Disorder; hair pulling in the presence of Trichotillomania; concern with appearance in the presence of Body Dysmorphic Disorder; preoccupation with drugs in the presence of a Substance Use Disorder; preoccupation with having a serious illness in the presence of Hypochondriasis; preoccupation with sexual urges or fantasies in the presence of a Paraphilia; or guilty ruminations in the presence of Major Depressive Disorder).

E. The disturbance is not due to the direct physiological effects of a substance (e.g., a drug of abuse, a medication) or a general medical condition.

Specify if:

With Poor Insight: if, for most of the time during the current episode, the person does not recognize that the obsessions and compulsions are excessive or unreasonable

Figure 6.2   Illustration of a DSM-IV diagnostic definition.

there is always a need for updating and perhaps for conceptual changes as new knowledge becomes available. Such progressions can be seen by examining the changes in the diagnostic categories for personality disorders and paraphilias (sexual deviations) across DSM-III, DSM-III-R, and DSM-IV. Overall, the definitional criteria are best viewed as structured guidelines for making clinical judgments on the diagnostic category or categories into which a patient best fits.

A full DSM diagnosis requires the clinician to consider the patient's characteristics in five separate areas, or *Axes*. Axes I and II contain the entire classification of mental disorders, Axis III refers to any physical disorders and conditions that might be relevant to the patient's mental condition, and Axis IV provides a seven-point rating scale for judging the severity of the patient's psychosocial stressors of the past year. Axis V utilizes the *Global Assessment of Functioning (GAF) Scale,* a rating scale for judging the patient's level of psychological, social, and occupational functioning currently and over the past year. The GAF scale from DSM-IV is shown in Figure 6.3.

There are fundamental similarities between the two basic directions—the development of objective instruments for collecting and processing biographical and interview information, and the increased formalization of diagnostic categories. Both involve greatly increased structure and definition of the important variables, plus the specification of objective procedures for gathering and processing the relevant information. One recent major advance, drawing directly on all of this work, is the development of structured interview guides for the collection and processing of data that enable DSM diagnoses to be made. The leading system is the *Structured Clinical Interview for DSM-III-R* or *SCID* (Spitzer, Williams, Gibbon, & First, 1990), an elaborate manual that presents "a semistructured interview for making the major Axis I and Axis II diagnoses" (p. 1).

Although the development of the SCID drew heavily on the work done in developing instruments such as the PAR and the CAPPS, there are two fundamental differences: (a) the SCID is not a computer-based instrument, and (b) its intended end product is not a normative description or scores on standardized scales, but a formal psychiatric diagnosis. It is expected that users of the SCID will be mental health professionals who are familiar with the DSM diagnostic criteria, experienced in asking useful questions to elicit relevant information, and specifically trained in the use of the SCID itself. In addition to the basic form of the SCID (the Patient Edition or SCID-P), there is an edition for nonpatients (the SCID-NP) and a separate instrument for evaluating personality disorders (the SCID-II). The SCID has an empirical basis of some 400 studies and is the subject of continuing research. It is not yet available for DSM-IV.

Another noteworthy interview guide for clinical purposes is the *Diagnostic Interview Schedule* (*DIS*; Robins, Helzer, Croughan, & Ratcliff, 1981). In contrast to the SCID, the DIS was explicitly designed to be administered by

| 100 | Superior functioning in a wide range of activities, life's problems never seem to get out of hand, is sought out by others because of his or her many positive qualities. No symptoms. |
| 91 | |

| 90 | Absent or minimal symptoms (e.g., mild anxiety before an exam), good functioning in all areas, interested and involved in a wide range of activities, socially effective, generally satisfied with life, no more than everyday problems or concerns (e.g., an occasional argument with family members). |
| 81 | |

| 80 | If symptoms are present, they are transient and expectable reactions to psychosocial stressors (e.g., difficulty concentrating after family argument); no more than slight impairment in social, occupational, or school functioning (e.g., temporarily falling behind in schoolwork). |
| 71 | |

| 70 | Some mild symptoms (e.g., depressed mood and mild insomnia) OR some difficulty in social, occupational, or school functioning (e.g., occasional truancy, or theft within the household), but generally functioning pretty well, has some meaningful interpersonal relationships. |
| 61 | |

| 60 | Moderate symptoms (e.g., flat affect and circumstantial speech, occasional panic attacks) OR moderate difficulty in social, occupational, or school functioning (e.g., few friends, conflicts with peers or co-workers). |
| 51 | |

| 50 | Serious symptoms (e.g., suicidal ideation, severe obsessional rituals, frequent shoplifting) OR any serious impairment in social, occupational, or school functioning (e.g., no friends, unable to keep a job). |
| 41 | |

| 40 | Some impairment in reality testing or communication (e.g., speech is at times illogical, obscure, or irrelevant) OR major impairment in several areas, such as work or school, family relations, judgment, thinking, or mood (e.g., depressed man avoids friends, neglects family, and is unable to work; child frequently beats up younger children, is defiant at home, and is failing at school). |
| 31 | |

| 30 | Behavior is considerably influenced by delusions or hallucinations OR serious impairment in communication or judgment (e.g., sometimes incoherent, acts grossly inappropriately, suicidal preoccupation) OR inability to function in almost all areas (e.g., stays in bed all day; no job, home, or friends). |
| 21 | |

| 20 | Some danger of hurting self or others (e.g., suicide attempts without clear expectation of death; frequently violent; manic excitement) Or occasionally fails to maintain minimal personal hygiene (e.g., smears feces) OR gross impairment in communication (e.g., largely incoherent or mute). |
| 11 | |

| 10 | Persistent danger of severely hurting self or others (e.g., recurrent violence) OR persistent inability to maintain minimal personal hygiene OR serious suicidal act with clear expectation of death. |
| 1 | |

| 0 | Inadequate information. |

Figure 6.3 The Global Assessment of Functioning scale from the DSM-IV.

laypersons who are specifically trained in its use. It is appropriate for studies involving very large numbers of subjects, such as in epidemiological research. Questions, which are asked verbatim, cover biographical aspects of the respondent's life, and events and symptoms experienced during recent years. Concerns have been raised about the appropriateness of using non-professional personnel for diagnostic interviewing. Some studies on the reliability of the DIS when compared with its use by professionals have tended to be satisfactory (e.g., Helzer & Robins, 1988), but questions about its reliability have been raised by other researchers (e.g., Folstein et al., 1985). Instruments similar to the DIS include the Diagnostic Interview Schedule for Children (DISC; Costello, Edelbrock, & Costello, 1985) and the Diagnostic Interview for Children and Adolescents (DICA; Herjanic & Campbell, 1977).

There have been similar developments for employment interviewing as well. A number of programs, such as SmartHire: Competency-Based Interviewing for Windows (Psychological Consultants to Management, 1995), assist the interviewer to systematically develop a structured employment interview. These programs typically start with a job analysis to determine the personal/interpersonal competencies required for on-the-job success. Once these skills have been identified, the program leads the interviewer through a choice of behaviorally based questions to be asked during the interview. In SmartHire, which is based on the "Big Five" personality traits, if Conscientiousness is determined to be a specially important personal skill for success on the job, the interviewer could select from 22 questions about facets of Conscientiousness. An example of such a question might be: "Tell about a time when you had to exert an extraordinary amount of energy to get a job done within a time frame." Virtually all of these programs, however, involve proprietary materials and have no published research.

QUANTIFICATION OF OBSERVATIONS

This chapter and the previous one have concentrated on a rather holistic approach to the data obtained in behavioral observations and interviews, and passing references have been made to rating procedures and other attempts at quantifying the data. Let us now examine in greater detail these quantification procedures and some of the inherent problems involved in using them.

A *rating scale* is a form or device by which observers can record their observations or judgments about the behavior of another person in some predetermined, ordered fashion. Rating scales may be filled out either during or after the observations, which can be complete and wide ranging or incomplete and circumscribed. In principle, just about any data can be quantified by rating procedures, although consideration must be given to issues such as interrater agreement and possible rater biases. The form of the rating scale for personality assessment may range from a simple list of adjectives to be checked (e.g., Gough & Heilbrun, 1983) to scales of generalized characteristics such as overall psychological adjustment or extraversion-introversion.

A common procedure for making such ratings employs a graphic rating scale. In its simplest form, shown in Figure 6.4, respondents mark a point on the line between two extremes that best correspond to the subject's characteristics. It is left to the rater to determine what is meant by different degrees of the dimension, in this case introversion-extraversion. Sometimes, as shown in Figure 6.4, each end of the rating scale is "anchored" with an extended description to characterize each extreme of the dimension. Raters may also be instructed that the different points between the extremes should be taken to represent equal intervals on the dimension. Sometimes the raters are asked to circle one of the numbers, and sometimes the instructions permit the raters to place a mark anywhere at all along the continuum. In the latter case, a number (either a fractional number or the nearest whole number) would be assigned later to each rating.

A rating scale can be unipolar or bipolar, depending on the dimension being assessed. The trait of introversion-extraversion is considered bipolar in nature, so that the "neutral" point of the rating scale (Figure 6.4) occurs in the middle. The numbers representing this dimension could also have appropriately been 2, 1, 0, 1, 2. Other concepts, such as anxiety, leadership, sales ability, and schizophrenia, may be unipolar. In these instances, there is no "neutral" point in the middle of the scale, and the low end of the dimension is simply the absence of the characteristic of interest. A more sophisticated form of rating scale contains anchoring descriptions along all parts of the scale. A good example is the Global Assessment of Functioning Scale (American Psychiatric Association, 1994), represented in Figure 6.3. The information needed to make the GAF rating can come from any

1	2	3	4	5
Introverted				*Extraverted*
Careful				Enjoys excitement
Thorough				Impulsive
Quiet				Loud
Thoughtful				Socially outgoing
Internalizes feelings				Active
Overcontrolled				Verbally facile
Contemplative				Externalizes feelings
Conscientious				Unreliable
Etc.				Etc.

Figure 6.4   Graphic rating scale for the trait of introversion-extraversion.

source, such as case records or a direct interview with the patient. Data reported by Endicott, Spitzer, Fleiss, and Cohen (1976) on an earlier version of the GAF scale showed satisfactory reliability and adequate sensitivity to change over time.

Ordinarily, a range of five to seven points on a structured rating scale is regarded as adequate to produce a sufficient dispersion of ratings for discriminating among subjects. If only a few judges are available, a rating technique allows more opportunity for differentiating among subjects than does a dichotomous task such as an adjective checklist. On the latter, items (such as "aggressive" or "flexible") are either endorsed or not endorsed as descriptive of the subject, without regard to different degrees of applicability. Satisfactory discrimination on an adjective checklist can be obtained when a larger number of judges are involved, and the subject's "score" on an item can be the number of times it is checked by the pool of judges.

Rating scales tend to produce fairly good interjudge agreement, and they are widely used in personality research because of the paucity of readily available measures of behaviors or traits under study. However, certain kinds of rater errors are particularly bothersome and should not be ignored. Similar errors are doubtless involved in all personality assessment, but they are seen most clearly in their effects on ratings. One is the tendency to produce *constant* errors or biases in filling out a rating scale. Thus, one rater may rarely or never use low ratings, and another may rarely use high ratings. A related problem is the *generosity error,* where raters systematically tend to give subjects highly favorable evaluations. Such ratings are of little value in discriminating satisfactorily between individuals. Another related problem exists when raters have only limited opportunities to observe the subject and therefore may not have enough data to make true ratings. Under these circumstances, the so-called *halo effect* may apply, where the rater overgeneralizes from the evidence available, especially if it tends to be positive.

A number of procedures have been developed to reduce rating errors. Constant errors can be reduced by statistically transforming raters' scores into some type of standard score that will compensate for their constant errors and, to a lesser degree, for their leniency errors. Asking for specific behavioral or anecdotal data to support a particular rating is also an effective technique for reducing these errors. The halo effect can be reduced in the same way, especially if there is an opportunity for the rater to use a category like "insufficient data to make this rating." The *forced-choice* technique (Edwards, 1959; Scott, 1968) also reduces rating errors. The rater is forced to choose which of two traits or phrases, closely matched on favorability, is the more descriptive of the subject.

When there are several subjects to evaluate, the observer can be asked to rank-order the individuals on the trait dimension under consideration. When the group to be ranked is rather large, they can be ordered into a specified distribution along the trait dimension, such as a seven- or nine-point forced-normal distribution. A "forced" distribution means that the number of individuals to be placed at each of the seven or nine points is specified in advance, and "forced normal" means that these numbers are specified in such way that the resulting distribution will be approximately the same shape as the normal curve, with relatively few subjects at the extreme points of the distribution and most of the group in the center. Such ranking procedures, however, are ipsative; that is, they only provide relative data about the group under study and do not indicate how the group would compare with any other group along some absolute dimension of the trait, or how an individual from the group would compare with an individual from another group.

An important use of forced-distribution ranking procedures is the *Q-sort* (Block, 1978, 1994; Stephenson, 1953). The observer is given a deck of cards, each of which contains a single statement, such as "is basically anxious" or "communicates ideas clearly and effectively." The judge, who may also be the subject (in which case the Q-sort becomes a self-report measure), is then asked to rank-order the statements from most descriptive to least descriptive of the subject, using a forced-normal distribution for the ranking.

The California Q-sort (Block, 1961, 1994) is a list of items specifically developed to assess personality and psychological adjustment. The items have themselves been rated (weighted) by trained clinicians for adjustment, so that a Q-sort for a particular person can be scored quantitatively for adjustment. A children's version of the California Q-sort has also been developed (Block & Block, 1980; Caspi et al., 1992).

In another use of the Q-sort to assess personality, the subject is asked to sort the cards once as "you actually are" and then again as "you would like to be." The discrepancy between these actual-self and ideal-self Q-sorts has been used in psychotherapy research as a criterion measure for personality change (Rogers & Dymond, 1954), with the expectation that successful psychotherapy would reduce the discrepancy. Marks, Seeman, and Haller (1974), in another interesting use of the Q-sort, developed an "atlas" of Q-sort statements that are empirically correlated with various MMPI profiles.

The Q-sort method is a useful technique for both clinical and research purposes, especially for the description of complex or global personality attributes, but several problems should be noted. One problem concerns whether any manageable group of short statements can satisfactorily describe complex behavior or personality functioning. Another problem is created by the assumption that the descriptive statements can be "forced" into a normal distribution without producing biases. A third problem involves the fact that unless the Q-sort employed offers a comprehensive and unbiased coverage of the personality domain of interest, comparisons among the Q-sorts of different subjects will not yield satisfactory results.

Peer assessment is the process by which people with the same status, such as classmates or fellow workers, judge each other on particular characteristics. Kane and Lawler (1978) identified three related methods of peer assessment: (a) rankings, (b) ratings, and (c) nominations. Peer *ranking* has been relatively little researched but has the potential for being the most discriminating method because of its particular psychometric properties.

Peer *rating*, a more commonly used procedure, is generally based on extended observation in real-life situations. Peer ratings often produce evaluations of the subject that may be rather different from other judgments, a situation that reflects the different values of the peer and superordinate (or subordinate) subcultures. A rebellious college student who leads student protests may be seen as a leader by peers but as a malcontent and troublemaker by professors. Both kinds of information are relevant, but perhaps for different purposes. Peer ratings appear to be particularly useful for feedback purposes but tend to be less valid and more subject to biases than the other methods (Kane & Lawler, 1978).

In the peer *nomination* technique, each member of the peer group is asked to list or nominate a fixed number of persons who are group members and who are most prominent or visible in particular ways. As part of Peace Corps selection procedures, for example, all members of a training group were asked to nominate the five trainees they would: (a) most like to be assigned with overseas, (b) least like to be assigned with overseas, (c) regard as the most successful, and so on. Unpublished research on Peace Corps peer ratings indicates that they consistently predicted overseas success. Similar findings of the predictive efficiency of peer nominations were reported for military personnel (Downey, Medland, & Yates, 1976) and a variety of other occupational groups. The peer nomination technique appears to have the highest reliability and validity of the three methods, but serious problems, especially in the context of selection, involve the high degree of anxiety about the task and the antagonism toward the investigator that may be aroused.

A close variant of the nomination technique is the sociometric rating, originally developed many years ago by Moreno (1934) and used to study the social structure of small groups. All persons in such a group are asked to choose one or more other group members whom they would like to work with, play with, sit near, and so forth. They also designate those whom they wish to avoid. The patterns of likes and dislikes are then given pictorial representation by plotting them on a sociogram. From the sociogram, the small cliques, the leader or "star," and the social isolates within the group can be identified.

For young children, nominations can be obtained by another early method, the "guess who" technique (Hartshorne & May, 1929). Members of the group are asked to "guess who" is the class athlete (the one who plays games best) or who is the class bully (the one who is always annoying or picking on the other children). The number of times each child is nominated under such rubrics constitutes his or her score on that dimension.

Peer ratings are readily obtainable, and they represent a quite useful approach to personality measurement. In the past, they have been employed primarily in research and in personnel selection. For other purposes, such as clinical assessment, they have rarely been used in spite of the important vantage they seem to offer in understanding individual behavior.

The *semantic differential* (Osgood, 1952; Osgood, Suci, & Tannenbaum, 1957) is a rating technique originally developed as a tool for assessing the meaning of concepts. The individual rates the concept or person on a series of seven-point bipolar adjective scales, such as simple–complicated or cruel–kind. Factor-analytic studies have shown that the majority of the adjective scales employed in these ratings can be summarized in three factors: (a) *evaluation* (which incorporates adjective scales such as good–bad and kind–cruel), (b) *activity* (e.g., fast–slow and active–passive), and (c) *potency* (e.g., strong–weak and large–small). Wide use has not been made of this tool as a means of clinical personality description; rather, it has been utilized as a research instrument. One early example of research use is Nunnally's (1961) extensive study of public attitudes toward concepts in the field of mental health. More recently, Intieri, von Eye, and Kelly (1995) demonstrated the utility of an Aging Semantic Differential, a semantic differential instrument developed to measure attitudes and negative stereotypes toward older people, and showed that its content was best represented by four factors rather than the traditional three-factor structure.

SUMMARY

Biographical data regarding recent and current events are utilized for assessment in a wide variety of applications. Research in the technology of assessment has demonstrated the great importance of using structured and objective procedures in gathering such data. Considerable use has been made of biographical data for personality assessment purposes, particularly in personnel selection. Personal history data as provided on a formal job application blank can be examined impressionistically as a basis for forming hypotheses about a candidate. The weighted biographical data sheet provides an empirical approach in which a score is determined from weights assigned to various personal and biographical items.

Personal history data have also been used empirically to predict the outcome of schizophrenia. Other specific uses include assessment of social competence, shyness, and children's problems, and understanding of the antecedents of sexually assaultive behavior. Stable relationships have been shown between stressful life events and mental health disorders. A number of structured, multiscale instruments based on biographical data were developed as an integral aspect of an attempt to use computerized assessment systems for mental health purposes on a large scale. Intuitive or projective interpretations can also be made from an individual's biographical data sheet, although the accuracy of such an approach is not proven. On-line computer procedures for self-report of biographical data have also been developed. The question of possible falsification of self-reports needs to be considered, although it is generally not thought to be a serious problem.

Interviews can provide two kinds of information, based on the content and the style of the subject's responses. The nature of the interview depends on the particular purpose for which it is designed. An interview may be preferred over self-report methods of gathering information because of its flexibility and its opportunities to establish rapport, to deal with unexpected situations, and to observe reactions and overall behavior. Interviewers should be aware of their own social stimulus value and possible biases. Extensive research findings have shown satisfactory validities from employment interviews, particularly structured procedures, in predicting on-the-job performances.

Two kinds of structured interview rating instruments are available. Summary instruments are designed to produce a capsule version of the interview after completion. A brief mental health instrument of this kind is the Brief Psychiatric Rating Scale; a more extensive one is the Missouri Automated Mental Status Examination Checklist. Interviewer guides, intended as structured guides to be utilized in conducting the interview, require trained interviewers but not necessarily professional personnel. The third and fourth editions of the *Diagnostic and Statistical Manual of Mental Disorders* (DSM) can be viewed as general interview guides for assessing psychopathology; a full DSM diagnosis may utilize additional information and requires summary ratings on five separate scales. More specific interview guides geared to the DSM system include the Structured Clinical Interview for DSM and the Diagnostic Interview Schedule. Similar guides are available for employment interviewing.

How are systematic observations quantified? Perhaps the most common technique is some variant of the rating scale, an approach that can be applied to just about any kind of data. Problems with rating scales include possible rater biases or constant errors, unwillingness to give low or undesirable ratings, and the "halo effect," where a rater overgeneralizes from little evidence. One method for reducing rater errors is the forced-choice technique, in which the rater is forced to choose which of two descriptions, matched on favorability, is the more applicable. A variant of this technique is the Q-sort, in which the rater arranges a series of cards, each containing a personality statement, in order from least to most descriptive of the individual. Peer assessment, the process by which people with the same status judge each other on particular characteristics, can involve rankings, ratings, or nominations. The semantic differential, another rating procedure originally developed as a tool for assessing the meaning of concepts, also has applicability in personality assessment.

CHAPTER SEVEN

Psychometric Considerations

The first six chapters have provided an overview of the nature of personality assessment, its history, and the common methods for performing it. This chapter deals in more detail with the concepts of *reliability* and *validity,* which are basic to an adequate understanding of the scope and limitations of different assessment methods. Also discussed are systematic irrelevancies, or *response distortions.* These distortions, which affect the utility of personality assessment procedures, include the problem of both deliberate and unconscious attempts to make a favorable (or unfavorable) impression.

Reliability, as its name implies, has to do with the reproducibility or dependability of a measure. As a very simple example, let us say that yesterday we have measured a child's height as 48.3 inches. Today, somebody else measures the same child and gives a report of 48.4 inches. The two measures are in good agreement with each other; that is, we would consider the initial measurement of the child's height to have been verified or reproduced. The .1-inch discrepancy reflects the fact that repeated measurements almost always will be slightly inconsistent or unreliable, and our acceptance of the result indicates that the inconsistency is not large enough to negate its usefulness. Thus, the discrepancy of .1 inch is so small under these circumstances that it can be regarded as inconsequential. In other physical measurements, however, where the tolerance levels are quite small, as in an engine cylinder, such a difference would be important and a higher level of reliability of measurement would be required.

Reliability is not the same as precision. Precision refers to the exactness with which the measurement can be specified; thus, a measuring procedure that permits us to report to the nearest one-thousandth of an inch would be more precise than one permitting a report only to the nearest one-tenth of an inch. A mechanical gauge that gave a reading of 2.432 inches would have precision to one-thousandth of an inch, but if the gauge gave a second reading of 2.381 inches under the same conditions, the reliability of the measurement would be nowhere near the precision of which the instrument is capable.

The requirement that measurements be made "accurately enough" is also applicable to personality assessment. Compared with the measurement of physical characteristics such as height, personality measurement has always been rather sloppy and therefore somewhat unreliable. Thus, any decision to utilize a personality assessment device should focus on its reliability. Such instruments ordinarily have some index of reliability available for potential users. We shall return to the matter of reliability in a moment.

Personality measurement has an additional difficulty that is not present with common physical measurements, which have generally agreed-on standards against which measurements are made. There is no question that a yardstick (or a meterstick) is appropriate for measuring linear distances, such as body height. In personality assessment, however, questions are frequently raised about the legitimacy of the measuring device for assessing or evaluating the dimension under scrutiny. For example, can one really measure depression by counting the number of achromatic color responses given on the Rorschach? In this case, not only is there a question involving a reliable count of these responses but there is a further and more serious problem of demonstrating that counting achromatic color responses results in a legitimate measure of depression, in the way that the markings on a yardstick result in a valid measure of height. (The legitimacy or validity of the measuring instruments employed also becomes a problem in physical measurement where very high degrees of precision are required.)

Because it is necessary to be able to measure something with adequate reliability before we can determine whether the measure is, in fact, related to the concept of concern, we discuss reliability first. A practical guide to both reliability and validity, the *Standards for Educational and Psychological Testing,* has been issued by the American Psychological Association for many years (e.g., American Educational Research Association/American Psychological Association/National Council on Measurement in Education, 1985), and this guide should be studied carefully by all persons who are actively engaged in either the construction or the use of personality assessment devices. An analogous guide for specific use in the area of personnel selection is published by the American Psychological Association's Division of Industrial-Organizational Psychology (1980). The latter guide pays particular attention to issues of validity and criterion development, and is a valuable reference source on those topics.

RELIABILITY

Reliability refers to the repeatability or dependability of measurement. In a hypothetical situation where the measuring procedure is known to be completely reliable, it would be assumed that any change in the obtained measure reflected a true change in the attribute under study. Thus, in such a system, an increase of one pound on a scale would indicate that the object has gained exactly one pound of weight; similarly, an increase in a score on a depression scale would indicate that the respondent now is more depressed. *Reliability* is the more generic term; the terms *consistency* and *stability* are employed to describe instrument-related and time-related reliability, respectively.

Consistency refers to the agreement that is obtained by simultaneously using two or more instruments (e.g., scales, rulers, or tests). Any measuring instrument or set of instruments may be regarded as being drawn from a large population of such instruments (real or hypothetical) that might have been used to measure this particular attribute. Consistency is usually evaluated by simultaneous testing with another instrument or instruments, preferably selected at random from the available population of such instruments. Although this poses little problem in the measurement of physical dimensions such as height or weight, it raises some difficult problems in personality assessment. We shall return to these problems shortly.

Stability refers to the accuracy of the obtained measurement over time. Retesting over time may involve consistency as well as stability, if another instrument is used to make the second measurement. If the same instrument is used on both occasions, a direct assessment of the stability of the measurement can be made. Failure to obtain complete reliability is thus a consequence of the inconsistencies or errors that are a function of changes occurring in the system over time, or of differences associated with the particular instrument used, or both.

In general, reliability refers to many kinds of evidence that attempt to describe the agreement among measurement operations. Each bit of evidence emphasizes or focuses on a certain source of disagreement or error and may overlook others. Personality measurement involves taking a sample of behavior at a particular time on a particular day in response to a particular set of stimuli, with the responses recorded by a particular examiner according to a particular system. Some sampling errors are associated with each of these "particulars." The particular occasion is a sample from a period of time, and the particular set of stimuli or questions is a sample from the previously mentioned real or hypothetical array of available stimuli. The particular test administrator, observer, or scorer, as well as the scoring system used, are likewise single instances from real or hypothetical populations. It is important to be able to identify how much a particular response or score is likely to change as a function of changes in each of these aspects of measurement. Unfortunately, this type of information is rarely available in personality assessment.

Examination of textbooks on psychometric theory (e.g., Ghiselli, 1964; Nunnally & Bernstein, 1994) shows that experts differ on the philosophical assumptions to be made about the basis of psychological measurement. These differences in philosophy give rise to some differences in defining exactly what is meant conceptually by reliability, and thus lead to differences in the recommended ways of assessing the reliability of a measure. In this chapter, we try to steer a middle course through the various approaches, while attempting to avoid inconsistencies as well as issues that are beyond the scope of the book.

We begin with the observation that reliability is closely related to the concept of measurement error. Errors of measurement can be considered to be *systematic* or *random*. If we observe the time from a clock that is always five minutes fast, we are making a systematic error. If, on the other hand, the clock is accurate but is always so distant from us that we are unable to read the minute hand precisely, we are making a random error. Systematic errors can be thought of as associated with correctable mistakes; random errors, which tend to average about the correct or absolute score, can be regarded as the "fuzziness" left in the observation when all the systematic biases have been identified and removed.

To put it another way, random measurement errors are "built into" the measuring procedure, as when we try to measure to the nearest tenth of an inch with a yardstick marked only in inches, or when we try to assess "depression" with an omnibus paper-and-pencil inventory scale that lacks the necessary reportable clinical aspects of depression. In contrast to these random types of error, which are difficult to avoid, systematic errors are more identifiable and more easily correctable. In a sense, systematic errors are the fault of the test developer or user rather than being inherent in the instrument. We would be risking systematic error if we administered a depression scale to subjects who lived in a different culture (or subculture) from that represented by the available norms, or if we used stressful instructions that were markedly different from those used with the normative population. These potential systematic errors can and should be corrected by developing new norms based on the appropriate cultural group or suitable for the alternate testing conditions.

In their attempts to quantify reliability, psychometric theorists traditionally have concentrated on specifying the contribution of *random errors* to low reliability. Opinions differ on whether and to what extent *systematic errors* also should be considered a source of unreliability of measurement, and hence reflected in a numerical index of reliability. Each of the several commonly used measures of reliability reflects random error; each may also reflect some (but not all) of the sources of systematic error. The most recent revision of the *Standards for Educational and Psychological Testing* (1985), in recognizing that different methods of estimating reliability take account of different sources of error, recommends that investigators make clear exactly what procedures were used to obtain the particular reliability measure being reported.

Let us now consider the common methods for assessing reliability. The traditional index of reliability is the *reliability coefficient,* which can be regarded either as the correlation between the actual test scores and hypothetical "true" scores, or as the average correlation between the actual test scores and all other possible tests measuring the same characteristic. The following practical approaches to assessing reliability attempt to approximate this definition.

As we have implied, reliability associated solely with random error (errors stemming from the fact that the content of the test is but one sample of the universe of content covering the characteristic of interest) is termed the consistency or internal consistency of a test. Consistency can be assessed in various ways. One method is to divide the test into two comparable halves and correlate one half with the other. The obtained correlation is then "corrected" to its expected value for the full length of the test by what is known as the Spearman-Brown prophecy formula. Such an estimate of consistency, often arrived at by contrasting the odd and the even items in a test, is known as the *split-half reliability coefficient*. Another method for determining consistency is through the use of similar or *alternate* (or *parallel*) *forms* of the test, if they are available. The correlation between the forms essentially matches the corrected correlation between the two halves of the same form. When alternate forms are not available, a common compromise has been the use of a retest with the same form. The correlation between the two sets of scores is termed the *test–retest reliability coefficient*.

A more statistically sophisticated procedure for assessing reliability is by means of the *Kuder-Richardson reliability formulas* (Kuder & Richardson, 1937). The most useful of these formulas involves the percentage of items scored in a particular way, the correlations between the items and the total score, and the standard deviation of the test. These data are entered into a formula that yields a good estimate of consistency—provided that the test measures only one statistical factor. The most common reliability coefficient of this type, known as *coefficient alpha* (Cronbach, 1951) is "the mean of all split-half coefficients resulting from different splitting of a test" (Anastasi, 1988), regardless of whether the items are dichotomous or involve more than two choices. The complexities of this approach are beyond our scope here but are considered in detail in most texts on psychometrics.

Test–retest and alternate-forms correlations express more than the test's consistency. If the subjects remember some of the items when taking a retest, they might give the same answers purely from memory, a systematic effect that would have the result of spuriously increasing the correlation. Or, as previously noted, conditions from one testing session to the next might change, giving rise to unknown sources of systematic error. Or, the subjects themselves might change in the characteristic being measured. Both of these last two circumstances would serve to reduce the size of the reliability coefficient.

What particular method of computing a reliability coefficient should be employed in practice? A simple answer is that the coefficient should reflect the different kinds of errors in which the user is interested. Thus, if we want to know a test's reliability in assessing a concept, a consistency measure (Cronbach's alpha or split-half) would be appropriate. If we are interested in the test's stability in repeated administrations and under diverse conditions, then test–retest or alternate-forms reliability would be more appropriate. Ideally, the test producer will provide both sets of data.

What are acceptable limits for reliability coefficients? To answer this question, we must look at the way in which these coefficients can be used practically. Ordinarily, the key would be the *standard error of measurement,* a quantity derived directly from the reliability coefficient and the standard deviation of the obtained scores. Representing the reliability coefficient by r, and the standard deviation by s, the standard error of measurement is the quantity $s\sqrt{1 - r}$. To illustrate the meaning and use of the standard error of measurement, let us utilize the Sc scale of the MMPI. Internal consistency estimates (split-half correlation coefficients) for this scale have been reported to be in the neighborhood of .91 (Dahlstrom, Welsh, & Dahlstrom, 1975, p. 260). The standard deviation of all MMPI scales is 10 for scaled scores. The standard error of measurement can now be calculated from the formula to be $10\sqrt{1 - .91}$, or 3. That is to say, if it were possible to carry out the same testing many times over, the Sc scores obtained would average out to be the "true" score, but they would be distributed about this average with a standard deviation of 3.

If a distribution of scores is not markedly asymmetrical, about two out of three scores fall within one standard deviation of the mean. Thus, the chances that the score obtained in any given test administration is within three points of the "true" score are about two out of three. To put it another way, if a respondent obtains a scale score of 55 on Sc, the chances are about two out of three that the "true" score is within three points of 55, that is, between 52 and 58. By similar reasoning, because about 95% of the scores in a reasonably symmetrical distribution fall within two standard deviations of its mean, the chances would be about 95%, or 19 in 20, that the respondent's true score would be within six points of 55, that is, between 49 and 61.

Suppose the reliability coefficient (split-half) were only .75 instead of .91, as appears to be somewhat nearer the case with the D scale of the MMPI (Dahlstrom, Welsh, & Dahlstrom, 1975, p. 260). With a standard deviation once again of 10, the formula shows the standard error of measurement to be $10\sqrt{1 - .75}$, or 5. In practical terms, if a respondent obtained a score of 60 on the D scale, and we wanted to establish a range that would be 95% certain to include the "true" score, that range would be 50 through 70. The lower the reliability coefficient, the less reliance can be placed on a score as an estimate of the "true" degree of the characteristic possessed by the respondent.

Generalizability Theory

In 1964, Raymond B. Cattell suggested three major ways in which "test consistency," the generic term he considered most preferable, might be measured. The first was the consistency or agreement of scores over occasions; that is, changes in the same test given to the same people at different times. Cattell called this consistency "reliability." The second type of consistency was across tests (or parts of a test, or, commonly, single items) and involved agreement on the same occasion, and by the same people, over the tests (or parts). This consistency was termed "homogeneity." The third kind of consistency was across people. It involved agreement as to the meaning of scores on the same test, applied at the same time to different sets of people. This third type was labeled "transferability" (or hardiness).

In a similar approach, Cronbach, Gleser, Nanda, and Rajaratnam (1972) proposed that the most basic issue in reliability is the question of being able to generalize from the observations or measurements involved to some other class of observations. In their view, the study of reliability should therefore be the study of the degree to which the obtained scores are representative of scores generated under other conditions, or from different "universes." Examples would include the study of scores across different scorers, test items, methods, observers, or occasions. As emphasized by Wiggins (1973) in a thorough discussion of this approach, a major advantage is that it forces investigators to be explicit about the particular "universe" to which they are interested in generalizing their observations. It also tends to blur somewhat the traditional distinction between reliability and validity. A good example of a quantitative study of generalizability was reported by Jones, Reid, and Patterson (1975) on their Behavioral Coding System. In this study, the universes of generalization studied were subjects, observers, and occasions.

Reliability and Projective Techniques

The quantitative scores derived from projective tests often have low reliabilities when assessed by the methods just described. Because the reliability of a measure sets an upper limit on its potential usefulness or validity, the low reliabilities often have been blamed for the low demonstrated validities in research investigations of these tests. On the other hand, it has also been argued that the usual methods for assessing reliability are not applicable to projective instruments. For example, the split-half method is said to be inappropriate for the Rorschach because it is impossible to divide the ten cards in such a way as to obtain comparable halves. Test–retest reliability has been held inapplicable because a retest is regarded as a different psychological experience from the original test, and because projective techniques are said to be particularly sensitive to slight changes in the subject. Indeed, some proponents of projective tests seem to assume that such instruments are completely reliable and that the observed changes in test responses over time reflect real changes in the individual. Many of the characteristics tapped by these tests, such as mood or energy level, do fluctuate over time, thereby giving a certain cogency to this assumption. However, any real appreciation of the problems of reliability of measurement must lead to the conclusion that many, if not most, of these fluctuations are a function of the marginal reliability of the instruments.

Measurement problems contribute to unreliability in any test, but some problems tend to be particularly troublesome with projective devices. One problem involves test construction. In general, the stimulus materials used in projective tests have not been chosen with any thought toward ensuring that the various scoring categories would be adequately represented by the stimuli. For example, the mean number of human movement responses (*M*) for nonpatients on the Rorschach is only four, with a standard deviation of nearly two, and the mean for rare details (*Dd*) is only one (Exner, 1990). The practical ceiling on the reliability of such measurements is so low as to make the demonstration of significant validities a virtually impossible task.

It is often true, as with the TAT, that scoring systems were not developed until some years after the stimulus materials were selected. In the TAT, examiners even have a choice as to which stimulus they will employ. This haphazard development of scoring categories has contributed to low reliabilities. Ratio (and difference) scores, as used in the Rorschach, are particularly vulnerable to low reliabilities. Holtzman, in developing the HIT, took care to select stimulus cards for their specific contribution to certain scoring quantities; as a consequence, the reliabilities of most of the HIT categories are more satisfactory.

Another problem involves standardization of instructions. Directions for the administration of most projective instruments are not standardized, allowing the examiner to significantly influence the subject's responses. Even though Exner's (1986) current system for the Rorschach emphasizes the use of standardized instructions, the examiner can still make a difference. For example, Gross (1959) administered the Rorschach to 30 patients. For 20 of them, he gave social reinforcement after every human content response by saying "good" or by nodding his head. The reinforced patients gave significantly more human content responses than the remaining 10 patients. The importance of such subtle examiner differences, of which the examiner may be unaware, should be clear to the reader.

Even more vexing is the problem that subjects are often permitted to give a varying number of responses, of varying lengths. The latter portion of a long response or a set of responses is probably different in psychological content from a short response. Short responses on the Rorschach or TAT often tend to contain mainly "popular" or banal material. Variability in response length also makes statistical comparisons extremely difficult.

Another problem is presented in scoring. In some tests, such as the MMPI, scoring is mechanical. That is, little or no subjective judgment of the categorization of a response is involved. The same is true for some of the scoring categories in tests like the Rorschach. For example, determining the total number of responses given involves little or no judgment, once the data have been collected. Similarly, measuring the height of a figure drawing, or its total area, is a rather mechanical procedure. But by far the majority of scores derived from projective tests involve some subjective judgment in their determination. For example, does this Rorschach response involve color or human movement? Does this TAT story reflect the need for achievement, or affiliation, or both? For those projective tests where several different but similar scoring systems are available, the problem is even more aggravating.

Although the question of scorer reliability is simply one of interjudge or intrajudge agreement, it must be remembered that unreliability of scoring contributes to overall test unreliability. Murstein (1963, pp. 144–146) presented a summary table of scorer reliabilities for characteristics scored from the TAT. Of the 45 studies where reliability was reported as a correlation, the median scorer reliability was .74. With scorer reliabilities as low as this, the problems of achieving acceptable levels of test reliability are indeed large. It is possible, however, to achieve higher scorer reliabilities. Thus, Holt (1978) reported TAT data from several sources that showed scorer reliabilities as high as .90. The achievement of high reliabilities usually involves rather elaborate manuals that define the categories carefully and give many scoring examples. Because the use of such manuals requires considerable care and effort to generate just a single score, they are the exception rather than the rule.

Reliability of Global Interpretation

Paying too close attention to the various approaches to reliability determination involves a danger of missing what is, for practical purposes, the main issue involved in reliability. Tests are techniques for gathering information about personality and, usually, for making predictions about future behavior based on personality functioning. Thus, our ultimate concern with reliability should center on the use to which the test is put. That is, if the Rorschach is employed to provide a comprehensive description of global personality functioning, then the issue is the reliability of the global descriptions, not the reliability of individual scoring categories.

What is involved in assessing global reliabilities? The procedures are similar to those discussed previously. For example, split-half reliability would be assessed by comparing the interpretations made by examining comparable halves of the test; test–retest reliability would involve comparison of interpretations made from two different administrations of the test; and interjudge reliability would be determined by comparing the interpretations made of the same test material by different judges. Interexaminer reliability could also be assessed in a similar fashion.

To make global personality descriptions that can be statistically compared with one another in this way, some common descriptive framework for personality is required. A typical procedure is to employ a series of rating scales or dimensions that are relevant to the test and to the kind of descriptive information required. Interpretation is then accomplished by having the examiner assign scores or positions on these scales to the subjects, following a study of the test protocol. Or, the examiners might answer a number of true–false or multiple-choice questions about the subject. Another common method is the use of the Q-sort technique. A typical Q-sort consists of 100 cards, each containing a personality statement.

The examiner is asked to study the test protocol and then to sort the descriptive statements into nine piles, representing equal intervals from least descriptive of the subject to most descriptive. The number of cards to be placed in each pile is determined in advance, so that every judge provides the same distribution of cards. In all these techniques, rank correlation or percentage agreement methods can be applied to determine a numerical index of reliability. (If one wishes to determine reliabilities involving a single examiner, the number of test protocols being judged should be sufficiently large that the examiner will not be able to remember, or guess, which ones came from the same subject.)

The reliability established for any assessment procedure should be appropriate for the use to which the procedure is to be put. If predictions about specific events are to be made, the reliability of these predictions should be examined. If global personality descriptions are sought, it is their reliabilities that are at issue. Although there will often be additional basic sources of reliability to consider (such as scorer reliability), on which the ultimate reliabilities may depend, the reliability of the procedure in use is the question of ultimate interest.

VALIDITY

In Chapter Three, we introduced the general notion of the *usefulness* of a test or assessment procedure, meaning the extent to which it permits us to understand and predict some of a person's nontest behavior. We have also used the word *validity* as more or less synonymous with usefulness. We now explore the concept of validity in greater detail.

The *Standards for Educational and Psychological Testing* (American Educational Research Association/American Psychological Association/National Council on Measurement in Education, 1985) emphasize that evidence for validity may be accumulated in many different ways. "Validity always refers to the degree to which that evidence supports the inferences that are made from the scores" (p. 9). It has long been recognized that, because different tests may have different types of aims, an approach that would be appropriate for demonstrating validity in one test might well be inappropriate for another. Three different kinds of evidence for validity are generally recognized: (a) *content validity,* (b) *criterion-related* (*predictive* and *concurrent*) validity, and (c) *construct* validity. This threefold division in the purposes of a test is somewhat artificial; the categories overlap somewhat, and it is generally necessary to demonstrate that a test possesses validity in more than one way. The establishment of validity requires much more than just the evaluation, by either the target person or the test user, of the personality description or prediction yielded by the test instrument. Forer (1949) clearly indicated the fallacy of such "testimonial" or "personal" validity in a study that demonstrated a uniformly high degree of acceptance by a sample of undergraduates of a single, identical personality description. The students were unaware that they all had received the same feedback. O'Dell (1972) went even further in showing that students believed that such "Barnum" reports were more accurate than real computer-generated test reports on themselves.

Content Validity

Content-related evidence for validity involves showing that the content of the test is representative of the behaviors that are of interest. Content evidence has special relevance for achievement and aptitude tests, where the responses to the test items presumably are samples of the behaviors of concern. Personality assessment by means of behavior samples and situational tests, as discussed in Chapter Five, also involves content validity through the direct elicitation of the relevant responses. For example, suppose we wish to develop a test of leadership, and we arrange for a series of behavioral samples that require the respondent to display behaviors characteristic of his or her responses to situational leadership demands. If these behavioral situations are a representative sample of leadership situations in general (or of some clearly identified subset of situations), and if the amount of artificiality introduced by the testing situation is minimized, we would have a valid test of leadership (or an aspect of it) simply by virtue of the fact that the *content* of the test is a representative sample of the behavior of interest. In a sense, the content validity of a test for a particular purpose is the same as the subjective evaluation of the criterion itself. If, however, the aim of a test is to predict behavior under somewhat modified real-life circumstances, such as leadership in combat, then more than content validity is required.

It sometimes is argued that paper-and-pencil personality inventories are valid simply if they appear to have content (or face) validity—that is, when they are rationally derived. Thus, the presence on a depression scale of items referring to the experience of mood disturbance, loss of motivation for daily activities, and psychomotor retardation would be taken as reasonable grounds for the usefulness of the scale. But the clinical behaviors of depression cannot be sampled by the marking of an IBM true–false answer sheet. It is the nontest or real-life correlates of these marking responses that are of interest, and these must be demonstrated. Fortunately for test developers, rationality (or content validity) of a scale appears to be a necessary though not a sufficient condition for its usefulness.

Criterion-Related Validity

In personality assessment, because of its practical orientation, we often are most concerned with predictive validity in its various forms. Predictive validity refers to "the accuracy with which we can make guesses about one characteristic of an individual from another characteristic" (Ghiselli, 1964, p. 338). The test or assessment measure is called the "predictor," and the characteristic we are guessing at is known as the "criterion." A straightforward numerical index of predictive validity is given by the correlation between predictor and criterion. Predictive validity is central to the criterion-groups approach to test construction. It would be the appropriate type of validity to be demonstrated if, for example, we wished to use patients' average elevations on the MMPI scales at the time of their admission to psychiatric treatment as an index of the length of time they would be hospitalized. The correlation between average elevation and days of subsequent hospitalization would be an index of the validity of average elevation as a predictor of hospitalization.

It is important to keep the criterion measure from becoming "contaminated" with the predictor, in order to ensure that the correlation is not spuriously high. In the previous example, the overall elevation of the patient's MMPI profile must be given no part in determining the length of his or her hospitalization. In both the original criterion research and the subsequent practical use of the predictor, extreme care must be exercised to maintain the confidentiality of the predictor scores. Otherwise, such scores become "self-fulfilling prophecies."

Evidence for the predictive validity of a test must be shown for every criterion that it is expected to predict. The fact that average MMPI elevation might be found to predict length of hospitalization does not ensure its success in predicting likelihood of rehospitalization, even though both criteria might be considered measures of "success of treatment." Moreover, the fact that average elevation is found to predict length of hospitalization in one particular location and with one particular population does not automatically mean that it will be successful in another location. In the latter case, cross-validation with the new population should be carried out. The procedures involved in cross-validation and the dangers of a failure to do so have been discussed in Chapter Four.

Criterion-related validity *may* but does not necessarily refer to prediction in the future. It is logical, and often useful, to consider prediction to a *concurrent* event, and *postdiction* to an event that has previously occurred but cannot be measured directly without considerable effort. For example, let us say we wish to determine the nature and degree of the interpersonal needs of a group of college students. In one method, trained observers would follow them around for a period of time, gathering information from real-life situations. In another method, a series of situational tests would be arranged. A third approach might administer a paper-and-pencil inventory or have the subjects judge themselves on a variety of rating scales. The inventory or self-ratings would represent attempts to make an economical determination of the students' characteristics at that particular time. Validity then would be determined by arranging the lengthier and costlier behavior

sample and situational test procedures, for which content validity has presumably been demonstrated, and using them as the criteria for comparison
with the paper-and-pencil procedure. If these behavior samples or situational measures are available only at some future time, then we would again
have future prediction.

Construct Validity

Construct-related evidence for validity is a concept that was introduced in
the American Psychological Association's (1954) original version of the
Standards, and elaborated by Cronbach and Meehl (1955). Its purpose was
to provide a label for a method of demonstrating validity that had been
used to some extent prior to that time, but without a complete understanding of the method's logic and implications. It is relevant where no single definitive or tangible criterion exists for the quality, trait, or characteristic to
be assessed.

Validity can be dimensionalized in a number of ways—for example, using
the concrete versus abstract (or particular versus conceptual) dimension.
Frequently, we are interested in the correlations between scores on a test and
particular or concrete criteria, such as the number of psychiatric hospital-
izations or the number of traffic offenses. Predictive validity studies of this
nature have considerable appeal because they are immediately useful and do
not require much methodological or theoretical sophistication.

Often, however, we are interested in the validity of relationships involving
constructs or abstract terms—ego strength, anxiety, or extroversion—for
which there are no single, commonly accepted measures. We can demonstrate the predictive validity of a psychiatric hospitalization scale or a criminal recidivism index by means of a single correlation, but it is far more
difficult to demonstrate the construct validity of an anxiety scale or a measure of any other generalized, abstract concept in the psychological domain.
Construct validity requires the gradual accumulation of supporting evidence
garnered from a variety of research findings and arranged to demonstrate a
network of relationships among the measure in question and other relevant concepts. The nature and strength of these relationships should be predictable
both from the theory or theories in which the concept is embedded and from
the generally understood meaning of the concept.

Thus, to establish construct validity of a measure of anxiety, as the term
is generally understood, one might set out to demonstrate positive relationships among the measure and behavior in temporary stress situations, most
forms of psychiatric difficulty, physiological indexes such as palmar sweating and heart rate, and certain other behaviors typically regarded as related to anxiety. In addition, it should be demonstrated that *no* relationship
exists between the measure and certain characteristics that are presumed
to be independent of anxiety, such as height or intelligence. Establishment

of construct validity for an instrument might best be thought of as a continuing program in which the meaning of the construct is gradually sharpened and reified by the nature of the relationships into which it is found to enter, and by which the meaning of the construct may become clarified as unexpected relationships are discovered. In the final analysis, because there is no single coefficient or specifiable group of coefficients that, a priori, is acceptable as clearly "demonstrating" the construct validity of a measure, judgments about the degree of construct validity possessed by the device must necessarily be subjective.

The notion of construct validity has been seriously questioned on the grounds that it contributes nothing to the theoretical understanding of human behavior or to the accuracy and utility of practical work. One central issue in the objections to construct validity is the danger that the postulated attribute or construct will be taken for a *real* entity, rather than a convenient explanatory fiction. Sarbin (1968), using the construct of anxiety as the focus of his discussion, cogently pointed out the pitfalls involved in assuming that such mental states or traits as anxiety exist. The major danger is an involvement in searching for a verbal answer to questions like "What is anxiety?"—a question that cannot meaningfully be answered. Sarbin argued that our attempts to construct scientific fictions or "myths" are a function of our language system and verbal habits, and that these tendencies need careful attention and control. Nevertheless, much of the current research literature involving personality assessment techniques does involve construct validation, and knowledgeable readers should be aware of what is involved and of the problems inherent in this approach.

Incremental Validity

When a test is used as the basis for prediction in a clinical situation, determining the usefulness of the test is not as simple as determining the accuracy of prediction—that is, the predictive validities. As Sechrest (1963) explained, tests such as the Rorschach are often "interpreted after interviews, reading of case reports, conferences, and the like. It seems clear that validity must be claimed for a test in terms of some *increment* in predictive efficiency over the information otherwise cheaply and easily available" (p. 154). Meehl (1959b) had earlier spoken of the "increment in valid and semantically clear information transmitted" (p. 114), and Cronbach and Gleser (1965) discussed the same topic at length in regard to personnel selection.

Because the notion of evaluating the usefulness of a test according to its incremental validity in that particular situation seems so obvious and relevant, it may come as a surprise that many of the diagnostic tests commonly used in clinical practice show poor incremental validity—partly because clinicians are not generally oriented toward constantly evaluating the efficiency of their behavior. Indeed, Hathaway (1959) estimated that if clinicians were to evaluate their testing activities from an efficiency viewpoint, more than 40% of these activities would be abandoned. Research that has evaluated different assessment procedures in terms of their incremental validities is discussed in Chapter Eight.

Hits and Misses

The predictive validity of an assessment device has traditionally been expressed in terms of a correlation coefficient between the predictor score and the criterion. If the criterion involves a hit-or-miss situation, such as whether parolees will or will not violate their parole, predictive validity is sometimes more appropriately expressed in terms of the percentage of correct predictions.

Working within the framework of hits and misses (or percentage correct) makes it possible to demonstrate the importance of taking into account the *base rate* of an event; that is, the proportion of times the event occurs in the population of interest. Let us use the example of parole violation. Suppose we know from past experience that 30% of the potential parolees are likely to violate their parole. The base rate for parole violation is thus 30%, or .30. If we were to predict the future behavior of parolees from this information alone, we would do best if we predict that *no* parolees will violate the conditions of their parole. Because 30% will in fact be violators (though we have no way of knowing which 30%), we will be wrong 30% of the time. That is, we will be 70% accurate in our prediction. Suppose now that we have developed a test that has been shown to identify potential parole violators with 65% accuracy. Even though the test enables us to do better than the completely chance rate of 50%, we would be ahead in terms of predictive accuracy to predict directly from the base rate of 70%.

Incidentally, once we know that the base rate of nonviolators is 70%, the "chance rate" of assignment is really higher than 50%. If we randomly assign *any* 70 out of 100 prisoners to the "nonviolator" category, we should be correct 70% of the time, or 49 times, on average. Likewise, randomly assigning the remaining 30 to the "violator" category should result in 9 correct placements. Thus, in making a chance 70/30 assignment, we would be correct 49 plus 9 or 58% of the time. Some psychologists would go one step further and consider that "chance" should be identified with the base rate of 70%. The first detailed analysis of the use of base rate data in evaluating predictive accuracy in personality assessment was provided by Meehl and Rosen (1955).

In the preceding analyses, we have ignored the relative costs of the alternative outcomes. To be more precise, we have taken for granted that both kinds of possible errors—failing to identify violators and mislabeling nonviolators—would be equally costly. In practice, it is likely that an error in one direction would be more costly than an error in the other. For example, we could imagine that the cost of placing on parole a criminal who later violates parole may be higher, all values considered, than refusing parole to a person who would not have violated it. More detailed analyses of the problems of taking into consideration values of alternate outcomes have been made by Cronbach and Gleser (1965) and by Wiggins (1973). These questions involve the efficiency or utility of predictions and are discussed further in Chapter Eight under the subheading of "Decision Making."

Utilization of base rate data provides insight into the danger of using automatic cutting scores on tests, regardless of the population being considered. For example, Hathaway (1956b) reported that, on the MMPI *K*-corrected *Sc* scale, about 60% of schizophrenic patients in his psychiatric cross-validation group achieved a *T* score of 70 or greater, whereas only 2% of the normal cross-validation subjects scored in that range. Suppose the scale is used for diagnosis in a clinic where approximately half the patients are schizophrenic and the other half are "normal." Simple calculation shows that calling schizophrenic all patients who score 70 or more will result in 79% of all patients being correctly diagnosed. The calculation is portrayed in Table 7.1. Of those patients diagnosed as schizophrenic by the test, 30 of 31 (or 97%), are in fact schizophrenic. Most of the errors made will be in the direction of mislabeling schizophrenics as nonschizophrenic, so that a *lower* cutting score (e.g., 65) would raise the overall diagnostic efficiency. The main point is that the use of 70 as a cutting score ensures that almost all patients labeled schizophrenic by the test are, in fact, schizophrenic. The *Sc* scale, in practice, is not quite so successful as portrayed here, because some of the 50% who are normal will achieve high *Sc* scores because of their other disorders.

Table 7.1   Percentage of Patients Diagnosed as Either Schizophrenic or Normal by the Sc *Scale, Using a Cutting Score of 70, Where Half Are Actually Schizophrenic and Half Are Actually Normal*

T Score	Actually Schizophrenic	Actually Normal	Total
T Score 70 or more (diagnosed as schizophrenic)	30[a,b]	1[c]	31
T Score below 70 (diagnosed as normal)	20[d]	49[a,e]	69
Total	50	50	100

[a] Correctly diagnosed.
[b] True positives.
[c] False positives.
[d] False negatives.
[e] True negatives.

Now suppose we give the test to apparently normal college students. Let us assume that 1% of these students are schizophrenic. If the same cutting score of 70 is used, the test will diagnose 2.6% of the students as schizophrenic. This situation is represented in Table 7.2. In other words, most of the students scoring 70 or more on the *Sc* scale are *not schizophrenic*. Conceptualizing the prediction in terms of hit-and-miss and base rates makes it clear that, although the predictive accuracy is much higher for college students (97.6%) than for patients (79%), the test entirely fails in its function when used with a population for which it was not intended. However, this is not to deny that the high *Sc* scoring college students would tend to be different in some way from the lower scoring students. These differences can be ascertained from specific validity studies conducted on college students.

The example illustrating the danger of using automatic cutting scores also points up the problem of predictive accuracy when predicting events that occur infrequently. Table 7.2 suggests that it would probably be wasted effort to try to employ the *Sc* scale for the efficient identification of the few schizophrenics who would be found among a college population. The problem of predicting infrequent events was identified by Rosen (1954), using suicide as the infrequent event of interest. Estimating the suicide rate among psychiatric patients as .0033, and assuming a "correct" prediction rate of 75%, Rosen presented hypothetical data to show that even if the cutting score on a suicide detection index were raised so high that only 2.5% of the actual suicide cases were correctly identified, more than 98% of those patients called "suicides" would have been incorrectly labeled. Needless to say, this problem is always present, though often unrecognized, in attempting to identify potential suicide patients by clinical or subjective judgment.

Because the necessity for identifying patients who are potentially suicidal exists regardless of the difficulty of the prediction, ways of dealing with it must be found. Rosen pointed out that when hospital administrators

Table 7.2   Percentage of Students Diagnosed as Schizophrenic or Normal by the Sc *Scale Using a Cutting Score of 70, Where 1 Percent Are Actually Schizophrenic and 99 Percent Are Actually Normal*

T Score	Actually Schizophrenic	Actually Normal	Total
T score 70 or more (diagnosed as schizophrenic)	0.6[a]	2.0	2.6
T score below 70 (diagnosed as normal)	0.4	97.0[a]	97.4
Total	1.0	99.0	100.0

[a] Correctly diagnosed.

take the attitude that suicide should be prevented at almost any cost, the usual procedure is to err on the side of safety by identifying an enormous number of "false positives." Thus, almost any patient who shows signs (whether clinical or on a psychometric index) regarded as suicidal will be treated as a potential suicide risk. Also, some improvement in psychometric prediction would result from the careful collection of detailed data over a number of years, in order to permit more precise classification and the identification of certain subgroups of patients for whom suicide might be relatively more frequent. Studies of this type were initiated by Farberow, Shneidman, and Neuringer (1966) and have been continued by a number of researchers. In particular, Beck (1986; Beck, Berchik, Stewart, & Steer, 1990) has found that hopelessness is a strong predictor of suicide, and, with colleagues, has developed the Suicide Intent Scale (Beck, Schuyler, & Herman, 1974) and the scale for suicide ideation (Beck, Kovacs, & Weissman, 1979).

Selection Ratios

In discussing criterion-related validities, we have assumed that predictions or decisions are to be made for every client examined. That is, we have had to make a decision for every person involved. Under some circumstances, we have a slightly different problem: *selection*, where an assignment does not have to be made for everybody. Suppose we are asked to select 10 schizophrenic patients from a ward of 200. We know from past experience that there are about 100 schizophrenics on the ward, but we do not know exactly who they are. Our chances of performing this selection successfully by administering a test for schizophrenia and selecting the 10 highest scores are quite high, even if the predictive validity of the test is mediocre. The reason is that we are not going to make a prediction for the majority of the patients. We only have to make a prediction about the few patients about whom we are most likely to be correct—those with extreme scores.

The *selection ratio* is defined as the number of people to be selected compared to the total number considered. In this example, the ratio is 10 to 200 or .05. The smaller the ratio, the more successful the selection will be, given the same predictive validity for the test. Another factor that influences accuracy of selection is the proportion of suitable patients in the group being considered—that is, the base rate. In this example, the base rate is 100 to 200 or .50. Tables are available (Taylor & Russell, 1939) to indicate the expected accuracy of selection, given a specific predictive validity, base rate, and selection ratio. In our example, suppose the schizophrenia test had a predictive validity correlation coefficient of .4. The Taylor-Russell tables show that we would most likely have successfully identified 8 schizophrenics out of 10. Suppose, however, that there were only 20 patients to select from, still assuming that half are really schizophrenic. The selection ratio would now be 10 to 20 or .50, and the Taylor-Russell tables indicate that our most likely selection would be 6 schizophrenics out of 10, or only slightly above the chance selection of 5 out of 10.

Selection ratios are important where many people are competing for a few openings. Under such circumstances, a test with low predictive validities can be used to provide fairly accurate selection. This situation often arises in the selection of a person, from among many candidates, to fill a desirable job. It would also arise where the available treatment services, such as psychotherapy, are limited, and many patients desire treatment.

Moderator Variables

From time to time, statisticians have discovered what appear to be tricks for making silk purses out of sows' ears. One of these tricks was seemingly embodied in the Taylor-Russell tables, just described, which are used for enhancing predictive validity when there is a favorable selection ratio. The use of *moderator variables* is another procedure for achieving enhanced predictive validities under specific circumstances.

The concept of moderator variables was originally identified by Ghiselli (1956, 1963) and by Saunders (1956). A moderator is a piece of information that can be used to predict, for a given respondent or set of respondents, the accuracy of another predictor. For example, if it is known that college grades for compulsive students can be effectively predicted from their aptitude test scores but grades for noncompulsive students cannot, then a measure of compulsivity could be used to moderate the prediction of grades from aptitude test scores—that is, to identify those students for whom the prediction will be relatively accurate and those for whom it will not. If we were to confine our interest to only the highly compulsive students, the predictive validity of college board scores would be higher than if we considered everybody. In other words, we have improved prediction at the expense of working only with those persons for whom we know prediction to be the most valid. A moderator variable is logically equivalent to the occurrence of a particular type of interaction in the use of analysis of variance to study the results of a research inquiry. The above situation is represented in Figure 7.1, which shows the results of the same hypothetical study. A clear relationship can be seen between aptitude test scores and college grades for compulsive students but not for noncompulsive students.

At first glance, the potentialities for improving prediction by the use of moderators in personality assessment seem considerable. The concept is undoubtedly used informally in many situations. For example, if Dr. Jones is known to be expert at recognizing borderline personality characteristics in acting-out individuals who come to the clinic, the intake interviewer may be more likely to send the acting-out clients to Dr. Jones for their diagnostic workup. To extend the principle, there is the possibility

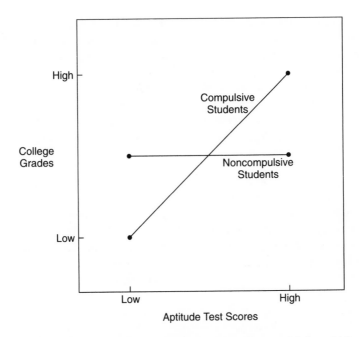

Figure 7.1. An interaction between college grades and compulsivity which serves to moderate the prediction of grades from aptitude test scores.

for devising a moderator to indicate how much attention should be paid to a patient's Rorschach protocol or MMPI profile in arriving at a psychiatric diagnosis. On a more complex level, it might be possible to determine whether, for a particular patient or group of patients, most attention should be paid to the Rorschach protocol, the Draw-a-Person, the MMPI, biographical information, or any other particular source of data.

To date, most of the research in developing moderator variables has been concerned with the prediction of success in academic or personnel areas. In attempting to enhance the prediction of earnings among cab drivers, Ghiselli (1960a) found that a moderator based on age and education could be used to indicate which of two ability measures (spatial and motor ability tests) was the better predictor. In this study, the spatial test was a better predictor for the older and less-educated drivers. Ghiselli (1960b) also showed that it was possible to develop a moderator variable empirically by using a criterion-groups approach. The characteristic to be predicted was sociability, as assessed by a questionnaire. The predictor, which showed a low correlation with sociability, was intelligence, defined by a rather arbitrary scale on a self-description inventory. To develop the moderator, two criterion groups were identified. The "predictable" group was composed of those persons whose scores fell at about the same point in the sociability and the intelligence distributions. The remainder constituted the "unpredictable" group. Responses to the self-description inventory were then examined to identify items that discriminated the two groups, and these items formed the moderator scale. Cross-validation on a new sample showed that the scale continued to identify the most predictable individuals.

Although the main area of research with moderator variables has been in enhancing prediction of academic or job success, clinically relevant research has also been done. Fulkerson (1959) demonstrated that the validity of a personality test for predicting general adjustment was related to the extroversion-introversion, or hysteric-psychasthenic, personality dimension, presumably because the introverted respondents were more careful in their responses. In a study of clinical judgment, Tomlinson (1967) showed, among other things, that the judges with high achievement needs made more accurate client predictions than other judges after interviewing a client directly, but *less* accurate predictions than other judges when observing the client through a one-way mirror. In a study involving psychiatric problems of men in a war combat zone, Clum and Hoiberg (1971) were able to improve their hit rate of successful decisions on whether to return a man to combat duty by using diagnostic categories as a moderator of prediction based on biographical variables.

What is the basis for the utility of moderator variables? In the first two examples above—the prediction of grades for college students and success among cab drivers—commonsense or rational explanations can be offered as to why certain subgroups should be more predictable than others. Thus, one would expect that compulsive students might be more likely to work to the limit of their abilities, and the less compulsive students would tend to devote time selectively to the courses that interested them. What is more difficult to explain is the fact that empirical moderator scales, with no obviously relevant content, can be developed in some instances. A discussion of possible psychometric explanations, though beyond our present scope, was offered by Hobert and Dunnette (1967). Zedeck (1971) provided an extensive review and discussion of the whole area.

There are several limitations to the use of moderators in enhancing prediction. First, it may not be possible to develop moderator variables for all predictions. Smith and Lanyon (1968) used biographical data to postdict juvenile offenders who violated their probation, and they then attempted to build an empirical moderator scale, based on MMPI items, to improve the postdiction. No improvement resulted, perhaps because the factors determining whether probation would be violated might have been circumstantial and not present or ascertainable until the probation period had begun. Another potential limitation was demonstrated by Bem and Allen (1974), whose work we have discussed in Chapter Two. They were able to show that people differed reliably in the consistency of their behavior in certain areas, and that "consistency" for each trait could be assessed by self-ratings.

As anticipated, highly consistent people were much more predictable by their peers than those who were low on self-rated consistency. Thus, it would appear that an overriding moderator might be "consistency," and that some people are simply more consistent or predictable than others, at least in specific areas. If it could be shown that this was a general personality characteristic, then the clinical potential of moderators would be severely limited, because the same person who scored high on a moderator for the MMPI, for example, would score high on moderators for all other sources of personality information.

Although the early promise of moderator variables as a significant aid to accuracy in personality assessment has not been fulfilled (e.g., Anastasi, 1988), there is continued research interest. For example, attempts have been made to discover moderators of the relationships between stressful life events and psychological disorders in adults (Johnson & Sarason, 1979) and children (Sandler, 1980). It is fair to say that the exploration of moderator variables represents an advance in the technology of personality assessment, because it goes beyond a global search for validity and explores the question of different degrees of validity for different kinds of persons under different circumstances.

RESPONSE DISTORTIONS

Responses to personality assessment procedures are influenced by other variables besides the personality characteristics of the respondents. Although an individual's personality characteristics are generally assumed to be the major determinants of his or her responses, we now know, on the basis of both research and theory, that these responses are complex products of a number of psychological, sociological, linguistic, and other variables, many of which have nothing to do with the purposes for which the assessment procedure was designed. For example, personality test responses may be influenced by a conscious desire to appear well adjusted, or by the obviousness of the "correct" answers to various items. Responses may also be influenced by recent prior experiences, such as viewing a dramatic motion picture. As a further example, subcultural differences in the use of evaluative words such as *often* and *very* may affect test answers. An understanding of how these systematic irrelevancies—typically termed *response biases, response sets,* or *response styles*—affect the responses to personality assessment devices is necessary both for improving effectiveness in utilizing current instruments and for developing new ones. Here, the generic term *response distortions* is employed.

Psychometricians' concern with the effects of response distortions began in the 1920s, when direct questionnaires were thought to be of little value because they could be easily faked. Cronbach (1941, 1942, 1946, 1950) was one of the first to direct formal attention to the general topic of response distortions. He was concerned with the distorting effects of students' tendencies to guess the answers on true–false classroom achievement examinations. Response distortions were also a concern of Hathaway and McKinley in developing the MMPI, and the conclusion was extended to other personality measurement instruments: the self-report variety, and then the Rorschach, TAT, and other projective tests.

Some critics have leaned toward the extreme position that answers to personality tests reflect little else besides response distortions, and that any efforts to use these tests for assessing the underlying response tendencies typically subsumed under the rubric of personality are doomed to failure. Another view, with which we are in accord, is that although efforts should be made during test construction to minimize the effects of response distortions, they are themselves consistencies in behavior that sometimes permit useful inferences about the personality and future behavior of the persons who evidence them. The major issue here, and throughout our discussion of personality assessment, is the degree to which inferences made from responses to assessment devices can be shown to have an empirical basis. Responses that are not related to any nontest behaviors of interest constitute, by definition, *error variance,* and strong efforts must be exerted to eliminate or to substantially reduce them. On the other hand, responses that are related to personality-relevant behaviors should be studied and understood, no matter what they are called or what brings them about.

There are two kinds of response distortion. The first, *response style* (Jackson & Messick, 1958), refers to the tendency to distort responses in a particular direction more or less regardless of the content of the stimulus. Examples of response styles are the tendency to answer "true" a disproportionate number of times on true–false inventories, and the tendency to choose a particular alternative, such as option (c), in a multiple-choice task. Extreme responding, discussed in Chapter Six in regard to rating scales, is a response style. On the Rorschach, the tendency to respond to the whole blot or the color rather than the shape of the blot would also be an example of response style. Because the content of a test stimulus is usually a powerful determiner of the response that will be given, the influence of response styles will become greater as the content becomes more ambiguous. Thus, we have the interesting situation that, with instruments whose stimulus content is relatively ambiguous, such as the Rorschach, response styles have been deliberately assessed and have been regarded as important indexes of personality factors. With self-report questionnaires, response style parameters are typically treated largely as error variance.

The second kind of response distortion, *response set,* refers to the "conscious or unconscious desire on the part of the respondent to answer in such a way as to produce a certain picture of himself. In this traditional usage, an individual may have a set to dissimulate, to malinger, to appear aggressive, to fake good, to get the job, etc." (Rorer, 1965, p. 133). As distinct from response styles, which may be regarded as relatively "contentless," response sets are largely determined by the stimulus content: the clearer or less ambiguous the content, the more susceptible it is to the influence of response sets. Because projective tests such as the Rorschach and the TAT are more ambiguous in stimulus content than self-report personality questionnaires, it has been assumed that projectives are less susceptible to the influence of response sets than inventories. Research evidence discussed later in the chapter, however, indicates that this assumption is not well supported.

It should be recognized that a particular response or pattern of responses could be evoked by a response style, a response set, or some simultaneous effect of both a set and a style. Thus, "guarded" respondents could employ the response set of generally revealing very little about themselves and the response style of choosing the "cannot say" or "uncertain" category on questionnaires that include such a choice. A well-designed program of personality assessment would include provisions for dealing with both aspects of response distortion.

There have been substantial differences of opinion regarding the importance of response styles and sets in the personality assessment enterprise. At one time, many psychologists believed that response distortions exerted such a powerful influence on test takers that the results of personality inventories showed little more than the influence of these irrelevant factors (e.g., Edwards, 1957; Jackson & Messick, 1958). Some aspects of the controversies of that time remain unresolved. However, to anticipate the conclusions arrived at here: these influences may be significant at times but can be satisfactorily managed through the use of careful test construction procedures. An exception is deliberate deception or faking, which is a problem in certain uses of personality assessment and is typically assessed separately. The current state of knowledge on response styles is reviewed first, starting with acquiescence.

Acquiescent Response Style

The most thoroughly researched response style is acquiescence, the tendency to respond "true" in a true–false questionnaire. In its most extreme form, an acquiescent response style would lead to a "true" response to all items, regardless of content, including such items as "I murdered my mother." It would also lead a respondent to answer affirmatively to two contradictory statements; for example, "I am happily married" and "I am unhappily married." Fortunately, extreme instances are rarely encountered, and concern about acquiescence has been mainly directed toward its influence on ambiguous items, such as "I often worry about unfulfilled responsibilities." On this item, a positive response may result from the fact that the respondent does indeed behave in that fashion; but it may also mean that the respondent is uncertain about this behavior and the response has been determined by an acquiescent response style. Whenever personality questionnaires contain many relatively ambiguous items on which the majority of the keyed responses are in the same direction, the scores are open to the influence of an acquiescent response style.

How significant is acquiescence response style in the practical use of inventories? Despite views such as those of Couch and Keniston (1960), who took the position that acquiescence was itself a useful personality variable, and Rorer (1965), who argued that it is an unavoidable part of our language structure and should be left alone, the best approach would seem to be a recognition that it can exert a small but bothersome influence in responding on personality inventories. It would therefore seem reasonable to make an effort to remove this influence by having a comparable number of "true"-keyed and "false"-keyed items, whenever this can be done without doing violence to the content of the items (e.g., Jackson, 1967, 1984; Lanyon, 1978).

Deviant Response Style

Another style of responding to personality test items has attracted considerable interest—the style of making atypical, unusual, or deviant responses. Certain modal or usual responses to personality test items are given by the general population; for example, an affirmative response to the inventory item "My father was a good man," the response of "a bat" to Card V of the Rorschach, or the drawing of a clothed figure on the Draw-a-Person test. Some psychologists have presumed that variations or deviations from these modal responses to test items are indicative of a general tendency toward deviance.

This position was formally articulated by Berg (1955, 1957, 1959) as the Deviation Hypothesis: "Deviant response patterns tend to be general; hence those deviant behavior patterns which are significant for abnormality and thus regarded as symptoms are associated with other deviant response patterns which are in noncritical areas of behavior and which are not regarded as symptoms of personality aberration" (1955, p. 62). Berg (1959) argued that deviant responding is better viewed as a response style, rather than a set, because the particular stimulus content was unimportant. Further, he believed that ambiguity of content heightened rather than reduced the operation of this factor. However, Hamilton (1968) took the position that item content was a significant factor in deviant responding, because each item had to be inspected individually to determine what would be a deviant response for that item.

It is interesting to note that Rorschach viewed deviant responding as an important consideration on his inkblot test. Rorschach initially noted (1942/1951, p. 23) that most responses to his inkblots were determined by the form of the blot, and "in order to avoid subjective evaluation," he developed the "definite range of normal form visualizations"—the so-called good-form, or F+ responses—based on the actual responses given by 100 normal persons. Rorschach noted that good-form perception was disturbed by various psychopathological states, especially schizophrenia, and he stated that "the more stable the emotions, the better the form visualization" (p. 31). The evaluation of form level accuracy of perception in Rorschach responses by means of the frequency of occurrence of these responses was more thoroughly studied and reported by Beck et al. (1961), Exner (1974), and others. In contemporary Rorschach interpretation (e.g., Exner, 1986, 1991), the form level, as determined by frequency tables and by the examiner's judgment and clinical experience, is considered to be an important index of the general level of deviance or psychopathology to be attributed to the subject. Deviant responding is also an important consideration on the MMPI; here again, it is considered to be a useful index of overall degree of psychological disturbance (e.g., Lachar, 1974). The MMPI scale for assessing deviant responding is, coincidentally, also designated *F* (for "frequency," in this case).

The Deviation Hypothesis has been severely criticized by a number of students of personality measurement (e.g., Rorer, 1965; Sechrest & Jackson, 1962, 1963) on a number of grounds. There appears to be little research evidence to support Berg's view that deviant responding in any response situation is predictive of deviant responding in all situations. However, it is clear that certain aspects of deviant responding, such as Rorschach form level and the MMPI *F* scale, are useful indexes of psychopathology. Because these indexes are indeed related to the content of the test stimuli, it would not seem appropriate to regard them simply as response styles. Rather, in view of the way they are used in the process of personality assessment, it may be best to view them as an integral aspect of the test procedure.

Extreme Response Style

One further response style is *extreme responding*. This style can operate only in tests whose items require subjects to respond on a rating scale or dimension, as discussed in Chapter Six. Some persons have a tendency to select the extreme categories (such as "strongly disagree" or "strongly agree") rather than the middle categories, regardless of the content of the item. Although extreme responding sounds rather like deviant responding, Hamilton (1968) differentiated them by pointing out that extreme responding is completely independent of content, while deviant responding involves a specific reaction to the content of the item. Hamilton's review of the research on extreme response style indicated that this phenomenon is a reliable characteristic of respondents and that it is consistently shown more by women than men, by persons with high anxiety, and by persons who have poor psychological adjustment. Thus, it would seem appropriate to take note of these small but significant effects when employing rating scales.

Favorable/Unfavorable Response Set

We concluded earlier that response styles (content-free distortions of responses to personality assessment devices) are relatively minor variables in most efforts to evaluate personality. The situation is rather different, however, when considering response *sets,* the tendency to systematically "slant" the content of one's responses to personality assessment items. The reader should recall that our definition of response set includes subjects' *deliberate* efforts to bias their answers in a particular direction and their subtle, *unconscious* tendencies to make biased responses.

The most widespread of all response sets is the portrayal of oneself in overly favorable or unfavorable terms. The original approach to understanding this problem was through the study of a special case, the *social desirability* response set. This term is now typically used to refer to the natural or unconscious production of socially desirable responses; the term *faking-good* is used for conscious, deliberately biased efforts in this direction. Anticipating the conclusion regarding the social desirability response set, persons who respond in a socially desirable fashion "naturally" or unconsciously are probably reflecting their personality characteristics accurately, but conscious, deliberate attempts to present oneself in favorable or unfavorable terms constitute an important source of response distortion. Figure 7.2 presents a summary of some of the most common terminology in the area of response styles and sets.

An important impetus for research on the social desirability response set in personality assessment was an early study by Edwards (1953). Edwards obtained college students' ratings on a variety of self-report inventory items on a nine-point scale, according to how desirable they regarded the behavior involved in each item. He then asked another group of students to take these same items as a self-report personality assessment device, and found a very high positive correlation (.87) between the frequency of endorsement of each item by the second group and the mean social desirability ratings given by the first group. In other words, these college students were, to an overwhelming degree, responding to the items in what they perceived as the socially desirable direction. Edwards (1964) went on to demonstrate that respondents' scores on the MMPI scales were so highly correlated with their social desirability ratings of the individual items that their actual MMPI profiles could be predicted moderately well from these ratings. He concluded that, at the least, social desirability interfered with accurate personality assessment; at worst, perhaps it made the use of inventories difficult or even impossible.

The conclusion that a social desirability response set seriously interferes with responses on personality questionnaires was challenged on

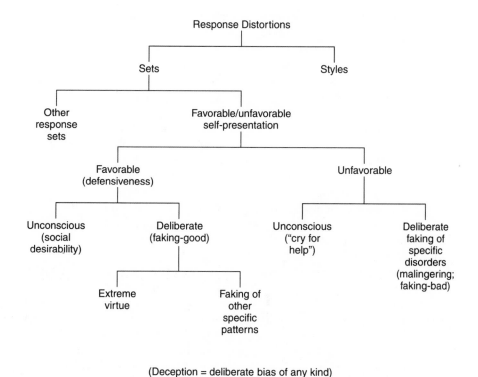

Figure 7.2   Summary of some terminology in the area of response distortions.

methodological, empirical, and theoretical grounds (e.g., Heilbrun & Good-stein, 1961a; Norman, 1967; Paulhus, 1984). At present, a widely accepted view is that social desirability is a normal part of responding and can be an important predictor variable in its own right. Normal individuals ordinar-ily behave in acceptable—that is, socially desirable ways; indeed, this is the typical meaning of "normal." Social undesirability of behavior is perhaps the most important criterion of psychopathology. Psychopathological per-sons' responses to questionnaire items, such as those on the MMPI, tend to be admissions that they are psychologically disturbed; the social undesir-ability of their disturbed behavior is also immediately obvious.

As Heilbrun (1964) noted, the tendency to make socially undesirable re-sponses to personality questionnaires would seem to be sufficiently related to the production of nontest undesirable behavior that a prediction from one to the other is possible. The conclusion that the production of socially desirable behavior is a correlate of adjustment or psychological health seems inescapable, and this conclusion precludes the relegation of social desirability to the category of response distortion. Indeed, for some of the newer tests, such as the Hogan Personality Inventory (Hogan & Hogan,

1992), the operation of a moderate social desirability response set is itself viewed as a social skill or competency.

It is generally agreed that *extreme* degrees of social desirability may mask or distort other aspects of responding on a test, and it is probably wise to take such extremes into consideration whenever possible. For personality inventories assessing characteristics within the normal domain, this can readily be done at the stage of item construction, by using items whose correlations with social desirability are relatively small (e.g., Jackson, 1967, 1976, 1984). Such an approach was originally advocated by Buss (1959) and Buss and Durkee (1957) in the assessment of hostility. For example, rather than presenting the item "Sometimes I lose my temper," to which an affirmative response would be undesirable, the item might be rewritten as "I'm afraid I sometimes lose my temper," or "Sometimes I cannot help losing my temper," or "I am concerned about losing my temper," all of which are worded in a less undesirable manner.

Another widely used approach to the control of social desirability is through the development of *forced-choice* items, with the items matched in pairs (or triplets) for social desirability. Each item in the pair is keyed empirically, or by some other means, as a significant predictor of a behavior of interest. (The EPPS, described in Chapter Three, employs this approach.) A number of problems are still unsolved in the forced-choice procedure. First, the subject is required to choose one of the alternatives, although neither of them may be descriptive of his or her behavior. This yields no information about the absolute strength of the preference or of the personality characteristic underlying it. Second, although the items in a pair are matched in a general way for desirability, many still differ enough that faking is possible (e.g., Dicken, 1959). Third, as noted earlier, efforts to eliminate social desirability may reduce the predictive power of the instrument while they are reducing the influence of defensiveness. Scott's (1968) review of studies comparing the validities of forced-choice and single-stimulus tests reached the more neutral conclusion that the validities achieved with the two approaches did not differ, and that there was no conclusive evidence for the advantage of the forced-choice approach in controlling defensiveness. Thus, it would seem that the forced-choice technique has not proved to be as advantageous a technique for personality questionnaires as had been initially anticipated.

There has been relatively little attempt to study the influence of social desirability in the functioning of projective approaches in personality assessment. Reznikoff (1961) reported insignificant correlations between the social desirability ratings of a series of common TAT themes and their frequency of endorsement, and concluded that social desirability is not an important source of variance in the production of the TAT themes. However, Exner (1978) showed in a Rorschach study that this element "does have a very significant effect on what is actually delivered by the subject"

(p. 45), although, in a later edition of the same book, he downplayed this finding (Exner, 1986). There is no reason to suppose that the general conclusions drawn here in regard to inventories should not also apply to projective techniques, but more research is needed before a definite statement can be made.

Deliberate Deception

A much more serious problem in the evaluation of personality is the tendency of persons to *deliberately slant* or bias their responses to personality assessment devices. The following discussion centers on two topics:

1. Deliberate efforts of individuals to present an unduly favorable picture of themselves as either excessively virtuous or excessively well-adjusted, both of which are loosely referred to in the literature as *defensiveness*. In common usage, this term also refers to individuals' efforts to slant their responses on other personality attributes, such as extroversion or sales ability.

2. Attempts to fake specific *disorders*, such as psychosis or posttraumatic stress disorder, or (outside the realm of personality assessment) memory disorder or mental retardation, for a particular reason.

Developers of the self-report inventory type of personality test have long been aware of these problems (e.g., Meehl & Hathaway, 1946), but could offer no effective solution. Indeed, the obviousness of the problems connected with personality inventories accounts in part for the popularity of the projective approaches to personality assessment, because it is widely believed that the projective approach obviates, or at least sharply reduces, the opportunity for deliberate deception. We shall shortly examine this belief in some detail.

Defensiveness is a deliberate attempt to create a favorable impression. Evidence on the prevalence of defensiveness as a problem in personality assessment comes from a variety of sources. First, normal-appearing personality test profiles are sometimes obtained from psychiatric patients and other deviant individuals who should not produce normal profiles. Second, there is much evidence that a variety of subject groups, such as college students and psychiatric patients, can alter their personality test responses upon request, especially on self-report questionnaires, in order to make a good (or better) impression. It is worth noting that even college students, who ordinarily produce rather normal personality questionnaire profiles, can produce more favorable profiles under "fake-good" instructions. This is especially true for inventories with mostly obvious items—that is, where the social desirability of responses is quite apparent. Many years ago, Fosberg (1941), using the Bernreuter Personality Inventory, was able to show that the correlation between scores obtained under normal instructions and those secured under "fake-good" instructions was quite modest (.11), clearly indicating how a defensiveness set can affect inventory responses of this sort.

On the other hand, there is considerable evidence to suggest that it is not possible for disturbed individuals, especially psychiatric patients, to completely simulate a normal profile. For example, Grayson and Olinger (1957) demonstrated that only 11% of a group of psychiatric patients could fake a normal MMPI profile. Some patients responded to the instructions by producing more deviant profiles, and others simply produced a different pattern of abnormality on their profiles. Canter (1963) found that the ability to "fake good" was itself linked to the relative adjustment of the individual. Using groups of alcoholics and applicants for employment, Canter found that the better-adjusted subjects were more successful in producing "fake-good" profiles on the California Psychological Inventory.

In regard to attempts to make a generally favorable impression on a personality test, it is becoming more common to distinguish between the pretense of superior mental health adjustment and the pretense of extreme personal virtue. Some authors (e.g., Paulhus, 1984, 1986) have tended to view the simulation of superior adjustment as strongly related to the traditional concept of social desirability—generally an unconscious characteristic—and simulation of extreme virtue as related to the concept of personal honesty versus deliberate lying. Thus, results of factor-analytic studies reported by Paulhus (1986) showed two distinct factors. Traditional measures of social desirability loaded on one, called *self-deception,* and measures of more deliberate bias loaded on the other, called *impression management.* Paulhus's (1991) instrument, the Balanced Inventory of Desirable Responding, was constructed to assess these two factors. Two scales developed for the Psychological Screening Inventory (Lanyon, 1970, 1993)—Endorsement of Superior Adjustment and Endorsement of Excessive Virtue—also distinguish between these two components of favorable deceptiveness.

Faking-bad or *malingering* is a deliberate attempt to create the impression of a particular disorder or disability. As with defensiveness, there is much evidence that pathological test profiles can be produced by persons who do not actually possess those characteristics. The developers of the Humm-Wadsworth Temperament Scale addressed this issue more than 60 years ago (Humm & Wadsworth, 1935). In a more recent study by one of the present writers, well-adjusted college students were shown to be able to simulate an MMPI pattern suggestive of psychopathic personality (Lanyon, 1967b). In their original writings on the MMPI, Meehl and Hathaway (1946) considered the existence of these distorting influences to be so obvious as to be self-evident.

Projective Techniques. There has been a traditional belief that projective techniques, especially the Rorschach, are not susceptible to conscious distortion (e.g., Rogers, 1988). However, even early studies, although not completely consistent, tended to show that the Rorschach was indeed vulnerable to faking in both the good and bad directions (Carp & Shavzin, 1950; Feldman & Graley, 1954; Fosberg, 1938, 1941; Henry & Rotter, 1956). These studies further suggested that, compared to psychiatric patients, normal subjects were more capable of distorting their responses, and that it was somewhat easier to "fake-bad" than to "fake-good." The results of more recent studies are mostly consistent with the earlier work. For example, Albert, Fox, and Kahn (1980) showed that experts were unable to detect malingering by either uninformed or informed malingerers. Mittman's (1983) study indicated that the Rorschach was susceptible to malingering when respondents were informed about their role. In regard to faking-good, Exner and Sherman found, in an unpublished study (Exner, 1991), that ten schizophrenic patients were unable to escape detection when asked to improve their performance.

Research on response distortions with other projective instruments, although quite sparse, tends to support these conclusions. For example, Weisskopf and Dieppa (1951) showed that subjects could successfully dissimulate in both positive and negative directions in producing TAT stories, and generally were more successful at "faking-bad," a conclusion also supported by the work of Kaplan and Eron (1965). Holmes (1974) instructed subjects to introduce false projections or to inhibit true projections on the TAT and found that judges were unable to identify either kind of faking. Brozovich (1970) demonstrated the fakability of scores on the Group Personality Projective Test. In a study using the Rosenzweig Picture Frustration Test, Schwartz, Cohen, and Pavlik (1964) found that instructional sets that were defensive or frank produced predictably different responses from their subjects. The main conclusion reached in a recent review of the research on defensiveness and malingering with projective tests is that there is not enough methodologically adequate research to permit firm conclusions (Stermac, 1988). However, the results do suggest that the problem of response distortion also exists for projective tests, and there is little evidence to the contrary.

Combating Deception

The conscious and deliberate efforts of some respondents to slant (especially in the positive direction) their responses to personality assessment devices of both the inventory and projective varieties constitute a serious problem. Perhaps the simplest and most direct approach in dealing with it is to appeal for the cooperation and honesty of respondents in making their responses. Such an approach is useful in situations where the evaluator and the respondent have the same goal: to obtain accurate information about the respondent. This is the case in most research situations and in evaluations related to counseling, mental health, and personal adjustment/development. But, in some common situations, the goal of the respondent is to secure a personal advantage. Examples are: law-related evaluations, whether for competence to stand trial, suitability as the custodial parent after divorce, or mental injury/disability related to a personal lawsuit or to a worker's compensation claim; and in personnel or job-related evaluations, whether for initial hiring, potential promotion, or other special advantage. In all of these situations, a personality-related evaluation will be of limited use unless the respondent's potential deceptiveness is taken into account.

Deceptiveness involves more than attempts to present a generally favorable or generally unfavorable picture. Respondents in a personnel situation may wish to present themselves as having a high degree of sales ability or leadership potential. In a court-related setting, a defendant may wish to deny any possible sign of deviant sexual tendencies. Efforts to malinger might involve the false representation of memory problems, brain damage, or chronic back pain. A fuller treatment of these topics is beyond the scope of this book, but may be found in a variety of sources (e.g., Rogers, 1988; Schretlen, Wilkins, Van Gorp, & Bobholz, 1992).

To understand the nature of contemporary procedures for assessing deliberate deception, a review of the field from a larger perspective is worthwhile. The traditional approach has relied on a *global-signs-of-lying* or *cues-to-deceit* model (Ekman, 1985). The major premise of this approach is that there are universal signs of lying, and they involve physiological and motor responses. These signs, which are usually held to be products of underlying changes in emotionality, are believed to be detectable by means of a polygraph and by careful behavioral observation. The model is fancifully portrayed by the story of Pinocchio, whose lies could be detected by changes in the length of his nose. However, as described in Chapter Five, there is now substantial empirical evidence that polygraph results, though better than chance, are nowhere near the level needed for practical utility (e.g., Bartol & Bartol, 1994). Likewise, the sparse research findings on the use of behavioral cues as global signs of lying suggest that this too is not a fruitful procedure (e.g., Ekman & O'Sullivan, 1991).

Over the past decade or so, another approach to detecting deception has gained increased prominence. In contrast to the traditional approach, which relied on the same global signs regardless of the context or target characteristics that are to be faked, the newer technology is *content-specific*. Because it relies on the respondent's lack of intimate familiarity with the target characteristic, it can be called the *accuracy-of-knowledge* model. As an example, Cornell and Hawk (1989) showed that prisoners attempting to malinger with functional psychosis could be distinguished from genuine psychotics in a number of observable ways. Most of the genuine psychotics showed a characteristic pattern of loose, circumstantial speech, and many were incoherent and/or used neologisms (private, made-up words). They showed flat, blunted, or otherwise inappropriate affect, and their symptom patterns were consistent with a particular disorder. Few malingerers showed these signs; however, malingerers showed signs that were *not* consistent with functional psychosis, such as visual hallucinations, dramatic and exaggerated behavior, and thoughts of suicide.

Similar findings have been reported in other areas. In assessing the genuineness of complaints of low back pain, Chapman and Brena (1990) found a detectable pattern for malingerers, including lower levels of physical activity, less interest in and attention to treatment, and too many symptoms. In regard to memory impairment, Wiggins and Brandt (1988) showed a variety of performance patterns on which true amnesiacs differed from malingerers.

The development of detection procedures based on the accuracy-of-knowledge approach is now occurring quite rapidly, and there is every indication that this approach will be reasonably successful in detecting deception in a wide variety of assessment areas. However, it is by no means new. More than 40 years ago, Gough (1954) developed the Dissimulation (*Ds*) scale to detect patients who were pretending to be more neurotic than they really were. He chose items that empirically distinguished a group of actual patients from persons who were merely pretending to be patients. This scale-construction procedure was successful because the deceptive group did not have accurate knowledge of what it was really like to be a patient. For those few persons who *do* have accurate knowledge of the target characteristic, measures of deceptiveness based on the accuracy-of-knowledge model would be unsuccessful.

The above discussion provides a background for understanding the procedures that have commonly been used for combating deception. This work has been done mainly in the context of mental health assessment and less frequently in the context of normal personality inventories. The three major approaches can be termed *detection, correction,* and *prevention.*

Detection Procedures.   Many inventories include special scales in an effort to assess the degree to which test takers are attempting to slant their responses. For example, the Verification scale of the Kuder Preference Record (Kuder, 1951) and the Lie (*L*) scale of the MMPI give a score indicating the number of times the individual has responded to certain items that are infrequently answered in this fashion. The Verification scale is primarily aimed at identifying subjects who are responding randomly, and the *L* scale attempts to identify persons who have naively defensive attitudes or who are faking-good. Most persons would truthfully endorse only a few of these excessively virtuous *L*-scale items (which are similiar to the item "I have never stolen anything"). Individuals who answer more than a few such items in the

defensive direction are typically regarded as faking-good, and their protocols are usually considered invalid for either clinical or research use.

Like the Kuder Verification scale, the *F* scale of the MMPI represents an
effort to identify those subjects who are responding in an irregular manner,
by utilizing items that are rarely answered in a particular direction. Because
most rare responses on the MMPI are socially undesirable or psychopathological, the *F* scale also serves to identify persons who are attempting to fake-
bad. Considerable research evidence shows that such scales are reasonably
effective in identifying dissimulation. The "*F − K* index," or the difference
between raw scores on the *F* and *K* scales, has also been successful in this regard (Dahlstrom, Welsh, & Dahlstrom, 1975; Gough, 1950).

Correction Procedures.   The authors of the MMPI attempted to go beyond simply detecting favorable or unfavorable response distortion. They
developed the *K* scale as a *correction* device, an attempt to assess the degree
of defensiveness present in a protocol and correct the profile accordingly.
As pointed out in Chapter Three, the *K* scale was developed empirically by
comparing the responses of normal persons with those of psychiatric patients whose scores on the clinical scales were in the normal range, and who
could thus be assumed to be underreporting their psychopathology. High
scores on this scale are obtained by answering "true" to items such as "I
have never felt better in my life."

The *K* score is used directly as a corrective variable and is added, in different fractions, to the respondent's scores on five of the clinical scales (*Hs,
Pd, Pt, Sc,* and *Ma*). The use of the *K* scale in this way was originally shown
to increase the discriminative power of these scales, particularly in the crucial middle range of score values (Dahlstrom, Welsh, & Dahlstrom, 1972, p.
128). It was originally believed by the MMPI authors that the optimal fractions of the *K* scale to be added would differ according to the population of
interest. Thus, Heilbrun (1963) reported a revised set of *K* correction fractions for improved validity of the MMPI among college students. However,
the original set of weights has long become an integral part of the test and
is used in virtually all applications. Nevertheless, the utility of using the *K*-
correction technique, and the particular corrections now in use, must be
viewed as uncertain. In the work of Marks, Seeman, and Haller (1974), who
developed an actuarial interpretation system for the MMPI profiles of adolescents, and in the more recent MMPI-A, it was found that greater validity
could be obtained if no *K* corrections were used at all.

Prevention Procedures.   The best known procedure for the *prevention* of
deception is the use of subtle items, that is, items with empirically demonstrable predictive or concurrent validity but with little or no face validity. It
is a common belief (see Chapter Three) that subtle items tend in general to
be less valid or useful than obvious items. For example, Norman (1963a),

who proposed a complex method for controlling dissimulation by carefully eliminating the most obvious items in his scales, concluded that the use of such scales "constructed for use in one setting with one class of respondents, may not generalize widely" (p. 240). This finding is, of course, consistent with the premise of the accuracy-of-knowledge model, in which successful items for detecting deception are specific to a particular context. When viewed in this light, the use of subtle items should be considered a promising approach. Thus, items such as those discovered by Cornell and Hawk (1989) to identify malingered psychosis, as described above, can appropriately be called subtle.

A rather radical procedure for preventing deception is suggested by the work of Wallace (1966, 1967). Instead of regarding personality in terms of traits or *habitual* performance, terms of abilities or *maximum* performance are substituted. Thus, a measure of dominance might involve a situational test where subjects would be required to respond as dominantly as possible and would be evaluated on their actual performance in meeting these task expectations. For a test of maximum rather than habitual performance, the problem of faking or defensiveness becomes somewhat irrelevant. An indirect version of this idea can be found in the personnel-oriented Comprehensive Personality Profile (Wonderlic Personnel Test, Inc., 1993), a questionnaire on which a candidate for a job is asked to respond to each item twice, once "to describe yourself and your feelings," and once to "put yourself in the shoes of the ideal/perfect candidate." A comparison between the two sets of scores is used to determine the applicant's self-perceived compatibility with the job. However, the validity of this or any other use of a maximum performance approach appears not to have been seriously studied as yet.

All these methods of attempting to handle defensiveness have some merit, and all have their supporters. At the same time, each has some clear-cut limitations and none is a completely satisfactory procedure for handling defensiveness in responding to personality questionnaires. Thus, the question of combating defensiveness will be a continuing one in personality assessment. As we will see in Chapter Twelve, some psychologists (e.g., Lovell, 1967) have expressed the view that personality tests should not be used at all under certain conditions of heightened defensiveness—for example, in personnel selection, a matter to which we will return in Chapter Nine.

SUMMARY

Reliability has to do with the repeatability of a measure. Reliability across presumably equivalent forms of a measuring instrument is called consistency. Stability refers to reliability over time. Lack of reliability, or measurement error, can be either systematic or random. Systematic errors, or biases, can be corrected for or allowed for. Random error can be regarded as stemming from the fact that the content of a test is simply one small sample of the universe of content covering the characteristic of interest. A number of different practical techniques are available for assessing reliability, and which one is used should depend on what sources of unreliability are to be assessed. The Kuder-Richardson formulas and Cronbach's coefficient alpha assess only random error and give an estimate of the internal consistency of a test. Split-half reliability also gives an estimate of random error; alternate-forms and test–retest reliabilities estimate varying degrees of random and systematic error. For practical use of reliabilities in determining the accuracy of a test score, the standard error of measurement can be determined from the reliability coefficient and the standard deviation of the obtained scores.

The special problems associated with determining reliabilities of some projective tests have often led to the inappropriate conclusion that reliability considerations should not apply to them. These problems stem from several sources: the fact that the tests were not constructed with the reliability of scoring categories in mind, the lack of standardization of instructions for administering and scoring the tests, and the subjective aspects of scoring. One approach has been to concentrate on the reliabilities of the various uses to which the test results are to be put; that is, the reliability of global interpretations. This approach, in spite of a number of difficulties, is probably the most appropriate for projective techniques.

Validity may be considered as the degree to which evidence supports the inferences that are made from the test scores. Because different tests may have different kinds of aims, an approach that is appropriate for demonstrating validity in one test or situation may be inappropriate for another. Content or face validity is claimed for a test whose content is a representative sample of the behaviors of interest. Criterion-related validity refers to the accuracy with which guesses about a certain characteristic of the individual, the criterion, can be made from another characteristic, the predictor. Construct validity is relevant where there exists no definitive criterion for the characteristic that is to be assessed, so that it is desirable to demonstrate a network of relationships between the measure of interest and a variety of relevant concepts.

In a clinical situation, the simple predictive accuracy of a test is less important than its incremental validity (the degree to which a test improves the accuracy of the prediction above the level achieved without the test). It is suspected that if closer attention were paid to incremental validities, much present-day routine clinical testing would be dispensed with.

As can be demonstrated when accuracy of prediction is evaluated in terms of hits and misses, it is important to know the base rate or frequency of the event of interest in the population. It is also important to know the cost or value associated with making an incorrect decision in one direction or the other. If the problem is one of selection rather than prediction—that is, if a prediction does not have to be made about every subject on whom information is available—then the selection ratio also becomes a factor in determining predictive efficiency.

A moderator is any piece of information that can be used to predict, for a given person, how accurate another prediction is going to be. Thus, increased accuracy in prediction is potentially possible at the cost of making the prediction only for some proportion of the respondents. The majority of the research and interest in moderator variables to date has been in the contexts of academic and personnel predictions, but it would seem potentially fruitful to explore their use further in clinical and personality assessment. Response distortions refer to any variables, other than the respondents' personality characteristics, that may influence responses to personality assessment procedures. Response styles have been defined as tendencies to select disproportionately some response category independently of the content of the test stimulus. Acquiescence, the most widely studied response style, is the tendency to overrespond "true" on true–false inventories. In an attempt to determine the degree to which acquiescence style distorts inventory responses, several research strategies have been used, including examination of the correlations between scores on original scales and "reversed" scales, factor-analytic studies, and comparison among various measures of acquiescence. The evidence seems to indicate that acquiescence does not exert an important distorting influence on inventory responses, and that previous conclusions to the contrary have not taken into account the contribution of item content. Deviant response style, the tendency to give responses in a deviant direction, has received somewhat less attention than acquiescence, and we have concluded that this style is likewise of little practical importance in personality assessment.

Response sets are tendencies, whether conscious or unconscious, to systematically slant responses to personality assessment devices. Social desirability, or the natural (unconscious) tendency to respond in a socially desirable direction, may not be such a distorting factor as was once supposed, but may instead reflect actual (socially desirable) characteristics of the respondent. Extreme degrees of social desirability are a valid concern, but their likelihood can often be minimized by appropriate wording of items during the initial stages of test construction. There is no conclusive evidence that forced-choice procedures are useful for controlling social desirability.

Deliberate deception, the conscious attempt to slant or bias personality test responses, poses a serious and unresolved problem for the validity of assessment devices. It refers to both faking-bad and faking-good, which themselves involve a number of different approaches, depending on what particular target characteristic is being faked. Considerable progress has been made in the development of specific, content-oriented procedures for detecting attempts at faking specific characteristics, based on the premise that would-be deceivers tend not to have accurate knowledge of the characteristic being faked. This accuracy-of-knowledge approach to deception can be contrasted with the more traditional global-signs-of-lying approach, in which there are believed to be certain universal signs that are independent of the content area being faked. Examples of content-oriented procedures for detecting deception include the MMPI *L* scale for detecting attempts to appear excessively virtuous. Contrary to popular belief, projective techniques are also vulnerable to respondents' efforts to slant their responses, although it appears to be more difficult to deliberately make a favorable impression than an unfavorable one.

There is no strong evidence that correction procedures such as the MMPI *K* scale are useful in combating response distortion. Further work is needed on the development of test construction technology that prevents defensiveness and other response distortions.

CHAPTER EIGHT

Factors Affecting Assessment Utility

We have surveyed many of the major procedures and devices involved in contemporary personality assessment and have attempted to explain their underlying rationale and their actual development. In this chapter, we discuss some of the principles and processes underlying their use in practical situations, the major challenges and problems involved, and research on ways of improving their accuracy in contemporary practice.

Because psychologists have been engaged in personality assessment for many years, it would be reasonable to suppose that standard assessment strategies have evolved for use in any particular situation. For example, there ought to be a relatively standard approach to the evaluation of executive potential, or psychopathology, or leadership in particular situations. Unfortunately, this is not the case. There tend to be rather substantial differences in opinion among practitioners as to which instruments are most useful in a given instance, and what should be done with the responses once they are obtained. In general, the behavior of psychologists in selecting assessment strategies seems to be governed as much by tradition and superstition as by relevance or evidence. Indeed, a survey of psychological assessment practices in acute inpatient settings by Sweeney, Clarkin, and Fitzgibbons (1987) showed that "psychologists typically continue to use the standard test battery developed by Rapaport, Gill, and Schafer in the 1940s" (p. 377). In a survey of outpatient services, Piotrowski and Keller (1989) concluded that "clinicians still rely on traditional assessment instruments" (p. 424). And in a recent survey of 412 clinical psychologists who were active in assessment, Watkins, Campbell, Nieberding, and Hallmark (1995) concluded that "psychological assessment as it is practiced now appears in many respects to be very similar to psychological assessment as it was practiced by psychologists 30 or more years ago" (p. 54). Watkins (1991) came to a similar conclusion.

CLINICIAN VERSUS ACTUARY

The many problems of how the scores derived from the chosen assessment instrument or instruments should be used have been of great interest to research-minded assessment psychologists. Readers may wonder why such problems exist, especially for those instruments with demonstrated empirical validity—that is, with known predictive usefulness. In making a specific prediction, one might presume that the size of the validity coefficient (the known correlation of the test score with the behavior to be predicted) should permit us to make a straightforward prediction by assuming a simple linear relationship between score and behavior. However, most contemporary assessment devices are multiphasic; they yield more than one score, and each of these scores has a different predictive relationship with the criterion behavior. The practitioner thus is faced with the decision of how these several scores should be combined into a single predictive statement.

Another aspect of this problem is that, in any given situation, most contemporary psychologists will want to use several different assessment devices, and these devices yield a melange of scores and responses that require integration before any predictions can be made. Still another problem is the fact that often the accumulated validity data involve a criterion situation that is somewhat different from the one now confronting the psychologist, so that existing validity coefficients are not directly applicable. How psychologists ought to go about using assessment data, how the scores ought to be combined, and how a specific prediction or decision should be made, have been the subjects of rather heated controversy, which crystallized some years ago around comparisons between the *clinical* and *actuarial* modes of operation.

Clinical versus Actuarial Prediction

In most practical situations, the professional psychologist has a great variety of data available on a client—test scores, interview impressions, and biographical information—and is asked to make one or more predictions from these data. Will this patient improve in intensive individual psychotherapy? Should this manager be promoted? Should this delinquent be paroled or imprisoned? In such situations, the psychologist's task is to integrate the available data and make a single overall prognostic or diagnostic statement. Readers may note that the same problem exists for the physician who is attempting a physical diagnosis or treatment regimen, the stockbroker advising a client whether to buy a stock, the potential bettor at the parimutuel window, and so on.

In the *actuarial approach,* the predictors (cues, scores, responses, data) are first quantified and then combined according to a set of rules that have been empirically determined and are to be scrupulously followed. On the basis of previously completed research, each of the obtained predictors is given some quantitative weight, and these predictors are then combined using a "best-fitting" actuarial model. The model may be a simple linear regression equation or a more complex configurational one. The important consideration is always that the actual process of decision making in the actuarial mode follows predetermined rules in a strictly mechanical fashion, requiring no human judgment once the procedure is established.

The *clinical approach* to prediction, in contrast to the actuarial approach, permits practitioners to assign their own weights to the predictors and to combine these predictors in a subjective fashion. The clinical approach refers to instances in which psychologists (or physicians, or stockbrokers, or weather forecasters) use their personal judgment or intuition in order to make what they feel are the appropriate adjustments in the given circumstances.

Examples of the two approaches are as follows. A clinical psychologist may note that a particular patient is depressed, rather agitated, somewhat seclusive, and preoccupied with themes of alienation and death. From these observations, the psychologist concludes that the patient is potentially suicidal and recommends that he or she should be watched carefully. This type of procedure, based largely on the informal accumulated experience of the clinician and his or her private conception of what is involved in suicide, is called the clinical (or case study) method of prediction.

Alternatively, the psychologist might observe the patient's age, marital status, and certain MMPI test scores. The psychologist then consults an actuarial table, which gives the statistical frequency of suicide in persons as a function of such characteristics, and obtains a figure indicating the probability of suicide by that particular patient. This type of procedure, where the prediction derives solely from prior statistical data, is called the actuarial (or statistical) method of prediction.

One of the earliest attempts to develop an actuarial prediction procedure for personality-related events involved the prediction of the likelihood that prisoners would violate their parole (Burgess, 1928; Glueck & Glueck, 1930; Hart, 1923). In the most comprehensive and influential of these studies, Burgess utilized the case files of over 3,000 parolees and was able to identify 21 factors in preparole history that were related to parole success. Burgess then "scored" each of the 3,000 case histories by assigning one point for every predictive factor that was present, yielding a "likelihood of nonviolation" score that could range from 0 to 21. Burgess was able to demonstrate that only 1.5% of those with scores of 16 through 21 were violators, but in the range of lowest scores (2 through 4), 76% were violators. The intermediate scores yielded corresponding intermediate results. These data appear to offer strong support for an actuarial approach to the prediction of parole success, although we shall see later in this chapter that Burgess's failure to deal with the problem of *base rates* flaws his conclusions and raises questions about the practical usefulness of the scores. Another limitation was that the two extreme groups together included less than 10% of the total number of parolees. Nevertheless, the actuarial approach has been successfully applied to a wide variety of other problems, including the prediction of academic success in various educational programs and response to different kinds of institutional and outpatient therapeutic treatments.

Note that the distinction between clinical and actuarial methods does not imply anything about the nature of the data utilized. Case history data, interview impressions, and formal personality assessment scores can be used in both the actuarial and the clinical approach. In the former, these data are quantified and interpreted according to established rules; in the latter, the interpretation is subjective and left to the assumed skill of the clinician. As Gough (1962) wrote:

> *The defining distinction between clinical and actuarial methods is instead to be found in the way in which the data, once specified, are combined for use in making the prediction. If the procedures, however complex mathematically, are in principle such that a clerk, or a machine, or anyone else could carry out the necessary operations and that the result would be the same in all instances, then the method is actuarial or statistical in the sense here being discussed. If the combining is done intuitively, if hypotheses and constructs are generated during the course of the analyses, and if the process is mediated by an individual's judgment and reflection, then the method is clinical. (p. 530)*

Thus, quantified responses to the ambiguous stimuli of projective techniques are a perfectly legitimate source of data for actuarial prediction, so that scores such as the number of Rorschach "whole" responses (W) or percentage of good-form responses (F + %) could be employed actuarially. More complex indexes could also be used. For example, Rorschach (1942) defined the *Erlebnistypus* (EB) as the ratio of the sum of human movement responses to the weighted sum of chromatic color responses (FC = 0.5, CF = 1.0, and C = 1.5). More recently, Exner (1986) listed a total of 30 additional objective ratios, percentages, and derivations to be computed from the basic scoring system, as part of his comprehensive approach to interpreting this test. In regard to specific predictions, Rose and Bitter (1980) developed the Palo Alto Destructive Content Scale as a means of predicting physical assaultiveness in men from their Rorschach responses, and Kendra (1979) used Rorschach scores to develop actuarial predictors for attempted and actual suicide. In each of these cases, the objectification of the data permitted the application of the actuarial method.

It should be obvious that the relative accuracy of the clinical and the actuarial approaches can be directly compared. Burgess (1928) compared his actuarial results with clinical predictions made by two prison psychiatrists and concluded that the overall advantage lay with the actuary. In his seminal work, *Clinical vs. Statistical Prediction*, Meehl (1954) was the first to draw attention to the fact that, although the two approaches arouse strong partisanship and affect, the question of their relative accuracy is, in the final analysis, a straightforward empirical one. After a full discussion of the logic involved in the two approaches, Meehl summarized all of the studies then available that attempted a direct comparison. These studies, not all of which were relevant to the personality domain, tended to fall into three categories: (a) success in training, (b) parole violation, and (c) recovery from psychosis. Meehl's conclusion was that "in all but one . . . the predictions made actuarially were either approximately equal or superior to those made by a clinician" (p. 119).

Meehl noted several qualifications: (a) too little was known about the skill of the clinicians involved in making the predictions; (b) some of the actuarial predictions were made on the data from which the original prediction rules had been derived (i.e., the prediction rules were not cross-validated); and (c) the predictive efficiencies for individual clinicians were rarely reported, so that it usually was not possible to determine the performance of the most accurate clinicians. Nevertheless, Meehl concluded that the studies favored the actuary over the clinician. He further noted that, in favor of the clinician, some clinical predictive activity (e.g., during psychotherapy) cannot in principle be duplicated by statistical procedures. On the other hand, the time saved by employing actuarial rather than clinical procedures is an important factor in favor of the actuarial method.

About a decade later, Meehl (1965) summarized the state of the controversy as follows:

> *Monitoring of the literature yields a current bibliography of some fifty empirical investigations in which the efficiency of a human judge in combining information is compared with that of a formalized ("mechanical," "statistical") procedure. The design and range of these investigations permits much more confident generalization than was true on the eighteen studies available to me in 1954. They range over such diverse substantive domains as success in training or schooling, criminal recidivism and parole violation, psychotherapy (stayability and outcome), recovery from psychosis, response to shock treatment, formal psychiatric nosology, job success or satisfaction, medical (nonpsychiatric) diagnosis, and general trait ascription or personality description. The current "box score" shows a significantly superior predictive efficiency in about two-thirds of the investigations, and substantially equal efficiency in the rest. . . . It would be difficult to mention any other domain of psychological controversy in which such uniformity of research outcome as this would be evident in the literature. (p. 27)*

Meehl revisited this topic yet again in 1986 and 1989, and came to the same conclusions. He stated that no more than 5% of what he said in 1954 needed to be retracted 30 years later (Dawes, Faust, & Meehl, 1989; Meehl, 1986).

Meehl's original work was extended in a review published by Sawyer (1966). Sawyer felt that an important part of the question had been neglected: how the data were *collected*—whether a clinical or a mechanical *measurement* procedure was employed. This neglect, according to Sawyer, had resulted in an incomplete picture of the issues involved in the clinical-statistical controversy. By Sawyer's criteria, data collection was statistical or mechanical "if rules can be prespecified so that no clinical judgment need be involved in the procedure" (p. 181). Thus, all self-report, biographical, psychometric, and clerically obtained data were regarded as statistical data. Information gained in interview or observation, on the other hand, was regarded as clinical data, because it involved subjective judgment. Allowing additional categories for composite methods, Sawyer classified 45 studies that compared the prediction of behavioral outcomes according to both the mode of data collection and the mode of combination of data.

In spite of methodological problems and equivocal results in many of these studies, Sawyer was able to conclude the following: (a) clinical combination of data was inferior to mechanical, no matter how the data were collected; (b) a synthesis between clinical and statistical methods, suggested by Holt (1958), did not appear promising; and (c) the clinician may serve a useful function in the data *collection* process "by providing, in objective form, judgments to be combined mechanically . . . that is, by assessing characteristics that otherwise would not enter the prediction." Thus, "improvement should result from devising better ways for the clinician to report objectively the broad range of possibly relevant behavior he perceives" (p. 193). In other words, Sawyer advocated that judges should act as measuring instruments, and objective procedures should be used to draw conclusions from the data. Parenthetically, we note that the reliability of judgment is greatly increased by averaging across multiple judges.

We have just concluded that, in a situation including a simple dichotomous judgment or prediction, objective rules should be used if they have been appropriately developed. The same conclusion would appear to apply in situations involving a series of decisions, such as a personality description, provided the actuarial rules are available. Why should this be so? Several authors (e.g., Dawes, Faust, & Meehl, 1989; Goldberg, 1991) have presented careful analyses of the reasons underlying the superiority of the actuarial approach. For one thing, clinicians are subject to factors such as fatigue, the biasing effects of recent experience, and other seemingly minor influences. Thus, they show fluctuations in judgmental accuracy. Second, the actuarial method can "ensure that variables contribute to conclusions based on their predictive power," and "include only the predictive variables and eliminate the nonpredictive ones" (p. 1671). Third, clinicians commonly develop false beliefs about the predictive power of their tests—beliefs that are quite resistant to change even when corrective information is available. This last difficulty, termed *illusory correlation* (see Chapter Twelve), is caused in part by "natural" but erroneous beliefs about associations between events, such as a belief that persons who perceive "eyes looking at me" in Rorschach cards are paranoid. Fourth, because particular clinicians may be exposed to a skewed sample of patients, it may be impossible for them to determine the true relationships among variables.

Dawes et al. (1989) also listed possible reasons why the findings regarding the superiority of actuarial approaches have not had more of an impact on clinicians. Perhaps the main reason is that clinicians tend not to be readily exposed to the relevant research findings; or, if they are exposed to them, such findings may not be taken seriously. After all, "the interview remains the *sine qua non* of entrance into mental health training programs" (p. 1672) and occupies a central role in all such professions. Thus, the use of actuarial data is not consonant with the interests or self-image of many persons in the helping professions, and it may even be viewed as dehumanizing. A second reason is based on the misconception that "group statistics do not apply to single individuals or events" (p. 1672). In this view, the uniqueness of the person under consideration is somehow believed to require a type of individual scrutiny for which normative or other group data are simply not relevant. A third reason has to do with possible overconfidence in one's ability to predict, a topic that is discussed later in this chapter.

The Clinician as Hypothesis Builder

A safe conclusion to be drawn from the foregoing discussion is that once empirical relationships have been established between cues and criteria, the clinician can profitably be supplanted by an actuarial model of the phenomenon to be predicted. This suggests that an important role for the assessment clinician, perhaps the most important role, is the identification or discovery of new predictors or cues that will enhance predictive accuracy.

An example of the role of the clinician as a hypothesis generator can be found in the work of Meehl and Dahlstrom (1960). Their project developed a set of rules for discriminating between the MMPI profiles of patients who, independently of the MMPI, had been unequivocally diagnosed as either neurotic or psychotic. Meehl and Dahlstrom initially used their clinical judgment to sort the profiles, and then wrote a series of sequential, mechanical rules that attempted to duplicate their clinical judgment. Using an essentially similar approach, Kleinmuntz (1963) was able to develop a computer program for distinguishing between the MMPI profiles of normal and maladjusted college students.

But even the hypothesis-generating role of the clinician can, in principle, be supplanted by the computer. L. R. Goldberg (1965), using the same MMPI profiles as Meehl and Dahlstrom (1960), compared their rules with 29 clinical judges and with a wide variety of other potentially discriminative rules and indexes, some based directly on clinical experience and some more or less arbitrary, with no known clinical significance. One of the more interesting findings was that one of the latter rules—the linear combination of scores ($L + Pa + Sc - Hy - Pt$)—proved to be the best discriminator between neurotics and psychotics. Goldberg (1970) also showed that simplified mathematical representations of the clinicians' judgments were more accurate than the original judgments themselves. However, the empirically developed rule given previously outperformed even these representations.

In principle, the Goldberg procedure—that is, the empirical study of predictive hypotheses—could be extended to any predictive situation. The efficiency of an assortment of different hypotheses or indexes—indeed, all possible indexes that could be generated—can be examined by computer, bypassing the need for the clinician even to generate hypotheses or offer judgments. This nontheoretical approach precisely corresponds to the empirical approach to test construction, discussed in Chapter Three, and embodies both the same advantages and the same disadvantages.

Development of Objective Interpretation Systems

The research findings showing the utility of actuarial modes of interpreting personality assessment data led to an interest in the possibility of developing objective code books (or "cookbooks") for test interpretations. In an early study, Halbower (1955) compared the accuracy of personality descriptions generated by clinicians from patients' MMPI profiles with descriptions generated from MMPI profiles by actuarial procedures. First, he identified, and defined by specific rules, four MMPI "types" that were relatively common in his patient sample. For example, the "code 13" type was defined by the following rules: *Hs* and *Hy* $\geq$ 70; *D* < *Hs* and *Hy* by at least 10 scale points; either *K* or *L* > both *?* and *F*; *F* $\leq$ 65; and scales *Pd, Mf, Pa, Pt, Sc, Ma,* and *Si* all < 70. To construct "cookbook" or actuarial descriptions of each profile type, he selected at random nine patients whose MMPI profiles fitted the type. Each patient's therapist then completed a 154-item Q-sort that involved the ranking of personality descriptive statements from "most like the patient" to "least like the patient." The mean of the five most similar Q-sorts was designated as the actuarial description of that type. To compare the accuracy of these cookbook descriptions with those made clinically, two additional patients fitting each MMPI profile type were selected, and therapists' Q-sorts were again used as the criterion. Not one of the individual clinicians' readings of an MMPI profile correlated as strongly with the criterion as did the cookbook reading. Halbower repeated the comparison using patients drawn from a different population and achieved similar results.

The finding that more accurate patient personality descriptions could apparently be obtained from an MMPI cookbook than from a clinician led Marks and Seeman (1963) to develop a much more comprehensive cookbook for describing the majority of psychiatric patients. Using MMPI profiles from the psychiatric patients of a midwestern medical center, they were able to develop 16 different profile types that accounted for 78% of the patients in their sample. The authors reported much normative information about their profile types (including other psychometric information, case history details, presenting symptoms, diagnosis, and course in treatment), expressing the data in terms of percent of occurrence and giving a comparison with patients in general. This cookbook was reissued in revised form a decade later with greatly simplified rules for classifying patients into the same 16 profile types (Marks, Seeman, & Haller, 1974). Although the change increased the percentage of patients whose profiles fitted the rules, thus countering a major criticism of the original cookbook (see following discussion), no new data were presented as to the validity of the simplified rules.

A similar handbook of MMPI profile interpretations was developed by Gilberstadt and Duker (1965). They developed 19 profile types, using an approach similar to the one employed by Halbower and by Marks and Seeman. Based on a careful reading of the case histories of the male VA psychiatric patients who fitted each of these profile types, Gilberstadt and Duker reported the most likely diagnosis and an extended clinical personality description of each type. They also reported a list of complaints, traits, and symptoms that statistically differentiated each type from patients in general.

A third MMPI interpretive cookbook was developed by Drake and Oetting (1959) for describing college students. Basing their analyses on the three highest and two lowest MMPI scales of the profiles of more than 4,000 college students who had sought counseling, they identified statistically nearly 700 different patterns. They then examined the counseling case materials and independently compiled a list of problems, descriptive phrases, and other items descriptive of these individuals. The cookbook lists the various code patterns, their frequencies, and the personality descriptions that were significantly associated with each pattern.

An interpretative MMPI cookbook for adolescents was developed by Marks, Seeman, and Haller (1974). These authors first developed eight new sets of MMPI norms (without *K* corrections), covering males and females separately in the following four age groups: 14 and below, 15, 16, and 17–18. The MMPI responses of approximately 1,800 "normal" adolescents from six different states were involved in establishing these norms. They then identified 834 White, nonretarded adolescent patients aged 12–18 from 74 different psychological treatment settings over 30 states, involving a total of 172 different therapists. All of these patients had been in treatment for at least 10 sessions.

To develop the cookbook, the profiles of the 834 treatment cases were determined using the new adolescent norms and were then categorized according to the two highest scales, regardless of the absolute values of these two scales. If a code type had less than 10 cases, the first and third highest scales were used. By this procedure, the authors were able to classify more than 98% of the 834 treatment cases. The cookbook presents descriptions of 29 different code types, based on a number of data sources such as adjective checklists filled out by both patients and therapists, a descriptive Q-sort and other data supplied by the therapist, and an objective case history form.

Another contribution to the MMPI literature on objective interpretation systems is the work of Megargee (1977, 1979) and his colleagues on a prison population. Megargee's primary aim was to develop a "reliable, valid, economical typology for classifying criminal offenders" (1979, p. 305). The first step in this project was to use Veldman's (1967) "hierarchical profile analysis" for the purpose of finding groups of profiles that were similar to one another. After identifying nine such groups, the researchers used a lengthy trial-and-error procedure to develop objective rules for defining each type. A wide variety of case information was available about each inmate, including presentence investigation reports, family data, educational and vocational achievement, adjustment reports while in prison, and postprison behavior. These data were used to develop modal descriptions of each of the nine code types. Megargee (1979) reported that more than 85% of offenders in a wide range of settings could be assigned a specific type within his system.

There are a number of more recent objective interpretation programs, for the MMPI and for other tests, but they exist within the context of automated or computerized interpretation systems that are offered commercially, and some of them are not based on empirical data. Because these systems are not available for use except through their commercial outlets, and because little or no information about their development or validity is available, they are discussed in Chapter Eleven in the context of automated interpretation and its associated problems. One exception is a cookbook for the Personality Inventory for Children (PIC) (Wirt, Lachar, Klinedinst, & Seat, 1977, 1990), which is based on a careful actuarial study by Lachar and Gdowski (1979). This study also forms the basis for a commercially available computer interpretation program.

There has been little research to cross-validate the various cookbooks by evaluating their adequacy in other populations. Most of the early research activity was directed at peripheral issues, such as showing that only relatively small percentages of patients could be covered by the 1963 Marks and Seeman rules and the Gilberstadt and Duker rules (e.g., Huff, 1965; Klett & Vestre, 1967; Payne & Wiggins, 1968; Sines, 1966). As we shall see in Chapter Eleven, the research efforts in the development of objective interpretation systems have tended to involve two areas: (a) the practical development of commercially available computer interpretation systems for a number of different tests, and (b) to a lesser extent, the objective use of interview and biographical data. There is also a body of research literature studying the relative merits of different actuarial strategies, to which we now turn.

Research on Actuarial Strategies

The first responses to Meehl's (1954) conclusion about the superiority of actuarial over clinical prediction were, understandably, objections that Meehl had not fairly represented the clinical side of the argument. These objections are exemplified by the writings of Holt (1958, 1970, 1986), who felt that it would be productive to attempt to understand the relative contributions of each approach. Holt described the process of prediction as involving several steps: a study of the criterion, choice of intervening variables, choice of measures of these variables, data collection, and data combination. Clinical or statistical approaches can be used at any of these steps, so that a prediction process should be characterized as "more clinical than statistical," or "more statistical than clinical."

Holt used the term *sophisticated clinical prediction* to describe a procedure employing all these steps but retaining the clinician as a prime instrument, and the term *naive clinical prediction* for a procedure in which the clinician does not make a systematic effort to collect the necessary preliminary information before making predictions. Most of the studies of clinical prediction reviewed by Meehl (1954) were, according to Holt, studies of the naive clinical method, and thus could not be expected to show what experienced clinicians could do if they really put their minds to it. Holt emphasized that there were prediction problems where it would make best sense to employ a more clinical approach *and* where a more actuarial approach would be the method of choice. Thus, for any problem, an attempt should be made to find the optimal combination of the methods.

Holt's challenge was taken up by a number of researchers. Over the years, a significant research literature has developed on the question of actuarial and clinical accuracy. One line of research made a closer study of actuarial procedures themselves. Is there one particular actuarial approach or model that consistently tends to result in more accurate outcomes? This research question was initially addressed in the simplest of contexts: dichotomous prediction situations. For example, L. R. Goldberg's (1965) study on the prediction of neurosis versus psychosis from MMPI profiles examined a wide variety of actuarial or objective predictors. Some of these predictors were *linear,* involving individual MMPI scales or simple additive combinations of scales, and some were *configural,* such as the sums of the squares of certain scale scores, the number of "signs" of a particular kind, and the Marks and Seeman profile types. Goldberg's conclusion from this aspect of his study was that "simple linear combinations of scale scores were more accurate than configural models" (p. 1). This conclusion directly contradicted Meehl's (1954) early hypothesis, in which he thought that because the judgment process of clinicians is believed to be highly configural in nature, the most accurate actuarial predictors would be configural.

Not content with his original findings, Goldberg (1969) tried out a variety of additional configural procedures. Once again, he was led to the same conclusion: "Neither . . . moderated regression analyses, profile typologies, the Perceptron algorithm, density estimation procedures, Bayesian techniques, nor sequential analyses . . . have been able to improve on a simple linear function" (p. 523). Further studies by Giannetti, Johnson, Klingler, and Williams (1978) and by Pritchard (1977), involving methodological improvements over earlier studies, reached the same conclusion regarding the superior accuracy of linear over configural predictors.

In a series of publications, Dawes (1979; Dawes & Corrigan, 1974; Dawes, Faust, & Meehl, 1989) demonstrated that the superiority of linear models in the prediction of complex events is widespread, not only in psychological predictions but on a much more general level, involving such disparate areas as business, violence, and politics. He and others have also questioned the importance of the individual weights given to each of the terms in the linear predictive function (e.g., Pruzek & Frederick, 1978; Wainer, 1978). Apparently, for situations where the ceiling on predictive accuracy is relatively low, it makes little practical difference whether these weights are selected with any particular care.

There is still a great deal to be learned about the technology of constructing actuarial prediction systems in personality assessment. Most of the research has been limited to consideration of simple dichotomous predictions, such as whether an MMPI profile reflects neurosis or psychosis. In real life, the problems facing psychologists who develop actuarial systems are more complex. For example, are the basic profile categories or "types" best formed on the basis of high-point profile codes (e.g., Marks, Seeman, & Haller, 1974), or of natural clusters of profiles that are then defined more precisely by complex rules (e.g., Marks & Seeman, 1963; Megargee, 1977), or by some other method? Lachar, DeHorn, and Gdowski (1979), addressing this question for the Personality Inventory for Children, concluded that both of these systems may be useful. In two of the most recent inventories, the NEO Personality Inventory (Costa & McCrae, 1992b) and the Personality Assessment Inventory (Morey, 1991), primary reliance for interpretation is placed on *facets* or subscales that were developed during test construction as an integral part of each scale. Another topic of considerable importance in constructing actuarial systems—the development of ways to include information about the population base rates of variables to be predicted—is discussed in Chapter Eleven.

Some General Considerations

There are several additional points to be made about actuarial and clinical approaches. First, it should not be forgotten that any instrument of demonstrated predictive usefulness (validity) can be used in either a clinical or an actuarial manner. Second, little is known about the degree to which actuarial or cookbook descriptions can be generalized from the original sample on which they were constructed. The research on the two major MMPI cookbooks that describe psychiatric patients, cited above, suggests that some caution may be necessary. However, the ultimate contribution of actuarial techniques to clinical psychology will depend on their generality, because the time and effort required to develop such cookbooks can be justified only when the results can be broadly applied.

Third, a general issue pertains to the clinician of exceptional predictive skill. In studies that have reported the success rates of individual clinicians, it is commonly found that some clinicians are consistently more accurate in their predictions than others. It has therefore been advocated that more effort should be directed toward identifying such clinicians and having them train others. Goldberg (1970), on the other hand, argued that it would be more useful to employ the most accurate clinicians in the development of actuarial formulas that would then supplant the clinicians altogether. His research evidence showed strong support for this position.

A related point was made by Pritchard (1980), who argued that, in certain situations, clinical input into a prediction might be desirable and justifiable. For example, in many instances, the costs or utilities associated with different sources of error should be taken into account (see later discussion). Pritchard also believed that clinical or subjective review of an actuarial prediction would be in order whenever a clinician had an ethical responsibility to an individual client. Dawes's (1980) response to these suggestions for using clinical input was that actuarial procedures would be superior to the subjective approaches in these situations also, and that clinical input was therefore still unjustified.

Our final comment concerns the relative economy of the clinical and actuarial procedures. Although one advantage claimed for actuarial over clinical methods is the ultimate savings in time, there are situations in which the clinical method will be more economical, especially if the two methods yield roughly comparable accuracy. Such a situation was described by Johnston and McNeal (1967), who compared methods of predicting length of stay in a psychiatric hospital. Actuarial prediction from case history and behavioral variables was about as accurate as clinical prediction made by the professional staff while handling their routine professional assignments. Because the clinical approach involved considerably less time and effort than the actuarial, the clinical approach was presumably the method of choice.

BASE RATES AND DECISION MAKING

The term *base rate*, or the relative frequency of an event (disorder, symptom, behavior) in the population of interest, was introduced in Chapter Seven, and examples were presented showing the importance of knowing the base rate of a disorder before making a prediction about its presence or absence for a particular individual. Although the intelligent understanding and use of base rate information greatly increases the effectiveness of personality assessment in practical situations, psychologists have been relatively slow to accept the importance of base rates and to incorporate this information into their clinical work.

The matter was first brought to prominence by Meehl and Rosen (1955) in their discussion of the hit-and-miss validity of predictive devices. Meehl and Rosen pointed out that the more the base rate diverges from .5 (i.e., a 50/50 division in the population), the greater will be the difficulty in prediction. In certain cases, the overall hit-and-miss success rate will be lower if the test is used than if all persons were simply regarded as belonging to the more frequent category. For example, in Table 7.2, the hit rate (correct diagnosis) was only 97.6%, as compared with 99% if everybody were to be called "normal."

Cureton (1950) showed that, for a valid predictor, it should always be possible to find a cutting score that will result in a greater overall proportion of correct predictions than would result from "using the base rate"— that is, by regarding everybody as belonging to the more frequent category. Thus, if the cutting score in Table 7.2 were to be raised to, let us say, 100, the result might well be depicted as in Table 8.1. The success rate (i.e., correct diagnosis) is 99.1%, a very modest improvement over the base rate of 99%, but an improvement nonetheless. However, it is doubtful whether a cutting score of 100 would be useful in practice; the great majority of the actual schizophrenics would not have been identified as such by the test. (We recognize that it *would* in fact be possible to identify situations where the base rate could never be exceeded no matter what cutting score was employed—for example, if the variability of scores in the less frequent condition was substantially smaller than the variability of scores in the more frequent condition. The point is, however, that hit-and-miss success rates can be manipulated simply by altering the cutting score.)

In making a particular prediction, it is probable that no single test will be uniformly optimal for all population base rates and relative outcome values. Satz, Fennel, and Reilly (1970) provided an excellent illustration of

Table 8.1   Hypothetical Percentage of Patients Diagnosed Schizophrenic or Normal by the Sc Scale, Using a Cutting Score of 100, Where 1 Percent Are Actually Schizophrenic and 99 Percent Are Actually Normal

T Score	Actually Schizophrenic	Actually Normal	Total
T score 100 or more (diagnosed as schizophrenic)	0.2[a]	0.1	0.3
T score below 100 (diagnosed as normal)	0.8	98.9[a]	99.7
Total	1.0	99.0	100.0

[a] Correctly diagnosed.

this point, reporting hit-and-miss percentages for the prediction of brain disease from five neurological tests and one neuropsychological test. Three different hypothetical base rates for brain disease were then considered (.8, .5, and .2). The data clearly showed that two of the tests that gave a relatively poor showing on overall percentage hit-and-miss figures were in fact the most effective when the base rate for brain disease was as low as .2. These tests, which made almost no "false positive" errors (calling normal persons brain-diseased) but correctly identified only a moderate percentage of the actual brain-diseased patients ("true positives"), proved most likely to be correct when the great majority of the subjects were not brain-diseased.

The need to consider base rates in making clinical discriminations based on tests was raised again by Elwood (1993), who introduced the concepts of *positive predictive power,* the ratio of true positives to all positives (0.2/0.3 in Table 8.1), and *negative predictive power,* the ratio of true negatives to all negatives. Using these concepts, Elwood was able to demonstrate that even when base rates are in the moderate range rather than very high or very low, they can still have a significant effect on accuracy.

Sensitivity and Specificity. In recent years it has become popular to approach questions of diagnostic accuracy through the language of signal detection theory, which was originally developed in psychophysics (Swets, 1961; Swets, Tanner, & Birdsall, 1961). Adapted for use in medicine and epidemiology by Lusted (1968) and others, concepts are available for describing two basic aspects of accuracy in a diagnostic or screening process:

1. *Sensitivity* is the ability of a test to give a positive finding for persons who actually have the disease (the true positives). Quantitatively, it is the proportion of all diseased persons who are currently identified by the test; or, in terms of the example in Table 7.1, the figure of 60%, which came from the Hathaway (1956a) study.

2. *Specificity* is the ability of a test to give a negative finding for those persons who do not have the disease (the true negatives). Quantitatively, it is the proportion of all nondiseased persons who are currently identified by the test; or, in terms of the Table 7.1 example, 49 of 50 or 98%, representing 100 minus the 2% figure from the Hathaway study.

In signal detection language, therefore, Hathaway's cutting point of 70 on the *Sc* scale has only moderate sensitivity, 60% (it misses a lot of schizophrenics), but high specificity, 98% (it correctly excludes nearly all normals). We remind readers that these figures are for illustrative purposes only. Hathaway's findings should not be considered applicable to other samples. Referring now to the figures on which Table 8.1 is based, raising the cutting point from 70 to 100 is accompanied by a decrease in sensitivity to as low as 20%. Specificity increases to 98.9/99% or 99.9%.

These terms offer a language to describe characteristics of the test itself. However, their practical application must take base rates into consideration. In a sophisticated study, Chen, Faraone, Biederman, and Tsuang (1994) introduced the signal detection theory concept of *receiver operating characteristic (ROC)* curves, which graphically represent the sensitivity rate against (one minus) the specificity rate. Chen et al. assessed the diagnostic accuracy of the Attention Problems scale of the Child Behavior Check List (see Chapter Ten). They demonstrated how base-rate data could be incorporated into the scheme by a simple formula, enabling them to compare diagnostic accuracy in samples with differing base rates. A similar study, demonstrating the use of receiver operating characteristics to optimize the prediction of violent crimes, was conducted by Rice and Harris (1995). Such studies demonstrate that when warranted by the availability of large samples, it may be possible to do significantly more than is currently being done to get the maximum performance out of existing tests and scales.

Decision Making

In a practical assessment situation, the interest is usually not so much in the hit-and-miss success rate as in the overall *usefulness* or *efficiency* of a test. Referring again to Table 7.2, for every 1,000 subjects tested, a cutting score of 70 on the *Sc* scale would identify a group of 26, but only 6 of them would actually be schizophrenic (i.e., "true positives"). However, we might well be willing to accept this state of affairs if we are planning to employ much more extensive and costly procedures for a further evaluation of the 26 thus identified. The benefit would be that we are saved the expense of evaluating the entire 1,000 in this manner. The price we pay consists of (a) failing to identify four pathological persons—the "false negatives," and (b) the cost of the screening procedure.

These questions involving costs and benefits fall in the area of *decision making*, a topic that is becoming increasingly important in personality assessment. The development of a decision-making orientation in the field of personality assessment came about in two ways. The first was an outcome of the Meehl and Rosen (1955) paper, which had implied, perhaps without intent, that percentage accuracy was the all-important criterion in diagnosis or classification. This paper elicited a number of rejoinders (e.g., Buchwald, 1965); they insisted that the *utility* of a classification, not its accuracy, should be used as the ultimate criterion for judging it. Taking account of utility involves a quantitative determination of the different consequences of the various possible classifications in terms of their costs to all concerned. For example, what would be the overall costs to the individual, the family, professionals concerned with the treatment, and society generally, of institutionalizing a patient at a given time; and, conversely, what would these costs be if the patient were to be maintained in the home?

The second important influence leading toward a decision-making orientation in personality assessment was the appearance of the first edition of the book *Psychological Tests and Personnel Decisions,* by Cronbach and Gleser (1957/1965), who offered a clear decision-making framework for the use of psychological tests as an alternative to more traditional orientations. Among the issues raised was the expected utility, or "payoff" relative to its yield in predictive accuracy, of a particular kind of information in terms of the cost of obtaining this information. In other words, the cost of the testing program must be weighed against the increased efficiency of the selection process. Further discussion of this and other practical applications of the decision-making approach have been provided by Chen, Faraone, Biederman, and Tsuang (1994), Elwood (1993), and Messick (1995).

The decision-making approach focuses on the consequences of various courses of action. Instead of describing a person according to such traditional personality dimensions as dominant, tolerant, and anxious, or classifying him or her according to traditional psychiatric categories, such as depressed, schizophrenic, and brain-damaged, the decision-making approach deals with the various courses of action open to the persons who are performing the assessment. For example, if a psychiatrist requests a "personality evaluation" of a psychiatric inpatient so that a decision can be made among discharge, an open unit, or a locked unit, these three options become the possible alternatives to be studied. There is no criterion for the accuracy of assessment, in the sense that a description of being high in dominance can be verified against peer ratings or the holding of leadership positions, or a diagnosis of schizophrenia can be checked for accuracy against a panel of expert judges, or a diagnosis of brain damage can be checked against physiological tests. Rather, the criterion is one of cost and utility—the *value* of the decision. The aim is to make the decision/assessment that results in the most useful outcome, all things considered. The technical aspects of decision-making strategies in psychological assessment situations (e.g., Cronbach & Gleser, 1957/1965; Wiggins, 1973) are quite complex and beyond the scope of this book. However, it is worth looking at one general approach to complex decision making, *operations research,* which developed in a quite different context.

Operations Research

During World War II, the British government was faced with the problem of allocating its limited war resources to a wide variety of possible activities. The criterion for allocation was simple in principle—maximize the effectiveness of these resources. Mathematical techniques were developed to assist in the kind of decisions that were necessary under such circumstances.

After the war, it was realized that the decisions that had been faced were essentially the same as those facing business and industry in countless ways. For example, how many salespeople should a company hire, and where should they be sent, to sell the maximum amount of the company's products at the least cost? Or, how many checkout counters should a supermarket have in order to preserve an optimal balance between saving on clerks' time and losing customers because of waiting too long? How many plants should a company have, and where should they be located, in order to strike an optimal balance between the cost of transporting raw materials and the cost of transporting finished goods to their markets? The field of expertise in the complex engineering, mathematical, and business approaches to such problems came to be known as *operations research*. For a classic account of some of the techniques of this field, readers are referred to Ackoff and Rivett (1963) for a brief introduction, and to Hillier and Lieberman (1967) for a more detailed treatment.

Ways in which the technology of operations research can be applied to personality assessment and to the broader context of decision making within mental health contexts have been described by Halpert, Horvath, and Young (1970) and by Lyons (1980). Although definite progress has been made in this area, the major difficulty continues to be the development of adequate criteria of *utility*, a task that involves quantification of the different values associated with the various possible decisions. In business and industry, *profit* is the criterion of utility traditionally employed. Relationships can be quantified in terms of the money involved, and a system that will result in the greatest profit can then be devised. A similar approach is possible in the context of psychological assessment; however, the situation is not quite so straightforward. The values will at times be financial, but a more important component is the social or cultural values involved. For example, how much is it worth to a person, socially, to avoid confinement in a psychiatric hospital? Or, how much is it worth to a community to have a particular person confined in a psychiatric hospital, where his or her bizarre actions will not threaten others? Despite an interesting collection of papers by Shelly and Bryan (1964) on the quantification of values, ways of determining such mental-health-related values and incorporating them into decision-making processes need still to be developed in order to make full use of the potential of operations research technology.

It can be argued that social and cultural values are too complex to be quantified, and that it is foolish to hope for any success along these lines. However, these values are implicitly estimated whenever an actual decision is made about a psychiatric patient, regardless of whether the decision maker is explicit about them. In other words, we cannot and do not avoid making judgments about these values in our actual behavior. The situation might be seen as analogous to skilled clinicians who integrate personality assessment information in their heads and make diagnoses or predictions about the respondent. They have combined certain specific pieces of information according to certain specific rules, even if they were not aware of doing so. On a broader level, administrators and policy makers constantly assign implicit quantitative values to human needs, desires, and conditions as they attempt to predict, for example, how much money the public will pay for admission to a concert or a baseball game, or how much of the country's limited budget should be spent on roads versus health care. A task for the future is to make explicit these implicit processes and values.

In conclusion, we refer back to the actuarial work of Burgess (1928) on parole violation. In his sample, 28.5% of all the parolees violated their parole; to put it a different way, the base rate for parole violation was 28.5%. Thus, we would have been correct 71.5% of the time if we had predicted that all parolees would be nonviolators. Gough (1962) reanalyzed Burgess's data and demonstrated that, if optimal cutting scores had been used (those that would give the greatest number of placements in the correct groups of violators and nonviolators), the overall predictive accuracy would have been 76%, or only 4% greater than the accuracy of predicting that all the parolees would be nonviolators. Whether the use of the actuarial data would have been justified in this setting (as opposed to following the base rate and predicting that there would be no violation at all) would depend on the efficiency or optimality of the decisions that would follow, or, more specifically, on the relative costs associated with each kind of predictive error.

COMPARISON OF DATA SOURCES

It may only be a slight exaggeration to say that many psychologists, when assigned a task in personality or clinical assessment, administer to the respondent a standard battery of psychological assessment instruments, and that they often follow the same procedure *no matter what* information is being sought or what question is to be answered. Findings to show that assessment practices have changed relatively little over the past 30 years have already been quoted (Watkins et al., 1995). Part of the reason for this continued behavior may be that referrals are often nonspecific as to the issues that are of concern; another is the traditional and now obsolete view that an understanding of any part of a person's problems requires an in-depth assessment of the entire personality.

There are at least two problems with this rigid approach. First, every patient is different; the task of finding things out about one patient is never quite the same as finding them out about another. Second, it would seem reasonable to expect that, for any given assessment task (regardless of whether we include the particular patient as part of the definition of the task), one particular combination of instruments and procedures would be optimal for the task.

In Chapters Three and Four, we discussed the various approaches to the construction of personality assessment devices (see also the Appendix). A significant part of that discussion was devoted to an examination of the ways in which individual items are selected to form a scale. The underlying principle was that each item should contribute something unique to the total product and should complement every other item, so that the concept or domain to be assessed would be fully represented.

The same principle should apply when a group of tests is assembled for the purpose of evaluating a particular patient. To do so, however, we would need to know exactly what is contributed by each test to the assessment task as a whole. For example, what patient characteristics are best assessed by the Rorschach? What does an interview contribute that cannot easily be learned by other methods? What are the strongest contributions of the MMPI? Unfortunately, there is no systematic body of research that addresses these questions directly, and such research would be an expensive and large-scale task. However, a number of individual studies are relevant to this area, and, indeed, permit us to draw some fairly firm conclusions. The findings are consistent with the general theme that the more *independent* the methods or sources of data that are employed, the more valid will be the resulting assessment. Let us now review the evidence in this area.

Contributions of Assessment Instruments

A number of studies have been carried out within an incremental validity framework to evaluate the different contributions of various assessment instruments to making a traditional clinical psychodiagnostic evaluation of psychiatric patients. Kostlan (1954) collected four kinds of information from each of five male psychiatric outpatients: social case history, the Rorschach, the MMPI, and a sentence completion test. Twenty clinicians were presented with different combinations of three out of the four kinds of data, and their analyses were compared with those of criterion judges, using a lengthy checklist of personality descriptive items. The surprising finding was that the clinicians who did not have access to the social case history gave personality descriptions that were no more accurate than those made on the basis of "minimal data" alone (age, occupation, education, marital status, and reason for referral to the clinic). It was also found that the "minimal data" permitted descriptions that were better than chance, and that the most accurate descriptions were those based on combinations that included both the social case history and the MMPI. Similar results were found by Sines (1959) in his study of biographical, interview, Rorschach, and MMPI data. Again, biographical data contributed significantly more than the test data; also, there was some evidence that, beyond a certain point, accuracy tended to *decrease* as more data were available.

The most extensive study of the ability of clinical psychologists to make traditional psychiatric diagnoses from assessment instruments was carried out by Little and Shneidman (1959). The instruments involved were the MMPI, the TAT, the Rorschach, and Shneidman's (1951) projective Make-a-Picture-Story Test. Each instrument was considered singly. Forty-eight psychologists—12 who were considered expert with each of the 4 tests—gave diagnoses and personality descriptions for 4 subjects. The criteria were diagnoses from extended case history data for each of the subjects. Although the results of this study were complex, findings of note were: the disappointingly low agreement of the test experts, both among themselves and with the criterion diagnoses, and the generally low accuracies of the experts' test interpretation. Golden (1964) utilized the same patient data in an attempt to determine whether descriptions based on clinical tests increased in accuracy as a function of the number of tests employed, and discovered that they did not. An independent study by Wildman and Wildman (1975) reported similar findings.

A related study in the area of normal personality characteristics was conducted by Scott and Johnson (1972). The aim was to compare the validity of assessments made from *direct* tests, such as self-report questionnaires, with those made from *indirect* tests, such as predicted consequences of hypothetical events and imaginative stories written about TAT pictures. Criteria for the predictions were provided by friends' ratings. The findings tended to support the superiority of the direct measures over indirect approaches to personality assessment. Mischel (1972) reached a similar conclusion after reviewing a variety of other evidence on the same topic.

What conclusions can be drawn from these studies? For one thing, the studies rather consistently demonstrate that, as sources of data for psychological prediction or description, personality tests do not fare as well as case history data. There is also the suggestion that a single test adds about as much to the case history data as do a number of tests, and that it does not much matter which test is utilized. To the extent that this is true, the economics of professional time and effort would favor self-report inventories such as the MMPI.

The above studies can be criticized on several grounds. First, some of them used relatively inexperienced diagnosticians, although it is shown below that the relationship between clinical experience and diagnostic accuracy is complex. In support of the studies, they did tend to mirror actual clinical practice for at least some clinical workers. Second, they were conducted before the ready availability of an organized objective research base for MMPI interpretation. Thus, one would expect that the MMPI (and any other test with actuarial interpretation data) would nowadays make a better showing than in the above results. (The more specific the actuarial rules, of course, the less relevant is the question of the clinician's degree of experience with the test.) Third, the studies were mainly concerned with general personality descriptions rather than with the assessment and prediction of specific traits and behaviors. The clinicians might have shown a higher level of predictive accuracy when dealing with specific behaviors. Fourth, because the criteria being predicted were often derived primarily from case history information, it should not be surprising that case history data consistently showed the best predictive accuracy; the predictor and the criterion may not have been fully independent.

Garb (1984) conducted a careful review of these and other studies on the incremental validity of information used in personality assessment. Despite the many thousands of studies on test validity, Garb was able to find only 32 that investigated incremental validity. However, his findings tended to confirm and extend those given above. Based on these findings, the following comments and recommendations can be made for practicing clinicians and for researchers. First, despite the possible contamination between predictors and criteria in the studies cited above, it would seem clear that biographical information should form the basis for a clinical assessment, and that other sources of data should be evaluated for their incremental contribution beyond this base. Second, the MMPI tended to perform better than projective tests and should be considered as the next addition. It is cautioned that this conclusion does not take into account the most recent developments in the validity of the tests studied, and it excludes promising recent instruments such as the Personality Assessment Inventory and tests based on the Big Five factors (see Chapter Nine).

The third point is that the ceiling on predictive or descriptive accuracy is reached relatively quickly, and the addition of further information sources beyond that ceiling may actually reduce accuracy. This effect is a product of the statistical truth that the lower the accuracy that is obtainable in absolute terms (due to limitations in reliability and validity of both the predictors and the criterion), the fewer predictors are needed in order to reach that ceiling. Fourth, considerations of cost efficiency favor the use of objectively administered and processed sources of data such as inventories and structured biographical questionnaires. Fifth, the interview may in some cases have a unique contribution, although there is a risk of misinterpreting visual and auditory cues. Sixth, little attention has yet been given to determining the unique advantages of each major test instrument and technique. Research in this area could yield information that would permit each test to be used for the particular questions (or on the particular types of patients) for which it is best suited. In effect, this is a call for the discovery of moderator variables (see Chapter Seven) to improve the predictiveness of different data sources.

Multimethod Assessment

The studies described in the preceding section have thrown some light on the question of the nature and optimal amount of data that should be collected in order to make a prediction or assessment in personality or psychodiagnosis. Let us now approach the question from a different angle, that of the literature on construct validity. In their classic paper on this topic, Campbell and Fiske (1959) pointed out that, in the assessment of any trait or characteristic, one can draw on a variety of different data sources, or *methods*. The greater the number of independent methods that yield interrelated data, the more substantial is the construct validity of the trait. Thus, the greater the variety of methods represented in the predictors, the more robust the prediction will be.

The data sources must be relatively independent, however. It is of little use to have a great deal of predictive data based on a single method or on highly similar methods, because the correlations among different trait scores based on a single method may at times be higher than correlations among different methods assessing the same trait. That is to say, each method is subject to its own characteristic biases, which could significantly influence all scores based on that method. For example, a person's scores on the scales of a normal personality inventory that assesses socially desirable traits could all be significantly correlated simply because of the influence of social desirability. Similarly, data gathered through interviews could be subject to a common bias because of the interviewer's positive (or negative) feelings about the client.

What is the meaning of the work of Campbell and Fiske for practical assessment situations? It means that much more emphasis should be placed on gathering data by different methods, rather than on the use of data gathered by a single method or by closely related methods. We are now in a position to understand better the disappointing results of the Kostlan (1954), Little and Shneidman (1959), and other studies reviewed by Garb (1984). Traditional tests might be viewed as representing a single method or a closely related group of methods. The unique contributions of biographical data and interview data to the accuracy of assessment can be understood by viewing these data sources as representing somewhat different methods. However, because all three methods are related in being self-report procedures, we might expect that the sum total of their contributions would still be fairly modest, as indeed it was.

The use of a traditional assessment battery appears to produce a redundancy of data within this rather narrow group of methods. One way to improve the efficiency of the assessment, if not its accuracy, would be to use abbreviated forms of each of the traditional data collection methods; for example, a brief, structured interview, a brief biographical data sheet, and a brief self-report inventory. Such an approach was suggested by Lanyon (1972). Also consistent with the multimethod philosophy is the *assessment center* method, which we described briefly in Chapter One and will cover more fully in Chapter Nine. Here, the assessors construct the entire assessment procedure around the goal of maximizing the number of different data collection methods that can be employed. A utility theory analysis of the assessment center method has demonstrated its efficiency even when individual validities are relatively low (Cascio & Silbey, 1979).

FACTORS AFFECTING CLINICAL ACCURACY

The core of the personality assessment enterprise is the validity or accuracy of the descriptions and predictions that are offered. There has been considerable interest in studying factors that may be related to accuracy independent of the particular assessment modality that is employed. A review of the research evidence regarding these factors follows.

Accuracy and Clinical Expertise

First, we consider the accuracy of judgments based on interpersonal cues—the cues available to all of us in our dealings with other people: content and style of speech, manner of dress, and all other subtleties regarded as contributing to our intuitive impressions about other people. The early research on clinical judgment based on interpersonal cues was summarized by Taft (1955) and by Vernon (1964). It would appear from their summaries that the ability to judge others is neither entirely general nor entirely specific; that is, there is no such person as a uniformly accurate judge of others, although there is some degree of generality to this ability. It is not related to age (in adults) nor strongly to gender, although there is a slight difference in favor of women. The ability to successfully judge others is positively related to intelligence, artistic and dramatic interests, good emotional adjustment, and social detachment, and is negatively related to authoritarian attitudes. Also, judgments are more accurate when the judges are motivated to make accurate judgments and when they come from cultural backgrounds that are similar to those of the persons being judged.

What about the effect of professional training in psychology or psychiatry? Although early studies were not encouraging in this regard, more recent findings are a little more favorable toward professional training (Garb, 1989, 1994). For example, graduate students in clinical psychology were more accurate than undergraduates in their ratings of depression from observing videotapes (Waxer, 1976), and a mixed group of mental health professionals were able to judge anxiety from tape-recorded therapy sessions more validly than a control group of nonclinical graduate students (Horowitz, Inouye, & Siegelman, 1979). Findings in regard to length of experience are not as positive, however. For example, in a study by Kendall (1973), where psychiatrists with four or more years of clinical experience made diagnoses after observing interviews with psychiatric inpatients, validity of diagnoses was not related to psychiatric experience. Thus, although persons in the mental health field do appear to have an edge, length of experience is not strongly related to accuracy.

What about the ability to make subjective judgments from formal assessment instruments? Approximately 30 studies in this area were reviewed by Garb (1994), including the use of various projective tests (Rorschach; TAT; projective drawings) and the MMPI. In this work, it was a common finding that clinicians' judgments of the patients, based on the projective tests, were no more accurate than those of graduate students in the mental health field, and that expert clinicians were no more accurate than nonexpert clinicians. Results with the MMPI were more mixed, however. For example, Walters, White, and Greene (1988) had graduate students, staff psychologists, and MMPI experts attempt to judge malingering of psychiatric disorder from the MMPI profiles of prison inmates. There was no relationship between presumed expertise and accuracy of judgments. But Oskamp (1962) found a positive relationship between accuracy of judgment and the amount of specific experience his judges had with the MMPI. And in a study where judges were asked to generate clinical descriptions from MMPI profiles, Aronson and Akamatsu (1981) reported that doctoral students significantly outperformed undergraduates who had received two hours of training.

These findings refer to the use of diagnostic tests when interpreted subjectively or clinically. As we have repeatedly seen, the use of objective interpretation rules, when available, is generally superior to the subjective approach. One reason why experienced clinicians have little edge over inexperienced clinicians may be that the overall accuracy of the subjective approach is rather low, and this level of accuracy tends to be reached rather quickly in training. Studies on consistency of clinical judgment among clinicians tend to support this view. Consistency is relatively low, which sets a low ceiling on attainable accuracy. For example, in their study of the reliability of clinicians using four data sources (MMPI, Rorschach, Wechsler-Bellevue Intelligence Scale, and a simple vocational history), Goldberg and Werts (1966) concluded that the "judgments of one clinician working from one data source bear no systematic relationship to those of another clinician working from another data source, even though both judges are ranking the same patient on the same trait" (p. 199). Similarly, Little and Shneidman (1959) found that their clinicians did not agree among themselves on the judgments made either from different data sources or from the same source.

Training in Judgmental Accuracy

Although the findings reviewed above do not provide much support for the value of clinical experience in making subjective judgments in mental health, they do offer some evidence for the value of training: fully trained professionals tended to do better than clinicians-in-training, in situations involving highly specific judgments. It is important, therefore, to understand the nature of training and to see whether there are grounds for possibly increasing accuracy through further training. In particular, could predictive accuracy be increased if clinicians were aware of the most predictive cues and used them in their predictions? Oskamp (1962) provided data to support this contention by showing that otherwise naive undergraduates who were given relevant training in the MMPI soon increased their judgmental accuracy to that of the most experienced judges. On the other hand, Goldberg (1968) reported that judges only demonstrated a stable increase in their ability to discriminate psychotic from neurotic MMPI profiles if they were given the values for a valid actuarial index for making this decision. Simply informing them of the existence and nature of the index resulted in only a temporary increase in accuracy.

Goldberg (1968) reported that another kind of training for increasing clinical predictive accuracy, involving immediate feedback about accuracy of prediction, was even less successful. Naive (undergraduate), middle (graduate), and expert (experienced doctoral level) judges were trained over a 17-week period in discriminating between psychotic and neurotic MMPI profiles. In this period, more than 4,000 training profiles were shown to the judges, who made a decision for each and were provided with immediate feedback about their accuracy. The judges also saw another 6,000 test profiles. The only group to show more than a negligible increase in accuracy as a result of this training were the naive judges, although the level of accuracy they reached was still substantially below that of the middle-level and expert judges, and even they were still below the ceiling of accuracy provided by actuarial prediction.

Sechrest, Gallimore, and Hersch (1967) studied several methods of improving clinical accuracy in naive (undergraduate) judges, who were asked to predict the traits of anxiety and pleasantness in subjects from their sentence completion responses. These authors showed that providing immediate feedback after each judgment did result in improved performance, but there was some evidence to indicate that this superiority may have been due to enhanced motivation rather than to any specific information imparted.

Schroeder (1972) believed that the effect of feedback would be enhanced if judges first developed explicit hypotheses about the nature of the person and the judgment task, and then applied the feedback to these hypothesized relationships. The results of this study showed that predictive accuracy was indeed greater when judges applied the feedback to the *basis* for prediction rather than simply to the predictor-outcome relationship. In a study involving the same principle, Strasburger and Jackson (1977) showed that accuracy of prediction increased when their judges were provided with information about valid constructs that mediated the relationship between the predictor and the target to be predicted.

These findings suggest several tentative generalizations that might be made regarding the relationship between accuracy of prediction and clinical training, and these generalizations could form the basis for training judges to be more accurate. (a) It would seem that a major source of inaccuracy is simply lack of information about the valid cues or predictors for the behavior to be judged. General clinical experience by itself is apparently not sufficient, nor is experience with a particular assessment device as a measure for general personality description. What appears to be minimally necessary is some awareness of the specific cues or "signs" that are predictive of the behavior under scrutiny. (b) Inexperienced judges who are provided the correct signs will improve their accuracy *if* they use the signs, but some motivation may be necessary in order to have the judges continue to use the signs. (c) In the absence of previously developed empirical signs, it is possible for judges to develop and "learn" signs by repeatedly making judgments and receiving feedback about the accuracy of these judgments; but, once again, they must be motivated to do so. However, there is a considerable danger that this learning will be illusory and erroneous in nature, as demonstrated by Chapman and Chapman (1971) and discussed in Chapter Twelve. (d) Knowledge or explicit hypotheses by the judges about the theoretical relationship between predictor and target result in improved accuracy.

So far, we have discussed the possibility of improving clinical judgment accuracy by teaching about the particular judgment made. A second avenue of teaching involves training in the judgment process itself. The findings in this area do not all stem from research in personality assessment or mental health, but they tend to be consistent in suggesting a number of things that clinicians can be trained to do in order to improve their accuracy (Arkes, 1981; Faust, 1986): (a) Clinicians should be attuned to the effect of base rates on accuracy of judgment, and should habitually attempt to estimate this information. (b) Alternatives to the answer being considered should be explicitly identified and explored. In fact, clinicians might be more likely to arrive at the correct conclusion if they actively try to *disconfirm* their hypotheses rather than support them. (c) Clinicians should decrease their reliance on memory by carefully preparing and freely consulting their records. (d) Clinicians should recognize that uncertainty is inevitable, and should live with it rather than believing that they should be able to reach a level of being right nearly all the time.

Two additional groups of variables are relevant to predictive accuracy: *amount of available information,* and *degree of confidence* in one's prediction. Each is reviewed below.

Accuracy and Amount of Information

It is a commonplace notion that the more information or data the clinician has available, the more accurate will be the prediction. Indeed, this rationale typically underlies the use of a battery of tests with a patient in order to make a comprehensive personality description. However, we have already seen that the breadth of range of the *methods* by which the data are gathered increases accuracy, not merely the fact of having a lot of data. This point was well made in a study by Turner (1966), who used only a single personality assessment device, the Rorschach. In this study, personality predictions were made about patients by clinicians who had varying amounts of the Rorschach protocol available to them, as follows: (a) free associations to the blots only; (b) free associations plus a marked location chart showing which areas of the blots were involved in the responses; (c) both of these plus inquiry information to help pinpoint the formal variables that determined the response; and (d) all of the foregoing plus a summary scoring sheet (psychogram) of all of the scoring results. The results showed that there were no increases in accuracy as a function of increased data for either experienced or inexperienced clinical judges. Presumably, the four data sources were so similar that the latter three did not add any information beyond what was contained in the first.

The major point that emerges from this and similar studies reviewed above is that it is important to identify the relevant sources of information for the particular descriptive or predictive task at hand, and, in routine practical situations, attention should be directed toward collecting only the data that are relevant. There is always the hope that extended data may contain further potentially useful predictors, but uncovering such predictors is a different task from routine practical assessment. On the basis of these conclusions, we should not be surprised to learn that certain aspects of personality assessment may be considerably simpler than we had earlier believed. In this connection, Peterson (1965) demonstrated that the two major personality dimensions of maladjustment and introversion-extraversion could be assessed as reliably by simple ratings as by more complicated measures such as personality inventories. Some characteristics can be optimally predicted from just a few pieces of data, or even from a single piece of information. For example, factor analyses reported in the manual for the 11-scale Marital Satisfaction Inventory (Snyder, 1981) indicate that marital satisfaction is a unitary concept that is readily assessed by any one of three scales (Global Distress, Affective Communication, or Problem Solving Communication). Assessment of life satisfaction and subjective well-being can be even simpler. For these concepts, the predictive power of single items is quite respectable (Andrews & Withey, 1976; Diener, 1984).

A word should be said about the effect of the reliability of the criterion to be predicted on the overall accuracy of prediction. In many prediction studies in mental health, the criterion measures themselves have been somewhat vague and unreliable, as are the traits and characteristics they have represented—for example, neurosis, psychosis, and anxiety. Naturally, the unreliability of a criterion measure sets a ceiling on the validities, or correlations with predictors, that can be achieved. It can be shown mathematically that the lower the ceiling on validity in any given prediction, the less useful it will be to have multiple predictors. In other words, if the best prediction that can be achieved is rather inaccurate to begin with, this ceiling on accuracy will usually be reached with the contributions of just one or two predictors. Thus, we should not be too surprised to find that multiple sources of predictive information did not add much to accuracy in the studies reviewed here. It has been stated above that, in Sines's (1959) study, accuracy actually appears to have declined as more data sources were added. On the other hand, the additional predictors would presumably be useful if the criteria could be made more reliable.

Accuracy and Confidence

Another issue that has concerned personality assessment investigators is the relationship between the accuracy of clinicians' judgments and their degree of confidence in the judgments. This question came to light as a result of an extensive study conducted by Kelly and Fiske (1951) to predict success in the Veterans Administration training program in clinical psychology. In trying to find reasons for their generally disappointing results, Kelly and Fiske discovered that the confidence of judges in a prediction was *inversely related* to the accuracy of that prediction.

Subsequent research on this issue has been summarized by Garb (1986, 1989, 1994) and by Wierzbicki (1993). In addition to personality assessment instruments, these studies have included judgments based on biographical data, interviews and therapy sessions, and neuropsychological test data. However, there were relatively few studies overall. The findings suggest that, contrary to the original Kelly and Fiske results, there tends to be a positive relationship between confidence in judgments and their accuracy, provided the information on which the judgments are based has relatively good validity. When the validity of the clinical information is low, however, the accuracy of judgments and confidence ratings tend to be unrelated. In regard to level of experience, the studies indicated that, if the judges received valid information, the confidence ratings of experienced judges were more appropriate than those of inexperienced judges, who tended to be overconfident.

These and other studies suggest that a low relationship between confidence in one's judgments and their accuracy could be related to a number of factors: lack of experience, lack of knowledge, lack of accurate input, or some combination of these interrelated factors. In a series of papers on the general topic of confidence in one's judgments, Fischhoff and his colleagues have shown that overconfidence is common in the judgment process in a wide variety of settings (Fischhoff, 1975; Fischhoff & Beyth, 1975; Fischhoff, Slovic, & Lichtenstein, 1977; Lichtenstein & Fischhoff, 1977). They also found that after people have knowledge of outcomes, they consistently over-estimate what they think they knew before they gained the outcome knowl-edge. A third finding was that, in some situations, with increasing knowledge comes decreasing overconfidence, until a point may be reached where very knowledgeable persons display a moderate degree of underconfidence.

Overall, these findings suggest a recommendation that clinicians-in-training should be made aware of a possible relationship between inexperi-ence and overconfidence, and should be taught to assess their level of confidence more realistically. It has been demonstrated that such training is indeed feasible (Oskamp, 1962)—for example, by having judges estimate their probability of success and then compare the estimate with their actual success. Further information on such procedures is available in the litera-ture of social judgment (Lichtenstein, Fischhoff, & Phillips, 1982).

THE PROCESS OF CLINICAL JUDGMENT

Thus far, the *outcome* or consequences of the clinical judgment process—that is, the effectiveness or accuracy of judgment—has been examined. There is also interest in the actual *process* of clinical judgment: How exactly does the clinician operate? Because it has been consistently documented that human judgment processes are not optimal when compared to predic-tions or decision processes made objectively, an understanding of *how* peo-ple make judgments could help to identify ways in which human judgment might be improved.

Meehl (1959a) had originally suggested that one potential advantage of clinicians was their ability to combine the available data in a complex, con-figural way that could not easily be reproduced mathematically. We now ex-amine the available evidence to see whether this is indeed how the process of clinical judgment operates. Because we have already seen that the most accurate actuarial predictors tend to be simple linear ones, we might sus-pect that Meehl's assertion about the clinical judgment process will be found wrong.

To determine whether clinicians utilize simple additive combinations of data in making predictions, or whether they employ complex config-ural combinations, it is necessary to make elaborate statistical analyses of the data available to the clinician. Basically, these analyses involve some measure of the amount of "nonlinearity" utilized by the judge in decision making, and several methods for doing so have been developed (Hammond, McClelland, & Mumpower, 1980; Hoffman, Slovic, & Rorer, 1968). One consistent finding (Hammond & Summers, 1965) has been that it is just as accurate to characterize the clinical judgment process as *linear* as to call it *nonlinear*. Using a different statistical procedure, Rorer, Hoffman, Dickman, and Slovic (1967) and Hoffman, Slovic, and Rorer (1968) were able to show that some judges *do* utilize configural combinations of signs in their judgments, but, in general, the contribution of these nonlinear elements is negligible when the contribution of the linear elements to the judgment is determined. Among the judgment tasks examined in these studies were decisions, based on behavioral data, whether to give weekend passes to psychiatric patients, and the differential diagnosis, from X-ray data, of malignancy of a gastric ulcer. These data clearly contradict Meehl's (1959a) position that clinical judgment typically involves the configural combination of data.

In another study, Wiggins and Hoffman (1968) used multiple correlation techniques to determine which of three "mathematical models" best described the judgment process used by each of the 29 clinical judges in discriminating psychotic and neurotic MMPI profiles. They reported that, although a configural or nonlinear model distinguished 16 of the 29 judges, the superiority over a linear model was small. In other words, what most of these judges used when making decisions could be described just as well by a simple additive combination of weighted signs as by a more complex configural combination. Goldberg (1971b) extended this study by examining five additional nonlinear models, including two that had been proposed by Einhorn and Bass (1971), of which one had been reported to outperform linear models. Once again, a "linear model provided a better representation of the judgments made by all clinicians than did either of Einhorn and Bass's models, and only the logarithmic provided the linear model with any real competition" (p. 458).

Earlier in this chapter, we saw that objectively derived linear models based on empirical data provide more accurate predictions than do nonlinear models. We have now seen that the clinical judgment process also appears to be better represented by linear rather than nonlinear models. Although we are not necessarily arguing that a simple linear model *explains* the behavior of the clinician in making a prediction, it seems clear that the linear model duplicates (or improves on) the *results* of the clinicians' behavior.

An extensive study of the process of human judgment has been made by Tversky and Kahnemann (1974, 1978; Kahnemann, Slovic, & Tversky, 1982). Although this work did not involve clinical subject matter, its findings are directly applicable in helping to understand the clinical judgment process. In particular, it offers insights into the human judgment process, showing how this process is inefficient and therefore capable of being outperformed by objective procedures.

Tversky and Kahnemann identified three important factors that typically operate in the human judgment process and serve to reduce its accuracy. The first is *representativeness*. In making judgments, people typically rely excessively on familiar associations between the predictor materials and the criterion targets. Thus, a student who is shy, meek, and orderly may be judged to be enrolled in library science rather than in psychology because those characteristics are stereotypical of librarians. However, a far more compelling factor in the judgment process should have been the fact that psychology majors outnumber library science majors 20 to 1, leading to the (more accurate) actuarial judgment that the student will almost certainly be a psychology major. The operation of the representativeness factor is another way of describing the failure of many judges to take into account the base rates of the criterion categories in the population.

The second factor identified by Tversky and Kahnemann, termed *availability*, refers to the process of basing a judgment on the ease with which instances can be brought to mind. For example, the decision of a clinician to call a new patient "schizophrenic" might be unduly influenced by the fact that the clinician had just interviewed several other schizophrenic patients. The third factor, *anchoring*, refers to the fact that judges typically select a preliminary judgment and then adjust it according to subsequent evidence. According to Tversky and Kahnemann, these adjustments are typically insufficient. Readers will note that similar factors have been previously listed as possible starting points for training clinicians to improve their subjective judgments.

Research on the process of clinical judgment has just begun. Yet, such research is essential for an understanding of this critically important process and for training others in it. In particular, researchers in this area need to become familiar with the overall psychological literature on the judgment process as a basis for developing hypotheses that can be tested within the context of personality assessment.

SOME CONCLUDING COMMENTS

This chapter has reviewed the contribution of quantitative research and technology to the accuracy and efficiency of the task of personality assessment. It began with a detailed consideration of the relative accuracy of actuarial versus clinical approaches, and then discussed what might be called the mechanics of each approach and the factors that affect their accuracy. This section makes some generalizations about the current state of the art in regard to the actual practice of assessment.

A middle ground was articulated by Sarbin (1986), who observed that few people today challenge the necessity for *both* approaches in seeking to develop and apply knowledge. In a more extensive review, Kleinmuntz (1990) carefully delineated what he considered to be the optimal application of each approach, singly or in combination. Kleinmuntz believed that the primary reason for continued reliance on clinical approaches to prediction, judgment, and decision making is that there are so few available actuarial formulas, and those that are available are often untested in the situation of interest. Within this set of constraints, the following suggestions are offered. First, people should identify the kinds of decisions that do *not* lend themselves easily to intuition and the kinds that are *not* readily converted to formulas. Examples of the latter might include open-ended predictions, special cases, urgent situations, and phenomena for which no theory exists. Using these guidelines, rules could then be developed for when to use the clinical approach, the actuarial approach, or a mixture of both.

Second, assessment psychologists should keep a systematic record of the accuracy of their work, noting what procedures were employed. Such a discipline would require careful attention to what actuarial procedures were used and how they were used, and also to the collection of feedback on accuracy, neither of which is easy to do.

Third, to counter the common tendency toward reaching a decision quickly and then attending selectively to information that is consistent with the decision, people should deliberately search for evidence that may disconfirm their initial formulation. This is equally true for clinical and actuarial approaches. People should also become aware of their other major biases and limitations, such as inaccurate calculations due to cognitive limitations, imperfect information processing, and faulty memory.

Fourth, records should be kept of overall cost-effectiveness, with and without using an actuarial aid.

Finally, Kleinmuntz called for serious study of those few experts who do seem to be consistently able to outperform the formula. The goal would be to aid "lesser mortals to become first-rate experts" (p. 304).

SUMMARY

Psychologists have made considerable progress in studying and comparing various aspects of personality assessment procedures in order to find out which are the most useful. Most of this research has involved comparisons of actuarial (mechanical, statistical, clerical) and clinical (subjective, intuitive, experiential) procedures for prediction. Meehl, who brought this research area before the public eye in 1954, concluded that, whenever it was possible to formulate them, mechanical predictive rules were generally equal to or superior in accuracy to the subjective predictions of clinicians using the same data. Subsequent research has not changed this conclusion, although it has suggested that a useful function of clinicians is in quantifying their behavioral observations; that is, in the domain of measurement rather than prediction. Actuarial techniques have also been applied to the description of personality, and "cookbooks" have been developed to yield personality descriptions of patients who possess certain types of profiles on the MMPI and other tests. Much of this work is available only in automated form and tends to lack the empirical rigor of the original research and development.

Research on actuarial strategies has shown consistently that linear models yield more accurate predictions than configural ones, and this finding has considerable generality beyond the field of personality assessment. Ultimately, the importance of actuarial procedures in personality assessment will depend on their generality; that is, the extent to which descriptive or predictive rules derived for one population are valid for another. Readers are again reminded that, in assessing the usefulness of an actuarial sign for prediction or description, it is essential to take into consideration the base rate of the event to be predicted or its frequency of occurrence in the population being considered.

The topic of decision making is becoming increasingly important in personality assessment. In psychological assessment, contrary to medical assessment, a diagnosis or description cannot usually be checked against any real or verifiable criterion. Therefore, interest has developed in making choices among the options or outcomes available; that is, concentrating on the decision to be made. The concepts of sensitivity and specificity, borrowed from signal detection theory, are useful in this regard. The adoption of a decision-making orientation makes available to psychologists the developments in decision-making technology from other fields and, in particular, the procedures utilized in business and industry known as *operations research*. A major problem with their application to personality assessment is that, associated with each possible outcome, there must be a quantifiable criterion of utility. In business and industry, these criteria may be specified in terms of monetary value; however, when decisions are to be made about people *qua* people, social and personal values become involved, and these are difficult to quantify.

Other aspects of the accuracy of personality assessment have also been studied. Whenever various data sources have been compared for their contribution to a valid comprehensive personality description, biographical information has been shown to be at least as powerful as the commonly used clinical tests. Further, it appears that there is a definite ceiling to the amount of data that is worthwhile to collect, and that the validity of the resulting assessment is not increased by just adding more data; in fact, the validity may even be lowered. Also, the more independent the methods or sources of data that are employed, the more valid will be the resulting assessment.

Contrary to early findings, more current research has shown that professional training in clinical psychology and psychiatry can lead to greater accuracy in making interpersonal judgments and judgments from test materials. However, length of professional experience does not seem to make a difference. A possible explanatory factor is the lack of reliability among clinical judges, which underscores the importance of identifying the particular cues that are relevant in making the judgments. Clinicians' confidence in their judgments may sometimes increase even though their accuracy does not; however, it appears that specific training could rectify this difficulty. Other important factors in the learning and making of more accurate judgments are the need for high motivation on the part of the judges and knowledge of the theoretical relationship between predictor and target results.

For a given assessment task, it is important to identify and collect only relevant data. Regarding the relationship between accuracy of judgments and clinicians' confidence in their judgments, it is shown that the relationship tends to be positive when the validity of the predictions is high. In general, inexperienced judges tend to be overconfident in their predictions. Research on the process of clinical judgment shows that this process is better represented by linear rather than nonlinear models. Overall, it is concluded that there are optimal applications for both the clinical and the actuarial approaches, depending on the assessment task, available data, and research base.

CHAPTER NINE

Applications to the Workplace

The initial chapter outlined the many influences that have shaped the development of personality-related psychological assessment, including the two that we regard as most central to this chapter—identification of psychopathology and prediction of behavior in the workplace. With little overlap between them, these two disparate influences have largely formed the content of current psychological assessment practice. Earlier chapters have focused mainly on the first of these two strands—clinical assessment—with only occasional reference to the workplace. We firmly believe that the underlying assumptions and methodologies apply equally to both areas of discussion, but application of these assumptions and methods differs substantially in each area. The purpose of this chapter is to bring together our understanding of contemporary assessment issues as applied to the world of work, including such important topics as the use of psychological testing in personnel selection, candidate interviewing, the measurement of leadership, the workplace use of assessment centers, and personality assessment in human resources training and development. Although several of these topics have been touched on in earlier chapters, this chapter will provide readers with an integrated and more comprehensive picture.

The Role of Hugo Münsterberg

Hugo Münsterberg (1863–1916) is widely recognized as the father of American industrial psychology. He received a Ph.D. degree from the University of Leipzig in 1885 and an M.D. degree in 1887. After several years as a faculty member at Freiberg University in Germany, he joined the faculty of Harvard University in 1892. He remained there for the rest of his life, serving as both professor and director of the Psychological Laboratory. Münsterberg's interests were broad and he wrote prolifically on a variety of subjects, authoring many books, journal articles, and articles for the popular press. He is an important historical figure because he was the first researcher to use both psychological measures and work samples as an aid in selecting persons for such diverse occupations as trolley car driver, telephone operator, and sea captain (Landy, 1992). His work in selecting telephone operators represents the first known example of test validation: operators who were chosen as being the best by the telephone company, but whose skill level was unknown to Münsterberg, scored best on his tests. Münsterberg is important not only for this pioneering experiment but also for establishing a strong empirical bias in industrial/organizational (I/O) psychology.

One way in which I/O psychology has differed from clinical psychology is that the bulk of I/O practitioners have retained strong linkages with academic psychology, at least until recently. The practice of clinical psychology has flourished more independently. Even when I/O psychologists have extensive consulting practices, most maintain academic appointments, an arrangement that is much less typical among clinical psychologists. An important consequence of these separate lines of development is that the practice of I/O psychology has been and continues to be more methodologically rigorous and more cautious in its claims, and thus perhaps is less attractive to some practitioners.

PERSONALITY ASSESSMENT IN PERSONNEL SELECTION

As one example of this caution, the conventional wisdom in I/O psychology has been that there is precious little evidence to support the use of personality measures in the personnel selection process. For example, Guion and Gottier (1965) concluded their comprehensive review of the research literature as follows: ". . . it is difficult to advocate, with a clear conscience, the use of personality measures in most situations as a basis for making employment decisions" (p. 106). Schmitt, Gooding, Noe, and Kirsch (1984) reached the same conclusion in their survey two decades later, as did a more recent survey by Hough, Eaton, Dunnette, Kamp, and McCloy (1990). This sorry state of affairs is hardly surprising. As we noted earlier, until quite recently, most of the focus in personality assessment has been on the identification of psychopathology.

The authors are quite aware that psychopathology is all too often present in the workplace—often with catastrophic consequences. However, the degree of psychopathology present in job applicants is usually not employers' most important consideration. The most seriously disturbed individuals rarely appear as applicants for employment. Instead, employers are concerned with more common problems: will the candidate show up regularly—and on time? How well will the candidate relate to his or her coworkers? What degree of potential leadership can the candidate be expected to exercise? It is hardly surprising that such clinically oriented instruments as the MMPI are not readily able to answer such questions reliably. Even instruments that are intended to answer these questions, like the CPI, often involve arcane scale names (e.g., Capacity for status, Communality, and so on), and require considerable clinical sophistication for interpretation. Furthermore, the standardization populations have often differed in many ways from the adult, employable persons who apply for jobs, and the use of these instruments has been restricted to trained clinicians. Given such conditions, the negative conclusions about the usefulness of personality assessment in the workplace would seem to be inescapable.

This state of affairs has substantially changed with the development and widespread adoption of the "five-factor" approach to personality assessment. This development (see Chapter Three) dramatically changed our understanding of the usefulness of personality testing in personnel selection. In view of its importance, we now examine the history of this line of research in some detail.

The Rise of the Big Five

Psychologists have long been interested in the issue of the number and nature of personality traits, but not until the widespread availability of computers was a resolution of differences, to a major degree, possible. The basic research approach was simple: develop a comprehensive list of adjectives and other descriptors, get knowledgeable observers to rate a group of target people on these descriptors, determine how the descriptors cluster together through the use of statistical procedures, and then determine the validity of each of the clusters through empirical research. (The Appendix gives a more detailed description of this process.)

As early as 1934, Thurstone described a study in which raters were provided a list of 60 trait adjectives "in common use for describing people." Each rater was asked to evaluate a person whom he or she knew well, using these 60 adjectives. Using the primitive statistical techniques of the day, Thurstone (1934) found that five common factors accounted for most of the intercorrelations among the 60 adjectives and concluded that "the scientific description of personality might not be so hopelessly complex as it is sometimes thought to be" (p. 14). What is most important is that Thurstone's conclusion of 60 years ago is now accepted as a fact by most psychologists, especially those who follow the research literature.

Thurstone's seminal research involved only 60 adjectives because a larger set could not have been accommodated by the statistical procedures of the day and the early hand-driven calculators that were just becoming available. Even in more recent research, both Norman (1963c) and Goldberg (1981) used reduced lists in order to simplify the task of the raters and make the statistical analysis more manageable, although most recent researchers have used more comprehensive lists (typically, about 200 descriptors) than Thurstone's.

In reviewing this research over the 50 years that followed the publication of Thurstone's 1934 paper, John, Goldberg, and Angleitner (1984) noted that most of the differences reported by subsequent investigators arose from methodological, not substantive, issues. They included: (a) the particular descriptors that were originally included; (b) the statistical procedures used; (c) the level of abstraction desired; and (d) the criteria for evaluating the clusters.

During the past half-century, these methodological differences led psychologists to a variety of conclusions about the nature and number of personality traits. Cattell (1945) identified 35 clusters as the "standard reduced personality sphere" with 12 underlying primary factors. Some years later, Fiske (1949), using ratings on Cattell's 35 clusters from several different sources—self, peer, and professional psychologists—found strong support for 5, not 12, factors, and those factors were the same from each of the three ratings sources. At the same time that Cattell was conducting his research, Eysenck (1947) and Guilford (1948) were working to develop their own models, which served largely to increase interest in this area of inquiry, particularly in the use of factor analysis—the dominant statistical procedure employed.

Based on the work of both Cattell and Guilford, Tupes and Christal (1958), using Air Force Academy cadets as their subjects, found clear and highly reliable evidence for five factors, which they labeled:

1. Surgency (Extroversion).
2. Agreeableness.
3. Conscientiousness.
4. Emotional Stability.
5. Culture.

More importantly, they found highly significant correlations between their five-factor scores and a variety of performance measures obtained on the cadets, ranging from .60 for Conscientiousness to .24 for Extroversion. These results can be seen as the basis for much of the subsequent interest in the Big Five, although with an inexplicably long lag time.

Tupes and Christal (1961) extended their research by using eight highly diverse samples. They concluded that the reliability of their five factors across the two studies was "remarkable." They went on to point out that the same five factors had been found on innumerable occasions in the past, but the generality of these findings had been obscured by the different labels that had been given to the factors.

An even more comprehensive extension of this work was reported by Norman (1963c), who decided to return to Thurstone's original approach and use a dictionary to develop a comprehensive list of descriptors. He developed a master list of 18,125 terms, which he was able to reduce, by application of a set of clear, predetermined rules, to 1,710. Norman again found that five factors, closely resembling those of Tupes and Christal, accounted for most of the significant relationships among the descriptors. Most important to note about Norman's work is that he focused simply on the terms themselves. Consequently, his comprehensive list of descriptors has served as the basis for most of the contemporary research in this area of inquiry. The fact that most researchers have started with a common list of comprehensive descriptors has done much to reduce the discrepancies in the reported findings from different research settings.

The work of Goldberg (1981, 1982, 1990a, 1990b, 1993) has served as a focus for the most recent work. Using Norman's list of 1,710 descriptors, Goldberg (1982) clearly demonstrated that five factors accounted for all the significant variance, regardless of which approach to factor analysis was used. He later (1990a) was able to obtain essentially the same results using only 100 carefully selected adjectives, which he labeled as the "markers for the Big Five." As Goldberg himself has pointed out about the necessity for using natural language, this line of research is based on one critical assumption: "[T]hose individual differences that are of most significance in the daily transactions of persons with each other will eventually become encoded in their language . . . . Moreover, this fundamental axiom has a highly significant corollary: *The more language is important in human transaction, the more the languages will have a term for it*" (Goldberg, 1981, pp. 141–142).

More recently, McCrae and Costa (1987) and Costa and McCrae (1992a) have been able to demonstrate clearly that the Big Five could account for most of the variability in both self-ratings and personality inventory responses, based on either self-ratings or ratings by persons who knew the target individuals well. McCrae and Costa (1987, 1990, 1994) have clearly shown the stability of individual profiles on the Big Five over extended periods of time—as long as several decades, in some instances—which has led them to conclude that personality is quite stable after age 30.

The bulk of the literature has labeled these five factors as follows:

1. Emotional Stability, or conversely, Neuroticism (calm, secure, and nonanxious).
2. Extroversion (sociable, talkative, assertive, ambitious, and active).
3. Openness to Experience (imaginative, artistically sensitive, and intellectual).
4. Agreeableness (good-natured, cooperative, and trusting).
5. Conscientiousness (responsible, dependable, organized, persistent, and achievement-oriented).

This is the order (NEOAC) in which they are presented in the Costa and McCrae (1992b) NEO Personality Inventory (Revised). But regardless of how they are labeled, there is widespread agreement among knowledgeable psychologists that the Big Five are the current key to understanding human personality, at least on the direct, pragmatic level that is required in the workplace.

What do we now know about the Big Five? First, theoretically, the Big Five are abstractions that represent consistencies in the ways that people experience their world and act, as well as the complex underlying causes of these patterns. Furthermore, the stronger the trait in a person, the more likely that person is to show trait-related behaviors—and thus, the more frequently we are able to observe that trait. Second, the research evidence, which is both extensive and rigorous, strongly supports the existence of five consistent and relatively independent traits. These conclusions are clearly spelled out in three recent comprehensive reviews of the research literature (Digman, 1990; Goldberg, 1993; Wiggins & Pincus, 1992).

It must be noted that there are serious, articulate objectors to the five-factor approach (e.g., Block, 1995) who insist that both assumptional and methodological limitations and uncertainties are ignored by its adherents. Block provided a comprehensive set of objections, including a denial of Goldberg's lexical hypothesis described above. Despite these objections, there is a strong consensus about the usefulness of the five factors in employee selection. This emerging consensus about the centrality of the Big Five in understanding and predicting human behavior was supported by Barrick and Mount's (1991) meta-analysis of 117 research studies that reported statistical relationships between measures of at least one of the five factors and actual job performance. Barrick and Mount differentiated three kinds of performance measures: (a) job proficiency measures, such as productivity indexes and performance ratings; (b) training proficiency measures, such as the number and quality of posttraining work samples and length of time to complete training; and (c) personnel data, such as salary level, length of service, and number of promotions. They also differentiated the studies by five job levels from skilled/semiskilled to managerial and professional. These performance and job level categories allowed Barrick and Mount to examine whether the Big Five could predict job success equally well regardless of job level, performance, or how performance was measured.

Not surprisingly, Conscientiousness, with an estimated true correlation of .22 with on-the-job performance, emerged as the most consistent predictor of job success among the five factors, regardless of the type of performance measure used or the level of the job involved. In all cases, people who were seen as conscientious by themselves and/or by others were the more effective workers! Extroversion was a valid predictor (across the criterion types) for two occupations, managers and sales (estimated true correlations of .18 and .15, respectively), but not for any other occupations. Extroversion was found to correlate well (.26) with success in training but only modestly with job proficiency (.10) and personnel data (.11). Openness to Experience also correlated well (.25) with training proficiency but was not a predictive factor for either job proficiency or personnel data.

Barrick and Mount attributed their finding that Extroversion and Openness to Experience were predictive of success in training to the fact that being gregarious, sociable, and active was important to training success, as was approaching training with a positive attitude. Quite interestingly, Emotional Stability showed only low, insignificant correlations (average correlation = .08) with any of the criteria. The authors speculated that persons with serious problems of emotional stability are not present in the workplace, being either self-selected out or unable to work regularly. Despite the limited nature of their findings, Barrick and Mount concluded that they had demonstrated the usefulness of the Big Five in making personnel selection decisions.

In a more comprehensive and more sophisticated study, Tett, Jackson, and Rothstein (1991) reported a meta-analysis of 86 studies selected from 494 that had been identified as reporting a positive relationship between measures of the Big Five and job performance. A critical difference between these two meta-analyses is that Tett et al. separated those studies in which the personality measures used were selected on the basis of a job analysis from others in which the measures used were selected without such an analysis, expecting better predictability from the studies where a job analysis was used to select the personality measures. They also analyzed studies of the following four groupings: (a) recruits v. incumbents, expecting that the criteria on which the incumbents were judged to be more reliable would produce better predictions; (b) age, expecting that older workers' performance would be more predictable; (c) length of tenure, expecting longer-term employees to be more predictable; and (d) civilian v. military job, expecting military job performance to be less predictable.

Agreeableness was the strongest predictor of job performance (.33), followed by Openness to Experience (.27), Emotional Stability (.22), Conscientiousness (.18), and Extroversion (.16). The overall estimated true correlation between the Big Five and job performance was .24—higher than that reported by Barrick and Mount. But, far more important, those studies in which the personality measures were selected on the basis of a job analysis yielded an estimated true average correlation of .38 as compared to .29 for those without. Not just any measure will do; the particular trait measured must be important for success in that job. Contrary to expectation, recruit performance was more predictable than incumbent performance (.30 vs. .21) and military job performance was more predictable than civilian job performance (.30 vs. .20). Neither age nor tenure mattered, nor did job level.

Although the pattern of results from these two studies is rather different, they both strongly confirmed the usefulness of using the Big Five as predictors of on-the-job performance, particularly when the personality measures are selected on the basis of a job analysis. The differences in the strength of the relationships in the two studies are presumably due to the different jobs that were involved. Different personality traits will be more or less predictive of on-the-job success, depending on what characteristics are necessary for success.

This point is dramatically illustrated by an original research study more recently reported by Barrick and Mount (1993). In a study of 146 civilian managers working at a number of different U. S. Army installations, they found that, of the Big Five, only two—Conscientiousness (.25) and Extroversion (.14)—were significantly correlated with ratings of success on eight different aspects of managerial performance. But when the jobs were sorted as being high or low in managerial autonomy, strikingly different results emerged. In those jobs with high autonomy, managers high on both

Conscientious and Extroversion did far better than did their counterparts in those jobs categorized as low in autonomy. Further, on those high-autonomy jobs, Agreeableness emerged as yet another strong predictor of success. Without close supervision, the manager's own sense of responsibility and his or her style of approaching work and other people became more important determinants of success. All jobs are not created equal, and, to be effective predictors of job performance, personality measures need to take those differences in the nature of the job into account. This can only be done by a careful job analysis that focuses on identifying the personal/interpersonal characteristics required for success as well as the technical ones.

Further evidence for the usefulness of a Big Five measure of Conscientiousness as a predictor of on-the-job performance is found in Barrick, Mount, and Strauss (1993). Using path analysis on the data obtained from a group of 91 sales representatives on the staff of a large appliance manufacturer, they reported a highly significant multiple correlation of .67 between a paper-and-pencil measure of intelligence ("can do") and Conscientiousness ("will do") on the one hand, and sales volume and supervisory ratings of performance on the other. Conscientiousness alone correlated .46 with supervisory ratings and .28 with sales volume; the correlation between the intelligence measure and supervisory ratings was .34 and .16 with sales volume. The two predictors, however, only correlated −.07 with each other, suggesting that each tapped different aspects of future performance—motivation *and* ability.

In a related study involving essentially the same sample, Mount, Barrick, and Strauss (1994) obtained supervisor, coworker, customer, and self ratings for each subject on each of the Big Five dimensions; the supervisors and coworkers also provided ratings of job performance. All the ratings on the two predicted job-relevant Big Five dimensions—Conscientiousness and Extroversion—were found to be valid predictors of rated job performance. Unexpectedly, Agreeableness was also found to be a valid predictor but only for supervisor and customer ratings. The nonself ratings were better predictors than the self ratings, *and* they added significantly unique variance to the prediction; the customer ratings yielded the highest validity coefficients. What is striking about these findings is that self ratings may actually provide underestimates of performance, even though the self ratings by and large were significantly higher than those of the other three rater groups.

This ever-growing research evidence for the usefulness of the Big Five in employment selection, as well as in understanding basic personality structure, supports a very different conclusion from the one reached three decades ago by Guion and Gottier (1965). Matarazzo (1995) concluded his recent predictions about the future of psychological assessment in general with this statement: "I believe tomorrow's offshoots of the NEO Personality

Inventory also will be broadband personality and character inventories for normal subjects comparable to what will be new generations of broadband MMPI-type tests for examining individuals with psychopathological conditions" (p. 1014). One can only hope that such predictions come to pass.

INTEGRITY TESTING

Of special concern in personnel selection is the evaluation of the integrity or honesty of candidates. Integrity tests—also known as honesty, trustworthiness, counterproductive behavior, dependability, or job behavior inventories—represent the most recent effort to provide organizations with a way to deal with a serious problem: employee theft of money and merchandise (sometimes termed "shrinkage"). The magnitude of this problem is enormous. Based on the then-available data, Sackett and Harris (1984) estimated the annual amount of such thefts at $10 billion—the most costly category of crimes against business organizations. In a survey of several thousand employees in a number of different businesses, Hollinger and Clark (1983) reported that, on average, the percentages of employees surveyed who admitted anonymously to theft were: 42% for retail store employees, 32% for hospital employees, and 26% for manufacturing employees. In a similar study, Slora (1989) reported that 62% of workers in the fast-food industry and 43% of supermarket workers admitted to theft of either money or company property. That such behavior is a serious societal problem is unquestionable. The main purpose of preemployment integrity testing is to screen out job applicants who have a propensity to steal or to engage in other counterproductive on-the-job behavior.

Prior to 1988, polygraph testing or lie detection (see Chapter Five for a discussion of this topic) was the principal technique used by organizations to screen out potentially risky applicants. But the Employee Polygraph Protection Act passed by the United States Congress in 1988 outlawed the use of such methods. This legislation was strongly supported by psychologists on three principal grounds: (a) no body of research supported the contention that polygraphs were valid indicators of past or future thefts; (b) the accuracy, fairness, and reliability of polygraph use were a function of the skills of the examiner; and (c) abuses of the procedure were rampant (Lykken, 1981). Since 1988, integrity testing has replaced the polygraph as the primary method of preemployment screening.

Besides the polygraph and the integrity questionnaire, other methods are used to tap these behaviors. One alternative method is on-the-job surveillance, but it is both expensive and highly invasive. Another is background checks to identify gross misrepresentations of educational and work history, criminal records, and financial information. However, background checks are unlikely to identify the majority of problem employees who have previously unblemished records. Reference checks among previous employers tend to yield little useful information on integrity because employers fear litigation if they provide any information other than the dates of employment. Work samples can provide applicants with an opportunity to steal or cheat but then the sticky legal problem of entrapment arises.

The employment interview, which is part of virtually all preemployment screening, provides another potential source of information about integrity. The interview, however, is not considered valid for such purposes because most employment interviewers tend to rely on invalid, stereotypical signs when making judgments about integrity—the absence of a firm handshake, shifty eyes, and type and style of clothing. Structured interviews offer a way to improve the validity of the employment interview for evaluating integrity, but there is little empirical evidence to support this practice. In any event, interviews are time-consuming and expensive to conduct—another reason for the popularity of integrity testing.

Are integrity tests widely used? Over a decade ago, Sackett and Harris (1984) estimated that as many as 5,000 companies, testing as many as 5 million job applicants annually, used integrity testing as part of their preemployment procedures. A plethora of publishers provide literally dozens of integrity tests to the employer marketplace. Many of these instruments are proprietary, and the publishers provide little or no information about their psychometric properties. Although both the American Psychological Association (APA; Goldberg, Grenier, Guion, Sechrest, & Wing, 1991) and the Association of Personnel Test Publishers (1991) have recommended strongly that such data be provided to examiners as an integral part of the manual of instructions, these recommendations have not had much effect. However, many responsible publishers do provide research reports on the psychometric characteristics of their instruments, and they give permission to external researchers to use their instruments for investigative purposes. Ones, Viswesaran, and Schmidt (1995) were able to identify 25 such publishers in their comprehensive meta-analysis, a subject to which we will return.

Integrity tests can be classified in a number of overlapping ways: (a) single-purpose vs. broadband; (b) subtle vs. obvious content; (c) based on predictive vs. concurrent validity; (d) based on applicant vs. employee validation sample; and (e) level of job complexity—low, medium, or high. The overt content tests typically are intended to directly assess dishonest behaviors, both past and present; the subtle content tests, which appear more like typical personality tests, are intended to tap a broader range of counterproductive behavior at work—chronic absenteeism, alcoholism, drug abuse, unsociable or antisocial behavior, and other counternormative behavior.

The obvious or overt content tests include the Personnel Selection Inventory (London House Press, 1980), the Stanton Survey (Reed, 1982) and the Reid Report (Reid Psychological Systems, 1951). These inventories ask such direct questions as "Have you ever taken, without permission, company merchandise or property?" or "Have you ever been tempted to steal?" Subtle or personality content measures include such statements as "I enjoy a great deal of excitement" (true–false) or "Have you ever been so upset that you wanted to leave home?" The Personal Outlook Inventory (Science Research Associates, 1983) and the Personnel Reaction Blank (Gough, 1972) are examples of covert content inventories. Detailed descriptions of these and other integrity tests can be found in the *Tenth Mental Measurements Yearbook* (Conoley & Kramer, 1989).

In the past decade, a number of literature reviews on integrity test research have appeared. Sackett and his colleagues (Sackett & Harris, 1984; Sackett, Burris, & Callahan, 1989) cited over 120 studies of different integrity tests, and concluded:

> *The present review found a large number of [criterion-related validity studies with external criteria] including large-scale predictive studies in which a substantial number of employees were subsequently dismissed for theft on the job, and studies utilizing a broad range of criteria, including absence, turnover, and supervisory ratings. Thus, a more compelling case that integrity tests can predict a number of outcomes can be made. (p. 520)*

In an independent review of 270 studies of integrity testing, O'Bannon, Goldinger, and Appleby (1989) came to much the same conclusion:

> *Studies of contrasted groups indicate that average honesty test scores differ for different groups . . . . A large body of research exists for admissions of wrong doing . . . . Several time-series studies have shown that an integrity test can have a positive impact on such organizational measures as inventory shrinkage and terminations for theft. (p. 92)*

In a meta-analysis of 23 studies of the Personnel Selection Inventory (PSI), involving 1,806 individuals, McDaniel and Jones (1988) found an estimated average validity coefficient of .50 (.53 for self-report criteria and .46 for all other criteria), suggesting that the PSI has a useful level of validity.

On the other hand, in their review of much of this same research, Guastello and Rieke (1991) came to a rather different conclusion. Because the multimillion-dollar integrity test market is dominated by only the PSI, the Reid report, and the Stanton Survey, they confined their analysis to these instruments. Guastello and Rieke tended to dismiss any positive correlations between integrity test scores and admission of theft as a result of the fakability of these instruments, even when the partial correlation between the Dishonest scores of the PSI and admissions of theft, when corrected for such distortion, was found to be .38. They similarly rejected any other positive results as artifacts of criteria contamination or other methodological flaws.

In addition to these research surveys, the U.S. Congressional Office of Technology Assessment (OTA; U.S. Congress, 1990) and the APA (Goldberg et al., 1991) have released reports on the status of integrity testing. Like Guastello and Rieke, the OTA review came to a negative conclusion about integrity testing. The OTA based its conclusions partly on the fact that, in five studies, there were high numbers of false positives; 73% to 97% of applicants who failed an integrity test but were hired anyway were *not* subsequently detected committing a theft on the job. On the other hand, the APA report, which was based on a much larger number of instruments, concluded that well-standardized, integrity tests are valid predictors of honest behavior in the workplace. Of particular note, the APA concluded that integrity tests reject fewer qualified applicants than any of the other available procedures; that is, integrity tests have a lower rate of false positives than the other procedures. The APA report called for caution in the actual use of integrity tests, suggesting that they be used only as part of a total selection process, and warning against overreliance on publisher-developed cutting scores.

The most comprehensive study of the validity of integrity testing is the meta-analysis reported by Ones, Viswesaran, and Schmidt (1993), who used a database of 665 validity coefficients based on 576,460 subjects. These authors estimated the true validity of all integrity tests to be .34 with overall job performance as the criterion, and .47 with counterproductive job behavior (both self-reported and observed) as the criterion. In the latter case, when the large standard deviation raised questions about the reliability of the estimate, further analyses revealed that overt intregity tests were much more reliable than subtle or personality-based instruments. For studies that used counterproductive job behavior as the criterion, integrity tests were better at predicting self-reported than externally measured counterproductive behaviors. Similar results had been reported by McDaniel and Jones (1988), who pointed out that not all counterproductive behaviors are detected and it often is difficult to identify the culprit. Theft as a criterion was slightly better predicted (.52) than broader measures of counterproductive behavior (.45), and concurrent measures of validity were higher than predictive measures. Ones et al. also found a slight difference between the validities using applicants (.44) and current employees (.55), and at different levels of job complexity—low (.43), medium (.40), and high (.68).

When overall job performance was used as the criterion, the validity was .33 for the overt integrity tests and .35 for the personality tests, leading to the conclusion that test type was not a moderator of integrity test validity. Likewise, there were no differences based on the criteria, whether supervisory ratings (.35) or production records (.28); or in predictive (.31) versus concurrent validity (.37); or by using applicants (.40) versus current employees (.29); or at different levels of job complexity (low, medium, and high).

Based on these and additional analyses, Ones et al. (1995) concluded that integrity tests have an estimated mean operational validity of .41, which is sufficient for predicting job performance and such counterproductivity on the job as theft, disciplinary problems, and absenteeism. Murphy (1993), in a comprehensive analysis of honesty in the workplace, came to much the same conclusion, as did the APA (Goldberg et al., 1991). We are in agreement with this evaluation as well.

Given the obvious nature of the items in the overt integrity tests, it is appropriate to wonder why respondents answer these items truthfully, especially when applying for a job. A number of hypotheses have been offered to account for this surprising level of candor (Jones & Terris, 1991). Most prevalent is the respondents' reported belief that "everybody steals" and that it would be foolish to deny it.

A related issue is the fakability of scores on integrity tests. Ones et al. (1993) concluded that "response distortion, to the extent that it does exist, does not seem to destroy the criterion-related validity of these tests" (p. 696). Also, most integrity tests contain a separate Distortion or "Lie" scale to determine the degree to which respondents are being candid in their answers (Jones & Terris, 1991). And, research on the actual fakability of integrity tests (Cunningham, Wong, & Barbee, 1994; Ryan & Sackett, 1987) suggests that their validity does not substantially decrease even if people make clear-cut efforts to present themselves in a more favorable light.

In another view of the success of integrity tests in predicting on-the-job counterproductivity, integrity is seen as a subset of Conscientiousness—one of the Big Five factors previously described as an important predictor of on-the-job success. Of the Big Five factors, Conscientiousness has the highest correlation with integrity test results, although Ones et al. (1995) reported that a linear combination of Conscientiousness, Agreeableness, and Emotional Stability describes integrity better than any one dimension alone. However, the bulk of research tends to support the use of single-purpose, obvious-content integrity tests in actual practice, at least for now.

From a practical point of view, the use of integrity tests as part of a selection test battery certainly seems justified. Indeed, businesses that actually have employed integrity tests in their employee selection program have shown multimillion-dollar annual savings from theft, as compared to businesses that have not employed such devices and to their pretesting base (Jones, 1991).

THE EMPLOYMENT INTERVIEW

Interviewing, for better or worse, is a universal personnel selection procedure. The one-on-one employment interview, in which the interviewer attempts to ascertain the candidate's personal suitability to fill a job vacancy, is part of virtually all employment processes. Ulrich and Trumbo (1965), in a survey of 852 organizations, found that 99% used interviews as an element in their selection process. Interviewing is then the second most commonly used selection tool; review of the resume or application was reported as being used by *all* organizations surveyed.

In an employment interview, the interviewer—whether a line manager, a human resources specialist, or a professional psychologist—attempts to predict future job performance on the basis of the content of the candidate's responses to oral inquiries and the style or manner of those responses. How successful are these predictions of on-the-job success? In an earlier review of the research literature on employment interviewing, Guion (1976) concluded that the potential for adequate validity existed, but there were wide differences in validity among interviewers, who are themselves fallible instruments. This point is illustrated by the research of Dougherty, Turban, and Callendar (1994), who conducted a field study of how employment interviewers' initial impressions of an applicant affected the conduct of the interview. The interviewers studied the completed application blank and the candidate's pre-interview test scores, and then rated each candidate on his or her potential for success. Audiotaped recordings of the actual interviews revealed that interviewers handled applicants whom they had rated highly in pre-interview testing rather differently from those they had viewed less favorably. The highly rated interviewees were shown more positive regard, received more "selling" of the company, and were asked more open-ended questions. Interestingly, the applicants receiving the higher ratings were more positive in their communications and established better rapport with the interviewer, suggesting the operation of a "self-fulfilling prophecy." Interviewers clearly are fallible instruments and often produce the results they wish to produce.

Given the observation that most employment interviews are little more than casual conversations and are more likely to serve a public relations purpose rather than an evaluative function (Guion, 1991), this result is hardly surprising. What is surprising, however, is the persistence of such conversational interviews in view of the many texts and training programs on how to conduct a proper employment interview, all intended for nonprofessional audiences (e.g., Janz, Hellervik, & Gilmore, 1986; Swan, 1989). Instead of mere chit-chat, an interview should focus on having the applicant provide behavioral examples that illustrate his or her personal and interpersonal competencies to fill the job. On the premise that the best predictor of future behavior is past behavior in similar circumstances, these *behavioral interviews* require the interviewer to ask a standardized series of questions about the applicant's past successes and failures in a number of different areas of job performance. For example, an interviewer might say: "Tell me about a time when you had to deal with a difficult coworker" or "Give me an example of when you had to use your ingenuity in solving a problem, either at work or anywhere else."

Guion (1991) implicitly supported such approaches when he concluded that "there is substantial evidence that well-planned, systematic job-oriented interviews will be more reliable and lead to better predictions of subsequent job behavior than will more conversational interviews" (p. 347). This conclusion is substantiated by a recent comprehensive meta-analysis involving 245 validity coefficients obtained from 86,311 persons (McDaniel, Whetzel, Schmidt, & Maurer, 1994). A surprisingly high level of validity for the employment interview was demonstrated, especially when a structured approach was used. The overall validity coefficient of the employment interview was .37, averaging several different criteria. The highest coefficient (.50) was obtained between structured interviews of situational behavior and on-the-job performance ratings (rather than training performance or length of tenure on the job). Structured interviews, regardless of content, were more valid (.44) than unstructured interviews (.33) for predicting job performance.

A similar conclusion about the validity of structured interviews was reached by Huffcutt and Arthur (1994). Using supervisory ratings of on-the-job performance, they conducted a meta-analysis of 114 interview validity coefficients involving 32,124 persons, all of whom were starting entry-level jobs. The overall validity coefficient of .37 was the same as that reported by McDaniel et al. (1994), but the most highly structured interviews yielded a validity coefficient (.57) comparable to those obtained for ability tests. The inescapable conclusion of these research findings is that well-structured employment interviews provide useful, valid information on which to base selection decisions.

There are two types of structured interviews: (a) behavioral and (b) situational. As noted above, the behavioral interview inquires about actual prior experience in job and in other life situations; the situational interview asks applicants to predict how they would handle a variety of hypothetical situations that could arise. In a carefully controlled field study that matched the behavioral and situational questions on content and length, with the skill level of the interviewers and a number of other factors held constant, Pulakos and Schmitt (1995) found that behavioral interviews yielded a correlation of .32 with later on-the-job success in a fairly complex, professional job as compared to −.02 for the situational interviews. Further, the interview ratings added incrementally to measures of cognitive skill in prediction. This study strongly supports the conclusion that self-descriptions of past behavior are better predictors of future behavior than are self-statements about future behavior. Whether this is generally true of all employment interviews or holds true only for more complex jobs will require additional research.

Another important factor affecting the validity of employment interviews is the availability of a comprehensive job analysis, one that clearly reveals both the technical and the personal/interpersonal competencies required for success. Campion, Pursell, and Brown (1988), in a study of

149 entry-level workers, reported a corrected correlation of .56 between interviewers' predictions and on-the-job performance when the interview questions were based on a comprehensive job analysis. This line of research supports a conclusion reached earlier in this chapter: many of the earlier studies that found little or no predictive validity failed to include a thorough job description, especially one that clearly identified the personal/interpersonal characteristics required for success.

The degree of structure in interviews has been shown to be an important determiner of reliability. In a meta-analysis of 160 reliability coefficients from a total sample of 20,636, Conway, Jako, and Goodman (1995) reported an estimated true reliability of .67 for highly structured interviews, .56 for moderately structured interviews, and only .34 for interviews with low structure. These results support those of Huffcutt and Arthur (1994), who found that higher validities were a function of greater structure. Given the well-established relationship between reliability and validity, any other results would have been surprising indeed.

The research discussed above offers strong evidence for the use of interviewing as a employment selection tool, provided that the interview protocol is standardized, is based on a comprehensive job analysis, and focuses on previous experience. A number of commercially developed programs, such as SmartHire: Competency-Based Interviewing for Windows (Psychological Consultants to Management, 1995), assist the interviewer in developing such interview schedules. These programs typically start with a job analysis, to determine both the technical and personal/interpersonal competencies required for on-the-job success. Once these skills have been identified, the program leads the interviewer through a choice of questions to be asked about prior experiences. In the case of SmartHire, which is based on the Big Five personality dimensions, if a high degree of Conscientiousness is determined to be a specially important characteristic for success in the particular job, the interviewer could select from 22 different questions, all behavioral in nature, about various facets of Consciousness. An example is, "Tell me about a time when you had to exert an extraordinary amount of energy to get a job done within a time frame." Virtually all such programs, however, involve proprietary materials and have no published research.

The present status of the employment interview as a candidate selection tool is a good bit more positive than described by Guion in 1976. But the nature of work is dramatically changing, as are the roles of the workers and managers. Self-directed work teams, temporary multidisciplinary task forces, flatter nonhierarchical organizations, and just-in-time inventory processes are only a few of these changes. Constant attention and many new initiatives will be required if the selection tools of the past are to work effectively in this new environment (Cascio, 1995).

MEASURING LEADERSHIP

No topic has perennially excited more interest among I/O psychologists, researchers, and practitioners than the assessment of leadership. What are the qualities that allow one person to direct the affairs of others, and how can these qualities be measured? Simple answers to these questions have been elusive. The extent of the literature is indicated by Bass's (1990) comprehensive review covering more than 7,000 books, articles, and presentations, and by the Clark and Clark (1990) volume of edited papers from the 1988 conference on leadership sponsored by the Center for Creative Leadership and the Psychological Corporation. Space limitations allow no more than a skim of the surface of this voluminous and complex literature. We begin with a brief introduction to the theoretical underpinnings of the measurement of leadership.

By what criteria is any leadership instrument validated? Five different categories of criteria have been identified by Hogan, Curphy, and Hogan (1994):

1. Actual organizational performance.
2. Supervisory, peer, and subordinate ratings.
3. Ratings by relative strangers in such settings as assessment centers.
4. Self-ratings.
5. Descriptions of leaders who failed, were failing, or were being "derailed."

Although actual organizational performance measures are clearly the truest measures of leadership, such data are usually impossible to obtain, particularly from comparable groups. Ratings by others who know a person well, especially subordinates, are a reasonable alternative. Ratings by strangers, which are widely used in assessment centers, give a good picture of the initial impression that the person makes. Self-ratings are of little use in predicting leadership effectiveness, but they can be useful in understanding how unsuccessful managers perceive themselves in contrast to successful ones. Similarly, descriptions of managers at the low end of the success continuum provide information about failures of leadership.

Most research on leadership has not dealt directly with leadership at all; instead, it has focused on what Sashkin and Burke (1990) termed "supervisory management"—the behavior of management people at the supervisory and middle levels of the organizational hierarchy. These people serve primarily as interpreters of organizational structure and policies to those below them. Supervisors operate within these defined structures, making certain that the policies developed at the top and modified in the middle are carried out. The seminal work of the distinguished political scientist

James McGregor Burns (1978) differentiated these two sets of behaviors as *transformational* and *transactional* leadership. Burns's research on effective political leaders (e.g., Ghandi, Franklin D. Roosevelt, Winston Churchill) indicated that such leaders used a transformational approach—one that raises the consciousness of followers by appealing to higher ideals and moral values such as liberty, justice, compassion, peace, and equality. Followers rise from their "everyday selves" to their "better selves." Transactional leaders (managers) motivate followers by appealing to their self-interest and offering rewards (within the scope of their bureaucratic authority) for following leadership directions.

Both kinds of behavior can be found at any level of an organization, but transformational leadership is more likely to be observed at the higher levels, and it is certainly more important for success at those levels. For convenience, we divide the remainder of our discussion of leadership into an assessment of leadership at the supervisory and middle management levels, and an assessment of leadership at the top. Our intent is clear, but readers will find that the literature itself is unclear: the two terms—leaders and managers—are used interchangeably. Some confusion will be unavoidable.

Measuring Management

Independent lines of research—the work of Bales and his associates at Harvard University; Stogdill's group at Ohio State University; and Mann and his colleagues at the University of Michigan (see Bass, 1990; Yukl, 1993; Yukl & Van Fleet, 1991)—have reached much the same conclusion. Two critical, independent types of behavior determine the quality of management: (a) behavior centered on task accomplishment ("initiation of structure"), and (b) behavior centered on relationships, the socioemotional factors involved in work ("consideration"). Effective managers show higher levels of *both* sets of these behaviors; poor managers will have low scores on one or both. Persons with low scores on both dimensions receive the lowest ratings.

Of the several questionnaires that have been developed over the years to tap these two dimensions, the Leader Behavior Description Questionnaire (LBDQ; Stogdill, 1963) has dominated the research literature, apparently because of the elegant simplicity of its two-factor approach. Unfortunately, later research on the relationship between scores on instruments like the LBDQ and managerial effectiveness has tended to be inconclusive or even contradictory (Yukl & Van Fleet, 1991).

Hersey and Blanchard (1988) proposed that situational factors—principally, the job maturity of the subordinate—determine the optimal amount of task and relationship behaviors required from the manager. Thus, low levels of job maturity (e.g., new employees, or those taking on new job responsibilities) require a high level of task structuring and little relation-oriented behavior; workers at increasing levels of job maturity (increasing levels of performance) require the reverse pattern; and experienced, proficient workers require little of either. These authors' instruments, LEAD-Self and LEAD-Other, are intended to assist managers in diagnosing the levels of each of the two dimensions (task and relationship behavior) that are required. In a comprehensive review, Sashkin and Burke (1990) concluded that little evidence existed overall to support the use of these instruments. Yukl and Van Fleet (1991) observed that the underlying theory is conceptually weak, overly simplistic, and conceptually ambiguous, especially the notion of job maturity. However, the primary emphasis of Hersey and Blanchard has been in training people in their approach rather than in advancing research and understanding.

Fiedler's (1967, 1986) contingency theory is concerned with how three situational variables (position power, task structure, and leader–follower relationships) affect leader effectiveness. An assessment instrument taps the dimension of least preferred coworker (LPC), which is the sum of the leader's ratings (on a set of bipolar adjectives) of the person with whom the leader would work least well. Fiedler's theory predicts that high LPC leaders would be more effective in some situations, and low LPC leaders would do well in others. However, the research evidence is inconclusive (Yukl, 1993; Yukl & Van Fleet, 1991), and several comparisons have found no differences between low and high LPC leaders. Further, the focus on a single leadership behavior, especially one that is still unclear in its meaning, has limited both the accessibility and the acceptance of this measure.

Are standardized personality instruments like the California Personality Inventory (CPI) useful for assessing managerial potential? Gough (1990) presented some evidence that rather complex combinations of the existing CPI scales, especially Dominance, Independence, and Empathy, do differentiate leaders from nonleaders in a variety of different settings, but relationships between these patterns and measures of leadership effectiveness have not been demonstrated. Goodstein and Schrader (1963) were able to empirically develop a managerial key, based on 206 CPI items, that reliably differentiated managers from workers in general. The key also was able to differentiate managers at three different levels of management—(a) top management, (b) middle management, and (c) first-line supervision. Some 20 years later, the key was cross-validated with a rather different sample of managers (Gough, 1984). But, once again, the relationship between these scores and management effectiveness was not studied.

A comprehensive, long-term set of studies to predict managerial effectiveness was conducted by Sparks (1990) and his colleagues at the Exxon Corporation. Their initial study of 443 managers utilized a number of predictors, including the Guilford-Zimmerman Temperament Survey (GZTS; see Chapter Three for a description) as well as several measures of general intelligence. Except for a background form consisting of biographical items, the highest correlations between the Success Index (a weighted index of managerial success involving final position attained, salary, and managerial effectiveness as rated by supervisors, with age and tenure statistically controlled) and the GZTS were .27 and .31 for two similar samples. The multiple correlation between all predictors and the Success Index was .70 in the initial study. Although this correlation shrank to .47 in subsequent studies, much of the shrinkage was explained by factors in the Exxon workplace.

Prediction of managerial success via personality tests has been reported by Bentz (1990), who used the Guilford-Martin Personnel Inventory (GMPI; see Chapter Three for a description) plus other predictors, and a number of different success criteria. Based on a study of 136 managerial trainees at Sears, Roebuck and Co., he reported multiple correlations of .37 and .61 between the predictors and success. The results were relatively stable over an extended time period.

These latter studies provide fairly strong support for the conclusion that personality tests do predict managerial success, particularly when used in combination with other psychological instruments. Why have psychologists been so reluctant to accept this conclusion? We believe that the lack of any unifying conceptual scheme has allowed psychologists to dismiss these results as trivial and inconsequential. The emergence of the Big Five provides a way of integrating these disparate lines of research, once it is understood that researchers have tended to use a variety of names for these variables. Hogan, Curphy, and Hogan (1994) noted that *Extroversion* is variously described as Surgency, Dominance, Capacity for Status, Social Presence, and Sociability; *Emotional Stability,* as Self-Acceptance, Self-Confidence, Neuroticism, and Achievement via Independence; *Conscientiousness,* as Ambition, Need for Achievement, Dependability, and Constraint; *Agreeableness,* as Likability, Friendly Compliance, Need for Affiliation, and Love; and *Openness to Experience,* as Intellectance and Culture. As psychologists begin to use a common vocabulary, consumers of psychological research will be able to recognize the agreements in the research and will make progress in its application.

Assessing Transformational Leadership

Following Burns's (1978) initial formulation, a number of questionnaires were developed to evaluate individual levels of transformational leadership—the capacity to transform organizations in these turbulent times. We review five such instruments, all of which have reported adequate reliability (typically, alpha coefficients > .80):

1. Burke's (1994) Leadership Assessment Inventory (LAI; originally called the Leadership Report).
2. Bass's (1985) Multifactor Leadership Questionnaire (MLQ).

3. Kouzes and Posner's (1987, 1988) Leadership Practices Inventory (LPI).
4. Sashkin's (1996) Leadership Behavior Questionnaire.
5. Campbell's (1991) Leadership Index.

We also will include the Executive Profile Survey of Lang and Krug (1983), which stems from an entirely different theoretical base but deserves consideration in this context.

Burke's (1994) Leadership Assessment Inventory (LAI) is based on the assumption that the best way of differentiating transformational and transactional leaders is to assess the manner in which subordinates are empowered. The LAI consists of 18 items in a modified forced-choice format. The respondent is asked to apportion 5 points between two alternatives, one of which represents transformational leadership, and the other, transactional leadership. A sample item follows:

As a leader I spend considerable energy in:

  (A) managing separate but related goals [transactional]
  (B) arousing hopes, expectations, and aspirations in my followers [transformational].

Factor analyses of scores on the LAI reveal five factors that provide information about how power is used by the respondent: (a) Determining Direction (5 items); (b) Influencing Followers (5 items); (c) Establishing Purpose (3 items); (d) Inspiring Followers (3 items); and (e) Making Things Happen (2 items). The LAI provides scores on each of the five dimensions as well as an overall score indicating how transformational the respondent is in his or her own view. These self-perceptions also can be compared with those of subordinates and others who complete the LAI using the respondent as the target, thereby providing a comprehensive picture of the individual. Sashkin and Burke (1990) reported clear differences in the responses of executives and managers: the executives scored higher on the transformational dimension. Several of Burke's students have completed research providing empirical support for the concurrent validity of his LAI. In one such study, Van Eron and Burke (1992) reported that, in a group of 128 senior executives in a global communications company, LAI self-report scores of transformational leadership were significantly associated with reports by subordinates of behavior typically associated with that approach to leadership.

Bass's (1985) Multifactor Leadership Questionnaire (MLQ) takes a somewhat different approach by viewing leadership in terms of the leader's effect on his or her followers. A leader "transforms" subordinates by activating their higher-order needs and inducing them to transcend self-interest in order to advance organizational goals. The MLQ is based on an assumption that transformational and transactional leadership approaches are independent dimensions (Bass & Avolio, 1990). Organizations need both—transformational leadership to establish the vision, and transactional leadership of an active kind to ensure that the vision is being followed. Like the Leadership Assessment Inventory, the MLQ is completed by the leader and by others who report to that person.

The MLQ consists of 76 items to be rated on a five-point scale in terms of frequency of occurrence. It yields three transactional or managerial scores—(a) Laissez-Faire (essentially, an absence of leadership); (b) Contingent Reward (leadership through contingent rewards and punishments); and (c) Management by Exception (taking a leadership role when things do not go according to plan)—plus four transformational or leadership scores—(a) Charisma (leading by providing emotional arousal, that is, a sense of mission, excitement, and pride); (b) Inspiration (setting high expectations, expressing important purposes in understandable ways, and communicating a vision); (c) Individualized Consideration (developing a personal relationship with each follower, based on that follower's needs); and (d) Intellectual Stimulation (providing new ideas, creating new ways of attacking problems, and inducing people to rethink old problems). Thus, the MLQ provides information on the degree to which a person's transactional style is active and how transformational he or she is, together with an identification of specific areas of strength and weakness.

The MLQ manual (Bass & Avolio, 1990) provides considerable data on the development, reliability, and norms, all of which meet expected psychometric standards. There are also reports of a number of validation studies showing that high transformational scores and active transactional (as contrasted to passive) scores are positively correlated with a variety of performance measures, including Sunday school attendance (for ministers), the performance of naval vessels (for naval officers), productivity with several groups of industrial managers, and various measures for teams of MBA students engaged in a semester-long complex business simulation. The research to validate the MLQ is still emerging, but the preliminary results are quite positive (Yukl & Van Fleet, 1991).

Another approach to identifying transformational leadership behavior was taken by Kouzes and Posner (1987, 1998) in developing their Leadership Practices Inventory (LPI), which yields information solely on transformational leadership behavior. These authors asked over 1,000 managers and executives to write detailed accounts of their own best, most positive leadership experience. Their accounts contributed to the construction of an extensive list of questions about leadership behavior, which, in turn, became the basis for the preliminary versions of the LPI. Based on factor analyses of the responses of a large pool of managers to the preliminary versions, they identified factors (or, as Campbell labels them, orientations), each of which involves concrete behaviors:

1. Challenging the process—searching for new ways of getting work done and even taking sensible risks to improve the organization.

2. Inspiring a shared vision—constructing a vision of a future state and building follower support for that vision.

3. Enabling others to act—fostering collaboration among followers, and supporting followers in their personal development.

4. Modeling the way—setting examples by their own behavior, and helping followers set step-by-step goals to accomplish major objectives.

5. Encouraging the heart—recognizing followers' contributions and celebrating their achievements.

Reliabilities of the factor-based scales were quite high. A more recent factor analysis of responses to the LPI with a new group of managers yielded essentially the same factors (Posner & Kouzes, 1992). As with the MLQ, the body of research on the LPI is still incomplete, but most of the available research supports its validity, based on both organizational performance measures and ratings of leader effectiveness. At the present time, the LPI appears to be the most widely used of the leadership instruments.

Another approach to measuring transformational leadership is Sashkin's (1996) Leadership Behavior Questionnaire/The Visionary Leader (LBQ), which consists of 50 items to be answered, on five-point scales, in terms of frequency of occurrence. There are ten scale scores, developed by factor analysis; each is composed of five items. The scales are:

1. Focused leadership—the degree to which the leader makes the mission or vision clear, primarily through the use of metaphors and analogies.

2. Communication—attending to both content and feelings; active listening, summarizing, and so on.

3. Trust—being consistent over time and between verbalizations and deeds.

4. Caring—expressing concern for subordinates on an individual basis, demonstrating respect for others, and having a sense of "fitting into" the organization.

5. Risk leadership—taking risks for task accomplishment and encouraging subordinates to do the same.

6. Bottom-line leadership—demonstrating a clear sense of self-assurance, a belief that one can personally influence the organization, and a high sense of self-efficacy.

7. Empowered leadership—demonstrating a need for socialized power, a willingness to use power and influence for task accomplishment, and a willingness to empower others.

8. Long-term leadership—demonstrating a clear vision of a better future state, and concentrating on long-term rather than short-term goals.
9. Culture building—effective change management, focusing on meeting customer needs, coordinating individual and team activities, and maintaining the system.
10. Cultural leadership—developing a common set of values, basing decisions on values, and focusing on teamwork.

Visionary Leadership Behavior, Visionary Leadership Characteristics, and Visionary Culture Building are the headings for the three summary scores. As with the other leadership questionnaires, the LBQ is completed by both the respondent and others who report their observations on the respondent, thus providing complementary views.

Of all the leadership instruments, the LBQ scales have the poorest reported reliabilities (Sashkin, 1996). This is not surprising; the scales are quite short. The reliabilities for the scales of the third edition of the LBQ range from .31 for Cultural leadership to .83 for Focused leadership.

The Campbell Leadership Index (CLI; Campbell, 1991) is a 100-item adjective checklist arranged in alphabetical order with brief definitions alongside, such as "Active—In motion, on the go" and "Witty—Clever and amusing with words." The CLI requires respondents to indicate, on a six-point scale ranging from "Always" to "Never," how descriptive each adjective is of them. To provide external data, three to five other persons are asked to rate each respondent on the same instrument. The CLI profile that results from this process compares self and observer ratings on 22 standard scores, grouped into five orientations: **L**eadership, **E**nergy, **A**ffability, **DE**pendability, and **R**esilience. The CLI is based on an elaborate rationale that defines leadership ("Actions which focus *resources* to create *desirable opportunities*"; Campbell, 1991, p. 3) and then focuses on the tasks of leadership (Vision, Management, Empowerment, Politics, Feedback, Entrepreneurship, and Personal Style) as well as the five orientations described earlier. The complexity of these scores and their interpretation to a respondent require a trained professional. This is the only leadership instrument with such a requirement.

The psychometrics of the CLI are exemplary. The adjectives were originally chosen from actual descriptions of leaders. Scales were constructed using an iterative approach in which clusters of adjectives were grouped into preliminary scales and then modified on the basis of further research. The assignment of the individual scales to the five orientations was done by factor analysis. The reliabilities of the CLI scales are acceptable, although some are as low as .70, suggesting that the broader orientation scores, which have considerably higher reliabilities, are more trustworthy for individual interpretation. The CLI manual reports a number of studies of managers, completed during the development of the CLI, that show reasonable correlations between CLI scores and different levels of managerial performance, all of which support the construct validity of the CLI. As yet, however, the research literature provides little independent empirical support for the validity of the CLI.

How would one choose among these different but clearly overlapping approaches to leadership assessment? The answer we have developed for ourselves is that the choice depends on the use to which the data are to be put. If one is simply interested in determining whether the individual tends to a more transactional or a more transformational approach to his or her subordinates, the Leadership Assessment Inventory will suffice. For a more in-depth analysis as to where an individual fits on the two dimensions of transactional and transformational leadership, the MLQ would be the choice. The LPI and the LBQ are strong contenders for answering questions about the specific elements of transformational leadership. The final choice depends on how well the resultant profile fits the specific concerns being addressed.

A rather different approach to assessing high-level executive performance is provided by Lang and Krug's (1983) Executive Profile Survey (EPS), which was published well before the current interest in transformational leadership arose. Lang and Krug based their instrument on the theoretical speculations of: Erich Fromm (1947), on the marketing, hoarding, receptive, and exploitive orientations; David Reisman (1950), on the inner–outer orientation; and Charles Morris (1956), on the values inherent in his 13 "ways to live." What makes the EPS unique is that both its standardization and validation samples consisted of corporation presidents. The original instrument was based on the responses of 234 bank presidents, 117 presidents of advertising agencies, and 215 certified public accountants. The revised instrument was based on the responses of 90 CEOs of *Fortune* Magazine's 500 industrial corporations, 145 editors-in-chief of daily newspapers, 114 CEOs obtaining MBA degrees at Harvard University School of Business, 173 college and university presidents, and 42 business school deans.

The resulting instrument is a 94-item questionnaire that compares the individual along 11 dimensions developed by factor analysis with over 2,000 presidents and very senior executives in American business and educational organizations. These dimensions are:

1. Ambitious.
2. Assertive.
3. Enthusiastic.
4. Creative.

5. Spontaneous.
6. Self-focused.
7. Considerate.
8. Open-minded.
9. Relaxed.
10. Practical.
11. Systematic.

Although the manual provides lengthy explanations of each scale, the only way in which the EPS can be scored and interpreted is by sending the answer sheets to National Computer Systems. The scoring is based on a process termed *variance reallocation* or *computer synthesis,* which gives each item fractional weight based on the factor analysis of the 11 dimensions, making hand scoring impossible. The profile is reported in standard scores, and only scores below 40 and above 60 are regarded as interpretable.

The EPS appears to be strong psychometrically. The reported reliabilities are quite high, and repeated factor analyses with two independent groups support the reported factor structure. Of considerable interest is the reported multiple correlation of .35 between EPS scale scores and annual income for the sample of bank presidents. Those whose scores indicate they are more Assertive, Ambitious, Spontaneous, Creative, and Self-focused, and less Considerate, have the higher incomes. In addition, those bankers who characterized themselves as more Creative, Self-focused, Assertive, Enthusiastic, and Ambitious have risen to the top faster. One of the problems with EPS, however, is the paucity of independent validity data, probably a result of the proprietary nature of the instrument and its scoring. It is interesting to recognize that the 11 EPS dimensions can easily be sorted into the Big Five categories, again supporting the potential use of the Big Five in assessing executive-level personnel.

The quality of the instruments available to assess managerial and leadership potential is significantly better than the quality of the instruments traditionally used in assessing personality more broadly or, especially, assessing clinical phenomena. How do we account for this contrast? The reasons seem relatively clear-cut. The developers of the present instruments, being quite aware of the challenges inherent in test development, avoided the most serious pitfalls by careful application of psychometric principles. Indeed, the path taken by each of these sets of investigators follows rather closely the paradigm of test development presented in the Appendix. They have also benefited by targeting a circumscribed set of behaviors—managerial behavior in the workplace—for which there are clear criterion measures. Nevertheless, we salute the commitment to psychometric excellence demonstrated by the researchers in this area of personality assessment.

ASSESSMENT CENTERS

Assessment centers provide psychologists and other professionals with opportunities to collect data on individuals, using multiple assessment procedures. As pointed out in Chapter Five, these centers were initially developed by the OSS (now the Central Intelligence Agency) in World War II to select espionage agents who would be operating behind enemy lines. The more recent and somewhat more prosaic function of assessment centers has been to select managers—both new hires and from among personnel within the organization—and to serve as a focal point for collecting and integrating information about employees for training and development. The assessment center method, using multiple methods and multiple observers, including some with different perspectives, would seem to be ideal for the in-depth assessment of personality.

Assessment centers may be commercial or in-house. Commercial assessment centers are owned and operated by independent consulting organizations that sell opportunities to participate in this experience to individuals, although participation is almost always paid for by employers and is frequently mandated. The typical commercially operated program is composed of 10 to 12 participants, almost always strangers to each other, and a staff of psychologists and senior executives from a variety of backgrounds. For in-house programs, participants usually are selected to maximize the heterogeneity of the group, and a strong effort is made to keep people who directly work with or for each other from participating at the same time. The staff of in-house programs typically consists of a group of human resource specialists, including psychologists, and senior managers drawn from a variety of functions. Given the cost of in-house programs, only large, successful corporations have routinely developed and used them. With the decentralization and downsizing of corporate human resource departments, many organizations are now using commercial firms to develop, install, and partially staff their in-house centers.

The typical assessment center program runs from 3 to 5 days and is residential (conducted in a conference center away from the workplace) to allow the staff to interact and observe the participants in informal encounters as well as during their assigned tasks. Each participant usually completes a comprehensive battery of psychological assessment procedures, including interviews, biographical forms, measures of high-level intellectual functioning, and a variety of personality assessment instruments, which almost always include one or more of the leadership measures discussed above. The test battery typically is completed prior to beginning the residential part of the process, so that the instruments can be scored and interpreted by a psychologist before any other data are available on the participant. If this is not possible, completing the battery is one of the first items on the agenda. The data from the assessment battery, however, is not shared with the observer/raters until the final evaluation sessions (Bray & Howard, 1983; Thornton, 1992).

There is no such thing as a standardized assessment center, but two elements, in addition to the assessment battery, are common to most centers: (a) one or more *leaderless group discussions* and (b) one or more *situational tests*. In a leaderless group discussion, a small group of participants is brought into a conference room, seated, and asked to discuss a topic for 20 to 30 minutes. The assigned topics vary greatly but never have a known answer and often have a business or economic focus. "What will be the long-term impact of the European Union on United States trade policy?" is an example. Each participant is closely observed during the discussion, sometimes from behind a one-way-vision mirror. Typically, trained observers carefully record their observations on a standard form that includes such factors as drive and initiative, organization and planning, persuasiveness, communication skills, listening and sensitivity, and judgment and decision making. Figure 9.1 shows an example of such a structured rating form used by observers to evaluate a participant, in this case on the dimension of initiative. Peer ratings from participants are often solicited as part of the data-collection process. From this description of assessment center technology, it should be clear that the assessment center represents an excellent example of Campbell and Fiske's (1959) multitrait–multimethod approach to assessment.

Although the reliability of the ratings on these variables is usually adequate, Bray and Byham (1991) have suggested that videotaping be used instead of direct observation. Videotaping allows ratings to be made at convenient times and at remote locations by more professionally trained and experienced assessors. Videotapes also can reduce rater fatigue, increase reliability of the ratings, and create a permanent record. Ryan et al. (1995), using a scripted leaderless group discussion, compared the ratings from direct observations with those from videotapes of the same group of participants, with and without the opportunity to pause and rewind in order to review a portion of the discussion. Surprisingly, there were few differences among the three conditions, except that the raters who could pause and rewind the tape were somewhat more accurate in their observations. Considering both the cost and the administrative difficulties in making such videotapes, we question the usefulness of this process.

Probably the most common of the situational tests is the "in-basket" simulation. Each participant is told that a senior colleague has been taken ill and is unavailable. The participant is to "fill in" for this person on a temporary basis, and the first task is to develop responses to the various letters, memos, faxes, and telephone messages that have accumulated. The assessee is expected to sort and prioritize the contents of the in-basket. Performance is rated on how well that task is accomplished in terms of such variables as priority setting, organization, and decision making. Howard and Bray (1988)

Leaderless Group Discussion Exercise

Initiative

_____ Proposes a viable method to organize the meeting

_____ Proposes to the members that an option be ruled out if all agree

_____ Proposes that the options initially chosen be discussed later

_____ Proposes various methods of organizing the discussion

_____ Proposes to the members that they begin by eliminating options

_____ Proposes that each member identify his or her priorities

_____ Proposes that each member choose one option he or she most prefers

_____ Keeps the discussion active by moving on to other options

_____ Proposes revisions of an option

_____ Introduces a vote before discussion has ended

_____ Proposes that if the members cannot decide between two options, they can choose the third option

_____ Introduces points that have already been mentioned

_____ Introduces the voting procedures

_____ Effectively leads the discussion

_____ Controls the discussion by speaking frequently

Figure 9.1   Example of an observer's rating form used to assess participants on the factor of initiative during a leaderless group discussion exercise. (Source: From Thornton, 1992, p. 125. Copyright © 1992 by Addison-Wesley Publishing Company, Inc. Reprinted by permission of Addison-Wesley Longman Publishing Company, Inc.)

provided a listing of many other business simulations that have been used as part of assessment center technology. In-house assessment centers have the singular advantage that the in-basket elements can be organizationally relevant and thus more valid. Many in-house centers have developed additional situational activities that reflect their own organizational issues that need to be addressed.

An important aspect of all assessment centers is the development of the final evaluation, based on the observations and ratings of a number of raters. When the assessment center is used for personnel selection, the simple issue is whether the assessee should be selected. Under these circumstances, the assessment center staff provide very little information to the candidates about their performance. They are usually told only that they will be contacted if and when a suitable opening occurs. When the purposes of the assessment center, however, are to assess the potential of a candidate for advancement to more senior levels of management and to promote the creation of a self-development plan, the task is much more difficult. This type of assessment is primarily done in in-house centers. The assessors need to know the culture of the organization and how the characteristics of a particular individual will enhance or inhibit advancement in this culture. An individual developmental plan is often prepared, and the key assignments that will enhance the individual's chances of success and develop his or her "flat sides," both technically and personally, are identified. These kinds of assessment center activities require an enormous commitment of time, energy, and other resources.

Assessment centers have a reasonable record of predicting success in complex environments and with complex criteria. In a comprehensive meta-analysis of the predictive validity of the evaluations produced by assessment centers, Gaugler, Rosenthal, Thornton, and Bentson (1987) estimated the mean corrected validity coefficient of these evaluations to be .37. They noted that the validity is moderated by the type of criteria employed, the use of peer evaluations, and the nature of the exercises.

Assessment centers have a good record of predicting success in large, hierarchical organizations. The most comprehensive, longitudinal evaluations of assessment center results have involved two AT&T systems gathered under the title Management Progress Study (Bray & Howard, 1983; Howard & Bray, 1988). The results revealed Need for Advancement and Inner Work Standards as motives that are important to success in these systems. Both are defined by comprehensive ratings derived from multiple assessment methods. Managers who were high on both of these characteristics were seen as independent, energetic, and optimistic. Those high in Need for Advancement but not in Inner Work Standards were seen as more impatient about their progress and more self-confident and forceful. Those high in Inner Work Standards but not in Need for Advancement were seen as less extroverted and more deliberative and reflective. By tracing variations in these dimensions over time and as a function of changes in managerial responsibility, these authors provided insight into personality changes during managerial careers.

One problem posed by assessment centers is that they evaluate managers for a world that no longer exists. The all-male, all-Caucasian, hierarchical management structure has largely disappeared. As Cascio (1995) has pointed out, the business world that managers now face involves global competition, requires a high level of technological competence, and is staffed by a multiracial, heterosexual workforce that will operate more and more in self-managed work teams. The traditional skills required for managerial success may or may not be useful in this new world. Howard and Bray (1988) warn that only by constantly attending to the emerging pattern of skills that are now required, and building these skills into templates for evaluating managers, will assessment centers (or any other procedure for evaluating managers) be successful.

USING PERSONALITY ASSESSMENT IN TRAINING
AND DEVELOPMENT

Probably the most widespread use of personality assessment in the workplace is in training seminars, especially those that are devoted to developing managers and executives. How can we account for this interest in psychological assessment by those engaged in management development?

The average literate adult can describe his or her physical environment in exquisite detail. People ordinarily can describe a room's dimensions, furnishings, decorations, and ambience without difficulty or hesitation, often in a variety of ways. But this verbal competence usually is lacking when they must describe themselves, others, and their interpersonal world.

Our educational system simply has not provided most adults with the vocabulary or conceptual tools to describe people adequately—neither their behavior nor their psychological states. Rather, substituted for objective, behavioral description is either lavish praise ("She's simply the best manager we've got") or scatological damnation ("He's nothing but a miserable S. O. B.").

This pervasive lack of widely accepted nomological nets for describing and understanding human behavior is probably the root cause of the intense interest in personality-related theory in organizational life. The typical questions asked are direct and simple, although the answers are rarely simple, at least to professional psychologists. "Why is Mary so conscientious while Sally is not?" "How can I motivate Fred to complete his assignments on time?" Group-level constructs such as work-group climate, organizational norms, and organizational reward systems provide some partial answers, but individual differences among people—differences in personality—are widely assumed to provide additional answers. Understanding and measuring these differences, especially differences in personality, is the special province of psychology, and psychology has earned its place at the organizational table because of its presumed expertise in doing exactly that.

In the best of all worlds, there would be a single, universally accepted approach to describing individual behavior in organizational settings, a *Gray's Anatomy* of the psyche. But there is not! An ideal personality theory would be readily comprehensible by psychologists *and* their clients. Further, it would have only a few, easy-to-remember dimensions that could be reliably measured and would have demonstrable heuristic value. Such a theory would enable managers in an organization to communicate more effectively about their human resources and the issues that arise in dealing with them.

Instead, the language of personality and its constructs is a veritable Tower of Babel. To remedy this lack of a single, readily used language for viewing human behavior, many organizations, especially larger ones, have instituted training programs intended to enhance their employees' understanding of human nature, especially workplace behavior. These programs, which can range from a few hours to several days, tend to take a single approach and then train the participants in the theoretical concepts underlying that approach and in their applications to real-life situations. Kouzes and Posner's (1987) Leadership Practices Inventory, discussed above, offers the basis for such an approach. Indeed, each of the leadership assessment approaches discussed above provides information on how to conduct such programs—in each case, based on a particular instrument.

Prior to its use in the seminar or training program, the instrument is completed by the participant and by at least five or six others—supervisors, peers, and subordinates—who know the participant well at work. The instruments are scored by the seminar leader prior to the actual session, and a profile is provided to the participant as part of the seminar. This comprehensive feedback process is intended to lead the participant to develop an action plan to improve his or her managerial or leadership behavior.

The degree to which an organization uses such a training approach will determine whether the supervisors and managers speak the same language. It is quite common to hear managers in organizations using the language of a particular training approach when describing themselves and others. Unfortunately, the human resource managers who decide which of these competing approaches to purchase for their organization are often more impressed by the slickness of the sales presentation and the packaging of the product, as well as its price, than by the quality and validity of its psychometrics. Thus, we find that the Myers-Briggs Type Indicator (MBTI) is probably the instrument most widely used in management training, despite its psychometric limitations (see Chapter Three). Managers may engage in this type of assessment-speak: "What can you expect from him; he's a strong J" or "She a ENFP and she just won't fit in that group." These muffled psychological descriptions are an improvement over the superficialities provided at the beginning of this section, but they probably do not offer more substance.

An alternative to this confusion would be to describe human behavior using dimensions that have direct application to the workplace, and to develop training programs around that set of descriptors. The instruments to tap these dimensions would have to be psychometrically sound and have good predictive validity. It appears to us that these dimensions already exist in the Big Five, and that instruments based on these dimensions are already available. The task for the future is how to sell this simple but elegant unifying approach to the marketplace.

SUMMARY

In contrast to the earlier chapters' clinical orientation, this chapter focuses on assessment issues relevant to the workplace: selection and promotion, training and development, and measurement of leadership. The character of today's industrial/organizational psychology—methodologically rigorous, cautious in its claims, and carrying strong academic linkages—may be traced to its founder, Hugo Münsterberg, who was the first researcher to use psychological tests and work samples to select individuals for a variety of jobs. Because of their clinical orientation, concepts, and standardization populations, however, most contemporary personality assessment instruments have been of limited value in the workplace. A dramatic shift in this situation is now underway, as a result of the emergence of the five-factor approach to personality assessment.

Initiated by the early work of Thurstone, and made possible by the development of modern statistical procedures and computers, successful study of the number and nature of basic personality traits is now possible. In 1963, Norman developed a comprehensive list of descriptors that has become the standard for work in this area, thereby reducing discrepancies reported by different researchers. Over the past 15 years, Goldberg has demonstrated that, regardless of statistical methodology, five particular factors best account for the variance in personality. Most psychologists now agree on the existence of these basic traits: Emotional Stability (or conversely, Neuroticism), Extroversion, Openness to Experience, Agreeableness, and Conscientiousness.

Consensus also exists on the usefulness of the Big Five in employee selection. Not surprisingly, Conscientiousness has emerged as the most consistent predictor of job success, and Emotional Stability as the least relevant, perhaps because genuinely unstable individuals are rarely present in the workplace. Some differences have been identified between traits associated with training proficiency and traits related to job proficiency. Recent studies and reviews that identify the traits relevant to a given job have underlined the linkage between job analysis and the Big Five. They have also illuminated relationships between Big Five factors and other types of measures, such as ability ("can do") and motivation ("will do").

Theft and other types of counterproductive employee behavior have become a major societal problem. The study of job-related integrity shows that it is an aspect of Conscientiousness, although research suggests that other Big Five factors are also involved. With the outlawing of preemployment polygraph testing in 1988, integrity testing has become a vast industry as other methods of addressing this problem have proven inefficient or ineffective. A useful distinction in integrity tests is between subtle content measures, which resemble typical personality tests, and obvious content measures, which contain explicit, overt items. Despite concerns about easy fakability and some reports of high numbers of false positives, research has shown that the operational validity of overt tests is adequate for predicting job performance and identifying serious types of counterproductivity. As for the question of why job applicants respond honestly to obvious test items, the most widely accepted answer is that people believe "everyone steals," and therefore denial would be foolish.

Employment interviews are used by essentially all organizations, but, because of interviewer fallibility, the interview varies widely in predictive effectiveness. The conversational interview persists, despite data on the effectiveness of structured interviews and the existence of many texts, training programs, and materials on this topic. Structured interviews are behavioral, in which the interviewee reports actual past behavior, or situational, in which the interviewee predicts future behavior in hypothetical situations. Research strongly supports use of the behavioral approach and the overall utility of interviews, provided they are highly structured, well standardized, and based on a comprehensive job analysis.

The perennial interest in identifying and measuring leadership characteristics has spawned a vast literature. In evaluating this research, it is important to consider what criteria were used and who did the assessing or rating. Even more important is the question of what is actually being measured. Burns's concepts designated behavior as leadership (transformational) or management (transactional) behavior.

Research has shown that management quality depends on two critical and independent types of behavior: (a) initiation of structure and (b) consideration. However, questionnaires designed to tap these two variables have yielded inconclusive and even contradictory results. Alternatively, evidence exists showing that standard personality tests can be useful in assessing management potential. But psychologists remain reluctant to take this approach, perhaps because it lacks a unifying conceptual scheme. Here again, the Big Five may well supply the needed integration, provided a common vocabulary can be agreed on.

The interest in Burns's formulation has led to the development of many instruments addressing transformational leadership. Those reviewed here all demonstrate adequate reliability and validity, and a particular choice depends on the specific purpose of the assessment, the depth and breadth of analysis desired, and the structure of the profile produced and its congruence with the needs of the assessment. In comparing the leadership and managerial assessment instruments reviewed in this chapter with the more general clinical instruments discussed elsewhere in this text, the present instruments have the advantage of focusing on a better-defined set of behaviors with commonly understood criteria measures. They also demonstrate a more rigorous application of psychometric principles, generally following the paradigm presented in the Appendix.

Assessment centers, which date from World War II research associated with the selection of espionage agents, are now used more prosaically for initial hiring and for promotion and career development planning. They are characterized by the use of multiple measures, observers, and viewpoints; a time frame of three to five days; and the use of leaderless group discussions, various situational tests, and a battery of questionnaires. Although the assessment center methodology has proved successful for evaluation in large hierarchical organizations over several decades, it has not yet been updated to reflect the emergence of global competition, workforce diversity, and the needs of self-managed teams.

The inability of most adults to describe and discuss behavior and psychological states clearly and comfortably creates problems for organizations as well as for individuals. This handicap is enhanced by the often technical language of professional psychology. For this reason, many organizations have turned to training programs designed to increase understanding of workplace behavior. Such training is usually based on an instrument similar to those reviewed in this chapter, but often selected with little regard for psychometric properties, especially validity. Nonetheless, this type of training and development represents a major use of personality assessment in the workplace.

CHAPTER TEN

Special Applications

There are a number of areas in mental health and related disciplines where personality assessment procedures have traditionally been used in certain accepted ways. Although some of these uses are valid and appropriate, for others there are questions as to whether the uses may have evolved out of necessity or opportunity without regard to validity. In this chapter, we briefly review four of these areas of application: (a) assessment involving special demographic factors, (b) assessment of children, (c) law-related applications, and (d) neuropsychological assessment. Anticipating our conclusions, we will see that some of the current uses of personality assessment procedures in these areas are not appropriate, but there may be other defensible ways, either potential or currently available, to handle the questions of concern.

DEMOGRAPHIC FACTORS

The utility of a personality assessment procedure can be affected by demographic variables in two ways. Different demographic groups might vary in (a) their *normative responses* and (b) the external *validity*, or empirical correlates, of their scores. Both sources of variation must be considered, whether the assessment procedure is an objective one, such as the MMPI code book interpretation, or a subjective one, such as the clinical interpretation of TAT stories. The literature regarding the effect of gender, age, and ethnic background on each of these factors is briefly reviewed. The examples given tend to involve inventories because only in inventories is relevant empirical information available.

Gender

Psychologists involved in developing objective tests have known for many years that males and females differ normatively on many aspects of responding that are not directly sex-related. These differences are reflected, for example, in the procedure for converting raw scores to scale scores on the MMPI-2. Thus, a raw score of 30 on the Depression scale is equivalent to a T score (standard score) of 74 for males but only 70 for females. Possible explanations for this and similar differences are that women and men differ in their willingness to admit or report certain kinds of behaviors, thoughts, and feelings; that there are valid normative differences between the sexes; or that the meaning of certain items is different for men and women. In any event, test users should be aware of these normative differences and should be sure to use the appropriate set of norms.

Another possibility for a difference is in validity. Do the valid correlates of inventory scales or projective test interpretations differ for men and women? Empirical studies involving psychodiagnostic instruments such as the MMPI suggest that they may. For example, the code book developed by Lachar and Gdowski (1979) for the actuarial interpretation of the Personality Inventory for Children contains separate lists of empirical correlates of each scale for boys, girls, and the combined sample. More recently, the empirical correlates of the MMPI-2 content scales have shown substantial differences between men and women (Butcher, Graham, Williams, & Ben-Porath, 1990). On the other hand, many researchers have chosen to emphasize those correlates of their scales that apply equally to men and women. In developing their actuarial code book for MMPI interpretation, Marks and Seeman (1963) found that their empirically developed interpretations tended to apply about equally well to men and women, and showed an overall validity correlation with external criteria of about .5. Likewise, the major empirical correlates of the facets of the NEO-PI-R scales are given for a combined sample of men and women (Costa & McCrae, 1992b).

In general, then, it would seem appropriate to expect that different norms will apply to males and females on many assessment devices. Empirical interpretive materials should be utilized cautiously unless they are known to apply specifically to the patient's gender.

Age

It is known that age, like sex, affects responses to personality assessment devices both normatively and in validity. For example, in regard to norms, the Psychological Screening Inventory (Lanyon, 1973, 1978) shows a small but steady decline in scores on the Social Nonconformity scale with increasing age from 16 to 60 for both males and females, and a smaller decline in scores on the Expression scale. Because these data are cross-sectional rather than longitudinal in nature, they cannot be said to represent potential changes that might take place with aging, but only currently existing differences between the generations. As with the gender variable, some test differences of this nature are presumably due to real-life differences as a function of age, and some are due to other factors. In regard to age-related differences in validity, there is no particular reason to expect significant variation within the middle-age adult ranges, although little or no research exists in this area. The younger age groups (adolescents and children) require special consideration, as discussed in a separate section of this chapter.

The elderly also require special consideration. The volume edited by Storandt, Siegler, and Elias (1978), on the clinical psychology of aging, documents specific changes in responses to certain tests with increasing age, but gives no systematic normative or validity data. Specific data related to the elderly are also absent from the manuals for most major tests. Much of the professional literature on assessment of the elderly deals with cognitive and physical capacity variables, such as capability for performing the ordinary activities of daily living (e.g., Kane & Kane, 1981; Morin & Colecchi, 1995). Although some reliable normative differences clearly exist between middle-age and older adults on measures of common clinical characteristics, the underlying rationales for these differences are not always easy to determine. For example, Blazer, George, and Hughes (1991) reported an apparent decline in anxiety syndromes for persons 65 or older relative to the 45–64 age group, but other studies have shown the opposite result (Himmelfarb & Murrell, 1984). Such symptoms could be confounded with medical problems, or perhaps are underreported by older adults (Morin & Colecchi, 1995).

There is general agreement that the incidence of depression is higher among the elderly, although, once again, the underlying reasons probably are varied and complex. It has been suggested that the most common instruments for assessing depression may not be as effective with the elderly, and that specially tailored procedures might be needed (e.g., Cresswell & Lanyon, 1981). The Geriatric Depression Scale is one such instrument (Olin, Schneider, Eaton, Zemensky, & Pollock, 1992). It was designed to be easy to complete, and, to avoid possible confounding with physical health status, it contains no somatic items.

Ethnic Background

As with the demographic variables of age and gender, by far the greatest amount of research on the effect of ethnic background on personality assessment devices has involved the MMPI. Much of the early work was done by Gynther (1981) in the investigation of test differences between Black and White respondents. Gynther's work demonstrated that Blacks differ in noteworthy ways from the MMPI normative group; most prominently, they appear to show more psychopathy. However, a careful analysis of these studies (Dahlstrom & Gynther, 1986), followed by examination of a considerable amount of new data gathered with careful attention to methodology, led to the conclusion that "The evidence . . . documents the lack of serious bias or distortion in the use of the MMPI in mental health settings for the assessment of the emotional status of black clients, since the relative accuracy of these scores was as good or better for this ethnic minority as it was for white clients" (Dahlstrom, Lachar, & Dahlstrom, 1986b, pp. 204–205). Obtained differences were viewed as being due to legitimate differences between the groups, of which one was a factor that was labeled distantiation, estrangement, or discontent.

Research with the MMPI involving Mexican Americans, Native Americans, and Asian Americans was summarized by Gynther (1979) and, more recently, by Dahlstrom (1986). On the basis of this work, Dahlstrom concluded that the adequacy of the MMPI for use with these groups cannot as yet be fairly judged, because the research picture is far from complete. Perhaps the most basic need is for the development of appropriate norm groups. This is itself a complex task because the United States "has an ethnically diverse population that is constantly growing and being assimilated at different rates" (p. 85). However, there is some research support for the conclusion that, in clinical populations, some of the differences between majority and minority groups tend to disappear when the groups are matched on relevant variables. Thus, for some minority individuals, the MMPI may tend to reflect the increased stresses and difficulties they face in their lives as compared to the majority population.

The *translation* of inventories into other languages is an entirely different matter. It requires considerable sophistication in the translation process as well as substantial study of the translated form, which should be regarded as a new and unvalidated instrument until proven otherwise. Technical information regarding the translation of inventories has been provided by Brislin, Lonner, and Thorndike (1973) and by Butcher and Pancheri (1976). Essentially, what is required for a satisfactory translation is the development of an initial foreign-language translation by a committee of bilingual persons, preferably psychologists, followed by back-translation into English by a similar committee, and the reconsideration of items that did not regain their original meaning. Further steps include the development of norms for the translated version, plus empirical confirmation of validity. These steps were followed in the development of a Spanish version of the Psychological Screening Inventory for use with Costa Rican adolescents (Gonzalez & Lanyon, 1982).

PERSONALITY ASSESSMENT WITH CHILDREN

The theory and the technology of assessment that are described throughout this book apply equally to adults and children, and some of the assessment procedures already described have been specifically applicable to children. However, we have chosen to discuss the topic separately because it requires two particular considerations that are less relevant with adults. First, the development of norms (whether explicit or implicit) and the demonstration of validity are complicated by the necessary assumption that there may be major differences among children at different age levels. Second, self-report devices would appear to be more limited in applicability, particularly with young children. The assessment of children has been approached in four different ways: (a) with *projective* techniques, (b) with *inventories,* (c) from a *behavioral* viewpoint, and (d) with *checklists* and *rating scales.*

Projective Techniques

The use of projective techniques, interpreted subjectively, has traditionally been the method of choice in the assessment of children. It has usually been supplemented by material gained through various play techniques and whatever other interactions the child could be persuaded to engage in, and the data have typically been integrated within a framework employing psychoanalytic concepts. Palmer's (1983) book, *The Psychological Assessment of Children*, illustrates this approach. Surveys of psychodiagnostic practices (e.g., Elbert & Holden, 1987; Watkins, Campbell, Nieberding, & Hallmark, 1995) show that personality or diagnostic assessments with children continue to rely heavily on projective instruments.

The problems of reliability and validity with projective tests, discussed in Chapters Four and Seven, are magnified in the assessment of children, because each age grouping might be viewed as involving a different application of the test—somewhat analogous, perhaps, to different ethnic groups. Thus, not only must it be expected that the norms will differ across age groupings, but there is no reason to suppose that a predictive or descriptive correlate that is valid for five-year-olds, for example, will also be valid for ten-year-olds.

One way of approaching the validity problem has been to adopt the theoretical viewpoint that children's personality development is systematic and progressive in a holistic sense, in the same way that the original construction of the Stanford-Binet Intelligence Scale was based on the assumption that intellectual development is systematic and progressive. Thus, administration of the traditional Stanford-Binet resulted in a "mental age," which might have been higher or lower than the child's chronological age. Developmental deficits could then be pinpointed, together with areas in which the child was mentally advanced for his or her age. The work of Ames, Learned, Metraux, and Walker (1952) represented an attempt to apply this approach to the Rorschach. Ames and her colleagues tabulated and discussed the Rorschach responses of 650 boys and girls between the ages of two and ten, reporting the mean number of responses in each formal scoring category at different ages. Some categories (such as *FM*, or animal movement) showed a systematic trend in frequency during a particular age range, and some did not. Even where age trends were apparent, however, they were for the most part too small to be significant. Further, the mean number of responses per child in most categories was so small that the reported differences between age groupings were highly unreliable.

A more global problem with the developmental approach to the interpretation of the child Rorschach responses of Ames and her colleagues is that there is little firm evidence that particular responses have valid meaning at any age level for children, let alone across different age levels. At most, the Ames norms can be regarded as portraying the typical responses of children at different ages as summarized by the traditional Rorschach scoring categories, information that is frequently used subjectively in offering clinical hypotheses about individual respondents. Koppitz (1963) presented a somewhat analogous approach to the use of the Bender-Gestalt test for personality assessment with children, and this work embodies the same difficulties and constraints as that of Ames.

To conclude, the use of most projective techniques with children tends to be a highly subjective enterprise. There are several exceptions to this conclusion, two of which involve structured procedures discussed earlier in this book: the Blacky Pictures Test and such structured sentence-completion procedures as the Rotter Incomplete Sentences Blank (Rotter & Rafferty, 1950) and the Incomplete Sentences Task (Lanyon, 1972). (The nature and validity of these instruments has been discussed in Chapter Four.)

Personality Inventories

This section discusses the use of inventories that are completed by the children themselves rather than by an informant. As with projective techniques, evidence of their validity for use with preadolescent children is sparse. For adolescents, adequate validity data exist for some instruments.

One early test is the California Test of Personality (Thorpe, Clark, & Tiegs, 1953), which was published in various forms over the years 1939–1953 for use with children from kindergarten through age 14. In view of its lack of published validity information and consistently poor reviews in the *Mental Measurements Yearbook,* it is not recommended for use. Another set of children's personality inventories is based on Cattell's Sixteen Personality Factors Questionnaire (16 PF): the Preschool Personality Questionnaire (PSPQ), for ages 4–6; the Early School Personality Questionnaire (ESPQ), for ages 6–8; the Children's Personality Questionnaire, for ages 8–12; and the High School Personality Questionnaire, for ages 12–18. All are similar in nature to the 16 PF and share its theoretical orientations and methodological perspective. The PSPQ and the ESPQ for 4- to 8-year-olds are read aloud to the children. All of these inventories suffer from the same problems as described in Chapter Three for the 16 PF test: lack of specificity as to the procedures involved in selecting the items for each scale, and a relative absence of empirical validity data.

MMPI and MMPI-A.   Use of the MMPI with adolescents was based on adult norms and validity data until 20 years ago. In 1974, Marks, Seeman, and Haller published an extensive actuarial MMPI study and code book for adolescents, similar to their earlier work for adults (Marks & Seeman, 1963). This 1974 adolescent cookbook, described in Chapter Eight, makes use of norms for adolescents that are different from the norms for adults, and abandons the use of the *K*-correction. Marks, Seeman, and Haller found these changes to be necessary in order to achieve valid interpretations for adolescents, although there has been little subsequent research beyond the original work (Graham, 1987). Nevertheless, the 1974 code types provided clinicians with a databased way to use the MMPI with adolescents without relying on research findings with adults.

A major advance occurred in 1992 with the publication of the MMPI-A, a revision of the MMPI for use with adolescents ages 14–18. It can be considered as parallel to the MMPI-2, the revision of the MMPI for adults, and it was undertaken for the same reasons, besides addressing the lack of item content and scales of specific relevance to adolescents.

Because the MMPI-2 was done first, most of the technical and policy decisions that needed to be made for the MMPI-A had already been worked through, and the basic strategy for revision was the same. An experimental Form TX was created with 704 items: the 550 MMPI items, plus the 58 new items written for the MMPI-2 and 96 items specific to adolescence (in the areas of identity formation, negative peer-group influence, school and teachers, relationships with parents and families, and sexuality). The format of the MMPI-A is virtually identical to that of MMPI-2: the original three "validity" scales (L, F, and K) and three new ones (F_2, VRIN, and TRIN); the original 10 basic scales; 15 new content scales; and 6 supplementary scales. All the items on the basic scales appear in the first 350 (of 478) items.

To develop norms for the MMPI-A, subjects were obtained through schools in eight states. The goal was to obtain a balanced sample according to geographic region, urban/rural residence, and ethnic background. These balances were satisfactorily achieved; however, like the MMPI-2, the MMPI-A normative sample is quite heavily skewed in the direction of higher education and occupational level. The intended age range for the MMPI-A is 14–18, although bright, mature 12- and 13-year-olds can also be tested, and 18-year-olds who have completed high school should be given the MMPI-2.

Three of the six supplementary scales are revised and shortened versions of the corresponding MMPI scales. Three additional scales that focus specifically on adolescents were included: ACK (Alcohol/Drug Problem Acknowledgment), PRO (Alcohol/Drug Problem Proneness), and IMM (Immaturity). A set of 15 content scales was also developed and validated for the MMPI-A; this work is documented in a separate, book-length report (Williams, Butcher, Ben-Porath, & Graham, 1992). Initial research toward establishing the external validity of the content scales has been presented in the Williams et al. volume, in the MMPI-A manual, and elsewhere.

As with the MMPI-A, the validity of the MMPI-2 basic scales is dependent to a considerable degree on the research database for the MMPI, although work that is specific to the MMPI-A is now appearing. For example, Archer, Belevich, and Elkins (1994) used factor analysis to develop an eight-factor framework, with the objective of representing underlying dimensions in the MMPI-A scales and subscales. The scales that correlated most strongly with each of the eight factors were then listed under that factor, providing an eight-part "structural summary" as a framework for interpreting the test. Empirical correlates of each factor have been reported by Archer et al. for both normal and clinical samples.

Millon Adolescent Personality Inventory. Two other relatively recent inventories are designed especially for adolescents. One is the Millon Adolescent Personality Inventory (MAPI; Millon, Green, & Meagher, 1982). The MAPI represents an adaptation for the adolescent population of the approach used in the development of the Millon Clinical Multiaxial Inventory (MCMI-III; Millon, Millon, & Davis,1994), described in Chapter Three. As with the MCMI, many of the 20 MAPI scales are highly correlated. Most of the variance in the test can be accounted for by two factors, whose content represents the two general problem areas of internalizing (e.g., inhibited; insecure) and externalizing (e.g., not respectful; family conflicts). Also available is a clinical test for adolescents, the Millon Adolescent Clinical Inventory (Millon, Millon, & Davis, 1993).

Personality Inventory for Youth. The final inventory to be discussed is the recently published Personality Inventory for Youth (PIY; Lachar & Gruber, 1994). Beginning with the items of the Personality Inventory for Children (PIC; Wirt, Lachar, Klinedinst, & Seat, 1977, 1990), the authors reworded the items in a self-report format to reflect the targeted age range of 9–18 years. Based on the responses of 585 clinical cases, a rational test construction strategy was used, involving a series of factor-analytic and other statistical steps. This procedure resulted in 9 nonoverlapping clinical scales, such as Delinquency, Somatic Concern, and Social Skills, plus 24 complementary facets or subscales, either 2 or 3 for each scale. Some initial validity data are presented in the PIY manual (Lachar & Gruber, 1994).

Behavioral Approaches

Behavioral assessment is an area of considerable importance (see Chapter Six). The major impetus to its development was the growth of behavior modification and behavior therapy, in both research applications and practical settings involving individual clinical cases and single-case experimental studies. Although there are no differences in principle between the application of behavioral assessment to adults and to children, it is more used with children than with adults, perhaps for two reasons. First, there are fewer viable alternative approaches to the assessment of children. Second, systematic observers—who are essential in behavioral assessment—are more readily available with children, in the form of parents and teachers. As emphasized in Chapter Six, although behavioral assessment is a promising approach for many topics and problems involving children, increased attention to psychometric considerations such as standardization, norms, validity, and reliability is needed in order to maximize its utility.

A number of other factors should be taken into consideration if child behavioral assessment is to contribute optimally to the assessment process (Ollendick & Meador, 1984). First, behavioral assessment must be viewed, like other assessment modalities, as just one of several sources of data to be integrated in a multimodal approach. Second, the obtained data should be understood within the context of age-related variables, sociocultural variables, and other factors that may influence the child. Third, attention should be paid to the relevance of internal states (thoughts, feelings) as behaviors in their own right and for their effects on what is overtly observable. Finally, it is emphasized that methodologically sound observations that are made in the naturalistic environment, particularly on an ongoing basis, represent the major and unique contribution of the behavioral approach to the assessment enterprise.

Structured Checklists and Rating Scales

In this section, we discuss procedures that require observers to make rating judgments or other types of judgments about a child. There is a fine line between what is typically called "behavioral assessment" and what is viewed as the use of structured checklists and rating scales. A convenient distinction is that checklists and rating scales are used to make global reports of the habitual occurrences of behaviors; the behavioral assessor observes and records *each instance* of behavior as it actually occurs.

Perhaps the best known instrument is the Personality Inventory for Children (PIC; Wirt, Lachar, Klinedinst, & Seat, 1990), originally published in 1977. Although termed an "inventory," the PIC is classified here as a checklist because it is completed by a person other than the child—typically, the mother. The development of the PIC was in many ways similar to that of the MMPI. Initially, 600 items were written to represent 11 content areas: those regarded as primary areas of personality functioning in children, and other areas that were thought to be useful to the practicing clinician. This item pool served, over a number of years, as the basis for the construction of a total of 33 scales. Some were constructed empirically, in the manner of the MMPI scales, and some were developed on a rational basis. Of the 33, a total of 16—4 validity scales and 12 clinical scales—were ultimately selected for inclusion in the published form of the test. The remaining 17 are regarded as supplemental scales to be used if desired. There are four separate PIC profile sheets: (a) separately by gender and (b) separately by ages 3–5 and 6–16. The development of norms involved nearly 2,400 children in the age range 6–16 and about 200 children aged 3–5. Three of the validity scales—Lie, F (deviant responding), and Defensiveness—are similar to those of the MMPI. The fourth scale (Adjustment) is an overall screening for poor psychological adjustment. The following descriptions of the clinical scales are paraphrased from the manual by Wirt et al. (1990):

Achievement (ACH): an empirical scale to identify children whose academic achievement is below expectation

Intellectual Screening (IS): an empirical scale to identify children whose difficulties could be due to impaired intellectual functioning

Development (DVL): a content-based scale to assess poor intellectual and physical development

Somatic Concern (SOM): a content-based scale to assess various health-related variables

Depression (D): a content-based scale composed of items judged to reflect childhood depression

Family Relations (FAM): a content-based scale designed to assess family effectiveness and cohesion

Delinquency (DQL): an empirical scale designed to assess delinquent tendencies

Withdrawal (WDL): a content-based scale to measure withdrawal from social contact

Anxiety (ANX): a content-based scale to assess various manifestations of anxiety

Psychosis (PSY): an empirical scale to discriminate children with psychotic symptoms from normals and from disturbed but nonpsychotic children

Hyperactivity (HPR): an empirical scale to identify children displaying symptoms typically associated with the "hyperkinetic syndrome"

Social skills (SSK): a content-based scale to measure characteristics that reflect effective social relations in childhood

Factor analysis of the PIC item pool (Lachar, Gdowski, & Snyder, 1982) led to the identification of four basic factors, which the authors labeled undisciplined/poor self-control, social incompetence, internalization/somatic symptoms, and cognitive development. The items that most directly represent these factors are placed first in the item booklet, so that the first 131 items can serve as a four-scale "short form" of the PIC. The standard version of the PIC can be completed if the first 280 items are answered; longer versions of the scales can be scored if the first 430 items are completed. The 17 supplementary scales require the full 600 items.

A considerable amount of information about the test, including empirical validity data, is given in the manual by Wirt et al. (1990). In particular, Lachar and Gdowski (1979) conducted a major validity study involving the development of an actuarial interpretation system for the PIC. Subjects were 200 children (mostly aged 6–12) and 231 adolescents (aged 13–17) evaluated at an urban university-affiliated clinic, over a 16-month period. Several hundred items of criterion information were available on these children, including a preappointment questionnaire (usually filled out by the child's mother), teacher ratings and school information, and diagnostic interview information. Lachar and Gdowski reported those criterion items that correlated significantly with high or low scores on each of the scales, separately by sex and age grouping and also in combination. Also reported was the range of scores on each of the scales where the relationship with a criterion variable was the strongest, and the results of the study were used as the basis for the development of an automated interpretation program. In addition to interpretation by means of the Lachar-Gdowski actuarial system, cluster-analytic techniques were employed to identify twelve different PIC profile "types" (Gdowski, Lachar, & Kline, 1985). Rules for classifying profiles into this typology were developed (Kline, Lachar, & Gdowski, 1987), and several kinds of empirical interpretive data for the types have been reported (e.g., LaCombe, Kline, Lachar, Butkus, & Hillman, 1991).

Because of its careful development and the availability of empirical data, the PIC would appear to be a useful instrument. Justification is needed for the decision to employ only two age categories—3–5 and 6–16 for the original test norms, and below-12 and 13–17 for the actuarial interpretation study of Lachar and Gdowski.

Another widely used checklist is the *Child Behavior Check List* (CBCL) and its accompanying Child Behavior Profile (CBP; Achenbach, 1978, 1991a). Designed to obtain parents' reports of their children's competencies, the CBCL consists of 118 behavior-problem items to be rated 0, 1, or 2, plus seven multidimensional items related to social competencies. The initial item pool for the CBCL was developed on the basis of existing literature on the assessment of children's problems plus the case histories of 1,000 psychiatric cases. Some items are quite specific in content (e.g., "runs away from home"; "sleeps less than most children"); others are inferential (e.g., "suspicious").

The behavior-problem items served as the basis for constructing six separate sets of scales—by gender, and by three different age groupings: 4–5, 6–11, and 12–16. Scales involve clusters of items identified through factor analyses of CBCL responses on several hundred children in each of the six age/gender groupings from mental health settings. Originally, the resulting six forms of the CBCL differed in the number of scales on each (either eight or nine), and some of the scale names differed, as did the particular items on scales of the same name. As of 1991, all forms have the same eight clinical scales—for example, Withdrawn, Anxiety/Depressed, and Delinquent Behavior. There are also two broadband scales, Internalizing and Externalizing. The social competence scales—Activities, Social, and School—are also the same for all six forms and consist of behavioral items that reflect each of the three categories. There are national norms for the 1991 version of the CBCL, and a variety of validity data is available in the manual.

Two other forms of this instrument have been developed. The Teacher Report Form (TRF; Achenbach, 1991b) is set up to obtain teachers' ratings, and it contains additional items appropriate for teachers. The Youth Self Report (Achenbach, 1991c) is appropriate for ages 11–18. It can be filled out by youths with fifth-grade reading skills, or administered orally. Overall, reviews of the CBCL have regarded it as a useful test with a satisfactory psychometric foundation (e.g., Kelley, 1985; Martin, 1988).

Besides the instruments already described, a number of others can be considered for use in appropriate settings. One is the Conners Ratings Scales (CRS; Conners, 1989), which consists of four parent and teacher scales involving 93 items to be rated on four-point dimensions. Others include the Social Skills Rating System (Gresham & Elliot, 1990), the Revised Behavior Problem Checklist (Quay & Peterson, 1983), and the Louisville Behavior Checklist (Miller, 1984).

The final category of instruments to be described involves *adaptive behavior*. The concept of social competence refers to "the child's ability to perform the social roles appropriate for persons of his or her age and sex in a manner that meets the expectations of the social systems in which he or she participates" (Mercer, 1979, p. 102). Although the concept is as much related to intelligence as to personality, such instruments do have some similarity to other procedures that are designed to assess overall adjustment. One example is the *Adaptive Behavior Inventory for Children* (ABIC; Mercer, 1979). The interviewer asks an informant, typically the mother, a series of age-graded questions about the degree to which the child currently engages in a wide variety of behaviors that are believed to be adaptive in one of five social systems. The six scales represent each of these social systems: family, community, peer relations, nonacademic school roles, and earner/consumer, plus a sixth nonspecific area of adaptation, termed *self-maintenance*. The 242 items were refined from a much larger pool developed from previous scales and from interviews with mothers of normal and retarded children. Norms are available for each of the six scales for age groupings at three-month intervals in the age range of 5–11. Separate tables for Black, Hispanic, and White children are also presented.

The ABIC is one part of a much larger assessment battery, the System of Multicultural Pluralistic Assessment (SOMPA), developed by Mercer (1979) to provide for the comprehensive or multidimensional evaluation of children in educational settings, taking sociocultural differences into account. However, the ABIC can be employed separately, and it appears to have the potential for satisfactory validity in the context of a social skills approach to general adjustment and mental health. Two other instruments that are similar to the ABIC in nature and purpose are the Vineland Adaptive Rating

Scales (Sparrow, Balla, & Cicchetti, 1984) and the Developmental Profile II (Alpern, Boll, & Shearer, 1984).

ASSESSMENT IN FORENSIC SETTINGS

The role of psychologists and other mental health professionals in the legal and correctional systems has increased substantially in recent years. These developments are reflected in the increased number of articles in professional journals and textbooks, and relevant courses and programs in college and university settings, dealing with topics in forensic psychology. This section reviews several specific uses of assessment in the forensic area, and attempts to put them in proper perspective.

Insanity Evaluation

Perhaps the best-known role of psychiatrists and psychologists in court settings is as expert witnesses testifying whether a defendant was insane at the time of committing an offense (and therefore worthy of special consideration). Although very few defendants indeed are ultimately found not guilty by reason of insanity, this issue has generated a great deal of scholarly activity over the years. Legal experts disagree on the exact nature of the concept of insanity, and on why special consideration should be given to defendants who are found to have suffered from it (e.g., Fingarette & Hasse, 1979; Melton, Petrila, Poythress, & Slobogin, 1987). Because the language and concepts of the law are different from those of behavioral science, it is doubtful that even a precise definition of insanity would have a clear counterpart in psychology or psychiatry. Thus, it should not be surprising that a great deal of subjectivity is often involved in the assessment of insanity.

Different legal jurisdictions have different definitions of insanity. The most conservative is the McNaughten Rule, which originated in England in 1843. Under this rule, the defendant must be shown to have been "labouring under such defect of reason, from disease of the mind, as not to know the nature and quality of the act he was doing; or, if he did know it, that he did not know he was doing what was wrong." The insanity laws in most states now include a broader definition of insanity (Wrightsman, Nietzel, & Fortune, 1994). For example, some states have included the irresistible impulse test, in which defendants are legally insane if they knew the difference between right and wrong at the time of an action but found themselves overwhelmed by an irresistible impulse.

The necessity for showing that the defendant was insane *at the time of the offense,* and not simply at the time of examination, presents additional difficulties. The most straightforward cases are those in which defendants have a history of psychosis, such as schizophrenia, accompanied by evidence (other than the offense itself) that they were psychotic at the time of the offense. In most cases, there is substantial ambiguity, and little can be said about the process of making the assessment except that those who do so rely heavily on the accumulation of their subjective or clinical experience. It is perhaps reassuring to know that despite the differing legal standards and the ambiguities for mental health professionals, juries tend to operate according to a fairly consistent general standard, regardless of the particular definition of insanity in their state (Finkel, 1989). This standard apparently includes consideration of both cognitive (McNaghten) and self-control or volitional (irresistible impulse) issues (Bailis, Darley, Waxman, & Robinson, 1995). These findings suggest that a conservative role is appropriate for the mental health professional—namely, to present mental health information to the jury but not to give an opinion on the ultimate legal issue (insanity) itself.

Competency to Stand Trial

The basic criteria for competency to stand trial were determined by the U.S. Supreme Court in *Dusky v. United States* (1960). They involve two basic standards: (a) the defendant's ability to consult with his or her attorney with a reasonable degree of rational understanding, and (b) a rational as well as factual understanding of the court proceedings. Additional criteria involve an understanding of the consequences of the proceedings and of the constitutional rights that the defendant would be giving up by entering a guilty plea (Roesch & Golding, 1981).

Readers should distinguish clearly between the evaluation of *competency*, which involves the defendant's general mental condition at the time of the trial, and *insanity*, which involves special aspects of the defendant's general mental condition at the time of the alleged offense. The assessment of competency, like the evaluation of insanity, has been traditionally approached from a psychiatric viewpoint. However, Sales (1980) and others have pointed out that the terms *competent* and *incompetent* are unfortunate designations because they imply a permanent illness or incapacity when the situation requires only the assessment of the person's *current ability* to stand trial, which may be temporarily, not permanently, affected by various factors.

Several noteworthy attempts have been made to develop structured, quantifiable procedures for assessing competency to stand trial. The Competency Screening Test (CST), a 22-item sentence-completion instrument with stems relevant to the legal criteria of competency, was designed to distinguish, "at the earliest possible stage, the competency issue from other legal and mental health issues" (Lipsitt, Lelos, & McGarry, 1971, p. 105). Responses, scored on a three-point scale (2, 1, 0) with the aid of a structured scoring manual, reflect different levels of competency. For example, with the sentence stem "When I go to court, the lawyer will . . . ," the response "defend me" would be scored 2, but the response "put me away" would be scored 0. Lipsitt et al. showed significant differences on the test between groups of men who had been judged incompetent and groups who had not, and concluded that the instrument could facilitate competency screening procedures. Subsequent research, summarized by Roesch, Ogloff, and Golding (1993), has shown some degree of support for the CST, although the level of reading and writing ability that is required makes it inappropriate for many defendants.

A much more elaborate instrument, the Competency Assessment Instrument (CAI), was developed by McGarry et al. (1973) in the context of a major project to clarify and improve theory and practice of the assessment of competency on a broad basis. The CAI consists of a 13-item interview schedule representing "functions related to the accused's ability to cope with the trial process in an adequately self-protective manner" (McGarry et al., 1973, p. 24), and is intended to cover all possible grounds for the finding of incompetency. The interview schedule is shown in Figure 10.1. The detailed manual that accompanies the CAI defines the intent of each item and gives sample interview questions and scoring examples. A subsequent study by the same authors showed that the manual could be successfully used to train personnel in administering and scoring the CAI with adequate reliability. McGarry et al. emphasized that the ultimate decision regarding the weight to be put on any or all of the items should be the responsibility of the court, taking into consideration all factors relevant to the particular defendant. The CAI should be considered a standardized interview rather than a test, and as such can be a useful guide for the clinician (Grisso, 1988).

Several other standardized procedures, such as the Interdisciplinary Fitness Interview (Schreiber, Roesch, & Golding, 1987) and the Georgia Court Competency Test (Wildman, White, & Brandenburg, 1990), have been developed to assist in evaluating competency to stand trial. Forensic psychologists may be called to assess many other kinds of legal competencies, such as competency to make a confession, to represent oneself in court, or to draw a will. The volume by Grisso (1986) discusses these and other competencies.

Dangerousness and Violence

One of the most common questions asked of mental health professionals in legal and correctional settings centers on whether a particular defendant or inmate is dangerous or potentially violent. *Dangerous* is another concept that is defined in legal terms but does not have a direct counterpart in the language of psychology. A useful definition has been offered by Shah (1978), who wrote that "dangerousness" refers to an increased likelihood of

		Degree of Incapacity				
	Total	Severe	Moderate	Mild	None	Unratable
1. Appraisal of available legal defenses	1	2	3	4	5	6
2. Unmanageable behavior	1	2	3	4	5	6
3. Quality of relating to attorney	1	2	3	4	5	6
4. Planning of legal strategy, including guilty plea to lesser charges where pertinent	1	2	3	4	5	6
5. Appraisal of role of:						
a. Defense counsel	1	2	3	4	5	6
b. Prosecuting attorney	1	2	3	4	5	6
c. Judge	1	2	3	4	5	6
d. Jury	1	2	3	4	5	6
e. Defendant	1	2	3	4	5	6
f. Witnesses	1	2	3	4	5	6
6. Understanding of court procedure	1	2	3	4	5	6
7. Appreciation of charges	1	2	3	4	5	6
8. Appreciation of range and nature of possible penalties	1	2	3	4	5	6
9. Appraisal of likely outcome	1	2	3	4	5	6
10. Capacity to disclose to attorney available pertinent facts surrounding the offense including the defendant's movements, timing, mental state, actions at the time of the offense	1	2	3	4	5	6
11. Capacity to realistically challenge prosecution witnesses	1	2	3	4	5	6
12. Capacity to testify relevantly	1	2	3	4	5	6
13. Self-defeating v. self-serving motivation (legal sense)	1	2	3	4	5	6

Examinee _____ Examiner _____

Date _____

Figure 10.1 Interview schedule and rating sheet for the Competency Assessment Instrument. From McGarry et al. (1973).

engaging in dangerous behavior or violence, defined as "acts that are characterized by the application of or the overt threat of force and that are likely to result in injury to other persons" (p. 224).

Traditionally, the origin of dangerous conduct has been assumed to lie within the individual. This view led to the evaluation of the likelihood of future violence by means of responses to traditional personality tests such as the Rorschach (e.g., Lerner, 1975), the MMPI (Gearing, 1979), or other inventory scales (e.g., Spielberger, Jacobs, Russell, & Crane, 1983). Considerable attention has been paid to the MMPI Overcontrolled Hostility (O-H) scale of Magargee and Mendelsohn (1962) and to the high 4–3 pattern, both of which have shown better than chance results but not the accuracy needed for satisfactory predictions on an individual basis.

More recent views focus on the interaction between the person and the particular environment or social situation (Monahan, 1981; Otto, 1992). Thus, people are more likely to engage in dangerous behavior in particular contexts, such as when their self-esteem is threatened in the presence of a member of the opposite sex. Several writers have presented detailed frameworks for assessing dangerousness within this expanded view, in which both the person's stable characteristics and the situational variables are assessed (e.g., Hall, 1984; Megargee, 1995; Monahan, 1981). Monahan's (1981, 1984) outline for such an evaluation is presented in Figure 10.2. The framework draws on data from a variety of sources, most of them referring to personal history of the subject and aspects of the current environment. Other relevant variables to be considered include the base rate of violence among persons similarly situated, and any factors that would predict the *absence* of violent behavior.

There is no intent here to give an impression that internal or personality factors are unimportant, but they were traditionally relied on to the exclusion of situational variables. In fact, Lykken's (1993) thoughtful analysis of the causes of violence strongly implicates internal factors that are deep-seated and perhaps biological in nature, such as fearlessness, stimulus seeking, impulsiveness, and aggressiveness.

A further difficulty with the assessment of dangerousness is that the behavior has relatively low base rates. Thus, the predictive problems associated with infrequent events, as discussed in Chapters Seven and Eight, apply here. In particular, the use of any cutting point that would correctly identify the majority of "dangerous" persons would also yield an extremely high false-positive rate, so that nearly everybody identified as dangerous would not in fact be dangerous. Therefore, the necessary conditions for the meaningful prediction of dangerous behavior would seem to involve populations (a) where the proportion of dangerous people is substantial and (b) for whom a large false-positive rate is acceptable. More detailed analyses of base rate issues in the prediction of violence have been provided by Otto (1992), Mossman (1994), and Bjorkly (1995).

In summary, the prediction of violence from traditional personality variables is not accurate enough to be useful in practice. The inclusion of a

1. Is it a prediction of violent behavior that is being requested?
2. Am I professionally competent to offer an estimate of the probability of future violence?
3. Are any issues of personal or professional ethics involved in this case?
4. Given my answers to the above questions, is this case an appropriate one in which to offer a prediction?
5. What events precipitated the question of the person's potential for violence being raised, and in what context did these events take place?
6. What are the person's relevant demographic characteristics?
7. What is the person's history of violent behavior?
8. What is the base rate of violent behavior among individuals of this person's background?
9. What are the sources of stress in the person's current environment?
10. What cognitive and affective factors indicate that the person may be predisposed to cope with stress in a nonviolent manner?
11. What cognitive and effective factors indicate that the person may be predisposed to cope with stress in a nonviolent manner?
12. How similar are the contexts in which the person has used violent coping mechanisms in the past to the contexts in which the person likely will function in the future?
13. In particular, who are the likely victims of the person's violent behavior, and how available are they?
14. What means does the person possess to commit violence?

Figure 10.2 Monahan's outline for an evaluation to predict violent behavior. (**Source:** *From Monahan, 1981, p. 160. Copyright © 1981 Sage Publications. Reprinted by permission of Sage Publications.*)

broader range of predictive variables—in particular, situational factors—leads to substantial improvement but does not yield enough accuracy for a high degree of confidence. Predictions in the short term (1–7 days) would be expected to be more accurate than longer-term predictions, because of a greater ability to know the situational factors, but, paradoxically, this result has not been found, at least according to one review (Mossman, 1994). Thus, there is still a lot to learn about predicting violence. On the positive side, studies since 1980 have yielded better results because of methodological improvements. Consistent with common sense, it appears that the best predictor of future violence is past behavior (Mossman, 1994).

Assessment in Child Custody Cases

Until the nineteenth century, children were generally regarded as the personal property of the father and automatically stayed with him if the marriage collapsed (Einhorn, 1986). With the development of equal rights for women, this custom gradually evolved into a preference for awarding custody to the mother, particularly if the children were young. More recently, courts have emphasized a responsibility to do whatever is in the best interests of the child, and judges have considerable discretion in interpreting this policy. Behavioral science professionals are often invited to contribute their expertise. Because the adversarial nature of the decision-making process often impedes the task of determining the child's best interests, it is recommended that behavioral scientists should represent the court, or the child, or both parties, rather than one side alone (Halleck, 1980).

The assessment—determining the child's best interests—is legal, sociological, and psychological. In many states, the legal criteria for the best interests of the child are based on the Model Standard of the 1970 Uniform Marriage and Divorce Act (Melton, Petrila, Poythress, & Slobogin, 1987). Figure 10.3 shows the criteria in the state of Arizona; items A-1 through A-5 constitute the Model Standard. Several of the criteria involve psychological matters: the love and affection between parent and child; the capacity

---

A. The court shall determine custody, either originally or upon petition for modification, in accordance with the best interests of the child. The court shall consider all relevant factors, including:

1. The wishes of the child's parent or parents as to custody.

2. The wishes of the child as to the custodian.

3. The interaction and interrelationship of the child with the child's parent or parents, the child's siblings and any other person who may significantly affect the child's best interest.

4. The child's adjustment to home, school and community.

5. The mental and physical health of all individuals involved.

6. Which parent is more likely to allow the child frequent and meaningful continuing contact with the other parent.

7. If one parent, both parents or neither parent has provided primary care of the child.

8. The nature and extent of coercion or duress used by a parent in obtaining an agreement regarding custody.

B. The court shall consider evidence of domestic violence as being contrary to the best interests of the child. If the court finds that domestic violence has occurred, the court shall make arrangements for visitation that best protect the child and the abused spouse from further harm. The person who has committed an act of domestic violence has the burden of proving that visitation will not endanger the child or significantly impair the child's emotional development.

Figure 10.3   State of Arizona legal criteria for determining the best interests of the child in regard to custody after divorce. From Arizona Revised Statutes, Section 25, Article 3.

and willingness of each parent to continue providing love, affection, and child-rearing guidance; the mental health of each parent; and the potential permanence of the custodial home.

Several researchers have surveyed the views of judges and mental health professionals as to the most important factors in determining the best interests of a child (Keilin & Bloom, 1986; Lowery, 1981; Woody, 1977). These surveys point to two general criteria: (a) the *quality of the relationship* between parent and child, and (b) the parent's *capacity to meet the child's needs.* Another relevant source of input for assessment comes from research findings about children's adjustment following divorce. This literature emphasizes the importance of a positive relationship (low conflict) between the divorced parents, a continuing positive relationship of the child with both parents, and the mental health of the custodial parent (Sales, Manber, & Rohman, 1992).

Many of the questions to be answered in a child custody evaluation are psychological; they involve the assessment of personality, mental health, and psychopathology. It is equally clear that the issues are complex and the evaluation must be wide-ranging. Data should include careful examination of records, interviews with family members (singly and in combination), contact with teachers and other relevant persons, psychological testing, home visits, and so on. For general guidance, the reader is referred to the American Psychological Association's (1994) Guidelines for Child Custody Evaluations in Divorce Proceedings. Sources such as Bushard and Howard (1995) give more detailed practical information. Custody assessments are most appropriately performed by psychologists who have specific training and experience in assessing parent–child relationships, plus a working knowledge of the empirical literature in child development. One final point must be emphasized. The psychologist's contribution is only part of the total question of "suitability"; the court retains responsibility for making the overall determination.

Classification in Correctional Settings

Administrators of prisons have traditionally utilized some systematic means of assigning inmates to various facilities, living quarters, and work and rehabilitation programs. There are two major ways in which classification is useful: (a) to facilitate *management,* and (b) to facilitate *rehabilitation.* In regard to management, the factors to be considered typically include whether the inmate can be placed in a large dormitory or whether a single or shared room is more appropriate; whether there is a suicide risk; whether there is an increased risk of harassment from other inmates, as may happen with child molesters, for example; whether the inmate is known to be militant and therefore requires careful management; and whether the inmate is known to be in physical danger from other inmates.

Factors that are relevant in classification for rehabilitation include, in addition to those already listed, educational level, skills and abilities, interests, and job-related personality patterns.

Much of the classification task involves demographic and educational factors, or aspects of behavior that are listed directly in court and correctional documents, rather than psychological variables. Thus, in many instances, the classification task is primarily clerical. However, some of the relevant factors—suicide potential, sexual deviance, and personal interest patterns—fall within the realm of personality assessment, broadly defined. Because the goals of classification differ from institution to institution, the first step in developing a classification system should be to determine exactly what the goals of the system are for that particular setting. Once that is done, sources of data to assess the variables of interest can be assembled, together with information about the base rates of these variables among the population at hand. The extent to which specific cutting points should be used depends on real-life constraints. For example, if there are only 50 single cells, they would be necessarily assigned to the 50 persons judged to need them most, in view of the system's goals. However, if single cells are unlimited, then an "optimal" cutting point is used, either explicitly or implicitly, in deciding which inmates to house singly and which ones in pairs or group settings.

Recently, classification systems have been developed that are based on a single personality inventory, such as the MMPI or the 16 PF Questionnaire. For example, as discussed in Chapter Eight, Megargee (1977) and his colleagues reported the painstaking development of a system involving 10 MMPI "types." Although there are definite demographic and personality-related differences among these types (Edinger, 1979; Megargee & Bohn, 1979), the use of test responses alone as predictors in building a classification system seems to be an indirect and inefficient method of approaching classification, except for factors that are strongly related to measurable personality variables.

NEUROPSYCHOLOGICAL ASSESSMENT

According to Benton (1994), "The primary purpose of neuropsychological assessment is to draw inferences about the structural and functional characteristics of a person's brain by evaluating an individual's behavior in defined stimulus–response situations" (p. 1). At one time, this procedure was called the assessment of "organicity," based on the belief that what was being assessed was the presence or absence of a simple unitary phenomenon. The results of traditional psychodiagnostic tests such as the Rorschach and the Bender-Gestalt were examined for "signs of organicity," and there was continuing interest in the search for the "best" single test of "organicity." With the development of the field of clinical neuropsychology as a separate subdiscipline came the recognition that there can be many different types of impairments, depending on what parts of the brain are damaged. A more scientific and differentiated approach to assessment followed. Lezak (1995) differentiated three areas of functioning that are relevant for neuropsychological assessment: (a) cognitive functioning, (b) personality/emotionality, and (c) executive functions. By far the greatest attention has been given to the assessment of cognitive functions, which Lezak designated as receptive functions, memory, thinking, expressive functions, and mental activity variables.

For the assessment of the cognitive and executive function areas (or, more accurately, the assessment of impairments in these areas), extensive neuropsychological test batteries such as the Halstead-Reitan and the Luria Tests have been developed (Lezak, 1995; Reitan & Wolfson, 1993). There is increasing evidence that such test batteries, and other individual test procedures, are useful in assessing impairments due to brain dysfunction, and that they may sometimes be of assistance in determining the location of the brain damage, and in discriminating organic disorders from functional disorders such as schizophrenia (e.g., Goldstein, 1986; Lezak, 1995).

Despite the highly specialized nature of assessment for cognitive and executive functions, the procedures for assessing personality and psychopathology in patients suspected of having sustained brain damage are no different from those that would be used in assessing these characteristics in other patients. However, distinguishing difficulties directly caused by the brain damage itself from the emotional effects of having an impairment is often a difficult task. For example, symptoms of depression can be both a direct effect of brain damage and a psychological reaction to its handicapping effects (Sweet, Newman, & Bell, 1992). And certain personality changes can be a direct result of damage of the frontal lobes (Prigatano, 1992). Overall, the assessment of persons suspected of being brain-damaged is a complex task that requires a working knowledge of brain function and the nature of possible impairments, plus familiarity with the available testing procedures and their strengths and weaknesses.

SUMMARY

The utility of personality assessment procedures can be affected by demographic variables in two ways: demographically different groups can vary in their normative responses and in the validity of their scores. For example, males and females differ normatively on many tests and also in their empirical correlates, although the overlap is great enough that, in many cases, a single set of interpretive material is sufficient. Age also affects responses, although variations within the middle-adult years is probably small. Assessment of the elderly requires special consideration, both because of differences in norms and validity, and because some of the problems requiring assessment in the elderly are somewhat specific to that age group. Another demographic variable affecting responses is ethnic background, and stable differences have been found on such tests as the MMPI between Whites and Blacks, and among other ethnic groups. Some of these differences appear to reflect legitimate group differences, but the meaning of others is not as easily understood.

Personality assessment with children is more complex than with adults, and there is no reason to expect that either the norms or the validity of a test developed for adults will be applicable to children and adolescents, or even that one childhood age group will be comparable to another in norms or validity. The most common procedure for the assessment of children has been through the use of projective tests, and this practice continues to be popular despite the fact that empirical validity data are lacking for all but a few instruments. Several relatively new personality inventories are available. The most prominent is the MMPI-A, a revision of the MMPI designed specifically for adolescents. The MMPI-A incorporates many of the same improvements as the MMPI-2, including content scales and balanced norms. Also available are the Millon Adolescent Personality Inventory and the Personality Inventory for Youth.

Behavioral approaches to the assessment of children employ the principles and procedures described in Chapter Six for behavioral assessment in general, and have recently increased in popularity. Considerations of reliability and validity need attention here also. The most rapidly growing personality assessment procedure for children is the use of structured checklists and rating scales that are completed by informants, such as parents and teachers. Two recent and potentially important instruments of this type are the Personality Inventory for Children and the Child Behavior Check List.

The use of psychological assessment in law-related settings has increased substantially in recent years. Perhaps the best-known use is in insanity evaluations. Because insanity is a legal concept and not a psychological one, and because there is disagreement as to even its legal meaning, its assessment is usually a highly subjective enterprise. Psychologists are also called on to assess competency to stand trial, which is perhaps best viewed as the defendant's current ability to cooperate with an attorney and to be aware of the nature and consequences of the court proceedings. A potentially useful device for guiding such evaluations is the Competency Assessment Instrument.

The assessment of dangerousness and potential for violence is another law-related question. Psychologists have had limited success in this area for several reasons: the concept of dangerousness has no consistent psychological definition; dangerous conduct is viewed by many psychologists as being a product of person–environment interactions; and the base rates of dangerous behavior are quite low, leading to high false-positive rates. It appears that the best predictor of future violence is past behavior.

Child custody decisions represent another area in which the input of psychological assessment is often sought. The relevant task is to determine the best interests of the child. Surveys point to several basic criteria: the quality of the relationship between parent and child, the parents' capacity to meet the child's needs, continuing positive relationships, and the mental health of the custodial parent. The development of classification systems for correctional settings is also viewed by many persons as involving personality assessment. However, more detailed study shows that classification is, in large part, a clerical task based on demographic data. Input from the area of personality assessment may be useful for certain classification questions such as sexual deviance, psychosis, and job-related interest patterns. Actuarial systems based on a single personality test are relatively inefficient.

Psychologists originally tried to assess problems in the neuropsychological area through the use of personality and intelligence tests, in an effort to determine the presence or extent of "organicity." Emphasis was placed on finding the single best test for this purpose. Clinical neuropsychology is now a separate area of inquiry, and it is recognized that brain damage can result in a great variety of deficits. Contemporary assessment procedures involve lengthy batteries to assess the many different areas of possible deficit, and they require a good working knowledge of brain functions on the part of the assessor.

CHAPTER ELEVEN

Automated Personality Assessment

Automated devices for the assessment of personality have been part of the entertainment industry for many years. In the penny arcades, for example, there were machines that would list a number of trait-descriptive adjectives. When the user inserted a penny and held the handles, some random combination of the traits would light up, calling the user "prudent, bashful, and aggressive" or something equally unlikely.

In this chapter, we consider the systematic use of automated procedures in personality assessment. This field has, of course, been made possible by the development of computers, although there were various early attempts to construct automated procedures through mechanical means. Automation in personality assessment has gained considerable popularity, after its early development in the 1960s and a period of relatively slow growth in the 1970s. Automation has been applied in three major ways: (a) to the *administration* of an assessment procedure, (b) to *scoring,* and (c) to *interpretation.* Following a discussion of the development of the field, each of these topics is reviewed in turn. There are two necessary bases for the successful application of automated procedures to personality assessment, both of which have been discussed in earlier chapters. The first is the availability of assessment devices that can yield objective scores, such as the MMPI. The second is the availability of research knowledge concerning the relative advantages of using objective (vs. subjective) interpretation systems and a technology for developing such systems. This material has been reviewed in Chapter Eight.

It is important to understand that the notion of actuarial description and prediction is independent of automation. The use of computers in personality assessment would not have been possible without the prior development of actuarial systems, but actuarial systems can be used without computers. The specific positive contribution of the computer has to do with the saving of time and effort, and the resultant economic advantages. There is also a qualitative difference between the manually applied objective rules of the actuarial code books and the rules developed for computer application. Because the rules for computer use can be many times more complex, and because the computer can search through a much larger library of statements than would be economical for a human researcher, a different type of product is possible—a whole interpretive system rather than a limited number of interpretive statements.

Psychologists and other mental health professionals began to become interested on a large scale in the possibilities for automation in the 1960s, as this technology began to filter into human service fields in general. In psychology and mental health, applications of automation were attempted in a rather wide variety of areas, including personality and ability testing, case history taking, interviewing, preparation of reports, record keeping, behavioral observations, ward nursing notes, aspects of psychotherapy and behavior therapy, vocational guidance, and personnel assessment. There is no single review of all this work, although accounts of some of it have been prepared by Bartram (1994), Butcher (1987a), Lanyon (1987), and Vieweg and Hedlund (1992).

The serious work on automated personality assessment began in the early 1960s. The necessary groundwork had been laid previously in regard to the validity of actuarial description and prediction (e.g., Meehl, 1954, 1956), and several actuarial description systems had already been developed (e.g., Drake & Oetting, 1959; Marks & Seeman, 1963). Around that time, psychologists at the Mayo Clinic were faced with the stereotyped and repetitive task of writing MMPI interpretations for patients referred for psychiatric screening (Rome et al., 1962; Swenson & Pearson, 1964, 1966). The volume of referrals was so high, with more than 170,000 patients registered annually at the clinic, that they felt it would be appropriate and convenient to program their interpretive statements and to have the computer score the MMPI responses and print out the appropriate interpretations.

Several factors about the Mayo Clinic situation made it particularly suited to an automated procedure, and possibly laid the groundwork for the overly ready acceptance of automated interpretation and the resulting difficulties for which it would later be criticized (Adair, 1978b; Matarazzo, 1986). First, the population was quite homogeneous, so that most of the interpretive needs could be covered with relatively few statements. Second, the procedure was designed for screening only, which further simplified the interpretive task because it meant that responsibility for decision making was not vested in the interpretations. The printout was designed to avoid technical and emotional words, underscoring the intention that the process was simply intended as a screening. Third, the psychology staff could easily police the use of the system, because they had control over the use of the printouts and could readily communicate with the referral sources. Fourth and perhaps most important, the setting was a medical one, in which physicians were accustomed to "ordering tests."

Several years after the Mayo developments, Fowler (1967, 1969) constructed a more complex program for the automated interpretation of the MMPI. His procedure was essentially a subjective one, involving approximately 2,000 cases over a four-year period. Contrary to the nature of the Mayo Clinic program, which was intended for its own population only, Fowler wished his program to have general applicability, and for that reason he included cases from a variety of other human service settings. The Fowler program was test-marketed through the pharmaceutical company Roche Laboratories before moving into full-scale commercial operation on a national basis (Fowler, 1966). Shortly afterward, the Mayo Clinic program began commercial operation through the Psychological Corporation (Pearson & Swenson, 1968). Several other commercial services soon appeared, and, within ten years, more than 150 computer applications could be identified for all forms of psychological assessment (Butcher, 1987b).

Examination of the recent catalogs of text publishers suggests that there currently may be two to three times that number. In addition to automated services related to personality inventories, there are automated case histories, personnel and career choice instruments, intelligence and neuropsychological tests, child assessment checklists, and even projective tests. Perhaps the most ambitious computerized effort is that of Exner and his colleagues, offering automated interpretations of the Rorschach test based on Exner's scoring system (Exner & Ona, 1995). The extent and breadth of these developments could be due to at least three influences: (a) a natural and legitimate progression toward greater technological sophistication in the mental health and human services industries, (b) the recognition that potential commercial profit exists in this area, and (c) the general movement in psychology toward applied and professional enterprises. Many psychologists, believing that more technical and professional knowledge is first needed, have reservations about the appropriateness of these developments. These reservations are discussed later in the chapter.

AUTOMATED ADMINISTRATION

Online administration software, often with the capability for immediate scoring and an interpretive printout if desired, is available for many personality inventories. Regarding other areas of assessment, there are several computerized neuropsychological tests for cognitive functioning (e.g., Berger, Chibnall, & Gfeller, 1994; Powell et al., 1993) and for attention deficit disorder (Greenberg & Dupuy, 1993). The use of online computer technology has also been developed for gathering biographical and case history data, as indicated in Chapter Six.

One area where automated administration has not been fully explored is with projective techniques. To date, the only such use appears to be the procedure designed by Veldman (1967) for his One-Word Sentence Completion Test, in conjunction with an automated scoring procedure. Each sentence stem is presented on the computer screen, and the subject responds by typing in a single word. The computer then conducts an inquiry by asking one of a number of specific questions about the subject's response. For example, if the subject is given the stem "What I want most is . . ." and responds "Happiness," the computer asks: "Are you unhappy now?" If the subject responds "Yes," the computer asks "Why?" The automated scoring procedure described below for the Holtzman Inkblot Technique also has the potential for use in conjunction with automated administration.

The problems and concerns that accompany the use of automated test administration procedures are the same as those that arise when any change is made in the standardized procedure for administering a test. Because the nature of the task is changed, norms must be reestablished, the validity of the scores must be questioned, and the reliability of the auto-mated procedure must be established. For personality inventories, the as-sumption that computer administration yields the same norms as scores based on written responses is largely unexamined. For computerized ad-ministration of existing neuropsychological tests, it seems clear that differ-ent norms are required for the computer version (Berger, Chibnall, & Gfeller, 1994). The question as to whether the same construct is being mea-sured by both forms of the test must also be considered carefully.

AUTOMATED SCORING

Procedures for automated scoring of personality assessment devices have been available for many years, in the form of machine scoring for personal-ity inventories. Other than the need to ensure the accuracy of scoring, which involves adequate preparation of the answer sheets and maintenance of the equipment, this would seem to be a noncontroversial area.

Developments in the automated scoring of projective techniques have not kept pace with the field. The obvious advantage of such procedures is time savings, both for clinical work and for the collection of large amounts of research data in a standard form. One significant problem has been that, because responses to projective stimuli are traditionally open-ended, any automated scoring system has the potential for violating the integrity of the procedure. Whether the result is indeed detrimental is, of course, a matter for empirical study.

Two major projects in this area have been those of Gorham, Holtzman, and their associates with the Holtzman Inkblot Technique (HIT; Gorham, 1967; Gorham, Moseley, & Holtzman, 1968) and the work of Veldman with his One-Word Sentence Completion Test (Veldman, 1967; Veldman, Menaker, & Peck, 1969). In each of these projects, the researchers began by setting a limit on the length of the response. For the HIT, each response was limited to six words; with Veldman's test, responses were limited to a single word. The next step in each case was to develop a library of possible response words and store them in a computer. For the HIT, each of the six words of a response was listed separately, without regard to order. For Veld-man's test, words were reduced to generic form or word stems, so that, for example, the words *love, loving, loves,* and *loved* were all represented by the stem *lov.* Gorham listed 6,100 words, accounting for 95% of his response material; Veldman's 4,336-item response dictionary included 98% of his material.

The next step was to use the computerized data as a basis for generating scores on relevant and potentially useful variables. For the HIT, Gorham employed a combination of empirical analyses and expert judgment to as-sign each of his 6,100 words a weight on 17 of the scoring categories of the test. Veldman followed a similar procedure in assigning weights on a rational basis to his items on 25 different variables. Both groups of researchers showed that the reliability of the computer-based scores was at least as good as that of hand scoring. That is to say, the correlations between computer scoring and hand scoring were about the same as (or better than) those between hand scorers (Gorham, 1967; Veldman, Menaker, & Peck, 1969). The utility of the scores and indexes is a matter to be approached empirically. It cannot be assumed that validity data that apply to scores generated through hand scoring are necessarily applicable to scores based on computer scoring, even though reliabilities may be comparable. Except for some unpublished data (Holtzman & Gorham, 1972), no validity information appears to be available for either of the systems.

AUTOMATED INTERPRETATION

The development and use of automated procedures for personality assessment is now a major industry; for tests with a significant user base, the availability of computer interpretation is the rule rather than the exception. The literature on automated interpretation should be viewed as including the literature on actuarial interpretation, such as the technology of developing actuarial programs and the assessment of their validity, as discussed in Chapter Eight and in a later section of the present chapter. Questions that are unique to automated interpretation have to do with large-scale application; these are both technical and professional/ethical questions.

The development of an automated interpretation system requires the following: a personality test whose responses are in a summary form that can be directly utilized as input to a computer; a library of interpretive statements and a program that selects those that are validly associated with particular responses; and a way of integrating the output and delivering it to the user. Let us examine the developments in each of these areas.

Input

For objective inventories, the input question has posed no problem; input simply consists of scores on the scales of the inventory. In addition, as many special scales can be scored as desired, and special indexes can be computed, such as the total T-score difference between obvious and subtle subscales (Butcher, 1989). Many programs also include indexes and scores that are unique to each program. In regard to projective techniques, the major work is that of Exner with the Rorschach (Exner & Ona, 1995). Here, the input is the completed scoring system for each response, as detailed elsewhere (Exner, 1990). Based on about 80 possible scores, plus derived ratios and indexes, the task of scoring Rorschach protocols in this manner is complex and time-consuming. An earlier attempt to automate Rorschach interpretation was made by Piotrowski (1964, 1969, 1980); in his system, coding the record in preparation for computer processing was said to take several hours.

Development of Interpretive Statements

The development of an interpretive statement library and a program for selecting specific statements according to the particular set of test scores is the core of actuarial personality assessment and its extension into automated personality assessment. There are two approaches to generating an interpretive program: (a) empirical or actuarial, and (b) subjective or clinical. *Empirical* development involves the objective determination, for a particular population, of the relationships between test indexes and patient characteristics. A number of sets of purely empirical data exist for the MMPI, some of them packaged for use in actuarial interpretation "by hand" (e.g., Drake & Oetting, 1959; Gilberstadt & Duker, 1965; Marks & Seeman, 1963; Marks, Seeman, & Haller, 1974; Megargee, 1977). However, none has been programmed for automated use in purely empirical form. Rather, the automated programs for the MMPI and the MMPI-2 that make use of these data do so in combination with a variety of subjectively developed material, so that the programs lack the desirable characteristics of a purely empirical program. An example of direct empirical interpretation is Lachar's program for the Personality Inventory for Children, which is based on the actuarial data of Lachar and Gdowski (1979).

The *subjective* approach to automated interpretation refers to the procedure of compiling an accumulation of interpretive statements about a test from all possible sources, and tying each statement to specific scores or cutting points on the basis of clinical judgment. This was the procedure employed by Piotrowski in developing his computerized percept-analytic Rorschach, and by Swenson and Pearson (1964, 1966) in developing their interpretive rules for the Mayo Clinic MMPI program. It appears also to have been the procedure used in developing most of the currently available interpretive programs, although the lack of published information on most of them makes this possibility difficult to verify. A more sophisticated way of employing the subjective approach was demonstrated for individual indexes by Meehl and Dahlstrom (1960) and by Kleinmuntz (1963), who coded their clinical expertise or that of other experts into objective rules for sorting MMPI profiles into two or more categories. Incidentally, Goldberg (1970) showed that objective predictions made from tidied-up versions of such rules could surpass the predictions made by the experts on cross-validation.

The term *subjective* development does not mean that none of the interpretive statements has known empirical correlates. It means that the program is based on a general pool of knowledge about the test and not on specific study of a given population. Thus, although it does not mean in any sense that subjectively developed programs are invalid, there is no built-in assurance that validity will exist for any particular population. Thus, validity cannot be taken for granted but must be demonstrated on a use-by-use basis. Just how rigorously this rule needs to be applied is discussed in a later section.

Output

The task of preparing and delivering output from an automated personality assessment program is, for the most part, a clerical one. The typical output consists of several pages of printed copy in a format that is more or less standardized. There are orienting statements with appropriate cautions and disclaimers; general descriptive materials, either in narrative form or as a series of short paragraphs or statements; standard scores; a plotted profile; and a variety of additional information involving such areas as critical items, supplemental scales, and perhaps diagnostic categories. The process of extending actuarial "by-hand" interpretations to computer-produced output is essentially clerical, although the added step of constructing narratives out of individual statements complicates the task of establishing validity and adds further nuances of meaning, some of which may be unintended.

Available Programs

Computer test interpretation programs are much too numerous to list individually. They are available, usually through the test publishers, for nearly all of the inventories in widespread use that are described in this book, including the MMPI-2 and MMPI-A, the Personality Research Form, Millon's tests, the 16 PF family of tests, the Personality Assessment Inventory, the NEO-PI-R, the Hogan Personality Inventory, the California Psychological Inventory, and others. Programs are also available for the assessment of vocational and career interests, and for personnel-related assessment.

Many of these programs have been subjectively developed and have no independently demonstrated validity basis for the uses that are offered. In most cases, there is not even a published description as to how the computer program was developed. Possible exceptions include Lachar's (1974) MMPI Automated Psychological Assessment program (see Adair, 1978a; Butcher, 1978a) and the Lachar and Gdowski (1979) program for the Personality Inventory for Children. The main use of the Millon Clinical Multiaxial Inventory is through computer scoring and interpretation, and although the manual contains a considerable amount of statistical information about the development of the automated interpretation program, validity data are essentially limited to the subjective judgments of clinicians who receive the reports. The question of validity and how it should be demonstrated for computer-based interpretive reports is controversial. It is considered next, in the context of the construction of such computer programs.

TECHNICAL CONSIDERATIONS

We now examine the major technical questions, mainly psychometric in nature, that underlie the development and use of automated personality assessment procedures. These questions relate to the methodology of constructing programs and the methodology of validating them. Except for the topic of clinical versus actuarial prediction, the amount of research in this area is quite modest, and many important questions remain unanswered. Once again, it should be noted that although this technology also forms the basis for actuarial "by-hand" interpretive programs, the addition of computers to the interpretive process magnifies its importance.

Technology of Program Construction

As reviewed in Chapter Eight, the earliest question historically in the technology of program construction was the one asked (and answered affirmatively) in the 1950s by Meehl (1954, 1956): Was actuarial interpretation a legitimate enterprise? The next set of questions were those raised in the 1960s by L. R. Goldberg (1965, 1968) and others; they queried the best kinds of actuarial strategies to follow in personality assessment and clinical diagnosis. Findings have continued to indicate that linear predictive indexes outperform nonlinear ones, and that predictions based on automating the clinical skill of the expert can outperform the expert, although empirically selected predictors do best of all. Similar findings have since been reported for a wide variety of other tasks in human prediction and decision making (Dawes & Corrigan, 1974; Dawes, Faust, & Meehl, 1989).

Questions regarding the relative merits of different kinds of indexes that might be used as a basis for interpretive statements have received relatively little research attention. MMPI researchers, after their initial disappointment that scores on individual scales did not provide the levels of predictive validity that had been originally hoped for, discovered that patterns of scales worked somewhat better (e.g., Marks & Seeman, 1963). These authors later chose to base interpretations simply on the two highest scales, or "two-point" codes (Marks, Seeman, & Haller, 1974). Nearly all of this work has involved the MMPI, and, quite possibly, it may not be as useful with other inventories (e.g., Lachar, DeHorn, & Gdowski, 1979). A more recent trend is to build scales as an integrated cluster of subscales, or facets; a wide variety of possibilities for automated interpretation is then available through the facet scores. The Personality Assessment Inventory (Morey, 1991) and the NEO-PI-R (Costa & McCrae, 1992b) have used this approach. There does not appear to be any research comparing its accuracy with that of other approaches, however.

Other relevant topics include the use of population *base rates* of relevant characteristics and *relative values* associated with different predictions or decisions. The massive differences that the use or omission of such data can make to interpretive utility were illustrated years ago by Meehl and Rosen (1955), Rimm (1963), and others. However, relatively few published prediction systems in personality assessment have employed base-rate data in an attempt to improve accuracy. Two that have done so are Millon's tests and the Personality Inventory for Children (Lachar & Gdowski, 1979). Ways of approaching the inclusion of data on the relative values of alternative predictions or outcomes have generated a small literature, and several authors have listed some of the necessary considerations (e.g., Elwood, 1993; Rice & Harris, 1995). Some possible applications of both types of data are suggested in the following section.

Validity

The reviewers of automated personality assessment in the *Eighth Mental Measurement Yearbook* (Buros, 1978) raised serious questions about the inadequate attention paid to validity by the developers of automated programs. To quote Butcher (1978b): "The validation efforts to date have not been very convincing, mostly because the methods employed will not produce uncontaminated and unambiguous results" (p. 944). These words are still applicable nearly 20 years later; in fact, they tend to understate the problem. For most programs, there have been no serious attempts to demonstrate validity.

Requirements for Demonstrating Validity. What would constitute an adequate demonstration of validity? This question is analogous to the validity question involved in constructing an individual scale consisting of separate items. In constructing a scale, if the item development procedures have involved both empirical and rational considerations, and if the sample sizes have been relatively large, then we can anticipate that the scale will continue to be valid when used with the same population, although there will be some shrinkage in validity from the initial correlations. A usual additional requirement in establishing adequate validity for a scale is to show that the scale has some generality; that is, to show that it also discriminates or predicts for several different populations.

The requirements for demonstrating the validity of an interpretive program that has been developed empirically are analogous to those for demonstrating the validity of an individual scale that has been developed by the empirical method. They were fully applied by Halbower (Meehl, 1956) in his initial demonstration of the feasibility of constructing actuarial interpretation programs. In Halbower's procedure, patients were selected whose MMPI profiles fitted one of several specific patterns. Judges who knew the patients then performed criterion Q-sorts describing them, and an average Q-sort pattern was established for each of the three MMPI patterns. Validity for the program was demonstrated by the significance of the correlations between MMPI-based Q-sorts and criterion-based Q-sorts for an independent sample of patients from the same institution. Halbower also did a second validity study, using patients from a different institution in the same city, and demonstrated validity for his program there also.

What would be the requirements for demonstrating the validity of an interpretive program that was developed by a subjective rather than an empirical procedure? Again, let us first examine how validity would be established for a subjectively developed individual scale. The procedure utilized to develop such a scale would probably consist of assembling a group of items that appear to be good candidates for validity on the basis of general accumulated folklore or clinical hunches, with little or no statistical refinement of these items. There would be no compelling basis for concluding that such an assemblage of items would be sufficiently valid for prediction with any *particular* population, and it would therefore be necessary to demonstrate empirical validity for every use to which the scale is to be put. Once we had consistently shown such validity in a variety of relevant settings, we could begin to have some confidence about validity in other relevant settings, without continued empirical demonstrations. But until substantial validity had been established in a number of different settings, a demonstration of validity would be required for each new application.

The same validity requirements should apply to automated interpretation programs that have been assembled on a subjective basis. Use with each different population should require a specific empirical demonstration of validity for that population, and only after a variety of successful demonstrations had been accomplished could we be confident about likely validity in other related settings.

Some approaches to the development of automated interpretation programs are best characterized as intermediate between the empirical approach and the subjective approach. Here, interpretive statements are selected nonstatistically, but on the basis of established empirical validity in related settings. We might call this the "sophisticated subjective approach." The primary basis for establishing validity for such a program would still involve an empirical demonstration of validity for each population with which the program is to be used. However, the stringency of these requirements would diminish toward those of the empirical approach, to the extent that both of the following conditions are met. (a) The population for which the interpretive statements have shown prior validity is highly similar to the one with which the program is going to be used. Two aspects of similarity need to be considered: demographic characteristics and base rates of relevant difficulties. (b) The interpretive statements that comprise the program simply embody the prior empirical findings and are not embellished in any way.

Under what circumstances might these conditions be met? The most likely would be when an automated program is developed in a large hospital, agency, or clinic for in-house use, and where the program personnel are able to exercise active control over the way it is used. The original use of the Mayo Clinic MMPI program within the institution itself is such an example. Another can be seen in the MMPI programs of the type that have been developed specifically for particular populations in Veterans Administration services and are coordinated and monitored through a single source (e.g., Gilberstadt, 1970). Each homogeneous type of VA population would require its own program, of course, and the question of what constitutes a homogeneous population would need to be addressed empirically.

Methods of Validation.   What techniques are appropriate for demonstrating the validity of automated interpretation programs? The most satisfactory procedure would be to compare programmed interpretations with independently developed patient descriptions, either statement by statement or on a global level. We have already seen that Halbower and Meehl used this approach on a global level. Studies of this type were reviewed by Moreland (1985, 1986), who reported that their methodologies tended not to be sound. Not surprisingly, validity correlations with external criteria were low, mainly in the .20s. Many of the studies suffered from problems of reliability of measurement, which would have spuriously lowered the observed relationships between predictors and criteria.

The most common approach taken in validation studies has simply been to ask clinicians to rate the accuracy of statements or reports about individual patients. A serious problem with such an approach is the lack of control for the personal biases of the raters, which could be a major determinant of their responses. One way of adding controls would be to submit to each rater two kinds of statements: those that the program has identified as applicable to a patient, and some that have been identified as irrelevant. The raters' task would be to judge the accuracy of both kinds of statements without knowing which is which, and the ratings of the irrelevant statements would serve as a baseline over which the relevant statements would be expected to show a significant increment in their correlations with the criteria.

A research design based on this principle was employed by Guastello and Rieke (1990) in evaluating a computer-generated report from the Sixteen Personality Factors Questionnaire. The rated accuracy of the real reports was not very high; it was only marginally higher than that of the bogus reports (76.3% and 71.1%, respectively). A somewhat better result was obtained by Hoover and Snyder (1991) in their evaluation of an automated report based on the Marital Satisfaction Inventory (Snyder, 1981). A more detailed discussion of the validation research designs that control for responder bias has been provided by Snyder, Widiger, and Hoover (1990).

Using Base-Rate and Relative Utility Data. We now address the troublesome question of how much generalized validity can be assumed for an interpretive program when applied in an unrestricted manner to new populations. It would seem clear that, in the absence of empirical evidence, there is no reason to assume that any interpretive program would be valid for a broad range of client populations across the country. Rather, in order to have an adequate chance of possessing acceptable validities, programs should be tailored to specific populations and decision situations. The technology for this tailoring would involve the use of base-rate data and information on relative utilities.

As an illustration, for automated interpretation programs that are designed for use with a particular population, a simple method for improving accuracy would be to tie cutting points directly to actual population base rates. For example, if 30% of the population of interest are known to lack adequate social skills, then the cutting point on the scale or index used for making statements about inadequate social skills would be chosen to separate out 30% of respondents. The use of population base-rate data could be further extended by expanding a computer interpretation program to include the capacity for responding differently to different population base rates. These data, together with the test scores, would be entered into the computer as input. Because most commercially available programs are intended for use with a variety of populations, their potential validity could be substantially increased if they could respond to the unique base-rate pattern of any given population in this manner. Such a procedure would represent a beginning toward the goal of "individualizing" automated interpretation programs.

The use of data on the relative utilities of different decisions or diagnoses, as discussed in Chapter Eight, has to do with the relative importance of different kinds of errors. It is relevant, for example, in dealing with the obvious fact that on a suicide prediction device, a false-negative error (a person whom the test failed to identify and who later suicided) is much more serious than a false-positive error (a person who was mistakenly tagged as a potential suicide). Rorer, Hoffmann, and Hsieh (1966) showed that the ratio of the relative "values" of the different types of errors, if quantified, can be directly viewed as a multiplier of the base rate, and can be entered directly into the calculation for determining the optimal cutting point. Thus, depending on the relative costs and benefits associated with different types of errors, an automated interpretation program might, at times, be deliberately designed to "overlabel" or to "underlabel." Such variations could either be written directly into the program or entered on a job-by-job basis.

PROBLEMS IN APPLYING AUTOMATION

Most recent reviewers of the current status of computers in personality test interpretations have reached the conclusion that was stated in the previous edition of this text and subsequently (Lanyon, 1984, 1987): Validity remains a serious problem, and little effort is being expended to rectify this situation. As noted by Cohen, Swerdlik, and Smith (1992), just about anybody with a computer, an entrepreneurial bent, and a product to offer can enter the field, and such operations "are getting into the publishing game in record numbers" (p. 736). However, even the interpretive programs for well-established and respected tests are usually not accompanied by the kinds of data that would allow a potential user to evaluate their quality. Practicing clinicians appear to share these concerns. In a survey of clinicians' attitudes toward computer-based testing (Spielberger & Piotrowski, 1990), it was reported that most respondents were "concerned about the lack of studies demonstrating the validity of automated narratives and computer-based test interpretation systems" (p. 62).

Responding to the types of concerns expressed here, the American Psychological Association in 1985 developed a careful and comprehensive statement on the development and use of computer-based test interpretation systems, addressing in particular the question of validity—how it should be established, and how that information should be made available to the user. For example: "The validity of the computer version of a test should be established by those developing the test" (Butcher, 1987a, p. 427); "Computer testing services should provide a manual reporting the rationale and evidence in support of computer-based interpretation of test scores" (p. 427); and "The manual or, in some cases, the interpretive reports, should describe how the interpretation statements are derived from the original scores" (p. 429). In addition, the guidelines strongly urge the test developer to make available to users the nature of the relationship between the test data and the interpretive statements—for example, by providing in the manual the library of interpretive statements and the scales and research on which they are based.

Because the field was well established before the guidelines were developed, they were explicitly intended to be advisory in nature and to provide a frame of reference for the future development of the field. However, in their ten years of existence they do not appear to have had a substantial impact on the field. Perhaps one of the reasons is that they can apply directly only to individual members of the American Psychological Association, and computer interpretation services are usually run by commercial enterprises.

It is generally agreed that the psychologist/user has the ethical (and perhaps legal) responsibility for the appropriate professional use of computer-based test interpretations. Indeed, it is usual for interpretive printouts to be accompanied by disclaimers that the interpretations should be regarded as only tentative hypotheses, should be regarded as only one of many sources of data to be considered by the clinician, may not be accurate, and so on. Matarazzo (1986) believed that the key issues of legal responsibility had not yet surfaced at that time, but also that "in litigation involving individuals who have been hurt by the uninformed use of such products, such product-liability disclaimers are of little help, either to the company or to the anonymous psychologist who developed the software . . ." (p. 23).

Some assessment psychologists have felt that the above criticisms are too harsh and do not fairly represent the true state of affairs regarding computerized test interpretations, and that the potential and the advantages of this technology have therefore been obscured (e.g., Butcher, 1987b; Fowler & Butcher, 1986). First, it is pointed out that many criticisms have been made indiscriminately, causing the best of the computer interpretation programs to be unfairly subjected to negative publicity. Second, the validity of computer-generated reports is typically studied on an absolute basis, whereas a more realistic comparison would be with clinical or subjective interpretations and reports. Viewed in this way, the validity of computer-based reports is said to be quite satisfactory. Third, once a program has been developed, reports can be generated for a fraction of the cost of traditional reports, leading to important cost advantages. Fourth, despite the concerns for abuse of the technology, no evidence of substantial legal or ethical violations could be found, either by psychologists or by nonpsychologists (Fowler & Butcher, 1986). Fifth, as the technology is further developed, computer-based reports have the potential for yielding substantially higher accuracies than traditional reports.

FUTURE DIRECTIONS

Let us try to assess the current state of this area of endeavor and offer suggestions for its future development. A balanced view would agree that computer interpretation and traditional interpretation both have their advantages and disadvantages, and the computer interpretation has the greater potential for cost efficiency but also for abuse. Cohen, Swerdlik, and Smith (1992) found no evidence that computer-based test interpretation products are being abused any more than conventional test products. Nevertheless, it seems apparent that some of the problems raised by computer interpretation may be rather different from those involved in traditional use of personality tests. For example, the computer assessment industry is, to a large extent, outside the ethical control of psychologists. Also, the question of whether a computer-generated report lacks validity may not be as readily answered as it would be for a traditional report. Third, despite the disclaimers included in many automated reports, their authoritative appearance may encourage users to view them as considerably more than just a series of hypotheses to be examined in the light of case history, interview, and other test and collateral data.

The above issues are general in nature and are not likely to be resolved quickly. However, a number of technical aspects in the development and use of computer-based reports *could* be engaged immediately and would significantly address the validity concerns expressed above (Lanyon, 1987).

1. *Reliability.* This is an important issue with regard to both criteria and predictor (test-related) variables. Perhaps one factor contributing to the success of the Meehl/Halbower study was the careful attention paid to ensuring reliable criteria. In regard to the predictors, some subscales, such as those of Harris and Lingoes for the MMPI (Graham, 1990), may be too short to demonstrate acceptable retest reliabilities. Demonstrations are also needed that high-point codes are reliable on retest.

2. *Bandwidth versus fidelity.* It would seem wise to focus on the careful development of test indexes that lead to single, focused predictions (the narrow-band/high-fidelity position), rather than trying to say a little about many topics (the broad-band/low-fidelity position). An example can be seen in the development of objective procedures for making standardized psychiatric diagnoses. In this work (see Hedlund & Vieweg, 1987), an extensive database is employed, usually involving case history and current status information, but the product is a single statement of diagnosis. Not surprisingly, the accuracies in this work are better than in test interpretation. Applying this recommendation to computer-based test interpretation systems means the separate development of each predictor geared to a single, specific prediction task.

3. *Degree of departure from the data.* If the automated interpretation is made strictly on the basis of the empirical validity data, without any attempt to group, cluster, polish, or otherwise alter them, problems with misinterpreting them are minimized. Possible disadvantages include a report that may not flow smoothly, some internal contradictions, and the lack of a professional appearance to the report. These disadvantages disappear if the printout is viewed as being a report to the assessment professional rather than to his or her client or to a professional who is not fully trained in psychological assessment.

4. *Generalizability.* The less the similarity between the population from which an objective interpretation system was derived and the population on which it is used, the greater is the shrinkage in validity that must be expected. However, almost no empirical data exist on this question. If a package developed for one population is to be generalizable to another, three conditions must hold: (a) the base rates of the characteristics to be assessed

must be the same; (b) the normative characteristics of the predictors (test scores) must be the same; and (c) the validity of each predictor must hold up. It is likely that unwarranted generalization is currently a major source of invalidity in using objective prediction systems—for example, applying to general medical patients a system that was derived on psychiatric patients. A few of the currently available programs do address this issue; thus, reports may be obtained from the MMPI-2 publisher for an adult clinical population, for an alcohol and drug treatment population, and for a personnel selection population.

5. *The selection/placement tradeoff.* It is obvious that accuracy is lower in placement tasks (where all subjects must be assigned) than in selection tasks (where not everybody is assigned). The opportunity to leave an "indeterminate" category in dichotomous prediction studies yields substantially higher validities for the remaining cases (e.g., L. R. Goldberg, 1965; Meehl & Dahlstrom, 1960). Thus, validities could be increased if statements were made only about extreme scorers, leading to shorter but more accurate reports.

6. *Accommodation of different base rates.* If the population on which the computer-based report is to be used is similar to the one on which it was developed, except for the base rates of the characteristics to be predicted or described, the cutting points (criteria for selecting particular interpretive statements) can be modified accordingly. To take such a step, the relevant base rates (e.g., frequency of schizophrenia) must be known in both populations, and the cutting point for the characteristic must be modified so that the percentage of "positives" (e.g., cases called schizophrenic by the objective rules) reflects the base rate in the new population.

OTHER APPLICATIONS OF AUTOMATION

We have thus far described automation in traditional personality test procedures. A number of attempts have been made to use automation in other procedures and tasks that are related to personality assessment. These are next reviewed briefly.

Automated Diagnosis and Progress Notes

Because one of the end products of a comprehensive assessment of a patient is often a psychiatric diagnosis, a major effort was made some years ago to develop actuarial programs that classify patients into diagnostic categories. One example was mentioned in Chapter Six—the diagnostic program (DIAGNO II) developed by Endicott and Spitzer (1972). This computer program employed a logical decision-tree model, and the output was one of 46 diagnoses based on the first edition of the American

Psychiatric Association's *Diagnostic and Statistical Manual of Mental Disorders* (DSM-I). This program was revised (DIAGNO III) to yield one or more of the 79 psychiatric diagnoses listed in the DSM-II (Spitzer & Endicott, 1974). Another computer diagnosis application involved the use of the decision-tree rules of the Research Diagnostic Criteria as the basis for decisions (Greist, Klein, & Erdman, 1976). A further example was seen in the Missouri Actuarial Report System (MARS; Altman, Evenson, Hedlund, & Cho, 1978), which yielded a comprehensive automated report including statements about the probabilities of different diagnostic categories. Although all of these efforts were technically successful, they were not readily accepted by the psychiatric and mental health community, and there is now relatively little activity in this area.

The same can be said of the use of computer-generated patient progress reports and automated nursing notes, which were developed during the same time period (Glueck, Gullotta, & Ericson, 1980; Rosenberg, Glueck, & Bennett, 1967). In a typical system, the nursing staff completed a daily checklist on each patient on a computer-readable form from which standardized scores on various dimensions were generated. Output consisted of a narrative report plus a printed or graphic display of standard scores on behavior factors.

Automated Interviews

The above developments were part of a general movement in the 1970s toward the widespread use of automation in the mental health industry. A major aspect of this movement was the development of comprehensive systems for gathering information on psychiatric inpatients on a large-scale basis, such as the Multi-State Information System (MSIS) centered at the Rockland State Hospital in New York, and the Standard System of Psychiatry of the State of Missouri. As stated above, systems of this type were technically successful but were not well received by the professional mental health community, and are little used nowadays. Nevertheless, some of the technology resulting from these research and development efforts forms the basis for currently available instruments, such as the Giannetti (1986, 1987) On-Line Psychosocial History form (GOLPH) (see Figure 11.1). To use this instrument, which is intended for ages 16 or older in a mental health context, the patient responds to computer-presented questions covering ten major psychosocial history categories. Branching questions follow up specific areas in an attempt to simulate live interviewing. The product is a comprehensive narrative that is said to correspond quite closely to what would have been obtained in a live interview (e.g., Grady & Ephross, 1977).

A number of other instruments for personal history or for current mental status are available commercially, but none appears to have been developed as carefully as the GOLPH. For example, the Personal History

Complications of pregnancy and birth	Eating/feeding problems
Presence of birth defects	Aggressive behavior
Developmental delays	Antisocial behavior
Manifestations of anxiety	Substance use/abuse
Manifestations of depression	General physical health
Activity levels/movement disorders	Sexual development/preference/abuse
Emotional lability	Peer relationships

Figure 11.1   Developmental history content areas covered in the automated Giannetti On-Line Psychosocial History (GOLPH). (Source: Giannetti, 1987, p. 135. Copyright © 1987 HarperCollins Publishers. Reprinted by permission.)

Checklist—Adult (Schinka, 1989) is available in both clinician interpretation and computer report forms, and parallel instruments are available for generating reports on current mental status of adolescents and children. These and similar instruments are outgrowths of such forms as the Mental Status Examination Record (Spitzer & Endicott, 1971) and the Current and Past Psychopathology scales (Endicott & Spitzer, 1972), discussed in Chapter Six.

SUMMARY

Automation of personality assessment procedures tends to be synonymous with the use of computers. This field received its impetus in the early 1960s as a response to routine high-volume assessment needs in particular institutional settings, but it is now a thriving commercial enterprise on a national basis, involving many other areas of psychological assessment besides personality. Automation is not a significant aspect of the administration of personality tests, mainly because its most ready application is with inventories, which already require minimal professional time and effort to administer. Some online computer procedures for administration have been proposed, however. Automated scoring has been available for inventories for many years. Some interesting beginnings in the automated scoring of projective tests involve the development of libraries of possible response words together with a limitation on the length of each response.

The bulk of the literature in automated personality assessment is in the area of interpretation. The development of an automated interpretation system requires three steps: (a) personality test responses in summary form, (b) a library of interpretive statements and a valid program for associating them with the test responses, and (c) a way of delivering the output. For inventories, the input can be a series of scales and indexes; for projective techniques, scores must first be developed through traditional hand-scoring procedures. Interpretation programs can be developed either empirically or subjectively. Empirical development involves the determination of interpretive statements that are known to be empirically related to particular test responses, in exactly the same manner as for the empirical selection of individual items to constitute a single scale. Few interpretation programs have been developed in this manner, however. Most have employed the subjective approach, in which interpretive statements about a test are accumulated from all possible sources and are then tied to specific scores or cutting points on the basis of subjective judgment. The task of preparing and delivering automated output is essentially a clerical one and may involve the use of additional computer programs for the construction of narrative prose.

Despite the popularity of automated personality assessment, relatively little research has been conducted on the technical aspects of developing and validating automated programs. It has been well established that linear predictors tend to outperform nonlinear ones, and whenever test profile patterns are used as input to the computer, the simplest patterns, such as high two-point codes, tend to be employed. Relatively little attention has been given to information on population base rates of relevant characteristics, to the relative values associated with different decisions, or to the generalizability of interpretations across different populations.

The lack of validity research on automated interpretation programs has been the subject of serious criticism directed toward the automated assessment enterprise. The same requirements should apply to establishing the validity of such programs as are needed to establish the validity of individual inventory scales or predictive indexes. However, the most common approach has been simply to rely on clinicians' ratings of the accuracy of statements in the automated report, a procedure that can be subject to obvious biases. Other criticisms have included the inappropriate readiness of commercial enterprises to offer services without the backing of adequate validity. Careful guidelines prepared by the American Psychological Association in 1985 do not appear to have had an impact on this industry. Some writers believe that the criticisms are too harsh and that the advantages of automated interpretation have not been fully appreciated. Validity could be improved by attending to issues of reliability, bandwidth versus fidelity, the degree to which the interpretive statements depart from empirical findings, and the selection versus placement tradeoff.

Other applications of automation in personality assessment include diagnostic programs such as DIAGNO II and the development of methods for generating routine reports on the progress of hospitalized psychiatric patients. Such procedures can form part of a comprehensive and interlocking set of instruments for use on a statewide or multistate basis, which might include the processing of case history data, mental status examination results, and a variety of instruments for more specific purposes. The popularity of comprehensive automated systems has declined in recent years, however.

CHAPTER TWELVE

Criticisms of Personality Assessment

Psychological tests, including those used for personality assessment, have been criticized throughout their existence. Some of these criticisms undoubtedly have arisen from the vague resentments that many of us feel toward being examined, and especially toward evaluations of any kind (Amrine, 1965, p. 859). Other criticisms have been based on misunderstandings. For example, Dahlstrom (1969) pointed out that some government employment application forms have required applicants to sign a statement that their answers are true to the best of their knowledge. But self-report personality inventories usually instruct respondents that there are no right or wrong answers; they are to give either their own opinions of themselves or the most appropriate response. Most projective devices are even more ambiguous: they require respondents to give their initial, unqualified impression. All such responses are treated simply as behaviors and not necessarily as "true" or factual information. With such conflicting instructions and attitudinal sets, one can easily understand why respondents could become confused as to whether there are supposed to be right answers, and cautious about their responses. Incidentally, such contradictions point up the importance of having the personality tests administered by, or at least supervised by, qualified professionals who can make certain that the respondents understand the nature of the task.

Most of the traditional criticisms are more serious than those just described. In 1965, in response to a gradual buildup in public sentiment against psychological testing, two sets of congressional hearings were held. The House Special Subcommittee on Invasion of Privacy of the Committee on Government Operations conducted an inquiry "because of a large body of evidence that certain activities and operations of federal agencies were being carried out concerning which serious questions could be raised. . . . There is the matter of psychological or personality testing of government employees and job applicants by federal agencies. Many federal workers are subjected to extensive tests on their sex life, family situations, religion, personal habits, childhood, and many other matters" (Gallagher, 1965, p. 955). The other inquiry was conducted by the Senate Subcommittee on Constitutional Rights of the Committee on the Judiciary, which made its investigation for similar reasons (Ervin, 1965). The testimony involved in these inquiries covered a much wider variety of issues than the avowed purposes of the hearings, and a broad range of dissatisfactions and criticisms was voiced by a variety of different people, including a number of psychologists. There might also be some truth in Dahlstrom's (1969) suggestion that psychological tests were to some extent used as a scapegoat for the public's concern and anxiety over the development of "an increasingly precise psychotechnology."

In the 1960s and 1970s, with the increased visibility of employment issues regarding minority groups, public concern also became focused on the discriminatory use of ability tests in job-related settings. These concerns led to the creation of the Equal Employment Opportunity Commission (EEOC), which issued guidelines for fair employee selection procedures (Equal Employment Opportunity Commission, Civil Service Commission, Department of Labor, & Department of Justice, 1978). The guidelines, which have been refined and updated, provided further constraints that are of relevance to the fair use of both ability tests and personality tests.

These actions at the federal level forced psychologists to face the many criticisms of psychological tests and testing practices that had previously been minimized, avoided, or denied (Novick, 1981). The hearings also had the effect of spurring psychologists to initiate a number of reforms that have now become part of the established expectations for psychologists involved in psychological assessment. Another positive outcome of the lengthy debates and soul searching generated by these actions has been the clarification of some complex ethical and moral issues in regard to psychological testing in general. In this chapter, we deal with some of the issues that are particularly relevant to personality assessment.

Criticisms of personality assessment might be grouped roughly under two general complaints: (a) that they are *inaccurate* and (b) that they are *immoral* (Gross, 1965). The use of personality tests in the past has been inaccurate *and* immoral in some instances. Other uses have been both accurate and moral, and were of obvious benefit to individuals and to society (Dahlstrom, 1993). A sorting of the accurate uses from the inaccurate, and the moral from the immoral, remains to be done. We discuss these two areas under the headings of *usage* and *moral* issues.

USAGE OF PERSONALITY ASSESSMENT DEVICES

Problems in the use of personality tests are of two kinds. First, there are the problems involved in the misuse of a valid test—for example, a test that has been shown to be valid for one purpose is used for another. Second, there are the problems involved in using a test that has no clearly demonstrated validity for any purpose. We deal first with the problems involved in using tests that have established valid uses. In these cases, the criticism would seem to be more appropriately directed at the test users than at the test itself.

Improper Usage

The improper application of otherwise valid tests has probably been, and undoubtedly will continue to be, among the most serious of all the abuses of personality assessment technology. In a sense, all such abuses should be considered to be a result of the test users' inadequate understanding of the nature of the test and the critical issues involved. Thus, frequently stated criticisms of testing include the use of particular tests in situations where they may not be applicable, and the production of unfavorable evaluations based on obsolete or otherwise inadequate information (e.g., Gordon & Terrell, 1981).

Use in Personnel Selection. One obvious and serious misuse of personality tests has been their employment by untrained users, in inappropriate circumstances, for personnel work in industry. This indictment applies particularly to the use of tests intended for use in psychiatric settings, such as the Rorschach and the MMPI. Some possible reasons for this practice are as follows. Directors of human resources (HR) must be able to identify persons with potential emotional disturbances. Also, the HR directors' formal academic training in personality measurement is quite likely to have stressed these instruments and their validity in identifying psychopathology, whereas, in practice, their concern is with assessing aspects of normal personality functioning, especially those related to job success and management potential. Further, some HR specialists may be indirectly motivated by a desire to gain some of the status of professional psychologists, or to engage in the psychological voyeurism that is legitimized in that profession. It is noteworthy that a basic cause of the 1965 congressional hearings was the use of the MMPI by the State Department in a limited, though routine, manner.

In response to this criticism, it must be agreed that abuses of personality tests certainly do occur. One direction for professional psychologists to take in counteracting them is to restrict the use of such tests to persons qualified to use them properly. Such a policy was formally adopted by the American Psychological Association (1970) in its statement that "decisions about what assessment procedures are to be used and how they are to be handled should be based on persons competent to make them" (p. 266). In the same vein, the formal *Standards for Educational and Psychological Testing*, published by the American Psychological Association and now in its fifth revision (American Educational Research Association/American Psychological Association/National Council on Measurement in Education, 1985), states:

> The test user, in selecting or interpreting a test, should know the purposes of the testing and the probable consequences. The user should know the procedures necessary to facilitate effectiveness and to reduce bias in test use. Although the test developer and publisher should provide information on the strengths and weaknesses of the test, the ultimate responsibility for appropriate test use lies with the test user. The user should become knowledgeable about the test and its appropriate uses and also communicate this information, as appropriate, to others. (p. 41)

In this publication, the 51 specific standards for the use of tests cover six general areas that include both testing for selection and many other uses. Responsible and ethical use of tests by psychologists requires a familiarity with these standards, as well as with the more general *Ethical Principles of Psychologists and Code of Conduct* (American Psychological Association, 1987).

The federal government has also developed laws and regulations for the proper use of tests. Although most of these regulations refer to ability tests in the context of schools and employment (Kaplan & Saccuzzo, 1993), some also apply to personality-related instruments. For example, the 1990 Americans with Disabilities Act bars employers from asking preemployment questions about an applicant's possible mental disabilities (DeAngelis, 1995). The law has the effect of barring tests of psychopathology, such as the MMPI, from use in preemployment screening, while apparently permitting tests assessing "normal" characteristics.

The problem of faking on personality tests is another focus for criticism, one that becomes especially important when tests are used in the workplace. The practical question is whether valid information can be elicited from respondents if they do not wish to reveal themselves. The discussion of this problem in Chapters Seven and Nine leads to a tentative answer: The validity of information gained under these circumstances cannot be assumed; it is a matter for research in each particular situation. Lovell (1967) took the extreme viewpoint that personality tests should not be used at all in personnel selection situations; Dahlstrom (1969) suggested that they could ethically be used because respondents are protected by having the opportunity to protect their privacy (through faking) if they so desire. Consistent with our own conclusions, the *Principles for the Validation and Use of Personnel Selection Procedures,* published by the Division of Industrial/ Organizational Psychology of the American Psychological Association (1980), subsumes the question of faking within an extensive and detailed discussion of validity in general. Thus, the view is implicitly taken that if the topic of validity, "the degree to which inferences from scores on tests or assessments are justified or supported by evidence" (p. 2), is properly addressed, the question of faking need not be considered separately.

It should be noted that the social value underlying the traditional workplace use of personality tests has related to their ability to identify and eliminate unconventional and difficult persons, and the validity of tests for accomplishing such a purpose is also a measure of their "bias" against such persons. Nevertheless, inability to "get along" with coworkers is an important cause of workplace problems, and most employers strongly prefer not to have "problem" workers. Resolution of this dilemma would appear to involve a reconsideration of the underlying social values rather than an attack on personality tests. In general, the issues with regard to personality (and other) tests and discrimination are difficult and complex, and the best current insurance against unfair practices is a thorough understanding of the underlying social, psychometric, and ethical principles by test users.

Mention should be made of the many volumes of the *Mental Measurements Yearbook* (e.g., Kramer & Conoley, 1992), an excellent series of handbooks dating from 1938, which have ironically played an unwitting role in aiding the test critics. Examination of these volumes will reveal an enormous number of personality assessment devices available for use, many of them unvalidated in any more than a rudimentary way. The majority of these tests, fortunately, are little used in practical situations. For the relatively few tests that are more widely used, the status of their validity, although not always what one might hope, tends to be somewhat better. These yearbooks, however, unwittingly provide abundant ammunition for those who wish to attack personality tests, because they imply (correctly, but misleadingly) that almost all existing published tests have limited demonstrable validity. A more accurate characterization would be that the validity of *some* of the more widely used tests, when employed by adequately trained persons under appropriate conditions, is satisfactory and appears to be improving, especially in the workplace.

Failure to Consider Base Rates.   A serious area of concern that seems to have been overlooked by the lay critics of personality tests is the problem posed by base rates, an issue discussed in Chapters Seven and Eight. The failure of unsophisticated critics to recognize and understand this complex, technical issue should not be surprising; many professional psychologists are also unaware of its importance.

At the risk of boring the reader, we again consider how the failure to take base rates into account may result in the misuse of an otherwise valid test. A clear example of this problem is offered by Seeman (1969) in his reanalysis of the results of Hall and LaDriere (1969), who reported that the number of "conceptually inadequate" responses given on the Similarities subtest of the Wechsler Intelligence Scale for Children had diagnostic usefulness in the detection of cerebral pathology. Seeman noted that, if it was assumed that approximately 25% of children seen in child guidance clinics were actually cerebrally damaged (almost certainly an overestimate) and the actual cutting score recommended by Hall and LaDriere was employed, accurate diagnoses would be made only 37% of the time and inaccurate ones would be made 63% of the time, even though there is no question about the "validity" of the "conceptually inadequate" sign. Thus, the failure to take into account the frequency of occurrence of the event to be predicted could result in an unwarranted application of an otherwise valid predictive sign. Once again, the ultimate choice of whether to use the sign should depend on the relative costs and values involved.

Discrimination against Particular Groups.   The proper use of tests in regard to specific groups has been the subject of controversy for years, and the controversy is likely to continue for some time to come. Although the main focus of concern is on tests of ability, the same basic issue applies to tests of personality and psychopathology: Do some test scores result in unfavorable treatment for minorities, women, and other groups? The issue can be illustrated by considering the hypothetical use of the Dominance scale to assess leadership potential. Examination of the norms for dominance-related scales on common personality tests shows that, on the average, men tend to score higher than women. As discussed in Chapter Ten, there are a variety of reasons for such differences, only one of which may be that men in general have more dominance than women in general. Even this position, if correct, would not answer the question of whether dominance is a valid predictor of leadership for women (or for men). Another possibility is that the amount of dominance required for a woman to be a successful leader is lower, on the average, than the amount required for a man.

These are complex issues, and although they have been extensively studied in relation to tests of abilities and aptitudes, there is little research in regard to tests of personality and psychopathology (Sackett & Wilk, 1994). For example, research reported in Chapter Ten leads to the tentative conclusion that MMPI indexes of psychopathology may mean the same thing for Blacks as for Whites, but such research is not yet available in regard to Native Americans (Dahlstrom, Lachar, & Dahlstrom, 1986a). Until adequate research is available, test users will require considerable understanding of the issues plus a willingness to be very tentative in their conclusions.

A careful analysis of this problem from a psychometric perspective has recently been provided by Messick (1995). In offering a broadened concept of construct validity, Messick emphasized the importance of evaluating "both the evidence for and the actual—as well as potential—consequences of score interpretation and use" (p. 742). Although the question of what should be done about tests with potentially adverse social consequences is a social policy issue, not a psychometric one, it is essential that the test actually should assess the particular construct that it is supposed to assess. At the test development level, there are two threats to this result. In the problem of *construct underrepresentation,* the test is too narrow; it fails to include critical dimensions or facets of the construct. In the problem of *construct-irrelevant variance,* the test is too broad; it includes other constructs that are not relevant to the interpreted construct. Both of these deficiencies will result in a test that does not correctly assess the construct of interest. Messick's conclusion is that extreme care is needed in test construction, especially at the stages of assembling item pools and selecting items from those pools, in order to ensure that the test fully and fairly represents the construct, and does not include irrelevant constructs. Only if this mandate is carried out can differences in test scores be confidently interpreted as caused by the construct in question, and not attributable to a different construct that might give one population group an unfair (and irrelevant) advantage over another.

The Experience Controversy.   One aspect of the argument concerning use of personality tests by technically unsophisticated persons is more controversial than those discussed above. In the context of clinical diagnosis, there are claims that expertise with such instruments as the Rorschach requires more than just training with that instrument; rather, intensive experience plus a comprehensive theoretical understanding of both general personality theory and the rationale of the particular test are needed. It follows from this position that many studies that have failed to demonstrate validity for these clinical instruments are inadmissible as evidence because inexperienced clinicians were employed in the study. The issue is not one of marginal versus moderate training (as was the case when the use of tests in personnel selection was discussed, and in the research reported in Chapter Eight), but moderate versus elaborate training and experience.

There is little research evidence on this question of the necessity for prolonged and intensive training, and the evidence that does exist is inconsistent. On the positive side, Goldberg (1959) demonstrated that a highly experienced expert in the Bender-Gestalt test did much better in diagnosing presence or absence of brain damage than did a number of other judges. However, in the extensive study of psychiatric diagnosis conducted by Little and Shneidman (1959), in which care was taken to select the country's leading practitioners of the tests studied, results were unimpressive. It may be significant that Goldberg's Bender-Gestalt expert spent some 20 hours on the 30 protocols in order to achieve his result, and this would be consistent with the conclusion offered in Chapter Eight that the motivation of the judges plays a significant part in their clinical accuracy. But even if it can be consistently demonstrated that highly trained clinicians are superior to those with minimal training, the question remains as to whether their superiority would be sufficient to justify the effort and expense of the additional training.

Unwarranted Applications.   Personality tests are widely used, albeit ethically and in good faith, for purposes for which they simply were not intended and for which they are inappropriate. For example, it is not uncommon for psychologists to make an estimate of intelligence from TAT stories or a Rorschach protocol. In a similar vein, the far-reaching attempts that have been made to extend the use of the MMPI can be seen from a scrutiny of Lanyon's (1968) collection of the mean MMPI profiles of a large variety of subject groups. It can also be clearly seen from this collection that the more psychopathological the subjects, the better the discriminations that could be made among their profiles. For example, the MMPI was almost completely ineffective in differentiating good and poor automobile drivers. On the other hand, there are wide and obvious differences between personality disorders and anxiety disorders. As noted earlier, this should surprise nobody, because the MMPI was built for the specific purpose of making the latter type of discriminations, not the former kind. A similar comment can be made about the TAT, which was devised to describe personality needs and traits, not psychopathology. Despite continuing claims for the utility of the TAT for this purpose (e.g., Sharkey & Ritzler, 1985), there are still no substantial data to contradict Eron's (1948) findings of relatively few differences between the TAT responses of college students and those of schizophrenic patients.

Another unwarranted application of personality tests is found in the routine development of careful psychodynamic formulations on patients in clinical settings. Such formulations might be of use in lengthy psychodynamically oriented treatment—although even this has been questioned (Meehl, 1960)—but the value of such a procedure in most settings, where briefer treatment approaches are the norm, is obscure. This point was viewed by some authors as heralding the "decline of psychological testing" (e.g., Cleveland, 1976; Lewandowski & Saccuzzo, 1976). Probably a more accurate view is that the nature of the assessment enterprise has changed somewhat, moving away from lengthy assessment batteries involving a number of projective tests and toward shorter, more objective instruments and the use of practically oriented computer-based interpretations. Nevertheless, the surveys of recent testing practices cited in previous chapters continue to show extensive use of projective methods.

Unwarranted Criticisms.   From time to time, criticisms of personality testing are offered in the popular press. Some of these criticisms can be attributed to the naïveté of the critics, who appear not to have understood the psychometric principles involved (e.g., Gross, 1962). Many of the complaints made by Gross about the MMPI fall into this category. For example, it was inexplicable to him that a correction score such as the K scale could improve validity, or that a high score on the Sc scale should not invariably indicate schizophrenia. Another criticism concerns the admissibility of subtle items. Gross found it somehow inequitable that a person who denies belief in the second coming of Christ should be, to use his term, "penalized" on the depression scale, and he was unable to comprehend the argument that the depressive patients in the original criterion group did in fact differ from the normal groups in their responses to this item. Dahlstrom (1993) and others have gone to considerable pains to explain and illustrate some of the psychometric points that may not be obvious to the uneducated.

A New Approach.   In 1984, a joint committee of several organizations concerned about the proper usage of psychological and related tests was formed to develop an empirical approach to assessing test-user qualifications (Fremer, Diamond, & Camera, 1989). Previous methods used by test publishers to determine who is competent to use particular tests had relied on an evaluation of credentials. In contrast, the new effort focused on identifying behavioral competencies that should be required of individual test users (Moreland, Eyde, Robertson, Primoff, & Most, 1995). An initial phase of the study used the critical incident procedure to develop a list of 86 test user competencies that were applicable to more than one test. A series of analyses reduced this list to "12 test user competencies that are minimum requirements for competence by all test users" (Moreland et al., 1995, p. 16). These 12 competencies are shown in Figure 12.1. They can be summarized by two broader, comprehensive elements: Knowledge of the test and its limitations, and accepting responsibility for competent use of the test. Also addressed in the study were issues of how this scheme might be put into practical use by test publishers.

Generalized Test Invalidity

We now turn to criticisms that are more appropriately directed at the tests (or their authors) rather than at the users. We shall concentrate on the

Item No.	Competency
1.	Avoiding errors in scoring and recording
2.	Refraining from labeling people with personally derogatory terms like *dishonest* on the basis of a test score that lacks perfect validity
3.	Keeping scoring keys and test materials secure
4.	Seeing that every examinee follows directions so that test scores are accurate
5.	Using settings for testing that allow for optimum performance by test takers (e.g., adequate room)
6.	Refraining from coaching or training individuals or groups on test items, which results in misrepresentation of the person's abilities and competencies
7.	Willingness to give interpretation and guidance to test takers in counseling situations
8.	Not making photocopies of copyrighted materials
9.	Refraining from using homemade answer sheets that do not align properly with scoring keys
10.	Establishing rapport with examinees to obtain accurate scores
11.	Refraining from answering questions from test takers in greater detail than the test manual permits
12.	Not assuming that a norm for one job applies to a different job (and not assuming that norms for one group automatically apply to other groups)

Figure 12.1   Twelve empirically determined competencies for the proper use of tests. (Source: *From Moreland et al., 1995, p. 16. Copyright © 1995 by the American Psychological Association. Reprinted with permission.*)

problems of validity that result from test development procedures that do not pay adequate attention to the usefulness of the test in some specific respect. Excellent discussions of this topic may be found in the *Principles for the Validation and Use of Personnel Selection Procedures,* second edition (American Psychological Association, Division of Industrial/Organizational Psychology, 1980) and in the *Standards for Educational and Psychological Testing* (American Education Research Association/American Psychological Association/National Council on Measurement in Education, 1985).

The Criterion Problem. We first discuss the problems that occur if a personality assessment device is developed without regard to any clear-cut criterion. Our earlier discussion stated that when the empirical approach to test construction is used, test developers have a clear idea of what dimensions of personality they want to assess, and they try to make these dimensions operational by specifying definite criterion groups or by some other clearly described procedure. If correctly applied, the rational and theoretical approaches to test construction also include a clear idea of what dimensions or attributes of personality are to be assessed (expressed in either rational or theoretical terms) plus reliable methods of defining these dimensions. In all of these cases, relatively clear-cut definitions lead to criteria against which the test can be evaluated. Problems arise for personality assessment when there is no clear-cut specification of the criterion that we are trying to assess.

The problem of criteria has been particularly acute with some of the projective devices and rationally based inventories, but it is by no means absent even for instruments with originally specified criteria. One example is the MMPI scales, which were constructed in order to predict patients' assignment to psychiatric diagnostic categories. The criteria originally employed were the diagnostic categories to which the patients had already been assigned. Hathaway (1959) and Meehl (1959b) both pointed out that because (at that time) psychiatric diagnosis was relatively unreliable and to some extent arbitrary, one might seriously question why so much attention should be given to these nebulous categories. That is, why attempt to develop an instrument that is concerned, from the first, with predicting an event that is arbitrary and unreliable? The ceiling for the predictive accuracy of such scales is set by the reliability of the criterion diagnosis, so that no further improvement in the instrument is possible beyond this level of accuracy.

There are at least two ways to resolve the dilemma of improving a test when no adequately clear-cut referent or criterion exists for what is being assessed. One solution, proposed by Hathaway (1959), would be to give the assessment result equal status with the criterion. Looking at the issue of psychiatric diagnosis in this light, a patient could then be called "schizophrenic" from a Rorschach or MMPI record just as validly as from a psychiatric examination. Incongruities among various sources of data would be resolved by clinical judgments. Another way to resolve the problem would be to employ factor-analytic procedures and then to adopt factor scales as "basic" psychological variables, recognizing that the initial construction had been based on fallible data. The merits of this procedure were examined in Chapter Three.

In general, persons engaged in developing techniques of personality assessment have paid far too little attention to the specific aims of their assessment procedures, and to the development of adequate criteria for what is to be assessed. With respect to the assessment of specific behaviors, Holt (1958) wrote:

> First, if we are to predict some kind of behavior, it is presupposed that we acquaint ourselves with what we are trying to predict. This may be called job analysis or a study of the criterion. Perhaps these terms sound a little fancy when their referent is something that seems so obvious to common sense. Nevertheless, it is surprising how often people expend a great deal of time and effort trying to predict a kind of behavior about which they know very little without even thinking that it might help if they could find out more. (p. 2)

This shortcoming was initially pointed out many years ago by Toops (1944), who suggested that comparable amounts of time should be given to developing the criterion and to perfecting the assessment instruments. Similar warnings and criticisms were offered by Taft (1959) and by Stern, Stein, and Bloom (1956). These writings discussed two large-scale personality assessment studies, the OSS study (OSS Assessment Staff, 1948) and the VA assessment study of training in clinical psychology (Kelly & Fiske, 1951; Kelly & Goldberg, 1959), respectively. Neither of the studies was particularly successful in its aims because of inability to specify clearly in advance the nature of the criterion behavior. A more sophisticated approach to a complex assessment problem was used by Laurent (1962), who wished to employ personality and other data to select management trainees with the greatest potential for success. To cope with the criterion problem, Laurent first developed a composite criterion for "success" by factor-analyzing a variety of available measures of success, such as position level and salary history. The resulting primary factor was adopted as a criterion of overall success and could be used as the target for the predictions.

The foregoing studies deal with complex or multiple assessment projects, but similar criterion problems are encountered in developing instruments to assess individual personality characteristics. Many researchers fail to demonstrate predictive validity for projective devices because the tests were constructed without reference to reliable and easily definable criteria. Rather, each investigator is free to choose whichever dimensions of personality are of interest in the investigation. The resulting melange of investigations has produced largely negative findings, but there can never be a "definitive" study if there is no definitive criterion.

This discussion perhaps can best be summarized by referring to Ebel's (1964b) viewpoint, in which tests that are clearly proposed to be shortcuts for avoiding more elaborate methods of behavioral assessment are distinguished from those that are not. For the shortcut tests, the criterion for test construction must be the "more elaborate method of assessment," and validity is assessed by the correspondence between the two measures. In such cases, the criterion scores would be produced by a measurement procedure that is superior in important ways (e.g., more comprehensive, more reliable) to the test, so that the test is a poorer but more convenient measure of the comprehensive method. In personality assessment, the major problem is usually that a more elaborate method for evaluating personality functioning does not exist or cannot feasibly be employed. It is also true, however, that appropriate criteria could sometimes be developed in the manner utilized by Laurent (1962). An example can be seen in the work of B. Lanyon (1972), who constructed careful criteria as a basis for the empirical aspects of developing a three-scale sentence-completion test, as described in Chapter Four; another example of the positive impact of clear-cut criteria is the development of integrity tests, discussed in Chapter Nine.

Illusory Correlation. Another serious problem that involves the validity of certain assessment procedures applies whenever tests are interpreted by common sense or by an accumulated fund of clinical information, as is the case with much interpretation of projective drawings and, to some extent, with the Rorschach and similar instruments. The problem was identified by Chapman (1967) and labeled "illusory correlation" (Chapman & Chapman, 1967). Is illusory correlation the reason that certain tests with doubtful empirical validities continue to be used and are supported enthusiastically by diagnosticians?

The Chapmans had observed that, when college students were shown a series of word pairs carefully arranged so that all possible pairings were presented equally often, they systematically but mistakenly reported that certain words tended to occur together more often than was actually the case. Specifically, there was an illusion that words with high associative strength for each other (e.g., table and chair, hungry and food) had occurred together more often than words with low associative strength. The Chapmans characterized this effect as "analogous to the well-known Muller-Lyer illusion, in that there is a widely shared systematic error of observation that is not dependent on the observer's having some exceptional prior experience or training" (Chapman & Chapman, 1967, p. 194).

Reasoning that this illusory correlation might also occur in clinical test interpretation, the Chapmans had college undergraduates observe a series of human figure drawings. On each drawing was arbitrarily written two contrived personality symptom statements that were said to describe the person who produced the drawing. There were six such symptom statements, and each was attached to several different drawings. This observational experience was purportedly designed to "teach" the subjects the relationship between drawings and symptoms. The subjects, having "learned" about figure drawings, were then given a written list of the six personality symptom statements and asked to list under each symptom statement the drawing characteristics they had observed to be related to it. The correct response in each case was, of course, that there was *no* systematic relationship between the personality symptom statements and any drawing characteristic whatever.

As expected, the subjects tended to list as related to each personality symptom those drawing characteristics that had high associative strength for the symptom. For example, the subjects overwhelmingly reported a connection between the personality symptom of suspiciousness and the drawing characteristic of atypical eyes, even though their "learning" experience had provided absolutely no basis for such a connection. Further investigation produced the following critical finding: the "personality interpretation" given by the naive undergraduate subjects corresponded closely to the interpretations given by experienced clinicians! Thus, there are indications that some of the "clinical lore" used to interpret projective tests is spurious, and presumably is perpetuated for the same reasons that it originally occurred—because such interpretations "make sense" or are "intuitively correct," although the empirical evidence for these relationships is simply not present.

How strong is the illusory correlation effect? Chapman and Chapman (1969) were able to show that it occurred in assessing homosexuality from the Rorschach, and Starr and Katkin (1969) also found the effect on the Incomplete Sentences Blank. A study by Dowling and Graham (1976) reported a similar phenomenon in using the MMPI, although their results are open to other interpretations. Two studies have shown that the illusory correlation effect persisted unchanged even where subjects received specific warnings about its effects plus training in avoiding it (Kurtz & Garfield, 1978; Waller & Keeley, 1978). In a study designed to provide further understanding of this phenomenon, Lueger and Petzel (1979) showed that the greater the amount of information to be processed by the judges, the greater was the illusory correlation effect.

It cannot be concluded that illusory correlation accounts entirely for the discrepancy between the positive claims made by many practicing clinicians for validity of the figure drawing technique and similar tests, and the meager empirical evidence that is available in their support. Nevertheless, the strength and consistency of the research findings is a potent condemnation of relying solely on one's "experience" in test interpretation, no matter how confident one might be. In his analysis of the accuracy of clinical judgment in general, Dawes (1989) pointed out that the problem of illusory correlation occurs in a much broader context than just test interpretation, and is almost certainly a significant factor in accounting for the limitations of clinicians' skills in clinical judgment and their difficulty in learning from experience.

MORAL ISSUES IN USING PERSONALITY ASSESSMENT DEVICES

The criticisms discussed under this heading do not apply only to personality assessment. They are relevant to many other aspects of psychology, including the experimental use of human subjects, as well as to many aspects of other social sciences, such as economics, education, and law. We are referring to situations in which individuals feel personally threatened with regard to either their personal rights and needs, or their social and civil rights. The threats are often so subtle that people may find it difficult to articulate their reasons for feeling concern or threat, and they may even explicitly deny that threat is the real cause for their actions. These concerns are the bedrock of the criticisms that have come to be identified with the term *invasion of privacy*.

Dahlstrom (1969) distinguished two meanings for the concept of invasion of privacy. The first involves the issue of *confidentiality*, where there may be "certain facts about a person that he would prefer to keep secret [that are] in danger of being revealed to someone who could then use them against him" (p. 268). The second is concerned with *inviolacy;* it involves people's unwillingness to have another person intrude on them in a significant way. In Dahlstrom's words, "They consider any intrusion upon their activities as a violation of their private pattern of living" (p. 268). Anastasi (1988) made a similar distinction.

Before considering these two aspects in detail, let us first examine reasons why invasion of privacy is a socially sensitive issue. Following Willingham (1967), we can list six possible contributing or underlying influences.

1. The concern for individual dignity and privacy, which was originally sensitized by the Civil Rights movement. Identification of personal characteristics may facilitate socially invidious comparisons.
2. Ironically incompatible with the first reason are the demands for social equality. Social scientists are asked to make careful studies and comparisons of social groups, so that inequalities can be investigated and changes can be initiated.
3. The demand for sound research on social issues.
4. The availability of highly sophisticated computer technology. Complex and extensive research projects are not only tempting for researchers but are seen as mandatory if behavioral scientists are to

maintain an image of competence and respectability in the scientific community.

5. The efforts by social scientists for greater involvement in socially meaningful research. These efforts might be seen as a reaction against criticisms leveled at much behavioral research in the past, especially against the charge that this research has been irrelevant to the real problems now confronting society.

6. The public has become highly sensitized to invasion of privacy in a number of areas that are not necessarily psychological in nature, but it has failed to make discriminations among them. Thus, some of the resentments against the use of electronic eavesdropping devices, the large-scale accumulation of personal credit histories, and the collection of personal data in the federal census, have spread to psychology in general and to personality assessment in particular.

Let us now return to our examination of the major complaints about invasion of privacy as they apply to personality assessment. We do so under the two headings suggested by Dahlstrom, although the two categories overlap to some extent.

Confidentiality

Problems relating to confidentiality are present not only with personality assessment data but with any personal information revealed to a clinical psychologist or counselor—or, for that matter, to a physician, lawyer, or minister. Confidentiality of client records, including the results of testing, is both an ethical and a legal requirement for psychologists (American Psychological Association, 1992; Stromberg et al., 1988). The term *privilege*, a much narrower concept than confidentiality, refers to laws (i.e., exceptions to privilege) that require disclosure of records under specific circumstances. For example, if a client requests a psychological evaluation to be used as support in a legal proceeding such as a child custody case or a criminal defense, the test records are usually not privileged, but are subject to subpoena by the court or by the opposing party. On a broader level, confidentiality and other related issues for psychologists involved with the criminal justice system are extensive and complex. In addition to the references cited above, the reader is referred to the textbook on psychological evaluations for the courts by Melton, Petrila, Poythress, and Slobogin (1987) and to the Specialty Guidelines for Forensic Psychologists (Committee on Ethical Guidelines for Forensic Psychologists, 1991). In general, the rules (laws and ethics) governing confidentiality of psychologists' records are quite stringent, and they vary from state to state. Test users are advised to become familiar with those aspects of the rules that are relevant for their own particular work setting.

Ethical Considerations. It seems unnecessary to state that individuals have the right to withhold whatever information they wish, unless they have entered into a contract (actual or implied) to the contrary. If, in addition, they have reason to believe that the information will be employed against their best interests, they would indeed be foolish to disclose it. The issues, however, are more complex. It may seem strange now to realize that, at the height of the public controversy over personality assessment, it was often seriously suggested that all personality tests should be outlawed! This failure to distinguish their many legitimate and apparently humanitarian uses from their abuses attests to the amount of emotion invested in the issues.

As stated above, many of the legal issues involved in confidentiality have been debated and codified (made into statutes) in recent years, perhaps as people realized that legal mechanisms could indeed exist to protect their rights. Together with increased legal activity has come more vigorous debate over what would be *ethically* appropriate from the professional's viewpoint in many different situations. Although most of the debate has involved psychological and psychiatric treatment rather than assessment, the issues are the same in both cases. In particular, legal imperatives have not always been consistent with ethical views (e.g., Siegel, 1979). It is perhaps fair to say that the issues that originally gave rise to the congressional hearings in 1965 are now being formulated, debated, and resolved both within the courts and within each of the helping professions, through the continued evolution of laws and ethical principles.

Under what circumstances in personality assessment situations have people been asked to provide personality information that might be used against them? Perhaps the most blameworthy practice—discussed earlier, in the context of validity criticisms—has been the use of psychopathologically oriented assessment devices in the context of personnel selection. The confidentiality problem has arisen here in two ways. First, some tests have included questions pertaining to sexual and religious practices, information that has little apparent relation to job suitability but presumably could afford much opportunity for personal embarrassment and the exercise of prejudices. (The MMPI-2 does not contain such items, but they were present in the original MMPI.) Second, and perhaps more important, the respondents may be revealing information of which they are not aware, and which they would not choose to reveal if given that choice. The person who is asked to respond to the Rorschach inkblots faces just such a possibility.

What are the ethics of the situation? Rather different views were proposed by Dahlstrom (1969) and Lovell (1967). The use of personality tests in a mental health or a counseling setting is not at issue. In those instances, clients are seeking professional help for their own problems, and the outcome of the intervention is clearly understood to be for the clients' own benefit. Lovell referred to this type of situation, where there is no conflict of interest between assessor and respondent, as the *client function* of personality testing. Whenever a potential conflict of interest does exist between assessor and respondent, such as in personnel selection, tests are being used in a *personnel function,* and it is this use that has caused concern. Lovell argued that the use of personality tests is inadmissible on three counts. First, on ethical grounds, it has no place in a free society. Second, on scientific grounds, it is doubtful that adequate validity is possible under these conditions, because of the difficulties of obtaining subject cooperation. Third, on grounds of community service, the public will be best served in the long run if personality tests are not used in this manner.

Dahlstrom (1969) drew attention to a similar dichotomy, initially proposed by Cronbach and Gleser (1965), referring to the use of personality tests in making decisions serving an *individual* and decisions serving an *institution.* Dahlstrom, however, saw no ethical dilemma in either type of decision under normal circumstances. As an example of an institutional use of tests, let us consider the case where a candidate is being screened for an executive position in a particular company. Because the psychologist's loyalties to the company are clear to the candidate, there should be no ethical problem. Further, the applicant can choose to invalidate the procedure, if he or she so desires, by subtle noncooperation. Conflicts of interest, however, might arise for the psychologist in the event that information of real concern to society in general, such as murder or pyromania, were revealed in the course of the examination. Dahlstrom offered another plausible reason why many persons are conflicted about the use of personality tests in personnel selection: The outcome of the testing session is often unfavorable to the respondent. In a sense, the information is used in a fashion that is at cross-purposes with the respondent's own interests. Regarding actual breaches of confidentiality with undesirable *general consequences* to the respondent—that is, the use of test results outside of the situation for which they were obtained—the 1965 congressional hearings uncovered little or no evidence of such practices (Brayfield, 1965).

Confidentiality and the question of having to violate it have been matters of great concern and considerable disagreement among psychologists. The appropriate principle in the *Ethical Principles of Psychologists and Code of Conduct* (American Psychological Association, 1992) states that "Psychologists disclose confidential information without the consent of the individual only as mandated by law, or where permitted by law for a valid purpose . . ." (Standard 5.05). This can include situations in which there is a clear and imminent danger to an individual or society. Such "duty to warn" laws are an outgrowth of the famous case of *Tarasoff v. the Regents of the University of California* (1974/1976), in which the university was held liable for not revealing that a student in counseling had stated (and subsequently carried out) his intention to kill a particular young lady. On the other hand, the view has been expressed by some psychologists that psychologists should *not* break the confidentiality of a client under any circumstances (e.g., Siegel, 1979). These issues will continue to be debated for some time to come.

The Client's Right to Know.   Another important issue regarding confidentiality is people's right to know their own test results. Psychologists have traditionally been very reluctant to share this information, reasoning that it might be misleading or harmful to the subject. However, as a result of the debate initiated by the 1965 congressional hearings and the widespread concern over the existence of inaccessible personal records, psychologists have acknowledged both the client's right to know and their own responsibility to present the information in a manner that can be understood and appreciated by the client. Thus, the *Ethical Standards of Psychologists and Code of Conduct* (American Psychological Association, 1992) includes the principle that "psychologists ensure that an explanation of the results [of assessment] is provided using language that is reasonably understandable to the person assessed or to another legally authorized person on behalf of the client. Regardless of whether the scoring and interpretations are done by the psychologist, by assistants, or by automated or other outside services, psychologists take reasonable steps to ensure that appropriate explanations or results are given" (Standard 2.09). Exceptions are possible if there is an explicit agreement to that effect in advance. Once again, the principle is not completely consistent with laws at the state level, which differ considerably in the degree of patient access that is mandated (Stromberg et al., 1988).

In concluding our discussion of the confidentiality issue, it must not be overlooked that some people *do* have things to hide that may or may not be related to the assessment task at hand, but would be potentially damaging to them if inadvertently revealed. Thus, in the context of a personality research program involving schoolchildren, Eron and Walder (1961) reported that one of the local citizens who had made efforts to harass the research team was later indicted for a sexual offense, though this was not in any way related to the research. How to permit such people to retain their right of privacy in situations where the cooperation of a whole group is sought is indeed a difficult dilemma. Even if it is made known that persons who would rather not cooperate need not do so, such persons may become a focus of attention merely by their action in not participating. The same problem is present whenever questionnaires or inventories are administered with the instructions that respondents may omit any items they would rather not answer. A glance at the answer sheet for omitted items reveals the areas of greatest personal sensitivity!

Inviolacy

Inviolacy involves situations where there is no threat that the information that people give as part of an assessment procedure will be used against them; rather, it involves the individual's right of personal privacy—the right not to have an intrusion of privacy. The question of inviolacy is relevant

when people are questioned about aspects of their daily living that traditionally are not openly discussed in Western culture. Thus, items on the
original MMPI regarding eliminative functions are hardly likely to provide material that might be self-incriminatory; however, in our society,
toilet functions are very private matters, and many people are embar-
rassed to discuss them. In fact, one reason for negative reactions to such
self-report items is that merely reading these items arouses anxiety about
"taboo" topics.

Another type of material that people object to discussing involves cher-
ished beliefs about human nature. Bennett (1967) stated that "A great
many people seem to take comfort in believing that all children love and
respect their parents, accept without question the teachings of their religion and live without sexual curiosity or urge until they attain the married
state" (p. 9). In discussing behavioral research, Brim (1967) made the related point that much of the general concern about such research appears
to come "not so much from the concern about methods and privacy, but
about the inroads that behavioral science is making on ideas" (p. 30). There
is an implication that security is found in the familiar, and that to be asked
even to consider alternatives raises anxieties that are turned into aggression toward the test.

Some personality psychologists have placed considerable importance on
the "need for inviolacy" as a personality characteristic. Brim (1965) suggested that such people may also be "authoritarian in interpersonal relations, intolerant of diversity in ideology or beliefs, and strongly opposed to
most forms of social change" (p. 128). Jourard (1964) wrote extensively on
the topic of self-disclosure, by which he meant one's readiness to be open
and share oneself with others. Murray (1938) listed and discussed the need
for inviolacy as one of the basic needs in his personality theory. And it was
reported that, for normal persons, the *K* (defensiveness) scale of the MMPI
appears to be related to personality needs to remain cool, aloof, and wary,
and to a general reluctance to reveal oneself (Dahlstrom & Welsh, 1960).

To state the issue simply, some people resent being asked certain questions, for a variety of reasons. These reasons do not necessarily concern the
use to which the information will be put, but principally involve the negative feelings that result from being forced to confront the anxiety-arousing
subject matter. In his excellent analysis of the problem, Bennett (1967)
noted that every society has established rules or norms under which its
members attain more benefits than would result from anarchy. These rules
periodically should be, and typically are, scrutinized and changed if found
lacking. Those people who wish to initiate these changes have the responsibility for considering the consequences that even thinking about change
would have on members of the society. Because such inquiry does cause
considerable apprehension and anxiety, a reasonable degree of restraint
must be exercised in asking members of a culture to give information

about, or even to think about, certain of its important rules. If this restraint is not exercised, the effectiveness and professional image of the would-be changers of a society are bound to suffer. In the case of our contemporary American society, however desirable it may appear in the long run to gather certain information, psychologists and other social scientists will be ineffective and perhaps will even seriously damage themselves if they do not recognize and respond to these very basic concerns and facts about social change.

Some positive responses to many of the criticisms previously discussed in this chapter suggest themselves when the public image of psychology, especially of personality assessment, is considered. A clear statement of the poor state of this public image was offered by Nettler (1959) in "Test Burning in Texas," an article that described the generalized unfavorable public reaction to a community-wide testing program. Eron and Walder (1961) reported, however, on another personality research program in which comprehensive and thoughtful procedures were instituted to prepare the community for the participation of both parents and children. Although some persons in the community produced publicity that was unfavorable and deliberately misleading, the foresight of the research team and their straightforwardness in dealing with community concerns and anxieties resulted in excellent cooperation from all but a handful of people. Psychologists might pay more careful attention to their public relations, particularly with regard to disseminating clear and accurate information about assessment procedures. This attention could do much to forestall unfavorable public reactions.

In positions involving public security, there should be no question about the legitimacy of gathering personal information about someone for selection purposes. Bennett (1967) identified three such situations: (a) where an individual may be susceptible to blackmail by unfriendly governments; (b) where a person may be assigned for important public duty overseas; and (c) where the position is that of a police officer or a security guard. Bennett also pointed out that the amount of investigation to which an individual is subjected is proportional to the seriousness of making a poor selection decision. Thus, applicants for loans or credit are often subjected to a detailed investigation in the relevant areas, however private those areas may be.

Perhaps the best example of personality evaluation of an applicant is the scrutiny given to a candidate for the presidency of the United States. First, his entire background is combed by his rivals for any information that could possibly reflect negatively on him. Then, under guise of determining his position on substantive issues, the candidate is made the target of a blistering stress interview lasting many months, in which a single major error could cost him his goal. The degree of personal stability required to survive such a test is possessed by few, and the candidate who makes the best showing in this lengthy situational test is elected. The same description applies, to some degree, to all political campaigns. In these circumstances, confidentiality or personal privacy traditionally has no meaning, and American society demands that the lives of important political figures be open to continual public scrutiny.

RESTRICTION OF FREEDOM

One further criticism of personality assessment that merits discussion involves procedures that are claimed to restrict a person's individual freedom. For example, with regard to ability assessment, the use of intelligence tests in schools has often been criticized on the grounds that opportunities tend to be restricted by the categories into which the test scores explicitly or implicitly place children (e.g., Ebel, 1964a). This restriction was documented in a series of research projects by Rosenthal (1966), who concluded that children tend to perform according to others' expectations of them, and that these expectations tend to get communicated regardless of efforts to control them. Because personality assessment interpretations lead us to develop expectations about others, we may subtly influence these others to fulfill our expectations. For example, if an assessment report suggests that a person is "untrustworthy," either our constant suspiciousness may produce ambiguous behavior, which we then interpret as justifying the label, or we may actually induce such behavior in the other person by our responses. One trend toward counteracting these effects can be seen in the current efforts to deemphasize the use of psychiatric diagnostic labels for patients in clinics and mental hospitals because they create strong expectations of patient behavior. This point of view is supported, in rather different ways, by the writings of Szasz (1961, 1984) and by the behavioral approach to personality assessment.

Regarding the restriction of freedom, a somewhat different criticism has been made of personality assessment in the context of selection: the problem of "prevention of progress by encouraging the mundane and prosaic" (Guion, 1965, p. 372). Suppose a large industrial organization wishes to select the best executive applicants. The organization might follow the time-honored empirical procedure of exhaustively studying the best persons it has recruited for some years and using the results of this study to set the standards for selection (Howard & Bray, 1988). Thus, a selection battery might be developed to choose applicants similar to the company's best executives over the past 15 years. Once the selection battery is in operation, the company has inadvertently assured itself of hiring executive trainees whose personality is currently adaptive and has been so in the recent past. Unfortunately, however, persons are needed who will best fit the company's configuration in the future. There may be a serious error in assuming that the kind of executives most suited for running the company yesterday and today will be optimal in the future (Cascio, 1995). At best, the talent pool becomes markedly narrowed by this procedure, and all executives in the company begin to look alike. At worst, if the management happens to be mediocre at the present time, this level of performance is perpetuated. People with new and different ideas are never given a chance.

Selection programs need not involve a narrowing of talent and perpetuation of the present state of affairs. Once the nature of the present management staff is determined, the selection team, in collaboration with the management, can decide whether to continue this pattern. A reasonable approach might be to determine what trends are occurring in the industry, and to orient the selection criteria toward persons with characteristics most suitable for dealing with or fulfilling these trends. Diversity can be deliberately built in. Once the present managers are described, a deliberate plan can be developed to detect persons who differ from them in specified ways. These plans capitalize on the advantages of a selection program—knowing what kinds of people are being selected—without falling into the trap of making the organization's managers increasingly narrow in their outlook.

SUMMARY

Personality assessment practices were subjected to a lengthy and careful scrutiny in 1965, when two sets of congressional hearings were held. Although the avowed purpose of the hearings was to investigate invasion of privacy through the use of personality tests in the federal government personnel selection practices, many more issues were explored. Complaints about personality assessment can be grouped under two headings: problems of use and problems involving moral issues.

Use problems are of two kinds: (a) test misuse, involving invalid use of an assessment procedure that has legitimate and validated uses; and (b) generalized test invalidity, involving the use of assessment procedures in which validity has not been established for any purpose. Test misuse is probably the most serious problem in the field of personality assessment, and some of the criticism delivered is traceable to selection practices in the workplace, particularly the use in this context of psychiatrically oriented instruments. Another potential misuse of personality tests is with cultural minority groups for whom the tests may not be valid, as has often been the case with the assessment of abilities. There is also a controversy over whether extensive training and experience are necessary for the valid use of projective instruments. A further misuse of personality assessment procedures is the tendency of clinical psychologists to try to derive from certain tests information that those tests were not designed to discover. In response to these concerns, the *Standards for Educational and Psychological*

Testing contains an extensive section on standards for the appropriate use of tests. A behavior/competency-based method for assessing user knowledge and responsibility has also been proposed.

Concerning generalized test invalidity, one troublesome problem is that some assessment instruments were not designed with reference to any criteria, so that there is no reasonably straightforward use to which one can point as the "purpose" of such an instrument. Another serious problem is illusory correlation, which applies to tests that have traditionally been interpreted by reference to an accumulated fund of "clinical lore" or commonsense principles, when many of these commonsense principles, although reliable, simply have no basis in fact.

There are two kinds of moral issues. One involves confidentiality—instances where test respondents are afraid that the information they give might be used in some way against their interests. Again, probably the most serious criticism arises in the context of personnel selection practices. Another problem arises when a respondent has something to hide that has nothing to do with the assessment at hand but may be damaging for other reasons if revealed. The legal issues involved in confidentiality and privilege have recently come to the forefront, as people have come to recognize that legal mechanisms do indeed exist to protect their rights. At times, laws governing confidentiality and psychologists' ethics in this regard may conflict. In a different aspect of confidentiality, the APA *Ethical Standards for Psychologists* has recently affirmed people's rights to know their own test results.

The second moral issue is connected with an individual's right to personal inviolacy, or privacy of thoughts and behaviors. Many persons do not wish to be required to even think about certain topics, and being asked for responses to controversial statements is seen as a definite and unwarranted intrusion into their thoughts. However, in personnel selection situations where the public security is involved, a candidate's privacy must often be invaded. This situation might apply in assessing a person's suitability to be a police officer or an armed guard; for candidates for political office, invasion of privacy has traditionally been the rule.

A final criticism of personality assessment procedures is that they tend to restrict an individual's freedom. This could happen through the "Rosenthal effect," in which a person's expectation of how another will behave sometimes influences the other's actual behavior. Assessment procedures can also cause restriction in the context of selection, if the criterion on which the selection procedure has been based is narrow and outmoded.

Developing a Personality Assessment Instrument: General Principles and Practical Considerations

How does one go about developing a useful personality inventory? The Appendix is intended to answer this question by providing a practical guide, with solid foundation and clear explanation, to the development of a reliable and valid inventory. The guidelines here are applicable for any concept representing "typical performance" as opposed to "maximum performance" (Cronbach, 1984). Although the guidelines are written to apply to the assessment of individual concepts (anxiety, depression, leadership, and so on) rather than to entire domains (personality, psychopathology, vocational interest, and so on), the same logic can be applied in developing sets of scales to assess domains as well.

Some of the material in this appendix summarizes material contained in the body of the book. In these instances, references to the relevant literature are not repeated. Where the material is new, however, appropriate references are provided.

Historical Summary

Early inventories were not "developed." They came about in an arbitrary or accidental manner. The Woodworth Personal Data sheet, later called the Woodworth Psychoneurotic Inventory, was simply a paper-and-pencil version of the questions that physicians asked World War I military recruits in order to screen out those who were at risk for emotional problems. As another example, Hermann Rorschach made the accidental discovery that the kinds of responses his mentally ill patients gave to inkblots used in his experimental studies of perception were related to the types of disorder they had.

But it was soon recognized that tests that originated in such arbitrary ways were not nearly valid enough for practical use. Two developments then occurred. First, a need for external or empirical cross-validity was recognized. For a test to be commercially acceptable, a demonstration of empirical accuracy was essential, using groups of subjects who were independent of those involved in the initial test construction procedures. The second development occurred in test construction technology. An increasingly sophisticated set of procedures evolved over the years to develop and refine test stimuli in order to increase the likelihood that they would accurately tap into the characteristic(s) of interest. The use of such procedures can be viewed as a process of *building into* the instrument the potential for obtaining external validity. To state it another way, each of the many steps now recognized as state-of-the-art processes in test development serve to reduce a particular source of error in the final product.

As the technology for developing personality-related scales has become increasingly precise, definitions of what is to be measured have had to be more specific. If a definition is fuzzy or obscure, the lack of clarity will set a statistical ceiling on the predictive accuracy that is achievable. For example, it is arguable that, in constructing the original scales of the MMPI, the lack of a precise definition of schizophrenia was the main factor that limited the ability of Hathaway and McKinley to produce a scale that had acceptable accuracy (Hathaway, 1956b).

Often, complex or broad concepts that we are interested in measuring prove to be composites of two or more concepts that can be more precisely defined. For example, the broad concept of "anxiety" is often conceptualized as having cognitive, affective, and behavioral components, and their relative prominence may vary from person to person and from group to group. Similarly, the concept of leadership has been shown to involve at least two major sets of behaviors: (a) leadership—setting a direction, energizing others, and establishing goals; and (b) management—establishing processes to implement the leadership vision. Some apparently broad concepts, after careful study, turn out to be unidimensional, a situation that facilitates measurement considerably. Life satisfaction and marital satisfaction are two such concepts (e.g., Diener, 1984; Snyder, 1981). Other concepts, such as intimacy, continue to defy researchers' efforts either to break them into components or to define them in a unidimensional manner (e.g., Monsour, 1992). An analysis of the evolution of broad and narrow concepts has been provided by Furnham (1990).

The Importance of Content Validity

From the 1930s through the 1960s, the role of the content validity or face validity of inventory items was a matter of debate. Psychodynamically oriented psychologists viewed the role as unimportant, for two reasons: (a) the most meaningful aspects of personality were believed to be unavailable to a person's conscious scrutiny; and (b) face-valid items could be easily faked. Psychologists who preferred the criterion-groups approach shared this view, but for a different reason. They believed that, provided an item was shown to be a valid predictor, the extent of its face validity was irrelevant; that is, any item could turn out to be valid, regardless of its content. On the other hand, trait-oriented psychologists regarded content validity as critically important, believing that persons could and would describe themselves accurately.

By the 1970s, there was strong evidence that accurate measurement devices did require relevant content (e.g., Jackson, 1971). The converse, that content validity *guaranteed* empirical accuracy, was not true. Thus, state-of-the-art procedures began to be viewed as including two broad steps: (a) the assemblage of a large number of items that comprehensively overrepresented the relevant content of the concept; and (b) a series of processes for ending up with a group of items that most accurately represented that content.

The objection that content-relevant items can be easily faked is important. In actual situations where the respondent's goals and the examiner's goals are the same, such as in a research or mental health setting, there is no problem. Difficulty arises when the two goals may be different, as they are in certain personnel or court-related settings. Thus, faking is far more a problem when a test is used in a hiring decision or in evaluating the mental status of a prisoner awaiting trial. Because all tests are fakable to some extent, this difficulty is not unique to inventory scales whose items are "obvious." The state of the art in dealing with potential faking situations is to use specially constructed scales to detect faking, such as the Balanced Inventory of Desirable Responding (Paulhus, 1986, 1994) or the MMPI *Ds-r* (Gough, 1954, 1957) and *L* and *K* scales. The use of "correction" procedures for the regular inventory scales, such as the *K*-correction of the MMPI, is not considered very successful and has been little used elsewhere.

Definition and Universe of Content

The inevitable first step in constructing a measure is to define what is to be measured. This step goes hand in hand with developing a *universe of content,* or a complete listing of all the characteristics (behavior, thoughts, feelings, and so on) that are integral parts of the concept. For well-researched concepts, little problem results, because the characteristics are already well delineated and adequate measures of such concepts may already exist. It is for the less well-studied concepts that one usually faces the task of developing a measure. In a related step, one must determine which of these characteristics the instrument will address—one, or several.

There is no substitute for studying the available empirical, clinical, and theoretical literature on the concept. To develop a measure of a concept, there must be a satisfactory definition, and if none of the existing definitions is adequate, one has to be developed from scratch. The assessment device will be created to mirror this definition; in other words, the test will be based on the definition and will be measuring the definition. The ultimate quality of the device can be no better than that of the definition.

The creation of a definition often coincides with the development of the measure. It is essential that the initial universe of content contain all of the content that will eventually be part of the definition. The content can and should be assembled from all sources that are believed to have some relevance to the concept. For example, in assembling the initial content pool for extraversion, one would include material reflecting the theories that are believed to be relevant, the subjective literature that impresses the test developer, and the relevant empirical research. Content reflecting items from other scales for extraversion can be included if it is considered relevant.

Item Preparation

The next step is to *sample representatively* the universe of content. It might first be helpful to cluster or organize the content in some manner. Items or other stimuli (e.g., dichotomous, multiple-choice, sentence stems, and so on) should then be prepared to representatively and comprehensively cover each element. As to how many items should be prepared, a good rule is to have at least twice as many as will ultimately be needed. For test developers who are unfamiliar with item preparation, and for concepts that are not straightforward, more (rather than fewer) initial items will be necessary.

There are many rules for preparing items. Some are arbitrary rules-of-thumb; some are supported by research. Here, we discuss item writing as it applies to dichotomous items, but the same or similar rules apply to other kinds of items. A basic point to remember is that the most reliable and valid initial items will survive the test-construction process. Reliability refers to the ability of the items to mean the same thing from one time to another, one setting to another. Important qualities include the use of unambiguous language. Items that are specific (e.g., "I get one headache or more per week, on the average") tend to be more reliable than items that are more general (e.g., "I often get headaches"). Items that are general in scope may have a place if the concept of interest involves generalities. For example, an appropriate item in an initial pool to assess life satisfaction might be "In general, I am satisfied with my life."

Items should be written in a manner that maximizes their potential for empirically demonstrable validity; that is, each item should clearly reflect the content that is intended. The response endorsement probability should not be extreme; the skewness should be relatively small. Items with a true–false response ratio between .25 and .75 have the greatest potential for contributing to validity. If an item has a ratio of 90/10 or 10/90, its ability to add much to the scale is statistically limited, and its potential contribution to validity must be weighed against its potential contribution to unreliability and other unwanted results.

An exception to this rule appears in assessing concepts whose defining characteristics are unusual, such as charisma or schizophrenia. Here, the true–false ratios of many of the items will necessarily be quite asymmetrical; it is then even more important that the items be potentially reliable. Reliability and validity can be enhanced by having a longer scale. Also, items that may offend some people, such as references to sex, religion, body elimination functions, and politically sensitive topics, should be avoided unless the scale is specifically designed to measure a concept in one of these areas. Respondents may refuse to take the test or, alternatively, may give invalid responses to those items. In view of current political and legal concerns, it may be difficult to obtain subjects for validation research.

Two other threats to external validity should be addressed at the item-writing level: (a) acquiescence and (b) social desirability. Acquiescence is the systematic tendency to respond "true" (or "false") regardless of the content of the item. In the late 1950s and the 1960s, this behavior was believed to be a quite serious obstacle to using true–false inventories; subsequently, its effects have been shown to be relatively modest in the assessment of most concepts. It can be satisfactorily dealt with by writing a comparable number of items keyed true and false. In the assessment of severe psychopathology or other statistically rare events, this tactic may not be possible because the respondent must be asked about the presence of unlikely but pathological symptoms; also, it may not be possible to prepare meaningful item reversals. In such a case, preference should be given to maintaining the clarity of the items.

Social desirability refers to the natural or unaware tendency of some respondents to put their best foot forward in answering items: they select the more socially desirable direction. Socially desirable responding should be distinguished from deliberate deception, in which respondents make a considerable effort to misrepresent themselves. Like acquiescence, social desirability was once considered to be a serious impediment to the accuracy of personality tests. However, most researchers now acknowledge that it is an inevitable part of the meaning of many concepts that are themselves socially desirable (e.g., conscientiousness) or undesirable (e.g., hostility).

It is common to avoid the use of items that are particularly high in social desirability (e.g., "I love my mother") or particularly low (e.g., "I often feel like hurting people"). Instead, they may be reworded to reflect the same meaning in less extreme forms (e.g., "I must admit that I have occasionally felt like hurting somebody"). Empirically, it is appropriate to compute the correlation of each item with some established measure of social desirability, such as the Marlowe-Crowne Social Desirability Scale (Crowne & Marlowe, 1960) and to exclude items whose correlation reaches an arbitrary level, such as .30. Jackson (1976) used a more sophisticated approach, retaining an item if its correlation with a preliminary measure of the concept being assessed was significantly higher than its correlation with social desirability. Thus, items were retained if their contribution to measuring the concept went beyond a shared relationship with social desirability.

To summarize thus far, the preparation of items involves the following stages:

1. A satisfactory definition is developed for the concept to be measured.
2. A universe of content is developed.

3. The universe of content is representatively sampled by writing items that are clear and unambiguous, specific rather than general, relatively free from skewness (as far as possible), not personally offensive or potentially threatening in language, balanced for acquiescence, and not at the extremes of social desirability.

Preliminary Screening of Items

Items must have several basic psychometric properties: adequate reliability, relative freedom from skewness, and a relatively low relationship with social desirability. These properties can be checked directly by administering the preliminary items to a group of subjects who are similar to those with whom the finished product will be used. For example, if the scale refers to health-related concerns such as attitudes toward the medical profession, the preliminary subjects should be persons in the context of receiving health care, such as family practice patients.

There is no firm rule for the number of subjects to be used, but the nature of the statistical procedures to be employed suggests that about 300 subjects is usually adequate. Skewness is evaluated by examining the true–false ratio, and/or a formal quantitative measure of skewness can be employed. In regard to social desirability, a scale such as the Marlowe-Crowne (see above) would be administered along with the preliminary items, and those with correlations higher than a predetermined level would be discarded. To assess reliability, the items would be readministered to some or all of the subjects after an arbitrary retest interval of perhaps 1–3 weeks. Items with test–retest correlations below an arbitrary level—say, .50—would be eliminated.

We have described the cutting points as "arbitrary" because they will differ according to the concepts involved and the type of subjects employed. But it is safe to say that the screening procedures described above permit the elimination of items that are obviously unsuitable. They are meant to be viewed as "deselection" rather than "selection" procedures; they leave a pool of items that will be subjected to content-based selection procedures, described below. Items that survive this multiple-screening process have real potential for contributing reliably to the validity of the measure, and are therefore psychometrically superior candidates for inclusion in the final scale.

The initial screening procedures also serve as an opportunity to solicit feedback from respondents: Are any items offensive, difficult to understand, or unsuitable for some other reason? On a global basis, they enable the test-development team to have an initial interaction with actual respondents, who may offer a variety of comments and other informative feedback that may not have been anticipated.

Addressing Content Suitability

The task of deciding which items most directly represent the nature of the content being assessed usually involves factor analysis. The specific procedure to be employed depends on the degree to which the nature or structure of the concept is understood. For example, if it is accepted that the concept of anxiety is best defined in terms of behavioral, cognitive, and affective behaviors, and if the universe of content has been prepared to reflect these three facets of anxiety, then the appropriate procedure would be a confirmatory factor analysis with the expectation of confirming this three-factor model as the most parsimonious structure. To the extent that confirmation (to an acceptable criterion) is not achieved, items would be dropped or reworded to make the factors more distinct, and the confirmatory factor analysis would be repeated until the required factor structure is obtained. Any reworded or added items would need to be screened for psychometric adequacy as described above.

If the concept being assessed is not well structured, so that there are no preconceived ideas as to its components or facets, an exploratory factor analysis should be conducted to see how many independent content clusters exist and to measure their relative strength. For these clusters to represent the concept, the pool of items that were the basis of the factor analysis must be representative of the original universe of content. If previous steps have resulted in the disproportionate elimination of certain content areas, they would need to be replaced with new, successfully screened items before proceeding.

The factor structure resulting from the exploratory analysis should be studied to determine whether it is sensible or logical according to the researcher's views about the nature of the concept. There does not always have to be an expectation that any clear factor structure will emerge—although, if one does not, the researcher has to decide whether the concept is very heterogeneous or whether the items did not adequately represent it. Efforts should be made to confirm the exploratory factor structure on a new sample of subjects. Other issues involve variables related to the factor analysis, such as what kind of rotation is advisable, and/or whether to rely on the unrotated factors. These technical issues, however, are beyond the scope of the present discussion.

Final Selection of Items

The step of determining which items are to be included in the final version of a scale or test inevitably involves subjective judgment. All the item and scale statistics are considered together, and decisions are made according to the multitude of priorities and criteria discussed above. One useful consideration not yet mentioned is the relationship of items to scales for which they were *not* written, and the correlations among the various scales and/or facets. Although there is often no logical reason why the scales should be statistically independent of each other, the presence of substantial correlations between scales suggests a degree of overlap in the underlying concepts that might be best handled by redefining the concepts.

Norms

Norms should be developed on the same group or population for which the test is intended. A choice must be made between developing a single general set of norms versus many specific sets of norms for population subgroups. The most common approach is to develop separate norms for males and females, and to determine the variation in mean values with respect to age, education, and other demographic characteristics. In interpreting test scores, a judgment is then made as to whether any significant variation represents an artifact or demographic characteristic, or whether it truly reflects the respondent's position on the scale of interest. Unfortunately, such judgments are easier said than made, and a full understanding must often await specific research on each demographic characteristic and each scale.

External Validity

As indicated above, the appropriate use of any psychometric instrument requires an empirical demonstration that it is valid for that particular purpose. External validation is an ongoing process; in practice, some uses of a test will inevitably be made before specific evidence exists. Such uses must be regarded as tentative and temporary.

Whenever a scale is used objectively to make a particular decision, cutting points should be based on actual information about the presence or absence of the target characteristic in the population of interest, and error rates should be stated. The selection of optimal cutting points also requires a knowledge of the relative costs of each type of error: failing to identify a target case (false negative), and mistakenly identifying a person who does *not* possess the target characteristic (false positive). For example, in identifying potential suicides, the cost of failing to identify a person who is actually suicidal is much higher than giving a false label to someone who is not; thus, a lower cutting score would be used, and more false positives would be tolerated in order to minimize false negatives. Conversely, higher cutting points would be used in assessing the dangerousness of sex offenders who are up for parole, because the cost to society of mistakenly releasing a dangerous person (false negative) is much higher than the cost of mistakenly retaining a nondangerous person (false positive).

Reliability

Questions of sample size and scale size (number of subjects and number of items) are directly related to the need for adequate reliability. To address the issue of items first, there is no directly relevant body of research on which to draw. However, based on writings, experiences, and recommendations in test construction in the past, the following guidelines are offered. The minimum number of items needed for adequate reliability in most dichotomous scales is probably about 20. Jackson (1974, 1976) found 16 to be too few, but 20 to be sufficient, given item-development procedures to enhance reliability. Hogan's (1992) dichotomous scales ranged in length from 14 through 37 items; subscales ranged down to as few as three items. Because of the brevity of many of these subscales, only extreme scores would be reliable enough for interpretation (see "Screening Instruments," below).

Likert-type rating scales have gained popularity in recent years, in part because fewer items are needed to achieve the same level of reliability as a dichotomous scale (Burish, 1984). Costa and McCrae (1992) used 24-item Likert scales (0–4), each with 3 facets of 8 items, making a score range of 0–32 possible for each facet. They viewed each facet as capable of reliable and independent interpretation.

What is considered adequate test–retest reliability? There is no firm guideline, but a rule of thumb puts the minimum at .80 over a one-week retest interval. Some concepts (e.g., rebelliousness, extraversion) are easier to assess reliably than others (e.g., defensiveness, dependency).

Scale Homogeneity and Subscales

Another meaning of the term *reliability* is linked to internal consistency, the extent to which all the items on a scale address the same concept. Some recent researchers have resolved the dilemma of developing concepts that are heterogeneous in content by independently defining each of the "subconcepts," and making the scale an aggregation of these more homogeneous subscales, or facets. The use of subscales offers the important advantage of a finer-grained interpretation; in a sense, a scale with several subscales is itself a multiscale test for that concept. For example, as indicated earlier, the concepts of anxiety and leadership are heterogeneous and are appropriately assessed through the use of subscales. The extent to which subscales are independently interpretable depends on the care put into their construction, the availability of independent external validity evidence, and (central to both of these issues) their test–retest reliability.

Screening Instruments

The development of screening instruments requires special comment. The aim of these instruments is to identify problems or characteristics that should receive further attention. There is no expectation that much meaningful information will be obtained for every subject. Thus, no final decision is to be made solely on the basis of the score or scores, which instead serve to signal whether further assessment is needed. Another aspect is that the decision to use a screening instrument should be based strictly on cost-effectiveness; that is, whether enough information is gained from the instrument to justify its use. High accuracy is not as important a goal as brevity, and retest reliabilities may be correspondingly lower. It is usually appropriate to note only high scores—that is, scores above a preselected cutting point—and to ignore the remainder. Objective cutting points are determined in the manner described above.

As an example, in using the Psychological Screening Inventory (Lanyon, 1978) to screen for severe mental disorder in a community mental health center population, the *Manual* presents the expected percentages of "hits" and "misses" that are associated with different cutting scores on the Alienation scale. Based on these data, a raw score of 11 or more would identify 94% of males who have a serious mental disorder, but would also misidentify 50% of normals as having such a disorder. A lower cutting score of 9 or more would correctly identify 86% of persons with a serious disorder and 75% of normals. The choice of a particular cutting score would depend on the *base rate*, or proportion of persons in the population who have the target characteristic, and (as discussed above) on the relative cost of the two types of errors.

References

Achenbach, T. M. (1978). The child behavior profile: I. Boys aged 6–11. *Journal of Consulting and Clinical Psychology, 46,* 478–488.

Achenbach, T. M. (1991a). *Manual for the Child Behavior Checklist/4–18 and 1991 Profile.* Burlington: University of Vermont, Department of Psychiatry.

Achenbach, T. M. (1991b). *Manual for the Teacher's Report Form and 1991 Profile.* Burlington: University of Vermont, Department of Psychiatry.

Achenbach, T. M. (1991c). *Manual for the Youth Self-Report and 1991 Profile.* Burlington: University of Vermont, Department of Psychiatry.

Achenbach, T. M., & Edelbrock, C. S. (1979). The child behavior profile: II. Boys aged 12–16 and girls aged 6–11 and 12–16. *Journal of Consulting and Clinical Psychology, 47,* 223–233.

Ackoff, R. L., & Rivett, P. (1963). *A manager's guide to operations research.* New York: Wiley.

Adair, F. L. (1978a). Review of MMPI automated psychological assessment. In O. K. Buros (Ed.), *Eighth mental measurements yearbook.* Highland Park, NJ: Gryphon.

Adair, F. L. (1978b). Review of MMPI computerized scoring and interpreting services. In O. K. Buros (Ed.), *Eighth mental measurements yearbook.* Highland Park, NJ: Gryphon.

Albert, S., Fox, H. M., & Kahn, M. W. (1980). Faking psychosis on the Rorschach: Can expert judges detect malingering? *Journal of Personality Assessment, 44,* 115–119.

Allen, L. (1985). Review of Law Enforcement Assessment and Development Report. In J. V. Mitchell, Jr. (Ed.), *The ninth mental measurements yearbook.* Lincoln: University of Nebraska, Buros Institute of Mental Measurements.

Allport, G. W. (1937). *Personality.* New York: Holt.

Allport, G. W. (1961). *Pattern and growth in personality.* New York: Holt, Rinehart and Winston.

Allport, G. W., & Odbert, H. S. (1936). Trait names: A psycho-lexical study. *Psychological Monographs, 47* (Whole No. 211).

Alpern, G. A., Boll, T. J., & Shearer, M. S. (1984). *Developmental Profile II: Manual.* Los Angeles: Western Psychological Services.

Altman, H., Evenson, R. C., Hedlund, J. L., & Cho, D. W. (1978). The Missouri Actuarial Report System (MARS). *Comprehensive Psychiatry, 19,* 185–192.

American Educational Research Association/American Psychological Association/National Council on Measurement in Education (1985). *Standards for educational and psychological testing.* Washington, DC: Author.

American Psychiatric Association. (1980). *Diagnostic and statistical manual of mental disorders* (3rd ed.). Washington, DC: Author.

American Psychiatric Association. (1987). *Diagnostic and statistical manual of mental disorders* (3rd ed., rev.). Washington, DC: Author.

American Psychiatric Association. (1994). *Diagnostic and statistical manual of mental disorders* (4th ed.). Washington, DC: Author.

American Psychological Association. (1954). Technical recommendations for psychological tests and diagnostic techniques. *Psychological Bulletin, 51,* (2, pt. 2).

American Psychological Association. (1970). Psychological assessment and public policy. *American Psychologist, 25,* 264–266.

American Psychological Association. (1987). *Casebook on ethical principles of psychologists.* Washington, DC: Author.

American Psychological Association. (1992). *Ethical principles of psychologists and code of conduct.* Washington, DC: Author.

American Psychological Association. (1994). Guidelines for custody evaluations in divorce proceedings. *American Psychologist, 49,* 677–680.

American Psychological Association, Division of Industrial/Organizational Psychology. (1980). *Principles for the validation and use of personnel selection procedures.* Berkeley, CA: Author.

Ames, L. B., Learned, J., Metraux, R. W., & Walker, R. N. (1952). *Child Rorschach responses.* New York: Hoeber.

Amrine, M. (1965). The 1965 congressional inquiry into testing: A commentary. *American Psychologist, 20,* 859–870.

Anastasi, A. (1988). *Psychological testing* (6th ed.). New York: Macmillan.

Andrews, F. M., & Withey, S. B. (1976). *Social indicators of well-being: America's perception of life quality.* New York: Plenum.

Angyal, A. (1941). *Foundations for a science of personality.* London: Commonwealth Fund and Oxford University Press.

Ansbacher, H. L. (1951). The history of the leaderless group discussion technique. *Psychological Bulletin, 48,* 383–391.

Archer, R. P., Belevich, J. K. S., & Elkins, D. E. (1994). Item-level and scale-level factor structures of the MMPI-A. *Journal of Personality Assessment, 62,* 332–345.

Argyle, M. (1972). Non-verbal communication in human social interaction. In R. Hinde (Ed.), *Non-verbal communication.* New York: Cambridge University Press.

Arkes, H. R. (1981). Impediments to accurate clinical judgment and possible ways to minimize their impact. *Journal of Consulting and Clinical Psychology, 49,* 323–330.

Aronson, D. E., & Akamatsu, T. J. (1981). Validation of a Q-sort task to assess MMPI skills. *Journal of Clinical Psychology, 37,* 831–836.

Aronson, M. L. (1953). A study of the Freudian theory of paranoia by means of the Blacky pictures. *Journal of Projective Techniques, 17,* 3–19.

Asch, S. E. (1946). Forming impressions of personality. *Journal of Abnormal and Social Psychology, 41,* 258–290.

Ashton, S. G., & Goldberg, L. R. (1973). In response to Jackson's challenge: The comparative validity of personality scales constructed by the external (empirical) strategy and scales developed intuitively by experts, novices, and laymen. *Journal of Research in Personality, 7,* 1–20.

Association of Personnel Test Publishers. (1991). *Model guidelines for pre-employment integrity testing programs.* Washington, DC: Author.

Bailis, D. S., Darley, J. M., Waxman, T. L., & Robinson, P. H. (1995). Community standards of liability and the insanity defense. *Law and Human Behavior, 19,* 425–446.

Bales, R. F. (1950). *Interaction process analysis.* Cambridge, MA: Addison-Wesley.

Bandura, A. (1986). *Social foundations of thought and action.* Englewoood Cliff, NJ: Prentice-Hall.

Bandura, A., Lipsher, D. H., & Miller, P. E. (1960). Psychotherapists' approach-avoidance reactions to patients' expressions of hostility. *Journal of Consulting Psychology, 24,* 1–8.

Barker, R., Kounin, J., & Wright, H. F. (Eds.). (1943). *Child behavior and development.* New York: McGraw-Hill.

Barker, R., & Wright, H. F. (1951). *One boy's day.* New York: Harper.

Barker, R., & Wright, H. F. (1955). *Midwest and its children: The psychological ecology of an American town.* New York: Harper & Row.

Barrick, M. R., & Mount, M. K. (1991). The Big Five personality dimensions and job performance: A meta-analysis. *Personnel Psychology, 44,* 1–26.

Barrick, M. R., & Mount, M. K. (1993). Autonomy as a moderator of the relationships between the Big Five personality dimensions and job performance. *Journal of Applied Psychology, 78,* 111–118.

Barrick, M. R., Mount, M. K., & Strauss, J. P. (1993). Conscientiousness and performance of sales representatives: Test of the mediating effects of goal setting. *Journal of Applied Psychology, 78,* 715–722.

Barthell, C. N., & Holmes, D. S. (1968). High school yearbooks: A nonreactive measure of social isolation in graduates who later become schizophrenics. *Journal of Abnormal Psychology, 73,* 313–316.

Bartol, C. R., & Bartol, A. M. (1994). *Psychology and law: Research and application* (2nd ed.). Pacific Grove, CA: Brooks/Cole.

Bartram, D. (1994). Computer-based assessment. *International Review of Industrial and Organizational Psychology, 9,* 31–69.

Bass, B. M. (1954). The leaderless group discussion. *Psychological Bulletin, 51,* 465–492.

Bass, B. M. (1960). *Leadership, psychology and organizational behavior.* New York: Harper & Row.

Bass, B. M. (1985). *Leadership beyond expectations.* New York: Free Press.

Bass, B. M. (1990). *Bass and Stogdill's handbook of leadership* (3rd ed.). New York: Free Press.

Bass, B. M., & Avolio, B. J. (1990). *Transformational leadership development: Manual for the Multifactor Leadership Questionnaire.* Palo Alto, CA: Consulting Psychologists Press.

Bass, B. M., & Coates, C. H. (1952). Forecasting officer potential using the leaderless group discussion. *Journal of Abnormal and Social Psychology, 47,* 321–325.

Beck, A. T. (1986). Hopelessness as a predictor of eventual suicide. In J. J. Mann & M. Stanley (Eds.), *Psychology of suicidal behaviors.* New York: New York Academy of Sciences.

Beck, A. T., Kovacs, M., & Weissman, A. (1979). Assessment of suicidal ideation: Scale for suicidal ideation. *Journal of Consulting and Clinical Psychology, 47,* 343–352.

Beck, A. T., Schuyler, D., & Herman, I. (1974). Development of suicidal intent scales. In A. T. Beck, H. L. P. Resnick, & D. J. Lettieri (Eds.), *The predictions of suicide.* Bowie, MD: Charles Press.

Beck, A. T., Brown, G., Berchik, R. J., Stewart, B. L., & Steer, R. A. (1990). Relationship between hopelessness and ultimate suicide: A replication with psychiatric outpatients. *American Journal of Psychiatry, 147,* 190–195.

Beck, S. J., Beck, A. G., Levitt, E. E., & Molish, H. B. (1961). *Rorschach's test: I. Basic processes* (3rd ed.). New York: Grune & Stratton.

Becker, J. V., & Kaplan, M. S. (1990). Assessment of the adult sex offender. In P. McReynolds, J. C. Rosen, & G. J. Chelune (Eds.), *Advances in psychological assessment* (Vol. 7). New York: Plenum.

Beidel, D. C., Turner, S. M., Jacob, R. G., & Cooley, M. R. (1989). Assessment of social phobia: Reliability of an impromptu speech task. *Journal of Anxiety Disorders, 3,* 149–158.

Bell, H. M. (1939). *The adjustment inventory.* Palo Alto, CA: Consulting Psychologists Press.

Bellack, A. S. (1979). A critical appraisal of strategies for assessing social skill. *Behavioral Assessment, 1,* 157–176.

Bellack, A. S., & Hersen, M. (Eds.). (1988). *Behavioral assessment* (3rd ed.). New York: Pergamon.

Bellak, L. (1954). *The Thematic Apperception Test and the Children's Apperception Test in clinical use.* New York: Grune & Stratton.

Bellak, L. (1975). *The TAT, CAT, and SAT in clinical use* (3rd ed.). New York: Grune & Stratton.

Bem, D. J., & Allen, A. (1974). On predicting some of the people some of the time: The search for cross-situational consistencies in behavior. *Psychological Review, 81,* 506–520.

Bender, L. (1938). A visual motor test and its clinical use. *American Journal of Orthopsychiatry,* Research Monograph No. 3.

Bender, L. (1946). *Instructions for the use of the Visual Motor Gestalt Test.* New York: American Orthopsychiatric Association.

Bennett, G. K. (1967). Testing and privacy. In W. W. Willingham (Ed.), Invasion of privacy in research and testing. *Journal of Educational Measurement, 4*(Suppl.), 7–10.

Benton, A. L. (1994). Neuropsychological assessment. *Annual Review of Psychology, 45,* 1–23.

Bentz, V. J. (1990). Contextual issues in predicting high-level leadership performance. In K. E. Clark & M. B. Clark (Eds.), *Measures of leadership.* West Orange, NJ: Leadership Library of America.

Berg, I. A. (1955). Response bias and personality: The Deviation Hypothesis. *Journal of Psychology, 40,* 60–71.

Berg, I. A. (1957). Deviant responses and deviant people: The formulation of the Deviation Hypothesis. *Journal of Counseling Psychology, 4,* 154–161.

Berg, I. A. (1959). The unimportance of test item content. In B. M. Bass & I. A. Berg (Eds.), *Objective approaches to personality assessment.* Princeton: Van Nostrand.

Berg, R., Franzen, M., & Wedding, D. (1987). *Screening for brain impairment: A manual for mental health practice.* New York: Springer.

Berger, S. G., Chibnall, J. T., & Gfeller, S. D. (1994). The Category Test: A comparison of computerized and standard versions. *Assessment, 1,* 255–258.

Bernreuter, R. N. (1939). *The Personality Inventory.* Palo Alto, CA: Consulting Psychologists Press.

Bersoff, D. N. (1973). Silk purses into sow's ears: The decline of psychological testing and a suggestion for its redemption. *American Psychologist, 28,* 892–899.

Billingslea, F. Y. (1963). The Bender-Gestalt: A review and perspective. *Psychological Bulletin, 60,* 233–251.

Bingham, W. V. D., & Moore, B. V. (1959). *How to interview* (4th ed.). New York: Harper & Row.

Bjorkly, S. (1995). Prediction of aggression in psychiatric patients: A review of prospective prediction studies. *Clinical Psychology Review, 15,* 475–502.

Blanchard, E. B., & Epstein, L. H. (1978). *A biofeedback primer.* Reading, MA: Addison-Wesley.

Blazer, D., George, L. K., & Hughes, D. (1991). The epidemiology of anxiety disorders: An age comparison. In C. Salzman & B. D. Lebowitz (Eds.), *Anxiety in the elderly: Treatment and research.* New York: Springer.

Block, J. (1961). *The Q-sort method in personality assessment and psychiatric research.* Springfield, IL: Thomas.

Block, J. (1965). *The challenge of response sets*. New York: Appleton-Century-Crofts.

Block, J. (1971). *Lives through time*. Berkeley, CA: Bancroft Books.

Block, J. (1978). *The Q-sort method in personality assessment and psychiatric research*. Palo Alto, CA: Consulting Psychologists Press.

Block, J. (1994). *California Q-Sort, Revised*. Palo Alto, CA: Mind Garden.

Block, J. (1995). A contrarian view of the five-factor approach to personality description. *Psychological Bulletin, 117*, 187–213.

Block, J. H., & Block, J. (1980). The role of ego-control and ego-resiliency in the organization of behavior. In W. A. Collins (Ed.), *Minnesota Symposium on Child Psychology* (Vol. 13). Hillsdale, NJ: Erlbaum.

Bloxom, B. M. (1978). Review of the Sixteen Personality Factors Questionnaire. In O. K. Buros (Ed.), *Eighth mental measurements yearbook*. Highland Park, NJ: Gryphon.

Blum, G. S. (1949). A study of the psychoanalytic theory of psychosexual development. *Genetic Psychology Monographs, 39*, 3–99.

Blum, G. S. (1950). *The Blacky Pictures*. New York: Psychological Corporation.

Blum, G. S. (1951). *Revised scoring system for the research use of the Blacky Pictures*. Unpublished manuscript.

Blum, G. S. (1962). A guide for research use of the Blacky Pictures. *Journal of Projective Techniques, 26*, 3–29.

Blum, G. S., & Kaufman, J. B. (1952). Two patterns of personality dynamics in male peptic ulcer patients as suggested by responses to the Blacky Pictures. *Journal of Clinical Psychology, 8*, 273–278.

Boring, E. G. (1929). *A history of experimental psychology*. New York: Appleton-Century-Crofts.

Bowers, K. S. (1973). Situationism in psychology: An analysis and a critique. *Psychological Review, 80*, 307–336.

Bray, D. W. (1982). The assessment center and the study of lives. *American Psychologist, 37*, 180–189.

Bray, D. W., & Byham, W. C. (1991). Assessment centers and their derivatives. *Journal of Continuing Higher Education, 39*, 8–11.

Bray, D. W., & Grant, D. L. (1966). The assessment center in the measurement of potential for business management. *Psychological Monographs, 80*, 1–17 (Whole No. 625).

Bray, D. W., & Howard, A. (1983). Personality and the assessment center method. In C. D. Spielberger & J. N. Butcher (Eds.), *Advances in personality assessment* (Vol. 3). Hillsdale, NJ: Erlbaum.

Brayfield, A. H. (Ed.). (1965). Testing and public policy. *American Psychologist, 20*, 867–1005.

Brehm, S. S. (1976). *The application of social psychology to clinical practice*. Washington, DC: Hemisphere.

Briggs, I. M. (1980). *Introduction to type*. Palo Alto, CA: Consulting Psychologists Press.

Briggs, K. C., & Myers, I. B. (1943). *Myers-Briggs Type Indicator*. Palo Alto, CA: Consulting Psychologists Press.

Briggs, K. C., & Myers, I. B. (1985). *Myers-Briggs Type Indicator*. Palo Alto, CA: Consulting Psychologists Press.

Briggs, P. F. (1959). Eight item clusters for use with the M-B History Record. *Journal of Clinical Psychology, 15*, 22–28.

Briggs, P. F., Rouzer, D. G., Hamburg, R. L., & Holman, T. R. (1972). Seven scales for the Minnesota-Briggs History Record with reference group data. *Journal of Clinical Psychology, 28*, 431–438.

Brim, O. G. (1965). American attitudes toward intelligence tests. *American Psychologist, 20*, 123–124.

Brim, O. G. (1967). Reaction to the papers. In W. W. Willingham (Ed.), Invasion of privacy in research and testing. *Journal of Educational Measurement, 4*(Suppl.), 29–31.

Brislin, R. W., Lonner, W. J., & Thorndike, R. M. (1973). *Cross-cultural research methods.* New York: Wiley.

Brock, T. C., & Guidice, C. D. (1963). Stealing and temporal orientation. *Journal of Abnormal and Social Psychology, 66,* 91–94.

Brown, S. H. (1978). Long term validity of a personal history item scoring procedure. *Journal of Applied Psychology, 63,* 673–676.

Brozovich, R. (1970). Fakability of scores on the group personality projection test. *Journal of Genetic Psychology, 117,* 143–148.

Buchwald, A. M. (1965). Values and the uses of tests. *Journal of Consulting Psychology, 29,* 49–54.

Buck, J. N. (1948a). The H-T-P test. *Journal of Clinical Psychology, 4,* 151–159.

Buck, J. N. (1948b). The H-T-P technique: A qualitative and scoring manual, part one. *Journal of Clinical Psychology, 4,* 319–396.

Buck, J. N. (1949). The H-T-P technique: A qualitative and scoring manual, part two. *Journal of Clinical Psychology, 5,* 37–76.

Burgess, E. W. (1928). Factors determining success or failure on parole. In A. A. Bruce (Ed.), *The workings of the indeterminate sentence law and the parole system in Illinois.* Springfield, IL: Illinois Board of Parole.

Burish, M. (1984). Approaches to personality inventory construction: A comparison of merits. *American Psychologist, 39,* 214–229.

Burke, W. W. (1994). *Leadership Assessment Inventory* (Rev. ed.). Pelham, NY: W. Warner Burke.

Burns, J. M. (1978). *Leadership.* New York: Harper & Brothers.

Buros, O. K. (Ed.). (1978). *Eighth mental measurements yearbook.* Highland Park, NJ: Gryphon.

Bushard, P., & Howard, D. A. (1995). *Resource guide for custody evaluators.* Madison, WI: Association of Family and Conciliation Courts.

Buss, A. H. (1959). The effect of item style on social desirability and frequency of endorsement. *Journal of Consulting Psychology, 23,* 510–513.

Buss, A. H., & Durkee, A. (1957). An inventory for assessing different kinds of hostility. *Journal of Consulting Psychology, 21,* 343–349.

Buss, A. H., & Plomin, R. (1975). *A temperament theory of personality development.* New York: Wiley.

Butcher, J. N. (1978a). Review of MMPI Automated Psychological Assessment. In O. K. Buros (Ed.), *Eighth mental measurements yearbook.* Highland Park, NJ: Gryphon.

Butcher, J. N. (1978b). Review of MMPI computerized scoring and interpretation services. In O. K. Buros (Ed.), *Eighth mental measurements yearbook.* Highland Park, NJ: Gryphon.

Butcher, J. N. (1987a). *Computerized psychological assessment: A practitioner's guide.* New York: Basic Books.

Butcher, J. N. (1987b). The use of computers in psychological assessment: An overview of practices and issues. In J. N. Butcher (Ed.), *Computerized psychological assessment: A practitioner's guide.* New York: Basic Books.

Butcher, J. N. (1989). *MMPI-2: User's guide: The Minnesota Report: Adult Clinical System.* Minneapolis, MN: National Computer Systems.

Butcher, J. N. (1990). *MMPI-2 in psychological treatment.* New York: Oxford University Press.

Butcher, J. N., Dahlstrom, W. G., Graham, J. R., Tellegen, A., & Kaemmer, B. (1989). *MMPI-2: Manual for administration and scoring.* Minneapolis: University of Minnesota Press.

Butcher, J. N., Graham, J. R., Williams, C. L., & Ben-Porath, Y. S. (1990). *Development and use of the MMPI-A content scales.* Minneapolis: University of Minnesota Press.

Butcher, J. N., Kendall, P. C., & Hoffman, N. (1980). MMPI short forms: Caution. *Journal of Consulting and Clinical Psychology, 48,* 275–278.

Butcher, J. N., & Pancheri, F. (1976). *A handbook of cross-national MMPI research.* Minneapolis: University of Minnesota Press.

Butcher, J. N., & Williams, C. L. (1992). *Essentials of MMPI-2 and MMPI-A interpretation.* Minneapolis: University of Minnesota Press.

Butcher, J. N., Williams, C. L., Graham, J. R., Archer, R. P., Tellegen, A., Ben-Porath, Y. S., & Kaemmer, B. (1992). *Minnesota Multiphasic Personality Inventory-A: Manual for administration, scoring, and interpretation.* Minneapolis: University of Minnesota Press.

Campbell, D. P. (1991). *Manual for the Campbell Leadership Index.* Minneapolis, MN: National Computer Systems.

Campbell, D. T. (1957). Factors relevant to the validity of experiments in social settings. *Psychological Bulletin, 54,* 297–312.

Campbell, D. T., & Fiske, D. W. (1959). Convergent and discriminant validation by the multitrait-multimethod matrix. *Psychological Bulletin, 56,* 81–105.

Campion, M. A., Pursell, E. D., & Brown, B. K. (1988). Structured interviewing: Raising the psychometric properties of the employment interview. *Personnel Psychology, 41,* 25–42.

Canter, F. M. (1963). Simulation on the California Psychological Inventory and the adjustment of the simulator. *Journal of Consulting Psychology, 27,* 252–256.

Carlson, J. G. (1985). Recent assessments of the Myers-Briggs Type Indicator. *Journal of Personality Assessment, 49,* 356–365.

Carp, A. L., & Shavzin, A. R. (1950). The susceptibility to falsification of the Rorschach psychodiagnostic technique. *Journal of Consulting Psychology, 14,* 230–233.

Cascio, W. F. (1995). Whither industrial and organizational psychology in a changing world of work. *American Psychologist, 50,* 928–939.

Cascio, W. L., & Silbey, V. (1979). Utility of the assessment center as a selection device. *Journal of Applied Psychology, 64,* 107–118.

Caspi, A., Block, J., Block, J. H., Klopp, B., Lynam, D., Moffitt, T. E., & Stouthamer-Loeber, M. (1992). A "common-language" version of the California Child Q-Set for personality assessment. *Psychological Assessment, 4,* 512–523.

Cattell, R. B. (1945). The principal trait clusters for describing personality. *Psychological Bulletin, 42,* 129–169.

Cattell, R. B. (1946). *Description and measurement of personality.* New York: World Book.

Cattell, R. B. (1950). *Personality: A systematic theoretical and factual study.* New York: McGraw-Hill.

Cattell, R. B. (1957). *Personality and motivation: Structure and measurement.* New York: World Book.

Cattell, R. B. (1964). Validity and reliability: A proposed more basic set of concepts. *Journal of Educational Psychology, 55,* 1–22.

Cattell, R. B. (1965). *The scientific analysis of personality.* Baltimore: Penguin.

Cattell, R. B., Eber, H. W., & Tatsuoka, M. M. (1970). *Handbook for the Sixteen Personality Factor Questionnaire (16 PF).* Champaign, IL: Institute for Personality and Ability Testing.

Chapman, L. J. (1967). Illusory correlation in observational report. *Journal of Verbal Learning and Verbal Behavior, 6,* 151–155.

Chapman, L. J., & Chapman, J. P. (1967). Genesis of popular but erroneous psychodiagnostic observations. *Journal of Abnormal Psychology, 72,* 193–204.

Chapman, L. J., & Chapman, J. P. (1969). Illusory correlation as an obstacle to the use of valid psychodiagnostic signs. *Journal of Abnormal Psychology, 74,* 271–280.

Chapman, L. J., & Chapman, J. P. (1971). Associatively based illusory correlation as a source of psychodiagnostic folklore. In L. D. Goodstein & R. I. Lanyon (Eds.), *Readings in personality assessment.* New York: Wiley.

Chapman, S. L., & Brena, S. F. (1990). Patterns of conscious failure to provide accurate self-report data in patients with low back pain. *Clinical Journal of Pain, 6,* 178–190.

Chen, W. J., Faraone, S. V., Biederman, J., & Tsuang, M. T. (1994). Diagnostic accuracy of the Child Behavior Checklist scales for attention-deficit hyperactivity disorder: A receiver-operating characteristic analysis. *Journal of Consulting and Clinical Psychology, 62,* 1017–1025.

Childs, A., & Kleinoski, R. J. (1986). Successfully predicting career success: An application of the biological inventory. *Journal of Applied Psychology, 71,* 3–8.

Choca, J. P., Shanley, L. A., & Van Denberg, E. V. (1992). *Interpretive guide to the Millon Clinical Multiaxial Inventory.* Washington, DC: American Psychological Association.

Clark, K. E., & Clark, M. B. (Eds.). (1990). *Measures of leadership.* West Orange, NJ: Leadership Library of America.

Cleveland, S. E. (1976). Reflections on the rise and fall of psychodiagnosis. *Professional Psychology, 8,* 309–318.

Clum, G. A., & Hoiberg, A. (1971). Diagnoses as moderators of the relationship between biographical variables and psychiatric decisions in a combat zone. *Journal of Consulting and Clinical Psychology, 37,* 209–214.

Coddington, R. D. (1972). The significance of life events as etiologic factors in the diseases of children: 1. A survey of professional workers. *Journal of Psychosomatic Research, 16,* 7–18.

Cohen, R. J., Swerdlik, M. E., & Smith, D. K. (1992). *Psychological assessment and testing.* Mountain View, CA: Mayfield.

Committee on Ethical Guidelines for Forensic Psychologists. (1991). Specialty guidelines for forensic psychologists. *Law and Human Behavior, 15,* 655–665.

Conners, C. K. (1989). *Manual for Conners' Rating Scales.* Toronto: Multi-Health Systems.

Conoley, J. C., & Kramer, J. J. (Eds.). (1989). *Tenth mental measurements yearbook.* Lincoln: University of Nebraska, Buros Institute of Mental Measurements.

Conway, J. M., Jako, R. A., & Goodman, D. F. (1995). A meta-analysis of inter-rater and internal consistency reliability of selection interviews. *Journal of Applied Psychology, 80,* 565–579.

Cooper, D. (1990). Factor structure of the Edwards Personal Preference Schedule in a vocational rehabilitation sample. *Journal of Clinical Psychology, 46,* 421–425.

Cornell, D. C., & Hawk, G. L. (1989). Clinical presentation of malingerers diagnosed by expert forensic psychologists. *Law and Human Behavior, 13,* 375–383.

Costa, P. T., Jr., & McCrae, R. R. (1986). Personality stability and its implications for clinical psychology. *Clinical Psychology Review, 6,* 407–423.

Costa, P. T., Jr., & McCrae, R. R. (1992a). Four ways five factors are basic. *Personality and Individual Differences, 13,* 653–665.

Costa, P. T., Jr., & McCrae, R. (1992b). *NEO PI-R professional manual.* Odessa, FL: Psychological Assessment Resources.

Costa, P. T., Jr., McCrae, R. R., & Arenberg, D. (1980). Enduring dispositions in adult males. *Journal of Personality and Social Psychology, 38,* 793–800.

Costa, P. T., Jr., & Widiger, T. A. (Eds.). (1992). *Personality disorders and the five-factor model of personality.* Washington, DC: American Psychological Association.

Costello, E. J., Edelbrock, C. S., & Costello, A. J. (1985). Validity of the NIMH Diagnostic Interview for Children: A comparison between psychiatric and pediatric referrals. *Journal of Abnormal Child Psychology, 13,* 579–595.

Couch, A., & Keniston, K. (1960). Yeasayers and naysayers: Agreeing response set as a personality variable. *Journal of Abnormal and Social Psychology, 60,* 151–174.

Cresswell, D. L., & Lanyon, R. I. (1981). Validation of a screening battery for psychogeriatric assessment. *Journal of Gerontology, 36,* 435–440.

Crites, J. O., Bechtoldt, H. P., Goodstein, L. D., & Heilbrun, A. B. (1961). A factor analysis of the California Psychological Inventory. *Journal of Applied Psychology, 45,* 408–414.

Cronbach, L. J. (1941). An experimental comparison of the multiple true-false and multiple multiple-choice tests. *Journal of Educational Psychology, 32,* 533–543.

Cronbach, L. J. (1942). Studies of acquiescence as a factor in the true-false test. *Journal of Educational Psychology, 32,* 401–415.

Cronbach, L. J. (1946). Response sets and test validity. *Educational and Psychological Measurement, 6,* 475–494.

Cronbach, L. J. (1950). Further evidence on response sets and test design. *Educational and Psychological Measurement, 10,* 3–31.

Cronbach, L. J. (1951). Coefficient alpha and the internal structure of tests. *Psychometrika, 16,* 297–334.

Cronbach, L. J. (1984). *Essentials of psychological testing* (4th ed.). New York: Harper & Row.

Cronbach, L. J., & Gleser, G. C. (1965). *Psychological tests and personnel decisions.* Urbana: University of Illinois Press. (Original work published 1957)

Cronbach, L. J., Gleser, G. C., Nanda, H., & Rajaratnam, N. (1972). *The dependability of behavioral measurement: Theory of generalizability for scores and profiles.* New York: Wiley.

Cronbach, L. J., & Meehl, P. E. (1955). Construct validity in psychological tests. *Psychological Bulletin, 52,* 281–302.

Crowne, D. P., & Marlowe, D. (1960). A new scale of social desirability independent of psychopathology. *Journal of Consulting Psychology, 24,* 349–354.

Cundick, B. P. (1985). Review of the Holtzman Inkblot Technique. In J. V. Mitchell, Jr. (Ed.), *Ninth mental measurements yearbook.* Lincoln: University of Nebraska, Buros Institute of Mental Measurements.

Cunningham, M. R., Wong, D. T., & Barbee, A. P. (1994). Self-presentation dynamics on overt integrity tests: Experimental studies of the Reid Report. *Journal of Applied Psychology, 79,* 643–658.

Cureton, E. E. (1950). Reliability, validity, and baloney. *Educational and Psychological Measurement, 10,* 94–96.

Dahlstrom, L. E. (1986). MMPI findings on other American minority groups. In W. G. Dahlstrom, D. Lachar, & L. E. Dahlstrom (Eds.), *MMPI patterns of American minorities.* Minneapolis: University of Minnesota Press.

Dahlstrom, W. G. (1969). Invasion of privacy: How legitimate is the current concern over this issue? In J. N. Butcher (Ed.), *MMPI: Research developments and clinical applications.* New York: McGraw-Hill.

Dahlstrom, W. G. (1993). Tests: Small samples, large consequences. *American Psychologist, 48,* 393–399.

Dahlstrom, W. G., & Gynther, M. D. (1986). Previous MMPI research on Black Americans. In W. G. Dahlstrom, D. Lachar, & L. E. Dahlstrom (Eds.), *MMPI patterns of American minorities.* Minneapolis: University of Minnesota Press.

Dahlstrom, W. G., Lachar, D., & Dahlstrom, L. E. (Eds.). (1986a). *MMPI patterns of American minorities.* Minneapolis: University of Minnesota Press.

Dahlstrom, W. G., Lachar, D., & Dahlstrom, L. E. (1986b). Overview and conclusions. In W. G. Dahlstrom, D. Lachar, & L. E. Dahlstrom (Eds.), *MMPI patterns of American minorities.* Minneapolis: University of Minnesota Press.

Dahlstrom, W. G., & Welsh, G. S. (1960). *An MMPI handbook.* Minneapolis: University of Minnesota Press.

Dahlstrom, W. G., Welsh, G. S., & Dahlstrom, L. E. (1972). *An MMPI handbook: Vol. 1. Clinical interpretation* (Rev. ed.). Minneapolis: University of Minnesota Press.

Dahlstrom, W. G., Welsh, G. S., & Dahlstrom, L. E. (1975). *An MMPI handbook: Vol. 2. Research applications* (Rev. ed.). Minneapolis: University of Minnesota Press.

Dana, R. H. (1978). Review of the Rorschach. In O. K. Buros (Ed.), *Eighth mental measurements yearbook.* Highland Park, NJ: Gryphon.

Dana, R. H., & Cantrell, J. D. (1988). An update on the Millon Clinical Multiaxial Inventory (MCMI). *Journal of Clinical Psychology, 44,* 760–762.

Davies, J. D. (1955). *Phrenology: Fad and science.* New Haven, CT: Yale University Press.

Dawes, R. M. (1979). The robust beauty of improper linear models in decision making. *American Psychologist, 34,* 571–582.

Dawes, R. M. (1980). Apologia for using what works. *American Psychologist, 35,* 678.

Dawes, R. M. (1989). Experience and validity of clinical judgment: The illusory correlation. *Behavioral Sciences and the Law, 7,* 457–468.

Dawes, R. M., & Corrigan, B. (1974). Linear models in decision making. *Psychological Bulletin, 81,* 95–106.

Dawes, R. M., Faust, D., & Meehl, P. E. (1989). Clinical versus actuarial judgment. *Science, 243,* 1668–1674.

Dean, E. F. (1972). A lengthened Mini-Mult: The Midi-Mult. *Journal of Clinical Psychology, 28,* 68–71.

DeAngelis, T. (1995, November). ADA confounds use of psychological testing. *APA Monitor, 26,* 12.

DeVito, A. J. (1985). Review of the Myers-Briggs Type Indicator. In J. V. Mitchell, Jr. (Ed.), *Ninth mental measurements yearbook.* Lincoln: University of Nebraska, Buros Institute of Mental Measurements.

Dicken, C. F. (1959). Simulated patterns on the Edwards Personal Preference Schedule. *Journal of Applied Psychology, 43,* 372–378.

Diener, E. (1984). Subjective well-being. *Psychological Bulletin, 95,* 542–575.

Digman, J. M. (1990). Personality structure: The emergence of the five-factor model. *Annual Review of Psychology, 41,* 417–440.

Dion, K. K., Berscheid, E., & Walster, E. (1972). What is beautiful is good. *Journal of Personality and Social Psychology, 24,* 285–290.

Dombrose, L. A., & Slobin, M. A. (1958). The IES Test. *Perceptual and Motor Skills, 8,* 347–389.

Dougherty, T. W., Turban, D. B., & Callendar, J. C. (1994). Confirming first impressions in the employment interview: A field study of interviewer behavior. *Journal of Applied Psychology, 79,* 659–665.

Dowling, J. F., & Graham, J. R. (1976). Illusory correlation and the MMPI. *Journal of Personality Assessment, 40,* 531–538.

Downey, R. G., Medland, F. F., & Yates, L. G. (1976). Evaluation of a peer rating system for predicting subsequent promotion of senior military officers. *Journal of Applied Psychology, 61,* 206–209.

Drake, L. E., & Oetting, E. R. (1959). *An MMPI codebook for counselors.* Minneapolis: University of Minnesota Press.

Drummond, R. J. (1984). Review of the Edwards Personal Preference Schedule. In D. J. Keyser & R. J. Sweetland (Eds.), *Test critiques* (Vol. 1). Kansas City, MO: Test Corporation of America.

Duckworth, J. C. (1991). Response to Caldwell and Graham. *Journal of Counseling and Development, 69,* 572–573.

Duff, F. L. (1965). Item subtlety in personality inventory scales. *Journal of Consulting Psychology, 28,* 565–570.

Dush, D. M. (1985). Review of the Holtzman Inkblot Technqiue. In J. V. Mitchell (Ed.), *Ninth mental measurements yearbook.* Lincoln: University of Nebraska, Buros Institute of Mental Measurements.

Dusky v. United States, 362 U. S. 402 (1960).

Eaton, M. E., Altman, H., Scheff, S., & Sletten, I. W. (1970). Missouri Automated Psychiatric History for relatives and other informants. *Diseases of the Nervous System, 31,* 198–202.

Eaton, M. E., Sletten, I. W., Kitchen, A. D., & Smith, R. J., II. (1971). The Missouri Automated Psychiatric History: Symptom frequencies, sex differences, use of weapons, and other findings. *Comprehensive Psychiatry, 12,* 264–276.

Ebel, R. L. (1964a). The social consequences of educational testing. *School and Society, 92,* 331–334.

Ebel, R. L. (1964b). Must all tests be valid? *American Psychologist, 19,* 640–647.

Eberhardt, B. J., & Muchinsky, P. M. (1984). Structural validation of Holland's hexagonal model: Vocational classification through the use of biodata. *Journal of Applied Psychology, 44,* 141–145.

Edinger, J. D. (1979). Cross-validation of the Megargee MMPI typology for prisoners. *Journal of Consulting and Clinical Psychology, 47,* 234–242.

Edwards, A. L. (1953). The relationship between the judged desirability of a trait and the probability that the trait will be endorsed. *Journal of Applied Psychology, 37,* 90–93.

Edwards, A. L. (1954). *Manual: Edwards Personal Preference Schedule.* New York: Psychological Corporation.

Edwards, A. L. (1957). *The social desirability variable in personality assessment and research.* New York: Dryden.

Edwards, A. L. (1959). *Manual: Edwards Personal Preference Schedule* (Rev. ed.). New York: Psychological Corporation.

Edwards, A. L. (1964). Social desirability and performance on the MMPI. *Psychometrika, 29,* 295–308.

Einhorn, H. J., & Bass, A. R. (1971). Methodological considerations relevant to discrimination in employment testing. *Psychological Bulletin, 75,* 261–269.

Einhorn, J. (1986). Child custody in historical perspective: A study of changing social perceptions of divorce and child custody in Anglo-American law. *Behavioral Sciences and the Law, 4,* 119–135.

Ekehammar, B. (1974). Interactionism in personality from a historical perspective. *Psychological Bulletin, 81,* 1026–1048.

Ekman, P. (1985). *Telling lies: Cues to deceit in the marketplace, politics, and marriage.* New York: Norton.

Ekman, P., & O'Sullivan, M. (1991). Who can catch a liar? *American Psychologist, 46,* 913–920.

Elbert, J. C., & Holden, E. W. (1987). Child diagnostic assessment: Current training practices in clinical psychology internships. *Professional Psychology: Research and Practice, 6,* 587–596.

Elwood, R. W. (1993). Psychological tests and clinical discriminations: Beginning to address the base rate problem. *Clinical Psychology Review, 13,* 409–419.

Endicott, J., & Spitzer, R. L. (1972). Current and Past Psychopathology Scales (CAPPS). *Archives of General Psychiatry, 27,* 678–687.

Endicott, J., Spitzer, R. L., Fleiss, J. L., & Cohen, J. (1976). The Global Assessment Scale: A procedure for measuring overall severity of psychiatric disturbances. *Archives of General Psychiatry, 33,* 766–771.

Endler, N. S., & Magnusson, D. (1976). Toward an interactional psychology of personality. *Psychological Bulletin, 83,* 956–974.

England, G. W. (1961). *Development and use of weighted application blanks.* Dubuque, IA: Brown.

Equal Employment Opportunity Commission, Civil Service Commission, Department of Labor, & Department of Justice. (1978). Adoption by four agencies of Uniform Guidelines on Employee Selection. *Federal Register, 43,* 38290–38315.

Eron, L. D. (1948). Frequencies of themes and identifications in the stories of schizophrenic patients and non-hospitalized college students. *Journal of Consulting Psychology, 12,* 387–395.

Eron, L. D., & Walder, L. (1961). Test burning: II. *American Psychologist, 16,* 237–244.

Ervin, S. J. (1965). Why Senate hearings on psychological tests in government? *American Psychologist, 20,* 879–880.

Evenson, R. C., Sletten, I. W., Hedlund, J. L., & Faintich, D. M. (1974). CAPS: An automated evaluation system. *American Journal of Psychiatry, 131,* 531–534.

Exner, J. E., Jr. (1974). *The Rorschach: A comprehensive system.* New York: Wiley.

Exner, J. E., Jr. (1978). *The Rorschach: A comprehensive system* (Vol. 2). New York: Wiley.

Exner, J. E., Jr. (1986). *The Rorschach: A comprehensive system* (2nd ed.). New York: Wiley.

Exner, J. E., Jr. (1990). *A Rorschach workbook for the comprehensive system*. Asheville, NC: Rorschach Workshops.

Exner, J. E., Jr. (1991). *The Rorschach: A comprehensive system* (Vol. 2, 2nd ed.). New York: Wiley.

Exner, J. E., Jr. (1993). *The Rorschach: A comprehensive system* (Vol. 1, 3rd ed.). New York: Wiley.

Exner, J. E., Jr., & Andronikof-Sanglade, A. (1992). Rorschach changes following brief and short-term therapy. *Journal of Personality Assessment, 59*, 59–71.

Exner, J. E., Jr., & Ona, N. (1995). *RIAP-3: Rorschach Interpretation Assistance Program version 3.1*. Odessa, FL: Psychological Assessment Resources.

Exner, J. E., Jr., & Weiner, I. B. (1982). *The Rorschach: A comprehensive system* (Vol. 3). New York: Wiley.

Eysenck, H. J. (1947). *Dimensions of personality*. London: Routledge & Kegan Paul.

Eysenck, H. J. (1952). *The scientific study of personality*. London: Routledge & Kegan Paul.

Eysenck, H. J. (1953a). The logical basis of factor analysis. *American Psychologist, 8*, 105–114.

Eysenck, H. J. (1953b). *The structure of human personality*. New York: Wiley.

Eysenck, H. J. (1960). *The structure of human personality* (2nd ed.). London: Methuen.

Farberow, N. L., Shneidman, E. S., & Neuringer, C. (1966). Case history and hospitalization factors in suicides of neuropsychiatric hospital patients. *Journal of Nervous and Mental Disease, 142*, 32–44.

Faschingbauer, T. R. (1974). A 166-item written short form of the group MMPI: The FAM. *Journal of Consulting and Clinical Psychology, 42*, 645–655.

Faust, D. (1986). Research on human judgment and its application to clinical practice. *Professional Psychology: Research and Practice, 5*, 420–430.

Fear, R. A. (1978). *The evaluation interview* (2nd ed., rev.). New York: McGraw-Hill.

Feldman, M. J., & Graley, J. (1954). The effects of an experimental set to simulate abnormality on group Rorschach performance. *Journal of Projective Techniques, 18*, 326–334.

Festinger, L., Riecken, H. W., & Schachter, S. (1956). *When prophecy fails*. Minneapolis: University of Minnesota Press.

Fiedler, F. E. (1967). *A theory of leadership effectiveness*. New York: McGraw-Hill.

Fiedler, F. E. (1986). The contribution of cognitive resources to leadership performance. *Journal of Applied Social Psychology, 16*, 532–548.

Fingarette, H., & Hasse, A. F. (1979). *Mental disabilities and criminal responsibility*. Berkeley: University of California Press.

Finkel, N. J. (1989). The Insanity Defense Reform Act of 1984: Much ado about nothing. *Behavioral Sciences and the Law, 7*, 403–419.

Fischhoff, B. (1975). Hindsight≠foresight: The effect of outcome knowledge on judgment under uncertainty. *Journal of Experimental Psychology: Human Perception and Performance, 1*, 288–299.

Fischhoff, B., & Beyth, R. (1975). "I knew it would happen": Remembered probabilities of once-future things. *Organizational Behavior and Human Performance, 13*, 1–16.

Fischhoff, B., Slovic, P., & Lichtenstein, S. (1977). Knowing with certainty: The appropriateness of extreme confidence. *Journal of Experimental Psychology: Human Perception and Performance, 3*, 552–564.

Fiske, D. W. (1949). Consistency of the factorial structures of personality ratings from different sources. *Journal of Personality and Social Psychology, 44*, 329–344.

Flanagan, J. C. (1954). The critical incident technique. *Psychological Bulletin, 51*, 327–358.

Folstein, M. F., Romanoski, A. J., Nestadt, G., Chahal, R., Merchant, A., Shapiro, S., Kramer, M., Anthony, J., Gruenberg, E. M., & McHugh, P. R. (1985). Brief report on the clinical reappraisal of the Diagnostic Interview Schedule carried out at the Johns Hopkins site of the Epidemiological Catchment Area Program of the NIMH. *Psychological Medicine, 15*, 809–814.

Forehand, R., & Scarboro, M. E. (1975). An analysis of children's oppositional behavior. *Journal of Abnormal Child Psychology, 3,* 27–31.

Forer, B. R. (1949). The fallacy of personal validation: A classroom demonstration of gullibility. *Journal of Abnormal and Social Psychology, 44,* 118–123.

Forer, B. R. (1950). A structured sentence completion test. *Journal of Projective Techniques, 14,* 15–29.

Forer, B. R. (1957). *The Forer Structured Sentence Completion Test: Manual.* Los Angeles: Western Psychological Services.

Fosberg, I. A. (1938). Rorschach reactions under varied instructions. *Rorschach Research Exchange, 3,* 12–20.

Fosberg, I. A. (1941). An experimental study of the reliability of the Rorschach psychodiagnostic technique. *Rorschach Research Exchange, 5,* 72–84.

Foster, S. L., Bell-Dolan, D. J., & Burge, D. A. (1988). Behavioral observation. In A. S. Bellack & M. Hersen (Eds.), *Behavioral assessment: A practical handbook.* New York: Pergamon.

Fowler, R. D. (1966). *The MMPI notebook: A guide to the clinical use of the automated MMPI.* Nutley, NJ: Roche Psychiatric Service Institute.

Fowler, R. D. (1967). Computer interpretation of personality tests: The automated psychologist. *Comprehensive Psychiatry, 8,* 455–467.

Fowler, R. D. (1969). The current status of computer interpretation of psychological tests. *Supplement to the American Journal of Psychiatry, 125,* 21–27.

Fowler, R. D., & Butcher, J. N. (1986). Critique of Matarazzo's views on computerized testing: All sigma and no meaning. *American Psychologist, 41,* 94–95.

Frank, L. K. (1939). Projective methods for the study of personality. *Journal of Psychology, 8,* 389–413.

Fremer, J., Diamond, E. E., & Camera, W. J. (1989). Developing a code of fair testing practices in education. *American Psychologist, 44,* 1062–1067.

Friedman, A. F., Webb, J. T., & Lewak, R. (1989). *Psychological assessment with the MMPI.* Hillsdale, NJ: Erlbaum.

Fromm, E. (1947). *Man for himself.* New York: Holt, Rinehart and Winston.

Fulkerson, S. C. (1959). Individual differences in response validity. *Journal of Clinical Psychology, 15,* 169–173.

Furnham, A. (1990). The development of single trait personality theories. *Personality and Individual Differences, 11,* 923–929.

Gallagher, C. E. (1965). Opening remarks. In testimony before House Special Subcommittee on Invasion of Privacy of the Committee on Government Operations. *American Psychologist, 20,* 955–988.

Galton, F. (1884). Measurement of character. *Fortnightly Review, 42,* 179–185.

Gamble, K. R. (1972). The Holtzman Inkblot Techniques: A review. *Psychological Bulletin, 77,* 172–194.

Garb, H. N. (1984). The incremental validity of information used in personality assessment. *Clinical Psychology Review, 4,* 641–655.

Garb, H. N. (1986). The appropriateness of confidence ratings in clinical judgment. *Journal of Clinical Psychology, 42,* 190–197.

Garb, H. N. (1989). Clinical judgment, clinical training, and professional experience. *Psychological Bulletin, 105,* 387–396.

Garb, H. N. (1994). Judgment research: Implications for clinical practice and testimony in court. *Applied and Preventive Psychology, 3,* 173–183.

Gaugler, B. B., Rosenthal, D. B., Thornton, G. C., & Bentson, C. (1987). Meta-analysis of assessment center validity. *Journal of Applied Psychology, 72,* 493–511.

Gauquelin, M. (1973). *Cosmic influences on human behavior.* New York: Stein and Day.

Gdowski, C. L., Lachar, D., & Kline, R. B. (1985). A PIC profile typology of children and adolescents: I. Empirically derived alternative to traditional diagnosis. *Journal of Abnormal Psychology, 94,* 346–361.

Gearing, M. L., II. (1979). The MMPI as a primary differentiator and predictor of behavior in prison: A methodological critique and review of the recent literature. *Psychological Bulletin, 86,* 929–963.

Geer, J. H. (1980). Measurement of genital arousal in human males and females. In I. Martin & P. H. Venables (Eds.), *Techniques in psychophysiology.* New York: Wiley.

Ghiselli, E. E. (1956). Differentiation of individuals in terms of their predictability. *Journal of Applied Psychology, 40,* 374–377.

Ghiselli, E. E. (1960a). Differentiation of tests in terms of the accuracy with which they predict for a given individual. *Educational and Psychological Measurement, 20,* 675–684.

Ghiselli, E. E. (1960b). The prediction of predictability. *Educational and Psychological Measurement, 20,* 3–8.

Ghiselli, E. E. (1963). Moderating effects and differential reliability and validity. *Journal of Applied Psychology, 47,* 81–86.

Ghiselli, E. E. (1964). *Theory of psychological measurement.* New York: McGraw-Hill.

Giannetti, R. A. (1986). *GOLPH: Giannetti On-Line Psychosocial History: User's guide.* Minneapolis, MN: National Computer Systems.

Giannetti, R. A. (1987). The GOLPH psychosocial history: Response-contingent data acquisition and reporting. In J. Butcher (Ed.), *Computerized psychological assessment: A practitioner's guide.* New York: Basic Books.

Giannetti, R. A., Johnson, J. H., Klingler, D. E., & Williams, T. A. (1978). Comparison of linear and configural MMPI diagnostic methods with an uncontaminated criterion. *Journal of Consulting and Clinical Psychology, 46,* 1046–1052.

Gilberstadt, H. (1970). *Comprehensive MMPI code book for males.* Minneapolis, MN: Veterans Administration Hospital.

Gilberstadt, H., & Duker, J. (1965). *A handbook for clinical and actuarial MMPI interpretation.* Philadelphia: Saunders.

Gleser, G. C., & Ihilevich, D. (1969). An objective instrument for measuring defense mechanisms. *Journal of Consulting and Clinical Psychology, 33,* 51–60.

Glueck, B. C., Gullotta, G. P., & Ericson, R. P. (1980). Automation of behavior assessments: The computer-produced nursing note. In J. B. Sidowski, J. H. Johnson, & T. A. Williams (Eds.), *Technology in mental health care delivery systems.* Norwood, NJ: Ablex.

Glueck, S., & Glueck, E. T. (1930). *500 criminal careers.* New York: Knopf.

Goffman, E. (1959). *The presentation of self in everyday life.* Garden City, NY: Doubleday.

Goheen, H. W., & Mosel, J. N. (1959). Validity of the Employment Recommendation Questionnaire: II. Comparison with field investigations. *Personnel Psychology, 12,* 297–302.

Goldberg, L. R. (1959). The effectiveness of clinicians' judgments: The diagnosis of organic brain damage from the Bender-Gestalt test. *Journal of Consulting Psychology, 23,* 24–33.

Goldberg, L. R. (1965). Diagnosticians vs. diagnostic signs: The diagnosis of psychosis vs. neurosis from the MMPI. *Psychological Monographs, 79,* (9, Whole No. 602).

Goldberg, L. R. (1968). Simple models or simple processes? Some research on clinical judgments. *American Psychologist, 23,* 483–496.

Goldberg, L. R. (1969). The search for configural relationships in personality assessment: The diagnosis of psychosis vs. neurosis from the MMPI. *Multivariate Behavioral Research, 4,* 523–536.

Goldberg, L. R. (1970). Man vs. model of man: A rationale, plus some evidence, for a method of improving on clinical inferences. *Psychological Bulletin, 73,* 422–432.

Goldberg, L. R. (1971a). A historical survey of personality scales and inventories. In P. McReynolds (Ed.), *Advances in psychological assessment* (Vol. 2). Palo Alto, CA: Science and Behavior Books.

Goldberg, L. R. (1971b). Five models of clinical judgment: An empirical comparison between linear and nonlinear representations of the human inference process. *Organizational Behavior and Human Performance, 6,* 458–479.

Goldberg, L. R. (1972). Man vs. mean: The exploitation of group profiles for the construction of diagnostic classification systems. *Journal of Abnormal Psychology, 79,* 121–131.

Goldberg, L. R. (1978a). Differential attribution of trait-descriptive terms to oneself as compared to well-liked, neutral, and disliked others: A psychometric analysis. *Journal of Personality and Social Psychology, 36,* 1012–1028.

Goldberg, L. R. (1978b). Review of the Jackson Personality Inventory. In O. K. Buros (Ed.), *Eighth mental measurements yearbook.* Highland Park, NJ: Gryphon.

Goldberg, L. R. (1981). Language and individual differences: The search for universals in personality lexicons. In L. Wheeler (Ed.), *Review of personality and social psychology* (Vol 2). Beverly Hills, CA: Sage.

Goldberg, L. R. (1982). From ace to zombie: Some explorations in the language of personality. In C. D. Spielberger & J. N. Butcher (Eds.), *Advances in personality assessment* (Vol. 1). Hillsdale, NJ: Erlbaum.

Goldberg, L. R. (1990a). The development of markers for the Big-Five factor structure. *Psychological Assessment, 4,* 26–42.

Goldberg, L. R. (1990b). An alternative "description of personality": The Big-Five factor structure. *Journal of Personality and Social Psychology, 59,* 1216–1229.

Goldberg, L. R. (1991). Human mind versus regression equation: Five contrasts. In D. Cicchetti & W. M. Grove (Eds.), *Thinking clearly about psychology: Vol. 1. Matters of public interest.* Minneapolis: University of Minnesota Press.

Goldberg, L. R. (1993). The structure of phenotypic personality traits. *American Psychologist, 48,* 26–34.

Goldberg, L. R., Grenier, J. R., Guion, R. M., Sechrest, L. B., & Wing, H. (1991). *Questionnaires used in the prediction of trustworthiness in pre-employment selection decisions: An APA task force report.* Washington, DC: American Psychological Association.

Goldberg, L. R., & Slovic, P. (1967). Importance of test item content: An analysis of a corollary of the deviation hypothesis. *Journal of Counseling Psychology, 14,* 462–472.

Goldberg, L. R., & Werts, C. E. (1966). The reliability of clinicians' judgments: A multitrait-multimethod approach. *Journal of Consulting Psychology, 30,* 199–206.

Goldberg, P. A. (1965). A review of sentence completion methods in personality assessment. *Journal of Projective Techniques and Personality Assessment, 29,* 12–45.

Golden, C. J. (1979). *Clinical interpretation of objective psychological tests.* New York: Grune & Stratton.

Golden, M. (1964). Some effects of combining psychological tests on clinical inferences. *Journal of Consulting Psychology, 28,* 440–446.

Goldfried, M. R. (1979). Behavioral assessment: Where do we go from here? *Behavioral Assessment, 1,* 19–22.

Goldsmith, D. B. (1922). The use of the personal history blank as a salesmanship test. *Journal of Applied Psychology, 6,* 149–155.

Goldstein, G. (1986). The neuropsychology of schizophrenia. In I. Grant & K. M. Adams (Eds.), *Neuropsychological assessment of neuropsychiatric disorders.* New York: Oxford University Press.

Gonzalez, J. R., & Lanyon, R. I. (1982). A Spanish Psychological Screening Inventory. *Journal of Cross-Cultural Psychology, 13,* 71–85.

Goodenough, F. L. (1926). *Measurement of intelligence by drawings.* Yonkers-on-Hudson, NY: World Book.

Goodstein, L. D., & Schrader, W. J. (1963). An empirically-derived managerial key for the California Psychological Inventory. *Journal of Applied Psychology, 47,* 42–45.

Gordon, E. W., & Terrell, M. D. (1981). The changed social context of testing. *American Psychologist, 36,* 1167–1171.

Gordon, L. V. (1967). Clinical, psychometric and work-sample approaches in the prediction of success in Peace Corps training. *Journal of Applied Psychology, 51,* 111–119.

Gorham, D. R. (1967). Validity and reliability studies of a computer-based scoring system for inkblot responses. *Journal of Consulting Psychology, 31,* 65–70.

Gorham, D. R., Moseley, E. C., & Holtzman, W. W. (1968). Norms for the computer-scored Holtzman Inkblot Technique. *Perceptual and Motor Skills, 26,* 1279–1305.

Gottschalk, L. A., & Gleser, G. C. (1969). *The measurement of psychological states through the content analysis of verbal behavior.* Berkeley: University of California Press.

Gough, H. G. (1950). The *F* minus *K* dissimulation index for the MMPI. *Journal of Consulting Psychology, 14,* 408–413.

Gough, H. G. (1953). The construction of a personality scale to predict scholastic achievement. *Journal of Applied Psychology, 37,* 361–366.

Gough, H. G. (1954). Some common misconceptions about neuroticism. *Journal of Consulting Psychology, 18,* 289–292.

Gough, H. G. (1957). *California Psychological Inventory: Manual* (Rev. ed.). Palo Alto, CA: Consulting Psychologists Press.

Gough, H. G. (1962). Clinical versus statistical prediction in psychology. In L. Postman (Ed.), *Psychology in the making.* New York: Knopf.

Gough, H. G. (1965). Conceptual analysis of psychological test scores and other diagnostic variables. *Journal of Abnormal Psychology, 70,* 294–302.

Gough, H. G. (1972). *Manual for the Personnel Reaction Blank.* Palo Alto, CA: Consulting Psychologists Press.

Gough, H. G. (1984). A managerial potential scale for the California Psychological Inventory. *Journal of Applied Psychology, 69,* 233–240.

Gough, H. G. (1987). *California Psychological Inventory: Administrator's guide.* Palo Alto, CA: Consulting Psychologists Press.

Gough, H. G. (1990). Testing for leadership with the California Psychological Inventory. In K. E. Clark & M. B. Clark (Eds.), *Measures of leadership.* West Orange, NJ: Leadership Library of America.

Gough, H. G., & Heilbrun, A. L., Jr. (1983). *The Adjective Check List manual.* Palo Alto, CA: Consulting Psychologists Press.

Gough, H. G., McClosky, H., & Meehl, P. E. (1951). A personality scale for dominance. *Journal of Abnormal and Social Psychology, 46,* 360–366.

Gough, H. G., & Peterson, D. R. (1952). The identification and measurement of predispositional factors in crime and delinquency. *Journal of Consulting Psychology, 16,* 207–212.

Grady, M., & Ephross, P. H. (1977). A comparison of two methods for collecting social histories of psychiatric hospital patients. *Military Medicine, 142,* 524–526.

Graham, J. R. (1987). *The MMPI: A practical guide* (2nd ed.). New York: Oxford University Press.

Graham, J. R. (1990). *MMPI-2: Assessing personality and psychopathology.* New York: Oxford University Press.

Grayson, H. M., & Olinger, L. B. (1957). Simulation of "normalcy" by psychiatric patients on the MMPI. *Journal of Consulting Psychology, 21,* 73–77.

Greenberg, L. M., & Dupuy, T. R. (1993). *Interpretative manual for the T.O.V.A.* Los Alamitos, CA: Universal Attention Disorders.

Greene, R. L. (1980). *The MMPI: An interpretive manual.* New York: Grune & Stratton.

Greist, J. H., Klein, M. H., & Erdman, H. P. (1976). Routine on-line psychiatric diagnosis by computer. *American Journal of Psychiatry, 133,* 1405.

Gresham, F. M., & Elliott, S. N. (1990). *Social Skills Rating System,* Circle Pines, MN: American Guidance Service.

Grisso, T. (1986). *Evaluating competencies: Forensic assessments and instruments.* New York: Plenum.

Grisso, T. (1988). *Competency to stand trial evaluations: A manual for practice.* Sarasota, FL: Professional Resource Exchange.

Gross, A. M., & Wixted, J. T. (1988). Assessment of child behavior problems. In A. S. Bellack & M. Hersen (Eds.), *Behavioral assessment: A practical handbook* (3rd ed.). New York: Pergamon.

Gross, L. R. (1959). Effects of verbal and nonverbal reinforcement on the Rorschach. *Journal of Consulting Psychology, 23,* 66–68.

Gross, M. L. (1962). *The brain watchers.* New York: Random House.

Gross, M. L. (1965). Testimony before House Special Subcommittee on Invasion of Privacy of the Committee on Government Operations. *American Psychologist, 20,* 958–960.

Groth-Marnat, G. (1990). *Handbook of psychological assessment* (2nd ed.). New York: Wiley.

Guastello, S. J., & Rieke, M. L. (1990). The Barnum effect and validity of computer-based test interpretations: The Human Resource Development Project. *Psychological Assessment: A Journal of Consulting and Clinical Psychology, 2,* 186–190.

Guastello, S. J., & Rieke, M. L. (1991). A review and critique of honesty testing research. *Behavioral Sciences and the Law, 9,* 501–523.

Guilford, J. P. (1940). *An inventory of factors STDCR.* Beverly Hills, CA: Sheridan Supply Company.

Guilford, J. P. (Ed.). (1947). *Printed classification tests.* Washington, DC: U.S. Government Printing Office.

Guilford, J. P. (1948). The principal trait clusters for describing personality. *Psychological Bulletin, 42,* 129–169.

Guilford, J. P. (1959). *Personality.* New York: McGraw-Hill.

Guilford, J. P., & Martin, H. G. (1943a). *Personnel Inventory: Manual of directions and norms.* Beverly Hills, CA: Sheridan Supply Company.

Guilford, J. P., & Martin, H. G. (1943b). *The Guilford-Martin Inventory of Factors GAMIN: Manual of directions and norms.* Beverly Hills, CA: Sheridan Supply Company.

Guilford, J. P., & Zimmerman, W. S. (1949). *The Guilford-Zimmerman Temperament Survey: Manual of instructions and interpretations.* Beverly Hills, CA: Sheridan Supply Company.

Guion, R. M. (1965). *Personnel testing.* New York: McGraw-Hill.

Guion, R. M. (1976). Recruiting, selection, and job placement. In M. D. Dunnette (Ed.), *Handbook of industrial and organizational psychology.* Chicago: Rand McNally.

Guion, R. M. (1991). Personnel assessment, selection, and placement. In M. D. Dunnette & L. M. Hough (Eds.), *Handbook of industrial and organizational psychology* (Vol. 2, 2nd ed.). Palo Alto, CA: Consulting Psychologists Press.

Guion, R. M., & Gottier, R. F. (1965). The validity of personality measures in personnel selection. *Personnel Psychology, 18,* 135–164.

Gynther, M. D. (1979). Ethnicity and personality: An update. In J. N. Butcher (Ed.), *New developments in the use of the MMPI.* Minneapolis: University of Minnesota Press.

Gynther, M. D. (1981). Is the MMPI an appropriate assessment device for Blacks? *Journal of Black Psychology, 7,* 67–75.

Halbower, C. C. (1955). *A comparison of actuarial versus clinical prediction to classes discriminated by MMPI.* Doctoral dissertation, University of Minnesota, Minneapolis.

Hall, C. S., & Lindzey, G. (1978). *Theories of personality* (3rd ed.). New York: Wiley.

Hall, H. V. (1984). Predicting dangerousness for the courts. *American Journal of Forensic Psychology, 2,* 5–25.

Hall, L. P., & LaDriere, L. (1969). Patterns of performance on WISC Similarities in emotionally disturbed and brain-damaged children. *Journal of Consulting and Clinical Psychology, 33,* 357–364.

Halleck, S. L. (1980). *Law in the practice of psychiatry: A handbook for professionals.* New York: Plenum.

Halpert, H. P., Horvath, W. J., & Young, J. P. (1970). *An administrator's handbook on the application of operations research to the management of mental health systems.* Washington, DC:

National Institute of Mental Health, National Clearinghouse for Mental Health Information.

Hamilton, D. L. (1968). Personality attributes associated with extreme response style. *Psychological Bulletin, 69*, 192–203.

Hammer, E. F. (Ed.). (1958). *The clinical application of projective drawings.* Springfield, IL: Thomas.

Hammer, E. F. (1968). Projective drawings. In A. I. Rabin (Ed.), *Projective techniques in personality assessment.* New York: Springer.

Hammond, K. R., McClelland, G. H., & Mumpower, J. (1980). *Human judgment and decision making: Theories, methods, and procedures.* New York: Praeger.

Hammond, K. R., & Summers, D. A. (1965). Cognitive dependence on linear and nonlinear cues. *Psychological Review, 72*, 215–224.

Hampson, S. E., John, O. P., & Goldberg, L. R. (1986). Category breadth and hierarchical structure in personality: Studies of asymmetries in judgments of trait implications. *Journal of Personality and Social Psychology, 51*, 37–54.

Hart, H. (1923). Prediciting parole success. *Journal of Criminal Law and Criminology, 14*, 405–413.

Hartmann, D. P., Roper, B. L., & Bradford, D. C. (1979). Some relationships between behavioral and traditional assessment. *Journal of Behavioral Assessment, 1*, 3–21.

Hartshorne, H., & May, M. A. (1928). *Studies in deceit.* New York: Macmillan.

Hartshorne, H., & May, M. A. (1929). *Studies in the nature of character: Vol. 2. Studies in service and self-control.* New York: Macmillan.

Hartshorne, H., May, M. A., & Shuttleworth, F. K. (1930). *Studies in the nature of character: Vol. 3. Studies in the organization of character.* New York: Macmillan.

Hartwell, S. W., Hutt, M. L., Andrew, G., & Walton, R. E. (1951). The Michigan Picture Test: Diagnostic and therapeutic possibilities of a new projective test for children. *American Journal of Orthopsychiatry, 21*, 124–137.

Hase, H. D., & Goldberg, L. R. (1967). Comparative validities of different strategies of constructing personality inventory scales. *Psychological Bulletin, 67*, 231–248.

Hathaway, S. R. (1956a). Clinical intuition and inferential accuracy. *Journal of Personality, 24*, 223–250.

Hathaway, S. R. (1956b). Scales 5 (masculinity-femininity), 6 (paranoia), and 8 (schizophrenia). In G. S. Welsh & W. G. Dahlstrom (Eds.), *Basic readings on the MMPI in psychology and medicine.* Minneapolis: University of Minnesota Press.

Hathaway, S. R. (1959). Increasing clinical efficiency. In B. M. Bass & I. A. Berg (Eds.), *Objective approaches to personality assessment.* Princeton, NJ: Van Nostrand.

Hathaway, S. R. (1964). MMPI: Professional use by professional people. *American Psychologist, 19*, 204–210.

Hathaway, S. R., & McKinley, J. C. (1940). A multiphasic personality schedule (Minnesota): I. Construction of the schedule. *Journal of Psychology, 10*, 249–254.

Hathaway, S. R., & McKinley, J. C. (1951). *Minnesota Multiphasic Personality Inventory: Manual.* New York: Psychological Corporation.

Hathaway, S. R., & McKinley, J. C. (1989). *Minnesota Multiphasic Personality Inventory—2.* Minneapolis: University of Minnesota Press.

Hawkins, R. P., Berler, E. S., & DeLawyer, D. D. (1984, May). *Defining units of verbal behavior for applied analytic research.* Paper presented at the Third Annual Convention of the Association for Behavior Analysis, Nashville, TN.

Hawton, R., Salkovskis, P. M., Kirk, J., & Clark, D. M. (Eds.). (1989). *Cognitive behavior therapy for psychiatric problems.* Oxford, England: Oxford University Press.

Haynes, S. N. (1978). *Principles of behavioral assessment.* New York: Gardner.

Haynes, S. N. (1991). Clinical applications of psychophysiological assessment: An introduction and overview. *Psychological Assessment: A Journal of Consulting and Clinical Psychology, 3*, 307–308.

Haynes, S. N., & Wilson, C. C. (1979). *Behavioral assessment*. San Francisco: Jossey-Bass.

Heath, A. C. (1991). The genetics of personality. *Contemporary Psychology, 36,* 1063–1064.

Hedlund, J. L., Sletten, I. W., Evenson, R. C., Altman, H., & Cho, D. W. (1977). Automated psychiatric information systems: A critical review of Missouri's Standard System of Psychiatry (SSOP). *Journal of Operational Psychiatry, 8,* 5–26.

Hedlund, J. L., & Vieweg, B. W. (1987). Computer generated diagnosis. In C. G. Last & M. Hersen (Eds.), *Issues in diagnostic research*. New York: Plenum.

Heider, F. (1958). *The psychology of interpersonal relations*. New York: Wiley.

Heilbrun, A. B. (1963). Revision of the MMPI *K* correction procedure for improved detection of maladjustment in a normal college population. *Journal of Consulting Psychology, 25,* 161–165.

Heilbrun, A. B. (1964). Social-learning theory, social desirability, and the MMPI. *Psychological Bulletin, 61,* 377–387.

Heilbrun, A. B., & Goodstein, L. D. (1961a). Social desirability response set: Error or predictor variable? *Journal of Psychology, 51,* 321–329.

Heilbrun, A. B., & Goodstein, L. D. (1961b). The relationships between individually defined and group defined social desirability and performance on the Edwards Personal Preference Schedule. *Journal of Consulting Psychology, 25,* 200–204.

Helmes, E., & Reddon, J. R. (1993). A perspective on developments in assessing psychopathology: A critical review of the MMPI and MMPI-2. *Personality Bulletin, 113,* 453–471.

Helmreich, R., Bakeman, R., & Radloff, R. (1973). The Life History Questionnaire as a predictor of performance in Navy divers training. *Journal of Applied Psychology, 57,* 148–153.

Helzer, J. E., & Robins, L. N. (1988). The Diagnostic Interview Schedule: Its development, evolution, and use. *Social Psychiatry and Psychiatric Epidemiology, 23,* 6–16.

Henry, E. M., & Rotter, J. B. (1956). Situational influences on Rorschach responses. *Journal of Consulting Psychology, 20,* 457–462.

Henry, W. E. (1956). *The analysis of fantasy*. New York: Wiley.

Herjanic, B., & Campbell, W. (1977). Differentiating psychiatrically disturbed children on the basis of a structured interview. *Journal of Abnormal Child Psychology, 31,* 127–134.

Herman, C. P. (1992). The shape of man. *Contemporary Psychology, 37,* 525–526.

Hersey, P., & Blanchard, K. H. (1988). *Management of organizational behavior* (5th ed.). Englewood Cliffs, NJ: Prentice-Hall.

Hess, A. K. (1992). Review of the NEO Personality Inventory. In J. J. Kramer & J. C. Conoley (Eds.), *Eleventh mental measurements yearbook*. Lincoln: University of Nebraska, Buros Institute of Mental Measurements.

Heymans, G., & Wiersma, E. (1906). Beitrage zur Speziellen Psychologie auf Grund einer Massenunterschung. *Zeitschrift fur Psychologie, 43,* 81–127.

Hill, E. F. (1972). *The Holtzman Inkblot Technique*. San Francisco: Jossey-Bass.

Hillier, F. S., & Lieberman, G. J. (1967). *Introduction to operations research*. San Francisco: Holden-Day.

Himmelfarb, S., & Murrell, S. A. (1984). The prevalence and correlates of anxiety symptoms in older adults. *Journal of Psychology, 116,* 159–167.

Hirsh, S. K., & Kummerow, J. M. (1990). *Introduction to type in organizations* (2nd ed.). Palo Alto, CA: Consulting Psychologists Press.

Hobert, R., & Dunnette, M. D. (1967). Development of moderator variables to enhance the prediction of managerial effectiveness. *Journal of Applied Psychology, 51,* 50–64.

Hoch, A., & Amsden, G. S. (1913). A guide to the descriptive study of personality. *Review of Neurology and Psychiatry, 11,* 577–587.

Hoffman, P. J., Slovic, P., & Rorer, L. G. (1968). An analysis-of-variance model for the assessment of configural cue utilization in clinical judgment. *Psychological Bulletin, 69,* 338–349.

Hogan, R. T. (1978). Review of Personality Research Form. In O. K. Buros (Ed.), *Eighth mental measurements yearbook*. Highland Park, NJ: Gryphon.

Hogan, R. T. (1983). A socioanalytic theory of personality. In M. M. Page (Ed.), *1982 Nebraska Symposium on Motivation*. Lincoln: University of Nebraska Press.

Hogan, R. T. (1986). *Manual for the Hogan Personality Inventory*. Minneapolis, MN: National Computer Systems.

Hogan, R. T. (1992). *Hogan Personality Inventory: Manual*. Tulsa, OK: Hogan Assessment Systems.

Hogan, R. T., Curphy, G. J., & Hogan, J. (1994). What we know about leadership: Effectiveness and personality. *American Psychologist, 49*, 493–504.

Hogan, R. T., DeSoto, C. B., & Solano, C. (1977). Traits, tests, and personality research. *American Psychologist, 32*, 255–264.

Hogan, R. T., & Hogan, J. (1992). *Hogan Personality Inventory manual* (Rev. ed.). Tulsa, OK: Hogan Assessment Systems.

Hollinger, R., & Clark, J. (1983). *Theft by employees*. Lexington, MA: Lexington Books.

Holmen, M. G., Katter, R. V., Jones, A. M., & Richardson, I. F. (1956). *An assessment program for OCS candidates* (HumRRO Technical Reports 1956–26). Alexandria, VA: Human Resources Research Organization.

Holmes, D. S. (1974). The conscious control of thematic projection. *Journal of Consulting and Clinical Psychology, 42*, 323–329.

Holmes, T. H., & Rahe, R. H. (1967). The Social Readjustment Rating Scale. *Journal of Psychosomatic Research, 11*, 213–218.

Holt, R. R. (1958). Clinical and statistical prediction: A reformulation and some new data. *Journal of Abnormal and Social Psychology, 56*, 1–12.

Holt, R. R. (1970). Yet another look at clinical and statistical prediction: Or, is clinical psychology worthwhile? *American Psychologist, 25*, 337–349.

Holt, R. R. (1978). *Methods in clinical psychology: Vol. 1. Projective assessment*. New York: Plenum.

Holt, R. R. (1986). Clinical and statistical prediction: A retrospective and would-be integrative perspective. *Journal of Personality Assessment, 50*, 376–386.

Holt, R. R., & Luborsky, L. (1958). *Personality patterns of psychiatrists*. New York: Basic Books.

Holtzman, W. H. (1961). *Holtzman Inkblot Technique: Guide to administration and scoring*. New York: Psychological Corporation.

Holtzman, W. H., & Gorham, D. R. (1972). *Automated scoring and interpretation of the group-administered Holtzman Inkblot Test by computer in group psychological assessment*. Symposium presented at the annual convention of the American Psychological Association, Honolulu, HI.

Holtzman, W. H., Thorpe, J. S., Swartz, J. D., & Herron, E. W. (1961). *Inkblot perception and personality: Holtzman Inkblot Technique*. Austin: University of Texas Press.

Hoover, D. W., & Snyder, D. V. (1991). Validity of the computerized interpretive report for the Marital Satisfaction Inventory: A customer satisfaction study. *Psychological Assessment: A Journal of Consulting and Clinical Psychology, 3*, 213–217.

Hops, H., Biglan, A., Sherman, L., Arthur, J., Friedman, I., & Osteen, V. (1987). Home observations of family interactions of depressed women. *Journal of Consulting and Clinical Psychology, 55*, 341–346.

Horowitz, L. M., Inouye, D., & Siegelman, E. Y. (1979). On averaging judges' ratings to increase their correlations with an external criterion. *Journal of Consulting and Clinical Psychology, 47*, 453–458.

Hough, L. H., Eaton, N. K., Dunnette, M. D., Kamp, J. D., & McCloy, R. A. (1990). Criterion-related validities of personality constructs and the effects of response distortions on those validities. *Journal of Applied Psychology, 75*, 581–595.

Hough, L. M. (1984). Development and evaluation of the "achievement record" method of selecting and promoting professionals. *Journal of Applied Psychology, 69*, 135–146.

Howard, A., & Bray, D. W. (1988). *Managerial lives in transition: Advancing age and changing times*. New York: Guilford.

Huff, F. W. (1965). Use of actuarial description of abnormal personality in a mental hospital. *Psychological Reports, 17,* 224.

Huffcutt, A. I., & Arthur, W., Jr. (1994). Hunter and Hunter (1984) revisited: Interview validity for entry-level jobs. *Journal of Applied Psychology, 79,* 184–190.

Hughes, J. F., Dunn, J. F., & Baxter, B. (1956). The validity of selection instruments under operating conditions (The Prudential Insurance Company of America). *Personnel Psychology, 9,* 321–324.

Humm, D. G., & Wadsworth, G. W. (1935). The Humm-Wadsworth Temperament Scale. *American Journal of Psychiatry, 92,* 163–200.

Hutt, M. L. (1977). *The Hutt adaptation of the Bender-Gestalt test* (3rd ed.). New York: Grune & Stratton.

Ihilevich, D., & Gleser, G. C. (1986). *Defense mechanisms: Their classification, correlates, and measurement with the Defense Mechanisms Inventory.* Oswosso, MI: DMI Associates.

Intrieri, R. C., von Eye, A., & Kelly, J. A. (1995). The aging semantic differential: A confirmatory factor analysis. *The Gerontologist, 35,* 616–621.

Jackson, D. N. (1967). *Personality Research Form: Manual.* Goshen, NY: Research Psychologists Press.

Jackson, D. N. (1969). *Personality Research Form: Manual* (Rev. ed.). Port Huron, MI: Research Psychologists Press.

Jackson, D. N. (1971). The dynamics of structured personality tests. *Psychological Review, 78,* 229–248.

Jackson, D. N. (1974). *Personality Research Form: Manual* (Rev. ed.). Port Huron, MI: Research Psychologists Press.

Jackson, D. N. (1976). *Jackson Personality Inventory: Manual.* Port Huron, MI: Research Psychologists Press/Sigma Assessment Systems.

Jackson, D. N. (1984). *Personality Research Form Manual* (3rd ed.). Port Huron, MI: Sigma Assessment Systems.

Jackson, D. N., & Messick, S. (1958). Content and style in personality assessment. *Psychological Bulletin, 55,* 243–252.

Jacobs, A., & Schlaff, A. (1955). *Falsification scales for the Guilford-Zimmerman Temperament Survey.* Beverly Hills, CA: Sheridan Supply Company.

James, L. R., Ellison, R. L., Fox, D. G., & Taylor, C. W. (1974). Prediction of artistic performance from biographical data. *Journal of Applied Psychology, 59,* 84–86.

Janz, T., Hellervik, L., & Gilmore, D. C. (1986). *Behavior descriptive interviewing: New, accurate, cost effective.* Newton, MA: Allyn & Bacon.

Jarnecke, R. W., & Chambers, E. D. (1977). MMPI content scales: Dimensional structure, construct validity, and interpretive norms in a psychiatric population. *Journal of Consulting and Clinical Psychology, 45,* 1126–1131.

John, O. P., Goldberg, L. R., & Angleitner, A. (1984). Better than the alphabet: Taxonomies of personality-descriptive terms in English, Dutch, and German. In H. C. J. Bonarius, G. L. M. Van Heck, & N. G. Smid (Eds.), *Personality psychology in Europe: Theoretical and empirical developments* (Vol. 1). Lisse, Germany: Swets & Zeitlinger.

Johnson, F. A., & Greenberg, R. P. (1978). Quality of drawing as a factor in the interpretation of figure drawings. *Journal of Personality Assessment, 42,* 485–495.

Johnson, J. H., & Sarason, I. G. (1979). Moderator variables in stress research. In I. G. Sarason & C. D. Spielberger (Eds.), *Stress and anxiety* (Vol. 6). New York: Halstead.

Johnston, R., & McNeal, B. F. (1967). Statistical versus clinical prediction: Length of neuropsychiatric hospital stay. *Journal of Abnormal Psychology, 72,* 335–340.

Jones, E. E., & Nisbett, R. E. (1971). *The actor and the observer: Divergent perceptions of the causes of behavior.* New York: General Learning Press.

Jones, J. W. (1991, March). *Personnel selection and corporate financial performance.* Paper presented at the 1991 Society for Human Resource Management Conference, Cincinnati, OH.

Jones, J. W., & Terris, W. (1991). Integrity testing for personnel selection: An overview. *Forensic Reports, 4,* 117–140.

Jones, R. R., Reid, J. B., & Patterson, G. R. (1975). Naturalistic observation in clinical assessment. In P. McReynolds (Ed.), *Advances in psychological assessment* (Vol. 3). San Francisco: Jossey-Bass.

Jourard, S. (1964). *The transparent self.* Princeton, NJ: Van Nostrand.

Jung, C. G. (1910). The accociation method. *American Journal of Psychology, 21,* 219–269.

Jung, C. G. (1923). *Psychological types.* New York: Harcourt Brace.

Kahnemann, D., Slovic, P., & Tversky, A. (Eds.). (1982). *Judgment under uncertainty: Heuristics and biases.* New York: Cambridge University Press.

Kane, J. S., & Lawler, E. E., III. (1978). Methods of peer assessment. *Psychological Bulletin, 85,* 555–586.

Kane, R. A., & Kane, R. L. (1981). *Assessing the elderly.* Lexington, MA: Heath.

Kanfer, F. H., & Phillips, J. S. (1970). *Learning foundations of behavior therapy.* New York: Wiley.

Kanfer, F. H., & Saslow, G. (1965). Behavioral analysis: An alternative to diagnostic classification. *Archives of General Psychiatry, 12,* 529–538.

Kaplan, M. F., & Eron, L. D. (1965). Test sophistication and faking in the TAT situation. *Journal of Projective Techniques, 29,* 498–503.

Kaplan, R. M., & Saccuzzo, D. P. (1993). *Psychological testing* (3rd ed.). Pacific Grove, CA: Brooks/Cole.

Karson, S., & O'Dell, J. W. (1976). *A guide to the clinical use of the 16PF.* Champaign, IL: Institute for Personality and Ability Testing.

Kazdin, A. E. (1974). Self-monitoring and behavior change. In M. J. Mahoney & C. E. Thoreson (Eds.), *Self-control: Power to the person.* Belmont, CA: Wadsworth.

Kazdin, A. E. (1979). *History of behavior modification.* Baltimore, MD: University Park Press.

Kazdin, A. E. (1994). *Behavior modification in applied settings* (5th ed.). Pacific Grove, CA: Brooks/Cole.

Keilin, W. G., & Bloom, L. S. (1986). Child custody evaluation practices: A survey of experienced professionals. *Professional Psychology: Research and Practice, 17,* 338–346.

Kelley, M. L. (1985). Review of the Child Behavior Checklist. In J. V. Mitchell (Ed.), *Ninth mental measurements yearbook.* Lincoln: University of Nebraska, Buros Institute of Mental Measurements.

Kelly, E. L., & Fiske, D. W. (1951). *The prediction of performance in clinical psychology.* Ann Arbor: University of Michigan Press.

Kelly, E. L., & Goldberg, L. R. (1959). Correlates of later performance and specialization in psychology. *Psychological Monographs, 73* (12, Whole No. 482).

Kelly, G. A. (1955). *The psychology of personal constructs.* New York: Norton.

Kendall, R. E. (1973). Psychiatric diagnoses: A study of how they are made. *British Journal of Psychiatry, 122,* 437–445.

Kendra, J. M. (1979). Predicting suicide using the Rorschach Inkblot Test. *Journal of Personality Assessment, 43,* 452–456.

Kent, G. H., & Rosanoff, A. J. (1910). A study of association in insanity. *American Journal of Insanity, 67,* 37–96, 317–390.

Kincannon, J. C. (1968). Prediction of the standard MMPI scale scores from 71 items: The Mini-Mult. *Journal of Consulting and Clinical Psychology, 32,* 319–325.

Kitay, P. M. (1972). Review of the Bender-Gestalt Test. In O. K. Buros (Ed.), *Seventh mental measurements yearbook.* Highland Park, NJ: Gryphon.

Kleinmuntz, B. (1963). MMPI decision rules for the identification of college maladjustment: A digital computer approach. *Psychological Monographs, 77* (14, Whole No. 577).

Kleinmuntz, B. (1990). Why we still use our heads instead of formulas: An integrative approach. *Psychological Bulletin, 107,* 296–310.

Klett, W. G., & Vestre, N. D. (1967). Demographic and prognostic characteristics of psychiatric patients classified by gross MMPI measures (Abstract). *American Psychologist, 22,* 562.

Kline, R. B., Lachar, D., & Gdowski, C. L. (1987). A Personality Inventory for Children (PIC) profile typology of children and adolescents: II. Classification rules and specific behavior correlates. *Journal of Child Clinical Psychology, 16,* 225–234.

Klopfer, B., Ainsworth, M. D., Klopfer, W. G., & Holt, R. R. (1954). *Developments in the Rorschach technique: Vol. 1. Technique and theory.* New York: Harcourt, Brace and World.

Klopfer, B., & Davidson, H. H. (1962). *The Rorschach technique: An introductory manual.* New York: Harcourt, Brace and World.

Klopfer, W. G., & Taulbee, E. S. (1976). Projective tests. *Annual Review of Psychology, 27,* 543–567.

Kobasa, S. (1979). Stressful life events, personality and health: An inquiry into hardiness. *Journal of Personality and Social Psychology, 37,* 1–10.

Komaki, J., Collins, R. L., & Thoene, T. J. F. (1980). Behavioral measurement in business, industry, and government. *Behavioral Assessment, 2,* 103–124.

Koppitz, E. M. (1963). *The Bender-Gestalt Test for young children.* New York: Grune & Stratton.

Koppitz, E. M. (1975). *The Bender-Gestalt Test for young children* (Vol. 2). New York: Grune & Stratton.

Kostlan, A. (1954). A method of the empirical study of psychodiagnosis. *Journal of Consulting Psychology, 18,* 82–88.

Kouzes, J. M., & Posner, B. Z. (1987). *The leadership challenge: How to get extraordinary things done in organizations.* San Francisco: Jossey-Bass.

Kouzes, J. M., & Posner, B. Z. (1988). *The leadership practices inventory.* San Diego, CA: Pfeiffer.

Kramer, J. J., & Conoley, J. C. (1992). *Eleventh mental measurements yearbook.* Lincoln: University of Nebraska, Buros Institute of Mental Measurements.

Kroeger, O., & Thuesen, J. M. (1988). *Type talk: Or how to determine your personality and change your life.* New York: Delacorte Press.

Krug, S. E. (1980). *Clinical Analysis Questionnaire manual.* Champaign, IL: Institute for Personality and Ability Testing.

Krug, S. E. (1982). *The Adult Personality Inventory manual.* Champaign, IL: Institute for Personality and Ability Testing.

Kuder, G. F. (1951). *Examiner manual for the Kuder Preference Record.* Chicago: Science Research Associates.

Kuder, G. F., & Richardson, M. W. (1937). The theory of the estimation of test reliability. *Psychometrika, 2,* 151–160.

Kurtz, R. M., & Garfield, S. L. (1978). Illusory correlation: A further exploration of Chapman's paradigm. *Journal of Consulting and Clinical Psychology, 46,* 1009–1015.

Lachar, D. (1974). *The MMPI: Clinical assessment and automated interpretation.* Los Angeles: Western Psychological Services.

Lachar, D., & Alexander, R. S. (1978). Veridicality of self-report: Replicated correlates of the Wiggins MMPI content scales. *Journal of Consulting and Clinical Psychology, 46,* 1349–1356.

Lachar, D., DeHorn, A. B., & Gdowski, C. L. (1979). Profile classification strategies for the Personality Inventory for Children. *Journal of Consulting and Clinical Psychology, 47,* 874–881.

Lachar, D., & Gdowski, C. L. (1979). *Actuarial assessment of child and adolescent personality: An interpretive guide to the Personality Inventory for Children.* Los Angeles: Western Psychological Services.

Lachar, D., Gdowski, C. L., & Snyder, D. K. (1982). Broad-band dimensions of psychopathology: Factor scales for the Personality Inventory for Children. *Journal of Consulting and Clinical Psychology, 50,* 634–642.

Lachar, D., & Gruber, C. P. (1994). *Personality Inventory for Youth: Manual.* Los Angeles: Western Psychological Services.

LaCombe, J. A., Kline, R. B., Lachar, D., Butkus, M., & Hillman, S. B. (1991). Case history correlates of a Personality Inventory for Children (PIC) profile typology. *Psychology Assessment: A Journal of Consulting and Clinical Psychology, 3,* 678–687.

Lah, M. I. (1989). New validity, normative, and scoring data for the Rotter Incomplete Sentences Blank. *Journal of Personality Assessment, 53,* 607–620.

Landy, F. J. (1992). Hugo Münsterberg: Victim or visionary. *American Psychologist, 77,* 787–802.

Lang, P. J. (1968). Fear reduction and fear behavior: Problems in treating a construct. In J. M. Schlien (Ed.), *Research in psychotherapy* (Vol. 3). Washington, DC: American Psychological Association.

Lang, P. J., & Lazovik, A. D. (1963). Experimental desensitization of a phobia. *Journal of Abnormal and Social Psychology, 66,* 519–525.

Lang, V. R., & Krug, S. E. (1983). *Perspectives on the executive personality: A manual for the Executive Profile Survey.* Champaign, IL: Institute for Personality and Ability Testing.

Langner, T. S., & Michael, S. T. (1963). *Life stress and mental health.* New York: Free Press of Glencoe.

Lanyon, B. P. (1972). Empirical construction and validation of a sentence completion test for hostility, anxiety, and dependency. *Journal of Consulting and Clinical Psychology, 39,* 420–428.

Lanyon, B. P., & Lanyon, R. I. (1980). *Incomplete Sentences Task: Manual.* Chicago: Stoelting.

Lanyon, R. I. (1967a). Measurement of social competence in college males. *Journal of Consulting Psychology, 31,* 495–498.

Lanyon, R. I. (1967b). Simulation of normal and psychopathic MMPI personality patterns. *Journal of Consulting Psychology, 31,* 94–97.

Lanyon, R. I. (1968). *A handbook of MMPI group profiles.* Minneapolis: University of Minnesota Press.

Lanyon, R. I. (1970). Development and validation of a psychological screening inventory. *Journal of Consulting and Clinical Psychology, 35* (1, pt. 2), 1–24.

Lanyon, R. I. (1972). A technological approach to the improvement of decision making in mental health services. *Journal of Consulting and Clinical Psychology, 39,* 43–48.

Lanyon, R. I. (1973). *Psychological Screening Inventory: Manual.* Goshen, NY: Research Psychologists Press.

Lanyon, R. I. (1978). *Psychological Screening Inventory: Manual* (2nd ed.). Port Huron, MI: Research Psychologists Press/Sigma Assessment Systems.

Lanyon, R. I. (1984). Personality assessment. *Annual Review of Psychology, 35,* 667–701.

Lanyon, R. I. (1987). The validity of computer-based assessment products: Recommendations for the future. *Computers in Human Behavior, 3,* 225–238.

Lanyon, R. I. (1993). Development of scales to assess specific deception strategies on the Psychological Screening Inventory. *Psychological Assessment, 5,* 324–329.

Lanyon, R. I., & Lanyon, B. P. (1976). Behavioral assessment and decision-making: The design of strategies for therapeutic behavior change. In M. P. Feldman & A. Broadhurst (Eds.), *Theoretical and experimental bases of the behavior therapies.* New York: Wiley.

Lanyon, R. I., & Lanyon, B. P. (1978). *Behavior therapy: A clinical introduction.* Reading, MA: Addison-Wesley.

Laurent, H. (1962, September). *The early identification of management potential.* Presented at the Annual Meeting of the American Psychological Association, St. Louis, MO.

Lerner, P. M. (Ed.). (1975). *Handbook of Rorschach scales.* New York: International Universities Press.

Levine, G., & Parkinson, S. (1994). *Experimental methods in psychology.* Hillsdale, NJ: Erlbaum.

Lewandowski, D. G., & Saccuzzo, D. P. (1976). The decline of psychological testing. *Professional Psychology, 7,* 177–184.

Lewin, L., Hops, H., Aubuschon, A., & Budlinger, T. (1988). Predictors of maternal satisfaction regarding clinic-referred children. *Journal of Child Clinical Psychology, 17,* 159–163.

Lezak, M. D. (1995). *Neuropsychological assessment* (3rd ed.). New York: Oxford University Press.

Lichtenstein, S., & Fischhoff, B. (1977). Do those who know more also know more about how much they know? The calibration of probability judgments. *Organizational Behaviors and Human Performance, 3,* 159–183.

Lichtenstein, S., Fischhoff, B., & Phillips, L. D. (1982). Calibration of probabilities: The state of the art to 1980. In D. Kahneman, P. Slovic, & A. Tversky (Eds.), *Judgment under uncertainty: Heuristics and biases.* New York: Cambridge University Press.

Lindsley, O. R. (1960). Operant conditioning methods applied to chronic schizophrenia [Monograph supplement]. *Diseases of the Nervous System, 21,* 66–78.

Lindzey, G. (1961). *Projective techniques and cross-cultural research.* New York: Appleton-Century-Crofts.

Lindzey, G., & Kalnins, D. (1958). Thematic Apperception Test: Some evidence bearing on the "hero assumption." *Journal of Abnormal and Social Psychology, 57,* 76–83.

Lipinski, D., & Nelson, R. O. (1974). Problems in the use of naturalistic observation as a means of behavioral assessment. *Behavior Therapy, 5,* 341–351.

Lippmann, W. (1922). *Public opinion.* New York: Harcourt, Brace.

Lipsitt, P. D., Lelos, D., & McGarry, A. L. (1971). Competency for trial: A screening instrument. *American Journal of Psychiatry, 128,* 105–109.

Little, K. B., & Shneidman, E. S. (1959). Congruencies among interpretations of psychological test and anamnestic data. *Psychological Monographs, 73* (6, Whole No. 476).

Loehlin, J. C., & Nichols, R. C. (1976). *Heredity, environment, and personality: A study of 850 sets of twins.* Austin: University of Texas Press.

Loevinger, J. (1957). Objective tests as instruments of psychological theory. *Psychological Reports, 33,* 635–694.

London House Press (1980). *Employee Attitude Inventory.* Park Ridge, IL: Author.

Lovell, V. R. (1967). The human use of personality tests: A dissenting view. *American Psychologist, 22,* 383–393.

Lowery, C. R. (1981). Child custody decisions in divorce proceedings: A survey of judges. *Professional Psychology, 12,* 492–498.

Lubin, B., Larsen, R. M., & Matarazzo, J. D. (1984). Patterns of psychological test usage in the United States. *American Psychologist, 39,* 451–454.

Lueger, R. L., & Petzel, T. P. (1979). Illusory correlation in clinical judgment: Effects of amount of information to be processed. *Journal of Consulting and Clinical Psychology, 47,* 1120–1121.

Lusted, L. B. (1968). *Introduction to medical decision making.* Springfield, IL: Thomas.

Lykken, D. T. (1981). *A tremor in the blood.* New York: McGraw-Hill.

Lykken, D. T. (1993). Predicting violence in the violent society. *Applied and Preventive Psychology, 2,* 13–20.

Lyons, J. P. (1980). Operations research in mental health service delivery systems. In J. B. Sidowski, J. H. Johnson, & T. A. Williams (Eds.), *Technology in mental health care delivery systems.* Norwood, NJ: Ablex.

Machover, K. (1949). *Personality projection in the drawing of the human figure.* Springfield, IL: Thomas.

MacKinnon, D. W. (1975). IPAR's contribution to the conceptualization and study of creativity. In I. A. Taylor & J. W. Gatzells (Eds.), *Perspectives in creativity.* Chicago: Aldine.

Maddi, S. R. (1989). *Personality theories: A comparative analysis* (5th ed.). Chicago: Dorsey.

Malamuth, N. M., Sockloskie, R. J., Koss, M. P., & Tanaka, J. (1991). Characteristics of aggressors against women: Testing a model using a national sample of college students. *Journal of Consulting and Clinical Psychology, 59,* 670–681.

Marks, P. A., & Seeman, W. (1963). *The actuarial description of abnormal personality.* Baltimore, MD: Williams & Wilkins.

Marks, P. A., Seeman, W., & Haller, D. L. (1974). *The actuarial use of the MMPI with adolescents and adults.* Baltimore, MD: Williams & Wilkins.

Marlatt, G. A. (1978). Behavioral assessment of social drinking and alcoholism. In G. A. Marlatt & P. E. Nathan (Eds.), *Behavioral approaches to alcoholism.* New Brunswick, NJ: Rutgers Center of Alcohol Studies.

Martin, R. D. (1988). *Assessment of personality and behavior problems: Infancy through adolescence.* New York: Guilford.

Marx, M. H., & Hillix, W. A. (1973). *Systems and theories in psychology* (2nd ed.). New York: McGraw-Hill.

Mash, E. J., & Terdal, L. G. (1976). *Behavior therapy assessment: Diagnosis, design, and evaluation.* New York: Springer.

Mash, E. J., & Terdal, L. G. (1981). Behavioral assessment of childhood disturbance. In E. J. Mash & L. G. Terdal (Eds.), *Behavioral assessment of childhood disorders.* New York: Guilford.

Matarazzo, J. D. (1986). Computerized clinical psychological test interpretations: Unvalidated plus all mean and no sigma. *American Psychologist, 41,* 14–24.

Matarazzo, J. D. (1995). Psychological testing and assessment in the 21st Century. *American Psychologist, 47,* 1007–1018.

McArthur, D. S., & Roberts, G. E. (1982). *Roberts Apperception Test for Children: Manual.* Los Angeles: Western Psychological Services.

McCallum, M., & Piper, W. E. (1990). The psychological mindedness assessment procedure. *Psychological Assessment: A Journal of Consulting and Clinical Psychology, 2,* 412–418.

McClelland, D. C., Atkinson, J. W., Clark, R. A., & Lowell, E. L. (1953). *The achievement motive.* New York: Appleton-Century-Crofts.

McCrae, R. R., & Costa, P. T., Jr. (1987). Validation of the five-factor model of personality across instruments and observers. *Journal of Personality and Social Psychology, 52,* 81–90.

McCrae, R. R., & Costa, P. T., Jr. (1990). *Personality and adulthood: Emerging lives, enduring dispositions.* New York: Guilford.

McCrae, R. R., & Costa, P. T., Jr. (1994). The stability of personality: Observations and evaluations. *Current Directions in Psychological Science, 3,* 173–175.

McDaniel, M. A., & Jones, J. W. (1988). A meta-analysis of the Employee Attitude Inventory theft scales. *Journal of Business and Psychology, 2,* 327–345.

McDaniel, M. A., Whetzel, D. L., Schmidt, F. L., & Maurer, S. D. (1994). The validity of employment interviews: A comprehensive review and meta-analysis. *Journal of Applied Psychology, 79,* 599–616.

McFall, R. M., & Marston, A. (1970). An experimental investigation of behavioral rehearsal in assertive training. *Journal of Abnormal Psychology, 76,* 295–303.

McGarry, A. L., Curran, W. J., Lipsitt, P. D., Lelos, D., Schwitzgebel, R. K., & Rosenberg, A. H. (1973). *Competency to stand trial and mental illness.* Rockville, MD: National Institute of Mental Health.

McKee, M. G. (1972). Review of the Edwards Personal Preference Schedule. In O. K. Buros (Ed.), *Seventh mental measurements yearbook.* Highland Park, NJ: Gryphon.

McLaughlin, J. F., Helms, E., & Howe, M. G. (1983). Note on the reliability of three MMPI short forms. *Journal of Personality Assessment, 47,* 357–358.

McMahon, R. J. (1994). Diagnosis, assessment, and treatment of externalizing problems in children: The role of longitudinal data. *Journal of Consulting and Clinical Psychology, 62,* 901–917.

Meehl, P. E. (1954). *Clinical vs. statistical prediction.* Minneapolis: University of Minnesota Press.

Meehl, P. E. (1956). Wanted—a good cookbook. *American Psychologist, 11,* 263–272.

Meehl, P. E. (1959a). A comparison of clinicians with five statistical methods of identifying psychotic MMPI profiles. *Journal of Counseling Psychology, 6,* 102–109.

Meehl, P. E. (1959b). Some ruminations on the validation of clinical procedures. *Canadian Journal of Psychology, 13,* 102–128.

Meehl, P. E. (1960). The cognitive activity of the clinician. *American Psychologist, 15,* 19–27.

Meehl, P. E. (1965). Seer over sign: The first good example. *Journal of Experimental Research in Personality, 1,* 27–32.

Meehl, P. E. (1979, February 23). *Making a new MMPI.* Memorandum to Robert R. Golden.

Meehl, P. E. (1986). Causes and effects of my disturbing little book. *Journal of Personality Assessment, 50,* 370–375.

Meehl, P. E., & Dahlstrom, W. G. (1960). Objective configural rules for discriminating psychotic from neurotic MMPI profiles. *Journal of Consulting Psychology, 24,* 375–387.

Meehl, P. E., & Hathaway, S. R. (1946). The *K* factor as a suppressor variable in the MMPI. *Journal of Applied Psychology, 30,* 525–564.

Meehl, P. E., & Rosen, A. (1955). Antecedent probability and the efficiency of psychometric signs, patterns, or cutting scores. *Psychological Bulletin, 52,* 194–216.

Megargee, E. I. (Ed.). (1977). A new classification system for criminal offenders. *Criminal Justice and Behavior, 4,* 107–216.

Megargee, E. I. (1979). Development and validation of an MMPI-based system for classifying criminal offenders. In J. N. Butcher (Ed.), *New developments in the use of the MMPI.* Minneapolis: University of Minnesota Press.

Megargee, E. I. (1995). Assessing and understanding aggressive and violent patients. In J. N. Butcher (Ed.), *Clinical personality assessment.* New York: Oxford University Press.

Megargee, E. I., & Bohn, M. J., Jr. (1979). *Classifying criminal offenders: A new system based on the MMPI.* Beverly Hills, CA: Sage.

Megargee, E. I., & Mendelsohn, G. A. (1962). A cross-validation of twelve MMPI indices of hostility and control. *Journal of Abnormal Psychology, 65,* 431–438.

Meichenbaum, D. (1986). Cognitive behavior modification. In F. H. Kanfer & A. P. Goldstein (Eds.), *Helping people change* (3rd ed.). New York: Pergamon.

Melton, G. B., Petrila, J., Poythress, N. G., & Slobogin, C. (1987). *Psychological evaluations for the courts.* New York: Guilford.

Mercer, J. R. (1979). *System of Multicultural Pluralistic Assessment: Technical manual.* New York: Psychological Corporation.

Messick, S. (1995). Validity of psychological assessment: Validation of inferences from persons' responses and performances as scientific inquiry into score meaning. *American Psychologist, 50,* 741–749.

Milgram, S. (1974). *Obedience to authority.* New York: Harper & Row.

Miller, L. C. (1984). *Louisville Behavior Checklist manual.* Los Angeles: Western Psychological Services.

Millon, T. (1987). *Manual for the MCMI-II* (2nd ed.). Minneapolis, MN: National Computer Systems.

Millon, T., Green, C. J., & Meagher, R. B. (1982). *Millon Adolescent Personality Inventory manual.* Minneapolis, MN: National Computer Systems.

Millon, T., Millon, C., & Davis, R. (1993). *The Millon Adolescent Clinical Inventory manual.* Minneapolis, MN: NCS Assessments.

Millon, T., Millon, C., & Davis, R. (1994). *The MCMI-III manual.* Minneapolis, MN: NCS Assessments.

Mills, R. B., McDevitt, R. J., & Tonkin, S. (1966). Situational tests in metropolitan police recruit selection. *Journal of Criminal Law, Criminology, and Police Science, 57,* 99–106.

Mischel, W. (1968). *Personality and assessment.* New York: Wiley.

Mischel, W. (1972). Direct versus indirect personality assessment: Evidence and implications. *Journal of Consulting and Clinical Psychology, 38,* 319–324.

Mischel, W. (1973). Toward a cognitive social learning reconceptualization of personality. *Psychological Review, 80,* 252–283.

Mischel, W. (1976). *Introduction to personality* (2nd ed.). New York: Holt, Rinehart and Winston.

Mischel, W. (1977). On the future of personality measurement. *American Psychologist, 32,* 246–254.

Mischel, W. (1979). On the interface of cognition and personality: Beyond the person-situation debate. *American Psychologist, 34,* 740–754.

Mitchell, J. V., Jr. (Ed.). (1985). *Ninth mental measurements yearbook* (Vols. 1–2). Lincoln: University of Nebraska, Buros Institute of Mental Measurements.

Mitchell, J. V., Jr., & Pierce-Jones, J. (1960). A factor analysis of Gough's California Psychological Inventory. *Journal of Consulting Psychology, 24,* 454–456.

Mittman, B. L. (1983). Judges' ability to diagnose schizophrenia on the Rorschach: The effect of malingering. *Dissertation Abstracts International, 44,* 2148-B.

Monahan, J. (Ed.). (1980). *Who is the client? The ethics of psychological intervention in the criminal justice system.* Washington, DC: American Psychological Association.

Monahan, J. (1981). *Predicting violent behavior.* Beverly Hills, CA: Sage.

Monahan, J. (1984). The prediction of violent behavior: Toward a second generation of theory and policy. *American Journal of Psychiatry, 141,* 10–15.

Monsour, M. (1992). Meanings of intimacy in cross-sex and same-sex friendships. *Journal of Social and Personal Relationships, 9,* 277–295.

Moore, T. (1987, March 30). Personality tests are back. *Fortune, 115,* 74–80.

Moos, R. H. (1968). Behavioral effects of being observed: Reactions to a wireless transmitter. *Journal of Consulting and Clinical Psychology, 32,* 383–388.

Moreland, K. L. (1985). Validation of computer-based test interpretations: Problems and prospects. *Journal of Consulting and Clinical Psychology, 53,* 816–825.

Moreland, K. L. (1986). Computer-based MMPI interpretations: External criterion studies. *Critical Items, 2,* 2–3.

Moreland, K. L., Eyde, L. D., Robertson, G. J., Primoff, E. J., & Most, R. B. (1995). Assessment of test use qualifications: A research-based measurement procedure. *American Psychologist, 50,* 14–23.

Moreno, J. L. (1934). *Who shall survive?* Washington, DC: Nervous and Mental Disease Publishing Company.

Morey, L. C. (1991). *Personality Assessment Inventory: Professional manual.* Odessa, FL: Psychological Assessment Resources.

Morgan, C. D., & Murray, H. A. (1935). A method for investigating fantasies: The Thematic Apperception Test. *Archives of Neurology and Psychiatry, 34,* 289–306.

Morin, C. M., & Colecchi, C. A. (1995). Psychological assessment of older adults. In J. N. Butcher (Ed.), *Clinical personality assessment.* New York: Oxford University Press.

Morris, C. (1956). *Varieties of human values.* Chicago: University of Chicago Press.

Mossman, D. (1994). Assessing predictions of violence: Being accurate about accuracy. *Journal of Consulting and Clinical Psychology, 62,* 783–792.

Mount, M. K., Barrick, M. R., & Strauss, J. P. (1994). Validity of observer ratings of Big Five personality factors. *Journal of Applied Psychology, 79,* 272–280.

MSIS (1973). *Multi-State Information System: A review.* Orangeburg, NY: Rockland State Hospital.

Murphy, K. R. (1993). *Honesty in the workplace.* Pacific Grove, CA: Brooks/Cole.

Murray, H. A. (1938). *Explorations in personality.* New York: Oxford University Press.

Murray, H. A. (1943). *Thematic Apperception Test manual.* Cambridge, MA: Harvard University Press.

Murstein, B. I. (1963). *Theory and research in projective techniques (emphasizing the TAT)*. New York: Wiley.

Myers, I. B., & McCaulley, M. H. (1985). *Manual: A guide to the development and use of the Myers-Briggs Type Indicator*. Palo Alto, CA: Consulting Psychologists Press.

Nelson, R. O. (1977). Methodological issues in assessment via self-monitoring. In J. D. Cone & R. P. Hawkins (Eds.), *Behavioral assessment*. New York: Brunner/Mazel.

Nelson, R. O., & Hayes, S. C. (1979). Some current dimensions of behavioral assessment. *Behavioral Assessment, 1*, 1–16.

Nettler, G. (1959). Test burning in Texas. *American Psychologist, 14*, 682–683.

Nisbett, R. E., Caputo, C., Legant, P., & Marecek, J. (1973). Behavior as seen by the actor and as seen by the observer. *Journal of Personality and Social Psychology, 27*, 154–164.

Norman, W. T. (1963a). Personality assessment, faking and detection: An assessment method for use in personnel selection. *Journal of Applied Psychology, 47*, 225–241.

Norman, W. T. (1963b). Relative importance of test item content. *Journal of Consulting Psychology, 27*, 166–174.

Norman, W. T. (1963c). Toward an adequate taxonomy of personality attributes: Replicated factor structure in peer nomination personality ratings. *Journal of Abnormal and Social Psychology, 66*, 547–583.

Norman, W. T. (1967). *2,800 personality trait descriptors: Normative operating characteristics for a university population*. Unpublished manuscript, University of Michigan, Ann Arbor.

Norman, W. T. (1972). Psychometric considerations for a revision of the MMPI. In J. N. Butcher (Ed.), *Objective personality assessment*. New York: Academic Press.

Norman, W. T., & Goldberg, L. R. (1966). Raters, ratees, and randomness in personality structure. *Journal of Personality and Social Psychology, 4*, 681–691.

Novick, M. R. (1981). Federal guidelines and professional standards. *American Psychologist, 36*, 1035–1046.

Nunnally, J. C. (1961). *Popular conceptions of mental health*. New York: Holt, Rinehart and Winston.

Nunnally, J. C. (1978). *Psychometic theory* (2nd ed.). New York: McGraw-Hill.

Nunnally, J. C., & Bernstein, I. H. (1994). *Psychometric theory* (3rd ed.). New York: McGraw-Hill.

Oas, P. (1984). Validity of the Draw-A-Person and Bender-Gestalt Tests as measures of impulsivity with adolescents. *Journal of Consulting and Clinical Psychology, 52*, 1011–1019.

O'Bannon, A. M., Goldinger, L. A., & Appleby, G. S. (1989). *Honesty and integrity testing: A practical guide*. Atlanta, GA: Applied Information Resources.

O'Dell, J. W. (1972). P. T. Barnum explores the computer. *Journal of Consulting and Clinical Psychology, 38*, 270–273.

Office of Technology Assessment. (1990). *The use of integrity tests for preemployment screening* (OTA-SET-442). Washington, DC: U.S. Government Printing Office.

O'Leary, K. D., & Wilson, G. T. (1987). *Behavior therapy: Application and outcome* (2nd ed.). Englewood Cliffs, NJ: Prentice-Hall.

Olin, J. T., Schneider, L. S., Eaton, E. M., Zemensky, M. F., & Pollack, V. E. (1992). The Geriatric Depression Scale and the Beck Depression Inventory as screening instruments in an older adult outpatient population. *Psychological Assessment, 4*, 190–192.

Ollendick, T. H., & King, N. (1994). Diagnosis, assessment and treatment of internalizing problems in children and the role of longitudinal data. *Journal of Consulting and Clinical Psychology, 62*, 918–927.

Ollendick, T. H., & Meador, A. E. (1984). Behavioral assessment of children. In G. Goldstein & M. Hersen (Eds.), *Handbook of psychological assessment*. New York: Pergamon.

Ones, D. S., Viswesaran, C., & Schmidt, F. L. (1993). Comprehensive meta-analysis of integrity test validities: Findings and implications for personnel selection and theories of job performance. *Journal of Applied Psychology, 78*, 679–703.

Ones, D. S., Viswesaran, C., & Schmidt, F. L. (1995). Integrity tests: Overlooked facts, resolved issues, and remaining questions. *American Psychologist, 49,* 456–457.

Osgood, C. E. (1952). The nature and measurement of meaning. *Psychological Bulletin, 49,* 197–237.

Osgood, C. E., Suci, G. J., & Tannenbaum, P. H. (1957). *The measurement of meaning.* Urbana: University of Illinois Press.

Oskamp, S. (1962). The relationship of clinical experience and training methods to several criteria of clinical prediction. *Psychological Monographs, 76* (28, Whole No. 547).

Oskamp, S., Mindick, B., Berger, D., & Motta, E. (1978). A longitudinal study of success versus failure in contraceptive planning. *Journal of Population, 1,* 69–83.

OSS Assessment Staff. (1948). *Assessment of men.* New York: Rinehart.

Otto, R. K. (1992). Prediction of dangerous behavior: A review and analysis of "second-generation" research. *Forensic Reports, 5,* 103–133.

Overall, J. E., & Gomez-Mont, F. (1974). The MMPI-168 for psychiatric screening. *Educational and Psychological Measurement, 34,* 315–319.

Overall, J. E., & Gorham, D. R. (1962). The Brief Psychiatric Rating Scale. *Psychological Reports, 10,* 799–812.

Overall, J. E., & Klett, C. J. (1972). *Applied multivariate analysis.* New York: McGraw-Hill.

Owens, W. A. (1983). Background data. In M. D. Dunnette (Ed.), *Handbook of industrial and organizational psychology.* New York: Wiley.

Owens, W. A., & Henry, E. R. (1966). *Biographical data in industrial psychology: A review and evaluation.* Greensboro, NC: Richardson Foundation.

Palmer, J. O. (1983). *The psychological assessment of children* (2nd ed.). New York: Wiley.

Pascal, G. R., & Suttell, B. J. (1951). *The Bender-Gestalt Test.* New York: Grune & Stratton.

Passini, F. T., & Norman, W. T. (1966). A universal conception of personality structure. *Journal of Personality and Social Psychology, 4,* 44–49.

Patterson, G. R., Hops, H., & Weiss, R. L. (1975). Interpersonal skills training for couples in the early stages of conflict. *Journal of Marriage and the Family, 37,* 295–303.

Patterson, G. R., Reid, J. B., Jones, R. R., & Conger, R. E. (1975). *A social-learning approach to family intervention: Vol. 1. Families with aggressive children.* Eugene, OR: Castalia.

Paul, G. L. (1966). *Insight versus desensitization in psychotherapy: An experiment in anxiety reduction.* Stanford, CA: Stanford University Press.

Paulhus, D. L. (1984). Two-component models of socially desirable responding. *Journal of Personality and Social Psychology, 46,* 598–609.

Paulhus, D. L. (1986). Self-deception and impression management in test responses. In A. Angleitner & J. S. Wiggins (Eds.), *Personality assessment via questionnaire.* New York: Springer-Verlag.

Paulhus, D. L. (1991). Balanced Inventory of Desirable Responding (BIDR). In J. P. Robinson, P. R. Shaver, & L. S. Wrightsman (Eds.), *Measures of personality and social psychological attitudes.* San Diego: Academic Press.

Paulhus, D. L. (1994). *Balanced Inventory of Desirable Responding: Reference manual for BIDR version 6.* Vancouver: University of British Columbia, Department of Psychology.

Payne, F. D., & Wiggins, J. S. (1968). Effects of rule relaxation and system combination on classification rates in two MMPI "cookbook" systems. *Journal of Consulting and Clinical Psychology, 32,* 734–736.

Peak, H. (1953). Problems of objective observation. In L. Festinger & D. Katz (Eds.), *Research methods in the behavioral sciences.* New York: Dryden.

Pearson, J. S., & Swenson, W. M. (1968). *A user's guide to the Mayo Clinic automated MMPI program.* New York: Psychological Corporation.

Pervin, L. A. (1989). *Personality: Theory and research* (5th ed.). New York: Wiley.

Peterson, D. R. (1965). Scope and generality of verbally defined personality factors. *Psychological Review, 72,* 48–59.

Peterson, D. R. (1968). *The clinical study of social behavior.* New York: Appleton-Century-Crofts.

Phillips, L. (1953). Case history data and prognosis in schizophrenia. *Journal of Nervous and Mental Disease, 117,* 515–525.

Pincus, A. L., & Wiggins, J. S. (1990). Interpersonal problems and conceptions of personality disorders. *Journal of Personality Disorders, 4,* 342–352.

Piotrowski, C., & Keller, J. W. (1989). Psychological testing in outpatient mental health facilities: A national survey. *Professional Psychology: Research and Practice, 20,* 423–425.

Piotrowski, Z. A. (1964). Digital-computer interpretation of inkblot test data. *Psychiatric Quarterly, 38,* 1–26.

Piotrowski, Z. A. (1969). Personal communication.

Piotrowski, Z. A. (1980). The psychological X-ray in mental disorders. In J. B. Sidowski, J. H. Johnson, & T. W. Williams (Eds.), *Technology in mental health care delivery systems.* Norwood, NJ: Ablex.

Plomin, R., Coon, H., Carey, G., DeFries, J. C., & Fulker, D. W. (1991). Parent-offspring and sibling adoption analyses of parental ratings of temperament in infancy and childhood. *Journal of Personality, 59,* 705–732.

Posner, B. Z., & Kouzes, J. M. (1992). *Psychometric properties of the Leadership Practices Inventory.* San Diego, CA: Pfeiffer.

Powell, D. H., Kaplan, E. F., Whitla, D., Weintraub, S., Katlin, R., & Funkenstein, H. H. (1993). *MicroCog: Assessment of cognitive functioning: Manual.* San Antonio, TX: Psychological Corporation.

Pressey, S. L., & Pressey, L. W. (1919). "Cross-out" tests, with suggestions as to a group scale of the emotions. *Journal of Applied Psychology, 3,* 138–150.

Prigatano, G. P. (1992). Personality disturbances associated with traumatic brain injury. *Journal of Consulting and Clinical Psychology, 60,* 360–368.

Pritchard, D. A. (1977). Linear versus configural statistical prediction. *Journal of Consulting and Clinical Psychology, 45,* 559–563.

Pritchard, D. A. (1980). Apologia for clinical/configural decision making. *American Psychologist, 35,* 676–678.

Pruzek, R. M., & Frederick, B. C. (1978). Weighting predictors in linear models: Alternatives to least squares and limitations of equal weights. *Psychological Bulletin, 85,* 254–266.

Psychological Consultants to Management. (1995). *SmartHire: Competency based interviewing for Windows.* San Diego, CA: Author.

Pulakos, E. D., & Schmitt, N. (1995). Experience-based and situational interview questions: Studies of validity. *Personnel Psychology, 48,* 289–308.

Quay, H. C., & Peterson, C. (1983). *Manual for the Revised Behavior Problem Checklist.* Coral Gables, FL: Authors.

Rabin, A. I., & Zltogorski, Z. (1985). The sentence completion method: Recent research. *Journal of Personality Assessment, 49,* 641–647.

Rand, S. W. (1979). Correspondence between psychological reports based on the Mini-Mult and the MMPI. *Journal of Personality Assessment, 43,* 160–163.

Reed, H. (1982). *The Stanton Survey: Description and validation manual.* Chicago: Stanton Corporation.

Reid Psychological Systems. (1951). *Reid Report.* Chicago: Author.

Reisman, D. (1950). *The lonely crowd.* New Haven: Yale University Press.

Reitan, R. M., & Wolfson, D. (1993). *The Halstead-Reitan Neuropsychological Test Battery* (3rd ed.). Tucson, AZ: Neuropsychology Press.

Reznikoff, M. (1961). Social desirability in TAT themes. *Journal of Projective Techniques, 25,* 87–89.

Rice, M. E., & Harris, G. T. (1995). Violent recidivism: Assessing predictive validity. *Journal of Consulting and Clinical Psychology, 65,* 737–748.

Richardson, S. A., Dohrenwend, B. S., & Klein, D. (1965). *Interviewing: Its forms and functions.* New York: Basic Books.

Rimm, D. C. (1963). Cost efficiency and test prediction. *Journal of Consulting Psychology, 27,* 89–91.

Roback, H. B. (1968). Human figure drawings: Their utility in the clinical psychologist's armentarium for personality assessment. *Psychological Bulletin, 70,* 1–19.

Robins, L. N., Helzer, J. E., Croughan, J. L., & Ratcliff, K. S. (1981). National Institute of Mental Health Diagnostic Interview Schedule. *Archives of General Psychiatry, 38,* 381–389.

Roesch, R., & Golding, S. L. (1981). *Competency to stand trial.* Urbana: University of Illinois Press.

Roesch, R., Ogloff, J. R. P., & Golding, S. L. (1993). Competency to stand trial: Legal and clinical issues. *Applied and Preventive Psychology, 2,* 43–51.

Rogers, C. R., & Dymond, R. F. (1954). *Psychotherapy and personality change.* Chicago: University of Chicago Press.

Rogers, R. (Ed.). (1988). *Clinical assessment of malingering and deception.* New York: Guilford.

Romanczyk, R. G., Kent, R. N., Diament, C., & O'Leary, K. D. (1973). Measuring the reliability of observational data: A reactive process. *Journal of Applied Behavior Analysis, 6,* 175–184.

Romano, J. M., Turner, J. A., Freidman, L. S., Bulcroft, R. A., Hensen, M. P., & Hops, H. (1991). Observational assessment of chronic pain in patient-spouse behavioral interactions. *Behavior Therapy, 22,* 549–567.

Rome, H. P., Swenson, W. M., Mataya, P., McCarthy, C. E., Pearson, J. S., Keating, F. R., & Hathaway, S. R. (1962). Symposium on automation techniques in personality assessment. *Proceedings of the Staff Meetings of the Mayo Clinic, 37,* 61–82.

Rorer, L. G. (1965). The great response-style myth. *Psychological Bulletin, 63,* 129–156.

Rorer, L. G., Hoffman, P. J., Dickman, H. R., & Slovic, P. (1967). Configural judgments revealed. *Proceedings of the 75th Annual Convention of the American Psychological Association, 2,* 195–196.

Rorer, L. G., Hoffman, P. J., & Hsieh, K. C. (1996). Utilities as base rate multipliers in the determination of optimum cutting scores for the discrimination of groups of unequal size and variance. *Journal of Applied Psychology, 50,* 364–368.

Rorschach, H. (1951). *Psychodiagnostics.* New York: Grune & Stratton. (Original work published in German 1921 and in English 1942)

Rose, D., & Bitter, E. J. (1980). The Palo Alto Content Scale as a predictor of physical assaultiveness in men. *Journal of Personality Assessment, 44,* 228–233.

Rosen, A. (1954). Detection of suicidal patients: An example of some limitations in the prediction of infrequent events. *Journal of Consulting Psychology, 18,* 397–403.

Rosenberg, M., Glueck, B. C., Jr., & Bennett, W. L. (1967). Automation of behavioral observation on hospitalized psychiatric patients. *American Journal of Psychiatry, 123,* 926–929.

Rosenberg, S., & Sedlak, A. (1972). Structural representations of implicit personality theory. In L. Berkowitz (Ed.), *Advances in experimental social psychology* (Vol. 6). New York: Academic Press.

Rosenthal, R. (1966). *Experimenter effects in behavioral research.* New York: Appleton-Century-Crofts.

Rotter, J. B., Lah, M. I., & Rafferty, J. E. (1992). *Rotter Incomplete Sentences Blank: Manual* (2nd ed.). San Antonio, TX: Psychological Corporation.

Rotter, J. B., & Rafferty, J. E. (1950). *Manual: The Rotter Incomplete Sentences Blank.* New York: Psychological Corporation.

Ryan, A. M., Daum, D., Bauman, T., Grisez, M., Mattimore, K., Naloda, T., & McCormick, S. (1995). Direct, indirect, and controlled observations and rating accuracy. *Journal of Applied Psychology, 80,* 664–670.

Ryan, A. M., & Sackett, P. R. (1987). Pre-employment honesty testing: Fakability, reactions to test takers, and company image. *Journal of Business and Psychology, 1,* 248–256.

Sackett, P. R., Burris, L. R., & Callahan, C. (1989). Integrity testing for personnel selection: An update. *Personnel Psychology, 42,* 491–529.

Sackett, P. R., & Harris, M. M. (1984). Honesty testing for personnel selection: A review and critique. In H. J. Bernadin & D. A. Bownes (Eds.), *Personnel assessment in organizations.* New York: Praeger.

Sackett, P. R., & Larson, J. R., Jr. (1990). Research strategies and tactics in industrial and organizational psychology. In M. D. Dunnette & L. M. Hough (Eds.), *Handbook of industrial and organizational psychology* (Vol. 1). Palo Alto, CA: Consulting Psychologists Press.

Sackett, P. R., & Wilk, S. L. (1994). Within-group norming and other forms of score adjustment in pre-employment testing. *American Psychologist, 49,* 929–954.

Sales, B. D. (1980). Law and attitudes toward the mentally ill. In J. G. Rabkin, L. Gelb, & J. B. Lazar (Eds.), *Attitudes toward the mentally ill: Research perspectives.* Rockville, MD: National Insitute of Mental Health.

Sales, B. D., Manber, R., & Rohman, L. (1992). Social science research and child-custody decision making. *Applied and Preventive Psychology, 1,* 23–40.

Sandler, I. N. (1980). Social support resources, stress, and maladjustment of poor children. *American Journal of Community Psychology, 8,* 41–52.

Sappenfield, B. R. (1965). Review of the Blacky Pictures. In O. K. Buros (Ed.), *Sixth mental measurements yearbook.* Highland Park, NJ: Gryphon.

Sarason, S. B. (1974). *The psychological sense of community.* San Francisco: Jossey-Bass.

Sarbin, T. R. (1968). Ontology recapitualates philosophy: The mythic nature of anxiety. *American Psychologist, 23,* 411–418.

Sarbin, T. R. (1986). Prediction and clinical inference: Forty years later. *Journal of Personality Assessment, 50,* 362–369.

Sarbin, T. R., Taft, R., & Bailey, D. E. (1960). *Clinical inference and cognitive theory.* New York: Holt, Rinehart and Winston.

Sashkin, M. (1990). *The visionary leadership behavior questionnaire trainer's guide.* King of Prussia, PA: Organization Design and Development.

Sashkin, M. (1996). *The visionary leader: Leadership behavior questionnaire trainer's guide.* Amherst, MA: HRD Press.

Sashkin, M., & Burke, W. W. (1990). Understanding and assessing organizational leadership. In K. E. Clark & M. B. Clark (Eds.), *Measures of leadership.* West Orange, NJ: Leadership Library of America.

Sattler, J. M. (1985). Review of the Hutt Adaptation of the Bender-Gestalt Test. In J. V. Mitchell (Ed.), *Ninth mental measurements yearbook.* Lincoln: University of Nebraska, Buros Institute of Mental Measurements.

Satz, P., Fennel, E., & Reilly, C. (1970). The predictive validity of six neurodiagnostic tests: A decision theory analysis. *Journal of Consulting and Clinical Psychology, 34,* 375–381.

Saunders, D. S. (1956). Moderator variables in prediction. *Education and Psychological Measurement, 16,* 209–222.

Sawyer, J. (1966). Measurement *and* prediction, clinical *and* statistical. *Psychological Bulletin, 66,* 178–200.

Saxe, L., Dougherty, D., & Cross, T. (1985). The validity of polygraph testing. *American Psychologist, 40,* 355–366.

Schaffer, J. W., Schmidt, C. W., Zlotowitz, H. I., & Fisher, R. S. (1978). Biorhythms and highway crashes. *Archives of General Psychiatry, 35,* 41–46.

Schinka, J. N. (1988). *Mental Status Checklist—Adult.* Odessa, FL: Psychological Assessment Resources.

Schinka, J. N. (1989). *Personal History Checklist—Adult: Computer report, version 3.0 manual.* Odessa, FL: Psychological Assessment Resources.

Schmitt, N. Gooding, R. Z., Noe, R. A., & Kirsch, M. (1984). Meta-analyses of validity studies published between 1964 and 1982 and the investigation of study characteristics. *Personnel Psychology, 37*, 407–421.

Schreiber, J., Roesch, R., & Golding, S. (1987). An evaluation of procedures for competency to stand trial. *Bulletin of the American Academy of Psychiatry and the Law, 15*, 187–203.

Schretlen, P., Wilkins, S. S., Van Gorp, W. G., & Bobholz, J. H. (1992). Cross-validation of a psychological test battery to detect faked insanity. *Psychological Assessment, 4*, 77–83.

Schroeder, H. E. (1972). Use of feedback in clinical prediction. *Journal of Consulting and Clinical Psychology, 38*, 265–269.

Schutz, W. (1967). *The FIRO Scales.* Palo Alto, CA: Consulting Psychologists Press.

Schwartz, L. A. (1932). Social-situation pictures in the psychiatric interview. *American Journal of Orthopsychiatry, 2*, 124–133.

Schwartz, M. M., Cohen, B. D., & Pavlik, W. B. (1964). The effects of subject- and experimenter-induced defensive response sets on Picture-Frustration Test reactions. *Journal of Projective Techniques, 28*, 341–345.

Science Research Associates. (1983). *Personal Outlook Inventory.* Park Ridge, IL: Author.

Scott, W. A. (1968). Comparative validites of forced-choice and single-stimulus tests. *Psychological Bulletin, 70*, 231–244.

Scott, W. A., & Johnson, R. C. (1972). Comparative validities of direct and indirect personality tests. *Journal of Consulting and Clinical Psychology, 38*, 301–318.

Sechrest, L. (1963). Incremental validity: A recommendation. *Educational and Psychological Measurement, 23*, 153–157.

Sechrest, L. (1976). Personality. *Annual Review of Psychology, 27*, 1–27.

Sechrest, L., Gallimore, R., & Hersch, P. D. (1967). Feedback and accuracy of clinical predictions. *Journal of Consulting Psychology, 31*, 1–11.

Sechrest, L., & Jackson, D. N. (1962). The generality of deviant response tendencies. *Journal of Consulting Psychology, 26*, 395–401.

Sechrest, L., & Jackson, D. N. (1963). Deviant response tendencies: Their measurement and interpretation. *Educational and Psychological Measurement, 23*, 33–53.

Seeman, W. (1952). "Subtlety" in structured personality tests. *Journal of Consulting Psychology, 16*, 278–283.

Seeman, W. (1953). Concept of "subtlety" in structured psychiatric and personality tests: An experimental approach. *Journal of Abnormal and Social Psychology, 48*, 239–247.

Seeman, W. (1969). *The complete clinician: Constituting some reflections on diagnostic decision-making and on theorizing.* Unpublished manuscript.

Shah, S. A. (1978). Dangerousness: A paradigm for exploring some issues in law and psychology. *American Psychologist, 33*, 224–238.

Sharkey, K. J., & Ritzler, B. A. (1985). Comparing diagnostic validity of the TAT and a new picture projective test. *Journal of Personality Assessment, 49*, 406–412.

Shaver, K. G. (1975). *An introduction to attribution processes.* Cambridge, MA: Winthrop.

Sheldon, W. H., Stevens, S. S., & Tucker, W. B. (1940). *The varieties of human physique.* New York: Harper & Row.

Shelly, M. W., & Bryan, G. L. (1964). *Human judgments and optimality.* New York: Wiley.

Shneidman, E. S. (1951). *Thematic test analysis.* New York: Grune & Stratton.

Siegel, M. (1979). Privacy, ethics, and confidentiality. *Professional Psychology, 10*, 249–258.

Sines, J. O. (1966). Actuarial methods in personality assessment. In B. A. Maher (Ed.), *Progress in experimental personality research* (Vol. 3). New York: Academic Press.

Sines, J. O. (1985). Review of the Roberts Apperception Test for Children. In J. V. Mitchell, Jr. (Ed.), *Ninth mental measurements yearbook.* Lincoln: University of Nebraska, Buros Institute of Mental Measurements.

Sines, L. K. (1959). The relative contribution of four kinds of data to accuracy in personality assessment. *Journal of Consulting Psychology, 23*, 483–492.

Sletten, I., Ernhart, C., & Ulett, G. (1970). The Missouri automated mental status examination: Its development, use, and reliability. *Comprehensive Psychiatry, 11,* 315–327.

Slora, K. (1989). An empirical approach to determining employee deviance base rates. *Journal of Business and Psychology, 4,* 199–219.

Smith, J., & Lanyon, R. I. (1968). Prediction of juvenile probation violators. *Journal of Consulting and Clinical Psychology, 32,* 54–58.

Snyder, D. K. (1981). *Marital Satisfaction Inventory: Manual.* Los Angeles: Western Psychological Services.

Snyder, D. K., Widiger, T. A., & Hoover, D. W. (1990). Methodological considerations in validating computer-based test interpretations: Controlling for response bias. *Psychological Assessment: A Journal of Consulting and Clinical Psychology, 2,* 470–477.

Sparks, C. P. (1990). Testing for management potential. In K. E. Clark & M. B. Clark (Eds.), *Measures of leadership.* West Orange, NJ: Leadership Library of America.

Sparrow, S. S., Balla, D. A., & Cicchetti, D. V. (1984). *Vineland Adaptive Behavior Scales: Survey form manual.* Circle Pines, MN: American Guidance Service.

Spencer, G. J., & Worthington, R. (1952). Validity of a projective technique in predicting sales effectiveness. *Personnel Psychology, 5,* 125–144.

Spielberger, C. D., Jacobs, G., Russell, S., & Crane, R. S. (1983). Assessment of anger: The State-Trait Anger Scale. In J. N. Butcher & C. D. Spielberger (Eds.), *Advances in personality assessment* (Vol. 2). Hillsdale, NJ: Erlbaum.

Spielberger, C. D., & Piotrowski, C. (1990). Clinicians' attitudes towards computer-based testing. *The Clinical Psychologist, 43,* 60–63.

Spitzer, R. L., & Endicott, J. (1971). An integrated group of forms for automated psychiatric case records: Progress report. *Archives of General Psychiatry, 24,* 540–547.

Spitzer, R. L., & Endicott, J. (1974). Can the computer assist clinicians in psychiatric diagnosis? *American Journal of Psychiatry, 131,* 523–530.

Spitzer, R. L., Williams, J. B. W., Gibbon, M., & First, M. D. (1990). *SCID: User's guide for the Structured Clinical Interview.* Washington, DC: American Psychiatric Press.

Spranger, E. (1928). *Types of men* (P. J. W. Pigors, Trans., *Lebensformen,* 5th German ed.). Halle: Max Niemeyer Verlag.

Starr, B. J., & Katkin, E. S. (1969). The clinician as aberrant actuary: Illusory correlation and the Incomplete Sentences Blank. *Journal of Abnormal Psychology, 74,* 670–675.

Stein, M. I. (1947). The use of a sentence completion test for the diagnosis of personality. *Journal of Clinical Psychology, 3,* 47–56.

Stein, M. I. (1966). *Volunteers for peace: The first group of Peace Corps volunteers in a rural community development in Colombia.* New York: Wiley.

Stephenson, W. (1953). *The study of behavior.* Chicago: University of Chicago Press.

Steptoe, A., & Johnston, D. (1991). Clinical application of cardivascular assessment. *Psychological Assessment: A Journal of Consulting and Clinical Psychology, 3,* 337–349.

Stermac, L. E. (1988). Projective testing and dissimulation. In R. Rogers (Ed.), *Clinical assessment of malingering and deception.* New York: Guilford.

Stermac, L. E., Segal, Z. W., & Gillis, R. (1990). Social and cultural factors in sexual assault. In W. L. Marshall, D. R. Laws, & H. E. Barbaree (Eds.), *Handbook of sexual assault.* New York: Plenum.

Stern, G. G., Stein, M. I., & Bloom, B. S. (1956). *Methods in personality assessment.* Glencoe, IL: Free Press.

Stodgill, R. M. (1963). *Manual for the Leader Behavior Description Questionnaire, Form XII.* Columbus: Ohio State University, Bureau of Business Research.

Stokes, G. S., Mumford, M. D., & Owens, W. A. (1989). Life history prototypes in the study of human individuality. *Journal of Personality, 57,* 507–543.

Storandt, M., Siegler, I. C., & Elias, M. F. (Eds.). (1978). *The clinical psychology of aging.* New York: Plenum.

Strasburger, E. L., & Jackson, D. N. (1977). Improving accuracy in a clinical judgment task. *Journal of Consulting and Clinical Psychology, 45,* 303–309.

Stromberg, C. D., Haggarty, D. J., Leibenluft, R. F., McMillan, M. H., Mishkin, B., Rubin, B. L., & Trilling, H. R. (1988). *The psychologist's legal handbook.* Washington, DC: Council for the National Register of Health Service Providers in Psychology.

Strong, E. K. (1927). A vocational interest test. *Educational Record, 8,* 107–121.

Strong, E. K. (1955). *Vocational interests 18 years after college.* Minneapolis: University of Minnesota Press.

Swan, W. S. (1989). *Swan's how to pick the right people program.* New York: Wiley.

Sweeney, J. A., Clarkin, J. F., & Fitzgibbon, M. L. (1987). Current practice of psychological assessment. *Professional Psychology: Research and Practice, 18,* 377–380.

Sweet, J. J., Newman, P., & Bell, B. (1992). Significance of depression in clinical neuropsychological assessment. *Clinical Psychology Review, 12,* 21–45.

Swenson, C. H. (1957). Empirical evaluations of human figure drawings. *Psychological Bulletin, 54,* 431–466.

Swenson, C. H. (1968). Empirical evaluations of human figure drawings, 1957–1966. *Psychological Bulletin, 70,* 20–44.

Swenson, W. M., & Pearson, J. S. (1964). Automation techniques in personality assessment: A frontier in behavioral science and medicine. *Methods of Information in Medicine, 3,* 34–36.

Swenson, W. M., & Pearson, J. S. (1966). Psychiatry—Psychiatric screening. *Journal of Chronic Diseases, 19,* 497–507.

Swets, J. A. (1961). Is there a sensory threshold? *Science, 134,* 168–177.

Swets, J. A., Tanner, W. P., & Birdsall, T. G. (1961). Decision processes in perception. *Psychological Review, 68,* 301–340.

Symonds, P. M. (1931). *Diagnosing personality and conduct.* New York: Appleton-Century.

Szasz, T. (1961). *The myth of mental illness.* New York: Hoeber.

Szasz, T. (1984). *The myth of mental illness.* New York: HarperCollins.

Taft, R. (1955). The ability to judge people. *Psychological Bulletin, 52,* 1–23.

Taft, R. (1959). Multiple methods of personality assessment. *Psychological Bulletin, 56,* 333–352.

Tallent, N. (1958). On individualizing the psychologist's clinical evaluation. *Journal of Clinical Psychology, 14,* 243–244.

Tarasoff v. Regents of the University of California, 529 P.2d 553 (Cal. 1974), 131 Cal. Rptr. 14, 551 P.2d 334 (1976).

Taylor, H. C., & Russell, J. T. (1939). The relationship of validity coefficients to the practical effectiveness of tests in selection: Discussion and tables. *Journal of Applied Psychology, 23,* 565–578.

Tellegen, A., Lykken, D. T., Bouchard, T. J., Jr., Wilcox, K. J., Segal, N. L., & Rich, S. (1988). Personality similarity in twins reared apart and together. *Journal of Personality and Social Psychology, 54,* 1031–1039.

Tett, R. P., Jackson, D. N., & Rothstein, M. (1991). Personality measures as predictors of job performance. *Personnel Psychology, 44,* 703–742.

Tharinger, D. J., & Stark, K. (1990). A qualitative versus quantitative approach to evaluating the Draw-A-Person and Kinetic Family Drawing: A study of mood- and anxiety-disorder children. *Psychological Assessment: A Journal of Consulting and Clinical Psychology, 2,* 365–375.

Thommen, G. (1973). *Is this your day? How biorhythm helps you determine your life cycle* (Rev. ed.). New York: Crown.

Thoreson, C. E., & Mahoney, M. J. (1974). *Behavioral self-control.* New York: Holt, Rinehart and Winston.

Thorne, A., & Gough, H. G. (1991). *Portraits of type: An MBTI compendium.* Palo Alto, CA: CPP Books.

Thornton, G. C., III. (1992). *Assessment centers in human resource management.* Reading, MA: Addison-Wesley.

Thornton, G. C., III, & Byham, W. C. (1982). *Assessment centers and managerial performance.* Orlando, FL: Academic Press.

Thorpe, L. P., Clarke, W. W., & Tiegs, E. W. (1953). *Manual. California Test of Personality.* Los Angeles: California Test Bureau.

Thurstone, L. L. (1934). The vectors of the mind. *Psychological Review, 41,* 1–32.

Thurstone, L. L. (1949). *Thurstone Temperament Schedule.* Chicago: Science Research Associates.

Thurstone, L. L. (1951). The dimensions of temperament. *Psychometrika, 16,* 11–20.

Tomlinson, J. R. (1967). Situational and personality correlates of predictive accuracy. *Journal of Consulting Psychology, 31,* 19–22.

Toops, H. A. (1944). The criterion. *Educational and Psychological Measurement, 4,* 271–297.

Travin, S., Cullen, K., & Melella, J. T. (1988). The use and abuse of erection measurements: A forensic perspective. *Bulletin of the American Academy of Psychiatry and the Law, 16,* 235–250.

Tupes, E. C., & Christal, R. E. (1958). *Stability of personality trait rating factors obtained under diverse conditions.* (*USAF WADC Technical Note,* No. 58-61).

Tupes, E. C., & Christal R. E. (1961). *Recrurrent personality factors based on trait ratings* (*USAF ASD Technical Report,* No. 61-97).

Turner, D. R. (1966). Predictive efficiency as a function of amount of information and level of professional experience. *Journal of Projective Techniques and Personality Assessment, 30,* 4–11.

Turpin, G. (1991). The psychophysiological assessment of anxiety disorders: Three-systems measurements and beyond. *Psychological Assessment: A Journal of Consulting and Clinical Psychology, 3,* 366–375.

Tversky, A., & Kahnemann, D. (1974). Judgment under uncertainty: Heuristics and biases. *Science, 185,* 1124–1131.

Tversky, A., & Kahnemann, N. D. (1978). Causal schemata in judgment under uncertainty. In M. Fishbein (Ed.), *Progress in social psychology.* Hillsdale, NJ: Erlbaum.

Twentyman, C. T., & McFall, R. M. (1975). Behavioral training of social skills in shy males. *Journal of Consulting and Clinical Psychology, 43,* 384–395.

Ulrich, L., & Trumbo, D. (1965). The selection interview since 1949. *Psychological Bulletin, 63,* 100–116.

Valins, S., & Nisbett, R. E. (1971). *Attribution processes in the development and treatment of emotional disorders.* New York: General Learning Press.

Van Eron, A. M., & Burke, W. W. (1992). The transformational/transactional leadership model: A study of critical components. In K. E. Clark & M. B. Clark (Eds.), *Impact of leadership.* Greensboro, NC: Center for Creative Leadership.

Van Lennep, D. J. (1951). The Four-Picture Test. In H. H. Anderson & G. L. Anderson (Eds.), *An introduction to projective techniques.* Englewood Cliffs, NJ: Prentice-Hall.

Veldman, D. J. (1967). Computer-based sentence completion interviews. *Journal of Counseling Psychology, 14,* 153–157.

Veldman, D. J., Menaker, S. L., & Peck, R. F. (1969). Computer scoring of sentence completion data. *Behavioral Science, 14,* 501–507.

Vernon, P. E. (1950). The validation of civil service selection board procedures. *Occupational Psychology, 24,* 75–95.

Vernon, P. E. (1964). *Personality assessment: A critical survey.* London: Methuen.

Vieweg, B. W., & Hedlund, J. L. (1992). *Competency in mental health: A selected bibliography.* University of Missouri, Department of Psychiatry.

Wade, C. (1991). *How to read palms.* Boca Raton, FL: Globe Communication Corp.

Wainer, H. (1978). On the sensitivity of regression and regressors. *Psychological Bulletin, 85,* 267–273.

Wallace, J. (1966). An abilities conception of personality: Some implications for personality measurement. *American Psychologist, 21,* 132–138.

Wallace, J. (1967). What units shall we employ? Allport's question revisited. *Journal of Consulting Psychology, 31,* 56–64.

Waller, R. W., & Keeley, S. M. (1978). Effects of explanation and information feedback on the illusory correlation phenomenon. *Journal of Consulting and Clinical Psychology, 46,* 342–343.

Walsh, J. A. (1978). Review of the Sixteen Personality Factors Questionnaire. In O. K. Buros (Ed.), *Eighth mental measurements yearbook.* Highland Park, NJ: Gryphon.

Walsh, W. B. (1967). Validity of self-reports. *Journal of Counseling Psychology, 14,* 18–23.

Walsh, W. B. (1968). Validity of self-reports: Another look. *Journal of Counseling Psychology, 15,* 180–186.

Walters, G. D., White, T. W., & Greene, R. L. (1988). Use of the MMPI to identify malingering and exaggeration of psychiatric symptomatology in male prison inmates. *Journal of Consulting and Clinical Psychology, 56,* 111–119.

Watkins, C. E., Jr. (1991). What have surveys taught us about the teaching and practice of psychological assessment? *Journal of Personality Assessment, 59,* 426–437.

Watkins, C. E., Jr., Campbell, V. L., Nieberding, R., & Hallmark, R. (1995). Contemporary practice of psychological assessment by clinical psychologists. *Professional Psychology: Research and Practice, 26,* 54–60.

Watson, L. (1973). *Supernature.* New York: Anchor/Doubleday.

Waxer, P. (1976). Nonverbal cues for depth of depression: Set versus no set. *Journal of Consulting and Clinical Psychology, 44,* 493.

Webb, E. (1915). Character and intelligence. *British Journal of Psychology Monograph Supplement, 3.*

Weideranders, M., & Choate, P. A. (1994). Beyond recidivism: Measuring community adjustments of conditionally released insanity acquittals. *Psychological Assessment, 6,* 61–66.

Weiner, I. B. (1977). Approaches to Rorschach validation. In M. A. Rickers-Ovsiankina (Ed.), *Rorschach psychology* (2nd ed.). Huntington, NY: Krieger.

Weiner, I. B. (1986). Conceptual and empirical perspectives on the Rorschach assessment of psychopathology. *Journal of Personality Assessment, 50,* 472–479.

Weisskopf, E. A., & Dieppa, J. J. (1951). Experimentally induced faking of TAT responses. *Journal of Consulting Psychology, 15,* 469–474.

Wells, F. L. (1914). The systematic observation of the personality—in its relation to the hygiene of the mind. *Psychological Review, 21,* 295–333.

Welsh, G. S., & Dahlstrom, W. G. (1956). *Basic readings on the MMPI in psychology and medicine.* Minneapolis: University of Minnesota Press.

Westover, S. A., & Lanyon, R. I. (1990). The maintenance of weight loss after behavioral treatment. *Behavior Modification, 14,* 123–137.

Widiger, T. A. (1992). Review of the NEO Personality Inventory. In J. J. Kramer & J. C. Conoley (Eds.), *Eleventh mental measurements yearbook.* Lincoln: University of Nebraska, Buros Institute of Mental Measurements.

Wierzbicki, M. (1993). *Issues of clinical psychology: Subjective versus objective approaches.* Boston: Allyn & Bacon.

Wiggins, E. C., & Brandt, J. (1988). The detection of simulated amnesia. *Law and Human Behavior, 12,* 57–78.

Wiggins, J. S. (1966). Substantive dimensions of self-report in the MMPI item pool. *Psychological Monographs, 80* (22, Whole No. 630).

Wiggins, J. S. (1973). *Personality and prediction: Principles of personality assessment.* Reading, MA: Addison-Wesley.

Wiggins, J. S. (1980). Circumplex models of interpersonal behavior. In L. Wheeler (Ed.), *Review of Personality and Social Psychology* (Vol. 1). Beverly Hills, CA: Sage.

Wiggins, J. S. (1982). Circumplex models of interpersonal behavior in clinical psychology. In P. C. Kendall & J. N. Butcher (Eds.), *Handbook of research methods in clinical psychology*. New York: Wiley.

Wiggins, J. S., Goldberg, L. R., & Appelbaum, M. (1971). MMPI content scales: Interpretive norms and correlations with other scales. *Journal of Consulting and Clinical Psychology, 37*, 403–410.

Wiggins, J. S., & Pincus, A. L. (1992). Personality: Structure and assessment. *Annual Review of Psychology, 43*, 473–504.

Wiggins, N. L., & Hoffman, P. J. (1968). Three models of clinical judgment. *Journal of Abnormal Psychology, 73*, 70–77.

Wildman, B. G., & Erickson, M. T. (1977). Methodological problems in behavioral observations. In J. D. Cone & R. P. Hawkins (Eds.), *Behavioral assessment*. New York: Brunner/Mazel.

Wildman, R. W., & Wildman, R. W., II (1975). An investigation into the comparative validity of several diagnostic tests and test batteries. *Journal of Clinical Psychology, 31*, 455–458.

Wildman, R. W., II, White, P. A., & Brandenburg, C. A. (1990). The Georgia Court Competency Test: The base rate problem. *Perceptual and Motor Skills, 70*, 1005–1058.

Williams, C. L., Butcher, J. N., Ben-Porath, Y. S., & Graham, J. R. (1992). *MMPI-A content scales: Assessing psychopathology in adolescents*. Minneapolis: University of Minnesota Press.

Willingham, W. W. (1967). Foreword. In W. W. Willingham (Ed.), Invasion of privacy in research and testing. *Journal of Educational Measurement, 4*(Suppl.), 1–31.

Wirt, R. D., Lachar, D., Klinedinst, J. K., & Seat, P. D. (1977). *Multidimensional description of child personality: A manual for the Personality Inventory for Children*. Los Angeles: Western Psychological Services.

Wirt, R. D., Lachar, D., Klinedinst, J. K., & Seat, P. D. (1990). *Multidimensional description of child personality: A manual for the Personality Inventory for Children*. Los Angeles: Western Psychological Services.

Wittman, P. (1941). A scale for measuring prognosis in schizophrenic patients. *Elgin State Hospital Papers, 4*, 20–33.

Wonderlic Personnel Test, Inc. (1993). *Comprehensive Personality Profile: Administrator's manual*. Libertyville, IL: Author.

Woodworth, R. S. (1919). Examination of emotional fitness for warfare. *Psychological Bulletion, 16*, 59–60.

Woodworth, R. S. (1920). *Dynamic psychology*. New York: Columbia University Press.

Woody, R. H. (1977). Psychologists in child custody. In B. D. Sales (Ed.), *Psychology in the legal process*. New York: Spectrum.

Wrightsman, L. S., Nietzel, M. T., & Fortune, W. H. (1994). *Psychology and the legal system* (3rd ed.). Pacific Grove, CA: Brooks/Cole.

Yates, B. T. (1985). *Self-management: The science of helping yourself*. Belmont, CA: Wadsworth.

Yukl, G. (1993). *Leadership in organizations* (3rd ed.). Englewood Cliffs, NJ: Prentice-Hall.

Yukl, G., & Van Fleet, D. D. (1991). Theory and research on leadership in organizations. In M. D. Dunnette & L. M. Hough (Eds.), *Handbook of industrial and organizational psychology* (Vol. 2, 2nd ed.). Palo Alto, CA: Consulting Psychologists Press.

Zebrowitz, L. A. (1990). *Social perception*. Pacific Grove, CA: Brooks/Cole.

Zedeck, S. (1971). Problems with the use of "moderator" variables. *Psychological Bulletin, 76*, 295–310.

Zedek, S., Tziner, A., & Middlestadt, S. E. (1983). Interviewer validity and reliability: An individual analysis approach. *Personnel Psychology, 36*, 355–370.

Zigler, E., & Phillips, L. (1960). Social effectiveness and symptomatic behaviors. *Journal of Abnormal and Social Psychology, 61*, 231–238.

Zigler, E., & Phillips, L. (1962). Social competence and the process-reactive distinction in schizophrenia. *Journal of Abnormal and Social Psychology, 65,* 215–222.

Zubin, J., Eron, L. D., & Schumer, F. (1965). *An experimental approach to projective techniques.* New York: Wiley.

Zuckerman, M. (1985). Review of Sixteen Personality Factors Questionnaire. In J. V. Mitchell, Jr. (Ed.), *Ninth mental measurements yearbook.* Lincoln: University of Nebraska, Buros Institute of Mental Measurements.

Zytowski, D. G., & Warman, R. W. (1982). The changing use of tests in counseling. *Measurement and Evaluation in Guidance, 15,* 147–152.

Author Index

Subject Index